BLACK ATHENA WRITES BACK

Black Athena Writes Back

MARTIN BERNAL RESPONDS TO HIS CRITICS

Martin Bernal

Edited by David Chioni Moore

Duke University Press Durham & London

2001

© 2001 DUKE UNIVERSITY PRESS

All rights reserved

Printed in the United States of America

on acid-free paper ∞

Designed by C. H. Westmoreland

Typeset in Quadraat

by Tseng Information Systems, Inc.

Library of Congress Cataloging-in-

Publication Data appear on the last

printed page of this book.

For Cyrus Gordon and Michael Astour,

who have led the way.

Contents

Preface

This book and its forthcoming companion volume, *Debating Black Athena*, have had a long gestation. They were conceived in August 1994 in a diner in Quebec City after a panel on *Black Athena* at the tenth conference of the International Federation of Societies of Classical Studies at Laval University. We panelists—Valentin Mudimbe, David Chioni Moore, Denise McCoskey, and I—ate and relaxed. In the course of the conversation, I expressed my frustration that Mary Lefkowitz and Guy Rogers were not allowing me to respond in their forthcoming edited volume *Black Athena Revisited* (BAR). What is more, they had refused to include the replies I had already published to many of the pieces to be contained in their volume.

I mentioned that I should like to bring out a collection of my scattered replies in a single book and I wondered whether any publisher would be interested in such a project. Mudimbe and Moore both said that the editors at Duke University Press might like the idea. They thought, however, that a book that moved away from the minutiae of Classics to discuss broader issues around *Black Athena* would be more interesting to them and to the Press. We agreed then that it should be possible to combine the two projects.

Valentin, David, and Denise put the idea to Reynolds Smith at Duke Press.

He was interested and asked to see what I had. I mailed him the very rough manuscript and he sent it on to readers. They gave it a mixed reception. Although they found Lefkowitz and Rogers's behavior disgraceful, the early readers were bored by the manuscript's many repetitions and were irritated by what they saw as its one-sidedness. I attempted to rectify the latter—with the kind aid of Geneva Cobb Moore, Professor of English at the University of Wisconsin–Whitewater—by asking the authors of BAR to contribute to our book. However, any chance of success in this endeavor was blocked by a circular from Lefkowitz informing all contributors that they were exclusively committed to the University of North Carolina Press.

After many months, a final letter of strong support tipped the balance and Duke University Press agreed to publish *Black Athena Writes Back*. Nevertheless, Reynolds Smith, the editor at Duke who took on the project, decided that I needed a coeditor. The obvious choices were either Denise McCoskey or David Chioni Moore, and the latter, despite an extraordinarily heavy workload of his own, very generously agreed not only to edit my pieces but to work with me in soliciting other contributions.

By the spring of 1998, we realized that because we had followed the two tracks of detailed response and broad-ranging discussion, we had far too much material to include in a single volume. Reynolds Smith agreed that we could have two books, one for each aspect of the project. Thus, this volume contains my replies, and *Debating Black Athena* is made up of essays from a wide range of distinguished scholars from many different disciplines.

In acknowledging the many women and men who have helped and encouraged me in this project, I should, once again, like to thank all those I have listed in the prefaces to the first two volumes of *Black Athena*. I shall restrict myself here to those with whom I have continued to work over the past five years. First, I must thank my editor, David Chioni Moore, for the enormous effort he has put into these books and for the superb mixture of patience and bluntness with which he has tackled me and my disorganized manuscript. I also want to express my deep gratitude to Mary Jo Powell, who when asked, at a late stage, to copyedit agreed immediately and has done a superb job, as has the copyeditor at the press. Thanks too to Judy Schulewitz, who was of enormous help in checking and correcting the bibliography. Finally, there is Reynolds Smith, our extremely able editor at Duke Press, who has helped, guided, and encouraged us at every step.

I should like to thank those without whom the intellectual and scholarly construction of this book would have been impossible: Nikos Axarlis, Gregory Blue, Stanley Burstein, Eric Cline, Molly Myerowitz Levine, Valentin Mudimbe, David Owen, and Gary Rendsburg. I must also thank the following for their great help and patient understanding: Anouar Abdel Malek, Lynne Abel, Fred Ahl, George Bass, Jacques Berlinerblau, Roger Blench, John Boardman, Walter Burkert, Paul Cartledge, Chen Yiyi, Geneva Cobb-Moore, Paddy Culligan, Peter Daniels, Robert Drews, Emmanuel Eze, Dan Flory, David Held, James Hoch, Ephraim Isaac, Susan James, Shomarka Keita, Isaac Kramnick, Peter Kuniholm, Saul Levin, David Levy, Hugh Lloyd-Jones, Beatrice Lumpkin, Fouad Makki, Denise McCoskey, Uday Mehta, Henry Mendell, Toni Morrison, John Pairman Brown, John Pappademos, Jacke Phillips, Jamil Ragep, Andrew Rammage, Nancy Rammage, Lori Reppetti, Stephen Scully, Barry Strauss, Wim van Binsbergen, Frans van Coetsem, Vance Watrous, Gayle Warhaft, and Linda Waugh.

The past seven years have been extremely strenuous emotionally but they have also been happy and satisfying. One reason for this is that I have had the support of the friends and colleagues listed above. Even more important, however, has been the great warmth and joy of our family life. This has been created by my sons Paul, Adam, and Patrick, my daughter Sophie, her husband Mark, my wonderful grandchildren, Charlotte and Ben, and my son William, his partner Vanessa, and their baby Kate. Finally, there is my amazing mother, Margaret, and all the time my wife, Leslie, who has given me both the intellectual stimulus and the emotional support necessary for carrying on the project.

Parts of chapters 4, 5, 10, 12, and 13 appeared in slightly different versions in the following journals, respectively: *Bookpress*, © 1992; *Arethusa*, © 1992 The Johns Hopkins University Press; *History of Science*, © 1994 Wellcome Trust; *Arethusa*, © 1995 The Johns Hopkins University Press; and *Arion*, © 1996 Boston University Press.

Transcriptions and Phonetics

Egyptian

The orthography used in Egyptian words is the standard one used by Anglo-American Egyptologists, the only exception being that the sign traditionally transcribed as ḳ is written q in this volume.

Whatever the exact sound of the 3 in Old and Middle Egyptian (3400–1600 B.C.E.), it was used where Semitic names contained r, l, or even n. This consonantal value was retained until the beginning of the New Kingdom. In Late Egyptian (spoken, 1600–700 B.C.E.), it appears to have become an ꜣaleph and later, like the Southern English r, it merely modified adjacent vowels. The Egyptian ỉ corresponded to the Semitic ꜣaleph and yōd. ꜣAleph is found in many languages and in nearly all Afroasiatic ones. It is a glottal stop before vowels, as in the Cockney "boꜣl" and "buꜣə" (bottle and butter). The Egyptian ꜥayin, which occurs in most Semitic languages, is a voiced or spoken ꜣaleph. The Egyptian form seems to have been associated with the back vowels o and u.

In early Egyptian, the sign w, written as a quail chick, may have originally had purely consonantal value. In Late Egyptian, the stage of the Egyptian spoken language that had most impact on Greek, it seems to have been frequently pronounced as a vowel, either o or u. The Egyptian sign transcribed as r was more usually rendered as l in Semitic and Greek. In later Egyptian, as with the 3, it weakened to become a mere modifier of vowels.

The Egyptian and Semitic ḥ was pronounced as an emphatic h. It appears that the sign conventionally transcribed in Egyptian as ḫ was originally a voiced ġ. In Middle and Late Egyptian, it was devoiced to become something approximating the Scottish ch in "loch." The sign transcribed as ẖ was pronounced as ẖy. In Middle and Late Egyptian, it was frequently confused with š. š is used to transcribe a sign that originally sounded something like ḫ. It later was pronounced as sh or skh.

As mentioned above, q represents an emphatic ḳ.

The letter ṯ was probably originally pronounced as tʸ. Even in Middle Egyptian it was already being confused with t. Similarly, ḏ was frequently alternated with d. In Late Egyptian, voiced and unvoiced stops tended to merge. Thus, there was confusion among ṯ, t, ḏ, and d.

EGYPTIAN NAMES

Egyptian divine names are vocalized according to the most common Greek transcriptions, for example, Amon for ꜣImn and Isis for St.

Royal names generally follow A. H. Gardiner's (1961) version of the Greek names for well-known pharaohs, for instance, *Ramesses*.

Coptic

Most of the letters in the Coptic alphabet come from Greek and the same transcriptions are used. Six other letters derived from Demotic are transcribed as follows:

ϣ š	ϧ ẖ	ϫ j
ϥ f	ϩ h	ϭ č

Semitic

The Semitic consonants are transcribed relatively conventionally. Several of the complications have been mentioned above in connection with Egyptian. Apart from these, one encounters the following.

In Canaanite, the sound ḫ merged with ḥ. Transcriptions here sometimes reflect an etymological ḫ rather than the later ḥ. ṭ is an emphatic t. The Arabic letter tḥā' usually transcribed as th is written here as tʸ. The same is true of the dhāl, which is written here as dʸ. The letter found in Ugaritic that corresponds to the Arabic ghain is transcribed as ġ.

The West Semitic tsade was almost certainly pronounced ts and the letter śin originally seems to have been a lateral fricative similar to the Welsh ll. In transcriptions of Hebrew from the first millennium B.C.E. the letter shin is rendered š. Elsewhere, it is transcribed simply as s because I question the antiquity and range of the pronunciation š.

Neither the dagesh nor begadkephat are indicated in the transcription. This is for reasons of simplicity as well as because of doubts about their range and occurrence in antiquity.

Vocalization

The Masoretic vocalization of the Bible, completed in the ninth and tenth centuries C.E. but reflecting much older pronunciation, is transcribed as follows:

Name of sign	Plain		with ʾ y		with ו w		with ה h	
Pataḥ	בַ	ba	—		—		—	—
Qåmeṣ	בָ	bå	בָי	bâ	—		בָ ה	båh
Ḥîreq	בִ	bi	בִי	bî	—		—	—
Ṣērê	בֵ	bē	בֵי	bê	—		בֵה	bēh
Sᵉgōl	בֶ	be	בֶי	bệ	—		בֶה	beh
Ḥōlem	בֹ	bō	—	—	בוֹ	bô	בֹה	bōh
Qibûṣ	בֻ	bu	—	—	בוּ	bû	—	—

The reduced vowels are rendered:

בְ bᵉ   חֲ ḥă   חֱ ḥĕ   חֳ ḥŏ.

Accentuation and cantillation are not normally marked.

Greek

The transcription of the consonants is orthodox; υ is transcribed as y; the long vowels η and ω are written as ē and ō, and where it is significant the long α is rendered as ā; accentuation is not normally marked.

GREEK NAMES

It is impossible to be consistent in transliterating these, because certain names are so well known that they have to be given in their Latin forms— Thucydides or Plato—as opposed to the Greek Thoukydidēs or Platōn. On the other hand, it would be absurd to make Latin forms for little-known people or places. Thus, the commoner names are given in their Latin forms and the rest simply transliterated from Greek. I have tried wherever possible to follow Peter Levi's translation of Pausanias, where the balance is to my taste well struck. This, however, means that many long vowels are not marked in the transcription of names.

Chapter 6

In chapter 6 some extra transcriptions are used. These are the International Phonetic Alphabet and the Pingyin system for Chinese characters. Also in this chapter, Greek accents are usually marked.

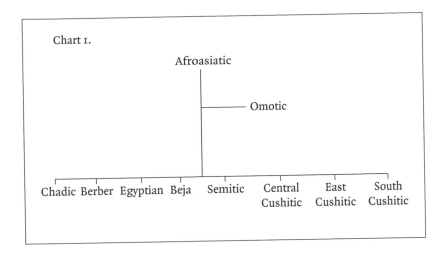

Chart 1.

Afroasiatic

— Omotic

Chadic Berber Egyptian Beja   Semitic   Central   East   South
                                              Cushitic   Cushitic   Cushitic

Maps and Charts

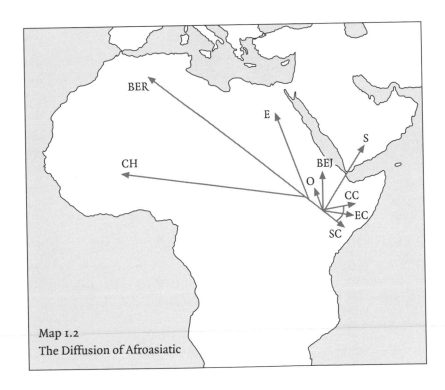

Map 1.2
The Diffusion of Afroasiatic

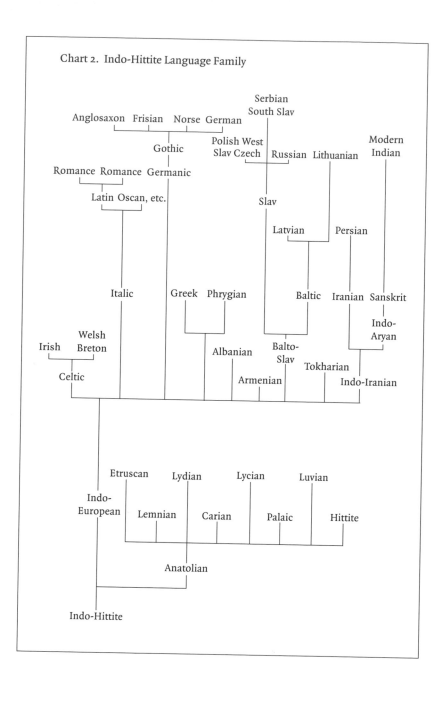

Chart 2. Indo-Hittite Language Family

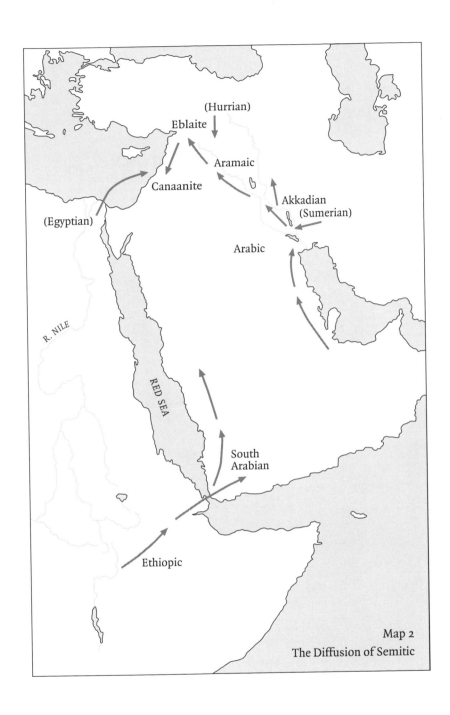

(Hurrian)

Eblaite

Aramaic

Canaanite

(Egyptian)

Akkadian
(Sumerian)

Arabic

R. NILE

RED SEA

South
Arabian

Ethiopic

Map 2
The Diffusion of Semitic

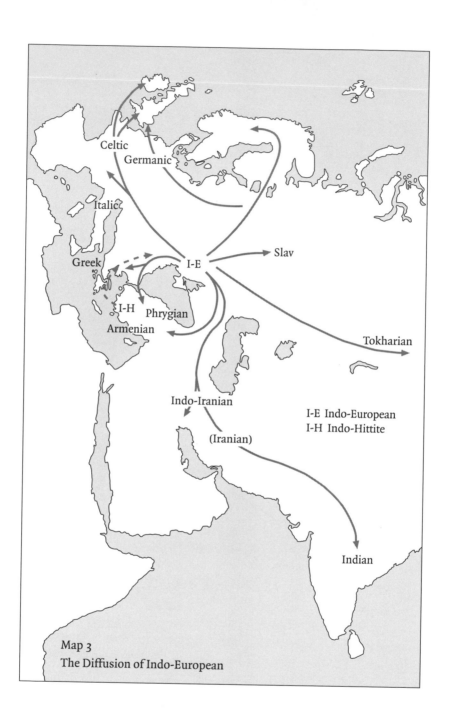

Celtic

Germanic

Italic

Greek

I-E → Slav

I-H

Phrygian

Armenian

Tokharian

Indo-Iranian

(Iranian)

I-E Indo-European
I-H Indo-Hittite

Indian

Map 3
The Diffusion of Indo-European

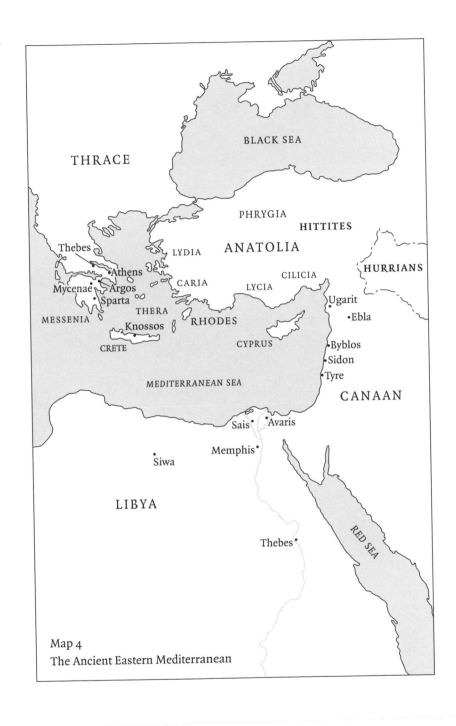

THRACE

BLACK SEA

PHRYGIA

HITTITES

ANATOLIA

Thebes

LYDIA

Athens

HURRIANS

Mycenae

Argos

CARIA

CILICIA

Sparta

LYCIA

Ugarit

MESSENIA

THERA

•Ebla

Knossos

RHODES

CYPRUS

•Byblos

CRETE

•Sidon

•Tyre

MEDITERRANEAN SEA

CANAAN

Sais•

•Avaris

Memphis•

•Siwa

LIBYA

RED SEA

Thebes•

Map 4
The Ancient Eastern Mediterranean

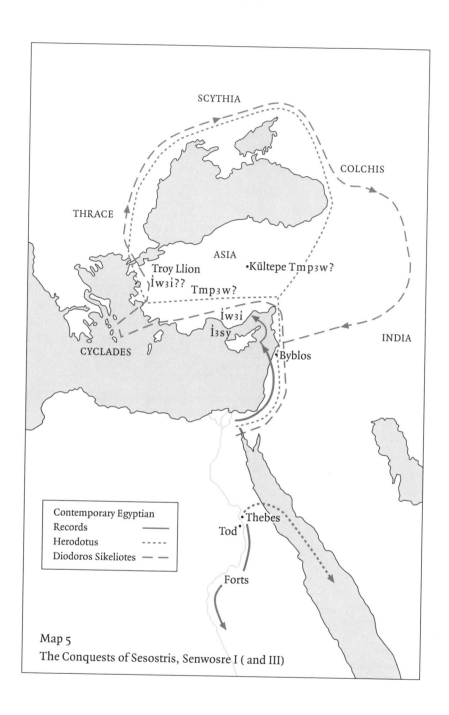

SCYTHIA

COLCHIS

THRACE

ASIA

Troy Llion   •Kültepe Tmp3w?
İw3i??   Tmp3w?

CYCLADES

İw3i
İ3sy

INDIA

•Byblos

Contemporary Egyptian
Records
Herodotus
Diodoros Sikeliotes

Thebes
Tod•
•

Forts

Map 5
The Conquests of Sesostris, Senwosre I (and III)

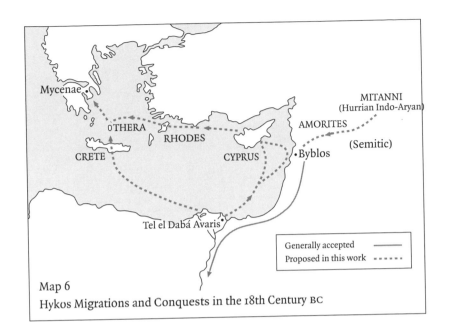

Map 6

Hykos Migrations and Conquests in the 18th Century BC

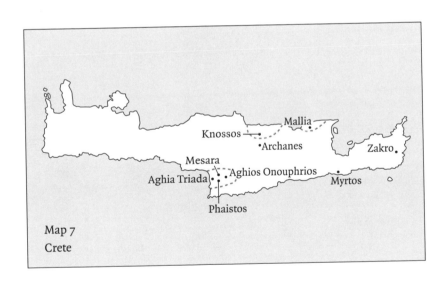

Map 7

Crete

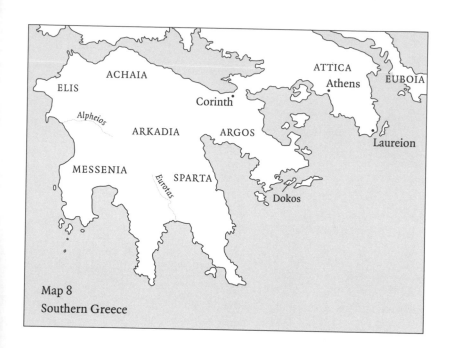

Map 8
Southern Greece

ACHAIA

ELIS

Alpheios

ARKADIA

MESSENIA

Eurotas

SPARTA

ARGOS

Corinth

ATTICA

Athens

EUBOIA

Laureion

Dokos

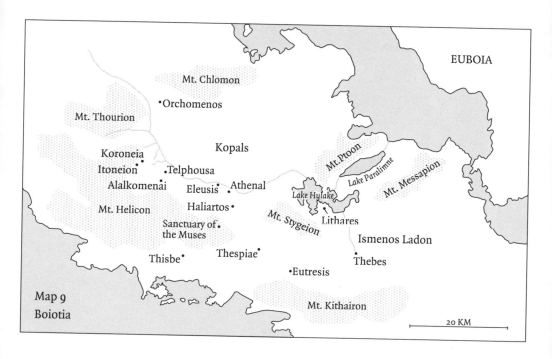

Map 9
Boiotia

EUBOIA

Mt. Chlomon

•Orchomenos

Mt. Thourion

Koroneia

Itoneion

Alalkomenai

Mt. Helicon

Kopals

Telphousa

Eleusis

Athenal

Haliartos•

Sanctuary of
the Muses

Thisbe•

Thespiae•

Mt. Ptoon

Lake Paralimne

Mt. Messapion

Lake Hylake

Mt. Stygeion

Lithares

Ismenos Ladon

•Eutresis

Thebes•

Mt. Kithairon

20 KM

Table 1 Egyptian chronologies

Dynasty	Breasted	Meyer	CAH	Helck	Mellaart	Bernal
1st	3400	3315±100	3100	2955	3400	3400
2nd			2900	2780	3200	3200
3rd	2980	2895±100	2730	2635	2950	3000
4th	2900	2840±100	2613	2570	2850	2920
5th	2750	2680±100	2494	2450	2725	2800
6th	2625	2540±100	2345	2290	2570	2630
7th	2475	—	2181	2155	2388	2470
8th	2475	—	—	—	2388	2470
9th	2445	2360±100	2160	—	—	2440
10th	—	—	2130	—	—	—
11th	2160	2160	2133	2134	2287	2140
12th	2000	2000/1997	1991	1991	2155	1979
13th	1788	1778	1786	?	1946	1801
14th	—	—	—	—	—	—
15th	—	—	1674	1655	1791	1750
16th	—	—	1684	—	—	—
17th	—	—	—	—	—	—
18th	1580	1580/75	1567	1552	1567	1567
19th	1315	1320	1320	1306	1320	1320
20th	1200	1200	1200	1196/86	1200	1200

Sources: Breasted (1906, 1: 40–45); Meyer (1907, pp. 68, 178); *Cambridge Ancient History* (charts at the end of vols I.2B, II.1, and II.2); Helck (1971, chart; 1979, pp. 146–148); Mellaart (1979, pp. 9, 19).

Table 2 Aegean chronology

Ceramic Period	CAH	K & M	Bet.	Bernal 1	Bernal 2
EMI	3000?				3300
EMII	2500?				3000
EMIII	2200				2400
MMIA	1900				2050
MMIB		2000			1950
MMII	1800				1820
MMIII	1700	1775–50		1730	1730
LMIA	1600	1675–50		1650	1675
LHI	1550				
LMIB/LHIIA	1500	1600–1575	1610	1550	1600
LMII	1450	1500–1475	1550	1450	1520
LHIIB	1430	1550			1520
LHIIIA1	1400		1490		1470
LMIIIA	1380		1490		1470
LMIIIA2/ LHIIIA2			1430–10		1410
LMIIIB/ LHIIIB	1275	1375–50	1365		1370
LMIIIC/ LHIIIC	1180		1200		1210

CAH = *Cambridge Ancient History*, 3d ed.
K & M = Kemp and Merrillees (1980).
Bet. = Betancourt (1989).
Bernal 1 = *Black Athena*, vol. 1.
Bernal 2 = *Black Athena*, vol. 2.

Introduction

Black Athena Writes Back is a direct response to another book, *Black Athena Revisited* (BAR). That volume, which came out in 1996, is a collection of essays written by some distinguished scholars from a number of disciplines. These writers, while conceding various merits to my work, are generally critical of it—sometimes violently so. Some of the contributors to BAR attack the general project of *Black Athena* for purely scholarly reasons, others from a mixture of scholarly and what I perceive to be right-wing political motives. The combination is powerful, and there is no doubt that a large number not merely of the experts but also of the cultivated lay public have been persuaded by the arguments set out in the book. The chapters of this book, *Black Athena Writes Back*, and its companion volume, the forthcoming *Debating Black Athena*, are attempts to challenge and debate the arguments in BAR both in detail and in general and, from our point of view, to right the balance.

BAR was largely made up of previously published reviews of the first two volumes of *Black Athena*. They have been contributed with very little alteration and with virtually no consideration to the replies to them I published at the time. Thus, about half of *Black Athena Writes Back* consists of revised versions of these replies. As some of the journals in which they first appeared are quite obscure, I believe that it is helpful to those interested in the debates around the *Black Athena* project to republish them in a single volume.

The rest of *Black Athena Writes Back* is made up of essays of three types. The first category consists of responses to a number of the critiques that appeared for the first time in BAR. The second category consists of three previously published articles on topics not directly covered in *Black Athena* but included here because of their bearing on the general debate. The third category is made up of reviews of recent important books by champions of a new, more hybrid brand of Classical studies, who maintain against the previous orthodoxy that Southwest Asia had a critical impact on important aspects of Greek civilization.

Outline of *Black Athena:*
The Afroasiatic Roots of Classical Culture
HISTORIOGRAPHY AND THE PROJECT AS A WHOLE

Black Athena is about the origins of Ancient Greece. This concern, then, is Eurocentric to the extent that Ancient Greece has been the most important single contributor to later Western European culture, either directly, or through Rome, Byzantium, and Islam. In investigating Greek origins, I have found it useful to set up two schemes, which I have called the "Ancient" and "Aryan" models. By "model" I merely mean a reduced representation, and this naturally involves oversimplification and distortion of some of the varied complexities of reality. The same can be said, however, of words themselves; just as with words, models are necessary symbols for a coherent representation of reality.

Most readers born before 1970 will have been educated in the Aryan model, which holds that ancient Greek culture developed as the result of one or more invasions from the north by Indo-European speakers or "Hellenes." These invaders are supposed to have conquered the native population, who are seen as having been sophisticated but soft. Their name having been lost, late-nineteenth-century promoters of the Aryan model called them "Pre-Hellenes." Although it is affirmed that the Pre-Hellenes were "white" or "Caucasian" and definitely not "Semitic" or "African," very little is known about them except for what can be reconstructed from supposed linguistic traces of their culture in Greek language and proper names.

Greek is an Indo-European language; its phonetic and grammatical structures conform with relative regularity to those of the other extant ancient members of the large linguistic family that includes Sanskrit, Latin, and many other languages. Greek, however, is unusual in the very high percentage of its vocabulary—more than 60 percent—that cannot be explained in terms of other Indo-European languages.[1] This pattern *can* be explained by the Aryan model, according to which most of the non-Indo-European words and names are attributed to the Pre-Hellenes. The serious difficulties presented by this scheme are discussed in my response to Jasanoff and Nussbaum.[2] The Aryan model does not claim that Greek as a language was homogeneous, or that the Greeks were pure "Indo-Europeans" or "Aryans." Instead, its proponents agree that there was linguistic mixing but insist that both invaders and natives were "Caucasian" or "European."

In this way, the picture produced of Ancient Greece is different from that of the Aryan conquest of India, because the original pre-Aryan inhabitants of the Indian subcontinent were "dark." Thus, despite what nineteenth-century historians saw as noble attempts to preserve their race through the caste system, the Aryans who conquered India suffered "racial degradation." The origin of Greece, in contrast, was imagined as having been more like the Germanic destruction of the Western Roman Empire, events that historians of the nineteenth and early twentieth centuries portrayed as Teutons infusing vigor into a Celtic and Roman *European* population. However, although the Germanic invasions were unquestionable historical events—and there is also strong legendary and linguistic evidence to suggest that there were Aryan conquests in Northern India—evidence for a similar conquest is completely lacking in the case of Greece.

The Ancient model, which is very different, was referred to by the playwrights Aeschylus and Euripides, the historians Herodotus and Diodorus Siculus, the orator Isocrates, the guidebook writer Pausanias, and the mythographers Apollodorus, Palaiphatos, and Konōn. It was omitted by one or two writers in contexts where they might have mentioned it, but was denied only by Plutarch in what is generally seen as an outburst of spleen against Herodotus. In other writings, Plutarch admitted Greece's deep cultural debts to Egypt; he took it as axiomatic, for instance, that Greek religion came from Egypt.

According to the Ancient model, Greece had once been inhabited by primitive tribes, Pelasgians and others. Certain regions, notably Boiotia and the Eastern Peloponnese, had then been settled by Egyptians and Phoenicians who had built cities and civilized the natives. The Phoenicians, for instance, had introduced the alphabet, and the Egyptians had taught the Pelasgians such things as irrigation, the names of the gods, and how to worship them.[3]

This Ancient model was not doubted until the end of the eighteenth century, and it was not seriously challenged until the 1820s. Only then did Northern European scholars begin to deny the ancient colonizations and play down Egyptian and Phoenician cultural influences on Greece. These historiographical developments cannot be linked to the availability of any new evidence. The great discoveries of the nineteenth century—the first archaeology of Bronze Age Greece by Heinrich Schliemann and the decipherment of cuneiform—took place many decades after the change of models. Jean-François Champollion had begun to decipher hieroglyphics in the 1820s, but the scholars who overthrew the Ancient model drew little from his work. Readings of Egyptian texts were not generally accepted by classicists until the 1850s. The reasons for the overthrow of the Ancient model are to be found not in internal developments within the disciplines, but in the intellectual milieu of the time.

The years from 1815 to 1830 were outstanding throughout Europe for political reaction and religious revival. Both of these movements were opposed to the Enlightenment and the French Revolution that was seen as its offspring. Thus, the reaction against Ancient Egypt during these years should be seen in the light of the Egypt's centrality to the beliefs of the Freemasons—see for example the Masonic trappings of Mozart's *Magic Flute*. The Enlightenment in general and the Freemasons in particular were seen by reactionaries to have been at the heart of the French Revolution and specifically to have been behind its anti-Christian "religion of reason."

In the long run, however, the Ancient model was destroyed not because of any threat to Christianity from the Freemasons but because of the predominance, in the nineteenth century, of the linked concepts of progress, romanticism, and racism. For the progressives, Ancient Egypt lost ground to Ancient Greece because the former was older and, hence, at an earlier stage of evolution. Egypt's stable centralized government did not appeal to the romantic love of small communities with turbulent histories. At first, the racism of the Enlightenment did not affect the reputation of the Egyptians because they were granted honorary European status. After the 1790s, however, both radicals and romantics began to view Egypt as increasingly African.[4]

In the new period of systematic racism, the eighteenth-century image of the Greeks changed progressively from that of intermediaries who had transmitted some part of the civilization and wisdom of the "East" to the "West" into that of the very creators of civilization. At the beginning of the eighteenth century, the Ancient Greeks were admired because of Homer and the later poets. In the middle of that century, cultivated Europeans, led by the connoisseur Johann Winkelmann, began to see Greek art as the highest ever achieved. Finally, in the 1780s, historians of philosophy came to agree that there had been no philosophy before the Greeks. This apparent triple achievement—of epic poetry characteristic of the "childhood of a race," art associated with flowering youth, and wisdom that came with its maturity—gave the Ancient Greeks a superhuman status as the models of balanced and integrated humanity.

This feeling was particularly strong in Germany. There, during the eighteenth century, intellectuals sought to preserve their cultural identity from French Zivilisation. The French threat was backed not only by the power and brilliance of contemporary Paris and Versailles but also by the Roman Catholic Church and Rome itself. In response, German thinkers turned to creating a sophisticated German language purged of Latinisms and to developing the romantic concept of an ineffable German Kultur seen as local, deep, and hidden as opposed to the superficial glitter of Zivilisation.[5]

German resistance to the supposed Rome-Paris axis also took the form of Neo-Hellenism. In the sixteenth century, Martin Luther had challenged the Latin Vulgate Bible with both the Greek New Testament and his German translation of the Bible, thereby undercutting the Roman monopoly of Western Christianity in two ways. In the political and cultural crises of the eighteenth century, enlightened German intellectuals like Christoph Martin Wieland and Johann Wolfgang von Goethe became passionately interested in pagan Greece. Many in their generation concluded that Germany, despite the efforts of Frederick the Great, could never be politically united or militarily powerful as a "New Rome." Nevertheless, with its many squabbling small states but high level of education and culture, it could become a "New Hellas."

German Neo-Hellenism became particularly passionate after 1789, when the French Revolution compounded the menace to Protestant Northern Germany, adding revolutionary ideas to its earlier Catholicism. In 1793, during the trial of Louis XVI, the brilliant young aristocrat and polymath Wilhelm von Humboldt sketched out a plan for a new education that would reintegrate men and women spiritually torn apart and alienated by modernity. This reintegration would be accomplished with the help of study of what Humboldt saw as the most perfectly integrated people of the past: the

Ancient Greeks. In 1806, the Prussian government, in panic after its military humiliation by Napoleon at Jena, appointed a reform cabinet. Humboldt was included and put in charge of national education. In this way, he was able to implement many of his earlier ideas, as well as establish the humanistic education of the *Gymnasium* and the university *Seminar* focused on *Altertumswissenschaft*, the "study/science of Antiquity and of the Greeks in particular." [6]

Humboldt seems to have intended his scheme to reach the whole population. Not surprisingly, this did not happen. Nevertheless, the new German educational system, as it was instituted, had clear meritocratic tendencies and was thus a threat to the aristocracy, many of whom opposed the new ideas.[7] Similarly, its English offshoot, "Classics," was seen as a middle way between reaction and revolution. From the beginning, however, the chief purpose of the Germans and English who advocated a humanistic education focused on Ancient Greece was not to attack the ruling class but to forestall or avoid revolution. Indeed, despite some trouble from the radicals associated with the Philhellenic movement in support of the Greek War of Independence, humanistic education has very effectively maintained the status quo.

The outbreak of the Greek War of Independence against the Turks in 1821 provided the only liberal outlet in an age of reaction. Academic and student circles thrilled to a passionate Philhellenism, intensified by the cult of the dead Philhellenic poets Byron and Shelley. The Greek revolt was seen by Philhellenes and much of the wider Northern European public as an apocalyptic struggle between freedom and tyranny, progress and reaction, youth and age, and, in particular, old corrupt Asia and Africa against young pure Europe. In this atmosphere, it is remarkable that the Ancient model survived as long as it did, but it was a tough nut to crack. Connop Thirlwall, the first writer—in either English or German—of a history of Greece in the "new" mode, wrote of the Ancient model in the 1830s: "It required no little boldness to venture even to throw out a doubt as to the truth of an opinion sanctioned by such authority and by the prescription of such a long and undisputed possession of the public mind, and perhaps it might never have been questioned, if the inferences drawn from it had not provoked a jealous enquiry into the grounds on which it rests." [8]

What were these "inferences"? It is impossible to be certain, but it is likely that they were formed by the ideas of two influential writers, Constantine Chassebeuf de Volney and Charles François Dupuis. Since the 1780s and 1790s, these two had promoted the notions, already present in

Antiquity, that the Ancient Egyptians had gained their higher civilization from the Upper Nile and that they themselves had been black. Abolitionists quickly picked up this idea to argue the immorality of enslaving the people who had given Europe civilization. The intellectual appeal of this position intensified the opposite desire among romantics and others who saw Europe and Europeans as the epitome of youth and progress. Thus, they saw a need to discredit the reputation of the Egyptians as the founders of Greek and, hence, European civilization.

The leading man who showed "no little boldness" in challenging the Ancient model was one of the first products of Humboldt's new educational system, Karl Otfried Müller. Claiming a base in "science" that his predecessors had lacked, Müller maintained that Classical reports of early Egyptian and Phoenician settlement and civilizing were the result of connivance among later Egyptian, Phoenician, and Greek priesthoods and were, therefore, untrustworthy. Furthermore, he argued, because none of the legends that made up the Ancient model could be proven, they should not be believed. Müller's approach pulled off two sleights of hand. First, it required "proof" in an area where the best that can be hoped for is competitive plausibility. Second, Müller placed the onus of proof on those who accepted the massive ancient testimony rather than on those who challenged it. The unspoken basis for the "modern" scholars seems to have been the new axiom that Europe was, and had always been, categorically separate from and superior to Asia and Africa. Thus, proof was required to justify something as unnatural as the Ancient model.[9]

The rapid general acceptance of Müller's discrediting of Egyptian colonization shows how well attuned his idea was to its times. Müller's denial of Phoenician influence on Greece, however, was not taken up so easily. During most of the nineteenth century, then, the predominant image of the origins of Greece was one that I call the "Broad Aryan model." This model denied the Greek traditions concerning the Egyptians, but accepted those about the Phoenicians. Indeed, the best-known colonization of Greece from Egypt—that of Danaos in Argos—was now attributed to the Phoenicians, for whom, indeed, a new boom arose in England. Men such as Prime Minister William Gladstone, who wrote extensively on Early Greece, clearly felt a sympathy for Phoenicians, who were typed as an upright manufacturing and trading people who spread civilization, sold cloth, and did a little slaving on the side. With this reputation it is not surprising that French and somewhat later German scholars also linked the Phoenicians with the English "nation of shopkeepers," which therefore caused a different result: they disliked the ancient people. The French term and image of perfide Albion arose from the Roman stereotype of the perfide Poene or Punica fides, the "bad faith" of Phoenician Carthage. Nevertheless, the Phoenicians were then, as they had been at least since the Renaissance, chiefly associated with Jews, with whom, in fact, they shared the common language of "Canaanite" and many religious and other customs. It is therefore significant that the peak of the Phoenicians' reputation in nineteenth-century historiography coincided with years of relative tolerance for Jews: between the dwindling of the traditional Christian religious hatred of Jews and the development of "racial" anti-Semitism at the end of the century.

In some ways, it is useful to see late-nineteenth-century "racial" anti-Semitism as a luxury that Gentile Europeans and their American "cousins" could afford only when the rest of the world was utterly crushed. One major factor behind the rise of Western anti-Semitism in the 1880s and 1890s was the massive migration of East European Jews into Western Europe and America. But another was the extraordinary arrogance associated with the triumphs of imperialism. It was during these decades that belief in the Phoenicians' formative role in the creation of Greek civilization plummeted. Concomitantly, this period saw not only the Dreyfus affair but also the publication of influential scholarly articles denying that there had ever been any significant extra-European influence on the formation of Greece. The Broad Aryan model survived, however, until the decade 1925–1935, when Western scholarship firmly put the "Semites," both Jews and Phoenicians, in their place: outside Europe. In contrast to the earlier period, the lessening of European self-confidence after the First World War now served to increase anti-Semitism. Furthermore, in 1917, anti-Semitism was driven to fever pitch by the perceived and actual importance of Jews in the Russian Revolution and world communism.[10]

Although I maintain that the "externalist" forces described above provided the chief impetus for the shift of models, and the only one for the destruction of the Ancient model, an important "internalist" impulse also lay behind the creation of the Aryan model in the 1830s and 1840s. This impulse came from the working out of the Indo-European language family and the plausible belief that at some time a single Proto-Indo-European language was spoken somewhere to the north of the Black Sea. Thus, as Greek was an Indo-European language, it must, at some stage, have been introduced from the north. Using this argument, advocates were able to postulate an "Aryan invasion"—despite the absence of any archaeological evidence or ancient authority—and thus satisfy externalist demands. The ideological forces behind the shift are shown by the increasing insistence of the proponents of the Aryan model that the northern and southern influences were mutually exclusive. I am convinced that this insistence came from the romantic desire for purity and the association of such purity with the north. No other reason can explain the inability to form the plausible hypothesis that Greece had been substantially influenced from both directions. This *dual* influence—and not a *sole* influence from the south and east—is what I propose in my "Revised Ancient model."

The situation has changed sharply since 1945, partly because of the moral revulsion at the consequences of anti-Semitism seen in the Holocaust. Sadly, I believe that the simultaneous rise of the "Third World" and of Israel as a bastion of the "First World" or "Western Civilization" has had an even greater impact on European and Euro-American academic opinion. Concretely, Israel's military triumphs have removed the stereotype, common at the beginning of this century, that "Semites," or at least Phoenicians and Jews (as it was never possible to include Arabs), were "racially" determined to be passive merchants and were, therefore, biologically incapable of the military actions attributed to them in Greek legends.

The events of the 1940s and 1950s led toward the readmission of Jews as Europeans. Among Jews in both the United States and Europe, the increased self-confidence has been largely reflected in Zionism and religious revival. At the same time, a very much smaller group has tried to restore the reputation of the Phoenicians. Thus, since the 1960s an attempt to bring back the Broad Aryan model for the origins of Greece has been reemerging. Resistance from the "extreme Aryanists" seems to result largely from inertia and respect for authority, which are naturally very high in such traditional disciplines as Classics and historical linguistics. Nevertheless, the defenders of the Extreme Aryan model have been weakened both by the changing intellectual climate and by increasing archaeological evidence of Egyptian and Levantine influence in the Aegean during the Late Bronze and Early Iron Ages. The Broad Aryanists are now gaining ground and will almost certainly succeed within the next five years. For instance, the editors of BAR now appear to accept the Broad Aryan model, although they still prefer Mesopotamian "East Semites" and the Northern Levant to the "West Semites" of the Southern Levant. The restoration of the Egyptian aspect of the Ancient model, in a revised form, will take somewhat longer; the principal debate is now beginning to be between the Broad Aryan and the Revised Ancient models.

At this stage, I should like to reiterate my respect for the achievements of the early-nineteenth-century Indo-European linguists and my conviction that, despite the presence of many foreign aspects and elements, Greek is fundamentally an Indo-European language. Equally, I do not believe that the legends of such heroic invaders as Danaos and Kadmos should be taken literally as referring to specific individuals. They should be seen, rather, as a general indication of Aegean settlements by Phoenicians and peoples from Egypt, or perhaps merely as markers of substantial cultural influences on Greece from the southeast. In sum, I do not argue for a complete restoration of the Ancient model but for a synthesis, incorporating the linguistic advances of the nineteenth century and adjusting some traditional dates in the light of archaeological evidence from the twentieth. Nevertheless, I believe that the new scheme or Revised Ancient model is closer to the Ancient than to the Aryan model.

Even if one accepts the argument put forward in the historiographical section of my work, that the Aryan model was conceived in what we should now consider to be the "sin" and error of racialism and anti-Semitism, the model is not invalidated by this argument alone. Many fruitful theories, such as Darwinism, have been developed for what would later seem, on factual or moral grounds, to have been dubious reasons. There is no doubt, however, that the Ancient model was discarded not because of any inherent defects but because it did not fit the nineteenth-century worldview. The Aryan model had the advantage that it made Greek history conform to what its proponents saw as the universal historical principle of perpetually unequal races.

This external "surplus explanatory value," to use the term of the philosopher of science Imre Lakatos, allowed the Aryan model to supersede the Ancient model.[11] Today, we should not abandon the Aryan model merely because we dislike the ideology behind its establishment. Nevertheless, we should remove such underpinnings and, as far as it is possible to do so, assess it simply in terms of its utility in explaining the data.

From the beginning of the Black Athena project, I saw competition between the Aryan and Revised Ancient models not in terms of certainty but in terms of competitive plausibility, to be judged in the light of evidence from contemporary documents of the Late Bronze Age (1500–1100 B.C.E.), archaeology, language, toponyms, divine and mythological names, religious ritual, and historical analogy or typology. In some cases, such as the documents and archaeology, the evidence merely tends toward the Revised

Ancient model. In the others, cult and language for instance, the evidence supports it strongly.

To some extent, competition of this kind can be measured by prediction: the ease with which new evidence can be fitted into one or other of the two models. In general, however, there are serious problems with prediction. In the years after the publication of the first volume of Black Athena (BA I) I came to realize the naïveté and logical impossibility of the idea that one could stand above or beyond the models and be given a "God's-eye view." All I now claim is that the "world" of the Revised Ancient model is more stimulating and exciting to inhabit than that of the Aryan model. That is to say, the Revised Ancient model generates more testable hypotheses; it enables one to check parallels among the civilizations around the Eastern Mediterranean and, when these parallels are found, it provides more interesting and intellectually provocative answers.

If on these or any other grounds one prefers the Revised Ancient model, the image of Ancient Greece must be reassessed. We should turn from the image of a civilization springing, like the conventional image of Athena from the head of Zeus, white, virgin, and fully formed, to an image of a new civilization growing up at the intersection of Europe and the Middle East as a thoroughly mixed and eclectic culture. The greatness and extraordinary brilliance of Greek civilization in Antiquity, and the central role it played in the formation of all later European cultures, was not the result of isolation and cultural purity but of frequent contact and stimulus from the many surrounding peoples with the already heterogeneous natives of the Aegean.

The Reception of Black Athena

I have told my version of the publication and early reception of Black Athena many times and I see no reason to repeat it here.[12] The only facts that need repeating are that, to my amazement and delight, and completely contradicting my sociology of knowledge, I found that a small number of experts were sympathetic to my project, and that an even larger fraction disagreed with most of my ideas but felt that the issues were important and believed that they should be debated. Scholars with these views made Black Athena the topic of the Presidential Panel of the 1989 annual meeting of the American Philological Association, the largest body of classicists in the world. This discussion was followed by invitations to panels at the annual meetings of other relevant disciplines; archaeometry, anthropology, Egyptology, and history. I found myself flooded with invitations to speak and debate at various universities and colleges around the country.

Another result of the APA Presidential Panel was that it convinced those who opposed my books that Black Athena would not evaporate from its own absurdity and would have to be confronted. This academic reaction coincided, and cooperated, with a much bigger political one. One of the side effects of the collapse of European communism in 1989 was that it opened an opportunity, particularly in the United States, for more attention to be paid to the so-called culture wars. Debates around Black Athena played an important role in these, and political objections to my work were added to the academic ones.

These different bases for opposing my work are reflected in BAR. Whereas its two editors object to Black Athena on both academic and political grounds, most of the contributors, many of whom see themselves as liberals if not socialists, object solely because of what they see as my bad or inadequate scholarship. Interestingly, however, a close reading of hostile reviews reveals that several of the reviewers, while objecting to my methods, accept many of my historiographic and archaeological conclusions, or at least agree that "they may well be right." [13]

This concession seriously undermines opposition to the theme of Black Athena. If archaeologists concede that relations around the Eastern Mediterranean in the Bronze Age had been far closer than previously supposed, and intellectual historians agree that the prevailing racism and anti-Semitism heavily influenced the work of nineteenth- and early-twentieth-century scholars, then the grounds for denying massive and fundamental Egyptian and West Semitic influences on Greek religion and language become extremely precarious.

At the 1989 meeting of the American Philological Association, I outlined a four-stage process through which I saw disciplines reacting to potentially fruitful radical new ideas: such ideas are ignored, dismissed, attacked, and then absorbed. The reception of volume 2 of Black Athena (BA II) when it was published in 1991 marked a shift from "ignore" to "dismiss." Where the first volume had received no attention from the U.S. mainstream and right-wing press, the second was given long reviews in the New York Times Book Review, the New York Review of Books, the Washington Post, and many other journals. Most, though by no means all, were hostile. [14] I can find two plausible explanations for the change. First, Black Athena was seen to have grown too important as a cult book and as a legitimizer of Afrocentrism to be ignored. It had to be confronted. Second, whereas at that stage the classicists and ancient historians had felt unable to deny my arguments on historiography, they sensed that the historical and archaeological arguments presented in volume 2 were more vulnerable.

Black Athena Revisited

By far the most important single reaction to Black Athena has been the publication of BAR. The title is brilliant, indicating as it does a calm objectivity. It is, however, misleading, as most of the reviews were written soon after the publication of BA I or BA II, and are not the products of long and mature thought. The book's objectivity is also compromised by the fact that hostility to my work was the main criterion in selecting the reviews. In disciplines where there were no sufficiently hostile reviews, new ones were commissioned. For instance, the editors of BAR did not select the two reviews that had already been published on my linguistic claims; these reviews were written by scholars who knew all three of the relevant languages: Ancient Egyptian, West Semitic, and Greek.[15] Instead, they commissioned a new chapter by two Indo-Europeanists with no knowledge of Ancient Egyptian and little interest in, or understanding of, language contact.[16] Similarly, new reviews were included on historiography, presumably to remedy the fact that earlier reviewers had tended to agree with that aspect of my work.

Initially, in 1993, I was not informed of the preparation of BAR. After it had been in preparation for some months, an uncomfortable contributor told me about it. My first reaction was one of dismay at having to write another article of response. Nevertheless, I dutifully emailed the senior editor Mary Lefkowitz, and asked when I could see the articles so that I could prepare my reply. She emailed back that the editors had decided not to include any response from me because, as she wrote, "most of the articles have appeared already and you have published replies to them." When I inquired whether my responses were to be included, Lefkowitz said no, adding that three authors had insisted that they would not contribute their articles if I were allowed to respond.

My first reaction was bewilderment. I had never heard of a scholarly volume devoted to the works of a living author not containing her or his response if she or he wished to write one. Within a few days, however, my disconcertion was compensated by a sense of the double honor Mary Lefkowitz and her colleague Guy Rogers were bestowing on me. I was flattered both because they felt it worthwhile to compile a book on my work and because their refusal to include my responses suggested that they believed my arguments were too compelling or persuasive to be included. As Emily Vermeule, one of the contributors, quoted Milton's *Paradise Lost* in reference to me:

> But all was false and hollow, though his tongue
> Dropp'd manna, and could make the worst appear
> The better reason, to perplex and dash
> Maturest counsels.[17]

PROFESSOR LEFKOWITZ'S PREFACE AND INTRODUCTION TO BLACK ATHENA REVISITED

Having summarized the *Black Athena* debates and my position in them and before outlining the contents of the present volume, I shall turn to an assessment of Mary Lefkowitz's preface and introduction to BAR. As most of the issues she raises are treated with more precision by other contributors to the volume, I respond to them in the body of this book. Here, therefore, I restrict myself to just a few of the points she brings out more clearly than her collaborators.

Lefkowitz gives BAR two openings—a preface and an introduction—and both provide excellent prefigurations of the book as a whole. She begins the preface with a quotation from a letter written in 1885 by the Catholic poet and Hellenist Gerard Manley Hopkins to a professor of Greek at Oxford. Hopkins suggested that the Greek legends about Egyptian colonizations of "Crete etc" should be taken seriously, and proposed an etymology for Aphrodite from an Egyptian form, *Nefrat-isi (BAR, p. ix).

Making this story the most prominent in BAR suggests that the editors would like it to be treated as a microcosm of the entire debate. In this way, the story serves a number of important purposes for Lefkowitz. First, Hopkins's suggestion demonstrates that my ideas are not original. Second, the reference to the poet shows that Lefkowitz is not a narrow specialist but a scholar of broad culture. Third, it implies that scholars on the periphery of a discipline (Hopkins was professor of Greek at Dublin), however respected they are in other fields, should not tell those at the center (Oxford) what to do. Fourth and fifth, the story shows how ridiculous it is to believe Greek traditions, and how easy it is to concoct etymologies.

The first suggestion is undoubtedly true. I have never claimed that my ideas are original, merely that I am reviving some neglected older views and bringing together some scattered contemporary ones. The second suggestion can stand on its own, but I believe that the last three points are thoroughly misleading. To begin with the third implication of the story of Hopkins's letter, I am convinced that all disciplines can profit from occasional marginal intervention. The study of Ancient Greece, in particular, has gained enormously from participants or even interlopers far further from the center of the discipline than Gerard Manley Hopkins: the banker George Grote, the tycoon Heinrich Schliemann, and the architect Michael Ventris, to name three.

On the fourth point, mistrusting Greek traditions, I believe that given the paucity of other information, Greek traditions should be used as *a* source of evidence about prehistory but used cautiously and in conjunction with material from other disciplines: archaeology, linguistics, studies of cult, and more. Finally, on the fifth point, concocting or fabricating etymologies is not an easy task. To be convincing, etymologies must have semantic congruence and follow certain regularities in their phonetic correspondences. It is simply not true to say, as Jasanoff and Nussbaum do in their chapter of BAR, that I maintain that in this area "anything goes." Thus, Lefkowitz's claim (p. xi) that my etymology of Athens "is intrinsically no more persuasive" than Hopkins's Egyptian derivation of Aphrodite is merely reductio ad absurdum. Jasanoff and Nussbaum's attempt to discredit the etymology of Athena and Athens from the Egyptian Ḥt Nt—for which I give abundant detailed evidence—heads a paragraph on it with the words: "This is not the place for a lengthy rebuttal of Bernal's case" (p. 194). I wonder where the correct place would be?

Lefkowitz's second beginning—that is, the introduction to BAR—is with an exaggeration. She heads the first section of the introduction "Are Ancient Historians Racist?" She writes: "Bernal himself ask[s] us to acknowledge that we have been racists and liars, the perpetrators of a vast intellectual and cultural cover-up, or at the very least the suppressors of an African past that, until our students and our colleagues began to mention it, we had ourselves known nothing about. Had our teachers deceived us, and their teachers deceived them?" (p. 4).

In the main clause before "or at the very least," Lefkowitz attempts to link two incompatible ideas, one of which is totally false and the other of which is partly so. In the first case, I have never accused contemporary classicists of being "racists and liars." As I have stated many times, I believe that modern classicists and historians of Antiquity are no more racist than other academics. Furthermore, modern classicists could not possibly "lie" about something of which they were unaware. For instance, in the 1960s, the brilliant scholars Cyrus Gordon and Michael Astour were driven beyond the pale of academic respectability. This was because conventional scholars then saw the intimate links between Semitic and Hellenic cultures that the two proposed as impossible within the framework of the Classics that that they had inherited. This reaction, in turn, was in many ways the result of the fact that several of the discipline's most influential founders were racist and anti-Semitic *and* that such prejudices had affected their scholarly approach.[18] Nevertheless, I have never suggested that either the creators or the defenders of this orthodoxy were insincere or "lying." They clearly believed in the ideological basis of their work. How could they have done otherwise?

Beyond these matters of contention, Mary Lefkowitz's introduction is marred by its sole focus on the specter of Africa and her consequent omission of the words "Southwest Asian" and "Semitic" in describing my work. In fact, *Black Athena* is substantially concerned with Levantine influences on the formation of Ancient Greece, and the role of anti-Semitism in their neglect. The Afrocentrist scholar Tony Martin, though problematic in other respects, is far closer to the mark when he writes: "If any of Bernal's Afrocentric followers had slowed down a bit in their speed reading of *Black Athena*, they would have noticed that he was as much or more concerned with a 'Semitic' origin for Greek civilization as for [*sic*] African influence over Greece."[19] Martin sees what Lefkowitz does not want to see: that I am interested in *both* Southwest Asian and African influences on Ancient Greece, in addition, of course, to Greece's indigenous sources of culture.

BLACK ATHENA AND AFROCENTRISM

At different times and in different places, Lefkowitz has expressed different views of my genuinely complex relationship to Afrocentrists. In BAR she scrupulously makes a distinction. At other times, as in a *questionnaire* sent out on her behalf to search out (and destroy?) Afrocentric influence in American schools, it is argued that my work "can be fairly listed with

Afrocentric literature."[20] This issue is discussed again in the chapter concerned with her popular book *Not Out of Africa*. At this stage, I merely want to point out that in BA I I made it clear that I disagreed with extreme Afrocentrists. Instead, I aligned myself on historical issues with more moderate historians, including George Washington Williams, W. E. B. Du Bois, John Hope Franklin, and Ali Mazrui, whom the more hardline Jacob Carruthers dismisses as "Negro Intellectuals."[21] Carruthers's view of my position is confirmed in his chapter in our forthcoming companion volume, *Debating Black Athena*.

Lefkowitz also overlooks the point that seeing Egypt as an important source of Greek higher culture is not necessarily an "Afrocentric" position. Such a position can also be taken by assimilationists looking for a common origin of African and European culture. Indeed, in what I might describe as a mirror image, her position is more compatible than mine with the extreme Afrocentrists. Both parties desire to keep Europe and Greece carefully separated from Egypt and Africa. The cases of intercontinental hybridity on which I focus are far more threatening to the view that Greece borrowed nothing of significance from Egypt than are Afrocentric notions of fundamental continental difference and separation.

WHERE ARE WE NOW?

To return to the four-stage scheme of ignore, dismiss, attack, and absorb mentioned above, BAR is on the cusp of the last two stages. The attack on *Black Athena* can be seen in the publisher's promotional material, which begins: "In this collection of twenty essays, leading scholars in a broad range of disciplines confront the claims made by Martin Bernal. The contributors to this volume argue that Bernal's claims are exaggerated and in many cases unjustified." Absorption appears in the blurb on the book's back, which states that, in their conclusion, Lefkowitz and Rogers "propose an entirely new scholarly framework for understanding the relationship between the cultures of the ancient Near East and Greece and the origins of Western civilization." The only positive suggestion I can find in their book is that one should avoid concentration on Egypt and Phoenicia and instead study "relations with the northern Levant, Anatolia, and, ultimately, Babylonia, which was much more influential culturally than Egypt generally in the Near East. Furthermore there were more geographical routes available by which that Babylonian influence could travel" (p. 450). Apart from the geographical argument that Egypt and the Levant were physically closer to Greece—and far more accessible to it—than Mesopotamia, I disagree with this proposal for many reasons, including, not least, that both the archaeological evidence and the Greek texts indicate that Egypt and Phoenicia provided much the most important outside influences on Greek culture.[22]

Nevertheless, the shift partway to the perspective of Black Athena made by Lefkowitz and Rogers is significant. Even self-proclaimed champions of the traditional disciplines now accept that Greece did not create itself and that one must look at its civilization in a much broader geographical and cultural context. As the classicist and recent president of the American Philological Association David Konstan put it in his review of Not Out of Africa and BAR: "In spite of a certain superficiality or tendentiousness in Bernal's history of philology, in which he ignores a good many scholars who have frankly acknowledged Greece's debt to its neighbours, Classicists as a whole (including those represented in Black Athena Revisited) have welcomed Bernal's forceful critique of the profession's implicit prejudices and its already palpable effect on the way the Classics are taught and studied." [23]

We are now at the stage of absorption.

The Structure of Black Athena Writes Back

Black Athena Writes Back is entirely my own work. Not all of the reviews that were reprinted in BAR receive responses here. Notably, I have excluded my many previously published replies to John Coleman because virtually all of the points he makes have been raised by other reviewers.[24] In revising my initial replies, I have tried to avoid excessive repetition. I use the word "excessive" because some repetition has been inevitable: different critics have leveled closely overlapping charges against Black Athena and I have responded to them in similar if not identical ways.

I also do not reply to some of the chapters of BAR that have not previously been published as reviews. We decided that it would be better to leave the response to Loring Braces's technical article to a professional physical anthropologist, Shomarka Keita; his extensive reply is included in Debating Black Athena. As my only substantial disagreements with Frank Yurco's chapter are specialized ones on chronology, we decided not to include a reply to his piece in either book. Katherine Bard's popular piece does not mention me and, therefore, does not require a direct response. I regret that I have not replied to professors Liverani and Jenkyns, from whose splendid book *The Victorians and Ancient Greece* I have learned a lot. However, my fellow editor David Moore and I felt it necessary to focus on the more substantial critics, notably Robert Palter, Jay Jasanoff, and Alan Nussbaum.[25] Palter is important as he is a powerful and interesting adversary both on questions of ancient science and on modern historiography. Jasanoff and Nussbaum require special attention not because of the quality of their linguistic arguments but because so many of the other contributors to BAR have relied on them.

At this point, I should note that Jasanoff and Nussbaum's contribution to BAR is anomalous in that they dislike my proposed etymologies from Semitic as much as, if not more than, they do those from Egyptian. In this reaction, as in other ways, they show their firm allegiance to the late-nineteenth-century tradition of the Neogrammarians, which I discuss in my reply. To put it in the terms set out in *Black Athena*, the editors and most of the contributors to BAR now work within a Broad Aryan model that denies Egyptian influences on Greece but accepts Semitic ones, though, within Southwest Asia, they prefer Mesopotamia to the Levant. By contrast, Jasanoff and Nussbaum continue to work within the Extreme Aryan model that denies suggestions of *any* Afroasiatic influences. This discrepancy produces an interesting anomaly in BAR as a whole. The editors Lefkowitz and Rogers, as well as other writers, now proclaim their open-mindedness to outside influences on Greece. By embracing Jasanoff and Nussbaum, however, they are forced to deny the obvious corollary that the close interaction in all other realms would lead to substantial linguistic borrowings.

As mentioned at the outset of this introduction, in addition to the responses to chapters in BAR we have included other articles relevant to the debate. Two of these are reviews of books written by contributors to BAR, Mary Lefkowitz and Sarah Morris. In the latter case, we thought it better to respond to her splendid book *Daidalos and the Origins of Greek Art* rather than to her less substantial chapter in BAR. We also include two reviews of books by Walter Burkert and Martin West, who since their student days have been in contact with the "Cologne school" dominated by Reinhold Merkelbach. For some decades, this school has emphasized the importance of Southwest Asian influences on Greek religion.

Burkert and West have been what one might call licensed deviants, licensed because their profound scholarship has never been questioned; until recently, however, their conclusions have been considered eccentric. Now, in the face of threats from outside, they are being hailed as pioneers of the direction that Classics as a discipline would have taken without all the brouhaha around *Black Athena*. I have the deepest admiration for Burkert and West and for Morris, who makes arguments similar to theirs, both for their courage in the face of the entrenched discipline and for their scholarship, which possesses depths that I could never possibly plumb. I disagree with them, however, on two important grounds. First, they focus largely on the Greek "Dark Ages" and Archaic Period, 900–500 B.C.E.; they tend not to look further back into the Bronze Age, when I am convinced much of the cultural borrowing took place. Second, they strikingly neglect Egyptian cultural influences, which I, like the Greeks of the Classical and Hellenistic Periods (500–50 B.C.E.), am convinced played if anything an even greater role in the formation of Greek civilization than did Southwest Asia.

The two areas of neglect are connected. Although Egypt played the larger role in the formation of Greek civilization in the Bronze Age and again in the late seventh and sixth centuries B.C.E., Southwest Asia in general and Phoenicia in particular had a greater impact on the Aegean from the eleventh to the early seventh centuries. For this reason we have also included an original article, "Phoenician Politics and Egyptian Justice in Ancient Greece." In this I tried to set out my views on the different types of cultural influence Egypt and the Levant exerted on the Aegean and the different periods in which one or other regional influence was predominant.

At this point, we should turn to the book itself and to the first part on Egyptology.

I

Egyptology

SOME OF MY CRITICS, notably the editors of BAR, desire to portray my work as exclusively focused on Egypt and Africa. These editors should have included an equivalent section on Syro-Palestine.[1] Nevertheless, it is true that I do see Egypt as central to the formation of Ancient Greece. Furthermore, much of my argument is based on Egyptian sources and I have spent a great deal of time and effort looking for evidence of Egyptian culture and language in Greece and Greek.

Though critical, the tone of the Egyptologists whose articles have been included in BAR is considerably more civil than that of the scholars from other disciplines. Much of this can be explained in purely personal terms. However, there are also structural reasons for this civility in that the ideas contained in *Black Athena* are less threatening to Egyptology than they are to Classics, Aegean archaeology, or the historiography of the ancient world. Before the fifth century B.C.E., Egypt had a far greater impact on Greece than vice versa. Thus, recognition of significantly closer relations between the two civilizations has a major impact on our understanding of Ancient Greece but a relatively minor one on the reconstruction of Ancient Egypt.

One reason I am particularly glad to be able to have calm debates with Egyptologists is because Egyptology was the first academic discipline with which I came into contact. My grandfather Alan Gardiner was not only an Egyptologist but he was a pioneer of Egyptology as a professional discipline. Having worked for many years in Berlin and in close contact with American colleagues, he introduced Germanic rigor and positivism into the previously amateurish Egyptology of France, England, and Wales. He used the Teutonic title Dr. when it was considered somehow foreign and vulgar at Oxford and Cambridge. He also made a clear demarcation between sound scholarship and unsound speculation. I experienced this personally when I was a child: he firmly warned me off reading "cranks" like Margaret Murray and "old-fashioned" scholars like Wallis Budge.

I now know that as a linguist, my grandfather had a bold and creative mind. However, as a child and a young man, I saw him as the model professional scholar, as opposed to my brilliant, wide-ranging, and controversial father, J. D. Bernal.[2] Knowing that I could not compete with my father, I found that my grandfather's professionalism had a considerable appeal to me as a strenuous but attainable goal. The fact that I never reached this in any discipline does not prevent me from feeling a fond familiarity with Egyptology and Egyptologists.

BAR contains three chapters by Egyptologists. I have replied to only two of them. The third, by Frank Yurco, contains some interesting challenges to the chronology I propose, but the bulk of the other issues he raises are covered in the chapters by John Baines and David O'Connor. More important, Yurco and I are largely in accord on the Africanity of Egypt. The writer Richard Poe, in his massive and fascinating work Black Spark, White Fire, which includes discussion of the struggles around Black Athena, finds it interesting that Yurco and I, with completely different backgrounds and diametrically opposed views on the Vietnam War, should be in such agreement about Egypt.[3]

Although we all agree that the issues are important and that there are significant differences between the two sides, as I have stated above, there is a civilized tone to the Egyptological debate. Baines, O'Connor, and I are, of course, united in our affection for if not love of Ancient Egypt. Furthermore, most Egyptologists acknowledge that the furor around Black Athena has increased general interest in their discipline. After years of decline, a number of new posts in Egyptology were created in the 1990s. Despite this growth, however, Egyptologists are terrified at nonprofessional interventions in their field, which has always been a fragile discipline set in a sea of "cranks." Many Egyptologists clearly put me in that category. As I went into the panel on my work at the annual conference of the American Research Center in Egypt (ARCE), I overheard someone say: "Now for some comic relief!" Others, like the contributors to BAR, take my work more seriously. They believe, however, that I have acted irresponsibly by encouraging cranks in general and Afrocentric cranks in particular.

Readers interested in the physical anthropology of the Ancient Egyptians will not find it in *Black Athena Writes Back*. For this they should turn to Shomarka Keita's substantial reply to the physical anthropologist Loring Brace's essay on the subject in BAR, which is included in *Debating Black Athena*. Although there is no discussion of bones and genes by the Egyptologists in BAR, these authors are unhappy at my use of the adjective "black." Unlike some critics, Baines and O'Connor have read my work carefully enough to realize that I have never suggested that the Ancient Egyptian population as a whole looked like stereotypical West Africans. Nevertheless, they find my statement that some dynasties and pharaohs can "usefully be described as black" to be distasteful. They argue that such categories make no sense biologically and were meaningless to the Ancient Egyptians themselves and, further, that my raising the issue exacerbates the tense situation between whites and blacks today.

As I have said and written a number of times, I should have preferred the title *African Athena*. On the other hand, I stand by my references to certain rulers as "usefully described as black." "Race" is certainly not a useful biological category, and until the Assyrian and Persian invasions in the first millennium B.C.E., it was not an issue for the Ancient Egyptians. However, it is a crucially important *social* classification for Europeans and North Americans today. Furthermore, *Black Athena* did not introduce the subject to Egyptology: it was always there. In later chapters of this book there are discussions of the nineteenth-century Abolitionists, who for their own political reasons insisted on the black pigmentation and "Negroid" features of the Ancient Egyptians.[4] By contrast, most Egyptologists formed before 1945 accepted the view held generally in the societies in which they lived that "Negroes" were categorically incapable of civilization. Thus, the extent to which the Ancient Egyptians were civilized was seen as the measure of their "whiteness." This belief has weakened since the 1960s, but it has not disappeared. It was for this reason that I have insisted that Ancient Egypt was both civilized and African and, further, that its population included some men and women of what we now think of as Central African appearance in politically and culturally important positions.

After this brief preamble, I should like to set out my individual replies, starting with that to the chapter by Professor Baines.

1 Can We Be Fair?

A REPLY TO JOHN BAINES

John Baines is not only professor of Egyptology at Oxford, more recently working at Harvard, but he had previously written two substantial essays on *Black Athena* II. The first of these appeared in the *New York Times* and the second was originally scheduled for a volume proposed as a publication for the American Research Center in Egypt on the basis of a session on *Black Athena* at the center's annual meeting in Berkeley in April 1990.[1] The volume, however, was scrapped at a late stage, and the editor, Antonio Loprieno, offered the papers responding to my work—though not my replies, which he also possessed—to Mary Lefkowitz and Guy Rogers for BAR. They accepted those by Baines and O'Connor.[2]

Baines's chapter in BAR is closely based on his second review. In his notes to the chapter, he scrupulously apologizes for reviewing the same book twice but justifies it by treating aspects of my work that he did not discuss in the earlier review. I must confess that I find this piece far more thoughtful and thought-provoking than the one in the *New York Times*. I am particularly impressed by the close attention to my work that this review shows. I shall respond to what I believe to be his main challenges in the order in which he raises them.

Baines's Introduction

In his introduction, Baines suggests that rather than attributing the apotheosis or idealization of the Ancient Greeks at the beginning of the nineteenth century to racism, one should attribute it to other factors. In general, as he puts it, "the emergence of Greece as an ideal was part of the incipient secularization of the Enlightenment and of Romanticism" (p. 28). In point of fact, I do not claim that racism was the sole factor in the downplaying of Egypt and the elevation of Greece in the early nineteenth century. I only maintain that it was one of many causes. I do, however, see racism as *a* significant initial factor and one that remained important until 1945. Furthermore, as I have stated in many places elsewhere, I believe that another of the initial factors was the revival of Christianity after 1815, which is precisely the opposite of the secularization that Baines proposes.

Furthermore, I do not accept the idea that many thinkers of the Enlightenment idealized Greece. Indeed, several of them preferred Egypt.[3] Love of Greece was very largely a romantic preserve. For some Romantics, like Shelley, this passion was linked to atheism, but for most eighteenth- and early-nineteenth-century Philhellenes, love of pagan Greece was paradoxically associated with passions for Europe as the Christian continent. With the general secularization from the end of the 1850s, Philhellenism became more detached from religion. Even after that period, Christian beliefs and a love of pagan Greece were quite compatible, as, for instance, in the English public schools (BA I: 320).

What I did underestimate was the appeal of a Greece of city states over the Roman and Egyptian "empires" to the progressive Northern European bourgeoisie; this appeal is epitomized by the work of George Grote.[4] However, here too one cannot dismiss the effect of romanticism and revived Christianity on the new historiography, not to mention the increasingly pervasive and systematic racism, which was particularly strong among the Northern European bourgeoisie.

The Argument of Black Athena, Volume 2

Immediately after his introduction, Baines sets out what he sees as the main points of BA II. Simplification is, of course, inevitable, but I find his restatement of some of my arguments too bald. For instance, I do not claim that "Egyptian temples were dedicated at Mycenae," I only refer to "possible foundations" (BA II: 478–479). Turning to another issue, he states, "In contrast with general practice, Bernal introduces authors with their ethnicity and often a sort of academic genealogy, and he frequently mobilizes these factors . . . in explaining, approving, or dismissing what they say. This quirk . . ." (p. 30). In point of fact, it is quite normal for historiographers to refer to a scholar's country of origin. John Baines himself is no exception. Take, for example, the three instances of this practice on a single page of his and Jaromir Málek's admirable *Atlas of Ancient Egypt*.[5] Presumably, these identifications are not merely mnemonic devices but are meant to convey something about the scholar concerned. It is also relatively common to refer to scholars' academic backgrounds. Indeed, most disciplines, including Egyptology, have biographical dictionaries in which nationality, academic formation, and the links among scholars are rightly emphasized.[6]

Where I go beyond the convention of Egyptology and Classics (though not that of other fields) is in stating publicly that I see the writing of history and other forms of scholarship as an intricate dialectic between the subjective predispositions of the scholar and the configuration of the object of study. Therefore, I believe one should attempt to take both into account. Naturally, I accept that my own situation and motives should also be scrutinized, and I have attempted to help in this analysis by making my conscious preferences clear. For example, I expressed my unhappiness at my conclusion that speakers of Hurrian and possibly even Indo-Aryan were present among the Hyksos when they conquered Egypt.

Methods and Theories

Baines shares the widespread uncertainty as to whether I believe contemporary classicists to be racist. I had thought that I had made my position clear on this point. For instance, in BA I, I wrote, "Muhly was undoubtedly right . . . to point out that the majority of modern Classicists do not share the racism and anti-Semitism endemic among their teachers and their teachers' teachers" (p. 422).

Baines raises the issue of the strategy, used by both conservatives and innovators, of legitimation through real or imagined ancestors. I certainly accept that some myths of origins are complete fictions (p. 31). I would agree, for instance, that it is unlikely that the Trojan prince Brutus sailed to South Devon and landed at Totnes, especially as the event was recorded by Geoffrey of Monmouth more than two thousand years after the alleged arrival. Other such myths, however, may contain genuine historical information. In the Eastern Mediterranean, given the relatively short distances involved together with the archaeological and, I would argue, linguistic evidence of contact, the stories of Hyksos settlements in Greece would seem plausible.

Many scholars today maintain that attempting to distinguish fact from fiction in myth is both futile and uninteresting.[7] They are concerned with the structure and contemporary function of myths. I do not challenge the significance of such concerns, but they are not mine. Given the unreliability and patchiness of other sources of information on the Bronze Age Aegean, I believe that one should use those elements of myths and legends with plausible historicity as aids in setting up working hypotheses to be tested in other ways. Obviously, I am not the first to do this. In the *Cambridge Ancient History*, for instance, Frank Stubbings uses precisely such a conjunction of tradition and archaeological evidence to set out his interpretation of the early Shaft Graves and the beginnings of the Mycenaean Period as the results of Hyksos conquests and settlements.[8]

On the issue of "blackness," Baines finds my attempts to establish the "paternity or maternity" of specific individuals distasteful, especially as this issue was of no concern to the Ancient Egyptians themselves. As I have written before, I am sympathetic to this view, especially because I too do not believe in the biological utility of the concept of "race."[9] As a social phenomenon, however, "race" is of overriding importance to anyone living at the turn of the twenty-first century. In particular, "blacks" are constantly being told explicitly or implicitly that "they" have never created a civilization and that, therefore, unless they accept European culture, they never will partake in civilization. Although I agree with Baines that Pharaonic Egypt was only one of a number of African civilizations, given the touted and real hegemony of European and Western civilization today, the role of Egypt in the formation of Ancient Greece gives Ancient Egypt a special significance. This fact is one reason why many American and British blacks are so eager to claim identification with Ancient Egypt. I believe that they are right to be indignant at the double standards applied to them and to the Ancient Egyptians. In the United States and Western Europe, "one drop of black blood" is enough to label someone a "black." However, when Ancient Egypt is viewed, no one is considered "black" unless he or she conforms to the European stereotype of a West African. Very few Ancient Egyptians would have been labeled "white" in nineteenth- or twentieth-century Britain or America.

I should have preferred this series of works to have been called "African Athena" because for Europeans and Euro-Americans, the word "black" conjures up a stereotype that is not appropriate for Egyptians. This, however, does not make them any less "African." [10] Hence, I accept that the title Black Athena is in some ways misleading. I do not, however, concede the same for my claim that the rulers of the Eleventh Dynasty were "black." The famous cult statue of Mentuhotpe II of that dynasty could have been painted black for many reasons. It could well have been to represent Osiris and the color of immortality, but that possibility does not rule out other factors. Before the rulers of the Eleventh Dynasty became pharaohs, the family had ruled the Theban nome or district in the south of Upper Egypt. As nomarchs or local rulers, the family had close relations with Nubia, and it is interesting to note that some of Mentuhotpe's wives are also represented as having black skin. [11] Thus, one cannot assume that the blackness of the pharaoh's miniature statue was purely the result of religious symbolism.

Baines's main question, however, is why I should have stressed the "blackness" of these pharaohs. I did it to counterbalance early-twentieth-century Egyptologists' emphasis on the image of Ancient Egyptians and their rulers as real or imagined northerners or "whites," and the continuing influence this image has in popular representations of Egyptians. [12] Take, for example, the straight-nosed sphinx at Las Vegas. At another level, there are the illustrations of the children's book Gods and Pharaohs from Egyptian Mythology by David O'Connor (not the Egyptologist of that name) with text by the Egyptologist Geraldine Harris, which consistently portray Egyptians as made-up Europeans. [13] Indeed, its striking cover and frontispiece is of a pharaoh with blue eyes and the features of the evangelist Billy Graham! The cover of the sophisticated board game Civilization, which was clearly developed in close consultation with archaeologists, features pyramids, a palm-fringed river with a felucca, the Acropolis, and Vesuvius. The center is dominated by the face of a bearded Greek Zeus/philosopher. Behind him to one side is a blond, blue-eyed Roman, and on the other side a gray-eyed, auburn-haired Cleopatra figure who makes Elizabeth Taylor look Mediterranean! In such a cultural environment, I believe it is useful to emphasize that the Ancient Egyptians were African.

Baines points out that my earlier work on China shows that I am extremely interested in some non-European civilizations for their own sake and not simply for their contributions to the development of "Western" civilization.[14] In general, I do not see why concern with the Egyptian and Phoenician roles in the emergence and flowering of Ancient Greece should be seen as diminishing respect for other African cultures. My books are not world histories; they are treatments of one particular historical theme. I concede that my choice of this theme is Eurocentric. Given the hegemonic position of European culture in the world today, I am convinced that this choice is a particularly important one.

Baines writes that I have "little to prove" and that "few will deny" that the Aegean was part of a wider cultural and economic Eastern Mediterranean region. I completely agree that recent archaeological discoveries are making denial of this position increasingly untenable. However, the isolationism of archaeologists and historians of the Ancient Aegean is deep-rooted and remarkably impervious to contrary evidence. The disgraceful treatment of the work of Gordon, Astour, and Bass on Semitic influences on the Aegean did not end in the 1960s.[15] Nevertheless, since the mid-1980s a movement, in which Black Athena has played a role, has opened up the possibility of substantial contacts around the Eastern Mediterranean during the Bronze Age. The one area where the old isolationist faith persists is that of language. If few now deny that Egypt and the Levant had close relations with the Aegean, the obdurate refusal to consider the possibility of substantial linguistic borrowing from Egyptian and West Semitic into Greek, seen clearly in the BAR chapter by Jasanoff and Nussbaum, becomes increasingly anomalous.

I agree with Baines (p. 41) that the "special relationship" between Byblos and Egypt indicates that Egyptian relations with other parts of Syro-Palestine were not equally close. I would maintain, however, that part of the difference lies in the length and continuity of the Byblian connection, whereas that between Egypt and other Canaanite cities was more episodic. When discussing the New Kingdom, we might differ on the semantic field of the word "colonial," but I would find it appropriate for the situation presupposed in the *Amarna Letters* as well as from evidence produced by excavations in Gaza, Aphek, Beth Shan, and elsewhere. Intense contact is also indicated linguistically by the Egyptian influence on Canaanite and vice versa.[16]

Although the situation in the Levant during the Middle Kingdom is less clear-cut, Baines states that most scholars now see more Egyptian influence there in this period "than would have been envisaged a generation ago" (p. 33). Naturally, I welcome this retreat from minimalism, but Baines is quite right to suppose that I find even the new cautious approach inadequate. It seems to me not only that Giveon's and Posener's maximalist views on Middle Kingdom influence in Syro-Palestine are plausible in themselves but also that, as the previous minimalist the late Wolfgang Helck generously conceded, their arguments have been powerfully reinforced by the Mit Rahineh inscription.[17] I do not, however, see a "colonial" situation at this stage; rather, I see a "zone of influence" within which some places such as Byblos and Sinai were under Egyptian administration but where most cities and districts were relatively independent, merely accepting Egyptian suzerainty. This position is not far from Baines's perception of "cultural dominance" (p. 33).

Incidentally, I do not understand why, in the absence of political or historical documents, Baines should maintain (p. 29) that it is reprehensible to seek information from contemporary fiction. In this case, I have referred to the well-known *Story of Sinuhe*, which, though fictional and unusual, resembles an official autobiography in form and contains at least some verifiable historical facts. As the Egyptologist and translator Miriam Lichtheim puts it, "It is the story of a life as it could have been lived. In fact it may be a true story. . . . Whether or not it relates the actual experience of an individual, the story reflects a true historical situation."[18]

I accept what Baines says about the relative fluidity of Mesopotamian cultural boundaries as compared to those of Egypt, but he goes too far when he links this to a belief that Mesopotamia "was much more generally influential in the ancient Near East" (p. 34). Mesopotamian influence was certainly strong in Anatolia and in some parts of the Levant. We should not forget, however, that most of our information from the Levant in the second millennium comes from Ugarit and the Israelite tradition, the two corners of the Levant with the least Egyptian influence. The cities on the coast, especially Byblos, were much more heavily Egyptianized. It was for this reason the Israelites saw them and the Canaanites as sons of Ham

(Genesis 10). The Egyptianized cities of the central Levant are particularly significant for my project because it was from, or through, them that most contact was made between the Aegean and the Near East.

I do not agree with Baines that as a partial consequence of Egyptian stability and homogeneity "many Egyptian cultural traits did not travel well" (p. 34). For most of its history, Chinese civilization has had a similar homogeneity and self-absorption. These characteristics, however, have not inhibited the spread of its culture to surrounding countries and, in some respects, around the world. It is also generally acknowledged that Egyptian culture spread south to Nubia and Meroe. The linguistic influence of Egyptian on the development of Canaanite was mentioned above. In later periods, it is universally agreed that such things as the calendar and Egyptian religion spread around the Mediterranean and beyond. Evidence of Egyptian cultural diffusion in the Bronze Age is also generally accepted. Few doubt that Egyptian influences on Minoan architecture and painting and later influences on Archaic and Classical Greek sculpture were substantial. Widely recognized Egyptian sources for significant Greek literary themes, notably the Trojan Horse and the blessings of Pandora, are discussed in chapter 14 below.

Furthermore, abundant Greek testimony specifies Egypt, rather than Mesopotamia, as the source of religion, justice, and knowledge. Though other factors have been involved, I believe that the most important reason for the de-emphasis of the Egyptian cultural effects on Greece in nineteenth- and twentieth-century scholarship comes from the sociology of knowledge. Babylonia has had its academic champions, especially since the discovery of the non-Semitic-speaking Sumerians (BA I: 354–366). Egypt, in contrast, apart from a flurry over Akhenaten, has not. Paradoxically, the very fact that Classical and Hellenistic Greeks emphasized the importance of Egypt in the formation of their culture has lessened credibility among modern scholars for whom *Besserwisserei* or "knowing better" than the Ancients has become a touchstone of their "scientific" status.[19]

Agendas and Methods of Ancient Near East Specialists

I find this section of John Baines's essay sensitive and thoughtful. Naturally, I agree with him that whether they are conscious of it or not, all scholars have preferences or "agendas." In this, of course, Baines's views are diametrically opposed to those of Lefkowitz and Rogers. I am also convinced that, on the whole, such preferences should be made explicit. I do not accept the contrary argument that the claim of objectivity and detachment and the need to keep up appearances on these fronts can help one move toward them. The losses from the basic falsehood of this latter position are greater than the gains, though the debate on this issue is not entirely one-sided.

Baines criticizes works by Edward Said and me for our treatment of earlier scholars and a tendency "to suffer from not adopting rules of interpretation that would normally apply to the study of alien periods or cultural contexts: that the interpreter should seek to comprehend evidence in context and to identify positive aspects of what the material under study was meant to achieve. Instead these works are often exercises in putting people from contexts other than those of today in the dock and judging them by anachronistic criteria" (p. 35).

To begin with a lesser point, I do not think it fair to accuse me of failing to appreciate the great achievements of earlier scholars, for I have spoken of my admiration for them in this volume and throughout my work. On the major issue, I think I can speak for both Said and myself when I insist that we are both acutely concerned with the historical, social, and political contexts of the earlier scholars. Indeed, as mentioned above, Baines has criticized me for overemphasizing such contexts. Said and I agree entirely with Baines's description of these scholars as belonging to "alien periods or cultural contexts." It is in fact precisely this issue that we try to bring out against the defenders of the traditional disciplines who want to portray the earlier scholars as dispassionate authorities who should be accepted as such in the contemporary world.

Despite this fundamental agreement with Said, there are also important differences between our approaches. In the first place, his work is literary and allusive, whereas mine is historical and pedestrian. More important, I do not accept his view that Orientalism, or, for that matter, ancient history, is almost entirely self-referential. As I stated above, although I believe in the critical importance of the sociology of knowledge, I am not a complete relativist. I do believe that there are objective constraints on what can be plausibly maintained, though I am convinced that the Aryan model has stretched such constraints to their utmost limits.

Baines suggests that I should not discriminate between the subjectivity of archaeologists and the observations of natural scientists on the issue of chronology. I am sorry that I did not make myself clear on this issue. The "naïve open-mindedness" I referred to applied only to the scientists' chronological conclusions. My impression is that the natural scientists are not very interested in the large stakes archaeologists and historians place on particular chronologies. I have no doubt that they are fighting their own methodological and technical battles with passions and prejudices equal to those of the archaeologists. They are, however, more detached about the resulting chronologies, which are not central to their concerns.

I concede that if I were to pronounce on the dating of the Middle Kingdom, I should have gone into the technicalities of the arguments between Krauss and Parker. Any cynical reader will have gathered my reasons for preferring the earlier chronology: I wanted a longer Second Intermediate Period. My general observation that the dates found by radiocarbon, dendrochronology, and other "scientific" measures generally tend to be "higher" or earlier than the conventional ones reinforced this desire. Baines dislikes my view that twentieth-century scholars feel pressure "to downdate" (p. 36). I developed the idea of a "minimalist ratchet," in which I saw scholars competing with each other to be more cautious and skeptical than their predecessors. This was to explain why the new datings from the natural sciences tend to correspond more closely with the chronologies set out at the beginning of the twentieth century than they do with those in fashion eighty years later. Therefore, I stand by my statement:

> Since the First World War, archaeologists and ancient historians have intensified their struggle to achieve "scientific" status. Their drive can be expressed as the desire to be "sounder than thou." Cautious and conservative scholars became terrified above all of the accusation of *being speculative*. At the same time, they were expected to be innovative. In this situation, the only room for innovation was to be hypercritical of every form of evidence but particularly of that from ancient documentary sources. Thus, they have tended to limit all ancient claims in both space and time. (BA II: p. 208)

This passage was written without any knowledge of the project that has resulted in the book *Centuries of Darkness*. In this volume, the editor Peter James and his colleagues propose an almost Velikovskyan attack on the concept of the so-called Dark Ages around the Eastern Mediterranean between the "Invasions of the Sea Peoples" in the thirteenth and twelfth centuries B.C.E. and the rise of Archaic Greece in the eighth. The young scholars attempt to cut out most of these centuries.[20] Scholarly authorities generally consider that the drastic lowering of dates undertaken by James and his colleagues went too far, and the conventional wisdom on chronology has been maintained, buttressed by radiocarbon dating and dendrochronology. Nevertheless, I see *Centuries of Darkness* as an extreme example of the "minimalist ratchet" at work. Its authors are Young Turks trying to be iconoclastic while not jeopardizing their professional and scientific status by being too "speculative."

In the short review of BA II in *Antiquity*, the anonymous reviewer complains rather charmingly, "Bernal has the alarming habit of being right for the wrong reasons." [21] Conversely, James and his colleagues could be seen by their seniors as having been wrong for the right reasons. In any event, as Baines states (p. 37), the minor arguments over a few decades in the Middle Kingdom are much less significant than my partial acceptance of the radical updating of the Old Kingdom made by Herbert Haas and his team. I do not go into the physics of the debate because I, like most Egyptologists, am not competent to do so. I did not, however, accept the conclusions of the Swiss and Texans merely because their dating was higher, coinciding with James Mellaart's interpretation of the radiocarbon dates, or because they were natural scientists "uncontaminated" by Egyptology—though I must confess that these factors inclined me in their direction. [22] I found them convincing for two reasons. First, higher Old Kingdom dates made sense of the synchronisms with Syro-Palestine and Mesopotamia. At the great Syrian city of Ebla, the higher Egyptian dating would resolve a bitter dispute on the date of destruction of the palace of level IIB1 and its sensational archive. The higher dates also would make better sense of synchronisms at Byblos, explaining why Fifth and Sixth Dynasty objects are found in level KIV, which is followed by a destruction. Only in level JI, which was reconstructed after an indeterminate period, have objects from the Sargon's empire at Akkad been found. [23] In contrast, the lack of synchronisms between Old Kingdom Egypt and Sargonic Mesopotamia would seem surprising if these two vast empires had been contemporary.

My second reason for preferring the views of Haas and his colleagues was the implausible degree to which twentieth-century Egyptology had compressed the First Intermediate Period. I have been pestering my Egyptological friends on this issue, and without exception they have replied that they would be quite happy to see it reinflated by one or two centuries. Such reinflation would explain the many pharaohs listed for the Ninth and Tenth Dynasties as well as the long dynasties of nomarchs between the end of the Old and the beginning of the Middle Kingdom. The artistic and other cultural changes between the two kingdoms are also difficult to explain in an intermission of less than a century. Thus, my choice of Haas's chronology was based on what seems to me to be a clear case of competitive plausibility.

I am delighted that Baines, with his infinitely greater knowledge of the field, agrees with me on the pernicious effects of evolutionism in the study of Egyptian literature, and I thank him for the references here (p. 37). As he surmises, I was unaware of most of them.

I do realize that fields are not monolithic and that scholars of the same generation may be working along very different lines. Nevertheless, I find it helpful to look for general trends in scholarship that often cut across perceived debates and personal feuds. Incidentally, I believe that offering the perspective given by distance is an important way an outsider can be of service to a specialized field.

Baines criticizes my inability or unwillingness to follow modern archaeologists in their sophisticated studies of social change. In particular, he appears to be concerned about my diffusionism. My second volume, however, is dedicated to Gordon Childe not as a diffusionist but "as a champion of modified diffusionism" (emphasis added). Of course, I accept that unless there is genocide, local selection and adaptation of the foreign culture must be taken into account.

I discuss my skepticism on the possibility of Egyptian colonization in third millennium Boiotia and second millennium Crete and my greater willingness to consider Hyksos settlements the Eastern Peloponnese and Eighteenth Dynasty suzerainty over the Aegean in chapters 3 and 4 below.[24] None of these trajectories, however, represents sustained Egyptian colonization of the type found in, for instance, Kerma, the Kushite states, Byblos at most times, and other parts of Syro-Palestine during the New Kingdom. As I see it, the sporadic nature of the Egyptian dominance in the Aegean, the frequent mediation of the Levant in Egyptian contacts with the Aegean, and the resilience of local culture made it possible for a hybrid and distinctive Greek civilization to emerge. Such a picture allows for substantial Egyptian cultural and linguistic influence without the massive archaeological testimony of Egyptian presence found in zones of sustained colonization.

As I mentioned earlier, the analogy I have found useful in looking at the relations of Egypt and the Levant with Greece is that of China and Japan. In the Japanese case, although it is possible that the imperial dynasty was established by Koreans, mainland influence on Japan after the dynasty's foundation was purely economic and cultural. The nature of this influence means that there are no substantial architectural Chinese remains on the archipelago comparable to those found in Korea and Vietnam, which for several centuries were incorporated into the Chinese empire. Furthermore, no one can claim that Japan is simply a reflection or projection of China. It would be absurd, however, to analyze or understand Japanese culture without constant reference to China. Yet, Hellenists and Aegeanists have, until very recently, employed this type of exclusion in the case of Greece.

Baines argues, "For the third millennium and early Iron Age Aegean, complex societies that would have assimilated more than stray items of high-cultural foreign influence are not apparent" (p. 38). I do not accept that EHII Greece of the mid–third millennium was a simple society.[25] It is true, however, that society in the Early Iron Age Aegean was less complex. Baines argues that "it would have had no use for writing and the alphabet" (p. 38). The breakdown in the Aegean at the end of the Bronze Age was certainly no greater than that after the fall of the Roman Empire in Western Europe, where, despite an undoubted increase in illiteracy, writing was preserved and continued to be used.

I maintain further that toward the end of the "Dark Ages" in the tenth and ninth centuries B.C.E. a massive cultural influence from Phoenicia led to the establishment of the new social order of the polis and the economic system of "Slave Society." [26] As I mentioned above, however, I believe that much of the Levantine and Egyptian material in Hesiod and Homer can be more plausibly explained as having arrived in the Late Bronze Age, when Greek society was undoubtedly more complex. Thus, one way or another, I see no reason to restrict "high-cultural foreign influence" on Greece to "stray items."

One key difference between Baines and me is precisely on the degree of cultural continuity across the "Dark Ages." No one contests the continuity of language and place-names. Many of the cities and religious cults remained the same throughout this period. Furthermore, I maintain— and Baines provides no reasons for denying it—that the alphabet survived throughout this period (p. 28).[27]

All in all, despite the undoubted breakdown of Mycenaean society and the many centuries of instability following, there was less of a cultural break in the Aegean between 1100 and 800 B.C.E. than there was in Western Europe between 540 and 800 C.E.[28] As considerable written records and memories survived the latter *coupure*, I see absolutely no case for maintaining a categorical disjuncture between the Bronze and Iron Age Aegean.

When Baines states, "Bernal requires Aegean societies to have assimilated and retained influences from abroad across changes that would have left those influences without meaning for the actors" (p. 38), he misses the meaning of the word "assimilated." The Egyptian and Semitic words and cultural features absorbed during the Bronze Age became *assimilated* to Mycenaean culture as a whole. Thus, for instance, if Greek cults had received Egyptian or Syro-Palestinian influences during the Bronze Age, why should these have been discarded and "native" ones retained? Of course, some rituals, symbols, and words, both native and "borrowed" or "copied," changed their meaning in the changed society. No sign of a movement for Hellenic purification, however, can be found in the early Iron Age analogous to the *katharevousa* ("purification") attempted for Modern Greek since the eighteenth century C.E.

It is all too true that I have not taken advantage of the sophisticated theoretical models now current in archaeology. At one level, I regret this lapse. On the other hand, I could never have begun, let alone carried out, this ambitious project if I had tried to incorporate all the complexities of modern archaeological theory into it. Furthermore, this failure is at least part of the complaint about my "alarming habit of being right for the wrong reasons." One reason for the "alarm" would seem to come from my apparent success with such crude methods and the extent to which they cast doubt on the superior utility of the sophisticated ones.[29]

In this regard, I am puzzled by Baines's question, "Is there . . . some crucial flaw in the approaches of specialists engaged with the Ancient Near East, who are often not self-critical in their examination of their own political or other agendas, that renders their work unsuited to studying Aegean–Near Eastern relations?" (p. 39). In the first place, I do not make such a blanket assertion. Gordon and Astour are specialists in the Middle East and I have an enormous admiration for their work. Likewise, I have great respect for the Egyptologist Siegfried Morenz's work on the relations between Egypt and Greece. On the second point, I think that Baines provides a partial explanation for the general failure among Near Eastern specialists to see connections with the Aegean, when he says that "this question is far from the research interests of many scholars." Baines continues: "To establish his case that their understanding of historical events has been fatally compromised, Bernal would need to show either that they [the Near Eastern scholars] were so thoroughly subjugated intellectually by Classicists that they could not use their evidence properly, or that their methods enacted the supremacist agendas of others." As he says, I try to set out the existence of such a dominance by the discipline of Classics in volume 1. It should be pointed out here that I do not see the development of the Aryan model as a "conspiracy" but as a broadly based intellectual movement. The few deviations have not blunted the general ideological thrust of the eighteenth, nineteenth, and twentieth centuries that "civilization" is and always has been a European monopoly.

Institutionally, there is an inherent plausibility that the establishment of Classics at the heart of the cult of Europe, and of the "humanities" as a whole, should have overawed the small communities of Semitists and Egyptologists studying "exotic" cultures at the fringes of the university. Thus, I do not take trivially the statement by the early-twentieth-century Egyptologist Alan Gardiner that "Classical scholars have not in the past taken kindly to the idea of Hellenic dependence on Egyptian civilization" (see BA I: 265). At an anecdotal level, Gardiner (who was my grandfather) told me I was not to study Egyptian until I had learned Greek, which I never did to his satisfaction! Gardiner was typical of his generation. The situation has clearly eased now, but I am not convinced that the imbalance has disappeared, and even today Egyptologists necessarily rely on the works of Gardiner and his generation formed in the period of the domination of Classics.

I shall not repeat all the examples of the scholarly and personal weakness of Semitists in the face of the Classical establishment in the late nineteenth and twentieth centuries. The success of Rhys Carpenter's amateurish and extreme views on the alphabet over those of the Semitic paleographers is merely the most striking example of this phenomenon.[30] A more recent example is the battering given to Cyrus Gordon and Michael Astour in the 1960s and 1970s, when they suggested that the Levant and Aegean cultures were fundamentally connected. I show elsewhere in this volume that George Bass still bears scars from the treatment he received when he tried to make the same case on archaeological grounds.[31]

In 1992 the broad-minded classicist Walter Burkert referred to the dominance of his discipline and the use of the power this position gave to minimize or exclude ideas of Oriental influence on Greece when he wrote in the preface of the English translation of his *Orientalizing Revolution*: "My thesis about the indebtedness of Greek civilization to eastern stimuli may appear less provocative today than it did eight years ago. This change may be partly an effect of the original publication, but mainly it reflects the fact that Classics has been losing more and more its status of a solitary model in our modern world."[32] If one takes Baines at his word, such indications of the inordinate power of Classics should explain scholars' failure to see the extent of relations between the Ancient Near East and the Aegean. I believe, however, that I can go beyond his requirements and provide internal reasons why specialists in the Ancient Near East should have wanted to keep the two regions separate. It is precisely because they have not, to use Baines's phrase, "been working in an intellectual vacuum." The academic environment puts a high value on "turf," or private scholarly property, and "poaching" is strictly sanctioned. Men and women from subordinate fields who encroach on the territories of superior disciplines are punished with particular severity.[33] Such defense of academic property has been reinforced by a general intellectual atmosphere of extreme isolationism, which is only now beginning to moderate.

I am inclined to see tight interconnections around the Eastern Mediterranean in the Bronze and Iron Ages simply because of their inherent plausibility. Additionally, the excesses of academic independent yeomanry and isolationism of such influential scholars as Colin Renfrew have added plausibility to this scheme.[34] Finally, I am more convinced by the work of Ullman, Gordon, Astour, Bass, and now scholars like Ruth Edwards, Patricia Bikai, Walter Burkert, Sarah Morris, and Eric Cline, who have emphasized early contact around the Eastern Mediterranean, than I am by the orthodox scholars of the mid–twentieth century who have played down such interconnections or denied them altogether.

Implications of Bernal's Methods

I have stated above and in many other places my position on the functions, uses, and limitations of myth.[35] In the case of Egypt, I am convinced that Egyptologists know things about Egyptian social structure, urban planning, and the early dynasties of which the Ancient Egyptians themselves were unaware. But the reverse is even more true: many features of Egyptian culture can never be reconstructed from this distance.

Baines argues that I am mistaken when I attempt to establish a narrative for such a long period of time and over such a wide area. As he describes this aspect of my work: "Narratives are what the evidence supports least effectively, so that he builds his edifice on the most difficult ground. His narrative spans well over a millennium—probably more than a narrative can effectively span and more than the actors can perceive as a coherent entity" (p. 42).

To deal with the second issue first, peoples living in more or less stable societies can perceive their societies in terms of millennia. This ability is true today in China and was true among the elite in Egypt. Even Romans were able to view their history with long-range perspective and celebrated the thousandth year of the city's foundation.

On the more general issue of my use of narrative as opposed to more "theoretically rigorous" approaches, first, I must plead that my narratives are always tentative and open to revision; second, I am convinced that narratives are more heuristically productive than theoretical models, which are often too intricate and complex to falsify. I am convinced by Francis Bacon's aphorism that "truth emerges more readily from error than from confusion." [36]

Baines also accuses me of Carlylean tendencies in my emphasis on great conquerors (p. 43). Although I do not shy from using the names of rulers and, sometimes, from speculating on their motives, I do not want to neglect economic, social, institutional, and political forces. Furthermore, although much historiography has exaggerated the importance of "great men," this does not mean that their historical significance should be dismissed. Though Lenin depended on the collapse of Russia in 1917, Mao on that of China in the 1920s and 1930s, and Hitler on the crisis in German sociopsychological culture, all three helped shape the events that followed. I stressed what I saw to be the role of Senwosret I.

Incidentally, I referred to the violence of Senwosret/Sesōstris' conquests and not that of other conquerors because, given the general, though mistaken, perception of my work as Afrocentric, I wanted to emphasize that I see being slaughtered by Africans as no better than being slaughtered by Europeans or Asians.

Egyptian Social and Intellectual Context

As I stated above, I do not contend that the Egyptians were particularly concerned with the Aegean or deny that, in general, they were more preoccupied with territories to the south. Nor do I disagree with Baines that during the Eighteenth Dynasty, Egyptian rulers relied as much on diplomacy as force of arms. Indeed, as I have stated, they also used economic carrots and sticks (BA II: 482–489). Egypt, however, did not have to focus its attention on the Aegean to have a major effect on the region. Think of the devastating influence of the United States on the Carribean during a century when its foreign policy has been focused on Europe and the Far East.

Baines argues that I should not claim that minor Egyptian deities could have influenced the Aegean. This argument raises a major issue of method, as did Baines's questions regarding whether Greek society at various stages was *sufficiently elaborate to absorb* Egyptian culture. Should one look for what an ancient people could have known, or for what they did know? Obviously, one cannot remove the first question entirely from one's mind. For instance, I should have to see remarkably strong evidence to convince me that the Ancient Egyptians possessed atomic power. On the other hand, the question of what a people *could have known* does interpose an unnecessary veil of subjectivity between the historian and the people she or he is studying. For instance, the understanding of Maya mathematics only came about when scholars stopped asking What could the Maya have known? and asked instead What did the Maya know?[37] The Greek cults and mythological names referring to lesser Egyptian deities indicate one of two things: the lesser deities may have been more popular at certain times and in certain places than modern scholars have supposed, or, if these deities really were relatively unimportant, the intimacy of cultural relations between Egypt and the Aegean is clearly indicated.

In the case Baines raises, Mont was not a second-rate deity in the twenty-first century B.C.E. when the Cretan bull cults first appeared, but one intimately connected both with the dynasty of the time (the Eleventh) and with northern conquest. Furthermore, the most probable reason why Rʿt/Ria was chiefly, though not exclusively, attested in the Theban nome was precisely because she was the consort of Mont, whose worship was also centered there. Rʿt/Ria was later assimilated to Nut, who in Hellenistic times was seen as the counterpart of Rhea. Baines wishes to dismiss this assimilation as a "crossword puzzle," but it is an intricate one that should be seen in the double context of known Cretan contact with Egypt in the Bronze Age and the absence of any Indo-European origin for the goddess or etymology for her name. I am interested to know why he should find the proposal so incredible or distressing.

Conclusion

I think Baines has put his finger on a basic contradiction in my work when he questions the "outrages" I list in the conclusion to the second volume of *Black Athena*. He asks whether I want to persuade scholars or to convince nonspecialists that I am overthrowing a model or paradigm. This inconsistency is related to my uncertainties about readership. Volume 1 was written with the "cultivated lay public" in mind, whereas volume 2 is clearly more specialized. Because of this, the tone of the latter is, in general, rather less polemical, as I aim to persuade some of the experts on specific points or at least shake their faith in conventional wisdom.

The listing of the "outrages" was, as I stated, to indicate to the nonspecialist the degree to which certain arguments in the book were orthodox and others went against the scholarly status quo. I must confess, however, that the list showed a certain amount of what I now see to have been unnecessary provocation to specialist readers. I did want to signal to them, however, that I am not content with promoting reform or incremental change. The new wine will not fit in the old bottles. Scholars cannot simply go on making exceptions to a pattern of basic isolation of the Aegean from Egypt and the Levant. From the outset of my project I was convinced that our thinking about the Eastern Mediterranean in the Bronze and Early Iron Ages had to change fundamentally, and that all aspects—material culture, art, religion, *and language*—of the three major civilizations on its shores should constantly be seen in conjunction with each other. Now, more than ten years after the publication of the first volume of *Black Athena*, such views are being widely expressed. As the classicist and archaeologist Paul Rehak put it in a review of recent works on connections around the Eastern Mediterranean in the second millennium B.C.E.: "We have much to rethink in the way we analyze evidence and construct models for interpreting these data. Contacts cannot simply be looked at in terms of unidirectional trade, or from the view of one culture alone. . . . Instead, the multidirectional nature of trade requires a different kind of scholarship, one in which students must become cognizant in several cultures without privileging one culture over another."[38]

Once again, I should like to thank John Baines for the obvious care and thought he has put into considering my work.

2 Greece Is Not Nubia

A REPLY TO DAVID O'CONNOR

David O'Connor is not merely an Egyptologist of distinction but also a specialist in relations between Ancient Egypt and the lands farther up the Nile. His knowledge of Egyptian relations with other cultures abundantly qualifies him to comment on my hypotheses on Egyptian contacts with Greece. I thank O'Connor for his generous and, from my point of view, constructive chapter. I especially appreciate the allowances he makes for constant changes in our understanding of the Ancient Near East and Eastern Mediterranean and the need to rethink our historical structures imposed by new discoveries (p. 50).

O'Connor questions what he sees as my general credulity. He is especially concerned with my consideration of the possibility of Twelfth Dynasty expeditions to Asia Minor and with my belief that there may be some substance to the reports by Herodotus, Manetho, and Diodorus Siculus that the pharaoh they called Sesōstris or Sesoôsis made extensive campaigns to the north beyond Syria. Sesōstris is generally agreed to be a conflation of

Senwosrets I and III, with emphasis on the former. In *Black Athena* I do not argue, as O'Connor claims (p. 51), that I see these expeditions as having reached, let alone affected, the Aegean. I see that merely as a possibility (BA II: 234–235).

The possibility of extensive campaigns in Southwest Asia has been a closed matter for two hundred years, but it was recently reopened by reports of the Mit Rahineh inscription. I am glad that O'Connor has joined Farag, Posener, Giveon, and Helck in accepting that the inscription is from the Twelfth Dynasty, rather than following Ward's improbable hypothesis that it was a Ramessid forgery.[1] The interesting and, to my mind, most impressive case is that of the previously minimalist Helck accepting, with the broadmindedness of a great scholar, evidence against his long-held convictions.

O'Connor does not mention that Helck identified the cities named in the inscription as i3sy and iw3i as Alashia and the Cilician port of Ura. The first would seem unexceptionable, although there is the unsolved problem of where Alashia was. I am orthodox in this respect in seeing it as Cyprus. In any event it, like Ura, is not in Syria.

I think there is another, admittedly remote, possibility that iw3i, like the later w3iwry on the statue base of Amenophis III, could be identified with Ilion/Troy. In any event, I believe that the metal-producing country of Ṯmp3w mentioned on the Mit Rahineh inscription should be identified with the biblical Tubal and the Assyrian Tabalum, the home of smiths, situated somewhere in central Anatolia. It is difficult to understand why O'Connor should describe it as "probably Levantine," as no similar name has been found in the extensive Egyptian and Syrian toponomy of Syro-Palestine. Finally, there is the name Stt; presumably, O'Connor means Ṣtt. Ṣtt is difficult to locate, but in the New Kingdom at least it was certainly placed to the north of Syro-Palestine.

In this way, the Twelfth Dynasty inscription would tend to back the Greek writers' contention that Sesōstris marched through "Asia" if one accepts as a reasonable assumption that in these contexts, Herodotus meant by Asia what we now call Asia Minor. Diodorus appears to have understood Asia in a continental sense, including Mesopotamia and lands further east. It would seem to be this understanding together with the Egyptian desire to outdo Alexander the Great that led to his claiming that Sesōstris had conquered India. Diodorus' Indian claim was contested in Antiquity, but, as far as we know, those of Herodotus were not.

The coincidence of evidence from Herodotus and the Mit Rahineh inscription by no means clinches the case, but it does justify trying it out as a working hypothesis. No doubt, marching through Anatolia and possibly around the Black Sea and through the western Caucasus would have been an immensely difficult undertaking, worth remembering for two thousand years. On the other hand, world history offers parallel long marches in the supposed conquests of Sargon the Great and the undoubted ones of Cyrus, Alexander, and the Chinese communists. None of these had transport superior to that possessed by Middle Kingdom Egypt, nor did they have equal possibilities of supply and reinforcement by sea. Furthermore, O'Connor and others have published evidence on the massive fortifications on the second cataract of the Nile, and expeditions to the south clearly demonstrate that Middle Kingdom armies had the military capacity to undertake such expeditions.

The geographical possibility and the military capability merely form a sine qua non; they do not demonstrate that the expeditions actually took place. Some pieces of evidence, apart from the tradition and the inscription, do suggest this, however. First is a series of destructions across central Anatolia and Thrace apparently in the late twentieth century B.C.E. These destructions can be dated both by synchronisms with correspondence between Assyria and its merchant colony at the city now known as Kültepe II and by Twelfth Dynasty objects found at the destruction levels of other sites (BA II: 218–223).

The second archaeological indication comes from the Tôd Treasure dating to the reign of Amenemḥet II, who was referred to on the Mit Rahineh inscription along with his father, Senwosret I (the Greek Sesōstris) as having carried out the expeditions by land and sea. The treasure consists of gold and silver, much of the latter coming from Anatolia and, as O'Connor has added, from the Aegean as well. The lapis lazuli in the treasure, almost certainly brought in through Assyria, and scores of flattened silver bowls of Anatolian and Aegean designs—some of the closest parallels seem to come from Kültepe II.[2] Possibly, these could have been acquired by trade, but circumstantial evidence indicates the bowls were military plunder. It is interesting and, I maintain, significant that the treasure was dedicated to Mont, the deity of northern conquest.[3]

The third indication of Egyptian activity so far afield is the shift in the center of metallurgy that took place in the late twentieth and early nineteenth centuries B.C.E. Before the shift, Anatolia and the Caucasus, with their abundant supplies of metals, had housed the most skillful metalworkers in the Middle East. After the shift, the center of such skills moved to the Levant. Furthermore, Egyptian metalwork developed greatly during this period. The archaeologist of Ugarit, Claude Schaeffer, once attributed the shift to a great earthquake in the southern Caucasus.[4] It is more likely to have come from a political upheaval of the type that would have been caused by Egyptian military campaigns passing through the region. Much of the booty reported on the Mit Rahineh inscription consisted of metal and slaves from these places, thus providing a possible explanation for the shift of the centers of metallurgy into areas of Egyptian control or influence.

The fourth indication of such expeditions comes from the figures of "Smiting Gods" wearing either the Heḍet (white) or the Seḫemty (double) crowns found throughout Syro-Palestine and Anatolia from the beginning of the second millennium. The similarity between representations of the Syrian Baˁal or the Anatolian Tarkhun and the iconography of Middle Kingdom pharaohs is—dare I say it—striking.[5] This could well be the result of Twelfth Dynasty campaigns in *both* regions.

The fifth indication comes from the well-attested tradition at Colchis, at the east end of the Black Sea, that their city had been founded by Sesōstris or another Egyptian pharaoh.

Finally, there is another mythological tradition, that of Memnōn. This tradition is complicated by an Elamite connection, but strong grounds exist for associating him with Upper Egypt and specifically with the pharaohs named Amenemḥet, and, as mentioned above, Amenemḥet II can be connected to the expeditions.

Thus, evidence from a contemporary inscription, archaeology in Egypt and Anatolia, iconography, and two other legendary traditions support Herodotus' story. I think it is less cumbersome to link these clues and accept the tradition than to deny it and leave the traditions and finds unexplained. Thus, although all this does not *prove* the historicity of Sesōstris' conquests, it would seem reasonable to accept them on grounds of "competitive plausibility."

O'Connor is skeptical about the possibility that the Hyksos reached the Aegean. In claiming this, I am not, of course, being original; I am merely following the interpretation of a significant minority of scholars, including Eduard Meyer and Frank Stubbings.[6] I differ from Stubbings, however, on two important points. First, I cannot agree with his acceptance of the Greek tradition that the Hyksos arrived in the Aegean *after* their expulsion from Egypt. Since the redating of the Thera eruption to 1628 B.C.E., it has become completely impossible—it was always difficult—to place the Shaft Graves in the sixteenth century. Thus, it would seem more plausible to place the Hyksos raids on the Aegean near the beginning of their rule in Lower Egypt in the late eighteenth century B.C.E. Suggesting their arrival then would also explain the destruction, at this time, of all the Cretan palaces and their rapid rebuilding along similar, though not identical, lines.

My second and more fundamental disagreement with Stubbings is with his claim that the Hyksos princes had no long-term impact on Greek culture. Although I agree that much of the substantial Egyptian and Levantine cultural influence came to Greece in the Late Bronze Age and Early Iron Age, and that some may have entered in the third millennium, I am convinced that the Hyksos played a major role in introducing West Semitic and Egyptian civilization to the Aegean.

The arrival of Hyksos in the Aegean in the late eighteenth century B.C.E. would seem to be indicated by the first appearance of many artifacts and techniques: Syrian weapons, including chariots, swords, and composite bows; the enameling technique of *niello*; and iconography associated with the Hyksos, namely, the winged sphinx and the griffin, the symbol of Cretan and Mycenaean royalty.[7]

Whatever the truth of the matter, the Thera murals leave no doubt that seventeenth-century Cycladic society was highly stratified and cosmopolitan. Furthermore, even if one does not accept Karen Pollinger Foster's claim that the Theran nautical festival is a version of the Egyptian royal ceremony of Heb Sed, there is no doubt that the paintings represent a society saturated with Egyptian influence.[8] The redating of the eruption to 1628 no longer allows one to see such influence as the result of the Pax Aegyptiaca in the Eastern Mediterranean in the fifteenth and fourteenth centuries B.C.E.

O' Connor has doubts about the early use of the term Ḥ3w nbw for the Aegean. Gardiner, who had earlier accepted the name "around or behind the islands" as "a sufficiently accurate description of the Aegean," was later convinced by Jean Vercoutter's minimalism to deny this.[9] Vercoutter thought it absurd that Egyptians of the Old Kingdom or earlier could have been aware of such a distant region. The Egyptian objects of these times found not merely in Crete but elsewhere in the Aegean, as well as the considerable irrigation schemes and granaries of Egyptian type found in Early Helladic Greece indicate that this attribution is not so absurd (BA II: 133–146).

When I accept the plausibility of Queen Aḥḥotpe's connections with the Ḥ3w nbw, I am again following a long line of scholars.[10] However, I now agree with O'Connor that it is unlikely that she came from the islands

(p. 55). Her active role in the war against the Hyksos reported on the Karnak stela makes it very unlikely that she was a foreigner.[11] On the other hand, evidence of her connections with the Aegean does not come merely from the statement on the stela that she was "Mistress of the shores of the Ḥ3w nbwt." It also derives from the Cretan style of her jewelry. Even more impressive is the discovery by Manfred Bietak that there are Minoan paintings not only in Hyksos Tel ed Daba'a but also in an early Eighteenth Dynasty palace built over the Hyksos fortifications. What is more, these include representations of griffins, which in the Aegean have been associated with queenship.[12]

Inscriptional evidence makes it clear that Aḥḥotpe wielded great power during and possibly after the reign of her son Aḥmose. Thus, it would seem extremely likely that the palace was hers. This greatly increases the probability of her connections with the Aegean. It also makes more plausible that there was some reality behind her son's claim that the Ḥ3w nbwt all served him.[13]

Finally, we come to O'Connor's arguments about the list of Aegean placenames on the statue base of Amenhotpe III. I agree that one need not take them at face value as indicating that these cities accepted Egyptian rule. On the other hand, the finds of objects inscribed with the pharaoh's name at most of the sites identified in the list do suggest some type of suzerainty. This suggestion can also be found in tomb paintings of what Egyptians took to be Aegean tribute being offered to the pharaoh.[14] Even before the discovery of the Kaş wreck, the finds from this period of Mycenaean pottery and metal in Egypt and the Egyptian Levant and of Egyptian and Levantine objects in the Aegean indicate close contact among the regions. But now the Kaş wreck leaves no doubt of it. At the height of the Eighteenth Dynasty, the economic and military power of Egypt was clearly far greater than that of any Greek state. Hence, any relation would tend to have been unequal. The possibility of Egyptian military involvement in the Aegean in the reign of Tuthmosis III is raised by his claim to have punished the Ḥ3w nbwt "in their islands." [15] It is also clear, as O'Connor agrees (p. 54), that the Egyptian state had ships easily capable of voyaging this far.

To sum up, I see many different Egyptian and Levantine interventions in and influences on the Aegean during the Bronze Age. I should like to insist that this is precisely what one should expect given the geographical proximity and the unequal levels of power and culture in the different regions.

Once again I should like to thank David O'Connor for the time and trouble he has taken with my work.

II

Classics

Black Athena Revisited contained three articles under the heading "Classics." My responses to two of these, those by Professors Tritle and Vermeule, are in this section of *Black Athena Writes Back*; however, I have chosen to include as my third response not yet another to John Coleman but rather one to Edith Hall. This is because although Professor Hall's review was classified in BAR under "Historiography," nearly all her criticisms are technical ones concerned with Ancient Greece.

The basic issues raised by all of these critics are familiar: that I am too credulous in my approach to ancient sources and too skeptical or hostile to modern ones. In this context, Vermeule, with some justification, refuses to accept BA II as archaeological because it has no plans or descriptions of archaeological sites. Hall does not believe that my work on Greek myths and legends should be taken seriously because I have not integrated it with—or even shown signs of having read—the advances in the study of myth made during the twentieth century. Tritle is even more sweeping in his objection to my work, for he maintains that as a political scientist, I simply do not have the basic qualifications of a historian and do not possess "historical method." I try to answer all these charges in the following chapters.

The discipline of Classics is clearly at the center of both my historical and my historiographical projects. I am not surprised that many classicists should react to my work with hostility. *Black Athena* is deeply offensive to them in at least three fundamental ways. First, there is the normal professional dislike of "poaching" by outsiders. In the case of *Black Athena*, this is compounded by my claims that the conventional isolationist treatment of the Aegean is utterly mistaken. Such resentment is doubled and redoubled by my argument that a principal reason for the rejection of the Ancient model was that the nineteenth-century founders of their discipline were heavily influenced *in their scholarship!* by the prevailing racism and anti-Semitism. Beyond all these offenses is the discomfort that my work has caused by politicizing fields that had previously provided refuge from the turmoil and uncertainty of the modern world. *Black Athena* has forced classicists and scholars in surrounding disciplines to make choices on general issues and take "political" positions for or against the status quo.

Because of these painful challenges to their disciplines, I originally expected all reviews of my work by classicists and classical archaeologists to be of the type represented in BAR. What has amazed and delighted me is that this kind of reaction has not been universal and, as I mentioned in the introduction, there have also been sympathetic and "balanced" responses to my work. None of these was included in BAR.

3 Who Is Qualified to Write Greek History?

A REPLY TO LAWRENCE A. TRITLE

When it first appeared, L. A. Tritle's review of BA II in the *Liverpool Classical Monthly* was much the longest: twelve tightly packed pages in small print. It also contained a mixture of learning and hostility to the work that convinced me that a response was necessary, and my reply was published in a later issue of the same journal.[1]

Apart from Tritle's conviction that I am not only wrong but incompetent, his review—which was not substantially revised for BAR—has no overarching scheme. It is a series of critical observations of varying quality and length on particular points or issues. Inevitably, therefore, my response too lacks cohesion and is merely a succession of unrelated attempts to answer his charges.

My Qualifications as a Historian

With the exception of that from Chester Starr, I find the quotations with which Tritle heads his sections quite admirable.[2] However, I cannot see that they have any bearing on his criticism of my work. Indeed, the passage by Keith Hopkins on the uncertainty of evidence agrees exactly with my principle that one cannot and should not require "proof" or "certainty" but merely "competitive plausibility" when considering the murky regions of Mediterranean prehistory. The fact that Hopkins and I see eye to eye on this is not surprising, as we were educated in the same college, King's Cambridge, in the same decade, the 1950s, and as fellows of the college, we have seen each other on and off since then.

This connection leads to Tritle's belief that I am "a political scientist rather than a historian" (p. 304). Although I have always emphasized that I came to Classics and the history of the Ancient Mediterranean as an outsider, I have never made the same claim about history in general. I shall respond later to Tritle's specific criticisms of my historical method. At this point, I should like to make it clear that I have had what would normally be judged to be a superb historical training. When I read Chinese at Cambridge, I was taught by excellent institutional historians. As a graduate student at Berkeley and Harvard, I took courses from two renowned intellectual historians, Joseph Levinson and Benjamin Schwartz. My dissertation, which gained me a research fellowship at King's College Cambridge, was read by a number of distinguished historians at that college. E. H. Carr was an examiner of my Ph.D. thesis, which was on intellectual history and cultural contact. He continued to keep in touch with me after the examination. Living in Cambridge as a fellow of King's, I was in more or less frequent contact with such historians as John Dunn, Mark Elvin, Moses Finley, Francis Haskell, Eric Hobsbawm, Nicholas Jardine, Geoffrey Lloyd, Joseph Needham, Quentin Skinner, and Robert Young, who was later to be my publisher.

What did I gain from such august company? No doubt this contact set me squarely in an Anglo-Saxon commonsensical tradition. Having lived through the 1960s, however, my contemporaries and I became aware of what we saw as the excesses of positivism. I suppose the basis was, as Tritle acutely hints, the historical approach set out in Carr's What Is History? Nevertheless, we glossed it in a number of ways, including that of Arthur

Marwick as cited by Tritle (p. 306). Indeed, in BA I, I paid special attention to what Marwick advocated, a "consideration of unspoken assumption(s) and shared values" of the scholars whose work I was attempting to analyze. At Cambridge in the 1960s, we all became very sensitive to the central importance of the sociology of knowledge. We also became acutely aware of the uncertainty of all historical claims and hence the futility of requiring *proof*. Nevertheless, my contemporaries and I did not retreat into absolute relativism; we believed and still believe that some historical narratives and explanations are better and some worse. We also tend to think that these should not be neatly labeled "true" or "false" but as falling along a scale of what I have come to call "competitive plausibility."

Having said all this, the chief lesson I have learned from twenty years at Cambridge and the further twenty-five at Cornell is that there is no one magic talisman of "historical method" and that there are many different ways in which one may reconstruct the past. Sometimes, excellent work can be done working rigorously in one field and disregarding all others; at other times, it is more helpful to be eclectic and combine information garnered from many approaches. Sometimes, it is helpful to be synchronic; at other times, it is best to be diachronic. The same goes for focusing on a small locality or sketching a wider geographical region, for splitting or lumping. My own work emphasizes the eclectic, the diachronic, wider regions, and lumping. But I am also concerned with other approaches and I would not dream of denying their utility in the work of other historians.

Although Tritle sees my lack of training as a crippling disadvantage, some very distinguished historians have not. When I began work in the new field, I circulated papers on it to a number of historians, including Michel de Certeau, Le Roy Ladurie, Edward Fox, and Moses Finley.[3] All of these expressed great interest in my project and gave me encouragement and positive help in pursuing it. I do not interpret this encouragement to mean that they were particularly impressed by my "method." In any case, they, unlike Tritle, did not have the talismanic image of a single historical method. What excited them about my work was not my professional skill, but that I was making interesting and important claims and that, in general, *I might well be right*.

In the early pages of his critique, Professor Tritle sees my approach as analogous to abandoning Einstein's relativity and returning to Newtonian physics (p. 304). Naturally, I believe that the analogy is misleading, especially as I do not accept for one moment that historiography has made advances in the twentieth century comparable to those in physics.

Incidentally, I take the latter very seriously, as my acceptance of twentieth-century techniques from natural sciences, such as carbon dating, lead isotope analysis, dendrochronology, and so on, is greater than that of most defenders of the conventional wisdom. I do not necessarily believe, as Tritle supposes, that natural scientists are dealing in certainties; rather, I merely suggest that their work is significantly less mushy than that of ancient historians and archaeologists. This assertion especially holds in the case of issues, such as chronology, on which the scientists have little or no prior commitment. Their calculations, therefore, other things being equal, should be preferred to those established before the new technologies were applied to ancient history.

Even accepting, for the sake of argument, Tritle's analogy between the emergence of Einsteinian relativity and contemporary developments in historiography, I believe that most of the flaws in the Aryan model are so obvious and straightforward that they can be analyzed simply, without recourse to the latest sophisticated methods employed in Classics. As I see it, many of the historiographical "advances" of the twentieth century have not been in areas that concern my project. New approaches to myths and legends may well tell us more than we knew previously about their structure or their functions in a given society, but apart from the collection of worldwide folk motifs, they do not help distinguish elements that have historical value from those that do not.

Some "advances" may, in fact, have been misleading. For instance, the extraordinary emphasis on Greek writings about "barbarians" as "projections" of Greek concerns, and the consequent propensity to deny that they might contain any objective information, have tended to remove important sources of evidence about the Greeks' neighbors.[4] I do not deny that "projection" is *an* element in such writings; I merely claim that other things are also going on in these texts.

Tritle sees himself as developing or continuing earlier criticisms of my method—or lack of it—by Frank Turner and Sturt Manning. It would seem useful, therefore, to consider their conclusions. Turner's statement on this reads as follows: "In summary, I would note that in many respects Professor Bernal and I disagree relatively little in our conclusions. . . . Where we differ is the manner in which we reach those conclusions. Professor Bernal discerns larger ideological sweeps that escape my discernment and, I believe, that of many intellectual historians. I would much prefer a more particularistic approach which seeks to understand the twists and turns of the lace before asserting the character of a larger pattern." [5] Although Turner clearly prefers a particularist approach, he does not deny the legitimacy of looking for larger ideological sweeps, as Tritle appears to do in his criticisms of my work. Furthermore, Turner agrees that both methods can reach similar conclusions.

Manning's criticism concludes, "Acceptance of a realist mode of thought within a wider acceptance of a relativist, or socially constructed, framework allows for Black Athena, and for satisfactory discussion of it. Uncritical positivism or relativism, does not." [6] As neither Tritle nor I can plausibly be accused of uncritical positivism or uncritical relativism, I think that Manning's elaborate strictures do not apply to us and that we should proceed with our discussion without invoking him.

Specific Criticisms

Having offered these preliminary remarks, I now turn to specifics. Tritle states that my "irritable and hypercritical" attacks on Besserwisserei (defined as "modern scholars knowing better than the ancients") "reveals a fundamental ignorance of the underlying methodological and historiographical concepts behind the Besserwisse[rei]. These are rooted in Italian (rather than German) thought, especially in Giambattista Vico's philosophy of history" (p. 304). [7]

In BA I, I attempt to set Besserwisserei in a general context of modern historiography, and of "source criticism" in particular, in which its practitioners select those sources that they see as representing the Zeitgeist and dismiss the others. [8] When describing the development of the Göttingen historians of the late eighteenth century, I write about one of the central figures in this movement, the historian and anthropologist C. Meiners: "Between 1770 and 1810 Meiners developed the earlier concept of the 'genius of the age' into an academic theory of Zeitgeist. Possibly unaware of Vico's earlier work along these lines, Meiners argued that each age and place had a special mentality determined by its situation and institutions" (BA I: 217). [9] The footnote on this passage reads: "For the degrees to which 18th century Germans were aware of Vico's work see Croce (1947 [Bibliographia Vichiana] vol. 1, pp. 504–515)." [10] It should be clear from this that I am not "fundamentally ignorant" of the Vichean aspects of "source criticism" and its corollary, Besserwisserei.

THE RELIABILITY OF ANCIENT SOURCES

Like many of my critics, Tritle maintains that I overestimate the credibility of the ancient historians and he raises the example of Plutarch's difficulties, as someone living in the age of Trajan, in understanding Athenian democracy five centuries earlier. This particular topic is not touched on in my work. Nevertheless, I willingly concede his general point that writers in "Late Antiquity" may have had difficulties in understanding or interpreting earlier history. He cites my response to Edith Hall in *Arethusa* as an example of what he sees as my uncritical acceptance of Hellenistic authors, and he repeats this charge throughout his review. I have stated my views on this many times in this volume and elsewhere.[11]

Tritle also accuses me of practicing Besserwisserei myself. In principle, he is clearly right to do so, because I do not advocate a return to the Ancient model but the establishment of a Revised Ancient model, which selectively accepts much of ancient historiography but takes into account a number of the "advances" made during the nineteenth and twentieth centuries.

Tritle (p. 305) gives a good example of my Besserwisserei when I dismiss, on the basis of modern archaeology and linguistics, Herodotus' belief that the Phrygians were the oldest people. Puzzlingly, however, the other examples he gives do not illustrate his case. He writes that I claim to know better than Herodotus when I set Homer in the ninth century B.C.E. Herodotus, writing about 450 B.C.E., maintained that he believed Homer lived "not more than four hundred years ago." This would place Homer in the second half of the ninth century. Herodotus' statement is, indeed, one of the reasons why I believe the poet to have lived in that century. Tritle may have been confused on this by missing my mention that I followed the ancient convention that Hesiod lived before Homer (BA I: 86). Tritle later states (p. 305) that my early dating of the two poets is "unsupported." I do, in fact, give arguments for my position on this over three pages (BA I: 86–88).

As an illustration of my "credulity," Tritle states that I "read Homer as a history book" (p. 306). This is a clear case of reductio ad absurdum. Throughout my work, I refer to Homer as an "epic poet" and maintain that poetry is inevitably written at many levels and is necessarily full of ambiguity (BA I: 125). I see the preeminent function of myth as an explanation of contemporary nature and social order and as a justification of the latter. I also believe, however, that poems and myths do quite often contain genuine historical data and that at times it is worth testing possible examples of these against evidence from other sources, such as archaeology, contemporary documents, later linguistic patterns, and other independent traditions. In the example Tritle raises, that of Odysseus' supposed raid on Egypt, I follow H. L. Lorimer and many other scholars who see this in the context of what we know from other sources about Egypt in the late thirteenth and twelfth centuries B.C.E. and I find it plausible.[12] Tritle is right, however, to call me to task for not having cited the scholars who oppose this view or having given the reasons why I disagree with them.

Tritle also refers to my credulity in accepting (BA II: 500) "without question (or discussion) that Herodotos saw 'alphabetic Cadmean script' of the thirteenth century B.C.E. in Thebes" and that I "simply omit . . . Herodotus' follow-up observation that the letters resembled the Ionic script" (p. 305). Tritle does not point out that the paragraph has a footnote referring to my book *Cadmean Letters*.[13] In this book, I give the reasons why I am inclined to believe that the pre–Trojan War inscriptions Herodotus claimed to have seen both existed and were genuine. One of these reasons is precisely his statement that "most of them were not very different from the Ionian." After forty pages of detailed discussion, I concluded on other grounds that the Ionian was the most archaic of all the Greek alphabets.[14]

Tritle contrasts my respect for Herodotus with what he sees as my suspicion of Thucydides, whom, he says, I view as a "nationalist and a hate-mongering foe of all non-Greek peoples" (p. 305). Though Tritle claims that the "preceding labels" may be found on pages 101–103 of BA I, a turn to these pages reveals that I do not there—or anywhere else in my work— apply the term "hate-mongering" to Thucydides or anybody. What I wrote in the section he cites was: "This kind of 'nationalism' would seem to be typical in the aftermath of the Persian Wars of the early fifth century and the subsequent expansion of Greek power: from this time on, one finds varying degrees of hatred of and contempt for 'barbarians' amongst most Greeks" (BA I: 102). This unexceptionable statement was not a personal attack on Thucydides but an attempt to describe the cultural environment in which he was living.

Tritle writes, "Thucydides' own Thracian connection could well undo all Bernal's opinions" (p. 305). This claim would seem too drastic even if Thucydides had boasted of his small component of Thracian ancestry, which he did not.[15] As we know that he went against his aristocratic Athenian family to follow Pericles with a convert's zeal, there is no reason to doubt that he shared the general attitudes of his fellow citizens toward "barbarians."

Tritle misstates another of my positions. He writes that I have argued that "historians in antiquity, just like their modern counterparts, have *systematically* engaged in understatement to appear 'sober and reasonable' to their readers, while at the same time wishing 'to astound their audiences with spectacularly high dates'" (p. 305). I emphasize the word *systematically* because I have never maintained that the ancient historians were more inclined to minimize than they were to maximize their stories. I merely claim that they exhibited both tendencies.

Tritle calls into question the reliability of ancient historians still further, when he refers to Arrian's clearly fantastic story of talking snakes leading Alexander to the oasis of Siwa (p. 305). Such absurdities should not lead one to dismiss all the works of Arrian or other ancient historian. The individual stories should be checked against natural science and other sources of evidence. Furthermore, it should be remembered that even the "more scientific" nineteenth-century historians held views that we cannot now take at all seriously. The most important of these are the notions of "racial" hierarchy and the desirability of "racial purity." These ideas have had a much more direct bearing on reconstructions of Greek relations with the Levant and Egypt than have any stories of guiding snakes.

PLUTARCH'S REPORT OF THE SPARTAN FINDS AT THE SO-CALLED TOMB OF ALKMENE

Tritle further criticizes my "credulity" on Plutarch's report of the Spartan finds at the so-called tomb of Alkmene and the inscribed bronze tablet found there. I argue that the inscription was probably "Linear B or possibly Linear A or cuneiform" (BA II: 127). Tritle (p. 306) states, "Bernal . . . rejects the possibility that Chonuphis [the Egyptian priest to whom the inscription was allegedly taken for elucidation] might have had *any difficulty*, like modern day scholars in making out an obscure but known text . . ." (my emphasis). In fact, I deny that the text could have been in Egyptian, because "if the inscription had been in any form of Egyptian hieroglyphics it would be impossible to explain Chonuphis' apparent difficulty in reading the tablet" (BA II: 127).

Tritle claims, "Bernal accepts the substance of the account as literally true" (p. 307). What I write is very different: "The least plausible part of the story is the report of Chonuphis' of the text's meaning" (BA II: 127). I go on to argue that although Chonuphis could not read the inscription, his "translation" of it could possibly have reflected knowledge of the political situation in Greece of his own day. Given the close relations between Greeks and Egyptians in the early fourth century B.C.E., I see no reason why an educated Egyptian should not have been aware of the complexities of contemporary Greek politics, which were of vital importance to Egyptians also facing the Persian menace.

Tritle continues with passionate hyperbole that "it is a pity that a text and its author should have been so abused" (p. 307). He sees my treatment of Plutarch's report as another example of my failure to grasp "historical method." It is only fair to point out that I am not the first to extract the report of the excavation of the tomb of Alkmene from Plutarch's essay *De genio Socratis*. Both J. G. Frazer and J. Schwartz did so.[16] Like them, I tried to assess the historicity of the discrete description. Tritle writes, "Bernal does not even consider that Plutarch's report might be a literary creation" (p. 307). In fact, I began my discussion of it with the words: "What if anything can be made of this passage?" Later I wrote: "The detailed description and the prosaic nature of the objects found make the report of their discovery seem very plausible. There is no tale here of serpents, gigantic bones or great treasures" (BA II: 125–126). Clearly, I did consider the possibility that it might be a literary creation, but to have gone into the details of the genre in which Plutarch was writing would have added considerable bulk to an already overburdened book. I have more sympathy with reviewers who claim that my writings contain too many digressions than with those, like Tritle, who say there are too few. No critic has claimed that my books are too short!

ANALOGY AS EVIDENCE?

Tritle attacks my use of analogy as "unsound," stating that "analogy is not a substitute for evidence" and that it "can distort rather than illuminate the past" (p. 308). Naturally, I am aware of this. When evidence is thoroughly ambiguous or entirely lacking, as is nearly always the case around the Eastern Mediterranean during the Bronze Age, one has to consider the possibility or plausibility of certain situations or sequences of events. In such situations, I believe, analogy can be helpful. Thus, for instance, in considering the possible historicity of the legendary conquests of Sesōstris, I looked at comparable campaigns or marches, taking into account the resources available, means of transport, and terrain covered. I also assessed what we know of the military capabilities of the Twelfth Dynasty. I then wrote: "There would seem no intrinsic reason why such a state with such a military machine should not have made considerable conquests in Asia. However, this ability does not mean that such conquests actually took place, for that we need more evidence" (BA II: 206).

All that analogy can do is clarify what is possible. Lack of analogies makes certain scenarios less likely and their existence makes other scenarios more plausible. Direct evidence is certainly of much greater importance than analogy in establishing competitive plausibility. As we have seen, Tritle himself is not above the use of analogy, as, for instance, when he claims that twentieth-century advances in Classics and ancient history of the Mediterranean were analogous to Einstein's modifications of Newtonian physics. In this regard, I should like to acknowledge Tritle's support of my position on competitive plausibility when he notes that since Einstein, "science has ceased to deal in certainties and looks now to probabilities" (p. 308).[17]

Tritle attacks what he sees as my "anachronistic" use of the term "pharaoh" when referring to rulers of the Old and Middle Kingdoms. This is petty and absurd. I am, of course, aware that the term pr ʿ3 ("Great House") came into use only in the New Kingdom. Because of its use in the Bible, however, the term is now the English word for "ruler of Ancient Egypt." For one of many instances, the Egyptologist Alan Gardiner entitled his history Egypt of the Pharaohs and referred to individual rulers of the Old and Middle Kingdoms as pharaohs.[18]

MORE METHODOLOGICAL PROBLEMS?

Tritle finds my "methodology" "more disturbing" because of what he sees as my "tendency to form rhetorical arguments and statements to support" my case (p. 308). This vague claim makes little sense in the context in which it now appears, because it is a watered-down version of the charge made in his original article. The original charge fits much better with the subsequent examples he offers. In the original text, he wrote that my "methodology" was most disturbing because of what he saw as my "misleading, even disingenuous statements."[19] He cited three examples of these statements. Here I shall try to demonstrate the inappropriateness of two of his charges; the first, on the dates of Homer and Hesiod, was discussed above.

The second charge concerns my reporting of the reception of George Bass's excavation of the wreck off Cape Gelidonya, with its conclusion that the crew were Levantines. Tritle thinks that my statement that "Bass's work was considered very startling and generally unwelcome" is misleading. He then takes up one of the references I give, the review of Bass's publication by G. Cadogan. He shows that in his review Cadogan wrote that Bass's study "was well worth buying and contains plenty to think over. It is a great achievement" (p. 308.). Tritle, however, also cites Cadogan as having used the word "startling" and writes that the review was "critical, though positive." However, nothing in Cadogan's published work since 1969 indicates that he *has* thought over Bass's conclusion. As for the validity of my statement that the "work was considered very startling and generally unwelcome," let me quote Bass's own view:

> When I published the Cape Gelidonya shipwreck (which may or may not be Canaanite . . .) I went over the external material and showed from Egyptian tomb paintings that Egyptians considered the copper trade a Canaanite or Semitic trade. They considered the ships Canaanite. Further the weights used on the Cape Gelidonya ship and throughout the Aegean were mostly of Near Eastern origin. These things have simply never been argued against. Yet I find that not one classical archaeologist who reviewed my book agreed with anything I said. . . . You can read entire articles on the copper trade that just ignore the Cape Gelidonya publication because it's a neat way of getting around it. No scholar has yet, twenty years later, ever gone point by point through the overwhelming evidence I presented and then said, "No this is not the case." [20]

Bass's statement "that not one classical archaeologist who reviewed my book agreed with anything I said" may have been hyperbolical. Nevertheless, the failure of Cadogan and other classicists and classical archaeologists to pay serious attention to Bass's monumental work for the next twenty years leaves no doubt about the generally "unwelcome" nature of his conclusions to the scholars who dominated these fields.

Tritle claims that I see such a response as the result of a "conspiracy." I have never used or even implied this narrow concept. I maintain that the hostility and neglect of Bass's work came from the fact that it did not fit the model or paradigm in which Graecocentric scholars were working.

The third example Tritle gives of my "manipulation of evidence" regards

Colin Renfrew's reference to *Rundbauten* (round buildings) in his *Emergence of Civilization*. He denies my claims that Renfrew is "equivocal" on the purpose of these structures or that Renfrew saw early Helladic Greece as having a subsistence economy (p. 309). Tritle does not mention the fact that I refer not to one but to two separate references to Rundbauten in Renfrew's book (BA II: 136). In the first, they are described as "probabl[e] . . . dwellings" and in the second, they are described as "possible granaries." [21] Because of this contradiction, I describe Renfrew as "equivocal" about the structures. Tritle does not mention the first reference but goes on from the second to cite Renfrew as having written that this gives "a picture of a subsistence economy expanding" (p. 309). This statement seems to me to be an equivocation, because the near certainty that the Rundbau at Tiryns was a massive granary indicates not merely expansion of a subsistence economy but the presence of a highly organized state in the Argolid in the ceramic period Early Helladic II, c. 3000–2400 B.C.E. Incidentally, my ideas here have been strengthened by geoarchaeological work indicating that cultivation of the Argive plain and its surroundings was as intense during EHII as at any other period in the Bronze Age, if not more so. [22]

GREECE OUT OF EGYPT?

Tritle begins his second section by claiming that in the light of criticism, I have made two revisions to my original scheme: first, that Greek is essentially Indo-European, and second, that Egypto-Levantine colonization occurred in the late eighteenth century B.C.E. rather than in the early sixteenth. If Tritle had read the first fourteen pages of the introduction to BA I, it would have been clear to him that from the start of my project, I have not proposed a revival of the Ancient model but a *"Revised Ancient model"* (BA I: 2). The latter has always included the agreement with conventional wisdom that Greek is essentially Indo-European and that the "colonizations" could not have taken place in the early sixteenth century. Though I have, of course, been influenced by criticisms, these fundamentals have remained unchanged. I sympathize with Tritle's difficulties in reading a work he detests. Nevertheless, I am surprised that he failed to grasp these points, which are central to my whole project.

Tritle goes on to suggest that I show traces of "staunch diffusionism" (p. 310). He then quotes a passage in which I strongly deny that Egyptians could have colonized Wessex in the third millennium B.C.E., a denial that is characteristic of modified diffusionism. Yet Tritle sees this as "obscuring rhetoric." I don't know how I can satisfy him on this: If I say I am a modified diffusionist and I write like a modified diffusionist, why not take the self-description at face value until there is evidence to the contrary?[23]

In my treatment of the legends surrounding Sesōstris, Tritle accuses me here too of taking Greek historians "literally" and not subjecting them to any sort of questioning or analysis (p. 310). A rejection of the general charge that I accept ancient writers literally and uncritically was given above. In this case, I take three pages (BA II: 200–202) to discuss *objections* to the Sesōstris stories, and in consequence, I *reject* as "fantastic" Herodotus' story of the Pharaoh's brother trying to burn him to death as well as Diodorus' claims that Sesōstris could have conquered Mesopotamia, India, or Persia. I also discuss what I describe as the "plausible" case that the Sesōstris legends were created to assuage Egyptian pride wounded by the Persian and Greek conquests. My tentative acceptance that the stories also contain information of historical value is not arbitrary or unexplained but, rather, arises from the congruence of some sections with archaeological and inscriptional evidence, which I describe at length. I am not alone in using this approach. In assessing the widespread anthropological approach that views myths purely as justifications of present structures, the Dutch historian of Africa J. Schoffeleers goes on to note that "more recently, however, voices have been raised, particularly among historians, which insist that a society's past is not manipulated at will but that it is treated circumspectly, the way one deals with any scarce resource."[24]

As for the newly available written evidence about Twelfth Dynasty conquests recently made available by the Mit Rahineh inscription, Tritle claims that I "would lead the unsuspecting reader to think that the inscription is trouble-free, its translation and interpretation only challenged by those scholars who think that they 'know better'" (p. 311). What I write is this:

Both the beginning and the end of the original inscription are missing, as are the tops of all the lines. The text is made still less clear by the fact that the left side of the photograph from which the transcription has been made was out of focus.... Nevertheless, Farag... and... Posener rightly believed that, despite these imperfections, it should be published as soon as possible.... Not surprisingly there has been no complete translation, but Posener and Farag have both written notes on some of the inscription's contents. (BA II: 188)

Tritle then writes, "Bernal claims that one word in the text, S̱tt, refers to Asia, which would support his view of Sesōstris' great campaign" (p. 311). This is not the only suggestive place-name on the inscription. There are several others that, with other corroborative evidence, have been detailed in the previous chapter.

RACISM

At this point in his review, Tritle turns to the ever charged question of "race." He follows F. M. Snowden in believing that I claim that because Herodotus had written that the Colchians were "black skinned and . . . [had] woolly hair just like the Egyptians," I accepted that the latter were indistinguishable from Ethiopians. I did no such thing. When I referred to the passage in BA I (p. 242), I was not discussing the actual but the "*perceived* 'racial' position of the Egyptians.*" Incidentally, I do not accept Snowden's argument that Greeks and Romans made a clear distinction between Egyptians and Ethiopians. The latter term was as uncertain in Classical Antiquity as "black" is today. At times, it was restricted to stereotypical West Africans—which is the way in which Snowden generally, though not always, interprets it.[25] Elsewhere, however, it was used much more broadly to include any people substantially darker than the Greeks or Romans themselves; see, for instance, Snowden's earlier *Blacks in Antiquity.*[26] For a physical anthropologist's opinion of Snowden's views as expressed in his attack on me, see Shomarka Keita's "Black Athena: 'Race,' Bernal and Snowden."[27]

In the footnotes to page 312 of his review, Tritle refers to the "full discussion" of the physical identity of the Ancient Egyptians in Yurco's "Were the Ancient Egyptians Black or White?" Yurco's article, which was written for the semipopular *Biblical Archaeology Review,* is not full, because it does not touch on the works on the subject by physical anthropologists.[28] Incidentally, Yurco has no doubt that it is useful to see the Egyptians as African (BAR, pp. 63–65). For a bibliography on these, see the notes to Keita's chapter in the forthcoming *Debating Black Athena.*

In his note 7, Tritle criticizes me for my suggestion that "racist attitudes" played a key role in the failure of historians in the nineteenth century C.E. to pay attention to the achievements of Mohamed Ali and Ibrahim Pasha in the Egyptian "Renaissance" and in Greece. He is right to fault me for not having looked at the relevant section of Finlay's 1877 *History of Greece.* I still maintain, however, that such Egypto-Greek episodes through the entire history of the Eastern Mediterranean have received remarkably little attention in nineteenth- and twentieth-century European historiography.

Tritle goes on to deplore as even "more troubling" my belief that white racism is more frightening than black racism. Here we have a profound difference on the significance of power. Tritle has correctly quoted me as having said, "I hate racism of any kind." Thus, for instance, I find contrasts between such supposed biological entities as "ice" and "sun" people nonsensical and thoroughly distasteful. On the other hand, the views of a tiny number of the poorest people in North America and Europe are not likely to have any significant impact intellectually, politically, or socially on the rest of the population.[29] Indeed, I do not think that such ethnic absolutism should be called "racism," which by many definitions is only possible when the discriminators hold power.[30] By contrast, the racial prejudices held by many of the majority and by far the most powerful element in the population of Europe and North America can have, have had, and are having devastating effects on the contemporary world. The situation is made still worse by the fact that such views are sanctioned by a substantial body of academic "knowledge," the outlines of which were established when racism and anti-Semitism were open and normal among scholars. These are the reasons I consider Eurocentrism a far more serious and pressing problem than Afrocentrism.[31]

Tritle faults me twice (pp. 311, 313) for failing to dwell on the significance of the Greek word *eleutheria* ("freedom") that appears in Herodotus' passage on Sesōstris. He has two complaints: that I fail to consider this important and, by implication, uniquely Greek concept, and that this failure indicates a "remarkable insensitivity" to the fact that Herodotus was writing in the fifth century. I have attempted to answer the second criticism above in discussions of my treatment of Herodotus and Thucydides. On the first criticism, I must again argue that I have made too many digressions from my main theme rather than too few. If he believes, as he seems to, that "freedom" was invented by Greeks in the fifth century B.C.E., we disagree fundamentally. Clearly, it had existed in many other societies including Ancient Mesopotamia, Syro-Palestine, and Egypt.[32]

Professor Tritle sees my acceptance of the identification of Osiris and Dionysos—unchallenged in Antiquity—as unpersuasive and superficial. He holds this view because I largely rely on "late," that is, Hellenistic and Roman sources for the identification and only touch on the considerable circumstantial evidence from earlier periods. In fact, the identification can be traced back to Herodotus. Given other early identifications of Ammon with Zeus and Isis with Demeter, there is no reason to suppose that the correspondence only began in the fifth century B.C.E.[33] I shall take up this topic in more detail in the forthcoming *Debating Black Athena*.

Tritle also accuses me of rejecting the Semitic traces in the origin of Herakles. In fact, I devote several pages to investigating this evidence before turning to the Egyptian material. The situation is extremely complicated. As I put it in the introduction to volume 2: "A long section in chapter 2 is devoted to looking at the many Mesopotamian, West Semitic and Egyptian strands that went to make up the greatest Greek and specifically Theban hero" (BA II: 16).

I am grateful to Professor Tritle for his reference to A. R. Schulman's "Battle Scenes of the Middle Kingdom," which I had missed. I do, however, write that Herakles' carrying out his labors on his own or with a single companion makes him resemble Gilgamesh, and then I continue: "This would seem to distinguish Herakles from the Egyptian pharaohs with their huge armies, except that Egyptian propaganda in texts—and even more strikingly in iconography—portrayed the conquests as if they were those of the pharaoh himself, with little or no support from his armies" (BA II: 116). Tritle cites the representation of a New Kingdom battle that "shows Egyptian infantry pressing its attack as the pharaoh, inscribed in a larger scale, casts his shadow over the whole scene" (p. 315). I do not think that we are so far apart on this.

On the other hand, Tritle sees Egyptian bull fighting as "altogether different" from the Cretan bull games, and therefore suggests that there can be no relation between the two. I do not deny the apparent differences, although we are not well-informed about the Egyptian rituals. There is a fundamental problem, however, in that the Cretan bull cult appears to have no precedents in the Neolithic and Early Bronze Age and seems to spring up suddenly, just before the first palaces around 2000 B.C.E. Walter Burkert suggests a connection with Çatal Hüyük some three to four thousand years earlier.[34] I think it is much more reasonable to link the Cretan bull cult to the contemporary bull cults of Egypt, because during this period, the Eleventh Dynasty, the royal cult of Mont, a hawk and a bull were especially prominent. We know that there were many other Egyptian and Levantine influences in Crete at this time. Evidence supports the association of the name M(i)n with bulls and founding rulers, and of bull cults with "winding walls," in both Egypt and Crete (BA II: 171–177).

As I show in my argument with Jasanoff and Nussbaum in chapter 6,

Tritle's semantic and phonetic objections to a derivation of the Greek kēr from the Egyptian k3 rely on misplaced precision.[35]

I am afraid that I cannot follow the logic of Tritle's statements in the final paragraph of his section 2:

> To establish evidence of linguistic influence, it is first of all necessary to show that 20 to 30 percent of words in one derive from another. The next step is to demonstrate phonetic similarity. . . . Finally the best method of revealing linguistic borrowing is to demonstrate parallelisms in the grammatic structures—and in this it would appear that there are none between Greek and Egyptian. Bernal, then, is working from the least satisfactory level of linguistic analysis, which should be sufficient cause to consider his linguistic arguments as at most tentative, and at worst tendentious. (pp. 316–317)

I do not know where Tritle found the arbitrary figure of "20 to 30 percent," and I am even less certain how one might quantify a thing called "influence." It happens that I do believe that Egyptian and Semitic loans in Greek amount to considerably more than 30 percent of the vocabulary, and I readily accept that the more accepted loans there are from language x to language y, the lower the threshold of acceptance should be for the next proposed etymology. I would go further and argue that geographical distance, temporal overlap, and other evidence of contacts should also be taken into account in assessing such possibilities. If, however, one wants to stay rigorously within linguistics, how can one *begin* to measure the extent of lexical loaning without assessing the plausibility of individual etymologies, the method used by Rendsburg and Ray and condemned by Tritle?[36] For further discussion on this issue, see chapter 6.

PROOF AND PERSUASION

Tritle heads his third section with a quotation from Chester Starr that I find quite unhelpful. Starr contrasts *historians* "seeking to restore past reality" with *authors* who use "intellectual skill and rhetorical dexterity" to "combine miscellaneous, inadequately criticized bits into a towering edifice of gossamer" (p. 317). Those of us who claim to be historians all seek to "restore past history"—as far as this is possible—and we all use "intellectual skill" to achieve this and "rhetorical dexterity" to persuade other scholars that our conclusions are closer to the truth than those we reject.

I find both Starr's sharp dichotomy between historical fact and fiction and Tritle's implication from the quotation that his views are true whereas mine are fanciful to be thoroughly misleading. Conventional history is full of loose connections that have to be bridged by constructions of gossamer. Similarly, although alternative schemes do also inevitably rely on untested hypotheses, some of them, such as the Revised Ancient model, are tied into external evidence of equal or greater reliability than that provided for conventional wisdom.

THERA AND ATLANTIS

Although Tritle claims to disagree with me, our differences on the dating of the massive eruption that blew the top off the island of Thera are very slight. We both accept the likelihood of a date in the seventeenth century B.C.E. and agree that dating from ice cores and tree rings is potentially more reliable than the methods or hunches previously used. Our disagreement is only on his claim that "Bernal's date for the Thera eruption can be no more secure than any other" (p. 318). Once again, I must reiterate that my whole project is based on the belief that one cannot and should not require *proof* on such topics. Thus, even though the period I suggest is based on evidence from ice cores, tree rings, and radiocarbon dating, I do not claim that a seventeenth-century date for the eruption is certain. I do maintain, however, that the bases for other dates in the third and second millennia B.C.E. are even more flimsy.

Tritle maintains that I have oversimplified the case in my acceptance of the widely held view that connects Plato's myth of Atlantis to the Thera eruption (p. 318). In the first place, my argument is much more complex than he suggests in that I claim that the myth contains allusions to at least three historical events: the Hyksos invasion of Egypt, the Thera eruption, and chaos at the end of the Bronze Age. Tritle is right to criticize me for not having added the Athenian role in the Persian Wars to this list. I do, however, refer to it in chapter 12 of my forthcoming popular book, *Moses and Muses*.

Tritle also criticizes me for having mistaken which Kritias Plato was referring to in the *Timaeus* (p. 318). He claims that J. K. Davies maintained that Plato's narrator was the tyrant Kritias IV. I do not believe that Davies was clear on the issue. In any event, I followed the later work of John Luce, who argued that the narrator was the tyrant's grandfather, Kritias III.[37]

EXCURSION TO CHINA

In his footnote 10, Tritle cites his former colleague Professor Xin Zhang as describing my discussion of the possible impact of the Thera eruption on China as "old timer's stuff." I find this description surprising because my work in this area is essentially based on that of K. D. Pang and H. H. Chou that was published between 1984 and 1988.[38]

In unpublished comments reported by Tritle, Xin Zhang also objects to my suggestion that there was shamanism in China. Shamanism is undoubtedly antithetical to Confucianism. In traditional belief, still powerful today, the absence of shamanism is one of the defining features of Chinese civilization. The chief characteristics of shamanism, including the possession of the priest or healer by a spirit and the medium's spiritual voyages away from the body, still occur frequently in Chinese folk religion.[39] Shamanism is also present in Chinese upper-class philosophy. In BA II (p. 313), I cited Joseph Needham's argument that shamanism is connected to the "gnosis" with which an enlightened saint or sage can rise to heaven. Such descriptions are found not merely in Taoist literature but also in the model statesman Qu Yuan's famous poem, Li sao.

Xin Zhang seems to suppose that I deny that rebellions occurred without signs from heaven or that successful usurpers could invent such signs to justify their rebellion. I do neither. I simply argue that the massive eruptions in the seventeenth and twelfth centuries B.C.E. were significant factors in the falls of the Xia and Shang Dynasties and that these falls were crucial in the formation of the political concept of the Mandate of Heaven, which could be both gained and lost. This concept, in turn, has been of central importance in Chinese political thought. As far as I am aware, however, there has been no correlation between such major climatic catastrophes and the many later popular risings and dynastic overthrows since approximately 1000 B.C.E.

THE POSSIBILITY OF HYKSOS SETTLEMENTS IN GREECE

To return to the Mediterranean and the possible Hyksos settlements in the Aegean: I am glad to see that Tritle, unlike some other reviewers of my work, recognizes that the Hyksos hypothesis is not an idiosyncratic heresy of my own but was earlier postulated by Frank Stubbings in the relevant chapter of the *Cambridge Ancient History*. This lineage does not prevent Tritle from remaining very hostile to the idea. He criticizes me by stating that the silver content of gold objects in Eighteenth Dynasty Egypt was significantly higher than that in those from Mycenae and that *tholoi* tombs existed around the Aegean and elsewhere long before the time of the Hyksos. The only trouble with these arguments is that I do not claim that the objects found in the Shaft Graves were made in Egypt or that tholoi first appeared in Crete and Greece at the end of the Middle Bronze Age. I see the grave goods of the early tombs at Mycenae as extremely eclectic but with a predominantly Cretan influence (BA II: 394–397). When mentioning the tholoi of early Mycenaean Greece (BA II: 393), I refer to the discussion in chapter 1 of the book of the far earlier tombs of this type found in Crete, which Arthur Evans and a number of other scholars have derived from Libya (BA II: 68, 551 n. 17). I make no claim that they were introduced by the Hyksos.

Tritle objects to my derivation of the place-name Mycenae on both semantic and phonetic grounds. His semantic objection is not to my derivation of the name from the common Canaanite toponym Mḫnm ("Two Camps").[40] Rather, he does not accept my skepticism of the traditional derivation from *mykos* ("mushroom"). He justifies what he appears to concede is a strange place-name—there is, to my knowledge, nothing like it elsewhere in the world—by citing what he holds are two other Greek town names: Sicyon, meaning "pumpkin," and Phlius, "spinach" (p. 319). As such toponyms do not appear in other cultures, it is much more likely that these were folk etymologies for names whose original meanings had been lost. Thus, it would seem less implausible to derive Phlius from one of the hundreds of Egyptian place-names beginning with Pr- ("House of-"). Sicyon looks very much like the Canaanite *škn* ("dwelling") found in the later Hebrew *šikūn* ("settlement" or "quarter").

Tritle's phonetic objection to the derivation of Myceneae from Mḫnm is that the Greek *kappa* was not related to the Semitic *kha* (p. 319). In fact, in many transcribed names the Semitic ḫ has appeared as k in Greek, without any positional restriction.[41]

As well as disbelieving my tentative acceptance of the views of the scholars who hold that Hyksos had settlements in Greece in the second millennium B.C.E., Tritle condemns me for maintaining that "Egyptian colonizers arrived in Greece" in the third millennium B.C.E. This is indeed the view of the archaeologist Theodore Spyropoulos. However, although I do see evidence of Egyptian contact with Boiotia at this time, I argue "that the chances that it took the form of a direct colonization are very low" (BA II: 152). Tritle seems to find the idea of noncolonial cultural contact difficult to understand (pp. 320–321). History, however, is full of examples of cultural diffusion without conquest. The saturation of Japanese culture by China, the spread of Christianity beyond the Roman Empire, and, for that matter, the worldwide Americanization going on today are all instances of this. On a technical level, Peter the Great introduced Western techniques and customs into Russia and the Meiji Emperor did the same in Japan.

Tritle maintains on the basis of photographs and a personal survey that the so-called hill of Amphion and Zethos is "simply a tumulus style mound found elsewhere in Greece" (pp. 321–322). Spyropoulos, who excavated it, saw the tomb as unique, carefully stepped and topped with brickwork. It also had a number of galleries cut into it that seemed to be associated with a funerary cult. All are remarkably reminiscent of Egyptian pyramids (see BA II: 130–133). The skeptical Sarantis Symeonoglou, who strongly objects to Spyropoulos' hypothesis of Egyptian colonization, has tried to associate the tomb with second millennium tumulus burials. To do this, he places the fragments of pottery and jewelry found in the tomb in the Middle Bronze Age.[42] Other specialists who have published on the issue accept Spyropoulos' dating to EHII (see BA II: 583 n. 29). No tombs from this earlier period remotely resemble that of Amphion and Zethos.[43]

Tritle raises the old argument that as the Egyptians were hostile to all barbarians, they never traveled and that this reluctance is proved by the passionate nostalgia for Egypt shown in the Story of Sinuhe (p. 320). On the first point, Greeks and Phoenicians, whose wide-ranging voyages no one would deny, were also hostile to barbarians. As for the idea that Egyptians never traveled, such a view was appropriate in the nineteenth century, when scholars believed in permanent national essences. Today, most scholars agree that peoples can and do change. Chinese have traditionally had a passionate attachment to living and dying in China, but they have frequently conquered Vietnam and Korea, and, during the Ming Dynasty, imperial fleets were sent as far as Sri Lanka and East Africa. For the past five hundred years Chinese have traveled and settled all over the world.

To return to the Story of Sinuhe: Nostalgia is not a uniquely Egyptian phenomenon; the literature of the far-flung British Empire is full of longing for "Blighty," and the concept of nostos ("return home") was extremely important in Ancient Greece. What is more, the popularity of the Story of Sinuhe would seem to come from two complementary aspects: its assertions that Egypt was best and the fascination of its exotic settings. The same is true of another favorite of the Middle Kingdom (2050–1750 B.C.E.), *The Shipwrecked Sailor*, as well as the later narration of the voyage of Wen Amun. We know that at least in the New Kingdom (1575–1200 B.C.E.) there were Egyptian war fleets, and we have details of the official expedition sent down the Red Sea and beyond (BA II: 426–427).

As the great classical epigrapher Paul Foucart pointed out almost ninety years ago, the bas reliefs at Deir el Bahri, showing Egyptian fleets in the second millennium traveling along the coast of Africa, well over a thousand miles to the south, make it "incredible" that scholars should deny that Egyptians could have sailed the much shorter distance to Greece.[44]

I am pleased to note that Tritle and I agree that there was extensive contact around the Eastern Mediterranean in the Late Bronze Age. This alone would seem to me to make the present denial of substantial linguistic borrowing from Egyptian and West Semitic into Greek extremely implausible. I am delighted, for instance, that he is open to the suggestion that *sitos* ("wheat") could have an Afroasiatic etymology. I should like to reassure him that in no way do I want to diminish what I see as the immense importance of West Semites in this trade and cultural exchange. Furthermore, although I do not treat it in BA, I argue elsewhere that in the Early Iron Age, Phoenician influence on the Aegean was far greater than that from Egypt.[45]

I was appalled when I became convinced that the relation between the Latin *simius* ("monkey") and the Greek *simos* ("snub-nosed") indicated that some Greeks and Romans associated black Africans with apes.[46] I should much prefer to believe with Snowden that the Greco-Roman Classical Age came, as he put it in the title of his book, *Before Color Prejudice*. Reluctantly, I came to the conclusion that St. Clair Drake in his *Black Folk Here and There* was right to state that, although Egyptians, early Israelites, and early Greeks did not have significant color prejudice, Greek, Jewish, and Roman attitudes changed during the sixth and fifth centuries B.C.E.[47] Lloyd Thompson treats this topic in his *Romans and Blacks*.[48] As I write, "There is no doubt that, while Greeks and Romans were by no means as obsessed with racism as Northern Europeans have been since the institution of racial slavery in the seventeenth century C.E., they were far from free of racial prejudice" (BA II: 444).[49] The disgusting association was made in this setting. Unfortunately, history is not always as we would wish it to be.

Should I have mentioned this association in print? Tritle thinks not. In fact, I hesitated for some time, even though Winthrop Jordan devoted a whole section of his magisterial work *White over Black* to European perceptions of links between Africans and apes.[50] I went ahead because, while accepting that in many ways the belief is naïve, I still work on the principle that the truth will make you free and that if we are to fight European racism (which I believe to be by far the greatest social problem in the world today), we should have as accurate an assessment of its depth and nature as possible.

In his criticisms of the last chapters of BA II on the end of the Bronze Age, Tritle is not convinced by the commonly accepted identification of the Egyptian Dene or Denyen (Dn[n]) with Homer's Danaans and the Achaians with the barbarian invaders of Egypt, the Ekwesh (iqwš) and the Aḫḫiyawa referred to in Hittite documents (p. 325). As I stress throughout my work, I do not attempt to achieve certainty or proof, merely competitive plausibility. In these cases, I think it overwhelmingly likely that these similar ethnic names of peoples in approximately the right places doing approximately the right things at the right time should be equated. I do not see the identifications as certain, and such equations should always be open to revision in the light of new evidence.

This last discussion raises, once more, the crucial difference between Tritle and me. He appears to think that unless one can *prove* connections one should not postulate them. I cannot accept this, at least for the epochs and areas with which we are concerned. The Eastern Mediterranean is small and the temporal overlap was long, and we now know that ships have been sailing around it at least since the Early Bronze Age. Therefore, I can see no reason why one should presume isolation. I should be very surprised if there had not been substantial contact between the Aegean and other shores of the Eastern Mediterranean during the two thousand years between 3000 and 1000 B.C.E. I think that those who seek to dissociate similar cultural features in Egypt, the Levant, and Greece have a greater requirement to justify their position than do those of us who want to relate them.

Finally, I should like to thank Lawrence Tritle for providing me with a number of references of which I was not aware and, more important, for having given the issues with which we are both concerned a substantial academic workout. I believe that the ongoing project of *Black Athena* is the stronger for it.

4 How Did the Egyptian Way of Death Reach Greece?

A REPLY TO EMILY VERMEULE

In her book *Aspects of Death in Early Greek Art and Poetry* published in 1979, Emily Vermeule wrote about outside influences on Greek views of death during the Bronze Age:

> These Bronze Age patterns of thought and representation, the tomb as a house for the body, the soul in a new home, the mourning in files and beside the coffin or bier, the *psyche*, the soul-bird and the sphinx-ker—were not all developed spontaneously on the Greek mainland, without influence from abroad. The natural source for such influence was Egypt, which had the grandest, most monumental, and the most detailed funerary tradition in the ancient world. The mechanics of transmitting some of the Egyptian ideas and some physical forms to Greece is not at all clear yet.[1]

I have tried to provide some clarification of this problem and Egyptian derivations for such concepts and crucial terms as *psyche* and *kēr*, and she is appalled.

Her distress would seem to be because *Black Athena* poses unacceptable threats both to her Classical educational background and to her archaeological professionalism. Until very recently, it was usual for conventional reviewers to give guarded praise to the description in volume 1, of the historiography and the ideology of the discipline of Classics, while they damned volume 2 and its treatment of archaeology. Vermeule appears to have wanted to follow this even-handed approach, but she cannot quite bring herself to do so. She writes: "Yet even for eager readers of the first volume of *Black Athena* it was not always easy to understand the nature of the anti-Semitism that so angered Bernal" (p. 269). She then cites some examples of what she sees as my exaggerated sensitivity on the subject. These included my disapproval of J. B. Bury, the writer of the best-known twentieth-century history of Ancient Greece in English, "when he described the Spartans as refusing to intermarry with their Helots, thus keeping their blood 'pure'" (pp. 269–270). Her summary given here would seem to me clear enough indication of Bury's racism. However, the longer quotation from Bury's book, which I gave in the volume, indicates other important aspects of his thought. He wrote: "The Dorians took possession of the rich vale of the Eurotas, and, keeping their own stock pure from the mixture of alien blood, reduced all the inhabitants to the condition of subjects. . . . The eminent quality which distinguished the Dorians . . . was that which we call 'character' and it was in Lakonia that this quality was most fully displayed and developed itself, for here the Dorian seems to have remained most purely Dorian."[2] This passage leaves no doubt of the writer's and the assumed readers' identification with a "master race." It is also significant because Bury was a Protestant from Ireland and he seems to have seen the Helots as similar to the native Catholic Irish.[3] This is not the only parallel taken from his own day to apply to Ancient Greece. "Character" was the code word used in Oxbridge through much of the nineteenth and twentieth centuries to justify admitting stupid upper-class English students while excluding "clever" members of the lower classes and Jews. If there is any doubt about Bury's preference for "racial" purity, if not anti-Semitism, it is dispelled by another passage (deleted only in the 1976 edition) from his standard history: "The Phoenicians doubtless had marts here and there on coast and island; but there is no reason to think that Canaanites ever made homes for themselves on Greek soil or introduced Semitic blood into the population of Greece."[4] I did not quote this (BA I: 387) as a personal attack on J. B. Bury, who, as it happens, was more liberal than many of his colleagues.[5] I cited it both as an example of attitudes common among classicists and others at the time and specifically to show how contemporary anti-Semitism and racism could affect and distort perceptions of contacts between the Levant and Egypt on the one hand and the Aegean on the other.

To return to Vermeule's review, this time to her anger at what she sees as my disregard for archaeology: "He in fact includes very little standard archaeology, in the sense of reference to excavated evidence, stratification of different civilizations, social organization, or cultural artifacts. There is far more about legends and linguistics and revised chronologies. Unfortunately Bernal handles most of his archaeological discussion by simple assertion" (p. 271). In one respect she is justified in making this claim. As I wrote in the introduction to volume 2:

> My intention to keep the different types of evidence neatly apart has broken down completely as I have found it impossible to indicate the significance of one type without reference to the others. For instance, I claim that the establishment of palaces in Crete in the 21st century B.C. was heavily influenced by the contemporary restoration of central power in Egypt at the beginning of the Middle Kingdom. I believe that this argument can be made convincingly only if one links it to the contemporary introduction of a bull cult to Crete and the latter's Egyptian precedents and parallels. Similarly, in examining the significance of the Mit Rahina inscription, I have felt obliged to look extensively at Classical and Hellenistic sources and at the archaeological evidence. Thus, I abandoned the attempt to apply disciplinary rigour to the material in favour of "thick description" involving many types of evidence simultaneously. (BA II: 2)

Looking back, I realize how naïve my earlier, idealistic view of relying exclusively on archaeological evidence was. However, few archaeologists anywhere and none in the Eastern Mediterranean can afford to disregard "non-archaeological" evidence. For instance, a student has written about Emily Vermeule, "Perhaps her most important lesson has been the value of an interdisciplinary approach to the study of this earliest stage of Greek history."[6] Vermeule's own book, *Greece in the Bronze Age*, is primarily archaeological, but it is full of references to documentary evidence from Linear B and Egyptian texts, to divinities and heroes known about largely from Homeric, Classical, and Hellenistic sources and descriptions, written hundreds of years after the collapse of the Bronze Age culture of Mycenaean Greece. Thus, in admitting other evidence, I am not going beyond conventional practice when I write about the archaeology of the Eastern Mediterranean in periods for which there are some written records and about which we have a considerable number of clues from cult, language, and later traditions. Nevertheless, I freely concede that I have introduced more nonarchaeological material than many other writers. On the other hand, I never claimed that volume 2 would be exclusively concerned with archaeology. After all, its subtitle is *The Archaeological and Documentary Evidence.*

Whether Vermeule likes it or not, other specialists in her field of archaeology have not considered my work beyond the pale and have spent considerable time thinking and arguing about it. These include some of the most eminent names in the profession: Paul Åström, George Bass, Patricia Bikai, Eric Cline, Sturt Manning, Ian Morris, Sarah Morris, James Muhly, and Theodore Spyropoulos.

Not all of these agree with my work, and I would not for a moment claim that the ideas expressed in it are mainstream or orthodox. I merely maintain that the archaeological aspects, sparse as Vermeule sees them to be, are considered sufficiently interesting to be worthy of discussion.

Vermeule argues that, in most cases, I use "simple assertion." The difference between an assertion and an argument is that, whereas an assertion is made in the void, a scholar gives the evidence for and against an argument. This is what I have attempted to do in all instances. It is true that in many cases, the evidence is exiguous and that in some, I may have "jumped the gun." However, I am convinced that it is often useful to set up working hypotheses based on what little evidence is available, even though these may later be refuted. Even so, I have tried to avoid reifying these working hypotheses and, as far as I am aware, I have always emphasized not merely the bases on which arguments are made but also the inadequacies of these bases.

Even "reasoned" arguments are bound to be influenced by subjectivity. This does not mean, however, that I believe that any opinion is as good as any other. Some conclusions clearly have much greater predictive and heuristic value than others. In looking at the archaeological aspects of the issues raised in *Black Athena*, I believe that the increasing archaeological evidence of contact around the Eastern Mediterranean during the Bronze Age that has been found during the decade or more since the publication of *Black Athena* volume 1 has increased the plausibility of many of my proposals.[7]

The strangest element in Vermeule's review is her quotation from Milton's *Paradise Lost:*

But all was false and hollow, though his tongue
Dropp'd manna, and could make the worst appear

The better reason, to perplex and dash
Maturest counsels. (p. 271) [8]

To begin with the subtext: Quoting Milton at all suggests to her readers that Vermeule is not a dry professional archaeologist but a woman of broad culture. This image was set out in the original essay in the *New York Review of Books*. It was only slightly tarnished when a Miltonist, Earl L. Dachslager, wrote to point out that although he completely agreed with her dismal assessment of my work, the devil referred to was not Lucifer, as she had implied, but Belial.[9] So far as I am aware, this is the first time since the seventeenth century that there has been a public discussion as to which devil was in possession of an academic opponent!

Since the initial publication, however, Vermeule has rectified her diabolical mistake, and in BAR she has firmly attached the passage to Belial (p. 271). Nevertheless, the Satanic implications of her original review have survived. She sees me both as the falsely persuasive Belial and as Lucifer, who challenged the divinity. According to Vermeule, I had initially been favored by the archaeological establishment and had then raised a standard of revolt against it. She apparently views me as a fallen angel who has had the hubris to challenge the hosts of classicists, ancient historians, and Mediterranean archaeologists. I see myself as much less of a rebel than she supposes, and throughout my volumes I have discussed my massive debts to professional archaeologists and ancient historians, including Vermeule herself.

Meanwhile, I should like to consider her attack on what she sees as my diabolical seductiveness, in which she echoes many other reviewers. The anonymous review in *Antiquity* concludes: "not for beginners or the gullible." [10] On one plane, the concern is political: the fear that blacks and the "politically correct" will be persuaded by my ideas because they fit their ideological preferences. However, the fear is not limited to these, as there is no doubt that students of all colors and shades of opinion as well as others new to the fields find my ideas inherently plausible. In their "innocence," they cannot see what is wrong with the proposition that Egypt and the Levant may have exerted substantial cultural and linguistic influences on Greek civilization and language.

Defenders of the academic status quo use two basic formulae to protect themselves from major challenges: "It's all rubbish" and "We all knew that anyhow." These can be combined in the single sentence I have overheard in Cambridge senior common rooms: "Some of what he says is new and some of what he says is true, but unfortunately what is new is not true and what's true is not new." This seems to be Vermeule's attitude to my work. The line she and other contributors to BAR are attempting to draw can be summarized as follows: Bernal exaggerates the extent of Oriental influences on Greece and it is untrue that classicists and ancient historians ever denied that there were some such influences.

Mary Lefkowitz seems to represent the majority when she concedes that until the mid-1960s there may not have been a full discussion of Oriental influences on Greece.[11] Vermeule is more hard-nosed: "First no one has ever doubted the Greek debt to Egypt and the East. Schliemann thought he had found a Chinese pot at Troy and was delighted; Sir Arthur Evans was equally pleased to see 'the Libyan codpiece' turn up in Crete, and confidently derived Cretan Tholos tombs from stone circles found in modern Libya. . . . Why on earth does Bernal claim that he is the first ever to look at Egypt and the East, when virtually all contemporary scholars have welcomed every sign of contact" (p. 272).

I have several responses to these sentences. In the first place, I have never written or stated that I was "the first ever to look at Egypt and the East." BA II is dedicated to Gordon Childe as "a champion of modified diffusionism." I make favorable if not flattering references to Arthur Evans throughout both volumes, and I have declared myself to be a great admirer of Cyrus Gordon and Michael Astour. Second, her statement that "virtually all contemporary scholars have welcomed every sign of contact" excludes the extremely influential school of archaeological thought led by Colin Renfrew, which maintains that there were no substantial influences on the Aegean from the East after the beginning of the Neolithic (see below and BA II: 69–77). Furthermore, Vermeule fails to make a crucial distinction in the thought of the more old-fashioned "modified diffusionists": that between the Aegean and the Greeks. Although Childe and the others have been quite happy to see early Oriental influences on the geographical region, they were much less willing to admit them directly on the Hellenes.

Let us consider the case of Arthur Evans, whose work Vermeule mentions approvingly and to which I refer (BA II: 67–68). Given the massive evidence of Egyptian and Levantine material he encountered in his excavation of Knossos, it would have been difficult for him to deny that Egyptian and "Oriental" civilizations had a major impact on Minoan Crete. Nevertheless, Vermeule is quite right to say that Evans welcomed such influences. However, Evans was not considering direct Egyptian or Levantine influences on Greek culture. Evans was adamant not merely that his Minoans were not Greek but that the Mycenaeans had been colonized by Minoans. Thus, any Oriental influence had been thoroughly filtered before it reached Greek civilization.

The problem of Oriental influences on Greeks became more acute when scholars like the historian of religion Martin Nilsson began to see—rightly, in my opinion—that Archaic and Classical Greek culture was based on that of the Mycenaeans, who in turn had borrowed substantially from the Minoans.

As Vermeule appears to have missed it, I shall repeat a long quotation from Renfrew initially included in BA II (p. 72). In his major work, significantly entitled *The Emergence of Civilization: The Cyclades and the Aegean in the Third Millennium* B.C., Renfrew wrote:

> I have come to believe that this widely held diffusionist view, that Aegean civilisation was something borrowed from the Orient, is inadequate. It fails to explain what is actually seen in the archaeological record. We can no longer accept that the sole unifying theme of European prehistory was, in the words of Gordon Childe, "the irradiation of European barbarism by Oriental civilisation." . . . Throughout the southern Aegean, for a thousand years [the third millennium B.C.], striking changes were taking place in every field. . . . *These developments evidently owed little to Oriental inspiration. Yet it was at this time that the basic features of the subsequent Minoan-Mycenaean civilisation were being determined* [my italics].[12]

It is also clear that Renfrew accepts the view of scholars such as the historian of religion and myth Martin Nilsson that the nature of Greek origins is important to European culture as a whole, hence his sweeping title *The Emergence of Civilization*. Where the archaeologists Oscar Montelius, Gordon Childe, and their followers tended to see significant breaks in the culture of the Aegean after 2000 B.C.E., Renfrew, like Nilsson, has maintained that there was an essential cultural continuity.

This notion of cultural continuity gained a great fillip in the 1950s with the acceptance of Michael Ventris's decipherment of Linear B and his demonstration that the Mycenaeans spoke Greek.[13] It was at this point that the earlier tolerance for Oriental influences on what had been thought to be the Pre-Hellenic Aegean was challenged. Although scholars like the Cambridge archaeologist Frank Stubbings continued to see considerable exchanges of material goods and even a Hyksos invasion of the Eastern Peloponnese, Stubbings was adamant that these had no long-term effect on Greek culture.[14]

Where some cultural exchanges were admitted, it was emphasized that these goods and ideas had been taken from the Orient by traveling Greeks. When George Bass, the leading underwater archaeologist of the Mediterranean, suggested on the basis of his excavation of the shipwreck at Cape Gelydonia off southern Turkey that Levantines might have played an active role in such contact, his work was systematically ignored.[15]

Not surprisingly, different subfields have been uneven in their openness on the issues of borrowing. The art historians have tended to focus on two periods, the Minoan in the first half of the second millennium B.C.E. and the so-called Orientalizing period in the seventh century, thereby avoiding what they see as the formative periods of Greek civilization of the centuries between. Nevertheless, they have been less closed-minded on these issues than most classicists and ancient historians. On mythology and literature, there has been a tendency to make general, worldwide comparisons with the Greek forms, and when dealing with the Near East, to start with the Hittites, then move to the Hurrians and Babylonians and only finally consider West Semitic speakers and the Egyptians. The Greeks of the Classical Period themselves had attributed most of their religion and mythology to the last of these.[16]

When, in the 1950s and 1960s, the Semitists Cyrus Gordon and Michael Astour put forward detailed arguments that Greek mythology had borrowed specific stories and names from the Semitic-speaking Levant, their work was largely dismissed by classicists.

The most rigid subfield of all has been that of philology, which is discussed in chapter 6. I shall be convinced of the openness that Vermeule sees in her discipline only when the philologists begin to examine the possibility of explaining the unknown 60 percent of the Greek vocabulary in terms of the two languages that were dominant in the Eastern Mediterranean during the Bronze and Early Iron Ages: Egyptian and West Semitic.

Vermeule argues that it was the Greeks of the Classical Period, not the nineteenth-century classicists, who invented the Aryan model: "[Bernal] has claimed that those who believe in some kind of natural and intellectual and artistic superiority of the Greeks did so because they were racist, probably anti-Semitic. Yet it was the Greeks themselves who first drew a sharp contrast between Asia and Europe, between 'Us' in the democratic West and the 'Barbarians' in the royal, imperial East" (p. 272). Naturally, I am fully aware of these Greek views, in particular those of Herodotus, whose *History* is explicitly based on the conflict between Greece and Asia. This theme and the general Greek pride or chauvinism after the Persian Wars make it all the more remarkable that Herodotus and most of his contemporaries should have maintained that they had been colonized and civilized by Phoenicians and Egyptians and had received their religion from the latter.

It is natural that Greeks themselves should have seen themselves as the best people of their time. However, until the end of the eighteenth century C.E., few other people accepted this at face value. Thus, the widespread Philhellenism, the denial of the Ancient model, and the rise of the Aryan model of the early nineteenth century must be seen as new phenomena. These should be put in the general context of European confidence in the nineteenth century and the sense of categorical superiority over peoples of other continents and of the then current historical belief in the eternal essences of "races." Hence, there was a widespread desire to project present triumphs into the past and stress both Greek achievements and Greek anti-Asiatic ideology for this purpose.

Vermeule maintains, "Bernal believes, or seems to believe, that there is no essential difference between Egyptian culture and language, written in hieroglyphs, and the languages of the ancient Near East, written in cuneiform. Large sections of his book consist of claims that words from one language derive from another" (p. 273). Although I cannot find these "large sections," I certainly accept the conventional wisdom that there are many cognates shared by Egyptian and Ancient Semitic languages. Vermeule exaggerates the significance of script. Both Egyptian and Semitic are branches of the Afroasiatic language family. Furthermore, there is ample evidence of loaning between them in both directions.[17] Contact between the two cultures was most intense in the Levant and especially in the great port city of Byblos, whose prince for many centuries was treated by the Egyptians as an Egyptian mayor. This region of mixed Egypto-Semitic culture was of particular importance because it was the one with the most direct contact with the Aegean.

Vermeule also claims, "Bernal believes there is no essential difference between Egypt and the city states and kingdoms of the Near East" (p. 273). How she could have come up with this idea completely baffles me. I have in fact published two articles in which I argue that the Phoenician city-states provided models for the Greek poleis.[18] These were beyond Vermeule's brief, but in Black Athena I frequently refer in both volumes to Canaanite and Levantine city states with their corporate structures, which are totally different from the pharaonic system of government. For instance, I quote Astour's description of the Bronze Age Syrian port of Ugarit: "In Ugarit, the big merchants were the upper class — they owned the largest land estates, they surrounded the throne as advisers and administrators, and they served in the elite corps of the army as *mariannu* — charioteers . . . if we look for a parallel to the Ugaritic *mariannu*, it would be the patriciate not of early Rome but of Medieval Venice, except that the social relations in Ugarit were far from the rigidity and exclusiveness of the Venetian mercantile oligarchy" (BA II: 437). Does Vermeule really believe that I see this as having "no essential difference" from the Egyptian monarchy?

Why did Vermeule make so many mistakes?

It is puzzling that a scholar of the distinction of Emily Vermeule should make so many mistakes in her review. Some of these are trivial and do not affect her overall argument. For example, she writes, in part quoting me: "Bernal adds Berber as an influential ancient language too; he claims a Berber linguistic root for 'Atlas, Atlantic' — the word *adrar*, mountain, which was not attested before the nineteenth century C.E., 'but there is no reason to suppose that it is not an ancient word'" (p. 273). In fact, after a long, not to say tedious, discussion, I do not accept the views of the scholars who have proposed *adrar* as the etymology for Atlas. I merely conclude that "in short it would seem quite possible that one source of the name Atlas/Atlantis was the Berber Adrar. It would seem unlikely to be the only source for Atlas as Adrar cannot explain a number of aspects of the name" (BA II: 298–299).

Thus, Vermeule attributes to me a position that I had noted had been accepted by some previous scholars but that I myself had explicitly rejected. Furthermore, where she says that I see Berber as "an influential language," I make no such claim and indeed refer to Berber etymologies only *once* — this time — in the 1,311 pages of *Black Athena* published so far. Like anybody who has read Fernand Braudel on the unity of the Mediterranean, I do not rule out the possibility of other Berber loans, although I do not have the linguistic competence to detect them. Such intellectual and cultural openness starkly contrasts with Vermeule, who appears to see the suggestion of any Berber etymology in Greek — even for a North African place-name — as inherently absurd; further, she assumes that her readers share that view.

Her general approach is to use reductio ad absurdum to exaggerate my position. For instance, at the end of a long sarcastic treatment of the idea of Hyksos being buried in the Shaft Graves of Mycenae, she concludes: "As they came, they shifted from being Egyptian *Hyksos* ('foreign princes') to being Greek *hiketai* ('suppliants') (2:364)—Although that word has a well-attested Greek root, *hikneomai*, *hiko*, 'I arrive as a suppliant after exile or murder'" (p. 277).

To put it simply, I do link the name Hyksos to the title of Zeus Hikesios, Zeus (the Suppliant), who dominates Aeschylus' play *The Suppliants*. I see the relation as one of punning or *paronomasia* in which Hyksos may have suggested Hikesios. I make absolutely no attempt to derive the root *hikō* from Egyptian, even though it lacks a clear Indo-European etymology.

At another point, Vermeule claims that I maintain that "the Greek god Pan is named for a Nile fish *pa in*" (p. 273). My actual account, however, is quite different. After raising the point that the name Pan probably involved sacred paronomasia and had several sources, I wrote: "Another and stronger possibility is that the development of the name Pan was influenced by the Egyptian *p3 ỉm* (the groan). A phonetic parallel comes in the derivation of the Greek word *pan*, *panos* (a Nile fish) from the Egyptian *p3 ỉn* (the fish)" (BA: II 171). Probably this was just carelessness on Vermeule's part, but it fits the general pattern of exaggeration.

Not surprisingly, the most systematic and significant examples of such misrepresentation are concerned with archaeology. She states, for instance (p. 275), that I believe there was an Egyptian conquest of Bootia during the Old Kingdom. This is not the case.[19] She claims (p. 275) that I view the Cretan palaces as solely Egyptian, whereas in fact, I refer repeatedly (BA II: 158–162) to influences from many parts of the Middle East. Vermeule also maintains (p. 274) that I do not consider the Egyptian sense of geographical polarity of north and south, but I do (see BA II: 251–253). More significantly, she states that I have "an endearingly childlike faith in the absolute historical value of Greek myths." As I have explained many times in this volume and elsewhere, this is simply not the case.

This observation leads to a much more serious objection to Vermeule's critique. It is against her statement that I see "the entire profession of Bronze Age Aegean and Classical archaeologists . . . as ignorant, prejudiced and racist" (p. 270). This assertion is followed by a quotation from my work that has absolutely nothing to do with her extraordinary claim. I am entirely opposed to the extreme isolationist views of Colin Renfrew and his supporters, but, though these ideas have been very influential during the past twenty-five years, they do not represent the more balanced views of the mainstream of Eastern Mediterranean archaeology of which Vermeule is a distinguished representative.

Indeed, my reliance on and respect for twentieth-century archaeology is clear from the very first page of BA II, as the volume is dedicated to the memory of the archaeologist V. Gordon Childe. Near the beginning of the book's conclusion I wrote: "There would seem to be a paradox here as the main thrust of my whole project has been against the influence of racism and anti-Semitism on scholarship. Yet in this volume I have frequently found myself championing the views of scholars working at the high tide of racism 1880–1940" (BA II: 522). With the single exception of my hypothesis about the conquests of the pharaoh Senwosret/Sesōstris in Anatolia and the Caucasus, all my major historical claims have been based on suggestions from professional archaeologists and ancient historians.

In earlier work, Vermeule herself has indicated that Egyptian officials were present in the Aegean during the Old Kingdom. On page 149 of BA II, I quoted her and Cornelius Vermeule's speculations on the origin of a gold hoard containing Egyptian objects of the Fifth Dynasty found in western Turkey: "Did they send an official as a diplomatic or commercial ambassador to the shores of the Mediterranean beyond Egypt . . . ? Did he carry his seal as credentials to be married, or murdered or perhaps robbed abroad?" [20] I seldom, if ever, rise to such imaginative heights.

The art historian and archaeologist Vance Watrous has suggested the Near Eastern colonization at the foundation of the Cretan palaces; I do not go so far. [21] I do, however, follow the encyclopedic and insightful early-twentieth-century German ancient historian Eduard Meyer, whom Vermeule and I both admire, when he maintained that the Hyksos had occupied Crete.

Vermeule is shocked by my suggestion that the warriors buried in the Shaft Graves may have been Hyksos princes. But, as stated above, this is a respectable minority position. [22] It is good to see that she is moving toward the early dating of the great Thera eruption to 1628 B.C.E. (p. 276). Thanks to my colleague, the dendrochronologist Peter Kuniholm, I have worked with this date since the beginning of my project. The redating from the previous convention of c. 1500 is significant, among other reasons because frescoes buried by the island's eruption now have to be seen as coming from the time of the Egyptian Second Intermediate Period rather than from the New Kingdom. This was a period when substantial contacts between the Aegean and the rest of the Eastern Mediterranean are generally admitted. The scholars who have published work on them agree that the Theran frescoes portray a highly sophisticated and cosmopolitan society reflecting Minoan, Egyptian, and Levantine influences. We now know that they were painted at a time when the Hyksos were the dominant power in the latter two regions.²³

This picture of considerable cultural contact around the Eastern Mediterranean in the seventeenth century B.C.E. has been confirmed by the frescoes of a Cretan type that were recently found at the Hyksos capital of Avaris and at Tel Kabri in the Galilee (p. 276). As I mention (BA II: 437), there is no doubt that during much of the second millennium B.C.E., Cretan art was admired throughout the Middle East. I do, however, also refer to the introduction to late-eighteenth-century Crete of important new artistic motifs: the "flying gallop," the winged sphinx, and the griffin. All of these have plausible origins in Syria (BA II: 364–365). Furthermore, we know that the chief language in use among the Hyksos was West Semitic, and it is quite likely that a Semitic language was spoken in Minoan Crete. We also know that the Hyksos rulers of Lower Egypt took on many aspects of Egyptian culture. Hence, it is not wildly speculative to suggest that Semitic and Egyptian vocabulary and religion could have been introduced to the Aegean during this period. Indeed, it would be surprising if it had not. The recent discovery that many of these paintings belong to a palace of the early Eighteenth Dynasty raises the strong possibility that they were commissioned by or for Queen Aḥḥotpe (mother of Aḥmose, the first pharaoh of that dynasty), who had other connections with the Aegean.²⁴

In concluding this lengthy response to Emily Vermeule's sharp critique, I should like to repeat that my work is not a rejection of the "entire profession," as she maintains. I merely follow early-twentieth-century scholars like Arthur Evans, Eduard Meyer, and Gordon Childe who worked on the very reasonable principle of modified diffusionism. Where I differ from them is in the belief that influences from the Near East continued long after the Aegean was inhabited by Indo-European-speaking "Hellenes," and therefore greatly affected later Greek civilization.

There are three major reasons for this difference and for my belief that we should update the work of these great scholars. First, we need to discount the racism and anti-Semitism to which they were inevitably exposed. I am convinced that although they were open to the idea of early Near Eastern influences on the Aegean, this racist atmosphere made them disinclined to see more specifically Semitic and Egyptian influences on Hellenes.

Second, the decipherment of Linear B in the 1950s made it clear that the language, proper names, and religion of the Late Bronze Age Aegean were Greek. Thus, there was clearly substantial cultural continuity through the so-called Dark Ages. We can therefore suppose that Near Eastern influences on the Aegean during the Mycenaean period would have affected the later civilization of Archaic and Classical Greece.

Third, there are the striking archaeological discoveries of the past quarter century, notably the Gelydonia and Kaş shipwrecks and the Theran and other frescoes. These discoveries indicate that during many centuries of the Bronze Age, the cultures of the Eastern Mediterranean were parts of an interlocking economic and political system that facilitated substantial cultural exchange. Furthermore, given the greater age, wealth, and political power of the civilizations of Egypt and the Levant, the predominant cultural flow would likely have been from the southeast to the Aegean.

5 Just Smoke and Mirrors?

A REPLY TO EDITH HALL

A reviewer inevitably simplifies the arguments she or he is considering. A boundary, however ill-defined, does exist beyond which criticism ceases to be interesting because distortion makes the object of the criticism into a straw man. I believe this is largely the case with Edith Hall's critique. In my reply, I shall refer to three major instances of this type of exaggeration. First is her claim that I advocate the Ancient model, implying that I dismiss all modern scholarship (p. 346). In fact, as I have stated in many places in this book and elsewhere, I propose a *Revised* Ancient model, which incorporates many modern academic achievements.

In the same spirit of exaggeration, Hall writes: "[Bernal] asks us to accept that the Greeks themselves genuinely believed that they were descended from Egyptians or Phoenicians" (p. 335), and further (p. 340): "Did the Greeks *all* believe they were descended from Egyptians and Phoenicians, *all* the time?" (her italics). At no point have I made these suggestions. All I have claimed is that conventional wisdom in Classical and Hellenistic Greece maintained that *some* Greek royal families were descended from Egyptians or Phoenicians.[1] I see no incompatibility between the legends of Egyptian and Phoenician settlement in Greece and other myths of origin claiming that the Greeks were of autochthonous or "Pelasgian" descent.

The third distortion is her suggestion that I take myths literally. In this, of course, she resembles many other contributors to BAR, but she adds that I reject the sophisticated work on mythology carried out during the twentieth century and refuse to see how confused and internally contradictory the myths are.

I believe that one reason for the variety and inconsistency of Greek myths and legends of origin was that the Greek past of the third and second millennia B.C.E. was in fact immensely complex. The other reason is that myths of origin are not merely histories. They serve, as Hall quite rightly emphasizes, many other aesthetic, ideological, and political purposes. The same purposes are also served in modern historiography. Thus, I maintain—and I state many times—in BA that *both* ancient and modern sources should be read critically with all these aspects in mind.

Acceptance of my work does not require, as Hall states, the abandonment of "the sophisticated theories of the twentieth century, which have helped us to understand how mythology works" (p. 347). The fact that myths have intricate and complicated structures and that some of these complexities can be explained interestingly by modern scholars has little or no bearing on the questions with which I am concerned as to what, if any, valid historical material they may contain.

Clearly, not every myth of origin contains a kernel of truth. Some myths are complete fictions and some are borrowed from other peoples. On the other hand, it is equally clear that many myths of origin do contain "historical" elements. It is possible that this is the case with Greek myths of origin. This possibility is increased by the fact that the myths and legends of settlement and cultural influence do not refer to anything that violates the rules of natural science, such as an origin in the sun or the moon.

These legends are not even very improbable. Greece is as close to Egypt and the Levant as Japan is to China, and the Mediterranean is much less dangerous than the Yellow Sea. At least since the fourth millennium B.C.E. Egypt and Canaan/Phoenicia had considerable periods of urbanization and prosperity and possessed the navigational means of reaching the Aegean. This inherent plausibility, as well as a respect for authority, led scholars to accept the basic truth of the Ancient model until the beginning of the nineteenth century, when there were pressing ideological needs not to do so.

Hall argues that in "a logical *non-sequitur* and a methodological flaw" I confuse what the Greeks may have believed about their "ethnic origins" with what actually happened (p. 336). This is not the case. I make the distinction throughout BA and I concluded BA I with the argument that the Ancient model could be wrong and modern scholarship right: "I insist that its [the Aryan model's] conception in sin, or even error, does not necessarily invalidate it" (BA I: 442). Nevertheless, I do believe that what would appear to be the historical kernel of the myths should not be taken, as Hall would have me claim, as "the most vital plank" (p. 335) of my argument. However, I do see it as an important source of information to be viewed in conjunction with others: archaeology, linguistics, and Bronze Age documents and paintings. Inquiry into these other sources has convinced me that the ancient traditions of settlement may well be right. Thus, in this case I am persuaded that the myths do contain a kernel of "truth." Nevertheless, any correspondence between what the Greeks believed about their past and "what actually happened" is contingent, not necessary, and I try to keep the two firmly distinguished both in my mind and in my books.

Hall is absolutely right when she claims that my knowledge of the secondary literature on ethnicity is sketchy and my use of the concept unsophisticated. Her counterproposal, however, is even worse, in that it relies on Max Weber's grossly outdated distinction between "objective" or "biological" and "subjective" ethnicity (p. 336). I do not find it at all helpful to make such a distinction. In 2000, as opposed to the first thirty years of the twentieth century, it is difficult to maintain that any *ethnos* is a "biological" entity. "Race" does not come into it. The only partial exception is the situation in Northern Europe and North America after the establishment of racial slavery and the resulting development of obsessional racism. In these societies, individuals of markedly different physical type have faced difficulties being accepted as members of the nation. Even in these societies, however, virtually no "objective biological" basis exists for, say, English, French, or German ethnicity. In the Ancient Eastern Mediterranean, there may have been awe and fear of, as well as jokes about, people with strange Northern European or Central African physical appearances. Egyptian, Phoenician, or Greek ethnicity, however, had very little objective or biological basis. These and nearly all ethnic groups were founded on a common language or dialect cluster, common customs, and a common ideology, among other similar commonalities. These are all more or less malleable. Thus, ethnicity is an essentially subjective category.

In any event, I do not accept that this issue impinges on the Revised Ancient model. Only in Hall's absurd exaggeration of my views, which I treat above, are the Greeks *as a people* supposed to be descendants of Egyptians and Phoenicians.

Kadmos

Now to some of Hall's specific sections: first, that concerning Kadmos and the foundation of Thebes (p. 337). I am sorry if my ellipse in BA I (p. 19) led readers to believe that Homer had referred to the Kadmean foundation of Thebes. As I read the passage, I only attribute the story of the foundation by Amphion and Zethos to him, but I see how confusion could arise. In any event, later on (BA I: 85), I state explicitly that "Homer did not mention the colonizations," referring to those of Kadmos and Danaos. I quite agree with the line of scholars stretching beyond professors Hall and Gomme to K. O. Müller that references to Phoinix or Phoinikes in connection with Kadmos and others *do not necessarily* indicate Phoenicians. However, given the frequent later associations between the Greek Thebes and Phoenicia and between Phoinix and Europa, plus very plausible Semitic etymologies for Kadmos and Europa and the iconographic evidence that Europa was seen as "Oriental" in the seventh century B.C.E., it is *overwhelmingly likely* that when Homer referred to "Kadmeans" at Thebes and Hesiod described Europa as "daughter of noble Phoinix" carried by Zeus over "salt water," they were already following the traditions for which we have so many later attestations.

Hall's discussion of the term "Aithiops," which she sees as a parallel term to "Phoinix," is of rather more consequence. She maintains that the name Athiopes was used only for a fabulous people living at the end of the world until what she sees as the "rise of ethnography in the late sixth century B.C.E." (p. 337). This argument raises a substantial and interesting division between classicists on the one hand, and archaeologists and other students of the Eastern Mediterranean on the other. Classicists still work within the model set up in the early and mid–nineteenth century according to which "Greece" began with Homer, Hesiod, and the Olympic Games in the eighth and seventh centuries B.C.E. and only rose to self-consciousness and consciousness of others in the following centuries.

Archaeologists working over a much longer time span now know that inhabitants of the Aegean had substantial knowledge of Africa and Africans in the Bronze Age. Spyridon Marinatos maintained that an African black

was portrayed on one of the Thera murals painted in the seventeenth century B.C.E.[2] Whether he was right about this particular case, the detailed
representation of African flora and fauna in the paintings makes it virtually
impossible that "Ethiopians" were unknown in the Aegean at the time. In
Cyprus too there are Late Bronze Age representations of blacks.[3]

The name Aithiopes would most probably have been used to describe
such people. Ventris and Chadwick plausibly linked the name A₃tijoqo,
which appears several times in Linear B, to the Homeric Aithiops.[4] They and
Chantraine also plausibly associated the Mycenaean names Sima and Simo
to the later ones, Simos, Simōn, Simmos, and Simmias, and to the word
simos ("snub-nosed").[5] The poet Xenophanes of the sixth century B.C.E.
referred to the Aithiopes as simoi.[6] Homer's Eastern Aithiopes can be explained in terms of the black and sometimes "negroid" population of Elam
in Eastern Mesopotamia, which had special associations with the Homeric
Ethiopian hero Memnōn. (I discuss this issue in excruciating detail in BA
II: 257–269.)

In other chapters, I have stated the grounds for many cultural continuities through what are misleadingly named the "Dark Ages" between the
end of the Bronze Age and the Greek revival during the Archaic Period.[7]
Thus, some aspects of previous knowledge of the outside world were undoubtedly preserved. Even during the Geometric and Archaic Periods of
the tenth to sixth centuries B.C.E., the idea that Greeks had only a foggy
sense of the wider world in general and Africa in particular is made still less
plausible by the substantial archaeological evidence of contact between the
Aegean and the Middle East not merely in the Late Bronze Age but also in
the Early Iron Age.[8] There was also continued contact with black Africans.
In the Odyssey, for instance, Odysseus' herald, Eurybates, was described as
black-skinned with curly hair, and Hesiod saw the Ethiopians as the polar
opposite of the northern Scythians.[9] All in all, although there is no doubt
that the term Aithiops was used in a utopian sense, I see no reason to believe that it ever lost its association with actual peoples whom we should
call black. Therefore, Hall is fundamentally mistaken when she argues: "It
is . . . just as plausible to argue that a fabulous people of Archaic epic, who
lived in the furthest East or West and whose name indicated a brilliance
in the eyes or face of reflected light from the rising or setting sun, were
identified during the period of the rise of ethnography in the sixth century
B.C.E. with real, outlying dark skinned peoples" (p. 337; my italics). Her
ingenious, though cumbersome, explanation is a remote possibility, but,
given the evidence cited above, it is absurd for her to claim against Profes-

sor Snowden and virtually all modern scholars that the name Aithiops had no connection with dark skin during the Bronze and Early Iron Ages.

Danaos

Moving away from Aithiops, Hall offers a different set of rebuttals on the issue of Danaos, the legendary founder of Argos. She is quite right to point out my sloppiness in stating baldly that Io was the daughter of Inachos, when this was merely the view of the annalist Kastor and many of the Tragedians. As she states, Hesiod and Akusilaos reported a tradition that her father was Pieren, whoever he was. While confessing to this omission, I should like to have another offense taken into account: my failure to state that Apollodorus (II.1.3) and Pausanias (II.16.1) maintained that Io's father was a certain Iasos. I cannot see, however, how these failures affect my general argument. Hesiod's statement that Io was impregnated near Euboia and not, as the mainstream tradition held, at the mouth of the Nile is more relevant. The Aegean location can be relatively easily explained, given the poet's close, if unfortunate, connections with the Greek island and the association between the cow Io and Euboia seen as coming from bous ("bovine"). Nevertheless, I concede Hall's argument here and agree that I should have raised this point. It does not, in my opinion, damage the case that the predominant Greek tradition associated Io and Danaos with Egypt.

I am more dubious about Hall's belief "that there *may have existed a whole alternative mythical tradition* about Io's descendants through Epaphos to the Danaids, and of course also to Herakles, which had a local mainland Greek color and very little to do with Egypt" (p. 338; my italics). Given the plausible Egyptian etymology for the name Epaphos (see BA I: 92), given the fact that Herakles had, as I have tried to show, *a great deal* to do with Egypt, and given the substantial attestation of a genealogy set outside Greece (BA II: 109–120), I see no basis for such speculation. I agree that there may well have been an Egyptianizing trend in Greece in the seventh and sixth centuries B.C.E., and I do not deal in *proof* but in *competitive plausibility*. Thus, I cannot *disprove* the idea that the connection of Danaos and Io with Egypt was constructed only in this late period. What I have tried to do is assemble evidence to suggest that it is extremely unlikely.

In pursuing her attack on my treatment of Danaos, Hall also refers to "the important process during this period (the 6th century), of which Bernal seems unaware, by which many traditional mythical figures were brought into connection with foreign peoples and places. This process was associated with *Greek* colonization" (p. 338).

Of course I am aware of this scheme, as it has been a staple of nineteenth- and twentieth-century Classics. Indeed, in *BA I* I explicitly refer to its beginnings (p. 310). Such a process may indeed have been one element in the construction of the myths of Oriental contacts, which are attested from after this time. What I argue throughout my whole project is that this kind of "late" syncretism was not a major element in the formation of the legends and that it has been blown completely out of proportion by nineteenth- and twentieth-century Graecocentrism and Besserwisserei.

Although we have many disagreements, I follow Martin Nilsson and Colin Renfrew on one essential point: The Greek religious and mythical traditions have strong and highly ramified roots going back to the Bronze Age. Where I disagree with them is in their attempt to maintain that the Aegean was isolated from the rest of the Near East in the formative second and third millennia with which they have been concerned. By contrast, considerable evidence suggests to me that for long stretches of both millennia, Egypt, the Levant, and the Aegean had substantial contacts. Material remains indicate that the predominant cultural flow was toward the northwest, a plausible view because of the greater wealth, power, and sophistication of Egypt and the Levant. Another reason I am inclined to believe the Greek claims of early connections with the rest of the Eastern Mediterranean is my distrust of the racism and anti-Semitism of the modern scholars who first denied such links. Hall concedes this last point when she writes: "There is, moreover, little doubt that Bernal is correct in arguing that modern racial prejudice has been one of the reasons why cultural contact between ancient Hellenophone communities and ancient Semitic and black peoples has been and is still being played down" (p. 335).

I do not, as Hall states, "consistently forget" that some Greek writers claimed autochthonous origin for heroes otherwise seen as foreign (see, for instance, *BA* I: 90). I do, however, see these stories as less remarkable than the legends of Oriental settlement and cultural influence. The admission that much of their civilization came from the southeast is striking because we know that Greeks in the fifth and fourth centuries B.C.E. were generally xenophobic and particularly hostile to Phoenicians and Egyptians, who were often allied with the Persians. The force that such feelings generated would seem to more than equal any desire to give Greece cultural depth by plugging it into older civilizations. The probable result would be a tendency to minimize cultural borrowings from the Near East rather than to exaggerate them, as indicated by the clear unhappiness of some writers in reporting foreign settlements (BA I: 90, 104).

This observation leads to another fundamental disagreement I have with Hall: the relative credibility of Greeks of the Classical, Hellenistic, and Roman periods on the one hand, versus nineteenth- and twentieth-century classicists on the other. She maintains that "credulity is stretched to the limit" when we use such "late" authors as Strabo, Pausanias, and Plutarch, who are "in little or no position better than we are to judge" (p. 339). As I have written many times, I believe that one should treat both the ancient and the modern writers with caution, but that on these issues one should be even more skeptical of the claims of the latter. In the first place, the scholarly framework that I have called the Aryan model was set up by scholars who saw no relevance in the great decipherments and archaeological advances made in the nineteenth and twentieth centuries. Thus, the creators of the Aryan model knew far less of the Bronze Age than even the "latest" ancient writers, who lived before the cumulative cultural breaks of the rise of Christianity and Islam and the collapse of the Western Roman Empire. The "late" writers lived when there were still many physical, linguistic, and institutional vestiges of the Bronze Age civilizations. Scholars working within the Aryan model in the twentieth century have had much more data than their nineteenth-century predecessors, and in some respects their knowledge may even exceed that of Late Antiquity, but I do not accept that this was true in general. Certainly Strabo, Pausanias, and Plutarch had a feel for the societies they were describing that cannot be equaled by modern scholars.

No doubt some modern scholars have been more systematic than the Ancients and have had the advantage of a general understanding of natural science. To my mind, this advantage is far outweighed, in the areas with which we are concerned, by the passionate faith in physical ethnicity and race held by the founders of the Aryan model and by the racism and anti-Semitism rampant in the societies in which the later nineteenth- and twentieth-century scholars have worked.

Raising an interesting issue, Hall implies that I am inconsistent when I maintain that the Ancient model contains a kernel of "historical truth" but have nothing good to say about the nineteenth-century "myth" of the Aryan model. In fact, however, I believe that the Aryan model too has a kernel of "truth." I accept its claims, for example, that once a Proto-Indo-European language or cluster of dialects existed somewhere to the north of Greece. Hence, as Greek is undoubtedly an Indo-European language, there must have been substantial cultural influence on, if not migrations to, the Aegean basin from the north. When, how, or in what ways these took place I do not know, except that I am convinced they must have taken place before 1900 B.C.E. Acceptance of these two kernels of historicity in the Aryan model is the most significant element of the "revision" of the Revised Ancient model.

Athenian Sources

Last, I should like to consider once again the charge that I have been taken in by Athenian propaganda.[10] This charge may be true to the extent that Athenian pride in what they saw as their autochthonous origins prevented me from giving the same emphasis to the legends of the Egyptian origins of Kekrops and Erechtheus that I gave to those around Danaos and Kadmos. Hall (p. 342) challenges me to find a text from the fifth century B.C.E. to back my statement that the story that Kekrops was an Egyptian was "probably current in Herodotus' day" (BA I: 79). She is quite right: I cannot. It was precisely for this reason that I used the word "probably."

My hypothesis, however, is not simply a projection backwards of the Egyptian claims reported to Diodorus Siculus in the first century B.C.E. (BA I: 28–29). It is based on a number of factors. First, Plato reported a special relationship between Sais and Athens in what was purported to be the beginning of the sixth century B.C.E.[11] Then, in the middle of that century, Peisistratos used Egypto-Libyan imagery in the propaganda for his tyranny. Furthermore, his promotion of the cult of Athena in Athens is almost certainly related to the promotion of the goddess's cult elsewhere in the Aegean by the tyrant's contemporary, the Saite pharaoh Amasis.[12] All of these suggest that in the sixth century B.C.E., Athens had a close relationship with Egypt and more specifically with the Egyptian capital of the Sais. Both cities worshipped the same goddess, called Nēith in Egypt and Athena in Greece (see BA I: 51–53). I believe such circumstantial evidence is enough to establish a *probable* case that stories of Kekrops' origin in Egypt were current in Greece during Herodotus' lifetime in the fifth century. If I am right, the contemporary political situation of the sixth and fifth centuries B.C.E. probably influenced these legends. I argue, however, that these stories were not merely the result of such pressures and that the forms in which the desired connection was established may well have had some historicity, which can be checked by other means.

Ample evidence suggests that Boiotians of Classical and Hellenistic times believed that the Theban Kadmos and his dynasty were connected with Phoenicia. This evidence is not restricted to the Athenian tragedies but includes toponyms, myths, and cults.[13] Thus, although the Athenian tragedies clearly had an anti-Theban bias, there is no reason to suppose that the material they used had no historical substance.

The position is equally clear in the Eastern Peloponnese, even if Hall arbitrarily rules Herodotus and the Athenians out of court. Here, the respectably Boiotian Hesiod offers evidence.[14] Pausanias provides detailed and specific references to local traditions concerning the arrival of "the Egyptians" in the Argolid and describes the cults they were supposed to have introduced.[15] There is a strong probability that the Spartan kings believed in their Heraklid "Syrian or Egyptian" descent as set out by Herodotus. This is indicated by the building in the seventh century B.C.E. of a national monument, the Menelaon, in the form of "a sort of small step pyramid." [16] Around 300 B.C.E. King Areios of Sparta wrote to the High Priest at Jerusalem claiming kinship between Spartans and Jews.[17] A century later, the last king of Sparta took the name Nabis. There is no doubt that he was a Spartan and quite probably from one of the two royal families. Nevertheless, Nabis is certainly not a Greek name but could derive either from the Canaanite *nåbîʾ* ("prophet") or from the Egyptian *neb* ("lord") or from both.[18] The Spartan attachment to the Libyo-Egyptian oracle of Ammon at Siwa is also amply attested.[19] I shall argue below that some special Spartan organizational terms have plausible Late Egyptian etymologies. This suggests that the Spartan rulers of the ninth and eighth centuries B.C.E. were eager to demonstrate their relationship with Egypt.[20] All this would seem to corroborate the conventionality of Herodotus' statement that the kings of the Eastern Peloponnese were of Egyptian or Syrian descent.[21]

Hall and I differ greatly over time scales. As mentioned above, she tends to follow the disciplinary tradition of Classics that places the beginning of Greece in the eighth century B.C.E. Looking at the Eastern Mediterranean as a whole, I prefer to look to the second or even the third millennium B.C.E. for its origins. This difference is brought out in our contrasting views of the legendary arrival of the god Dionysos in Greece from the east. In Antiquity, Dionysos was generally viewed as the latest of the gods. Therefore, modern scholars have tended to believe that his cult had begun in the Archaic Period (750–500 B.C.E.). This hypothesis, however, has been destroyed by the discovery of the name on two thirteenth-century tablets from Pylos, one of which has the sign for "wine" on the obverse.[22] In my opinion, the legendary arrival from the east by sea, after the establishment of the other gods, could just as well refer to the arrival of an ecstatic cult of Osiris, Thammuz, or Attis in the Late Bronze Age. The situation is made more complicated, however, by the discovery of traces of the cult of Dionysos in the Aegean from the turn of the second millennium B.C.E.[23]

Conclusion

I end this chapter by stating my fundamental disagreement with Hall's conclusion that "what we need to do is to reject the historical validity of both myths [the Ancient and Aryan models] and turn to the three really important questions: Who on earth did the Greeks think they were? Why did they think it? And what is it about the late twentieth century which renders the issue so important to us?" (p. 347).

We should not be so restricted. I see no reason why Hall's interesting questions should be incompatible with those posed in BA. We should ask both sets. Refusal to examine the historical as well as the structural-functional aspects of Greek myths and legends leaves in place the myth of a purely European Greece that I am convinced is not merely politically undesirable but historically wrong. I believe that both the Ancient model and the Aryan model contain elements that may well have historical value and that these possibilities should be examined in the light of evidence from other sources.

For several reasons, the cultural origins and makeup of Ancient Greek civilization are important to us in the late twentieth century. First, European culture is dominant in the world today, and directly or indirectly, the civilization of Ancient Greece has been central to the formation of this culture. Furthermore, Europeans holding a gamut of political views from fascist to liberal to communist agree that Ancient Greece gave the world philosophy, art, science, and democracy. This myth of origin has been widely used to give Europeans and their descendants elsewhere the exclusive possession of such desirable cultural artifacts. This monopoly has been used to bolster and justify the extension of European military, political, and cultural power into other continents.

Suppose that it is accepted that the greatness of Ancient Greek civilization came from its eclecticism, that it was not a purely "European" culture, that it had strong African and Asian components, and that many crucial elements of "Greek" philosophy, art, science, and democracy had been introduced from the Near East. Such an understanding would have a fundamental and, to my mind, beneficial effect on all peoples, *including those of Europe* and not merely on those of Southwest Asia and Northeast Africa. However, an empty or groundless "myth of an eclectic Greece" would be worse than useless, as it would lead to disillusion and a still greater sense of cultural inferiority among non-Europeans. For this reason I would not have published BA if I had not been convinced that on the issue of contacts between the Aegean and the rest of the Near East, the Greek traditions are generally more reliable than modern scholarship.

III

Linguistics

THE FACT THAT CHAPTER 6 is the longest in this book is overdetermined. In the first place, the essay by Jay H. Jasanoff and Alan Nussbaum in BAR, to which it is responding, is substantial and contains many specific challenges, to most of which I feel the need to reply. Second, their chapter has been relied on not only by other contributors to BAR but also by many reviewers. More important than either of these, however, is the fact that arguments on language are central to my whole historical project. If the contacts between Egypt and the Levant on the one hand, and the Aegean on the other, were as frequent and intimate as I maintain, linguistic exchange would surely reflect these contacts. I also claim that what I see as the great extent of linguistic borrowings into Greek from the two Afroasiatic languages, Ancient Egyptian and West Semitic, indicates the intensity of cultural contact. I admit that there is some circularity in this argument, but I am convinced that each prop supporting my case—archaeology, documents, Greek tradition and language—can stand on its own, and that together they are irrefutable.

Scholars now generally agree that the first three types of evidence do indicate a far greater degree of contact around the Eastern Mediterranean during the Bronze and Early Iron Ages than was supposed twenty-five years ago. This is not the case with language—at least as very traditional historical linguists like Jasanoff and Nussbaum describe the situation. Their claim that it is absurd to see substantial numbers of Egyptian and Semitic words in Greek makes language anomalous in what is now becoming the generally accepted reconstruction of cultural relations around the Eastern Mediterranean during the Bronze Age.

The chief reason their review was commissioned for BAR has been mentioned in my introduction to this book. The two previous reviewers of this aspect of my work were clearly sympathetic toward the project. Jasanoff and Nussbaum cannot be accused of this. When I first met Jay Jasanoff in the late 1970s, I was fascinated by a man who knew so many languages—even if they were all Indo-European. He was attracted to me because I came from Cambridge at a time when he was feeling lonely in Cornell, in exile from his Cambridge (Massachusetts). For some months he helped me in my researches, because, I believe, he thought that my project was merely a jeu d'esprit, an attempt to see how far one could develop an absurd hypothesis. He even attended a number of meetings of a discussion group I organized consisting of historical linguists from nearby universities, including Saul Levin, Joseph Pia, and Paul Hopper. When Jasanoff realized that I was serious, however, he first cooled toward my project and then became bitterly hostile to it, doing all he could to block any recognition of my work by colleagues at Cornell. He was joined in this by Alan Nussbaum when the latter arrived on campus a few years later.

However, the animosity is not purely personal. The reader may recall that, in the introduction to the Egyptological section, I gratefully noted the courtesy of the Egyptologists' criticisms. Unfortunately, the same spirit does not pervade this debate. One reason for the courteous tone of the Egyptologists is that they are sensitive to the uncertainties of their own positions. Jasanoff and Nussbaum could hardly be more different in this respect. The two men see themselves as professionals and they know "scientifically" that my work, in their area at least, is nonsense.

They see me as a mischievous amateur who does not, or will not, understand the basic principles of "scientific" linguistics. They accuse me of violating the cardinal rule of historical linguistics: that simple similarities between words in different languages do not show that they are related. To prove such a relationship, they insist, one must demonstrate regular phonetic correspondences. Jasanoff and Nussbaum give examples of the elegant precision with which studies within the Indo-European language family have achieved this degree of regularity. They go further and argue that loaning from one language to another has its own regularities. Therefore, for instance, they maintain that it is illegitimate for me to propose four or more different Greek renditions of a single Egyptian word or phoneme. They accuse me of having further widened the range of possibilities for myself by ignoring scholars' reconstructions of Ancient Egyptian vowels. They also complain that I have exaggerated my own originality and the blindness of classicists by playing down the fact that a number of Semitic words have long been recognized as having entered Greek and that some words have even been admitted from Egyptian.

Interestingly, Jasanoff and Nussbaum can provide Indo-European sources for only two or three examples of the Afroasiatic etymologies I propose. They admit that no Indo-European or other alternative derivations exist for the rest. They do not believe, however, that this void matters, as they do not accept my claim that Greek is unusual in having less than 40 percent of its vocabulary explicable in terms of other Indo-European languages. According to Jasanoff and Nussbaum, the non-Indo-European elements in Greek do not need to be explained unless or until the many other dead languages that have existed around the Eastern Mediterranean have been discovered and deciphered.

I attempt to respond to these challenges in the following chapter.

6 Ausnahmslosigkeit über Alles

A REPLY TO JAY H. JASANOFF AND ALAN NUSSBAUM

Before beginning this response, I should like to consider Jasanoff and Nussbaum's heading "Word Games." Word games are the stuff not merely of my proposals but of the discipline of philology or historical linguistics itself. Apparent phonetic and semantic similarities between words of different languages have led scholars to look for the relationships among them.[1] At times, helped by parallels, these relationships can be postulated with exquisite precision. At others, reconstruction of imaginary forms and massive phonetic and semantic shifts are required to explain the links. Word games provide Jasanoff, Nussbaum, and me with endless fascination, delight, and frustration.

As this chapter is by far the longest in *Black Athena Writes Back*, I feel a need to justify its size. First, as many commentators have observed, the linguistic argument is central to my hypothesis that Egypt and the Levant had a massive cultural impact on the formation of Ancient Greek civilization.

When, in the 1970s, I first read the works of Cyrus Gordon and Michael Astour, I concluded that if their claims of close mythological parallels between Southwest Asia and the Aegean were correct—as they seemed to be—close linguistic contacts should also be clearly evident. This is indeed what I have found over the past twenty years. Thus, linguistic arguments have always been central to my work.

Despite the importance of the subject to my project, BAR contains only one chapter on language, whereas, for example, another whole chapter is devoted to the dozen or so scattered sentences in which I mentioned the German writer J. G. Herder. Most of the other contributors refer to and defer to Jasanoff and Nussbaum's chapter on language. This fact alone provides reason enough to reply to the chapter in some detail. What is more, the nature of the article makes the reply still more necessary because the other contributors—and presumably many readers—appear unaware of the extent to which Jasanoff and Nussbaum are out of touch with twentieth-century linguistics.

The Egyptologist John Ray described Jasanoff and Nussbaum's article as an "elegant thrust" (into my bleeding corpse).[2] In his review of "Word Games," which is by no means favorable to me, the Semitist Peter T. Daniels portrayed it very differently. He wrote: "The tone of this article is more appropriate to an unmoderated discussion list . . . than to a published review . . . perhaps he [Jasanoff] wants to be remembered as the pit bull of the right wing of linguistics."[3] This comment may be exaggerated but there is no doubt that Jasanoff and Nussbaum remain close to the most rigid nineteenth-century traditions of their discipline, that of the Neogrammarians.[4] Their chapter is written de haut en bas using such statements as "on the basis of facts which *we control* " (p. 178; my emphasis). It is also buttressed in a very traditional way with such ponderous jokes as "What others do with lost continents Bernal accomplishes just as successfully—or unsuccessfully—with lost consonants" (p. 201).

Like many of the other BAR authors, Jasanoff and Nussbaum use the technique of reductio ad absurdum; finding my ideas, as I state them, difficult to attack, the two Indo-Europeanists exaggerate them to create false but easy targets. They argue, for instance, that I have an inordinate respect for myth and Herodotus' *History*, which they put in the same realm, and that I distrust every modern scholar who had "the misfortune to be born after 1750" (p. 177). As I have stated many times, however, I believe that one should be critical of all sources, even, unlike most of my reviewers, nineteenth-

and twentieth-century scholarship. My attitudes toward the Ancients and myth and legend are discussed elsewhere in this volume.[5]

As to the second charge, it should be clear to any reader that my books are based on modern scholarship. The ideas and information I use do not always come from the champions of conventional wisdom, but very few of the historical hypotheses put forward in BA are original. The series' originality comes from bringing together and making central information that has previously been scattered and peripheral. I have frequently expressed great respect for many twentieth-century scholars, not only those with whom I generally agree, such as Michael Astour, Victor Bérard, Walter Burkert, Gordon Childe, Arthur Evans, Paul Foucart, Cyrus Gordon, Eduard Meyer, Oscar Montelius, Peter Walcot, and Martin West, but also those whose views I often oppose, such as Martin Nilsson and Colin Renfrew. More to the point, I have a great admiration not merely for William Jones, Rasmus Rask, and Franz Bopp—the founders of Indo-European linguistics—but also for the original Neogrammarians to whom Jasanoff and Nussbaum are so closely attached.

The Neogrammarians

August Leskien, Karl Bruggmann, Hermann Osthoff, Berthold Delbruck, and the other Neogrammarians were mostly based in Leipzig and flourished between 1870 and 1900. They were very much part of the nineteenth century. The Neogrammarian method was based on Auguste Comte's positivism and their most important model came from Charles Lyell's "uniformitarian" geology. Lyell's scheme projected processes observable in the present onto the past and emphasized steady progress and regularity.[6] For the Neogrammarians, linguistics *was* linguistic history and linguistic history *was* that of the Indo-European "family." These German scholars maintained that every aspect of language change could be explained rationally by "the exceptionlessness of sound laws" (*Ausnahmslosigkeit der Lautgesetze*).[7] This approach has generally been very successful, and together with such "laws" has been able to explain approximately 70 to 80 percent of cases within language families.

The Neogrammarian approach, however, has significant limitations. Jasanoff and Nussbaum admit that these "laws" are not universal but "language-specific" (p. 181). They fail to point out, however, that the laws apply to to phonetics, not to semantics. Even leaving this limitation aside, it should be noted that the regularity found in phonology is not found in morphology, where analogy from other forms frequently interferes with the predicted regular sound changes.[8] Furthermore, even accepting analogy, application of the "laws" always leaves a substantial "residue" of inexplicable shifts or resistances to change, another point Jasanoff and Nussbaum do not mention.

This residue is the result of a number of factors that disturb the regularity of sound shifts. One is what has been called "phonesthemics." Phonesthemes associate certain experiences or states with specific phonemes. These can be partially onomatopoeic, as with the series slip, slide, slop, and sleasy, or flash, splash, dash, crash, clash, mash, and hash. Onomatopoeia is not necessary, and one finds such clusters as fly, flow, and flutter, or, even more distantly, glitter, gleam, glow, and gold, or the inconstant or iterative meanings of flutter, fritter, putter, glitter. All of these forms can best be described as "sound symbols," phonetic clustering around meanings. These associations thus tend to form even though they may come from different sources or would "regularly" have diverged.[9] In such cases, semantics, for which, as stated above, there is much less regularity, impinges on phonetic "certainty." Naturally, English is not the only language in which this phenomenon occurs. Specifically, in Ancient Greek there are such phonesthemic morphemes as "loi-" found in loigós ("loss, destruction, death"); loidoréô ("insult"); loimós ("plague"); loipós ("stay behind"); and loîsthos ("last"). Some of these forms can be explained paradigmatically but others cannot, and there was an ancient view that loimós was a cross between loigós and līmós ("famine").[10] Neogrammarians merely referred to this kind of mixture pejoratively as "contamination."

Another source of the residue that cannot be explained is what has been described by modern scholars as "lexical diffusion." According to this, some words undergo regular sound shifts, whereas others, for no clear phonetic reason, remain unaffected or go in different directions. For example, the word "meat" now rhymes with "meet," but "great," which originally seems to have had the same dipthong -ea-, now rhymes with "mate."[11] In "Word Games," however, Jasanoff and Nussbaum continue to work within the old framework and imply that there is complete conformity; as they put it, "'Sporadic' changes of this kind are precisely what the regularity principle disallows" (p. 181).

The Neogrammarians focused exclusively on Indo-European and paid no attention to its possible contacts with other languages except for those arising from what they called—using their geological model—"the substrate." This substrate consisted of the real, or supposed, influences on Indo-European languages from the non-Indo-European languages of peoples conquered by Indo-European speakers.[12] The Neogrammarians' lack of interest in non-European languages is easy to explain. First, living in an intensely Romantic age, they believed in the creative power of purity and the overriding importance of internal developments. Although they denounced the "organicism" or biological analogies used by some of their predecessors, "they continued to treat language as a 'thing' independent of the speaker and his social context" and, further, believed that languages as "independent things" did not mix.[13] Second, the Neogrammarians saw the speakers of Indo-European languages as the most active people in history; therefore, they did not believe that their languages could have been substantially influenced by those of less dynamic populations. Third, study of language contact risked confusing the image of geologically slow developments because contact could lead to acceleration of change and, even worse, to irregularity.

Like their academic forefathers, Jasanoff and Nussbaum focus almost exclusively on the Indo-European family, and much of "Word Games" is devoted to rehearsing the traditional and plausible historical reconstructions of developments within language families and in Indo-European in particular. They devote relatively little space to theories of language contact, especially those between unrelated or very distantly related languages. This emphasis may seem surprising given the topic of the review, but it is natural in light of the tradition within which they are working.

Walter Burkert, the leading modern authority on Greek religion, wrote about this traditional Indo-Europeanist spirit as it affects Greek:

Greek linguistics has been the domain of Indo-Europeanists for nearly two centuries; yet its success threatens to distort reality. In all the standard lexicons, to give the etymology of a Greek word means *per definitionem* to give an Indo-European etymology. Even the remotest references—say, to Armenian or Lithuanian—are faithfully recorded; possible borrowings from the Semitic, however, are judged uninteresting and either discarded or mentioned only in passing, without adequate documentation. It is well known that a large part of the Greek vocabulary lacks any adequate Indo-European etymology; but it has become a fashion to prefer connections with a putative Aegean substratum or with Anatolian parallels, which involves dealing with largely unknown spheres, instead of pursuing connections to well-known Semitic languages. Beloch even wanted to separate the Rhodian Zeus Atabyrios from Mount Atabyrion=Tabor, the mountain in Palestine, in favor of vague Anatolian resonances. Anti-Semitism was manifest in this case; elsewhere it was often operating on an unseen level. Even first-rank Indo-Europeanists have made astonishing misjudgments.[14]

Burkert's description rightly draws attention to the widespread tendency in traditional historical linguistics to use the model of a ramifying tree from a single bole rather than a complex lattice or mangrove, and to a preference for self-generating developments within languages or language families.[15] It would be much better for Indo-Europeanists to consider sociolinguistics and therefore be open to the possibility or likelihood of interference from other languages.

Jasanoff and Nussbaum have worked entirely within the Neogrammarian tradition. Jasanoff's one small book is entitled *Stative and Middle in Indo-European*; Nussbaum's more substantial volume is *Head and Horn in Indo-European*.[16] The latter's cultural blinkers, as well as those of his teachers, colleagues, and referees, are clearly and significantly indicated in this study of the Indo-European root $*\hat{k}^{[h]}er$ ("head") and $*\hat{k}^{[h]}\underset{.}{r}$-n- ("horn"). He does not mention, let alone discuss, the fact that the Semitic root for "horn" is *qarn.[17]

REGULARITY OF BORROWING?

When Jasanoff and Nussbaum do treat language contact, they insist on the "high degree of consistency" of loaning. They give the examples of the English "chant" and "chamber," which they see as regular modifications of the Old French nasalized vowels *chant* (čăt) and *chambre* (čăbrə) (p. 185). The historical sequence is not as clear as they suggest. It may well be that Middle English influences on Anglo-Norman merely retarded or prevented the development of consistent nasalization of vowels and the disappearance of nasal consonants taking place in other French dialects during these centuries.[18] Nevertheless, there is no doubt that English "chant" and "chamber" do correspond to the Old French *chant* (čăt) and *chambre* (čăbrə) in a regular way. Other borrowings from Latin and Romance forms of the Vulgar Latin *cantare* and *camera* do not fit this phonetic pattern, however. From the Latin *camera* we have the legal *in camera*, and from *camera obscura* (darkened room with a double lens as the only source of light) there is the modern photographic apparatus we call the camera. There are even more phonetically distinct derivations from *cantare*: whining "cant" from the Northern French; "cantata" from the Italian; "chant" and finally sea "shanty," said to be from the Modern French imperative *chantez* (ʃã'te).[19]

It is perfectly true that loans tend to be adapted with phonetic consistency *but only when they take place over the same period and between the same dialects*.[20] In the real world, languages change and regional dialects vary. Furthermore, loans come through various channels: literary language, popular contact, religious ritual, trade, slavery, and warfare. Loans made at different times or by different routes frequently do not follow the same patterns. In the cases described above, we have a reasonably detailed knowledge of the development of Romance dialects and the periods of borrowings. If all we knew were the Latin *canere* ("sing") and *camera* ("vault") and the English "chant," "cant," "cantata," "shanty," "chamber," and "camera," we would merely have groups of words with vague semantic and phonetic similarities without the precise regularities that traditional Indo-Europeanists require. Yet, they are all certain borrowings from Romance languages! In fact, because of difficulties of script, we have even less information about possible loans from Ancient Egyptian and West Semitic into Greek, which would have taken place in many different ways and over at least 1,500 years. Thus, the "irregularities" or "lack of rigor" in my proposals of which Jasanoff and Nussbaum complain are altogether to be expected.

As mentioned above, the Neogrammarians were concerned with the sounds of words, not their meanings, which they and their descendants admit were not amenable to the same "scientific" rigor. Thus, while there are regularities of phonetic change within language families, semantics follow no such clear-cut guidelines and often show considerable and largely unpredictable shifts of meaning. Take, for example, the Classical Chinese *hǎo*, which has changed its meaning from "love" to "good" in the modern language. Drastic semantic changes within the Germanic languages can be seen in the pattern found in the English shift relating "think" to "thank" or the derivation of "silly" from an older *sælig* ("happy, blessed"). With lexical relations between or among languages, semantics have even greater opportunities for semantic alteration. French and English contain scores of *faux amis* ("false friends"), similar words with significantly different meanings. See, for example, the French *prétendre* (primarily "to claim") and the English "pretend," "deceive," or the French *smoking* as a "dinner jacket." The Scots, then the English "glamour," "enchantment" comes from the Old French *gramarye, grammaire* ("learning, magic"), which itself was derived *irregularly* from the Latin *grammatica* and the Greek *grammatikos* ("knowing one's letters; good scholar"). Nevertheless, in their criticism of my proposals, Jasanoff and Nussbaum are remarkably restrictive on the semantic side.

EAST ASIAN PARALLELS

At several points in "Word Games" Jasanoff and Nussbaum note that I am competent in some East Asian languages. Therefore, I am impressed that for good comparativist reasons they should take an example from East Asia. They write: "Our knowledge of the pronunciation of Ancient Chinese depends in large part on the systematic way in which Chinese words were rendered into Japanese and Korean in the third century C.E." (p. 185).

Apart from being off by four centuries—the crucial period was the seventh, not the third century—their claim is generally justified. As a wonderful example of the exception that proves the rule, however, it is worth looking at in some detail. In the first place, because the Japanese, Korean, and Vietnamese languages all adopted Chinese characters (unlike the situations where borrowed words appear only in phonetic representations), the precise lexical sources of the loans can be identified without difficulty. Second, although borrowings took place before and after the seventh century, it was then that Japan was flooded with Chinese culture and Japanese with Chinese vocabulary.

At this point, we need to look at the political and linguistic situation in China in the late sixth and early seventh centuries C.E., about which a great deal is firmly known and even more has been plausibly reconstructed. After several centuries of disunity, China was reunited in 589 C.E. under Sui Wendi, the founder of the Sui Dynasty. This powerful but short-lived dynasty originated in northwestern China and established its capital at Changan, the present Xian in Shensi.[21] However, the unification stressed links with the center and south of China; it was at this time that the Grand Canal between the Yellow River and the Yangtze was dug. Culturally, Sui Wendi brought eastern and southern literati to the new capital, and their dialect became the standard of pronunciation. In 601, this pronunciation was codified, as a political act, in a massive rhyming dictionary, the *Qieyun*. Within two or three generations, however, the local northern dialect of Changan had reasserted itself. This dialect then became the standard language of the Tang Dynasty, which overthrew the Sui in 618 C.E.[22] Many Chinese words were taken into Japanese, through the Japanese Court, at the end of the Sui. But it was during the long-lived and powerful Tang Dynasty that most loans were made into Japanese and the languages of other surrounding territories.[23] The language of the Tang Court can be reconstructed in two important ways from within Chinese: first, through rhyming dictionaries; second, through the fact that nearly all the surviving Chinese dialects can be traced back to it.

On the Japanese side, we are particularly fortunate in that within a century of the words' introduction, Japanese scholars had classified the different pronunciations of these loans into two classes: *go'on* and *kan'on*. The former were older pronunciations more or less based on the Sui standard, as set out in the *Qieyun*, and the latter were the later borrowings from the Tang Court language.[24] Thus, in conjunction with the Chinese sources, the loans into Japanese and other languages do indeed, as Jasanoff and Nussbaum claim, provide very useful evidence for the reconstruction of these stages of Chinese.

Nevertheless, many *on* (or Chinese) readings in Japanese cannot be classified under these two headings, Sui or Tang. Although the written characters make the precise lexical provenance certain, it is difficult or impossible to tell at which periods these were introduced, by what means, and through what intermediaries.[25] For instance, no one knows why the second syllable in the name of the Chinese board game *weiqi* should be pronounced *go* in Japanese.

Thus, in the seventh century, there was undoubted regularity of loaning between two specific languages that can be dated to a few decades. This fact and its pinpointing by ancient and modern scholars have created a doubly extraordinary situation that is completely unlike any found in the Ancient Eastern Mediterranean. If we had as little information about Sino-Japanese cultural and linguistic relations as we do for the Egyptian-Levantine-Greek, we should be left with a far vaguer and more confused picture. For instance, the character for "lark" or "pipit," pronounced *lìu* in modern Chinese, has eight different *on* (Chinese) readings in Japanese: *ryū, ru, bō, hyū, mu, kyu, gu,* and *ryō*. Thus, unlike Jasanoff and Nussbaum (p. 187), I have no difficulty in believing that the Egyptian *nt̠r*, which is more complicated phonetically than the prototype of *lìu*, could have had "five distinct phonetic treatments" in Greek. Jasanoff and Nussbaum make a similar and equally unfounded objection to my proposals that the so-called vulture aleph, represented by

Egyptologists as 3, could have been borrowed into Greek in a number of different ways. I shall return to both nt̲r and 3 in the second part of this chapter.

In general, then, the parallel between China, Korea, and Japan on the one hand, and Egypt, the Levant, and Greece on the other seems a useful one, but in a different way from that suggested by Jasanoff and Nussbaum. As I see it, in both cases, the ultimate recipient culture initially used a language that was unrelated or, at most, only distantly related to those of the outside sources. In both cases, we have substantial archaeological, iconographic, and historical evidence of contact between the two regions. Both Japanese and Greek cultures retained and developed their distinctiveness. Nevertheless, both were saturated with elements from the older, more elaborate, continental civilizations. In both cases, the basic structure of their original languages remained, but more than 50 percent of the lexicon came from elsewhere.[26] In Japan, we know that nearly all of this outside vocabulary came directly or indirectly from China. I have argued, and shall argue below, that the parallel goes beyond this, and I claim that most of the non-Indo-European elements in Greek came from Ancient Egyptian and West Semitic.

RETURN TO THE MEDITERRANEAN

As loyal followers of the Neogrammarians, Jasanoff and Nussbaum use the old-fashioned and positivist terminology of "scientific," "prescientific," and "nonscientific" linguistics.[27] Their use of these words is based on the exquisite phonetic precision that has been successful in the majority of cases within Indo-European and other language families. They take these achievements much further, however, and put historical linguistics as a whole on a plane with "hard" observational sciences like geology or astronomy. They write, for instance, "To say that linguists 'prefer' to compare *érebos* with its IE cognates is, in its way, a bit like saying that geographers prefer to believe that the world is round" (p. 183). Jasanoff and Nussbaum do not mention the fact that scholars have been debating and asserting the relative merits of the Semitic and Indo-European etymologies of *Érebos* for well over a century.[28] This kind of positivist arrogance allows the two authors to reify their unattested reconstructed forms and turn long chains of hypothetical changes into irrefutable facts. Some of their propositions may indeed be true, but others are much less certain and should be discarded if challenged by more plausible explanations. It is right to point out the inadequacies and uncertainties arising from the scripts in which the Ancient Afroasiatic languages were written. Equally, however, the scores of varied Indo-European languages allow Indo-Europeanists to find phonetic and semantic parallels (the latter are often extremely loose) between words that may or may not be related to each other in fact. Thus, when facing, say, a Hebrew and an Old Prussian parallel to a Greek word, it is not automatically more certain or "scientific" to choose the Old Prussian. One has to balance the probabilities.

As emphasized above, the most misleading result of such Indo-Europeanist scientism is the requirement that the phonetic correspondences of proposed loans should be as precise as those for strong etymologies within a language family. The inappropriateness of applying this kind of stringency to contact between languages has been evident ever since the nineteenth century. Eduard Meyer, the polymath who dominated studies of the Ancient Eastern Mediterranean during the first third of the 1900s, was quite explicit about the danger of such rigidity, at least as it affected names: "We should never expect the renderings of such proper names in foreign languages and scripts to be correct from the point of linguistic science." [29]

As an example of their tendency to misplaced precision, Jasanoff and Nussbaum argue that in convincing etymologies, voiced stops in Semitic and Egyptian were "systematically represented by voiced stops in Greek," and that the same was true "*mutatis mutandis*" for unvoiced ones (p. 188). A glance at the Greek transcriptions of Hebrew names either in the *Septuagint* or in Josephus' writings, or at the Greek transcriptions and renderings of acknowledged loans from Egyptian found in Erman and Grapow's standard *Wörterbuch der Aegyptischen Sprache* (1926–1931), would have shown them that this statement was completely untrue. To give a couple of well-known examples, no one doubts that the West Semitic *gåmål* became the Greek *kámēlos* ("camel"), or that the Egyptian city name Ḥt k3 Ptḥ ("House of the Ka of Ptah"), Memphis, became *Aíguptos* ("Egypt").[30] In fact, it is well-known that in Late Egyptian from 1500 B.C.E., "oppositions between voiced and voiceless phonemes became gradually neutralized." [31]

To return for a moment to the Neogrammarians and their modern epigones: Within a language family, the "exceptionlessness of sound laws" has been a "noble lie." Although it is in fact untrue, it has been extremely helpful in encouraging historical linguists to look for regularities where they are not immediately apparent. When looking at contact between languages, however, the drawbacks of the *Ausnahmslosigkeit der Lautgesetze* equal or surpass its benefits. Recently, Walter Burkert has developed this theme, attacking Indo-Europeanists' challenges to proposals of loans from other languages:

> The negative statements of critics enjoy the advantage of seeming caution and strict methodology: Linguists can keep to well-established laws of phonetic evolution within a closed system, whereas borrowings are mostly inferred from similarities of sounds that may be fortuitous. But it is precisely methodology which is the problem. Greek language, at any rate the literary Greek that we know, absolutely rejects the use of unadapted foreign words; they are accepted only in perfectly assimilated form as to phonetics and inflexion. Thus there can be no method to discover borrowed words: They imitate and go into hiding, adapting themselves to the roots and suffixes of native Greek. . . . Popular etymology plays its role in this metamorphosis; no rules for phonetic evolution can be established.[32]

I am in general agreement with this statement, but my own position is less extreme. First, as I stated above, I believe that limited regularities exist and, hence, that there are methods of discovering borrowed words. Second, some foreign loans into Greek did remain unassimilated. Take, for instance, the letter names *alpha*, *beta*, and so on, or *onar* ("vision, dream"), all of which are indeclinable. This fact in itself strongly indicates that they were borrowings. Nevertheless, Burkert is quite right to claim that the vast majority of foreign loans did become thoroughly absorbed into the structures of Greek phonetics and morphology. This sensible notion, which fits all modern theories of language contact, undercuts Jasanoff and Nussbaum's claim: "Genuine loan words in Greek are for the most part isolated, not only in the sense that they lack convincing IE etymologies but also in the sense that they are not visibly derived from other simpler Greek words or roots" (p. 189).

All this passage indicates is that, when considering the possibility of borrowings, lexicographers of Ancient Greek have generally looked only for isolated and clearly exotic words. Newly introduced words retain their foreign appearance and some remain "exotic" for long periods. As Burkert points out, others are absorbed, "go native," and develop compounds and derivations.[33] Thus the "simpler . . . words or roots" may themselves be loans. Jasanoff and Nussbaum continue: "It is characteristic that there is no verb *khrū́sō 'I shine' beside the borrowed word for gold." Specifically, this is the case, but Liddell and Scott's standard *Greek-English Lexicon* contains scores of compounds from the Greek *khrūsos* ("gold") with its undoubted

Semitic origin.[34] Verbs are also formed in combination with prepositions on this base, such as *enkhrūsóō* ("gild") and *epikhrūsóō* ("overlay with gold"). Similarly, the Greek *býssos* ("tissue or cloth") from the Canaanite *bûṣ* ("fine Egyptian linen") has formed verbs *býō*, *embýō*, and *epibýō* ("stuff in, up") in which the final consonant of the Afroasiatic root has been dropped in the Greek present tense as if it were a morphological feature.

It is universally agreed that the Greek *kádos* ("jar") derives from the West Semitic *kad* ("jar").[35] Greek has many similar words: *kētharion* or *kēthis* ("voting urn"), *keithion*, *kheition*, *keition*, and the Mycenean *kati*. All are apparently vases of differing types and lack Indo-European etymologies.[36] Many of the most productive Greek roots, such as those found in *árkhō* ("lead, begin") and *xenos* ("stranger"), have no plausible Indo-European etyma and could well be derived from loans. Thus, Jasanoff and Nussbaum are quite wrong when they argue that we should restrict our searches for loans to obvious exotica and isolates, and Burkert is quite right when he says we should look more widely.

He is also right to conclude, "In any case, the kind of minimalism that rejects all connections with Semitic that are not crystal clear, remains, on the whole, the most unlikely of possible hypotheses."[37]

GREEK: THE RESULT OF A LINGUISTIC SHIFT
OR OF LANGUAGE CONTACT?

At this point, I should like to consider the relationship of Egyptian and West Semitic to Greek in the context of modern theories of language contact. Historians of Greek have worked out the phonetic relationships among Greek dialects in exquisite detail. Apart from showing the descent from Proto-Indo-European, however, they are much more vague when they consider the origins of the Greek language as a whole.[38] One reason for this vagueness is simply the lack of evidence. Nevertheless, the failure to apply modern approaches to the problem has a long tradition that I see as having an ideological basis. One of the founding fathers of Classics in the late eighteenth and early nineteenth centuries was Wilhelm von Humboldt. Among many other accomplishments, Humboldt was a great linguist, specializing in the intricacies of language mixture. Humboldt, however, was convinced that the "Sanscritic," that is to say, Indo-European languages, were qualitatively different from and superior to all others.[39] Furthermore, in an outline of the new discipline, later known as *Altertumswissenschaft* or

"Classics," he declared that the excellence of Greek lay in its being un-contaminated by foreign elements.[40] Elsewhere, he maintained that Greek history and culture as a whole were categorically above that of all other cultures and that "from the Greeks we take something more than earthly—almost godlike."[41]

Now, at the beginning of the twenty-first century, we should no longer set Greek apart as a special case but should treat it like any other language and compare it with other mixed languages. A good way to do this is to examine it within the framework proposed in *Language Contact, Creolization, and Genetic Linguistics* by Sarah Grey Thomason and Terrence Kaufman. This work has been widely accepted as the best survey of the subject so far; it has been endorsed enthusiastically by Jasanoff, among many others.[42] Thomason wrote the first section of the book, which deals with language contact in general, and she found it useful to set up a scale of languages that appear to be mixed. It begins with cases in which increasing degrees of *contact* have occurred. The culmination of this process is a linguistic *shift* in which a population gives up its language and takes on another.[43] The distinction between *contact* and *shift* comes essentially from the perspective of the observer: what had been viewed as the exotic language that has influenced the native one now itself becomes the focus of attention and is seen as having been influenced by the language it replaced. Typically, the context for such changes is the imposition of a colonizing language on a politically or socially subordinate but numerically larger population. Let me illustrate this schematically:

Generation 1: Monolingual speakers of the native language X and incomers speaking language Y, each possibly with a passive knowledge of the other language.

Generation 2: At least one group becomes bilingual. The speakers of X speak their own language natively and Y with an X accent (and structure), and the Ys speak their own language natively and possibly X with a Y accent (and structure).

Generation 3: Everyone speaks Y and X is dead. Two discernable accents, X and Y, still exist.

Generation 4: Y speakers with an X accent become dominant (possibly because of greater numbers), and this pronunciation becomes standard among the whole population.[44]

Thus, looked at retrospectively, mixed languages resulting from contact differ from those where a shift has taken place in the aspects of language affected. In most cases, the changes brought about through *contact* begin with vocabulary; first nouns, then verbs and modifiers change, and then the change goes on to particles, prepositions, and postpositions. After that, syntax and morphology, and, finally, phonology are transformed. In languages where a *shift* has largely taken place, the old intonation, phonology, and syntax tend to be retained long after the new vocabulary has been accepted. Examples of this can be seen in the Orkney and Shetland Islands where, during the fifteenth, sixteenth, and seventeenth centuries C.E., Aberdonian Scots replaced the old Norn. A few Norse words survive, but the only significant difference between the dialects of the islands and those of the Scottish mainland is now in the former's strikingly Scandinavian intonation. By contrast, during the same period, while Sweden ruled Finland, some Finnish speakers adopted every aspect of Swedish except the flat intonation of their original language, which was then adopted by the Swedish settlers themselves. Similarly, Irish English has absorbed remarkably few Irish words but still has a heavily Irish intonation and phonetic structure and some Irish syntax, as shown in the line from the song "If it's thinking in your inner heart." [45]

With language *contact*, in the sense supplied by Thomason and Kaufman, the native linguistic structures being maintained while much or most of the vocabulary has been imported is extremely common. It can be seen in Korean, Vietnamese, and Japanese as well as in Swahili, English, and many other languages. [46] Two other particularly striking examples of this pattern are found in Old Javanese or Kawi and Coptic. Kawi was the language to which Humboldt, who insisted on the purity of Greek, devoted the last years of his life. It was, as he rightly perceived, a Malay language with a massive infusion of Sanskrit and Pali vocabulary. [47] Coptic is the last form of Egyptian. Coptic phonology, morphology, syntax, and basic vocabulary are fundamentally native, but a high proportion of the nouns and verbs, as well as many particles, come from Greek. [48] If we lacked a knowledge of Egyptian history of the relevant period, we could still deduce that a minority of Greek speakers had dominated a larger Egyptian-speaking population for some centuries. It would be extremely implausible to use the linguistic evidence to propose that Egyptian speakers had dominated Greeks, but this kind of assertion is precisely what supporters of the Aryan model ask us to do when looking at the very similar pattern of mixing found in Greek.

No one doubts that Greek contains linguistic mixture. The question is whether it is the result of *shift* or *contact*. Although they do not spell out their position on the subject, supporters of the Aryan model of Greek origins implicitly posit a shift from Pre-Hellenic to Greek. By contrast, using the Revised Ancient model, I see the mixture as the result of contact.

Some of the phonetic modifications that Proto-Indo-European underwent before becoming Greek could conceivably be the result of an Aegean substrate, but this explanation is not very likely because many of these changes, such as the shift from the emphatic stops of Proto-Indo-European p′, t′, and k′ to the voiced ones b, d, and g of Greek, were shared by many other Indo-European dialects.[49] Other changes, such as the breakdown of labiovelars and the shift from initial and intervocalic s>h, were real phenomena affecting both Indo-Hittite and non-Indo-Hittite languages around the Eastern Mediterranean in the mid–second millennium B.C.E., too late to be plausibly associated with any Aegean substrate.

Beyond lexical items on their borrowing scale, Thomason and Kaufman see structural and morphological influences arising from more intense contact.[50] In fact, Greek morphology has a few anomalies not found elsewhere in Indo-European: the oblique dual ending -(o)iin, the suffix -eus ("the one who"), and the locatives -de and -then, and so on. Nevertheless, what is striking about Greek phonology and morphology as a whole is how well they fit into Indo-European. At the same time, however, the language has a very substantial non-Indo-European vocabulary. Jasanoff and Nussbaum agree that "a large number of Greek words . . . lack good Indo-European etymologies" (p. 185). Their Indo-Europeanist colleague at Oxford, Anna Morpurgo-Davies, estimates the proportion of Indo-European words in Greek at "less than 40%."[51] It is difficult to see this pattern as the result of a *shift* because it would require the hypothetical Pre-Hellenic, non-Indo-European-speaking, Aegean population to have given up the phonology and morphology of their language while retaining a considerable proportion of its vocabulary. Such a development would go against the usual pattern of shifts, as set out above.

Let us look at the situation in northern India, where Indo-European speakers appear to have overwhelmed indigenous populations that did not speak an Indo-European language. Sanskrit and the other related languages indicate that a shift had taken place in which native speakers had accepted most of the Indo-European morphology and nearly all of its vocabulary.[52] However, they retained their phonology to such an extent that the invaders themselves adopted it. By contrast, the Dravidian languages that survived in southern India indicate that there, there was contact but no shift. These languages accepted large numbers of Indic words and some morphosyntactical patterns, but retained their basic grammatical structure and pronunciation.[53] The Indo-European aspects of Greek are the opposite of those found in Sanskrit in that Greek has an Indo-European phonology and a large non-Indo-European vocabulary, while Sanskrit has a non-Indo-European phonology and an overwhelmingly Indo-European vocabulary. In fact, taking Indo-European as the base, the pattern found in Greek shows a striking resemblance to that of the Dravidian languages. Thus, the Greek mixture too should probably be seen as the result of contact, not of a shift.

In a very few situations a bilingual minority has retained its basic vocabulary in order to maintain its identity, while giving up most of its phonology and syntax. From a teleological perspective, such a language can be described as "dying," but the process can last several centuries.[54] Examples can be found in English Romany and the Modern Greek spoken in Turkey before the expulsions from Asia Minor of 1921–1922, where, as an author put it in 1916, "the body has remained Greek, but the soul has become Turkish."[55] Could this have been the case in Ancient Greece with the Pre-Hellenes as equivalents of the English Roma (Gypsies), abandoning nearly all aspects of their language except for their vocabulary?

I maintain that the answer is no. In such situations, the minority or socially subordinate population retains the words of everyday life, which is not the case for the hypothetical speakers of Pre-Hellenic. In fact, Greek shows a stark contrast between Morpurgo-Davies's estimated Indo-European component of less than 40 percent of the total vocabulary and the 79 percent found in the shorter hundred-word list of basic items drawn up by the linguist Morris Swadesh, in theory at least, applicable to all languages.[56] Still more remarkable, in three cases on the Swadesh list where there are both Indo-European and apparently non-Indo-European synonyms, the Indo-European word is thought to be older.[57]

All in all, the linguistic shift suggested by the Aryan model is extremely unlikely because it would require the Pre-Hellenic population to have given up its phonology, morphology, and everyday vocabulary for those of its Indo-European-speaking conquerors while retaining much of its sophisticated lexicon. On the other hand, the pattern found in Ancient Greek is exactly what one would expect after linguistic contact. Even the discrepancy between the vocabulary as a whole and that of the basic hundred-word list is the same as that found in England after the Norman Conquest. Estimates vary, but it seems clear that while more than 75 percent of the Middle English vocabulary derived from French, less than 10 percent of the Swadesh list came from that language.[58]

If the mixed origin of Greek is to be seen as the result of *contact*, not *shift*, by far the most likely languages to have had substantial influences on it in its formative period during the second millennium B.C.E. are Ancient Egyptian and West Semitic. These were the languages of the peoples we know, both from documents and from archaeological evidence, to have been dominant in the Eastern Mediterranean over those centuries.[59]

To return to the objections put forward by Jasanoff and Nussbaum: They agree that many Greek words cannot be explained in terms of other Indo-European languages, but they deny that this is unusual because, they maintain, all branches of Indo-European have many unexplained words. Here they go against a view expressed by Morpurgo-Davies. After her research on the proportion of Indo-European words in the Greek vocabulary, she found the small figure of "less than 40 percent" "remarkable."[60]

Jasanoff and Nussbaum concede that the proportion of "inherited IE words in Greek is lower than in the highly conservative Sanskrit of the *Rig-Veda*, it is probably about the same in Latin, and vastly higher than in the earliest attested IE language, Hittite" (p. 185). To begin with the last: Hittite was spoken in central and eastern Anatolia, a territory of great linguistic diversity that included some non-Indo-Hittite languages. Furthermore, the land of Hatti, the core of the Hittite Empire, was part of the Southwest Asian economic and cultural world for many millennia. The major Hittite writing system was cuneiform, and no one doubts that the language was heavily influenced by Semitic. As for Latin, Jasanoff and Nussbaum's statement that the proportion of Indo-European words was "probably about the same" is very vague. The authors are like me in that they have obviously not carried out any research on the issue. Nevertheless, substantial borrowing is quite possible in this case, as it is known that Roman civilization incorporated many religious rites, customs, and words from the Etruscans, non-Indo-European speakers.[61] Furthermore, given contacts with Phoenicians and especially with Carthage, it is also probable that like Hittite (and, I argue, like Greek), the Latin vocabulary was heavily influenced by Semitic. In any event, it is clear that both Hittite and Latin borrowed substantially from non-Indo-European languages as a result of contact.

I fully agree with Jasanoff and Nussbaum's general point, that all languages contain words that cannot be explained in terms of their own language family or acknowledged loans. Since less than 40 percent of the Greek vocabulary has Indo-European etymologies and I only claim that 40 percent of that vocabulary comes from Afroasiatic, a further 20 percent is still unexplained. This residue may or may not be as great as, say, that of the Germanic branch of Indo-European. However, although we have virtually no knowledge of the non-Indo-European languages with which the speakers of Proto-Germanic came into contact, we know a great deal about Ancient Egyptian and West Semitic.

INTERMEDIATE CONCLUSIONS

This section of my reply has five conclusions. First, Indo-European linguistics, as it developed in the nineteenth century, was influenced by the prevailing racism, anti-Semitism, and Romantic desire for purity, as manifested in the model of a self-generating tree. Therefore, substantial outside influences were considered only reluctantly. The sole exception to this was through the ideologically acceptable mode of a substrate influence from the languages of the conquered peoples on the language of the conquering Indo-European speakers. This reluctance was particularly strong in the case of Greek, which, since the early nineteenth century, was generally considered the most perfect or, at least, the most perfectly balanced European language.

My second intermediate conclusion is that the phonetic precision generally achieved by historical linguists within language families is inappropriate when dealing with language *contacts*, except when the time, place, and mode of borrowings can be closely documented. The third conclusion is that the development of semantics is never clear-cut or precisely predictable. My fourth point is that the linguistic mixture universally acknowledged to exist in Ancient Greek can be far more plausibly explained as the result of contact than as coming from a substrate following a shift. Fifth, if contact is accepted, the most likely sources of the non-Indo-European elements in Greek are Egypt and the Levant. The archaeological and documentary evidence clearly indicates that these areas had considerable interaction with the Aegean Basin during the appropriate periods.

All in all, rather than finding loans from Ancient Egyptian or Semitic into Greek surprising and requiring rigorous, one-sided proof (even if there are no, or only weak, etymologies from within Indo-European), it would be surprising if such loans were not abundant. Therefore, they should be tentatively accepted or rejected not on the grounds of certainty, but on those of competitive plausibility.

The Individual Challenges

At this point I have finished my general critique of Jasanoff and Nussbaum's overall framework and now turn to specific cases. As reasoned responses are always longer than original statements, I am unable to take up all of them. Just as Jasanoff and Nussbaum do not accept those of my proposed Afroasiatic etymologies that they have not challenged, I do not concede the validity of their challenges to which I do not respond here. Even so, I think it worthwhile in this part of the chapter to consider some examples that I find particularly significant. It is up to the reader to decide whether she or he wants to follow these detailed arguments.

I should also mention at this point that Jasanoff and Nussbaum are as scornful of my proposed Semitic etymologies as they are of Egyptian ones.[62] As I wrote in the introduction, this double denial puts them at odds with most of the rest of the contributors to BAR who, though they strongly oppose any suggestion of large-scale influences from Egypt, now claim to be quite open to the idea of Southwestern Asian influences. The contributors' reliance on Jasanoff and Nussbaum's linguistic arguments creates a serious discrepancy among the contributors between their treatment of linguistic transmission and that of all other aspects of culture. The only way the authors of BAR and classicists sympathetic to other Greek cultural borrowings from Southwest Asia can avoid this contradiction is to repeat the mantra "We do not use etymological arguments." It is unclear why, however, given the general shortage of information, such a potentially valuable source should be disregarded.

-NTHOS, -SSOS/-TTOS

Jasanoff and Nussbaum accept the conventional wisdom of the nineteenth and early twentieth centuries that Greek was the result of a linguistic shift following a conquest of Pre-Hellenes by Indo-European-speaking Hellenes. Thus, they follow the classicist J. Haley and the archaeologist Carl Blegen, who argued in a well-known article published in 1927 that the distribution of place-names with the elements -nthos and -ssos/-ttos corresponded with Early Bronze Age settlements (i.e., before the supposed conquest) and, hence, were indicators of Pre-Hellenic settlements (p. 186).[63]

Archaeologically, the theory is very flimsy, as the correspondences would hold up as well for Late Bronze Age as for Early Bronze Age sites. More important, the toponymic aspect is equally feeble as the hypothesis was abandoned by its creator, Paul Kretschmer, in 1924 when he pointed out that -nthos is found attached to Indo-European stems.[64] Thus, although it is possible to hypothesize that these survived from earlier, Pre-Hellenic, waves of Indo-European speakers, they cannot in themselves indicate a Pre-Indo-European language stratum. Jasanoff and Nussbaum's traditionalism in defending the older hypothesis is all the more remarkable because it has generally been discarded. As the broad-minded Indo-Europeanist Oswald Szemerényi wrote in 1958:

> In 1916, two main theses seemed well established. First, the great number of place names in -νθος (-νδα) and -σσος, scattered throughout the Greek mainland and archipelago *were* Pre-Greek, more precisely Aegaean-Asianic, certainly not Indo-European. Secondly, the "Minoan" culture as a whole was non-Greek, and non IE. . . . Since then, however, the exponents of both these theses have had increasing difficulties in defending their views. The linguistic foundations for the assumption of a non-IE, Aegaean-Asianic substratum have, largely through Professor Kretschmer's untiring research, been almost completely eliminated.[65]

Eight years later, Szemerényi reiterated:

> As we have seen above, the Semitic influence was minimalised in the first half of our century, especially by such leading scholars as Meillet and Debrunner. . . . This so-called Aegaean stratum was held to be the main, if not exclusive, source of all the foreign elements in the Greek vocabulary. The main shibboleths of this stratum were the suffixes -ssos/ttos and -nthos. . . . Today it seems more likely than not that these formations are in origin Anatolian, i.e. Indo-European.[66]

Earlier in the same article, however, Szemerényi had derived the Greek *asaminthos* ("bath") from the Akkadian *namasitu* ("bath"), and *plinthos* ("brick") from the Akkadian *libintu* ("brick").[67] There is no doubt in my mind that many other words and names with these suffixes can be plausibly derived from Semitic and Egyptian. Thus, whatever their origin, the suffixes were "alive" when Indo-European, Semitic, and Egyptian were in use around the Aegean. Therefore, -ssos and -nthos and the stems to which they are attached cannot be used, as Jasanoff and Nussbaum suggest, to locate a mysterious lost language that was neither Indo-European nor Afroasiatic.

Jasanoff and Nussbaum sympathize with the suggestion that the mysterious independent substrate language was that written in the Linear A syllabary found in Crete and other places around the Aegean. They write that it "cannot be read" (p. 186). Here again, they are mistaken. Even the staunchly orthodox John Chadwick tended to accept "the argument in favor of assigning closely similar, if not identical values to Linear A and Linear B syllabic signs."[68] Incidentally, the legibility of Linear A removes one of the two substantive arguments against Cyrus Gordon's interpretation of it as a script for a Semitic language. The other objection that East and West Semitic words could not occur in the same language has been removed by the discovery of the North Syrian Semitic language of Eblaite. Eblaite contains words that had previously been seen as restricted to either East or West Semitic.[69] Thus, at least in the third millennium B.C.E. from which the Eblaite texts come, the distinction between East and West Semitic was far less hard and fast than scholars, with their natural desire for clear classification, have wanted to suppose.

Many problems remain in the interpretation of the Linear A texts, and there may well be Anatolian, Egyptian, or other elements in the language or languages of Middle and Late Bronze Age Crete. However, Gordon has convincingly demonstrated the presence of a number of Semitic words on the Linear A tablets.[70] This is altogether to be expected, given the presence of Semitic words in the Greek inscribed on tablets written with Linear B: the archaeological and documentary evidence of contacts between Southwest Asia and Crete during the third and second millennia B.C.E. and the fact that the bureaucratic structures in Crete and on Mainland Greece show remarkably precise correspondences with those of Mesopotamia and Syria.[71] All in all, the scorn Jasanoff and Nussbaum show for Gordon and his followers is thoroughly misplaced. Gordon's pupils now dominate Semitic studies in the United States. Though few of them follow their teacher when he maintains that there were Ancient Semitic voyages to America, nearly all accept his view of close cultural connections around the Eastern Mediterranean in the Middle and Late Bronze Ages.

I have no explanation for the suffixes -ssos/ttos, which may or may not be a single entity. However, I believe that -nthos can be explained in a number of different ways. Sometimes, it is as a simple introduction of a nasal before a dental, such as in Korinthos, Korito in Linear B.[72] At other times, I see it is as a rendering of the Egyptian nṭr. Jasanoff and Nussbaum (p. 187) find my proposal that nṭr was "given five different phonetic treatments in Greek" absurd and outrageous. As mentioned above, parallels from varying manifestations of Chinese loans into Japanese or Romance loans into English make the number in itself unexceptional.

Therefore, we need to look at the proposed etymologies individually. There is one on which we all agree: ntr > nítron ("niter"). Ntr > ánthos requires some explanation. The Indo-European etymology claimed for ánthos is from a hypothetical root *andh or *anedh ("stand out, sprout, bloom"). The lexicographer of Indo-European Julius Pokorny derived this root from ánthos itself and such far-fetched forms as the Tocharian ānt ("plain").[73] The only member of the cluster that has a possible semantic parallel with ánthos is the Sanskrit ándhah, the magic "soma plant" that was supposed to confer immortality. Pierre Chantraine, the author of the latest etymological dictionary of Greek, doubts any connection between ánthos and ándhah.[74]

The case for a derivation of ánthos from the Egyptian ntr is much stronger. On the phonetic side, final -r was unstable even in Middle Egyptian.[75] The -r in ntr vanished altogether in the Coptic nute. Nevertheless, the final -r may possibly have originally existed in Greek. The word cluster around anthos contains several forms with a final -r: antharion ("pimple"), antheros ("flowery"), antherikos ("asphodel" and "ear of wheat"). The last was a sacred symbol of Osiris in Egypt and of the Eleusinian Mysteries in Greece. Thus, the root ntr ("divine") would be entirely appropriate. Despite the fact that in most of these cases the -r- could be morphological, a possibility remains that it is part of the root that has been dropped elsewhere.

A prothetic ì (a/i) was also common in Egyptian, where, as in this case, a word would otherwise begin with a double consonant.[76] A trace of this can be seen in the Coptic form enthēr for the plural "gods."[77] There are no problems with the rendering n as n and t as th.

Semantically, the fit between ntr and anthos is excellent. On the Egyptian side, the nineteenth-century Egyptologist Heinrich Brugsch maintained that ntr was "The operative power which created and produced things by periodical occurrence and gave them new life and restored them to the freshness of youth."[78] This view continues to be endorsed by twentieth-century Egyptologists.[79] In Greek, the accepted meaning of ánthos is "growth, young shoot, flower, flower of youth."

There are, moreover, many indications that Egyptians saw flowers as having deep religious significance. Virtually every representation of a sacrifice or offering shows flowers in prominent positions, often tied to the head of the sarcophagus being adored. It is also clear from Egyptian religious texts that flowers could represent the gods or the blessed dead. Furthermore, as the Egyptologist Hans Bonnet put it, "their significance does not stop here. It goes deeper. The gods themselves are present in the bouquets."[80]

Flowers and the blessed dead were also linked in Archaic and Classical Greece. The Ionian festival of Anthesteria was held when flowers began to bloom in February. While it was celebrated, the dead *Kēres* ("spirits of the dead," the Egyptian etymology of which will be discussed below) were supposed to rise from their graves and walk the streets.[81] This illustrates the associations with renewal and immortality.

A derivation of *ánthos* < *ntr* is strengthened by another proposed etymology, that of *xanthós* from *sntr* (*sonte*, in Coptic).[82] *Sntr* is the causative *s*- attached to the root *ntr*; hence, it meant "make holy." However, *sntr* took on the specific meaning of "consecrate through fire and incense" and, even more specifically, the resin of the Syrian terebinth tree, which was used as incense.[83] We can then turn to the etymological procedure of *Wörter und Sachen* ("words and things"), relating language to other types of evidence, advocated by the historical linguist Jacob Grimm.[84] We know from the famous shipwreck of the fourteenth century B.C.E. at Ulu Burun off the southern coast of Turkey that *sntr* was imported into Greece in large quantities during the Bronze Age.[85] The resin varies in color from brown to yellow.

Xanthós in Greek means "brown, yellow" and "sacred," particularly of hair. It also has connotations of fragrance, especially of cooked meats, and of *latax*, the last drops thrown with a splash into a basin. The phonetic objection comes from the initial *x* and from the possibility that the Mycenaean name Kasato means Xánthos. The initial *k* in *ks*, however, may have been a soft fricative rather than a plosive.[86] Thus, the transcription of loans from words with uncertain Egyptian and Semitic sibilants as *ks*, or for that matter *ps*, in Greek can by no means be ruled out.[87] In the case of *sntr* > *xanthos* the semantic fit is good and there is no known Indo-European competitor.

Other proposed derivations from *sntr* are Satyroi ("Satyrs") and Satrai ("a tribe in Thrace"). The lexicographer Hjalmar Frisk made a number of tentative suggestions that these names came from within Greek or were loans from Illyrian to the north. Pierre Chantraine saw the two names as linked and as loans into Greek; more cautiously, he stated that they have no assured etymology. All scholars agree that both Satyrs and the Satrai were linked to the cult of Dionysos and are connected with phallic or priapic cults. The idea of Egyptian influences on names around the Northern Aegean is made less absurd by the place-name Abydos on the Dardenelles. The original Abydos in Egypt was the cult center of Osiris, the Egyptian counterpart of Dionysos. Sixty miles along the Anatolian coast from Abydos was the ancient city of Príapos, which has been linked to the priapic cult there and at Lampsakos, halfway between Príapos and Abydos. Príapos has no Indo-European etymology. An extremely plausible one, however, can be construed from the Egyptian Pr 3b(t), an alternative name for the Egyptian Abydos and specifically the name of the giant phallic fetish of Osiris in that city.[88]

Thus, not only do Egyptian place-names occur in and near the Northern Aegean but some are specifically associated with Osiris-Dionysos and with phallic cults. These connections remove any surprise that Satyr and Satrai should have Egyptian etymologies.

No great phonetic objections exist to this etymology. The medial -n- was often dropped in Greek transcriptions of Egyptian words or names.[89] It was also sometimes assimilated to a following dental within Greek.[90] An alternation between retention and loss of this -n- can be seen in the two semantically related words katharós and kántharos. Chantraine provides no etymologies for them, though he tentatively proposes that kántharos comes from "the substrate." Katharós means "clean, purge, pure"; kántharos signifies "a scarab, a type of fish, a type of boat, plant, the mark on the tongue of an Apis bull and a cup with large handles." Szemerényi plausibly derives kántharos in the last sense, from the Akkadian kanduru ("cup with large handles").[91] Accepting this etymology, however, still leaves a bewildering number of other meanings unexplained. Two of these, "a scarab" and "the mark on the tongue of an Apis bull," have clear connections not merely with Egypt but with Egyptian religion. Thus, the semantics of the Greek word would seem to require an Egyptian etymon that is both vague and religious. I believe that this can be found in the Egyptian *k3 ntr ("holy spirit"). The asterisk is there because Egyptologists do not recognize such a form. A frequently used hieroglyph, ⊔, however, is conventionally read simply as an alternative for k3⊔ ("soul" or "spirit"). The bottom section, ⊤ (i3t, "standard"), is a sign widely used to designate divinities for which ntr is the usual word. Thus, ⊔ as a sign for the combination *k3 ntr would seem very likely. This hypothesis is strengthened by a Coptic word, ktēr or kater ("calf"), possibly linked to the Apis bull. An etymology from *k3 ntr ("holy spirit") would also seem very plausible for katharós and such derivatives as kathársis.

Finally, there is the suffix -nthos itself. Ntr was used as a suffix in Egyptian, and a number of the Greek words with the suffix, such as huákinthos ("hyacinth") and terébinthos ("terebinth") have plausible Egyptian etymologies.[92]

To conclude this section, I see no objection to there being five distinct renderings of the Egyptian nṯr, and I find each one of them competitively plausible; that is to say, a relationship between the Egyptian and Greek words is more likely than not.

THE LETTER , 3

Jasanoff and Nussbaum are appalled again by what they see as my lack of rigor in proposing different values for the letter 3, or "double aleph," in Greek words deriving from the Egyptian. They write in reference to my derivation of the Greek kắr/kếr from the Egyptian k3: "From the phonetic point of view the equation is hopeless: neither here nor anywhere else is there a shred of evidence to support Bernal's oft repeated claim that Eg. 3 was sometimes borrowed as r in Greek" (p. 195).

Here again, one must ask whether the difference lies with the observers or in the situation itself. We now know from cognates in other Afroasiatic languages, and from Egyptian renderings of Semitic names, that 3 was originally heard as a trilled liquid l, r, and sometimes even n.[93] We also know that at some point, probably during the New Kingdom in the second half of the second millennium B.C.E., it lost its consonantal force and merely modified vowels.[94]

Earlier scholars never considered the possibility that the liquids in Greek words could be derived from 3, for two reasons. First, until some twenty years ago, most Egyptologists still thought of 3 as a glottal stop.[95] Second, despite their acknowledgment that the name Aigyptos was present in Mycenaean Greece, linguists have not considered the possibility of loans from Egyptian into Greek during the second millennium B.C.E. Thus, in establishing etymologies of Greek words, they used the sound values only of very late Egyptian. We now know from both texts and archaeology that there was frequent contact around the Eastern Mediterranean during the second millennium and that Semitic loan words have been found in Linear B tablets from that period. Thus, the possibility of early loans from Egyptian words *both* during the period when 3 was a liquid and when it was merely vocalic cannot be ruled out.

As for Jasanoff and Nussbaum's objections to the derivation of the Greek kắr / kếr from the Egyptian k3, they refer to what they call the "standard assumption of a PIE 'root noun' *kếr ... literally a cutting (off) termination (cf. keírō ... I cut)" (p. 196). In fact, the "standard assumption" is not so

simple. In 1961, the classicist D. J. N. Lee compiled a history of the interpretations of kḗr and argued that the traditional interpretation had been
"fate and death." According to Lee, the emphasis on death and termination
that arose in the late nineteenth century came about only "by the word's
being put in an etymologist's bed of Procrustes." The new emphasis, Lee
argued, was developed to link kḗr to keírō ("termination") and keraḯzō ("de-
molish"). Lee maintained that the emphasis should be put on "fate," good
or bad, which he derived from keírō in the sense of "cut" or of "drawing
lots." [96] Chantraine accepted the first half of Lee's argument and the importance of the meaning "fate." However, he did not follow the rest of his
proposals and concluded that the etymology of kḗr "remained obscure."

In BA II (pp. 263–264) I wrote:

> The Greek kḗr . . . is a term of rich and complex religious significance. There
> is no doubt that it came to mean "fate, doom, or violent death." However, . . .
> Homer was also using it in a different sense of individual fate or "soul." This,
> according to one passage in the *Iliad*, was appointed to a man at birth to
> meet him at his death.[97] This same sense was preserved in the ancient for-
> mula used in the Athenian festival of Anthesteria—in which the souls of the
> dead revisit the living—"get out kḗres the Anthesteria is over."[98] Thus, this
> sense of kḗr as an individual soul would seem to be central to its original
> meaning. . . .
>
>   The concept of k3, commonly written ka, which is central to Egyptian the-
> ology, has an even richer semantic field. As the hieroglyph ⊔, represented
> open or embracing arms, the original meaning of k3 would seem to be one
> of relations between beings: god and god; god and man; man and man. In
> the sense of father and son it gained connotations of personal and institu-
> tional continuity and immortality, especially in royal contexts. It seems to be
> from this that the later sense of k3 as a ghost came about. Even in the Old
> Kingdom k3 had developed the sense of spiritual companion or *doppelganger*
> whom one met at the point of death, and it is from here that its widespread
> use to denote "fate" seems to have arisen.[99]

Thus, though the phonetic claims of a derivation of kḗr from keírō and kḗr
from k3 are approximately equal, the semantic fields of the Egyptian k3 and
the Greek kḗr are remarkably close and clearly favor the Afroasiatic over the
Indo-European etymology.

ÉREBOS

A few words have two equally plausible etymologies. One such is well-known today: "typhoon." Etymologists see it as coming either from the Arabic and Persian ṭūfān ("whirlwind, deluge") or the Cantonese tai fung ("great wind"). Possibly the word has a single origin, but the one meaning has become so "contaminated" (referenced above) by the other source that it is impossible to distinguish which came first. The Greek Érebos ("place of nether darkness, dusk") would seem to be a similar case. The fact that there have been debates over the relative merits of the Semitic and Indo-European etymologies of Érebos for well over a century was mentioned above.[100] I follow the first tradition and Jasanoff and Nussbaum follow the other.

Jasanoff and Nussbaum derive Érebos from an Indo-European root, *$h_1 reg^w os$ (or, as most modern scholars would put it *$H_1 rek'^w os$), meaning "darkness" (p. 183). They establish this hypothetical root on the basis of forms found in Sanskrit, Germanic, and Armenian. The Armenian is most important because they see its form, erek ("evening"), as providing evidence of a laryngeal consonant lost in other Indo-European languages and therefore explaining the prothetic e- in Érebos. Other scholars do not explain the parallel in the same way. James Clackson, in his recent Linguistic Relationship between Armenian and Greek, denies that the two prothetic vowels are directly related, either as a preservation of a laryngeal or as a common innovation. He sees them simply as coming from an Anatolian (and Aegean?) tendency to avoid initial r-. Presumably because many Greek words of undoubted Indo-European origin begin with r-, Jasanoff and Nussbaum prefer to postulate a laryngeal.[101]

The question of the origin of Érebos is further complicated by the existence of another Indo-European root, *erebh, *orebh ("dark," "swarthy," or "stormy"), found in Slavic and Old English. Julius Pokorny does not include érebos in this cluster.[102] However, Allan Bomhard, who promotes the macrolinguistic grouping of "Nostratic," a hypothetical proto-family that includes among others Indo-European and Afroasiatic, links *erebh to the Semitic ʿrb ("to set as the sun" or "become dark").[103] He sees both of them as coming from a single Nostratic root.

There is no doubt that ʿrb is deeply rooted in Semitic. Furthermore, the words araba ("black") and orbā ("cow with black spots") found in the Central Cushitic languages of Bilen and Saho make it possible that it is common to Afroasiatic as a whole. This makes the suggestion that it is an Indo-European loan into Semitic less likely.[104]

Jasanoff and Nussbaum object to my using the Akkadian form *erebu* ("setting of the sun"). In contrast, they construct a Canaanite form: **ʿaribu. I suppose they derive this form from the Arabic vocalic pattern found in *ġariba* ("be black"). Many other vocalizations of the triconsonantal root, such as *ġaraba* ("to set, of the sun"), *ġarb* ("west"), can also be found. In fact, the standard reconstruction of the Canaanite vocalization that preceded the Hebrew *ʿereb* ("evening") is **ʿarb*.

The initial *e*- in Érebos could be derived from the Semitic in two ways. John Pairman Brown suggests the first: that it comes from the segholate West Semitic form *ʿereb* itself.[105] Segholation, which in this case involved a development, *ʿarb > ʿereb*, is generally thought to be late in Hebrew, but the evidence from other Canaanite dialects is not clear. In any event, as Jasanoff and Nussbaum point out, I prefer Astour's derivation from the Akkadian *erebu*.[106] The appearance of Akkadian forms in Greek can be explained in two ways. First, Akkadian texts may have preserved words in use in Syro-Palestine that have not been attested. Second, as stated above, the discovery of the ancient Syrian language Eblaite indicates that hard and fast distinctions should not be made between the East and West Semitic. Third, Akkadian was the diplomatic language in Syro-Palestine during the relevant second millennium B.C.E. and an important literary language as well.

In short, as I stated in (BA II (p. 93), two plausible etymologies exist for *erebos*. I prefer the Semitic one for semantic reasons. There is little doubt of the existence of an Indo-European root **regʷos* (**rekʲʷos*). The arguments made by Clackson and Michel Lejeune that the initial *e*- is simply to avoid an initial *r*- lessen the certainty of Jasanoff and Nussbaum's proposal that it is a reflex of the ancient laryngeal **h_1*. Nevertheless, the Greek prothetic vowel in *erebos* is explicable in terms of both Indo-European and Semitic.

The semantic reason for preferring a Semitic etymology is the clear association of Érebos with the dark, western underworld of the dead. This is a semantic field where there are very few words of Indo-European origin but a considerable number with plausible derivations from Semitic and Egyptian.[107]

HÁRMA

If Érebos has two strong etymologies, hárma ("chariot") has two very weak ones or none. Ten years after making this claim in BA I, I still maintain that such words as hórmos ("chain, necklace") come from the West Semitic ḥrm in the sense of "net, filigree" and that such place-names as Hermióne, a mountain sanctuary, come from the Canaanite Hermon, also a mountain sanctuary. I am no longer so sure, however, of ḥrm as an etymology for hárma ("chariot"). Equally, however, I do not accept Jasanoff and Nussbaum's claim that hárma is "a Greek word whose form, inflection, and meaning are utterly unproblematic in IE terms" (p. 195). In fact, after a series of hypothetical maneuvers, all they can come up with is an Indo-European root, *ar ("to fit, join together").

DEILÓS, DOÛLOS

Jasanoff and Nussbaum do not mention the fact that doûlos is generally agreed to be a non-Indo-European loan into Greek. Even if one recognizes a relationship between deilós and deídō ("I fear"), the proposed Indo-European etymology is highly insecure.[108] They strongly object to my glossing doûlos as "client or slave." In fact, the standard Greek dictionary, Liddel and Scott, defines the doûlos as "born bond man or slave." This would seem close enough, but Chantraine in his more detailed description of the word's semantics writes, "The uses in Th.8.28 and E. Iph. A 330 do not show that the word means 'slave from birth.' The word has a general sense: and its frequent use on Mycenaean tablets does not provide precise meanings."

Once again, Jasanoff and Nussbaum have succumbed to the Indo-Europeanist's occupational hazard of misplaced precision. The Semitic root dl(l) means "to hang or be suspended" but also "brought low, weak, poor, and miserable." A plausible link between the two meanings is the sense of "dependent." Thus, one finds dl ("poor") in Phoenician and dal ("low, weak, poor"; as opposed to the rich) and dallâh ("the poor") in Hebrew. The semantic parallel with doûlos ("someone in servitude") is quite strong, especially in the absence of an Indo-European competitor.

The "primary" meaning given for deilós in most dictionaries is "cowardly," but even in Hesiod and Homer it is much more frequently used in the distantly related sense of "miserable, wretched, vile, low born."[109] The lexicographers' preference is most easily explained by the fact that the meaning "cowardly" fits better with the verb deídō ("I fear"), to which Frisk, Chantraine, and others (as well as Jasanoff and Nussbaum) want to attach deilós. Here, the semantics favor the Semitic over the Indo-European etymology.

Now, turning to the phonetics, Jasanoff and Nussbaum maintain, and I agree, that the initial in doûlos was d^w. They go on from that statement, however, to claim the Mycenaean form doero indicates that doûlos derived from a "*do(h)elos (<*doselos?)." The brackets Jasanoff and Nussbaum put around the earlier hypothetical form give a spurious solidity to the unbracketed *do(h)elos. John Chadwick proposed a sequence similar to doelos <(dohelos?) to make a connection with dahā ("man") in Khotanese (one of the many Iranian languages) and the Sanskrit dāsah, equally "man." Apart from the semantic looseness, the actual, as opposed to the hypothetical, forms provide no explanation either for the o or "rounding" or for the final r/l in doero/doûlos.

Explaining the "rounding" from Semitic faces fewer difficulties. The existence of a phoneme, d^we, in the languages represented by Linears B and A is strengthened by a sign for that sound. This, however, was not used in doero. The possibility of rounded stops in Semitic is increased by their continued presence in Ethiopic Semitic languages. The distinguished Russian historical linguist I. M. Diakonoff maintained that rounded labials and labiovelars existed in Proto-Semitic.[110] Alternations in Eblaite and the Assyrian dialect of Akkadian second- and third-person pronouns and the inflection of the verb kuānum ("be, be firm") suggest that this rounding survived in Asiatic Semitic into the second millennium B.C.E., later than it did in Greek.[111] Whether there were rounded dentals to match the palatalized ones known to exist is more difficult to say. The specialist in Afroasiatic linguistics Carleton Hodge reconstructed them, at least in the medial position, for Proto-Semitic.[112] Traces of rounded dentals seem to be present in Amharic and other Ethiopic Semitic languages.[113] West Semitic alphabets could sometimes indicate rounding in "hollow" verbs by using the letter vav or w.[114] This practice, however, was clearly not systematic. There is some evidence to suggest that dl(l) was sometimes rounded. In the basic sense of "hanging, especially in water," dl is found in the forms dålåh ("draw water") and dᵉlî ("bucket"). The presence of a d^w in this case is suggested by the alternation of the Akkadian forms dalū, dūlu ("bucket") and the Syriac daulå, which may have been copied from it. These meanings involve dangling ropes that could possibly lead to entanglement. Even the name of the entrapping temptress Delilah would seem to be linked to the Arabic *dalāl* ("coquetry") and could be derived from *dll*. *Dll* would also seem to be reflected in plausible Greek loans with the vowels *o* and *e*, such as *dólos* ("fish trap, trick") with no Indo-European etymology and *délear* ("fish by bait, trap").[115] Thus, an origin for both *doûlos* and *deilós* in a hypothetical Semitic form *d^welo* would be perfectly plausible.

Apart from the two Indo-Europeanists' failure to explain the initial *d^w*, the reasons for preferring the Semitic etymology for *doûlos* and *deilós* are, first, that it provides an excellent semantic fit, whereas derivation from an Indo-European word for "man" is vague. Phonetically, the Semitic etymology provides an explanation for the *l*, which the Indo-European etymology fails to do. The *l* and the semantics of the words lead me to believe that *deilós*, with a basic meaning of "wretched miserable, low class," should be separated from *deídō* ("fear") and linked to *doûlos* ("slave").

BASILEUS

Jasanoff and Nussbaum object strongly to my derivation of the Greek *basileús* from the Egyptian *p3 sr* ("the official"). Because of a cuneiform transcription, we happen to know that *p3 sr* was vocalized *pasiyara* in the thirteenth century B.C.E.[116] The two authors appear to have no difficulty with the semantics of this etymology, as in both New Kingdom Egypt and contemporary Late Mycenaean Greece the word appears to have meant "high official" rather than the later Greek "king." Their problems are with the phonetics. In the first place, Jasanoff and Nussbaum state that "the Egyptian *p* is never represented as a *b* in uncontroversial loan words" (p. 196). The unreliability of the distinction between voiced and unvoiced stops has been discussed above. Specifically, the Egyptian city name Pr w3y.t was rendered Boutō and the Egyptian God ʾInpw was Anubis to the Greeks.[117] Their second objection is to rendering *p3* followed by an *s*- as *bas-* . It is true that in all acknowledged loans, *p3-s* appears as *ps* in Greek. In these instances, however, the Egyptian definite article appears to have been reduced to *p*. In the case in point, however, we know from the form *pasiyara* that the vowel had been retained. Thus, the influence of the unvoiced *s* on the initial stop would have been lessened. Here too, Jasanoff and Nussbaum's precision is misplaced.

Their most serious objection is that the title in question is written *qasireu* in Linear B. That is to say, Jasanoff and Nussbaum see the initial as a labiovelar k^w rather than a labial p. No doubt the sign in Linear B transcribed as q originally represented a labiovelar. Equally, however, the poems of Hesiod and Homer indicate that the labiovelars had completely broken down before they were composed in the tenth and ninth centuries. John Chadwick has admitted "the pronunciation of the labiovelars remains a matter of conjecture, but the consensus of opinion favors their retention in Mycenaean." [118] Szemerényi expressed more uncertainty when he wrote: "A much more difficult question is whether the sounds so denoted were still labiovelars [when the texts were written]." [119] Jasanoff and Nussbaum are reduced to claiming "that there is no empirical support for his [my] assertion that the PIE labiovelars had already broken down in Linear B" (p. 196). In addition to Jasanoff and Nussbaum's slip in stating that Linear B was a language (and not the script that represented it), their position is oversimplified. In the first place, my "assertion" was backed by what they describe as a "long excursus." They dismiss this on the grounds that "not a single instance is known in which the labiovelar signs are used to write a demonstrably old labial, or in which labial signs are used to write a demonstrably old labiovelar" (p. 196). I have never questioned the fact that no labials with demonstrable Indo-European etymologies have been written with labiovelars. Jasanoff and Nussbaum, however, are being disingenuous when they refer to no "labial signs [being] used to write a demonstrably old labiovelar." Examples exist of labiovelars before u and y having been delabialized to become a velar k.[120] There is also an instance, which Jasanoff and Nussbaum relegate to a footnote, of an alternation ke/pe, which they explain in the orthodox way as a develarization as a result two labiovelars being in one term (pp. 204–205 n. 18).

Since I last wrote on this topic, a new Linear B text dated to the seventeenth century B.C.E. has been discovered at Kafkania near Olympia.[121] This text confirms the conventional view, which I have always followed, that the script was devised (or rather, adapted to Greek) in that century or earlier.[122] During the centuries between this period and that in which the bulk of the Linear B corpus was written, the orthography could have been fixed and the spoken language changed. Specifically, the labiovelars could have broken down in speech while still being preserved in writing. If this were the case, the sign qa would have been an alternative to pa during the fifteenth and fourteenth centuries B.C.E. and the Egyptian title pasiyara could have been pronounced *pasireu in the Aegean but written *qasireu. As I mentioned in my "excursus," it is quite common, if not normal, in such other languages as Japanese and Hebrew for the less common sign—or sign system—to be used to represent a foreign loan word (BA II: 506).[123] All in all, I do not accept that a conventionally sanctioned speculation that the labiovelars were intact in the fourteenth and thirteenth centuries B.C.E. is sufficient to dismiss the plausible etymologies of loan words that are possible if one accepts the labialization of *qa> pa* by this time.

The problem of the final *-eu(s)* in *qasireu / basieleus* can be solved relatively easily. The origin of the suffix *-eus*, with the Greek meaning "the one or the man who," is hotly debated. The classicist Joachim Schindler has written on the subject and admits both that there are no direct parallels to it in the rest of Indo-European and that most of the stems to which it is attached are non-Indo-European. Nevertheless, he maintains that the suffix is Indo-European.[124] Szemerényi and Perpillou, faced with the same problems, see it as an innovation within Greek.[125] Such an innovation can easily be explained if it is seen as a loan from the suffix *-w* found on Egyptian participles and "relative forms" that, when standing as nouns, mean "the one or ones who." [126]

The suffix has been reconstructed specifically on the word *sr* ("official"). The Egyptologists Adolf Erman and Elmar Edel have seen the full reading of it as *sirw* or *sriw*.[127] In 1923, the "Orientalist" William Albright maintained that sometime before 1300 B.C.E. the Egyptian *û* became *ew*.[128] This view would fit as an early stage of the shift from long stressed *u* to long stressed *e* seen by modern scholars as having taken place from around 1200 B.C.E.[129] Thus, the final *-sileus* could come directly from *sirw* or simply as *sil* and the Greek suffix *eus*.[130] The case for deriving *qasireu/basileus* from *pasiyara +w* is particularly attractive because of its semantic excellence and because all other attempts to find its source have failed spectacularly. As Chantraine put it: "Il est vain de chercher une etymologie pour βασιλεύς."

KUDOS

Jasanoff and Nussbaum come out swinging at the beginning of this item: "Bernal glosses [this] as 'divine glory,' [it] is said to come from the Semitic root *qdš* 'sacred.' But here again the deck has been stacked: there is nothing essentially 'sacred' or 'holy' about the Greek word which simply means 'renown'" (p. 196).

This definition is what one will find if one looks the word up in Liddell and Scott, the standard dictionary. If one checks its use in epic texts, however, one discovers something rather different; as Chantraine put it,

"Kudos . . . magic force, shining forth of force . . . a divinity gives kudos to a warrior . . . to a king . . . the idea of a shining forth of power appears in kúdei gaíōn applied to Zeus . . . an old word which expresses the shining forth of the force of the gods or those upon whom they confer it."

The semantic fit between kudos and the Semitic qds ("sacred" or "divine power, sometimes used for military victory" and "to set apart") is excellent.[131] Gary Rendsburg pointed out the strength of the phonetic parallel, showing that "the Hebrew qadōš 'holy' is a u-class segholate whose protoform can be reconstructed as *qudš."[132]

Despite its apparent excellence, Jasanoff and Nussbaum object to seeing kudos as a loan because, as they put it (p. 196): "Comparison with Sanskrit and other languages shows that the synchronically irregular alternation pattern kûd-os: kūd-ró: kūd-i results from the archaic set of PIE derivational rules known collectively as Caland's Law. Alternations of this type became obsolete so early in the history of Greek that word families which exhibit Caland behavior are virtually always direct inheritances from the parent language" (p. 196). Nussbaum's Ph.D. dissertation was entirely concerned with Caland's "law." Apart from a pattern of alternations common to different branches of Indo-European, the dissertation makes no temporal claims. Furthermore, in it, Nussbaum emphasizes the "law's" immense complications.[133] Probably for this reason, Nussbaum in his thesis places quotation marks around "law." These are dropped in the chapter but even there he refers to it merely as a "set of PIE derivational rules." According to his dissertation, all that is involved in the "law" is a set of correlated morphological properties of considerable regularity in certain words. According to Nussbaum, no diachronic priority can be stated between the alternates.[134]

As the situation around Caland's "law" is extremely confused, it is difficult to say when it was violated, let alone provide a date when these modifications became obsolete. The frequent alternations between C(onsonant)/C(onsonant) and C/C/r or C/C/i seem to have survived well into the first millennium B.C.E., as one sees in such late loans as alábaston/alábastron (alabaster) and balaústion/balaústrion ("flower of a wild pomegranate"). Almost equally common is the alternation C/Ci found in the admitted loan from Afroasiatic Kádos/káddikhos, or the non-Indo-European example cited by Jasanoff and Nussbaum, erébinthos/erebinthiaìos. Even if one insists on the limited number of cases with both alternations, Nussbaum's formula "virtually always" allows for loans. Indeed, one of the best-known of these ancient alternations, aîskhos/aîskhros ("ugly, ignoble"), has what Chantraine calls an "uncertain" etymology.[135] In short, there is no cutoff date for the end of the regularities found in Caland's "law."

As systematic exclusion on this basis is impossible, the etymology should be judged on its own merits. *Quds* is a common Semitic form dating back at least to the third millennium B.C.E. This history and the known contacts between the Levant and the Aegean make it easily possible for the form to have been loaned into Greek in the first half of the second millennium, which is generally acknowledged to be the formative period of the Greek language. Jasanoff and Nussbaum claim that "*kudos* has a perfectly good IE etymology: it is cognate with the Old Church Slavonic *čudo* (*gen. čudese*) 'wonder, marvel'" (pp. 196–197). Here, in their eagerness to have at me, Jasanoff and Nussbaum have tripped over themselves by having previously insisted that "there is nothing essentially 'sacred' or 'holy' about the Greek word." This, of course, does not affect Chantraine, who agrees that "the sense leads one to the Old Church Slavonic *čudo* . . . however, the Slav word would suppose a vocalism **qeu* (not found in the Greek *kudos*)."[136] Chantraine then turns to still less likely Indo-European etymologies.

TĪMÁ, TĪMÉ

One of the difficulties of this debate, for which I must take most of the responsibility, is that it is taking place before the publication of the third volume of *Black Athena*, which will be concerned with language. Therefore, in a number of instances, my claims in volumes 1 and 2 are merely made in passing without the full arguments behind them. This is the case with my derivation of tīmé from the Egyptian **dìt m3ʿ* and the Demotic *tym3ʿ*, which I describe as "render true, justify" (BA I: 61).

Jasanoff and Nussbaum object to this etymology on both semantic and formal grounds. Semantically, they claim that the meanings "truth" and "justification" have nothing to do with the Greek tīmé. According to them, "its meanings are 'honor(s) accorded to gods and kings . . . reward, compensation'" (p. 198). I did not mention the Coptic form *tma(e)io*, which generally had the meaning "justify, praise." However, *tma(e)io* was also used to translate the Greek *makariousi* ("blessed"; honors from God) and *timân* ("to honor") and *timian poein* ("to make honor").

Jasanoff and Nussbaum also fail to consider the central and wide-ranging importance of the concept of *m3ʿt* in Egyptian culture. This word means not merely "truth" and "justice" but also the order of the universe. Offering or giving m3ʿt, dì(t) m3ʿt was a royal ritual with many functions, one of which was to establish and reaffirm the legitimacy of the pharaoh's rule.[137] Tīmḗ has a meaning, found in the writings of Hesiod, of "a present or offering to the Gods." Greek words related to tīmḗ also overlap with dì(t) m3ʿt. Tímēsis has a meaning of "estimation, assessment," and tīmōréō "avenge" or "punish," which fits well with the basic sense of dì(t) m3ʿ ("cause to become just"). The sense of "praise" fits well with tīmḗ as "honors." All in all, even though both the Egyptian and Greek words are very wide-ranging, the semantic fits are remarkably good.

I quite agree with Chantraine, Jasanoff, and Nussbaum that tīmḗ and tíō ("I honor") are fundamentally related, but we see very different connections. The three see both words as deriving from a hypothetical *kʷī linked to a Sanskrit root, ci/cāy ("note, observe, respect"). In fact, as Chantraine and the Danish lexicographer Hjalmar Frisk pointed out, the proposed relationship is rather more complicated and dubious. This is partly because of confusion with another verb, tínō, which the two scholars interpret as having a basic meaning of "vengeance." They link this word in form to the Sanskrit cinute ("observe, notice") and in meaning to cáyate ("revenge, punish"). Elsewhere in the same entry, Chantraine concedes another original sense of tínō, "pay, ransom, fines," from which the meaning "punish, revenge" derived.[138] Here again there is a Late Egyptian parallel, the verb dìt ìnw, Demotic ty ìnw, Coptic tnnou, meaning "cause that they should bring."[139]

Jasanoff and Nussbaum suggest ironically that I might derive tíō from the Egyptian(r)dì(t) ("give") itself. They are not far off. I do in fact see tíō as coming from the attested Middle Egyptian terms dìt ʿ3, ty ʿ3 in Demotic, and Coptic taeio ("cause to become great, honor"). The Egyptian etymologies explain the links and differences among tīmḗ, tíō, and tínō, and they are certainly semantically and phonetically superior, as well as more direct, to the uncertain and tangled hypothetical gossamer linking them to Sanskrit and Proto-Indo-European.

XÍPHOS

Jasanoff and Nussbaum agree that the culturally central word xíphos ("sword") has no known Indo-European etymology and "that it is not impossible that . . . [it] has been borrowed into Greek from some other language" (p. 199). They also acknowledge that the idea that it is borrowed from the Egyptian sft, Coptic sēfe ("sword"), is an old one, although they do not mention that modern scholars still maintain this idea.[140] Jasanoff and Nussbaum deny this apparently plausible etymology on technical grounds set out by the Egyptologist R. H. Pierce. Pierce's first reason is that the Coptic form indicates that the vowel in Middle Egyptian was stressed and long, whereas that of xíphos is short. Jasanoff and Nussbaum strongly object (p. 199) to my use in this connection of a quotation from Alan Gardiner, which concludes, "The vowels and consonants of the older language have usually become modified in the course of time, so that the more recent can at best only serve as the basis for inference" (BA II: 371).[141] They deny that this was Gardiner's "true position" and choose another quotation: "Scholars have succeeded in determining from the Coptic the position and quantity [their italics] of original values in a large number of words; but the quality is far less easily ascertainable." [142] They do not mention that Gardiner began this observation with the words "By an elaborate process of inference. . . ." Gardiner's suspicion of "inference" can be seen from the quotation I give above. The entry in his index reads: "Vocalization of Middle Egyptian for the most part unknown." [143]

Even today, the precariousness of the reconstruction of Middle Egyptian pronunciation is illustrated by Antonio Loprieno, who is devoting his scholarly life to its study and systematization. He writes that the

divorce between methodological requirements and philological evidence has urged modern scholars to draw a distinction between two realities underlying our historical study of Egyptian: (1) the linguistic system resulting from a regular application of the morphophonological rules of derivation of Coptic forms from Egyptian antecedents, conventionally called "pre-Coptic Egyptian"; (2) the forms which emerge from the actual reality of Egyptian texts, i.e. "hieroglyphic Egyptian." The reasons for the fact that "hieroglyphic Egyptian" appears much less regular than "pre-Coptic" are twofold. First . . . the Egyptian graphic system. . . . There is also another aspect to this issue. . . . The reconstructed "pre-Coptic Egyptian" is an idealized linguistic system: even if the rules for its reconstruction were all correct, which is in itself very doubtful, this redundant system would still not be a mirror of an actual historical reality. . . . the actual historical manifestations of Egyptian were probably less regular than reconstructed "pre-Coptic," but more diversified than is betrayed by "hieroglyphic Egyptian." [144]

Loprieno's concern here is with morphophonology, but his strictures on the artificial or idealized nature of "pre-Coptic" hold for phonology itself.

Thus, the length of the vowel in the "pre-Coptic" reconstruction of *sft* does not provide a serious objection to the etymology.

Chantraine rightly does not refer to the argument on vowel length in his denial of the Egyptian origin. His objection is the more serious one, taken up by Jasanoff and Nussbaum, that there is a Mycenaean form of *xíphos* in the dual *qisipee* and that therefore it could not derive from *sft*. As I pointed out in BA II, interpreting this too strictly presents a problem (pp. 369, 605). The labiovelar indicated, $*k^w s$, should be expected to break down to form *psíphos*. Szemerényi tries to explain away this anomaly by saying that it is the result of a "post-Mycenaean dissimilation of the labial element in k^w caused by the following labial." The one parallel he gives for this is, as he admits, very uncertain.[145] The initial *qi* in *qisipee* may simply be a rhyming velar and sibilant, indicating an uncertain sibilant in the loaning language.

Given the perfect semantic fit between *xiphos* and *sft*, the general agreement that *xiphos* is a loan, and the archaeological evidence suggesting that swords came to the Aegean from the southeast, I am not the only scholar to believe that the phonetic difficulty provided by the Linear B form is far too uncertain to block the thoroughly plausible derivation of *xíphos* from *sft*. Bertrand Hemmerdinger is equally unimpressed.[146] Finally, I should like to repeat Burkert's statement: "In any case, the kind of minimalism that rejects all connections with Semitic [and, I would add, Egyptian] that are not crystal clear remains, on the whole, the most unlikely of possible hypotheses." [147]

KHÍLIOI

Burkert's statement should be born in mind when considering my derivation of the Greek *khílioi* ("thousand") from the Egyptian *ḫꜣ* with the same meaning. Jasanoff and Nussbaum admit that "the semantics are, for once, unexceptionable" (p. 199). The phonetics are reasonable but not perfect in that, though the parallel between the consonantal structures is exact, the standard Coptic form *šo* would suggest an earlier Egyptian or rather "Pre-Coptic" *ḫal/r*, or, as Loprieno expresses it, $*\chi$aR.[148] Nevertheless, the complex impact of *ꜣ* on later Egyptian vocalization and the uncertainty of borrowing make the barrier of the difference of vowels surmountable.[149] Jasanoff and Nussbaum do not attack me on this ground; they base their objections on what they see as the strength of the Indo-European etymology. They state (p. 199): "The Greek dialect forms . . . *point unequivocally to Proto-*

Greek *khéhliyo-<*khésliyo- . . . the correspondence is exact with a Skt. *sa-hasríya* 'thousandfold' . . . which taken together with the prototype of the Greek forms establishes a PIE adjective *ĝheslíyo. . . . The derivation of khílioi *is absolutely straightforward* " (my italics).

They then accuse me of misrepresenting Chantraine's dictionary by saying that the author of this section, who, in this case, as they correctly point out, was Chantraine's pupil J.-L Perpillou, "finds many formal difficulties" with this derivation. In fact, the phrase "formally very difficult" appears in the entry itself. Jasanoff and Nussbaum deny my claim on the strange grounds that the only difficulties seen are within Indo-European. This does not alter the fact that if there are competitive explanations *of any kind,* the etymology is not "absolutely straightforward." In any event, Jasanoff and Nussbaum disagree with Perpillou and claim that theirs is the sole true derivation (p. 200).

Jasanoff and Nussbaum's disagreement with the lexicographer goes further when they claim that the dialect forms of khílioi *point unequivocally to* Proto-Greek *khéhliyo <*khésliyo; Perpillou merely writes that *"they permit proposing"* these protoforms (my italics). Presumably, the reconstruction *khésliyo was encouraged by a knowledge of the Sanskrit *sa-hasríya.* As we have seen, it was in combination with this, its Avestan cognate, and the hypothetical Proto-Greek *khésliyo that the doubly hypothetical *ĝheslíyo was constructed. Thus, the imaginary structure forms a circular argument and becomes still more flimsy. The Egyptian etymology is far more straightforward. Jasanoff, Nussbaum, and I agree that the semantic fit between ḥ3 and khilioi is "unexceptionable." When put together with Egyptian parallels with both the kh and the l of khilioi, the case for this derivation becomes overwhelmingly plausible.

NĀOS, NEŌS AND NAÍO

With generous condescension Jasanoff and Nussbaum write that this word for "temple" is "connected by Bernal—correctly as it happens—with the verb naíō 'I dwell.' " I derive both words from the Semitic root nwh ("dwell"). They concede that "neōs and naíō happen to lack problem-free cognates in the other IE languages" (p. 200).[150] They object to my deriving these Greek words from Semitic because, they maintain, the words "must" derive from a root *nas or stem *naswos. Here again Jasanoff and Nussbaum have been trapped by the reification of their own imaginary constructs. No such forms are actually attested and the variety of dialect forms can equally well be explained as resulting from a loan. Gary Rendsburg has pointed out that in Hebrew, not only does *nåwåh* have the meaning "dwell, abide" and *naweh* that of "dwelling, abode," but also *naweh* is used with the specialized meaning "temple, shrine." [151] As the semantic and phonetic correspondences of the Semitic etymology for *nãos*, *neõs*, and *naíõ* are excellent and there is no Indo-European competitor, it is perverse to prefer a purely hypothetical construction.

PROPER NOUNS

Jasanoff and Nussbaum criticize my proposed etymologies for Greek place-names as "capricious" and "undisciplined" (p. 190). To which I reply, "People in glass houses . . ." Conventional views of Aegean toponymy are in total chaos. No book-length study has appeared on the subject since Fick's *Vorgriechische Ortsnamen als Quelle für die Vorgeschichte Griechenlands* came out in 1905. Fick's book has very little phonetic and absolutely no semantic discipline. His only detectable system was a refusal to consider the most obvious Semitic etymologies, as with, for instance, his denial that the Greek river name Iárdanos could be derived from the Canaanite Yardēn, Jordan.[152] For Jasanoff and Nussbaum's attempt to discredit this obvious loan, see below. Since Fick's attempt, apart from Blegen and Haley's ill-fated venture, classicists have left Greek place-names strictly alone.

Jasanoff and Nussbaum justify this failure when they write, "Names, in principle, can mean almost anything" (p. 190). I cannot accept this approach because I believe that although names are often repeated simply as names, the originals nearly always had a meaning, particularly in the case of place-names. Frequently, we fail to understand the meaning of a place-name simply because we do not know, or are not aware that we know, the language from which it was constructed. Nevertheless, before supposing that a certain name derives from an unknown language, we should check to see if it can be explained in terms of one that is known and understood.

I am convinced that the reason there has been no progress in Greek toponymy is that nineteenth- and twentieth-century scholars have seen these place-names as remnants of the lost Pre-Hellenic language and have not considered the possibility that many of them can be plausibly explained in terms of Ancient Egyptian or Semitic.

My approach is not "undisciplined." I insist on three criteria: There must be a good phonetic fit, the proposed Afroasiatic etymon must be attested as a place-name, and the etymon should fit the physical features of the place named. This last criterion has not been taken into account by previous scholars.

Telphoûsa/Thelpoûsa

Jasanoff and Nussbaum often dismiss my proposals by simply stating that a proposed etymology "might as well mean" without providing any serious alternative. For instance, they claim that the names Telphoûsa and Thelpoûsa for cataracts or springs in Boiotia and Arkadia might as well mean "'Cataract,' 'Travelers Rest,' or any of a thousand other possibilities" (p. 191). My phonetically plausible etymology from the attested place name T3lbyw, "Libya," has several bases. It is based not merely, as they say, on the fact that Libya contains cliffs, cataracts, and oases, but also on strong mythological and toponymic parallels of the Greek place-names with Libya. There are the role of the tumultuous god Poseidon, and the place-name Tritōn that is associated with him and found both as the name of a lake in Libya and as a stream flowing from Telphoûsa. Near the Libyan Tritōn there was a river Lathōn or Lēton. The Arkadian Thelpoûsa was sited on a river Ladōn. Ladōn was also an alternative name for the river Ismenos that flowed past Thebes in Boiotia. In BA II (pp. 92–98), I give many other mythological and toponymic parallels between Libya and these areas of Boiotia and Arkadia.[153]

Iárdanos

Jasanoff and Nussbaum attempt to discredit the etymology of this name of two Greek rivers called Iárdanos or Iárdēnos from the Canaanite river name Yardēn, the Jordan. Their grounds for this are that the Greek shift y>h generally dated to c. 1300 B.C.E. This would have meant that an earlier loan into Greek should have been rendered *Hardanos. Even if their dubiously established date for the shift is accurate, a later introduction presents little problem. We know that Elis in the Northwestern Peloponnese, the site of one Iárdanos, was very much influenced from the East toward the end of the Bronze Age, and that Eastern Crete, where the other was situated, received considerable Phoenician influence in the early Iron Age.

The early-twentieth-century classicist J. G. Frazer, author of *The Golden Bough*, was convinced of this Semitic etymology of Iárdanos. He reinforced this derivation by pointing out that Iárdanos was also the old name for two short rivers feeding into the lagoon of Kaiápha on the coast of Elis. These rivers were later known as the Akidas and the Anigros; the Anigros stunk of volcanic gases. Frazer showed that the leprosy cure described by Pausanias in the nearby cave of the Anigrian nymphs resembled the biblical cure of the leper Haaman the Syrian in the Jordan.[154] The name Anigros has a clear Semitic etymology from the root ŋgr ("spring, stream or oasis") found in a large number of place-names—Nagara, Nigira, Nigrai, and so on—in Southwest Asia and Northern Africa.[155]

Kōpā́ïs

The lagoon of Kaiápha leads us naturally to the similar toponym Kōpā́ïs. I derive the names of both Kaiápha and Kōpā́ïs, the name of a large shallow lake in Boiotia (where, before it was drained, there were plentiful wildfowl), from the Egyptian root qbḥ ("cool, fresh, spring, purify") and from a series of place-names: Qbḥ ("marsh country," "town of cool/fresh water") and Qbḥw ("lakes, ponds, or marshes with wildfowl").

Jasanoff and Nussbaum contest this etymology on the grounds that Kōpā́ï is the name of the town on the lake shore from which the body of water gets its name (p. 193). They agree that Kōpā́ïs límnē is "conventionally glossed" "Copaean Lake," but, according to them, it really means "lake near Copae." They have no idea of the meaning of Copae. This discussion seems to me to be absurd niggling. The names of lakes and the towns set on their shores are frequently confused, as in Erie, Windermere, and Geneva. The most obvious origin of the name Kōpā́ï is from the Egyptian Qbḥ, attested both as "marsh country" and "town of cool/fresh water." The derivation from Qbḥ would link Kōpā́ïs to the lake's other title, Kēphisian, from the river Kēphisiás that flowed into it. The common river name Kēphis(s)ós frequently is used for streams that go underground and were used for purification.[156] Qbḥ was also an Egyptian term for "purify." The cluster is completed with the lagoon of Kaiápha itself.

Methṓnē, Mothṓnē, and Méthana

Jasanoff and Nussbaum apply the same withering scorn to my proposal to derive these three city names from the Egyptian mṯwn ("bullfight, bull arena"), which they claim I propose simply because all are set on bays that could be described as theatrical. This coincidence and the excellent phonetic fit seem to me remarkable enough, but in fact I give more evidence for a connection. First, the two Greek words *móthos/móthon* ("battle din, fight between animals") and *mothṓn* ("licentious dance") suggest that the Egyptian *mṯwn* was known in Greece.[157] Second, Mṯwn is attested as an Egyptian city name, probably the modern Meidum. And third—as I point out in BA I (p. 50) but which Jasanoff and Nussbaum fail to mention—the theatrical association of the Greek names is greatly strengthened by coins from the Methṓne/Mothṓnē in Messenia, in which the city's harbor is represented as a theater.[158]

Láris(s)a

In the case of "Lárisa," Jasanoff and Nussbaum have been particularly sloppy. They write: "The 'fertile' Lárisa mentioned by Bernal was not the only town to bear this name in antiquity. Another Lárisa, likewise in Thessaly, was located high on a mountainside" (p. 191).

In fact, I refer (BA I: 76) to "many" Laris(s)ai. I also stress that the Homeric epithet *eribṓlax* ("deep-soiled") was attached to two of them. Furthermore, the second Thessalian Lárisa (Kremasté) was not situated "high on a mountainside" but, according to Pausanias, "by the sea." [159] It was almost certainly on slopes overlooking a small coastal plain. In addition, as Strabo, the geographer of the first century B.C.E./C.E., noted, all the Laris(s)ai were situated on rich alluvial soil.[160] Earlier, Xenophon reported that the Lárisa in Anatolian Ionia on the edge of the rich plain north of Smyrna was also known as Aigyptia.[161] The northern section of the largest plain on the Peloponnese, along the boundary between Elis and Akhaia, was drained by a river Lárisos. It was a land that brought the Nile Delta to Pausanias' mind.[162] Lárisa is a city name and, as such, it was associated with walls and heights, most strikingly as the name of the acropolis at Argos, which dominated the fertile Argive Plain. For this reason, not because of any association with mountain ranges, Stephanos Byzantios wrote that the name originally meant "citadel." [163]

The Egyptian R-ȝḫt is also a city name meaning "entry into the fertile lands," which seems to have been a name of the Hyksos capital Avaris that dominated much of the fertile Eastern Delta. Jasanoff and Nussbaum do not challenge the phonetics of the etymology, but in any event, these are good. R- ("mouth" or "entry") is *ro* in Coptic, indicating a Middle Egyptian or Pre-Coptic *la or *ʀa. It appears this way in the strong etymology of the

Greek laúra ("lane") from the Egyptian r-w3t ("path, way"). The equation of 3 with l or r was discussed above. To return to R-3ḫt: The disappearance of initial and medial ḥ is extremely frequent in transcriptions and acknowledged loans, and final -t s in Egyptian were often rendered as -is in Greek (see irt/Iris, St/Isis). Both shifts are seen in the universally accepted derivation of the Greek oasis from the Egyptian wḥ3t ("oasis"). Thus, we can tentatively reconstruct R-3ḫt as rendered *Lar is in Greek.

Lakedaímōn

In this case, I do not propose a loan from Egyptian or Semitic but a calque, in which the form and meaning of a foreign word is not transferred to the recipient language, which merely provides a model for a native formation. I propose that Lakedaímōn derives from lake ("howling" or "gnawing") plus daimōn ("spirit").[164] Greek contains two verbs with the root lak: laskō ("scream, cry out") and lakízō ("rend"). Both are associated with animals and lakízō specifically with wolves. Therefore, I see Lakedaímōn as a calque of the Egyptian K3 inpw or Kanōbos/Kanopos ("spirit of the jackal god Anubis"). "Kanopic" was the name used by the Greeks for the westernmost mouth of the Nile closest to Sparta. The Egyptians simply called the distributary K3. Alan Gardiner drew a parallel between this K3 and the name Agathodaímōn, which the geographer Ptolemy gave to this branch.[165] In Greek mythology, the Kanōbos was the helmsman of the Spartan king Menelaus, and that king was driven by storm to the Canopic mouth on his return from Troy.

Jasanoff and Nussbaum have three objections to my etymology for Lakedaímōn. First, they state that compounds consisting of verb + noun are always adjectives. Even if one accepts this assertion, the attested adjectives lakedaímonos and lakedaimónios could have preceded Lakedaímōn. Similarly, their objection that the second element -daimōn had to be the object as opposed to the subject of the verb is another example of misplaced precision. As the authoritative grammarian of Greek H. W. Smyth wrote, "The Greeks did not think of any actual case relation as existing in these compounds, and the case relation that exists is purely logical." [166]

Jasanoff and Nussbaum's third, and major, objection is to the segmentation Lake-daímōn. They argue that "the Mycenaean personal name ra-ke-da-no . . . is almost surely to be read as Laked-ānōr . . . showing that the correct segmentation of Lakedaímōn is not Lake-daímōn but Laked-aímōn" (p. 193).

Jasanoff and Nussbaum's failure to acknowledge Oswald Szemerényi as the author of this hypothesis gives it a spurious "scientific" validity. In fact, Szemerényi's hypothesis is generally seen as idiosyncratic. Jasanoff and Nussbaum wisely do not venture an etymology of their own, but Szemerényi proposed that the first segment was originally not Laked- but Laken-, related to Lakōn, Laconian, and that Aimōn should be linked to Haimōnes, a people Stephanos Byzantios reported to be living in Thessaly and other parts of Greece.[167] Chadwick hesitated on the proposal, and Chantraine stated that it was "ingenious" but remains doubtful. Before setting out his hypothesis, Szemerényi admitted that "all interpreters, both ancient and modern, agree that the division is $\Lambda\alpha\kappa\epsilon\text{-}\delta\alpha\iota\mu\omega\nu$."[168]

The idea of associating Lakedaimonians with tearing dogs and foxes fits well with many aspects of Spartan life. There is, for instance, Plutarch's strange story of the typical Spartan boy who, having stolen a young fox, allowed it to tear out his bowels rather than reveal the theft.[169] This tale suggests both a respect for canines and for Anubis' Greek counterpart, Hermes, as the god of thieves. A statue of Hermes carrying the infant Dionysos was set in the central market place of Sparta and was used as an emblem for the city on coins of the Roman period.[170]

According to the mythographers, Lakedaímōn was the son of Taïgétos, the name of the mountain range west of Sparta. It has a plausible late Egyptian etymology in T3(w) igrt: "Realm of the Dead," "necropolis," the territory of Anubis. The mountains are not only appropriately immediately west of the city, but at least one of the peaks looks remarkably like a pyramid.[171] A few of the many cultic and linguistic connections between Sparta on the one hand and Egypt, dogs, and death on the other were mentioned in BA I, and more will be elaborated in BA III.[172] The most striking connection, however, is that of the name parallel to Lakedaímōn—Sparta itself. This has a very strong etymology from the Egyptian sp3t ("district" or "nome"). The association with Anubis comes from his ancient title as the "Lord of Sp3(t)."[173] In this dense cultic, iconographic, and linguistic context, the generally accepted segmentation of Lakedaímōn as Lake-daímōn and the canine associations of lake-, the explanation I propose, would seem to be far more plausible than the derivation proposed by Szemerényi. Furthermore, although individual elements may be mistaken, the general sense I make of the cluster is preferable to the chaotic mystery in which Jasanoff and Nussbaum leave Spartan or Lakedaimonian nomenclature.

Mŭkênai, Mŭkénē

The ancient etymology for the great Late Bronze Age city Mycenae was from *múkēs* ("mushroom"). Amazingly, this notion is still maintained by some modern scholars.[174] Jasanoff and Nussbaum are more cautious; they simply attack the proposal that it derives from **Maḥănáyim* ("double camp"). *Maḥănáyim* occurs frequently in the Bible and is found as Mḥnm in Ugaritic. Jasanoff and Nussbaum object first on the grounds that there is no reason why the city should have such a name; they continue: "But more to the point is Bernal's failure—or refusal—to notice that the ending *-ēnai/-ēnē* older (<older *-ānai/-āna*) is a recurring element in Greek place names. No credence can be attached to an analysis of 'Mycenae' which separates the termination *-ēnai/-ēnē* from the corresponding *-ānai/-ānā* of names like Messáná 'Messene' and Kuráná 'Cyrene'" (p. 193).

Presumably because they insist on the integrity of the whole name, they do not propose the etymology from *múkēs*. And as with every place-name they discuss, they provide no alternative derivation. Here again, responding to their criticism has been made more difficult because my volume on language has not yet been published. In fact, I am aware of the ending *-ēnai*, but I do not think that it can be separated from a wider class of Greek city names, which are conventionally and puzzlingly seen as plurals with the ending *-ai* as in Thêbai or *-oi* as in Delphoi.[175] I believe that all of these derive directly or by analogy from the Semitic dual *-áyim* or in the reduced construct form *-ê*.[176] The ones with *-ēnai* are simply those in which the stem has a final *-n*.

Cyrus Gordon has shown that in Bronze Age Canaan, the duality of cities was important, and he has plausibly associated this with the double nature of the acropolis and the lower town, a feature that was found around the Eastern Mediterranean at that time.[177] Hence such names as Qîryrátáyim ("double city") and Maḥănáyim ("double camp") are frequently attested in the Bible. The phonetic correspondence of **Maḥanáyim* with Mŭkênai is good. The name also fits the city's military connotations, and the fact that it was situated above and beyond the Argive Plain with its older cities—Argos, Tiryns, and Lerna—makes for an excellent semantic match. The etymology is certainly competitively plausible when the only competition comes from a mushroom!

Thêbai

I admit that I did not clearly set out my etymology for the cities with this name, partly because the situation is intrinsically confusing. Middle Egyptian has two apparently different words: dbt ("shrine" or "coffin") and ḏbꜣt ("chest" or "box"). The Canaanite "ark of bull rushes" or "chest" derived from the latter. Ḏbꜣt was written tbt in Demotic, and dbt was also rendered tbỉ in that script. Both became taibe or tēēbe in Coptic. Ḏbꜣt also had a special sense of "palace," and Ḏbꜣ (Tbo in Coptic) became a place-name most notably of Edfu in Upper Egypt, but also of cities in the Delta, possibly including the Hyksos capital at Avaris/Tel ed Daba'a.[178]

As I wrote in BA I (p. 51), the idea that Thêbai means "palace" or "seat of a monarch" would explain its uses throughout Greece and in Boiotia in particular. Furthermore, if Thêbai had been seen as "capital of Egypt" during the Hyksos period, this would explain the puzzle of why Greeks should have called the capital of the new Eighteenth Dynasty Thebes, even though the name was never used for that city by Egyptians themselves.

The situation has been confused by Greek myths playing on the Canaanite stories of Têbåh in the sense of "ark." Astour has shown intricate parallels between legends about the foundation of Thebes with the wanderings of unyoked heifers and stories of the movement of the Israelite ark.[179] Thus, pace Jasanoff and Nussbaum (p. 191), one does not have to rely on Hesychios in the fifth century C.E. to make the association. They write that Bernal "tacitly assumes the identity of the name Thebes with the barely attested Greek noun thîbis 'basket' was 'generally accepted' before the advent of the Aryan Model" (p. 190). In fact, all I "assume" is that both the word thîbis and the toponym Thêbai come directly or indirectly from ḏbꜣt and dbt.

Jasanoff and Nussbaum's major objection to the etymology is that the city name was written Teqa in Linear B (p. 192). Above, I made the argument that qa was read as pa in Late Mycenean times. I admit, however (BA II: 506), that this case could cause problems, because the city name may have been introduced rather earlier than pasiyara/basileus.

Athḗnē, Athḗnai

Interestingly, although Jasanoff and Nussbaum rightly emphasize the importance of this example, they argue that their chapter "is not the place for a lengthy rebuttal of Bernal's case" (p. 194).[180] Thus, I can only argue against what apparently is only an outline of their attack on my derivation of the name of the Greek city and divine name from the Egyptian Ḥt Nt. Ḥt Nt, literally "Temple of Nëïth," was the name of the temple of the goddess Nëïth, and by extension it became the religious name of her cult center in Lower Egypt, the city of Sais, in the Western Delta. It should be noted, furthermore, that during the late seventh and sixth centuries B.C.E., Sais was the capital of Egypt.[181]

The two authors begin by criticizing what they see as my failure to explain the final -ēnai/ēnē, which I discussed above. The only phonetic similarity between Ḥt Nt and Athénē/Athénai that they recognize is that an n is preceded by a t. They claim that even this is deceptive because, although the two are not separated in Egyptian, there is a long accented vowel between them in Greek.

I shall come back to this last point after listing some of the phonetic correspondences. Ḥt ("house or temple") was originally pronounced Ḥwt. Jasanoff and Nussbaum, however, agree that the name Aikupitiyo found in Linear B is from the Egyptian Ḥt k3 Ptḥ. This suggests that by the second millennium the ḥ could be neutralized and the vowel heard as simply a-. In this case, the final -t- disappeared, but in some other renderings, it was preserved as t or tḥ, at least in front of sonorants: see, for example, Ḥt (t3) ḥr ỉb>Athribis in Greek and Ḥt Rpyt>Atrēpe or Athrēbe in Coptic, or the Goddess Ḥt Ḥr ("House of Horus") rendered in Coptic as Ḥathôr or Athôr and in Greek as Athur.[182] Thus, the initial vowel and the first consonant of Ḥt Nt correspond with those of Athénē/Athénai. As Jasanoff and Nussbaum point out, the following long vowel—it is not accented in the Homeric Athēnaíē—does present a problem, but not an insuperable one. Egyptian frequently had prothetic vowels that were unwritten. The likelihood in this case is increased by the name ʿAnât, given to a very similar West Semitic goddess.[183] Alternatively, the length of the vowel may come from a development within Greek, possibly as a result of what is sometimes known as Wackernagel's Second Law. According to this, the initial vowel in the second element of a compound word was lengthened.[184]

There is no problem with the -n-. The original vocalization of Nt would seem to have been -ā-. The vowel's quality is suggested by the biblical name of Joseph's Egyptian wife, ʾAsᵉnat, which was probably from the Egyptian n(y) s(y) Nt, "She belongs to Nt."[185] The quantity is indicated by Plato's rendering of Nt as Nēïth. This and other renditions of Nt as Nit- or Neth also indicate an original form *Nāi̯t with an off-glide.

The glide does not always appear in Greek. It is not present in the Doric Athánā and the Mycenaean Atana. However, Homer, whose language was sometimes more archaic than that written in Linear B, uses Athēnaíē, and there is an Attic form, Athēnaía.[186]

To work in the spirit of Jasanoff and Nussbaum, and in severe danger of misplaced precision, I tentatively propose the following sequence: A Middle Egyptian form *ḤataNāit was introduced into Proto-Greek as *H₂atanāit c. 2000 B.C.E.[187] With the disappearance of the Proto-Indo-European laryngeals, this form became *Atanāit and then *Atanāi(a), with the elimination of final stops. Following Wackernagel's Second Law, the second -a- became ā, giving *Atānāi(a). The Attic form Athēnaía and the Homeric Athēnaíē developed with the Ionic shift ā>ē. Given the awkwardness of Linear B, it is impossible to know precisely what sound was conveyed by Atana, but the Doric Athā́nā suggests that in this case, the spelling could be an accurate phonetic representation. Nevertheless, the forms Athēnā and Athēnē could derive from Athēnaía and Athēnaíē by normal contraction. The only feature left unexplained is the theta. The city name was formed in the same way but retaining the "plural/dual" ending for cities, -ai.

Although this sequence may not be precisely accurate, the phonetic correspondences between Ḥt Nt/(Ḥ)atNāit and Athēnaía would be remarkable even if there were not perfect semantic and iconographic parallels. As these exist, the etymology is logically unassailable. Jasanoff and Nussbaum attempt to bluster their way through by raising absurd countersuggestions. They write, "No principle is given for why we should take Athā́nā from Ḥt Nt rather than, say, from the Anatolian city name Adana which is attested in exactly this form from the middle of the second millennium" (p. 194).

Once again, Jasanoff and Nussbaum's skewing of my arguments is apparent, as I do discuss the name Adana in BA II (pp. 418–420). Ḥt Nt is to be preferred for phonetic reasons because it can explain the early forms Athēnaía and Athēnaíē much more easily than can the name Adana.[188] This point is trivial, however, compared to the mass of historical, semantic, cultic, and iconographic evidence linking Ḥt Nt to Athens and Athena, whereas this kind and scope of evidence is completely lacking with Adana.

Jasanoff and Nussbaum claim: "'Temple of Nēit' is no more likely, a priori, than 'olive grove,' 'rocky crag,' or countless other possible glosses" (p. 194). This is true, but they provide no words for these in any language and no reason to link such place-names with the name of any female divinity.

Thrashing around still more wildly, they write that because St. Augustine portrayed the pagan gods as demons, "Under Bernal's logic, it would seem perfectly legitimate to contemplate a direct borrowing of 'Athena' from a feminized variant of Hebr. śâṭân 'Satan' (older spelling Sathan)" (p. 194).[189]

Here we are dealing with competitive plausibility. First, strong semantic reasons exist for preferring Ḥt Nt as a source for the names Athena and Athens. Both Nēith and Athena were divinities of warfare, weaving, and wisdom. Herodotus and Plato saw Nēith and Athena as two names for the same deity, and the former did not exclude Athena from the list of Greek divinities whose names he saw as coming from Egypt.[190]

As mentioned above, Ḥt Nt was the religious name of Sais; thus, this etymology can elegantly explain why the Greek goddess should share a name with her cult city. Although Ḥt Nt is not attested as a name for Nt herself in pharaonic texts, an ambiguous example can be found in an inscription from the Roman period.[191] More significantly, as in many other cultures, it was normal in Egypt for a divinity to be addressed by the name of her or his dwelling. See, for instance, Pr ʿ3 ("Great House," the divine Pharaoh) and Pr W3ḏyt ("House of the goddess W3ḏyt"). Pr W3ḏyt was both the city called Bouto by the Greeks and a name used for the goddess herself.[192] Similarly, Pr B3styt, the Greek Boubastis, was the name of the cult center in the Eastern Delta of the lion goddess Bast and of the goddess herself.[193]

In Lower Egypt, as I stated earlier, the cult of Nēith was centered in Sais, whose citizens felt a special affinity with the Athenians. The historian Kharax of Pergamon made the correspondence explicit in the second century C.E., when he wrote that "the Saitians called their city Athēnai," a statement that makes excellent sense if they saw Ḥt Nt as a name for Sais.[194]

My etymological proposal is merely a complement to an iconographic connection established by Percy Newberry and Arthur Evans with great clarity early in the last century. They demonstrated that the sign of Neith, a figure 8 shield associated with weapons, was the origin of the so-called Shield Goddess represented widely in Minoan Crete.[195] The clearest evidence for this divinity comes from the ceramic period Middle Minoan III c. 1730–1675 B.C.E. Evans, however, made a plausible case for her symbols having been present in Early Minoan III 2050–1950 B.C.E.[196] Assuming rapid transmission from Crete to Proto-Greek speakers, this period would correspond to the original date of the linguistic loan given above.

The divinity behind the shield is known to be a goddess because of a painted limestone plaque, found at Mycenae, showing white arms and neck, which, according to Minoan (following Egyptian) convention, indicated a female. Even before Newberry and Evans, the classicist Edward Gardiner had seen this plaque as an early representation of the Palladion, a standing suit of armor associated with the cult of Athena, and had identified the Shield Goddess as Athena herself.[197] This connection was clinched by the more recent find at Knossos of a number of remains of burned children's bones clearly associated with the Shield Goddess. The most remarkable find of all was a pot decorated with three motifs: a gorgoneion, the face of the Gorgon, Athena's fearful double, who in Archaic and Classical times was always represented on the goddess's breastplate; the same shape without a face; and the figure 8 shield.[198]

In this way, one can trace an iconographic development from Egypt in the fourth and third millennia B.C.E., through Crete and Mycenae in the second, to the well-known Greek goddess of the first. This process corresponds precisely both to the legendary association between Nēith and Athena and to the etymology I propose.

There is, however, an interesting addition to this sequence. Newberry and Evans did not merely set the iconographic connections between the Egyptian Nēith and Athena; they also demonstrated iconographic links between Nēith and Libyan cultures, ancient and modern.[199] Sais was on the frontier of Egypt and Libya, and Herodotus explicitly associated Athena with Libya and such institutions as wrestling among women.[200] Partly because of this association, I did not set out to name my work *Egyptian Athena* but preferred something more inclusive: *African Athena*. As I have said a number of times, although I was the first to propose the title, it was my publisher who insisted on the title *Black Athena*.

Now I should like to turn to this Libyan connection. Arthur Evans paid particular attention to Libyan people known to the Egyptians as Ṯhnw. The Ṯhnw, who lived to the west of the Nile Delta, were known for their "Ṯhnw oil," which Newberry identified with olive oil (providing yet another association with Athena, whose sacred tree was the olive), and for faience, which in Egyptian was called ṯhn. Evans explained the connection by the supplies of natron (sodium carbonate) necessary for the manufacture of faience, found in the Libyan oases.[201] Alan Gardiner too, wrote about the Ṯhnw. He pointed out that although they were Libyans living in Cyrenaica and had been previously thought to have been "white," in Egyptian paintings, though dressed barbarically, they were represented as physically resembling Egyptians.[202] Gardiner further considered the possibility that the Ṯhnw also lived further south, in or near the Fayum.[203] In his note on the subject, he mentioned that there was a reference from the Old Kingdom to a Nt Ṯhnw.[204]

Five years ago I found another piece of evidence, which helps my thesis but confuses the title "Black" Athena. It was the attestation in Sais of a temple with the title Pr ṯḥn. Henri Gauthier, the geographer of Ancient Egypt, interpreted this as "House of Crystal" or "House of Faience."[205] The name was used elsewhere, but this temple of Osiris at Sais was the most famous instance. The phonetic and semantic parallel of Pr ṯḥn with Parthénōn is striking. Furthermore, there is a reference from the Twenty-sixth (Saitian) Dynasty to Nt ṯḥn in this sense. Clearly, through sacred paronomasia, Nēith was associated both with the Ṯḥnw and with the product of their land, ṯḥn ("faience").[206] As an adjective, ṯḥn.t is defined as "brilliant," "flashing," "jewels," and "blue green," the color of faience. It also seems to have been the color of the bright sky and fragments of the firmament as they appeared on Earth in the form of the green mineral malachite.[207] Parthénos in Greek means, "young woman, virgin" and was especially used for the virgin goddesses Artemis and Athena. The Egyptian and Greek words share a number of specific meanings. Both convey "blooming" and "happy." Ṯḥn(t) was also used for "bright eyes of divinities" and for a part of the eye. The Greek parthénos has a special sense of "pupil."

Athena had a number of epicleses concerning eyes: Ophthalmîtis and Oxyderkîs. Above all, the Homeric epithet Glaukōpis applied to her and other frightening creatures, and meant "pale and brilliant eyes." This obviously derives from the word glaukós ("gray" or "light blue, terrible, brilliant"). Indeed, glaukós is another word that Jasanoff and Nussbaum admit (p. 185) lacks an Indo-European etymology. It has a good Egyptian one, however, in g3g3 ("dazzle, amaze"), which is written with the eye determinative.[208] Glaukós is also related to glaûx ("owl") the large-eyed, ferocious bird of Athena, parallel as a bird of prey to Nēith's vulture. G3g3 also provides an excellent etymology for Gorgô, which also had the combined form Gorgōpis. The face and eyes of the Gorgon petrified all who saw them; her close and ancient association with Athena was referred to above.[209]

In Utterence 317 of the Pyramid Texts, the crocodile god Sobek, son of Neith, brings "greenness to the eye of the great one (feminine)."[210] This description plausibly refers to Neith herself. In the Fifth Dynasty inscription referred to above, the term Nt Ṯḥnw is followed by "Eye of Nt." The Egyptian Egyptologist Ramadan El Sayed plausibly suggests that "this is perhaps an aspect of Neith worshipped in this period by the Libyans."[211] Plato described the eyes of Pheidias' statue of Athena in the Parthénōn as set with pale jewels, and Cicero saw light blue flashing eyes in the ideal type of Athena's Roman counterpart, Minerva.[212] Diodorus rejected the "Greek idea" that Athena had blue eyes as "a silly explanation." According to him, the real reason why the goddess was called Glaukōpis was because "the air has a bluish cast." [213] In fact, the two images are not mutually exclusive and there is no reason to deny that Athena was sometimes represented as having flashing blue eyes. In many societies, such as Mongolia and China, where the overwhelming majority of the population is brown-eyed, blue eyes have been traditionally seen as a sign of ferocity. In Ancient as in Modern Greece, blue eyes were associated with the "evil eye," indicating all kinds of bad characteristics. Specifically, the connotation of Glaukōpis was that the paleness of Athena's eyes added to the terror she inspired. [214] The same could well have been true of Nēith in Egypt. In any event, her associations with blue-green "faience" and the bright sky and the association of t̠ḥn(t) with eyes suggest that—though in late tradition, hidden by a veil—her eyes too could be seen as blue. [215] Pausanias explicitly stated that the story of Athena's blue eyes came from Libya. [216] Thus, we may have the paradox that the goddess's blue eyes came from Africa. This certainly complicates the name *Black Athena*, but it strengthens my overall case and that of my preferred title, *African Athena*. Specifically, it provides further evidence of the extraordinarily rich network of associations linking the two goddesses and the two names Ḥt Nt and Athēnaía.

Conclusion

Jasanoff and Nussbaum begin with and emphasize their etymology of Érebos. They do this because, even though it also has a clear Semitic origin, it is the only instance they can produce of a genuinely straightforward Indo-European etymology for the words I put forward as deriving from Afroasiatic. All the others they propose have flaws or at least complications. They themselves admit that most of the words and all of the place-names discussed have no explanation whatsoever in terms of Indo-European.

In the first section of this reply, I made the argument that the linguistic mixture found in Greek is far more plausibly explained as the result of contact than through language shift. Furthermore, if this argument holds, the most likely sources of loans into Greek were Egyptian and West Semitic, the two languages that we know from legend and historical records have dominated the Eastern Mediterranean during most of the last two millennia B.C.E.

I also referred to the arguments made by Oswald Szemerényi, Walter Burkert, and others that at least by the second half of the nineteenth century, traditional Indo-European linguists were heavily influenced by the prevailing racism and anti-Semitism and the desire for European purity. Apart from obvious trade goods and exotica, the leading scholars were extremely reluctant to consider the possibility of loans into Greek from Semitic or Egyptian.

Finally, we should note again that Jasanoff and Nussbaum are among the last defenders of the Neogrammarian tradition in its pure and most rigorously isolationist form. Nussbaum was one of the three authors who said that he would not contribute to BAR if I were allowed to respond in it. I think that, on balance, he was right.

IV

Historiography

THE HISTORIOGRAPHY OF the origins of Ancient Greece is essential to my project, and the first volume of *Black Athena* is devoted to it. Only by situating the nineteenth-century philologists and classicists in their social and intellectual matrices can I explain why they should have made such fundamental errors in their descriptions and explanations of Greek origins. Previously, this aspect of my work had been generally accepted, and apparently for this reason the editors of BAR felt that they needed new pieces, those by Robert Palter and Robert Norton. Palter's piece is massive and wide-ranging; Norton's is shorter and deals with one topic, my treatment of Johann Gottfried Herder. My response to these criticisms is coupled with a reaction to a critique by Josine Blok, which is not in BAR. It was published first in the *Journal of the History of Ideas* and then in the special issue of *Talanta* on *Black Athena*.

All three scholars object to what they see as the superficiality of my work and my reliance on secondary sources. Norton and Blok attribute this to what they view as my propagandist and "political" approach. Palter, more accurately to my mind, sees it as coming from ignorance. I willingly admit that I have relied on secondary sources more than I should like. I think, however, that this problem is inevitable in any wide-ranging work and should not be used in itself to discredit my research, unless, that is, my failure to consult primary sources has led me to make mistakes. Norton and Blok have both found minor examples of such mistakes, but, to my mind at least, they do not affect my general scheme.

Palter's other great objection to my work is against what he sees as my failure to appreciate the full complexity of intellectual history. Specifically, he criticizes what he sees as my failure to recognize that the eighteenth and early nineteenth centuries saw antiracism as well as racism. He implies that antiracism was somehow equivalent to racism and should be treated with equal respect.

The third chapter in this section is a reprint of the article "The British Utilitarians, Imperialism, and the Fall of the Ancient Model," first published in the Danish journal *Culture and History*. It is a tale of two histories: the first is *The History of British India* by James Mill and the second George Grote's *History of Greece*.

In his chapter on historiography, Guy Rogers attacked my treatment of Grote in BA I (unfortunately, he had not read the article discussed above, which was first published in 1988). Rogers rightly emphasizes Grote's radical politics and progressive attitudes and is shocked that I should have called Grote an anti-Semite and a racist. I reply in detail to this charge in chapter 8. Rogers ends his chapter and the conclusion of BAR with some comments on my personality and psychological needs, to which I respond briefly in the same chapter.

In their criticism of my work that appeared after the publication of BAR, the intellectual historians Suzanne Marchand and Anthony Grafton have written: "Up to now Bernal has made noise, not historical argument."[1] I find it difficult to understand how mere *noise* could have stimulated the interesting and detailed *historical arguments* of the critics, to some of which I respond here.

7 Accuracy and/or Coherence?

A REPLY TO ROBERT NORTON, ROBERT PALTER,

AND JOSINE BLOK

When I make my work public, the fear comes over me that many will consider it an insufficiently documented improvisation, in spite of all the labor that went into it. It is the fate of anyone who wants to deal with cultural topics that he is compelled to make incursions into all sorts of provinces which he has not sufficiently explored. To fill all the gaps in my knowledge beforehand was out of the question for me, and by using references to justify details, I made it easy on myself. I had to write now or not at all. It was something very close to my heart. So I wrote. — JOHAN HUIZINGA, introduction to *Homo Ludens*, 1938[1]

Most chapters of BAR are concerned with ancient topics and events that took place many millennia ago. By contrast, the three essays by Norton, Palter, and Blok, which I consider here, criticize my claims about European writing of history in the modern era. Robert Norton's short chapter focuses exclusively on my account of the German thinker Johann Gottfried Herder (1744–1803). Responding to Robert Palter's much more substantial and wide-ranging piece will take up much more space and forms the long middle section of this reply. Finally, I turn to the critique of my treatment of the German classicist Karl Ottfried Müller (1797–1840) by Josine Blok, which was published after the appearance of BAR. I discuss below the reasons for replying to her in this book.

All of these critical essays are intelligent, erudite, and penetrating. Nevertheless, most of the issues they raise are relatively minor and, as a whole, they do not affect the overall structure of my argument. Thus, where the authors see their arguments as destroying my case, I see them as providing it with depth and subtlety.

Before beginning my detailed responses, I should like to consider some general issues. In essence, most of the criticisms attempt to rebut the charges of "racism" I have made or am supposed to have made against various figures of the eighteenth and nineteenth centuries. It may surprise readers of this book to learn that in Black Athena, I do not see racism as the sole cause of the historiographical shift from the Ancient to the Aryan model. Both the eighteenth-century Egyptophils and the nineteenth-century Philhellenes were affected by racism. The essential difference between the two groups tended to be their classification along "racial" lines of the Ancient Egyptians. Most of those who admired them saw them as at least "honorary" Europeans, whereas those who disliked them portrayed them as Africans or Orientals and, therefore, beyond the pale of civilization. I do not maintain that it was always the "racial" classification that determined the degree of respect. Sometimes, it was the other way around, the "racial" classification following a positive or negative opinion formed on other grounds. Either way, however, the removal of "European" status from the Ancient Egyptians was always accompanied by a drastic fall in their reputation. Thus, if we are to understand any of the ideas of the eighteenth and nineteenth centuries we must take "race" into serious account.

From the late seventeenth century, European thinkers shifted the basis of the perceived superiority of Europe over other continents away from its Christianity toward what they saw as its peculiarly blessed landform, climate, and "white" inhabitants. Later in this chapter, I discuss the links between these views and both the extermination of Native North Americans and the institution of race-based slavery in the same period. At this point, all that needs to be emphasized is that, from the 1680s, nearly all upper-class Europeans saw their continent as the unique site of the three new and related concepts of civilization, science, and enlightenment.

The turn from the Enlightenment of the seventeenth and eighteenth centuries to the romanticism and positivism of the nineteenth century only increased the intensity and salience of the newly "scientific" racism, which was less and less constrained either by Christianity or by the enlightened beliefs in the brotherhood of mankind and the universality of reason. Interestingly, however, Norton and Palter, the first two critics to whom I reply in this chapter, are generally more concerned with the Enlightenment of the eighteenth century than with its nineteenth-century aftermath.

Robert Norton

Robert Norton's piece on my treatment of Herder is the most civil of the three essays. Indeed, I think relatively little divides us. Brilliant and influential though Herder was, I do not see him as being in the foreground of the history with which I am concerned. In the first and principal reference to him (BA I: 206) I wrote:

> According to the new Romantic and progressive views . . . [t]he racial genius or spirit belonging to the land and its people changed its forms according to the spirit of the age . . . , but a people always retained its immutable essence. The most powerful figure concerned with this aspect of the Romantic movement was Johann Gottfried Herder, who was also important in relation both to Neo-Hellenism and the development of linguistics. Herder himself stayed within the universalist bounds of the Enlightenment, maintaining that all peoples, not merely Germans, should be encouraged to discover and develop their own genii. Nevertheless, the concern with history and local particularity, and the disdain for rationality or "pure reason" apparent in his views and those of other late-18th- and early-19th-century German thinkers including Kant, Fichte, Hegel and the Schlegels, *provided a firm basis for the chauvinism and racism of the following centuries* [emphasis supplied in this volume].

This view of Herder is by no means original. Before beginning his defense of Herder, the intellectual historian Isaiah Berlin wrote of him:

In the course of this propaganda against rationalism, scientific method, and the universal authority of intelligible laws, he is held to have stimulated the growth of particularism, nationalism and literary, religious and political irrationalism, and thereby to have played a major role in transforming human thought and action in the generation that followed.

This account, which is to be found in some of the best known monographs on Herder's thought, is broadly true, but oversimplified.[2]

Basing his attack on the passage from BA I quoted above, Norton argues that I have suggested that Herder's "real motives . . . [were] his opposition to foreign influences, foremost—among them the French—in Germany. What Herder promoted as a program of tolerance and independence really amounted therefore to nothing more than hostility and aggressive nationalism in a clever disguise" (p. 405).

I suggest nothing of the kind. I believe that Herder, like virtually all of his generation of German intellectuals, was frightened of cultural absorption by France and that he was, therefore, *defensively* a cultural nationalist, but I trust that the passage from my book makes it clear that I do not doubt Herder's sincerity in his theoretical promotion of tolerance and cultural independence for all peoples.[3] Furthermore, my statement that Herder's work, and that of some of his contemporaries, "provided a firm basis" for later "chauvinism and racism" does not mean—as Norton claims—that I believe that "racism . . . was the implicit and unavoidable consequence of the kind of historiography that saw Herder as its progenitor" (p. 405). That consequence was contingent and by no means necessary.

Norton writes, "Yet contrary to what we might expect after reading Bernal, Herder has nothing but the highest praise for the Egyptians" (p. 406). Norton's need for periphrasis here reveals that I had, in fact, written nothing on the subject of Herder's attitude toward the Egyptians one way or the other. Viewing Herder as a transitional figure between the Enlightenment, in which the Egyptians were usually included among civilized peoples, and the even more Eurocentric Romantic Age, in which they were excluded from civilization, I could not predict what Herder's attitude toward the Ancient Egyptians would be. In fact, not surprisingly, his position on the issue fluctuated. Indeed, Norton's fellow contributor Palter contradicts Norton's claims that Herder was an Egyptophil by quoting other passages in which the German philosopher was contemptuous of the Egyptians (p. 374)—a clear example of the many contradictions to be found among the contributions to BAR.

Norton, Palter, and Blok all complain that I have relied too heavily on secondary sources. If I had written a monograph they would undoubtedly be right. The writer of a general or synoptic work, however, cannot produce exhaustive studies on all the topics to be studied. I am relatively unconcerned when the charge is simply my failure to consult primary sources, but I take such charges seriously when they show that my failure to use primary sources has led me into error. Norton provides such a case, citing my statement, "Even in the 18th century, Herder *is reported as having said* that Carthage was so flawed by its abominations that it should be compared to a jackal" (BA I: 359; but the italics appear in Norton).

Norton has found the original passage, which shows clearly that, although the term "jackal" is not flattering, Herder's purpose was to condemn Roman, not Carthaginian, barbarity (p. 409). My fault here was to trust my secondary source, the academic journalist Gerhard Herm, who wrote, after referring to Gustave Flaubert's description of Moloch: "It is a grisly description and a reflection of the flawed image the world has had up till now of the Phoenicians and Carthaginians. Johann Gottfried Herder was so struck by this that he compared the Tyrian colony to a jackal, which the Roman she-wolf had to destroy."[4]

Naturally, I knew that Flaubert had written long after Herder's death, but I assumed that Herm was referring to the Classical sources on which Flaubert's work was closely based. Nevertheless, my failure to find Herder's own words indicates considerable sloppiness, but it does not demonstrate dishonesty, for, as I wrote in the footnote: "While I have no reason to doubt it, I have not been able to find the original" (BA I: 499 n. 80).

Norton then suggests that I link the total annihilation of Carthage as a precedent to the "final solution of the Jewish Problem." The whole paragraph of my book, of which Norton cites only a fragment, is concerned with the Prussian identification with Rome after 1870 and the contrary identification of England with Carthage. The paragraph goes on to consider the untrue platitude of the late nineteenth century, that "Carthage, which was destroyed by the Romans, was never rebuilt."

Norton goes on to claim that I was suggesting that "Herder obliquely endorsed the destruction of the entire continent's black inhabitants, and, even worse, Herder is by extension made to seem vaguely responsible for the twentieth century events" (p. 408). His leap from my mistaken claim that Herder thought that Carthage deserved to be destroyed, to Herder's "obliquely endorsing" genocide of the entire African population is both extraordinary and absurd. I agree with the contemporary Swedish writer Sven

Lindquist that the Northern European theoretical desire for, and actual extermination of, "lesser breeds" in Africa, the Americas, and Australia in
the nineteenth century provide far more direct precedents for the Holocaust than—as some German historians have claimed—Stalin's brutal col-
lectivization in Russia and the Ukraine.[5] But all this occurred long after
Herder's death.

I also believe that Isaiah Berlin has not completely overturned earlier
views of Herder's irrationalism and their consequences. Furthermore, I
accept that—in a book to which Norton pays scant attention—Paul Rose
has removed some of the gloss from the received view of Herder's philo-
Semitism.[6] Having conceded all this, I am convinced that it would be ludicrous to suggest that Herder proposed—even obliquely—the genocide of
any living people. While I unreservedly withdraw my mistaken reference to
his attitude toward Carthage and thank Norton for bringing it to my attention, I stand by the general assessment of Herder in BA I as quoted above.

Robert Palter

Unlike Norton, who is concerned with a single issue, Palter attacks on many
fronts. He has clearly expended immense passion and labor in criticizing
my work, and, as a broad-ranging and intelligent scholar, he has found a
number of flaws—some serious, some not. Furthermore, as an intellectual
he has been unable to resist making a number of digressions that, though
not directly concerned with my work, are fascinating in themselves.

Before beginning my response to his article, I should like to set out a
fundamental agreement. He is absolutely right to state that I have "certainly not 'fully investigated' the relevant history of classical historiography" (p. 350). I never claimed to have done so. My defense is that set out
by Huizinger in the epigraph of this chapter, partly, of course, because it
is pleasant to associate oneself with a great scholar, but largely because
Huizinger described my predicament more eloquently than I could.

Similarly, without wishing to give my ideas the status of a scientific paradigm, I believe Thomas Kuhn was right when he argued that to be effective and interesting a new set of ideas should be "sufficiently open ended
to leave all sorts of problems for the redefined group of practitioners to
solve."[7] Naturally, in my case, the incompleteness has not been a deliberate
strategy; it was the inevitable outcome of attempting to paint with a broad
brush on a huge canvas.

Palter correctly and repeatedly condemns me for my arbitrary selection of sources and lack of system. His own article, however, is not a model of rational order. For instance, he describes Newton's views on the Ancient Egyptians in the late seventeenth century *after* considering in some detail those of other writers of the middle and late eighteenth century (pp. 361–363). The reason for both sets of inconsistencies is that it is difficult to order and categorize intellectual history neatly; it is far too subtle and slippery. Furthermore, as Palter rightly emphasizes, in any given period, men and women can have very different and often contradictory thoughts.

As Palter makes so many and varied points, I feel obliged in my reply to classify them, with inevitable crudeness, under four headings: arguments that I do not accept; arguments where, I believe, he is picking a quarrel where none exists; points where he has found small faults; and issues where he has found major flaws in my work.

ARGUMENTS I DO NOT ACCEPT

Palter attacks my claim that there was "a massive ancient and modern tradition which saw Egypt and the Orient as the seats of philosophy." He maintains that this is "a figment of his imagination: we should not expect to find in *any* period of European history a uniform set of attitudes towards Egypt and Greece" (p. 377).

I quite agree that we should expect this, and clearly it is normal for there to be many varied opinions. Nevertheless, it is not by chance that Palter is unable to cite any doubt from Medieval or Renaissance sources that the Greeks had derived their wisdom and philosophy from "Egypt and the Orient."[8] Orthodox Christians maintained that Israel was prior to and therefore superior to Egypt, but the relative lateness of Greek civilization was never seriously in question. Therefore, the eighteenth-century claims that philosophy had originated in Greece were, as I described, "daring" (BA I: 216).[9]

In assessing these competing claims over early modern thought, it is important to consider Sir Isaac Newton. Both Palter and I accept that Newton's ideas on Ancient Egypt are extremely difficult to understand, and we agree that he always saw Greece as indebted to Egypt (p. 363). Where we disagree is on whether Newton's attitude toward Ancient Egypt shifted perceptibly.[10] I see a swing from youthful Egyptophilia to something close to Egyptophobia in old age. I link Newton's increasing hostility toward Egypt to a reaction against Spinoza and the "Radical Enlightenment" promoted by John Toland and others. Against this interpretation, Palter refers to R. S. Westfall, the modern biographer of Newton who has pointed out some of the extreme heretical beliefs held by Newton in his old age.[11] Westfall, however, is unable to explain the purpose of the chronological studies that preoccupied Newton in his later years. Westfall feelingly describes the most important of these, *The Chronology of Antient Kingdoms Amended*, as "a work of colossal tedium" and as a book "with no evident point and no evident form" (see BA I: 191). My interpretation of Newton's changing attitudes does not remove the tedium of his last work but does argue that its purpose was to downdate the Egyptians and establish priority and superiority for Israelite history.

Newton, I maintain, was unfashionable in this view. Palter, however, objects (p. 352) to my claim "that the mainstream of fashionable opinion in England and France [in the eighteenth century] seems to have been . . . unequivocally enthusiastic about Egypt" (BA I: 170). Even so, he later (pp. 361–362) accepts as a plausibly "representative sampling of opinion" a list of thirteen scholars who favored the Egyptians over the Jews. Palter continues: "There does seem to be a growing tendency in Britain during the eighteenth century to focus on the Egyptians versus the Jews." (As mentioned above, on the whole, scholars in both camps did not consider the Greeks a truly ancient people.) With this sentence, Palter contradicts his own claim made *on the same page* that "Bernal's only real evidence of Egyptophilia in the British context is the work of the English historian William Mitford" (p. 361).[12]

Palter criticizes what he sees as my failure to recognize intellectual countercurrents in general, and in particular that there was antiracism as well as racism in the eighteenth century. He objects to my attempts to point out the opposing forces of Egyptophilia and Egyptophobia. Where I write "By 1767 Britons were even beginning to assert Greek superiority over the Egyptians" (BA I: 211); he comments that Bernal "never clearly identifies just who was subscribing to these shifting attitudes toward Ancient Egypt and Ancient Greece" (p. 352). In fact, I could hardly have been more specific. In the next sentence, I write "As another Aberdonian, William Duff, wrote in that year. . . ." So I not only specify an individual but also a school in Eastern Scotland that experienced a particular affinity to the Greeks and a contempt for "decadent" southern societies.[13]

Just as Newton's ideas are essential in any consideration of early modern thought, those of Edward Gibbon are central to the historiography of the ancient world in the later eighteenth century. When considering Gibbon's early interest in the legendary conquests of the Egyptian pharaoh Sesōstris and his later dismissal of such speculation, Palter writes: "As an aging scholar myself, I find quite admirable Gibbon's mature stance of 'rational ignorance'" (p. 360). My position, as expressed in BA II, is that there was a good deal to be said for Gibbon's statement: "I no longer presume to connect the Greek, the Jewish and the Egyptian antiquities which are lost in a distant cloud." However, I add: "This cloud has been at least partially dispelled by linguistic and archaeological advances since the 1770s" (BA II: 273). Although it is clear that Gibbon developed a distaste for the Ancient Egyptians, I have found no later recantation of other passages from his early works: "Unfortunate inhabitants of the forests, these proud Greeks took everything from strangers. The Phoenicians taught them the use of letters; the arts, the laws, all that elevates man above animals, they owed to the Egyptians. These last brought them their religion, and the Greeks in adopting it paid the tribute that ignorance owes to wisdom. . . . The Greeks misconstrued this religion in many regards. They altered it with foreign admixtures, but the basis remained and this Egyptian basis was consequently allegorical."[14] Such sentiments, which ultimately derived from many similar statements in Late Antiquity, were perfectly orthodox in the mid–eighteenth century. Gibbon was equally orthodox in his racism. For instance, he wrote: "It is curious to observe on that first interview [of the Portuguese in West Africa] the superiority of the whites was felt and acknowledged by the blacks."[15] He also made somewhat shamefaced defenses of slavery and was ambivalent about the abolition of the slave trade. In a letter of May 1792 about a parliamentary bill just passed in favor of abolition, he wrote: "If it proceeded only from an impulse of humanity, I cannot be displeased even with an error, since it is very likely that my own vote (had I possessed one) would have been added to the majority. But in this rage against slavery, in the numerous petitions against the slave trade, was there no leaven of the new democratic principles? no ideas of the rights and natural equality of man? It is these I fear."[16] Thus, Gibbon showed a combination of respect for Ancient Egypt, elitism, and racism that appears to have been typical of his age.

Turning to German attitudes, Palter attacks from two somewhat contradictory angles my treatment of the relationship of the racist Göttingen professor Christoph Meiners to "source criticism." First, he writes that I have "perhaps exaggerated" Meiners's role in the formation of the new Göttingen historiography. He points out that Herbert Butterfield did not mention Meiners in his study of the "Scientific Revolution of Historical Study" (p. 382). This is not surprising, because Butterfield had good reason not to mention a scholar who had been used by the Nazis. Josine Blok suggests, in her article, that I focused on Meiners precisely because he had been praised by the Nazis as a pioneer of racism in order to smear Göttingen and source criticism.[17] Palter, however, recognizes that I portrayed Meiners as the central figure in the development of source criticism because I relied heavily on the secondary work of Lucien Braun, who attributed the method to Meiners (p. 383). Nevertheless, although I do describe source criticism as one of "Meiners's innovations," this statement is set in the context of the Göttingen school as a whole (BA I: 217).

Palter also accuses me of inconsistency in having referred "to Heyne as the scholar who promoted the new technique of source criticism" (p. 382). Palter's reading here is uncharacteristically sloppy. What I wrote was: "Heyne developed the seminar from the Socratic method and promoted the new technique of 'source criticism.' "[18] This is a small but significant difference in that I made no claim that it was Heyne himself who had developed source criticism.

At a more fundamental level, Palter questions my treatment of source criticism itself. In fact, the difference between our positions on this is slight. He quotes me as having written that these procedures " 'do seem essential to a historian as opposed to a chronicler: it is inevitable that one should give different weight to different sources.' [Palter then paraphrases my words:] The trouble comes when certain sources are neglected or rejected as being inconsistent with the spirit of the age; in this manner [Palter reverts to direct quotation] 'the historian can impose almost any pattern he chooses' " (BA I: 218; Palter, p. 384).

He continues: "One may agree with Bernal that the introduction of a subjectively defined or intuitively grasped 'spirit of the age' is open to abuse" (p. 384).[19] In other words, Palter and I concur that source criticism can be useful but also that the choice of historical texts to be selected or rejected is seldom, if ever, innocent. Where we differ is on the example he gives of the method's productive use. He states that one should be "suspicious of an 'expanding' tradition of texts in which the later ones claim to know more about a certain event than the earlier ones" (p. 384). I believe that we should treat all historical material with caution, if not skepticism. However, what appears to be elaboration of earlier sources may, in fact, be the result of the "later" writers' having had other texts or oral traditions at their disposal. The idea that the only sources available in Hellenistic or Roman times were those that are still extant today is obviously absurd.[20]

To return to Meiners: He may have been extreme in his views on racial inequality but, as Palter concedes, he was a central and well-known member of the Göttingen community. For instance, in 1787, the chemist and radical Thomas Beddoes wrote to the librarian of the Bodleian Library in Oxford deploring its failure to acquire "the important Continental works" by "Haller, Meiners and Heyne." [21] The brilliant Swiss anatomist Albrecht Haller had dominated Göttingen natural science during the middle of the century but had died ten years earlier, in 1777. Thus, in a period in which Eichhorn, Michaelis, Schlötzer, Gatterer, Spittler, and Blumenbach were all flourishing, the Englishman saw Meiners and Heyne as the two outstanding living Göttingen scholars. Meiners cannot and should not be excluded from any historical assessment of late-eighteenth-century Göttingen (p. 380).

On another important issue, Palter challenges my statement that "The intensity and pervasiveness of Northern European, American and other colonial racism since the 17th century have been . . . much greater than the norm" (BA I: 201). He comments scornfully, "What norm? That of all earlier European history? Of all previously recorded history? How is the degree of racism to be estimated?" (p. 365).

It is interesting that this could appear in a book to which Frank Snowden has contributed. Snowden's life's work has been to show that racism began in the seventeenth century and did not exist in Greco-Roman antiquity. As Snowden puts it: "It has often been noted that anti-black racism developed or increased in intensity after black and slave had become synonymous." [22] Sadly, I am not able to go as far as Snowden in his positive descriptions of "race" relations in Classical Antiquity. I state: "All cultures have some degree of prejudice for, or more often against, people whose appearance is unusual. . . . By the 15th century . . . there is no doubt that [in Northern Europe] clear links were seen between dark skin color and evil and inferiority" (BA I: 201). In this critique, therefore, Palter is unusual—and I am perfectly conventional—in arguing that late-seventeenth- and eighteenth-century racism was new and unprecedentedly intense.

Attempts at systematic "racial" classification and the concept of "Enlightenment" began at the same time, in the last quarter of the seventeenth century.[23] This was not a chance coincidence, because that era witnessed a growing European prosperity and expansion into other continents after the bloody turmoil of the first half of the century. In this epoch of increased confidence, Europeans began to shift the basis of their sense of superiority, and their right to enslave or destroy other populations, from a basis in Christianity to a secular image of Europe as the continent that epitomized the three new concepts of civilization, science, and enlightenment. The sociologist Norbert Elias wrote about these:

> But when one examines what the general function of the concept of civilization really is, and what common quality causes all these various human attitudes and activities to be described as civilized, one starts with a very simple discovery: this concept expresses the self-consciousness of the West: one can even say: the national consciousness. It sums up everything in which Western society of the last two or three centuries believes itself superior to earlier societies or "more primitive" contemporary ones. By this term, Western Society seeks to describe what constitutes its special character and what it is proud of: the level of its technology, the nature of its manners, the development of its scientific knowledge, or view of the world.[24]

Precisely in these decades European slavery became totally and indelibly linked to color, and the color "white" began to be attributed to the supposedly free and civilized inhabitants of "Europe," as it was variously defined. These pervasive ideas may go by many names, but I believe "racism" is perfectly appropriate. Harold Pagliaro, the editor of the volume on racism issued by the American Society for Eighteenth-Century Studies, wrote, "The essays on racism in the present volume indicate clearly that in the eighteenth century groups of whites—and individual whites as well—whenever they were faced with the social necessity of regarding persons of color en masse, found ways of denying them equality of whites and found theoretical support for such denial."[25]

In the discussion on "Racism in the Eighteenth Century," which followed in this volume, Winthrop Jordan argued against employing the word "racism," preferring "racial attitudes" or "ethnocentrism," though he admitted that the latter "is extremely likely to lead to racism." Richard Popkin disagreed, and stated that if by "racism" one meant a "systematic body of justification" for such beliefs, then it was present in the eighteenth century. While accepting this, Herbert Marcuse added the important dimension of power in the same discussion, when he stated, "I would say that racism is any 'theory' which assumes that a race other than the *dominant* white race is, by this very fact, naturally inferior. . . . The group discriminated against cannot be equal in power to the dominant white group."[26] At this stage, it should also be emphasized that Robert Palter is exceptional when he implies (p. 367) that racism and antiracism were forces of equal magnitude in the eighteenth century. The majority of scholars today side with Popkin when he writes, "Historians of philosophy are just beginning to become aware that many of the philosophical heroes of the Enlightenment, such as Locke, Berkeley, Hume, Voltaire, Franklin, Jefferson and Kant, expressed views that sound shockingly racist today."[27]

Palter has tried elsewhere to mitigate the racism of one of the worst of these, David Hume, who claimed in a notorious footnote:

> I am apt to suspect the negroes and in general all other species of men (for there are four or five different kinds) to be naturally inferior to the whites. There never was a civilised nation of any other complexion than white, nor even any individual eminent either in action or speculation. No ingenious manufactures amongst them, no arts, no sciences. On the other hand, the most rude and barbarous of the whites, such as the ancient Germans and present Tartars, have still something eminent about them, in their valour, form of government or some other particular. Such a uniform and constant difference could not happen in so many countries and ages if nature had not made an original distinction between these breeds of men.[28]

Palter attempts to play this statement down by saying that Hume was opposed to slavery and that the impact of the footnote was not as great as modern scholars have supposed.[29] I shall return later to the frequent combination of racist and abolitionist views. Regarding Hume's footnote, however, Palter mistakes quantity with quality. It is true, as he says, that James Beattie and others opposed Hume's assertion, that there is no doubt that Hume's towering intellectual authority allowed that footnote to remain the great justification of racism and slavery for the next century.[30] In the first decade of the nineteenth century, the courageous opponent of both racism and slavery, the Abbé Grégoire, singled out Hume and Jefferson as his chief antagonists. North American slaveholders continued to rely on the two until emancipation, if not beyond.[31]

The evidence is still more damning against the epitome of "pure" philosophy, Immanuel Kant, the last on Popkin's list cited above. Kant, who taught many more courses on "anthropology" than he did on logic, metaphysics, or moral philosophy, maintained that only Europeans were reflective and that unreflective non-Europeans were not "properly" human.[32]

However, for Kant, these "inferior" races differed from one another. Whereas he saw the Native Americans as uneducable, he believed that Negroes could be trained, "though only as servants."[33] For Kant, training involved beating, and he advised the use of "a split bamboo cane instead of a whip," so that the "negro will suffer a great deal of pain [because of the 'negro's' thick skin, he would not be racked with sufficient agonies through a whip] but without dying."[34] When Popkin writes that these thinkers were "shockingly racist," he means "*shockingly* racist."

Having studied several different societies and having read a number of studies of the problem, I do indeed believe that modern European racism is extreme. However, as my book is not a study of racism in general, I do not go into detail on this issue. If Palter seriously doubts this proposition, I can only ask him to read St. Clair Drake's excellent *Black Folk Here and There* and reread Jordan's *White over Black*.[35]

Palter also suggests that I am guilty of economic determinism when I state that after 1650, racism was "intensified" by "the increased colonization of North America, with its twin policies of extermination of the Native Americans and enslavement of Africans," which "presented moral problems" that could be eased only by "strong racism." Palter continues: "Here he [Bernal] takes a stand—apparently without realizing it—on a hotly debated issue in the historiography of American slavery, namely, whether slavery led to racism or racism to slavery" (p. 366).

Palter maintains that I simplemindedly believe that slavery led to racism. This is not so. My use of the word "intensified" was deliberate, and by definition, "intensification" cannot begin ex nihilo. If Palter had read this section of my work with any care—or rather, without wanting to pick a fight—he would have seen that I am fully aware of the chicken-and-egg nature of the issue and of Jordan's work. Furthermore, I have never stated—or believed for a moment—the absurd contention that all slavery was based on "racial" differences. I merely maintain that this was the case by the late seventeenth century in Northern Europe and its colonies. Thus, Palter's choosing, among all the many societies in which slavery without "racist ideology" has been practiced, the "widespread and large scale slavery *within Africa*" (p. 366; his italics) is completely gratuitous.

Having responded to a number of Palter's critiques of my writings that I do not accept, I now turn to some where I am unable to see a significant disagreement between us.

ARGUMENTS WHERE NO QUARREL EXISTS

Palter takes issue with my description of the historian William Mitford as "a consistent conservative [who] rejected the idea of progress" (BA I: 187). According to him, I should have followed Arnaldo Momigliano, who, "more forthrightly," refers to Mitford as "a determined supporter of the rights of kings . . . respectfully hated by Byron and the young Macauley" (p. 361). The negligible distance between my position on Mitford and that of Momigliano is narrowed still further by my description of the ferocious criticism of Mitford published by Macauley in 1824 in *Knight's Quarterly*, about which I wrote: "Mitford's conservative scorn for Greek democracy made his work 'A five volume tract' for the Tory Party" (BA I: 323–324).

Palter also objects to my quotation from Montesquieu: "The Egyptians were the best philosophers in the world." He points out that the context makes it clear that this statement was meant ironically (p. 353). I made it equally clear, however, that I view Montesquieu's statement as anomalous because I see him as having been essentially Eurocentric (BA I: 170). The brief passage is interesting not because it expressed Montesquieu's own opinions but because it represented the conventional wisdom of the time.

Palter and I agree that Christian Gottlob Heyne was the "central figure" in late-eighteenth-century Göttingen. Palter, however, suggests that I claim Heyne was a racist, and he takes pains to show how Heyne "strenuously rejected," though in a "surreptitious" way, the undoubtedly racist ideas of his colleague Christoph Meiners (p. 380). Palter misrepresents my argument here. My charge is less severe. I quote Frank Manuel's estimate of Heyne: "His scholarship was impeccable, his editing of texts in the great tradition, but for all the appurtenances of learning, the spirit that animated him and generations of German *Gelehrte* was the same Romantic Hellenism which possessed his literary compatriots in the 18th century." This does not constitute a charge against Heyne of racism, merely one of deep concern with ethnicity and race. What is more, I continue: "Heyne was fascinated by overseas travel and by exotic peoples. Given the importance in German academic life, of marrying the professor's daughter, the fact that Blumenbach was his brother-in-law was less significant than the fact that both of Heyne's sons-in-law were concerned with extra-European travel" (BA I: 222). Heyne showed none of the European provincialism so common in the nineteenth century, and charges of Eurocentrism are considerably mitigated. I cannot see where Palter and I differ on this central figure.

POINTS WHERE PALTER HAS FOUND MINOR FAULTS

Having discussed at length some of Palter's mistaken criticisms and non-disputes, I shall now turn to a number of his valuable, though minor, corrections to some of my assertions. Palter points out that I was wrong to state that one of the founders of the University of Göttingen, Kristophe August Heumann, was fifty years ahead of his time *both* in his belief that Greeks were the first to practice philosophy *and* in his theoretical promotion of German as a philosophical language. The first claim, which is the one important to my case, stands, but Palter rightly points out that Heumann's contemporary Christian Wolff also advocated the use of German to write philosophy, while in practice, both men continued to publish their own works in Latin (p. 377).

I was also wrong to claim that Charles François Dupuis had demonstrated "a series of astounding correspondences or coincidences between . . . the twelve labors of Herakles . . . and the twelve houses of the Zodiac" (BA I: 183). Palter quite rightly points out that only three do coincide (p. 357).

Palter criticizes me for having characterized Benjamin Franklin as a "racist." He observes that in the 1770s Franklin wrote that Negroes "were not deficient in natural understanding." [36] My claim, which is not unusual, was based on Franklin's much more famous *Observations Concerning the Increase of Mankind* published in 1751, where he noted that "the Number of White People in the World is proportionably very small." According to him, even most Europeans, including the Germans, were "of what we call a swarthy complexion." He wanted what would become the United States to belong to the "White People": "Why import the Sons of Africa, by Planting them in America, where we have so fair an opportunity, by excluding all Blacks and Tawneys, of increasing the lovely White and Red." [37]

Although Franklin was opposed to slavery, at least by the 1770s, the question remains whether he had reversed the views he expressed twenty years earlier. Winthrop Jordan has noted that by the 1770s "outright denials of Negro mental inferiority had become common." [38] Racism, however, was not dead among Franklin's enlightened contemporaries. Take, for example, the entry "Negro" in the third edition of the *Encyclopedia Britannica* (1794), which was hardly altered for the following four editions. It begins with a description of the most "notorious vices" of this "unhappy race . . . [known for its] idleness, treachery, revenge, cruelty, impudence, stealing, lying, profanity, debauchery, nastiness and intemperance." It continues in this vein for many hundred words until, after mentioning the beauty of some West African cloths and the skill of some slave watchmakers in the West Indies, it concludes piously: "God, who made the world, hath made of one blood all nations of men and animated them with minds equally rational."

Thus, although the entry contains both racism and antiracism, the balance is clearly on the side of the former. Nevertheless, although I still hold to the present consensus that Benjamin Franklin was one of those who expressed views that sound "shockingly racist today," describing him simply as a "racist" was an oversimplification.[39]

Palter begins his article (p. 350) with an attack on what I describe in a footnote as "a nice illustration of the Aryan Model at work." The richly furnished tomb of the last pagan Frankish king, Childeric, was discovered in 1653 and was described and illustrated in great detail and care in the seventeenth and eighteenth centuries. In the nineteenth century, many of the goods were lost. The problem arises because one of the early descriptions of the grave goods includes and illustrates a number of Egyptian scarabs, but nineteenth- and twentieth-century historians, including the modern scholar Françoise Dumas, have denied their presence in the tomb, claiming that the very distinguished earlier scholars Jean Jacques Chiflet and Bernard de Montfaucon had made a crude error by mistakenly adding them. Given the accuracy of the early reports, where they can be checked, I believe that it is the denial rather than the alleged "howler" that requires special explanation.[40]

As I could find no scholarly reason for the denial, I turned to the sociology of knowledge, arguing that the Frankish kings had been dear to the heart of the French right and particularly to those believing in the collaboration of France and Germany during the Second World War. The symbol of the Vichy regime was the *francisque*, the double-headed Frankish axe, a splendid example of which was found in Childeric's tomb (BA I p. 466 n. 88).

Palter is indignant that I present no evidence at all that Dumas was influenced by "Aryan prejudice in general, or by the French right wing in particular; and I would add, drag in the Vichy regime" (p. 351). I completely concede the particular point, which, though minor at a scholarly level, is important at a personal one, and I unreservedly apologize to Françoise

Dumas for the implication of the passage. I remain convinced, however, that her and her immediate predecessors' refusal to accept the clear reports of Egyptian scarabs in the tomb—when we know that Egyptian religion was influential in Central Europe during the fourth and fifth centuries C.E. and that Egyptian objects continued to be valued for their magical properties in early Christian France—can be most plausibly explained as a result of a general belief that north is north and south is south and never the twain shall meet.

Another person to whom I owe an apology, in this case posthumous, is the late-eighteenth- and early-nineteenth-century scholar Johann Friedrich Blumenbach. The case of Blumenbach is interesting and complex, and consequently I shall spend some time discussing it. I should begin by noting that I owe my apology to this scholar for reasons rather different from those demanded by Palter.

As Palter concedes, I do distinguish between Blumenbach's "scientific" classification of races and the crudely racialist ideas of Christoph Meiners (p. 378). Palter rightly criticizes me for failing to note Blumenbach's later short work on the biographies of "Ethiopians" who had succeeded in European or North American society.

I agree that Blumenbach was always more cautious than many of his contemporaries, yet his racism in the 1770s, when he published the first edition of his *De Generis Humani Varietate Nativa*, cannot be doubted. In an appendix to his chapter, Palter agrees that Blumenbach believed that the Caucasian "race" was the earliest, was the norm by which all others should be measured, and was the most beautiful. Palter denies, however, that this norm was ever moral or intellectual (pp. 392–394). As I pointed out, Blumenbach's scheme was an application to humans of the general plan set out, in the middle of the century, for other species by the naturalist Georges Louis Leclerc Buffon (BA I: 219). The concept of *degeneration* in other continents and climates was essential to both intellectual structures and, as Palter also concedes, Blumenbach saw the "Mongolians" and "Ethiopians" as having "degenerated farthest from the human norm" (p. 394). An English translation of his earlier editions described the latter: "Ethiopian variety: color black, hair black and curly, head narrow, compressed at the sides; forehead knotty, uneven, molar bones protruding outwards; eyes very prominent; nose thick, mixed up as it were with the wide jaws; alveolar edge narrow, elongated in front; upper primaries obliquely prominent; lips very puffy;

chin retreating. Many are bandy-legged. To this variety belong all the Africans except those of the north."[41] Elsewhere, Blumenbach combined a belief in the innate superiority of Europeans over Africans, with a visceral hatred of slavery: "Nearly all the facts demonstrate a greater affinity of the Negro than of the European to brute creation. But so slightly inferior to the Caucasians and so immensely superior to the intelligent animals, the poor negro might justly class those of us, who *philosophically* view him as merely a poor monkey, or who desire to traffic in his blood, not only below himself, but below the apes in intellect, and tigers in feeling and propensity."[42]

Blumenbach's early racism is most clearly demonstrated by the violence of his turn away from it. Before 1786 he had accepted the ideas of the Dutch traveler and anatomist Pieter Camper, who maintained that high foreheads indicated better aesthetic appearance and, *pace* Palter, greater intelligence.[43] Africans were reputed to have the smallest "Camper's facial angle" and were therefore the lowest human variety.[44] In 1786 or 1787 Blumenbach saw the famous painting of four African heads by Van Dyck.[45] In fact, the four portraits were of the same man from different angles. Blumenbach did not know this, but he realized immediately that two of the heads had remarkably wide "Camper's facial angle[s]." Camper himself had explained the problem away by claiming that the painter had simply asked Europeans to blacken their faces. Blumenbach was puzzled but still accepted Camper's theory.

In 1787, however, when Blumenbach was traveling in Switzerland, he stopped at Yverdon on Lake Neuchâtel. As he himself described the scene, he was approaching a residence when he saw from behind a female form that struck him by its "harmonious and beautiful shape." When she turned around, he was amazed to see "the features of an African lady . . . in complete accord to her bodily figure."[46] She reminded him at once of the Van Dyck painting. He soon realized that the lady was not only beautiful but witty and sensible. As a doctor, Blumenbach was impressed that she was "extremely well informed and expert in the obstetric art" and was the best-known midwife in that part of Switzerland.[47] It is quite clear that he was very attracted to the lovely "Négresse von Yverdon."

In this connection, a sentence quoted by Palter should be noted. In 1789 the German traveler and Jacobin Georg Forster wrote to his father-in-law Heyne: "The black wet nurse truly represents a victory over prejudice in dear enlightened Göttingen." As Palter points out, both the word *amme* ("wet nurse") used by Forster and the context make it clear that this was not a hospital nurse but a wet nurse brought in for one of Heyne's granddaughters.[48] One cannot help wondering whether Forster was not also obliquely referring to Blumenbach's flirtation with the midwife or *hebamme* of Yverdon.

In any event, 1787 marked a striking reversal of Blumenbach's attitude toward Africans, and in this new frame of mind he compiled the biographies that Palter quite rightly condemns me for not mentioning. It should be noted that, despite the clear liberal humanism of the project, Blumenbach took it for granted that the only measure of civilization was that of Europe.

The question remains which Blumenbach was the more influential. The first two editions of his great work, *De Generis Humani Variatet Nativa*, appeared in 1775 and 1781, before his "conversion." His great collection of human skulls first appeared after the change in 1790, as did the third edition of *De Generis*, which was published in 1795. Blumenbach also continued to teach for many years into the nineteenth century.

Some of his later students continued to receive the earlier message. Samuel Taylor Coleridge, for instance, studied at Göttingen in 1799, attended Blumenbach's lectures, became one of the professor's favorites, and had many talks with him. Blumenbach even gave a farewell party for the young Englishman.[49] Coleridge wrote a number of notes and speculations on the subject of "race." He clearly understood Blumenbach's categorical distinction between "race" and "species" and did not accept polygenesis. He used Blumenbach's scale of degeneration, with Caucasians at the top and Chinese and Negroes at the bottom.[50] He also followed Blumenbach's argument that races shade into one another. Nevertheless, he took off from this to argue that "there will gradually arise two classes of men in Families—the one distinguished by comparative approximation to the ideal of his being, and in more perfect isolation from and antithesis to Circumstantial Nature—the other by a degeneracy from the exponents of his proper humanity & comparative assimilation to & dependence on Circumstantial Nature."[51] This construct is part of Coleridge's scheme of the development of the notion of what he called "A(n) Historic Race." It was axiomatic in early-nineteenth-century Europe that only Europeans possessed true *history*. Elsewhere Coleridge wrote, "We may unhesitatingly assert—the Human species consists of an Historic Race—and other Races."[52] This master race would dominate all humanity, improve the others, and leave them in their own distinctive inferior orbits.[53]

So, despite Blumenbach's own change of attitude, even students who attended his later classes were able to use their interpretation of his ideas to buttress their own Romantic racism. In general, Blumenbach's later writings received relatively little attention, and throughout the nineteenth century he was seen simply as the first "scientific" classifier of races. For the majority in Europe and North America who were racists, that meant the inequality of races.[54]

In closing this section on Palter's less than major but still significant critiques, I turn again to Georg Forster, the late-eighteenth-century German traveler, Jacobin, and son-in-law of Heyne. In BA I (p. 222) I claimed that Heyne and Forster quarreled for two reasons: first, because Forster had supported the French Revolution, and second, because Forster had left his wife, Heyne's daughter, for her best friend, Caroline Böhmer. Palter objects to both of these explanations. He claims that Heyne's objection was not to the Revolution itself but to Forster's attempt to have the territory of Mainz incorporated into France. Second, he doubts that Caroline was the cause of the breakup of the marriage—although in a footnote, he admits that there was a tradition to this effect (p. 401 n. 67). If Palter is correct on the second score, this would remove the personal aspect of the quarrel and put greater emphasis on the political issues. Nevertheless, as Momigliano put it, "Thus Heyne—when he was deprecating 'those . . . French fanatics made furious by political strife,' who were thinking of grabbing land not belonging to them—was in fact addressing a member of his own family."[55]

Forster's proposal to cede a German city to France must certainly have enraged Heyne and other patriotic Germans. On the other hand, Heyne never showed any disloyalty to his Hanoverian sovereign, and, despite his later collaboration with Napoleonic armies to protect his city and university, there is no doubt that he detested the French Revolution.

All in all, Palter's specific criticisms here are minor if not niggling and give me no reason to alter the general conclusions of my discussion of Göttingen. I describe the university as having "desire for reform rather than revolution . . . profound concerns with ethnicity and race, and . . . exhaustive scholarship. Furthermore . . . [its scholars] shared the reaction to the French Revolution and its challenge to traditional order and religion and the concern with the differences and inequalities between different races. They also shared the passionate Romanticism and Neo-Hellenism of progressive German circles of the late 18th century" (BA I: 223).

ISSUES WITH MAJOR FLAWS

In concluding my discussion of Robert Palter's chapter on historiography, I should like to gratefully acknowledge those points on which he has made substantial and justified criticisms of my work. Even here, however, I think that his insights have helped me correct and formulate my arguments more clearly rather than damaged my general case.

On a general level, he is justified in criticizing my failure to consider the hostility toward Egypt expressed by Diderot and Voltaire. However, with typical scrupulousness, Palter qualifies the latter's attitude by quoting Voltaire's saying: "Nothing is truer than the old Latin proverb: 'The Egyptians learnt from the Babylonians, and the Greeks from the Egyptians'" (p. 354).[56] Palter is quite justified in requiring me to have discussed the attitudes of such centrally important figures. He might also have mentioned my omission of Adam Smith's dislike of the Egyptians, although I had touched on this elsewhere.[57]

In his second appendix, Palter argues convincingly that I have exaggerated my claims that Egyptology went into a recession between Champollion's death in 1831 and the late 1850s. He refers specifically to the work of Karl Richard Lepsius. Lepsius studied hieroglyphs in the 1830s, although, as Palter agrees, not from living professors (who could not read them) but from the posthumously published writings of Champollion. In any event, patronized by Christian Bunsen and the Prussian government, Lepsius carried out major expeditions to Egypt and Ethiopia in the 1840s, which produced important scholarly results. In fact, I do mention Lepsius in connection with Bunsen, whom I describe as having "learnt hieroglyphics and championed Egyptology during the '30s and '40s . . . keeping the discipline alive during its doldrums" (BA I: 254). Having said all this, Palter is right to condemn me for not having paid sufficient attention to Lepsius's scholarly achievements.

The issue remains, however, whether this neglect invalidates my two arguments: that there was a recession of scholarly interest in Ancient Egypt in the decades after 1831, and that the founders of the Aryan model did not rely on the decipherment of hieroglyphics and the reading of Egyptian texts to dismiss the traditions of Greek cultural dependence on Egypt. On the first question, I stressed (BA I: 267) that from the 1820s there was "intense" popular interest in Ancient Egypt following the Napoleonic Expedition and the publications resulting from it. I argued and still maintain, however, that a critical change was taking place: where Ancient Egypt had previously been regarded as the cultural ancestor of Europe, it now became a fascinating exotic civilization (BA I: 257).

Despite Lepsius's brilliant work and Bunsen's pedestrian writings, I still believe that the twenty-five years after Champollion's death can accurately be described as a "recession" in Egyptology. In the 1820s, Barthold Niebuhr and the Humboldt brothers had been fascinated by Champollion's work, but the German scholars who dominated ancient history in the 1830s and 1840s treated Bunsen's work on Ancient Egypt with, as his widow put it, "resolute mistrust and indifference" (BA I: 254). Bunsen was better connected politically than he was with academic circles. This explains the apparent contradiction between the lavish funding he was able to gain from the Prussian government for Lepsius's expeditions and the fact that no new chairs in the subject were created until the 1850s. Furthermore, Egyptian texts were not considered reliable by ancient historians until late in that decade.

Palter, following Erik Iversen, emphasizes one reason for the belated acceptance of Champollion's system: that it was only in the 1840s that Lepsius demonstrated that there were not merely monoconsonantal but bi- and triconsonantal signs in hieroglyphics and that earlier forms of Egyptian differed substantially from Coptic (p. 390).[58] Thus, paradoxically, Palter's modification of my first case, that there was a "recession" of interest in Egyptology between 1831 and 1855, strengthens my second and more important claim that the founders of the Aryan model did not rely on the decipherment of hieroglyphics and the reading of Egyptian texts to dismiss the traditions of Greek cultural dependence on Egypt.

CONCLUSION OF DISCUSSION OF PALTER

Palter's overall criticism of my work is that I oversimplify. There are two main issues on which he thinks this is important: racism, and the relationship between Ancient Egypt and Ancient Greece. On the first he writes, "*If racist beliefs and practices were centrally important in eighteenth-century British and American society, so was opposition to such beliefs and practices*" (p. 367; his italics). He is certainly right that my work would have been enriched if I had included more on antiracism. As I set out at the beginning of this chapter, I have never suggested that there were no European antiracists. However, there is every reason to accept the modern scholarly consensus that racism was the dominant trend of both the eighteenth and the nineteenth centuries.[59]

It would also have been interesting to discuss the abolition of slavery and, in particular, the abolitionists' creation and preservation of the Ancient model in its extreme African form at least until the 1850s.[60] For all its undoubted humanitarianism, however, abolitionism was not necessarily antiracist.[61] Palter himself points out that Hume, whose racism he cannot deny, was also opposed to slavery (p. 367).[62] Many American abolitionists advocated emancipation in order to keep blacks out of their state or to send them "back" to Africa.[63] Furthermore, many of the Romantics, who sympathized passionately with the sufferings of the black slaves, still perceived them as fundamentally "other." [64] Palter does not seriously confront the literature showing that, despite undoubted exceptions, racism and the concept of Europe as the one civilized continent, inhabited by whites, was central to the whole cultural project of the Enlightenment.[65] In the eighteenth century, racism was much more influential than antiracism and, tied in with ethnicity, its influence increased still further during the nineteenth.

Though very important, racism is not one of the two central themes of my work, which are the relationships of Ancient Egypt and Ancient Canaan (Phoenicia) to Ancient Greece and the historiographical interpretations of these relationships, which, naturally, since the end of the seventeenth century have involved racism. Thus, I discuss racism in this period without giving details of the lesser strand of antiracism. When considering the specific relationships and interpretations of them, I have attempted to provide both sides of the argument, as for instance in the chapters entitled "The Triumph of Egypt in the 17th and 18th Centuries," "Hostilities to Egypt in the 18th Century," "The Rise and Fall of the Phoenicians in the 19th Century," and "The Final Solution of the Phoenician Problem."

In 1989, the historian of Classics Frank Turner objected to my "larger ideological sweeps," preferring "a more particularist approach which seeks to understand the twists and turns of the lace before asserting the character of the larger pattern." [66] No doubt, Palter agrees with this quotation, though he would not subscribe to the mildness with which Turner expressed his views. Interestingly, Palter's insistence on the complexity and ambiguity of the evidence leads him into a position close to that of some postmodernists. Both he and they insist on a full representation of the intricacies of any situation in all their shifting chaos. Inevitably, such a position leads to intellectual and political paralysis. Where most postmodernists tend to regret this outcome, Palter, as a conservative, is very happy to use "full representation" as a tool to preserve the academic status quo. I fundamentally disagree with both groups because the only truly accurate representation of reality is the one-to-one map of reality itself. Thus, despite the inevitable distortion it entails, I am convinced that some degree of simplification and the establishment of models is necessary both for coherent thought and for effective political action.

Specifically, I do not accept that contradictory forces are necessarily countervailing. I am convinced that, with very few exceptions, at any given time or place hierarchies of power or influence exist and that certain ideas or ideologies predominate over others. The imbalance of racism over anti-racism in the entry "Negro" in the third edition of the *Encyclopedia Britannica* was mentioned above. For another instance, William Gladstone, a politician of central importance in mid- and late-nineteenth-century British life, made passionate and articulate speeches against British expansion abroad throughout most of his career. Nevertheless, most of the British Empire was acquired in the sixty years from the 1830s to the 1890s. Any serious historian should report significant countertrends, as I have tried to do, but at the same time he or she should focus on the dominant trend. Indeed, the historical enterprise cannot be reduced to a mere restatement of all the known "facts." "Facts" must be selected, assembled, and ordered within some sort of coherent framework.

In the case of racism, despite interesting eddies, I do not know of a single historian who doubts that between 1670 and 1920 the general tide of European thought and feeling was increasingly racist.[67] It is also generally accepted that although there were important anomalies before the early nineteenth century, European scholars saw Egypt and the Orient as the source of Western wisdom and philosophy and that after that period, they insisted on a categorical break with Greece, which now became seen as the cradle of true civilization. Despite the mass of detail and contradictory data, long-term trends and significant disjunctures can and should be detected. Without neglecting the trees, one should not lose sight of the forest.

I am convinced that there is room for both the small-scale and the broader approaches as set out by Professor Turner. Turner himself stated that both could have the same result when he wrote: "In many respects Professor Bernal and I differ relatively little in our conclusions."[68] I would go further and say that the two approaches are necessary. Large-scale historical schemes painted with a broad brush are needed to stimulate cautious specialists into coherent thought, but, without building on the latter and seriously considering their criticisms, generalists can all too easily take off into theoretical thin air.

Josine Blok

Josine Blok's critical essay appeared in the *Journal of the History of Ideas* after the publication of *Black Athena Revisited.*[69] I think her work is sufficiently important for me to respond to it here. Blok has pointed out several serious gaps and misinterpretations in my treatment of the early-nineteenth-century classicist and ancient historian Karl Otfried Müller. Nevertheless, I am convinced that her criticisms do not affect my overall assessment of his work and its significance. Thus, where Blok believes that my errors destroy my scholarly credentials, I see her criticisms as helpfully providing my case with rich texture.

When I first heard Blok's paper at a seminar on my work held in Leiden in June 1996, I experienced a powerful mixture of emotions: intense alarm combined with equally intense interest. The alarm came from the fact that unlike previous critics, she had found some serious flaws in my study of historiography. The interest came from the additional depth and complexity she brought to a topic that I had treated very superficially.

My fundamental disagreement with her paper is with the beginning of its title, "Proof and Persuasion in *Black Athena*: The Case of K. O. Müller," and the words in the last sentence of the conclusion, "decency in proof." I am convinced that "proof" is unattainable not merely in ancient history but also in modern historiography. In neither subject will there ever be a "final word" based on "proof." There is always room for further interpretation; all we can hope for is competitive plausibility or persuasion. Once again, I must insist that I am not a complete relativist who believes that "anything goes." If I were not convinced that there are better and worse approximations of the past, I should never have written *Black Athena*.

K.O. MÜLLER: MY DISAGREEMENTS WITH BLOK

Some of Blok's criticisms of my treatment of Müller seem unwarranted. For a trivial instance, she objects to my citing Ernst Curtius's observation that Müller's thesis on the island of Aegina resembled the local history of Osnabrück written by the Romantic conservative Justus Möser (p. 710). Her grounds for the objection are that Möser's book had been published in 1768, whereas Müller's thesis was not completed until 1817. In a footnote, she concedes that a revised edition of Möser's book appeared in 1780, but even without this, there is no reason to suppose that books and the traditions they represent have a time limit on their effectiveness.

More seriously, Blok claims that I maintain that "the Ancient Model fell because of racism" (p. 715). What I state many times is that in the early nineteenth century, racism was only one of many factors behind the shift from the Ancient to the Aryan model. I maintain that the Christian reaction to Egyptophil Freemasonry, attempts to find a middle way between revolution and reaction, Romanticism, and the paradigm of progress and positivism were all influential in this transformation (BA I: 281–336).

Although I see racism and the notion of progress as growing intellectual trends in the eighteenth and nineteenth centuries, I do not, as Blok supposes (pp. 722–733), see the two as indissolubly linked. As I stated above, I completely accept the conventional view that Blumenbach's classification of human races was based on Buffon's scheme for a natural history of "degeneration" (BA I: 219).

At a more fundamental level, Blok exaggerates the extent to which I separate the intricately intertwined "internalist" and "externalist" forces on scientific or scholarly developments. She also completely misunderstands me to say that the "internalist" forces are good and externalist ones bad. As I try to make clear, "externalist" forces are neutral in themselves and can be either good or bad according to our contemporary standards. They are, however, inevitable because science and scholarship are the products of scientists and scholars who live in societies. Thus, science and scholarship are socially embedded, though scientists and scholars—sometimes helped by internalist forces—can partially transcend their environments.

SIGNIFICANT ERRORS

Blok calls attention to factual errors in my treatment of K. O. Müller. What is more, as she rightly points out, these errors are particularly disturbing because I portray Müller as having played a central role in the destruction of the Ancient model. Most of my mistakes come from my failure to read Müller's correspondence, which has been published. Blok has demonstrated from this that although I had insisted on his hostility to Ancient Egypt *and had found no trace of his having been interested in it,* it was clear that as a young man Müller had been enthusiastic about Egyptology and Champollion's decipherment. Even more important, where I had claimed that Müller was anti-Semitic, a close reading of his correspondence and a study of the treatment of its publication in the twentieth century reveals convincingly that he was no more anti-Semitic than his contemporaries.

Blok attributes my failure to refer to the correspondence to my "political" desire to condemn the Aryan model as deriving from racism and anti-Semitism.[70] Here, as elsewhere, I believe she overestimates my villainy and underestimates my incompetence. Looking back at the reasons for my failure to consult the correspondence and other, less well-known writings, I find two factors involved, neither of them creditable to me. First, for a long time I focused my attention on Barthold Niebuhr because I was convinced that he had led the attack on the Ancient model. He was the leading ancient historian in the critical decade from 1820 to 1830, and he was a racist and a Romantic positivist. Nevertheless, when, at a late stage in my research, I read the lectures that Niebuhr gave toward the end of his life, I found that he had explicitly defended the Ancient model against "Wolf's" refusal to admit Greek relations with, and early dependence on, "the Eastern Nations" (BA I: 306).

The second reason for my failure to consult his letters was that, while the correspondence of Niebuhr and Bunsen has been translated into English, Müller's has not. As I read German with much more difficulty than English, laziness at a stage when I was hoping to complete my work contributed to my lapse. I must finally appeal to Huizinger's justification of the necessity of shortcuts for anyone working on a broad synthetic study.

Why did I assume that Müller was uninterested in or hostile to Egypt? In the published works I read he never referred to Champollion's decipherment and he condemned the Egyptians as "xenophobic and bigoted" (BA I: 312).[71] In fact, Blok condemns me for failing to unearth further evidence of his contempt for the Egyptians in a lecture "On the Alleged Egyptian Origins of Greek Art" (p. 718).[72] As she points out, Müller saw Egyptian art as inferior to Greek art, not as Winkelmann did, because Egypt was lower on an evolutionary scale, but for a Herderian reason that it was the product of a qualitatively different and, according to Müller, inferior people.

As I tried to show, Müller's enthusiasm for the Greeks and disdain for the Egyptians was a product of the Zeitgeist after 1815. The systematic nature of his passionate attack on the traditions of colonization of Greece, however, led him further to challenge, though with slightly more caution, the legends of Phoenician colonization. In this, he was ahead of his time. That is why he was praised as a pioneer by the notoriously anti-Semitic Julius Beloch at the end of the nineteenth century and by Rhys Carpenter, who worked during the apogee of anti-Semitism in the 1920s and 1930s.[73] The support of these later scholars, and his pioneering attack on the notion of Phoenician colonization, together with my misunderstanding of the complex passage she quotes (p. 712), led me to portray him as anti-Semitic. I apologize to his memory on this. Nevertheless, whatever his own feelings on the issue, Müller's work was seen by some contemporaries as rejecting the possibility of Jewish influences on Greece. A friend congratulated Müller for his defense of Greek autochthony in *Orchomenos* and his writing against influences by "Jewish, Phoenician, Egyptian, Indian and God knows what other bases."[74]

Blok criticizes me for having underrated Müller's breadth of scholarship and in particular for having omitted mention of his history of Antioch, which required some knowledge of Arabic. I plead guilty to the particular charge but not to the general one. In *Black Athena I*, I wrote: "Müller's scholarly range was prodigious. He was able to round out philology in the approved new manner, and as well as producing a major work on the Etruscans he wrote voluminously on ancient art and archaeology" (p. 309).

Blok also accuses me of having exaggerated Müller's Romanticism. All in all, the warmth with which the secondary sources praise Müller as a Romantic fits very well with his own published works. He insisted that Greek culture was autochthonous, and his most famous work, *The Dorians*, was described by historian of Classics Rudolf Pfeiffer as "more an impressive hymn on the excellence of everything Doric than a narration of history." Moses Finley was even more damning. He described *The Dorians* as "That perniciously influential 1,000 page fantasia."[75]

Blok's attack on this aspect of my interpretation is puzzling, as she herself attacks those who want to link Müller too closely to rationalism and the Enlightenment. She stresses Müller's Protestant Pietist background and his surprising convergences with the views of the Romantic superidealist Friedrich Kreutzer. This was despite Müller's fundamental objections to Kreutzer's beliefs in Oriental influences.[76]

Although Blok has revealed the sloppiness of my scholarship, I do not believe that the revelation affects my assessment of Müller's role in the destruction of the Ancient model. He not only vehemently attacked the legends of the colonization of Greece from the southeast but also fiercely rejected Ancient traditions and descriptions of early cultic and cultural con-

.tact between the Aegean and the rest of the Eastern Mediterranean. This denial was set in a Romantic framework in which ethnicity and the virtues and vigor of the Dorians coming from the north played an important part. Müller also used the Kantian language of Wissenschaft or "science" to dismiss all earlier scholarship on Greek origins and required "proof" of anyone who challenged his isolationism.[77]

While Blok is able to show that Müller's work was criticized during his lifetime, it was also highly regarded and very influential in Germany and throughout Europe.[78] It is true that Niebuhr mentioned only Wolf in his defense of the Ancient model, but Wolf's major work, *Prolegomena ad Homerum*, had appeared in 1795 and he had died in 1824, five years before Niebuhr's lectures. It would therefore seem plausible to suppose that Niebuhr was also considering Wolf's follower Müller.[79] Similarly, I do not see who, apart from Wolf and Müller, could have been on Connop Thirlwall's mind when he wrote in 1835 of the recent historians who, with "no little boldness . . . venture[d] . . . to throw out a doubt as to the truth of an opinion [the Ancient model] sanctioned by such authority and by prescription of such a long and undisputed possession of the public mind."[80]

CONCLUSION OF DISCUSSION OF BLOK

To my mind, the key passage in Josine Blok's paper is found on pages 707–708: "My aim is not just to clear Müller's name of Bernal's accusations and far less to criticize Bernal's views by presenting a 'true' reading of Müller. Rather, focusing on this essential case, I will show why *Black Athena* conveys Bernal's political views but cannot be regarded as acceptable history."

The two of us disagree profoundly on the issue of the relations of politics to scholarship. In the first place, it is a truism in social science that the label "political" is almost always restricted to studies that challenge authority and is not applied to those that uphold or defend it. A good example of this principle can be found in the ostensibly balanced opening paragraph of Marchand and Grafton's attack on my work. In it they contrast the "politically-minded Afrocentrists" with the merely "self-righteous classicists."[81] Like the majority of contemporary historians, I do not believe in the possibility of an apolitical history. Sometimes, as in the case of such coherent historians as Edward Gibbon, William Mitford, James Mill, George Grote, George Motley, and Julius Beloch, the political and/or religious agenda is obvious; among less coherent ones, like Connop Thirlwall and J. B. Bury, the agenda is more obscure.[82] But even obscurity can serve a political purpose. In any event, the charge that my political and other views have affected my writing of history is undoubtedly true but, to my mind, not in itself damning.

Interestingly, Blok does not mention in this passage the more dangerous charges against me: those against my sloppiness and my failure to read all the relevant texts. No doubt, I should have done much better. That failure, however, does not deal with the question of whether my general conclusions about Müller are in fact correct. Here, I believe, Blok's refusal in this essay to "present . . . a 'true' reading of Müller" is significant. It is interesting to note that her fellow specialist in nineteenth-century German classical studies, Suzanne L. Marchand—who is no fan of mine—joins Blok in deploring my reliance "almost exclusively on secondary sources" but goes on to declare, "Martin Bernal is undoubtedly right in underlining Müller's role in the narrowing of classical scholarship in the mid–nineteenth century." She continues, "His mistake, however, is to attribute this narrowing exclusively to 'racism' rather than to a similarly fateful combination of cultural nationalism, philological skepticism, institutionalized philhellenism *and* the beginnings of racialist thought."[83]

In the introduction to *BA I*, I refer to "the intensity of [Müller's] racism" (p. 33).[84] However, the word "racism" does not appear in the text on him, which is in fact concerned precisely with the "cultural nationalism, philological skepticism, [and] institutionalized philhellenism" to which Marchand refers. Thus, although she does not want to be contaminated by too close contact with my work, I can see no difference at all between our positions.

Does Blok share Marchand's assessment of Müller? Her text attacking me does not give any indication one way or the other. However, her later essay, "K. O. Müller's Understanding of History and Myth," indicates that our views on him are remarkably similar. As mentioned above, she stresses the religious and Romantic aspects of his thought and his insistence on the essential autochthony of all cultures and especially that of Greece and his fierce opposition to any suggestion of Eastern influences.[85] The real difference between us is that she has reached these conclusions through massive and meticulous scholarship, whereas mine were the result of a much more superficial approach.

This distinction places her paper "Proof and Persuasion in *Black Athena*: The Case of K. O. Müller" among the many that have deplored my methods while coming to the same conclusions.[86] See, for instance, Frank Turner's conclusion referred to above and quoted in full in the chapter responding to Laurence Tritle.[87] As I mentioned above, I am convinced that far from being mutually exclusive or damaging, the two types of historiography are not merely complementary but are necessary to each other.

Blok states in her conclusion: "There are today few ancient historians who do not deplore the former Hellenomania of classical studies. In particular the Eurocentrism and its frequent racism, the impact of which increased in the second half of the nineteenth century until far into the twentieth century. . . . The search for different approaches including a systematic interest in the interconnections between Greece, Egypt and the Near East has now been going on for several decades" (p. 724). The last sentence is disingenuous. As I have argued elsewhere, the openness essentially came about only in the 1980s, when I was preparing BA.[88]

"Eurocentrism" is a recent term, and I felt very daring when I coined the word "Hellenomania." I have no doubt that Blok sincerely believes in the motto of her paper, *non tali auxilio* ("not with such help"), in reference to me. The trouble is, she has received such help already.

General Conclusion

All three critics have demonstrated lacunae and errors in my scholarship. Norton and Blok attribute this very largely to my "demagoguery" and ruthlessly "political" agenda. Palter admits there is also a substantial element of incompetence and overreliance on secondary sources. My work, however, is not the only one to suffer from these failings. I do not know whether politics or incompetence is more important in explaining the mistakes that abound in BAR, but there is no doubt that both are important factors.

I cannot deny that subconsciously I may well have been influenced both politically and narratologically, to make the story simple and attractive, but I believe that most of my mistakes and flaws resulted simply from insufficient work. Once again, I must appeal to Huizinga's defense. Such shortcomings are inevitable in any project with as large a range as the one I have attempted. The writing of history cannot consist simply of monographic studies of great depth; despite their inevitable errors, wide-ranging studies with broader perspectives are equally necessary. However, the two must keep in touch with each other, as Palter sees when he writes, "The possibility of a more cogent reworking of Bernal's project, utilizing some of the newer cultural and historical methodologies, remains open" (p. 352).

I put it only slightly differently at the end of the introduction to BA I (p. 73): "The scholarly purpose of . . . [Black Athena] is . . . to open up new areas of research to women and men with far better qualifications than I have."

Having said this, I must insist that in their rush to condemn my work, all three writers have allowed or encouraged the trees to obscure the forest. There is no doubt that the leading thinkers of both the eighteenth-century Enlightenment and the dominant Romantic positivist current of the nineteenth century saw Europe as the only civilized continent and its "white" inhabitants as the only people capable of civilization. Initially, this view did not seriously affect perceptions of the origins of Ancient Greece. The Ancient model became problematic only when first the Ancient Egyptians and then the "Semites" were reclassified as non-European.

8 Passion and Politics

As well as being a joint editor of *Black Athena Revisited*, Guy Rogers has written two sections of the book: its last regular chapter and its conclusion. The chapter begins with a reference to the letter published by the Orientalist Bernard Lewis in the *New York Review of Books* aimed at destroying Edward Said's book *Orientalism*.[1] Lewis's technique was one of reductio ad absurdum. He claimed that it was as ridiculous for Arabs to protest about "Orientalism" as it would be for contemporary Greeks to object to the classicists' version of their history. Now, according to Rogers, Lewis's ludicrous vision has come to pass, for "Bernal . . . has constructed such a fantasy about Hellas and classical scholarship" (p. 429). It so happens that I too have referred to Lewis's letter. For me, however, the boot is on the other foot and I see that the fantasy is that of the Aryan model, not mine.[2]

   As so many of the other contributors to BAR have done, Rogers needs to establish an exaggerated representation of my position in order to attack my work: "In that [Bernal's] myth, the Egyptians and Phoenicians are revealed as the true and sole founders of classical and Western civilization: they taught the early Greeks religion, philosophy, literature, in fact, civilization itself" (p. 430).

In the introduction to BA I, however, I express things very differently: "The Revised Ancient Model . . . accepts that there is a real basis to the stories of Egyptian and Phoenician colonization of Greece set out in the Ancient Model . . . it also agrees that Greek civilization is the result of cultural mixtures created by these colonizations and by later borrowings from across the East Mediterranean. On the other hand it tentatively accepts the Aryan Model's hypothesis of invasions—or infiltrations—from the north by Indo-European speakers" (p. 2).

I have insisted throughout the Black Athena project that Greek is fundamentally an Indo-European language, though with massive lexical influence from the two Afroasiatic languages, Ancient Egyptian and West Semitic. I have perpetrated an inconsistency in that, though I have objected to the Romantic image of a culture as a tree, I have used the term "roots." My justification for this inconsistency is that, although a tree has a single bole or stem, roots are multiple, and I am convinced that all innovative civilizations are or, at least originally, were multicultural, with many different sources. Thus, when I subtitled my book The Afroasiatic Roots of Classical Civilization, I was referring to two crucially important and neglected sources of Greek culture. I have never suggested, as Guy Rogers claims, that they were the "sole" foundations of Classical civilization. There were also Indo-European, possibly Indo-Hittite roots as well as other influences.

It is also important to note in this regard that although it is true that I emphasize the role of Phoenicia and Egypt, I never insist that Greek civilization was a mere reflection of these continental prototypes. Rather, I see it as made up of distinctive forms created through fruitful interaction between the foreign and the native cultures.

The theme that runs through Rogers's writing appears at the end of his introductory passage: "The irony (and indeed the tragedy) about the impact that Black Athena has made upon the general public is that considerable ancient evidence supports exactly the multicultural foundation story of classical civilization, which Bernal's supporters have mistakenly attributed to him" (p. 430).

I have never claimed that my ideas were new. What he refers to as "considerable ancient evidence" I call the Ancient model. My originality consists precisely in my attempt to draw attention to this ancient evidence and to challenge its rejection in the nineteenth and twentieth centuries by the discipline of Classics, which has emphasized the purity and autochthony of Greek civilization. Clear traces of the discipline's absolute refusal to recognize the significance of Semitic and Egyptian influences on Greece can still be seen in BAR itself in the chapter on language by Jasanoff and Nussbaum. This topic cannot be considered trivial because language is central both to Greek culture and to the discipline of Classics.

Rogers implies that Classics and related disciplines have always been open to the idea of substantial cultural influences on Greece from the southeast. In fact, such openness is a very recent phenomenon brought about very largely—though not entirely—by pressures from outside the discipline.[3]

I shall reply to points raised by Rogers in the order in which he sets them out. In particular, I look closely at his sections "Historiography," "The Historical Argument," and what he entitles "The Myth of Martin Bernal." After that, I turn my attention to Rogers's eight-question "conclusion" to BAR as a whole.

Historiography

At one point in this section, in a spirit very different from that of the rest of his article, Rogers generously acknowledges the outline of my historiography. He writes: "Bernal's reconstruction of how some European scholars in an atmosphere of racism and anti-Semitism (especially during the nineteenth century), attempted to root out the contributions of the Ancient Egyptians and the Phoenicians to early Greek civilization seems to me beyond dispute" (p. 431). However, he continues in the very next sentence: "Racism and anti-Semitism pervaded *some* lines of European historical enquiry about the ancient world. Some nineteenth century scholars of antiquity did understand what we might today call cultural differences in terms of 'race.' But not all nineteenth century scholars of the ancient world were racists or anti-Semites" (p. 431; his italics).

This passage places the whole issue in the past, neatly side-stepping two additional and important issues. First, although the majority of twentieth-century scholars of Classics and related fields have been no more racist and anti-Semitic than most educated people, as in academia at large a significant minority have held such distasteful views, which at least in some cases affected their scholarship.[4] Still more important is the fact that until very recently the discipline as a whole has continued to work within the Aryan model, which was set up by men who were acutely conscious of "race" and categorical racial distinctions.

I quite agree with Rogers that a number of nineteenth- and twentieth-century historians of the Ancient Mediterranean were not exceptionally racist or anti-Semitic, or at least did not allow these prejudices to vitiate their academic work. Indeed, I discuss some of these, such as Victor Bérard, in BA I. Incidentally, Rogers is confused when he refers to Bérard's having "argued for fundamental Egyptian and/or Phoenician contribution to early Greek civilization at exactly the time when 'Aryanist' scholars . . . promoted what Bernal terms the 'Aryan Model'" (p. 430). In fact, Bérard focused exclusively on the Phoenicians (BA I: 377–383). It was Paul Foucart who emphasized the centrality of Egyptian civilization in the formation of the Eleusinian Mysteries and Greek culture as a whole (BA I: 264–265). Despite Rogers's muddle, the important point here is his concession that I have never seen the situation as simple or denied significant countercurrents.

Rogers argues, in particular, that I have done great injustice to one centrally important historian of Greece, George Grote. Apparently to rebut statements he mistakenly attributes to me, Rogers describes Grote's "commitment to higher education for Jews, dissidents and Nonconformists, and his principled stand on the separation of religious doctrine and scientific knowledge" (p. 434). In fact, I refer to these specific views on educational opportunities as held by Grote's near contemporary at school and fellow historian of Greece, Connop Thirwall, with whom I say Grote was "in general agreement" (BA I: 321–322). On Grote himself, I quote Momigliano with approval when he writes about circles of the two historians of Ancient Greece: "Both societies disliked Mitford, read German and were attacked by the *Quarterly Review.* Both aimed at a liberalization of English political and intellectual habits and wanted them to be founded on firm philosophical principles" (BA I: 326–327).[5]

I also describe Grote as a "Radical and a Utilitarian . . . naturally in sympathy with the scientific spirit which, in the 1830s was being articulated in France in the positivism of Comte" (BA I: 327). Nevertheless, Rogers is outraged because he sees me as implying that Grote was "guilty of anti-Semitism, racism and romanticism" (p. 432). Here again, Rogers has been slightly inaccurate. I have never in any way suggested that Grote was anti-Semitic. It is true that I did portray him as a Romantic, although I do not see this as a criminal or even a moral offense. Nevertheless, there is something to the nub of Rogers's charge, in that I did describe Grote as a "racist" (BA I: 336). The typeface of the passage in the last two printings of *Black Athena* in which the statement occurs indicates that the text has been altered.[6] In fact, in earlier printings, I had written "with the possible exception of Grote." The reason for this caution was that, despite his living in an intensely racist age, I had seen no evidence to suggest that Grote shared this aspect of the prevailing ethos. One cannot expect Rogers to have investigated such a nuance. Before devoting five pages to attacking me on this issue, however, he might have noticed that in 1988 I published "The British Utilitarians, Imperialism and the Fall of the Ancient Model."[7] This article is devoted to George Grote and his guru James Mill, the father of John Stuart Mill. In it, I attempted to reconcile the paradox that men who were among the most progressive of their time in Britain and Europe should have held "Orientals" and especially Indians and Ancient Egyptians in such contempt. They saw them not merely as at a lower stage of civilization but, in the spirit of Hume, as inherently inferior. For this reason I removed my earlier exception of Grote.

The gist of the article is that the paradox between the two views is apparent and not real and comes about only because today we associate the word "progressive" with hostility to Eurocentrism. Utilitarians such as James Mill and George Grote, however, saw Europe as the epitome of progress and believed that much, if not all, of its dynamism came from its racial essence. Therefore, they saw non-European cultures as relics of the past that should be swept away. However, such progress required two preconditions: first, it was possible only under European guidance, and second, it required that the people who lived in such "backward" societies were inherently capable of adapting to the modern world of the nineteenth century. It was this that led me to add George Grote to the list of "racists."

In 1998, however, I modified my views again as the result of a correspondence with David Levy on John Stuart Mill's support for the Ancient model in its African form.[8] At the same time, Mill was in charge of the East India Company's relations with Indian states during the twenty years before the Great Revolt of 1857–1858, and one of the major causes of the revolt was the company's extreme contempt for Indian culture. By contrast, for both good and dubious reasons, East India Company merchants were frequently outraged by the behavior of those of the West Indies.[9] On the dubious side, the East India merchants undoubtedly allied themselves to the movement for the abolition of the slave trade and even more to the later one for the emancipation of slaves because they were eager to limit the privileges of their rivals in the West Indies. The most striking example of this comes from Zachary Macauley (the father of historian Thomas Babington Macauley), an actively abolitionist friend of William Wilberforce. Macauley was sufficiently influential with the East India Company to ensure the appointment of James Mill to the high office of Examiner of the company. In 1822, James and his sixteen-year-old son, John Stuart, helped the elder Macauley prepare for a parliamentary debate on the preferential treatment given to West Indian sugar and slavery and advocating the removal of tariffs on the East Indian commodity. John Stuart Mill then published his first article which supported the proposal.[10]

Thus, both of the Mills and Grote were utterly contemptuous of non-European civilizations, especially India and Ancient Egypt. What is more, James Mill attributed this inferiority to the innate nature of their populations. At the same time, at least John Stuart Mill was antiracist in regard to the West Indies. Therefore, I should like to accept this part of Rogers's criticism and to return to my earlier description of Grote as a "possible exception" to the intense racism of his age. Nevertheless, I am still convinced that his extreme disdain for non-European cultures, which was altogether typical of his age, affected his discounting the Ancient model.

The Historical Argument

Rogers states under this heading that he does not want to get into the argument of whether there was Egyptian and Phoenician colonization of later Greek lands (p. 435).[11] He leaves that to others, notably Vermeule, Coleman, and Morris. He first objects to what he mistakenly supposes to be my argument here: he attributes to me a claim that most scholars today doubt that such settlements took place solely out of, as Rogers puts it, "a desire to exclude Egyptians and Phoenicians from the foundation story of the West (as Bernal implies)" (p. 435). As I have pointed out in other instances, Rogers can say only that I imply this, as I have never said or written any such thing. I do believe that this has been an element behind the denial, and I am not the only person to claim this. Walter Burkert has shown the impact of anti-Semitism on the work of Julius Beloch and other late-nineteenth- and twentieth-century scholars. There is also no doubt that one of the most revered ancestors of Classics, K. O. Müller (1797–1840), the man who first systematically challenged the legends of settlement, was clearly prejudiced against Ancient Egyptians as inherently inferior.[12]

It is not merely the fact that most of the predecessors of contemporary classicists denied the legends of settlement that has led scholars such as

Sarah Morris and John Coleman to the same conclusion. There are at least two other factors behind the modern skepticism. The first is the deep caution, minimalism, and requirement of proof for new ideas that has permeated the training and later careers of these scholars. The second is a liberal dislike of the notions of conquest and colonization. I have argued at length in BA and elsewhere that minimalism and the requirement of proof can lead one astray in understanding prehistory, because in their absence a conventional wisdom is left in place that may be far less plausible than a likely but unproven alternative.

The second objection, which has been made before, is the allegation that I maintain that conquest is the *only* way in which cultures can be diffused.[13] This is simply not the case. I merely maintain that the historical record shows us that it is *one way* in which diffusion can take place, and it is overwhelmingly likely that the same was true in prehistory. In this case, I do not believe that either invasion or settlement is necessary to explain what I see as the massive cultural influence of Egypt and the Levant on Greek civilization. As discussed above, my reason for maintaining that such settlements probably took place is the same as that of Frank Stubbings in the relevant article in the *Cambridge Ancient History,* that is, the congruence of the Greek tradition with the archaeological evidence from the Shaft Graves.[14]

At another point, Rogers attempts to turn the tables by chiding me for failing to acknowledge the significance of Mesopotamian civilization in the formation of Greece, which he argues has been widely recognized by scholars even in general histories. This is the case, but the references to "Near Eastern" influences are nearly always brief, vague, and general, whereas mine are specific.[15]

I shall reply to this criticism on a number of different levels. In the first place, my concern is not with a competition between Egypt and Mesopotamia over which was the greater or more creative civilization. I am interested merely in which had the greater impact on the formation of Ancient Greece. Here, archaeological evidence and Greek tradition overwhelmingly prefer Egypt, and this would seem obvious from a geographical point of view.

Second, it is not true that, as Rogers states, I maintain that "only the Egyptians and Phoenicians" had "significantly influenced early Greek civilization" (pp. 434–435; emphasis in the original). In a number of places, which I now briefly review, I have raised the possibility or likelihood of influences on the Aegean from other parts of Southwest Asia, including

Mesopotamia. Near the beginning of BA II, I accept the idea that the Agios Onouphrios style of pottery of Early Bronze Age Crete derived from Syro-Palestine. I also state that the fast wheel for pottery probably came to the Aegean from Mesopotamia, probably through Anatolia (BA II: 70–72). I see Syrian influence on Cretan pottery and metallurgy at the end of the Early Bronze Age (BA II: 156). I also describe the Minoan palaces as like other "Middle Eastern palaces: Mesopotamia, Syria, Anatolia etc." (BA II: 161).

Later, in the same volume, I quote with approval Ventris and Chadwick's reference to the great similarities of palatial organization record-keeping, and even the sexagesimal system between Mesopotamia and Syria on the one hand, and the Mycenaean Aegean on the other. I also claim that the derivation of the latter from the former was probably more direct than Ventris and Chadwick suppose. I conclude: "The best explanation for the striking parallels between the Mycenaean Aegean and Syro-Mesopotamia is to suppose that, along with the palaces and the script, the Mycenaean rulers took over the bureaucratic traditions of their predecessors in Crete, which in turn belonged to the general institutional patterns of the Near East" (BA II: 442).

Near the end of BA II, I discuss and accept Edith Porada's complex explanation for the presence of some splendid Kassite seals from Mesopotamia discovered in the palace of the Greek Thebes and discuss possible trade relations between the Aegean and Mesopotamia in the thirteenth century B.C.E. (BA II: 509–510).

Black Athena is focused on the Bronze Age. Nevertheless, I have written elsewhere on Iron Age contacts. In fact, in two articles, one published in 1989 but written much earlier and the other in 1993, I stress the influence of Mesopotamian social and economic structures on those of Greece, though I see these as having been transmitted and modified by Phoenicians.[16] I have also written about Mesopotamian influences on Greek mathematics and astronomy, though I have noted that these transmissions went largely through Egypt.[17]

Here again, I do not emphasize Phoenician and Egyptian transmission and modification in both of these instances through any hostility to, or lack of admiration for, Mesopotamian civilization. Geography is the simple reason for this emphasis. The difficulties of traversing the mountains of Anatolia made it much more convenient to travel from Mesopotamia to the Aegean through the Levant or Egypt.[18] Thus, the particular forms of Near Eastern culture received by the Greeks tended to be Egyptian or Phoeni-

cian or both. My descriptions of the remarkable *mixed* set of cultural influences on Ancient Greece could not be in greater contradiction to the
narrow transmissions that Rogers attributes to me.

The Myth of Martin Bernal

The intricate confusion of subject and object makes it difficult for me to
assess Rogers's section "The Myth of Martin Bernal." Naturally, I can have
few objections to his restating parts of the autobiographical section of my
introduction to BA I. Nevertheless, Rogers is mistaken on a number of factual points. For instance, he supposes that my project was "conceived during the years of the Vietnam War and the civil rights movement in America"
(p. 441). Although, in general, these processes reinforced my sympathy
with the oppressed, I gave no thought at all to the origins of Ancient Greece
or the foundations of Western Civilization before 1975.

Another misinterpretation is his supposition that I became more interested in my Jewish roots as a consequence of the Israeli military triumphs
in the 1970s. This mistake illustrates how difficult it is for a conservative to
understand a liberal. The Israeli victories made me less, not more sympathetic toward Israel because they completely removed its status as a victim.
As I stated in the preface to volume 1, I became interested in my Jewish
heritage in 1975 because "roots" were in fashion and because in the United
States I was encountering Jewish culture for the first time.

Leaving my supposed biography behind, Rogers also maintains that I
have neglected Hittite, Hurrian, and Mesopotamian contributions to Greek
civilization. I have already discussed this, and, as I have not published on
Iron Age Greek religion except when it has had clear connections with that
of the Bronze Age, I have not looked at the plausible connections from the
Babylonian *Enuma Elish* and the Hurrian pantheon to Hesiod's *Cosmogony*.
On the other hand, as I mentioned in the preface to BA I, long before I considered the possibility of Egyptian influences on the Greek language, I had
tried to discover Hurrian ones and was disappointed not to find any (BA
I: xiv). Elsewhere, I write at some length about the possible role of Hurrian
speakers among the Hyksos, and I have mentioned the occurrence of the
Hurrian divine name Teššub in the Greek city names Thisbe and Thespiai
(BA II: 119–120, 346–350, 499).[19]

I accept Eric Cline's assessment of the paucity of Anatolian finds at Mycenae in comparison to those from Egypt and the Levant.[20] An ideological

preference has long existed, I believe, for seeing "Oriental" influence as coming to Greece from or through the Indo-Hittite–speaking Hittites (BA I: 391–392). Nevertheless, I do discuss Anatolian influences on the Aegean in the Late Bronze Age (BA II: 452–462).

Returning to my biography, Rogers admits "(. . . it is perhaps to Bernal's credit that he has openly laid out what he wants the world to believe about the story behind Black Athena.) But if, after due consideration, the results of a project appear to be closely linked to its origins, scholars are obligated—as Bernal himself has felt obliged—to examine the relationship between the two." This statement is, of course, quite reasonable. But then, Rogers continues: "Given the stated social and personal contexts from which Black Athena evolved, it is hard in retrospect not to see the entire enterprise of Black Athena as a massive, fundamentally misguided projection onto the 2nd millennium B.C.E. of Martin Bernal's personal struggle to establish an identity in the later 20th century" (p. 441). I think his image of a "personal struggle to establish an identity" is exaggerated. Looking back, I do not think that curiosity about my Jewish "roots" reflected any serious doubts as to who I was.[21] The ethnic and cultural mixture in my background may have inclined me to see a similar pattern in the origins of Ancient Greece, but I should never have devoted so much of my life to such a project if I had not found what I considered to be ample evidence of its validity.

Rogers's view of this projection of my "personal struggle" as "fundamentally misguided" can apply only to the historical as opposed to the historiographical aspect of my work because, as mentioned earlier, he agreed that "Bernal's reconstruction of how some European scholars . . . attempted to root out the contributions of the Ancient Egyptians and the Phoenicians to early Greek civilization seems to me beyond dispute" (p. 431). In this area, then, he must concede that what he sees as my "personal struggle" has not harmed my scholarship.

In general, although I maintain that scholarship is socially and psychologically embedded, I do not believe that it is socially or psychologically determined. Furthermore, many of the best histories have been written with contemporary circumstances in mind. Arnaldo Momigliano, to whom BAR is dedicated, has written an elegant essay on the tight relationship between Grote's radical politics and his History of Greece.[22] Thus, a relationship between a historian and her or his subject is not in itself necessarily harmful and can sometimes help. Indeed, most historians would agree with Wilhelm von Humboldt, who maintained that a relationship between a historian and the object of "his" historical inquiry is both inevitable and desirable.²³ In sum, Rogers's view of my project as "fundamentally mis-guided"—like his description of me as "only a false prophet"—must stand on its own, simply as his opinion.

Rogers's Conclusion

Having discussed Rogers's penultimate chapter in BAR in some detail, I now wish to turn to his brief conclusion to the volume with the title "Quo vadis?" This section consists of eight questions about my work, followed by a summary of the answers provided by the contributors. It is constructed on the assumption that the authors selected for *Black Athena Revisited* fully represent their disciplines and that, therefore, their assessments of my work should be accepted as final. I think this scheme can be questioned at three levels. In the first place, as discussed in the introduction to this book, the selection of authors was skewed. Second, the assessments of challenges to disciplines—all disciplines—should not be left entirely in the hands of the practitioners themselves. Third, some of Rogers's simplifications of the responses in BAR exaggerate the contributors' hostility to my work. Let me consider Rogers's eight questions one by one.

WHO WERE THE EGYPTIANS?

A clear example of Rogers's third tendency appears in the treatment of the first question. Rogers simplifies Loring Brace's arguments to suggest that Brace and I are in complete disagreement. In fact, we share a number of views, notably that there is a skin color cline as one goes down the Nile Valley and that the Predynastic population of Upper Egypt (who were the founders of Pharaonic civilization) "differs less from the Somali to the South than do [from?] the Late Dynastic people from Lower Egypt" (p. 154). The latter do indeed resemble other peoples around the Mediter-ranean, but I accept the view of the physical anthropologist Shomarka Keita that both populations were African: East African and North African.²⁴ This is because, although there are clear signs of cultural influence from Meso-potamia at the beginning of the Dynastic Period, I accept the Egyptological consensus that there is no trace of an invading race from outside Africa.

WERE THE ANCIENT EGYPTIANS "BLACK"?

Rogers implies that I have used the racial terms "Caucasoid" and "Negroid" in reference to the Ancient Egyptians. Let me repeat—yet again—what I wrote about the subject in BA I:

> To what "race" then, did the Ancient Egyptians belong? I am very dubious of the utility of the concept "race" in general because it is impossible to achieve any anatomical precision on the subject. Moreover, even if one accepts it for the sake of argument I am even more skeptical about the possibility of finding an answer in this particular case. Research on the question usually reveals far more about the predisposition of the researcher than about the question itself. Nevertheless, I am convinced that at least for the last 7,000 years, the population of Egypt has contained African, South West Asian and Mediterranean types. It is also clear that the further South, or up the Nile one goes, the blacker and more negroid the population becomes and that this has been the case for the same length of time. As I stated in the Introduction, I believe that Egyptian civilization was fundamentally African, and that the African element was stronger in the Old and Middle Kingdoms, before the Hyksos invasion, than it later became. Furthermore, I am convinced that many of the most powerful Egyptian Dynasties which were based in Upper Egypt—the 1st, 11th, 12th and 18th—were made up of pharaohs whom one can usefully call black. (BA I: 241–242)

As it has been more than ten years since I wrote this, I would now modify the passage in the direction of a greater continuity of the physical types in Egypt and stress that North Africa was the source of the Mediterranean populations rather than the other way around. I also admit that in the final sentence, I used the term "black" in a more restrictive way than at some other places. This problem points to the fundamental difficulty surrounding the semantic field of the word "black." I have never employed it to suggest that the Ancient Egyptian population looked like the European stereotype of West Africans. I have used the word in the sense that it is used in contemporary North America to designate anyone with an evident trace of African ancestry. In Britain today it is used still more widely to include South Asians.

WAS EGYPT AFRICAN?

As I have written elsewhere, I should have preferred the title *African Athena* for my work.²⁵ Here I disagree strongly with Rogers, who wants to make a clear distinction between the Egyptians and other inhabitants of the African continent. For him, "Essentially the Egyptians were Egyptians" (p. 448). I follow Frank Yurco, who in his chapter expresses the views of the vast majority of Egyptologists when he writes, "Certainly there was some foreign admixture, but basically a homogeneous African population had lived in the Nile Valley from ancient to modern times" (p. 65).

There are two reasons for stressing the Africanity of the Ancient Egyptian population. The first is to right the misapprehension that it was somehow Asian or European. This myth was accepted by specialists in the early twentieth century. Later in that century, though experts knew this was a myth, they did not broadcast the fact and it has persisted in popular opinion. One can instructively contrast the noise now being made against Afrocentrist claims with the silence with which classicists and ancient historians have greeted the frequent popular representations of Ancient Egyptians as Europeans, sometimes even as Northern Europeans.²⁶

The second reason for associating Egypt with the rest of Africa is the simple fact that both the country and its inhabitants *were* related to the rest of Africa. Geographically, during the formative Predynastic Period (5000–3400 B.C.E.) Egypt was linked to West and Central Africa by the open savanna that later desiccated to become large regions of the Sahara. Then as later, Egypt was connected to East Central Africa by the Nile. The physiological links of the Egyptians with East and North Africans, acknowledged by both Keita and Brace, were mentioned earlier in this chapter. In material culture, the leading Egyptian prehistorian Fekhry Hassan and others have shown the relations between the Sahara (then savanna) and the Upper Nile with Upper Egypt in the Predynastic Period.²⁷ Linguistically, the Egyptian language belongs to the Afroasiatic superfamily and there is little doubt that this linguistic grouping originated in Africa, to the south of Egypt.²⁸ Though there is no doubt that a very distinctive and individual culture was formed in Egypt, it is extremely misleading to separate it from the rest of the continent.

DID THE ANCIENT EGYPTIANS OR HYKSOS COLONIZE GREECE?

Rogers begins this response with two mistakes. He states, "Bernal claims that Greece was colonized from Egypt not once, but twice: first during the third millennium B.C.E. . . . and second during the eighteenth/seventeenth centuries B.C.E., when the Hyksos having been driven out of Egypt, invaded the Argolid and ruled there" (p. 449). Here, as in other cases mentioned above, it seems that Rogers has been too busy damning my books to have read them with any care. Rogers's first slip is his claim that I maintain that Egyptians colonized or settled Greece during the third millennium B.C.E. Although I argue that there are signs of Egyptian influence in parts of Greece at this time, I conclude: "Unfortunately, it is impossible to determine the type of relationship that existed between Boiotia and Egypt in the period with which we are concerned. The chances that it took the form of direct colonization are very low: despite the dangers of the argument from silence, it has to be noted that not only is there a lack of Egyptian objects and Egyptian attestation of such colonies, but there is the strong likelihood that Boiotia's writing system was an Aegean one rather than hieroglyphics or hieratic" (BA II: 152). I do, however, go on to recognize that there is enough evidence of Egyptian presence in the Aegean in the middle of the third millennium to make some kind of "suzerainty quite possible."

Rogers's second slip is that he believes that I see a Hyksos colonization in the Argolid as the result of the expulsion of the Hyksos that took place in the sixteenth century B.C.E. In fact, early in the introduction to BA I (p. 20), I make it clear that archaeological evidence has made it impossible to sustain the traditional view that Danaos had arrived at the end of the Hyksos period. Therefore, one of my revisions of the Ancient model has been to put the settlements near the period's beginning (BA I: 20). Like a number of earlier scholars who accepted the later date, I am inclined to believe the traditions and the admittedly ambiguous archaeological evidence that there were Hyksos settlements on Mainland Greece beginning not in the sixteenth, but earlier in the eighteenth and seventeenth centuries B.C.E.[29]

DID THE ANCIENT EGYPTIANS AND/OR THE PHOENICIANS
MASSIVELY INFLUENCE THE EARLY GREEKS IN THE AREAS OF
LANGUAGE, RELIGION, SCIENCE, AND/OR PHILOSOPHY?

Rogers begins, "No expert in the field doubts that there was a Greek cultural debt to the ancient Near East" (p. 449). As I mentioned earlier, this statement is extremely misleading because such openness is a very recent phenomenon. Writing in 1992, Walter Burkert, whose work on the topic is now so much admired, stated: "My thesis on the indebtedness of Greek civilization to eastern stimuli may appear less provocative today than it did eight years ago."[30] Cyrus Gordon and Michael Astour received very harsh treatment for suggesting such stimuli in the 1960s.[31] The distinguished maritime archaeologist George Bass has spoken passionately about the way he and others were treated for claiming significant Semitic influence in the Eastern Mediterranean in the Late Bronze Age.[32] As I mentioned above, the article by Jasanoff and Nussbaum in BAR shows that the nineteenth-century spirit of Indo-European and Greek isolation from Near Eastern influences is far from dead. The fact that they were selected to write on a crucial subject, for which they were so badly prepared, indicates that the editors of BAR retain some sympathy with the extreme isolationist views of these two Indo-Europeanists.

Rogers continues: "The real questions are: How large was the debt? was it massive, as Bernal claims? and was it restricted to Egyptians and Phoenicians?" (p. 449). He claims that "the consensus of the contributors to this volume" denies both of these claims. This result is not surprising because the editors did not solicit articles from scholars of the caliber of Walter Burkert, Martin West, Cyrus Gordon, Michael Astour, George Bass, and Patricia Bikai, who have insisted on the massive influence of Semitic speakers on the Aegean.[33]

Nevertheless, Rogers does agree that "Certainly the evidence shows that the Eighteenth Dynasty and the Aegean were in close contact at certain levels" (p. 449). He could hardly do otherwise, given the mass of archaeological and documentary evidence of such contact. This has led Donald Redford, the eminent Egyptologist and expert in cultural relations around the Eastern Mediterranean, to write, "There is no reason to doubt that the Egyptian court was at all times during the Mycenaean age in correspondence with the court at Mycenae, although the letters have not as yet been recovered."[34] Rogers continues: "But such contacts are not equivalent to 'suzerainty' and do not imply the substantial cultural impact upon the Aegean that is required by Bernal's claims" (p. 449).

Permit me here to go over the argument for the term "suzerainty" that Rogers finds inadmissible. An objection has been raised against the standard translation of the Egyptian term *inw* as "tribute."[35] Redford describes the people from the Aegean carrying rich local products to the pharaoh both as "benevolence bearers" and "tribute bearers."[36] All that I claimed in BA II was that "the [repeated] ceremony of bringing rich gifts . . . was interpreted by the Egyptians as an act of submission" (p. 428). Similarly, the portrayal on the base of a statue of Amenhotep III of the names of several Aegean cities as subjects of the pharaoh does not necessarily mean that the cities' rulers saw themselves as such (BA II: 432–434). Nor do we know how much weight to put on the claim by Tuthmosis III that he had sent an expedition to the Aegean and that the inhabitants had been overawed (BA II: 426–427). Given the disproportion of wealth and power between united Egypt and the squabbling Mycenaean states facing a Hittite threat to the Aegean after 1440 B.C.E., I think that some form of "suzerainty" is more likely than not. My chief interest in the issue is why it should be so passionately denied.

Whether or not there was suzerainty, the intimacy of the relations between the two regions would lead one to expect substantial cultural exchange, and, other things being equal, this would have been predominantly from Egypt and the Levant to the Aegean. Other things are not equal, however, for we know that hundreds of Egyptian objects have been found in Late Bronze Age contexts in Greece and that such artistic motifs as the sphinx and the *ba* bird have also been found there from that period. Emily Vermeule has shown that some of the oldest Greek beliefs about death come from Egypt.[37] On top of all this, we have the Greek tradition that much of Greek religion came from Egypt. Given this accumulation of evidence, I am convinced that, at least for the Late Bronze Age, the burden should be on those who want to deny "a considerable [Egyptian] cultural impact" on Greece rather than on those who want to accept what the Ancient Greeks wrote on this subject.

Rogers makes a petty, though ideologically revealing, mistake when he states that "in the area of religion, Egyptian and Canaanite deities were never worshipped on Greek soil in their indigenous forms" (p. 449). In fact, in Hellenistic and Roman times, cults of Isis and Serapis were found all over Greece. Pausanias mentions one in particular, at Tithoreia, where Egyptian rites were meticulously followed.[38] I have never claimed that Greek religion or culture in general were mere projections of those of Egypt and the Levant. Clearly, important adaptations were made, with both innovations and preservations of archaic features lost in the Near East. Nevertheless, I disagree profoundly with Rogers's statement, "Nor does the abundant archaeological evidence support the claims of pervasive influence in the area of cult" (pp. 449–450).

Vermeule's arguments in favor of Egyptian influences (dating back to the Bronze Age) on the cults surrounding death were mentioned above. A detailed case for an Egyptian origin of the most important Greek mystery system, that of Eleusis, has been made in my review of *Not Out of Africa*, included as chapter 16 in this volume.[39]

The French scholar, journalist, and politician Victor Bérard demonstrated extensive Semitic influences on the cults of Arkadia, the most conservative region of southern Greece, which to my knowledge have never been challenged in detail, let alone refuted.[40]

Continuing his summaries, Rogers then writes, "In terms of language, the evidence that Bernal has presented thus far for the influence of Egyptian and Phoenician on the Greek language has failed to meet any of the standard tests which are required for the proof of extensive influence" (p. 449). I have argued at length that it is inappropriate to demand "proof" rather than competitive plausibility in such areas, and that if it should be required the burden should be on those who want to deny Greek tradition and the constraints of history and geography (BA I: 314). By "standard tests," Rogers can only be referring to the article by Jasanoff and Nussbaum in BAR. I have discussed in chapter 6, at some length, their incompetence to treat this subject. Suffice it to say here that scholars who both know the three relevant languages and the nature of linguistic loans consider my proposals critically but very seriously.[41]

Rogers makes two mistakes when he writes, "All of the contributors agree that the early Greeks got their alphabet from the Phoenicians; but little else. . . . the fact remains that Egyptian and Canaanite scripts were never used widely in historical Greece" (p. 449). In the first place, Sarah Morris, the only one of the BAR contributors who has studied the topic in any detail, is firmly convinced of a massive West Semitic influence on Greece.[42] Second, even if one rejects my proposal that a Canaanite alphabet was introduced to the Aegean in the Bronze Age, the distinction between "Canaanite" and "Phoenician" is both modern and arbitrary. What is the "Phoenician" alphabet other than a "Canaanite" one?

Rogers is inconsistent when he turns to the question of science. He states both that "the case for Egyptian influence on Greek mathematical astronomy, mathematics, and medicine is only somewhat stronger" and that "in these areas the Egyptians definitely influenced the Greeks." As the articles on science in this volume and in DBA show, a number of us agree with the second sentence and have little problem with his continuation: "but Greek achievements, especially in the fields of mathematics and medicine, became quite distinct and original" (p. 450).

In this section too Rogers repeats his contention that Greece derived more from "relations with the northern Levant, Anatolia and ultimately Babylonia, which was much more influential culturally than Egypt generally in the Near East. Furthermore there were more geographical routes available by which that Babylonian influence could travel" (p. 450). The last sentence is quite extraordinary. The geographical facts that, whereas Egypt and Phoenicia were in direct contact with the Aegean by sea Mesopotamia was not, have been touched on above. The archaeological, documentary, and traditional evidence for both the Bronze and Iron Ages all indicate that this geographical imperative was followed in history. As I wrote in BA I, I am convinced that the reason for emphasizing Anatolian or "Asianic" sources was essentially to avoid giving credit to the Semitic-speaking Phoenicians (pp. 391–392). It might appear that anti-Semitism could not explain an emphasis on the largely Semitic-speaking Mesopotamians. The Assyriologist Mogens Trolle Larsen, however, has shown how a desire to diminish the intellectual creativity of West Semitic speakers in general and Jews in particular was a central factor in the Pan-Babylonianism popular around 1900.[43] Once again, I want to make it clear that I am not imputing anti-Semitism to scholars who propose similar ideas today but merely to some of those in whose academic tradition they are working.

I have no substantial difficulty with Rogers's final point that cultural relations between the Near East and Greece were not "a one-way street." Indeed, I emphasize the economic importance of the Aegean in the trade of the Late Bronze Age and I devote an appendix to BA I to arguing that the Philistines came from the Aegean (BA II: 479–482; BA I: 445–450). Nevertheless, I am convinced that the predominant cultural flow came from the older, more elaborate, continental civilizations of Egypt and the Levant to the initially far less developed Aegean.

DID THE GREEKS BELIEVE THEY WERE DESCENDED FROM THE EGYPTIANS AND THE PHOENICIANS?

The answer is obviously no, and I have never said that they did.[44] This question is yet another attempt to exaggerate my ideas in order to give them a vulnerability that my actual views lack. All that some Ancients claimed was that certain royal dynasties had Egyptian or Syrian or both, as well as divine, ancestors. Though not believing in such persons as the mythical Kadmos, Danaos, and Pelops, I do consider that some of the royal dynasties in the Mycenaean period may well have had Southwest Asian and Anatolian origins. I argued earlier in this volume and elsewhere against the claim that I have been taken in by the Athenian propaganda that tried to portray other cities, notably Thebes, Argos, and Sparta, as being foreign, while portraying the Athenians themselves as autochthonous.[45] It is clear that the Thebans were as proud of their Kadmean (Phoenician) foundation as the Argives were of their association with Danaos from Egypt.[46] To my mind, it is the Athenian traditions of autochthony that require inquiry rather than traditions of foreign associations with Boiotia and the Eastern Peloponnese.

DID EIGHTEENTH- AND NINETEENTH-CENTURY SCHOLARS OBSCURE THE AFRO-ASIATIC ROOTS FOR REASONS OF RACISM AND ANTI-SEMITISM?

First, let me repeat that I never claimed that racism was the only reason earlier scholars dismissed this possibility. I have given a number of other reasons, which I believe were also significant in the early nineteenth century.[47] Rogers claims that racism and anti-Semitism were less important to these scholars than the fact that "they saw little evidence for the kind of massive influence that Bernal has argued for" (p. 451). I do not deny that positivism was a factor in the nineteenth-century requirement of proof (which, in any event, I believe to be inappropriate). As stated above, the fact that the proof was required of the ancient tradition and not of those who challenged it clearly indicates that the scholars had extra-academic ideological preferences, one of which was racism and another, somewhat later, was anti-Semitism.

Although the working out of the Indo-European language family was an important internalist cause of the rise of the Aryan model, it was not a factor in the destruction of the Ancient one. K. O. Müller's major attack on the earlier model was made in the 1820s, without the aid of the new historical linguistics. Second, as I have emphasized at many points in my work, I have always accepted the fact that Greek is fundamentally an Indo-European language and that this indicates that at some early period significant northern influences were at work in the Aegean. I insist, however, that this in no way invalidates the ancient views on Egyptian and Levantine influences on Greece (BA I: 439). The denial of such ancient traditions cannot simply be attributed to the identification of Greek as an Indo-European language.

ARE THE SCHOLARLY METHODS OF BLACK ATHENA CREDIBLE?

In chapter 3, I discuss the mystique of "method" and its use to defend otherwise indefensible orthodoxies.[48] Rogers refers to archaeologists' complaints that I "constantly misconstrue . . . such archaeological evidence as there is" (p. 451–52). I agree that the archaeological evidence is sparse before the Late Bronze Age and that, even in that period, it is open to many interpretations. None of the archaeologists who contributed to BAR specialize in Greek contacts with the rest of the Eastern Mediterranean. Eric Cline, the leading American expert in Egypto-Aegean relations, and George Bass, the outstanding archaeologist of relations between the Levant and the Aegean, have no major objections to my interpretations.[49]

Archaeologists and others are divided on my use of "competitive plausibility" as a method of reconstructing the distant past. Rogers prefers Mary Lefkowitz's formulation of "contextualised evaluation of all the available evidence" (p. 452). The difficulty comes when, as is often the case, scholars differ in their conclusions. As I stated above, I find competitive plausibility preferable to the requirement of proof for new ideas, though not for old ones. Waiting until all the evidence is in, which it never can be, leaves a conventional wisdom in place even though it may well be less likely or plausible than a new model or paradigm.

Like the conclusion as a whole, Rogers's final section has the strange heading "Quo vadis": Whither art thou going? Is it addressed to me personally, or to the readers individually? Or is it merely an inappropriate use of a well-known Latin tag? In this section Rogers maintains that any benefit I may have brought about by raising "legitimate, important and interesting" questions is vitiated by my encouraging the "racist theories" of the Afro-centrists. As I have stated many times, describing the extreme ethnocentric views of some Afrocentrists as "racist" is not useful. The term "racism" should be restricted to such views in conjunction with institutional and cultural power.[50] Even so, I am not happy to have my work used to promote any wholly or falsely "purist" views. However, I should be far more unhappy to support the status quo in Classics and ancient history of the Mediterranean. The author Richard Poe reports that neo-Nazi supporters of William Pierce, the author of the *Turner Diaries* (the inspiration for the Oklahoma bombing), are using Colin Renfrew's archaeological writings emphasizing the creativity and cultural independence of northwestern Europe.[51] This extreme example shows that those who insist on the separation of a "white" European Greece from the rest of the Eastern Mediterranean are giving comfort and encouragement to white racism, which is one of the most powerful and pernicious forces in the United States and the world today.

9 The British Utilitarians, Imperialism,

and the Fall of the Ancient Model

In this chapter, I attempt to tighten the connection between social forces in modern Europe and the shift among intellectuals from the Ancient model to the Aryan model. To do this, I look at the roles of some British Utilitarians in the historiography of Ancient Greece.[1] I barely mentioned the Utilitarian James Mill in BA I, and I offered only a few pages on George Grote, who wrote the most learned and influential history of Ancient Greece of the nineteenth century. I focused, rather, on social, intellectual, and educational developments in Germany and on the transmission of German Altertumswissenschaft as "Classics" to England in the 1830s and 1840s. I maintain that this emphasis was justified and that German Romanticism was the mainspring of both the Aryan model and Classics as we know them today. Nevertheless, in my eagerness to attack the late Arnaldo Momigliano's attempts to establish an Enlightenment as opposed to a Romantic pedigree for his discipline, I undoubtedly underplayed the indigenous British and "enlightened" forces behind the dismissal of non-European formative elements in Greek civilization. This chapter, which is an attempt to rectify that imbalance, focuses on two close friends who in many ways were two of the most progressive and enlightened figures of their times: James Mill and George Grote.

Part 1: James Mill (1773–1836)

Looked at from the twentieth century, James Mill's most famous product was his son, John Stuart. John Stuart Mill himself almost certainly shared this view. Nevertheless, James Mill had another major product, to which his son referred in the famous sentence near the beginning of his auto-biography: "I was born in London, on the 20th of May, 1806, and was the eldest son of James Mill, the author of the *History of British India*." [2]

In his biography of the younger Mill, Bruce Mazlish discusses this extraordinary, motherless trinity from the point of view of psychohistory. [3] Here, however, I am concerned with two of its more concrete aspects. The first of these is the centrality of the *History of British India* to James Mill's intellectual life, and the related fact that both he and his son became high officials of the East India Company. The second is the extraordinary attention that James Mill paid to the education of his eldest son and the fact that this education was centered on the learning of Greek, which started when he was three. Thus, by his eighth year, John Stuart Mill had read (in the original) Aesop's *Fables*, Xenophon's *Anabasis*, the whole of Herodotus, and "was acquainted with Lucian, Diogenes Laertius, Isocrates and six dialogues of Plato." [4] In this chapter, I attempt to relate James Mill's passions for Ancient Greece, social progress, and British imperialism.

James Mill's concern with Greece came earlier and remained more fundamental than his interest in India. Its origins are relatively easy to discern. Mill was born in the Mearns in eastern Scotland, which in the eighteenth century in many ways more resembled northern Germany than England. The cultural situation of Scotland, threatened with political and cultural absorption by England, paralleled that of Germany, where many thinkers saw their country as equally menaced by France and French culture (BA I: 204–207). In eastern Scotland, where the Reformation had been completely successful, there was acute awareness of the partially Catholic Highlanders above them. Hence, the parallel with Protestant North Germany threatened by Roman Catholics and Romance speakers was even closer.

Despite their economic and political weaknesses, Germany and Scotland both possessed strong school and university systems closely involved with both medicine and theology and geared to the production of doctors and ministers.[5] The Scottish system, unlike the English, allowed for considerable social mobility through education. The two English universities provided a polishing for gentlemen and emphasized the reading of ancient, mainly Latin, authors, and the writing of Latin and Greek verse, a useless qualification eminently suitable for marking status. This contrasted with the more "practical" education in Scotland.[6] Nevertheless, training for the ministry in Scotland had reasonably required Latin and New Testament Greek. Since the sixteenth century in Scotland, as elsewhere in Northern Europe, there had been what one might call an "alliance" among Protestantism, the Teutonic languages, and Greek against Roman Catholicism, the Romance languages, and Latin. Luther had used the Greek Testament to combat the Latin Vulgate and the Church of Rome (BA I: 193–194). As happened in Germany, the study of Greek declined in Scotland during the eighteenth century. But there were survivals. For instance, at Montrose Academy, where James Mill went to school, Greek seems to have been taught continuously since its introduction in the sixteenth century.[7] In the Scottish academies, Greek appears to have remained a prestigious subject suitable for outstanding students.

The poetry of Homer, generally admired by Protestants, was particularly central in eastern Scotland (BA I: 207–208). In the 1730s an Aberdonian, Thomas Blackwell, pioneered the notion that Homer was the poet or expression of the primitive age of Greece, which was, in turn, the childhood of Europe. Blackwell, like his successors Robert Wood and Friedrich August Wolf, also implied that Homer and his "folkish" culture were somehow "northern." It is also interesting to note that Blackwell was the teacher of James MacPherson, the creator of the fictitious third-century Scottish bard Ossian. In the later eighteenth century, MacPherson's "translations" of Ossian's poems were considered similar, though superior, to the works of Homer. Ossian's epics epitomized the Romantic cult of the cold and mountainous north, which could draw on the tradition going back to Aristotle, Tacitus, and Machiavelli that such environments produced "virtuous" and free peoples. Furthermore, among Protestants and Deists there was a natural association of Roman Catholicism with tyranny and of their own beliefs with freedom. Thus, there was a widespread desire among Romantics in general, and Scots in particular, to see early Greece—like Scotland—as free, poor, and pure. These Romantic views were also associated with a predisposition to see the arts, if not the sciences, as having derived from such temperate or cool geographical environments (BA I: 216–20). Thus, there was a natural propensity in eighteenth-century eastern Scotland to deny the conventional beliefs of the time that Greek civilization had come from the Middle East. The young Adam Smith from Kirkaldy in Fife, wrestling with these distasteful notions in the 1740s, wrote in his "Essay on the History of Astronomy":

> It was . . . in them [Greece and the Grecian colonies], that the first philosophers of whose doctrine we have any distinct account, appeared. Law and order seem indeed to have been established in the great monarchies of Asia and Egypt, long before they had any footing in Greece: Yet, after all that has been said concerning the learning of the Chaldeans and Egyptians, whether there ever was in those nations anything which deserved the name of science, or whether that despotism which is more destructive of security and leisure than anarchy itself, and which prevailed over all the East, prevented the growth of philosophy, is a question which, for want of monuments cannot be determined with any degree of precision.[8]

In the 1760s William Duff, who, like Blackwell, came from Aberdeen, wrote along the same lines, "In Greece the sciences made rapid progress and reached a very high degree of improvement . . . if the Egyptians were the inventors, this proves them to have been ingenious, but the Greeks have showed themselves to possess superior genius . . . arts and sciences have been known to the Chinese for many ages yet they have not. . . ."[9]

James Mill's career shows the possibilities of upward mobility in Scotland. The son of a cobbler, driven on by an ambitious mother and helped by scholarships for training for the ministry, he was able not merely to attend Montrose Academy but also to go to university. In the eighteenth century, four universities—Aberdeen, St. Andrews, Edinburgh, and Glasgow—were within a hundred miles of Mill's native village, while Oxford and Cambridge served the whole of England. Mill's social mobility or, seen from another point of view, his incorporation into the British establishment would have been impossible in England. Leslie Stephen, the editor of the (British) Dictionary of National Biography and father of Virginia Woolf, made an interesting comparison between Mill and his friend, the equally able Francis Place. Place was blocked by the inaccessibility of English education and was never accepted as a gentleman. Thus, where Mill became a reformer from within the establishment, Place as a radical attacked it powerfully from the outside.[10]

Thanks to the patronage of a local landowner, Sir John Stuart, in 1790 Mill went to Edinburgh University, then at its prime as a center of the Scottish Enlightenment. His selection of academic courses appears rather strange for the future Utilitarian. His biographer, the logician Alexander Bain, was puzzled that he failed to take courses in mathematics.[11] What Mill did study was Greek, for which he took every possible course. From the records of the library we know that "he made a dead set at Plato" and read massively from his works.[12] H. O. Pappé has shown that Mill's love of Plato, which he imparted to his son, established a British Platonism long before Benjamin Jowett introduced the new German Platonism to Oxford after 1870.[13] Mill passed the rigorous tests for the Scottish ministry, but his sermons being incomprehensible, he failed to find a living, and in 1802 he left for London to become a "man of letters."

There, to make ends meet, Mill had to take on extraordinary quantities of writing and editorial work on a huge range of subjects. Much of this work provided bases for his Utilitarianism after 1808, when he became a disciple of Jeremy Bentham. Among these was an interesting attack on the image of Plato presented by Thomas Taylor.

THOMAS TAYLOR (1758–1835)

Thomas Taylor, a brilliant autodidact, came to Plato by the interesting route of natural science, mathematics, and Aristotle.[14] He became fascinated by Neoplatonism and Hermeticism and read Plato according to these traditions. Becoming full of this idealism and mysticism himself, he rejected Christianity as a vulgar superstition of the masses and declared himself to be a Platonist, a member of the elite dedicated to "the Sacred Majesty of Truth." Before the French Revolution, Taylor's free thinking allied him to such political and sexual radicals of the time as Mary Wollstonecraft and the "Pythagorean" Marquis de Valady.[15] Taylor, however, was a more consistent Platonist than the latter. He argued against democracy and, as he grew older, became increasingly conservative in the general reaction against the French Revolution. Thus, although he remained a passionate Platonist and a prodigious translator of Plato, Aristotle, and the Neoplatonists, his challenge to the status quo was, if anything, from the right. It is possibly because of this that the reaction to his work was rather different from the response to his older contemporary, the Frenchman Charles

François Dupuis. Both men interpreted mythology as allegory and both saw Greek mythology and philosophy as deriving very closely from Egypt. As Taylor put it:

> That sublime wisdom which first arose in the colleges of the Egyptian priests, and flourished afterwards in Greece. Which was there cultivated by Pythagoras, under the mysterious veil of numbers; by Plato, in the graceful dress of poetry; and was systematized by Aristotle, as far as it could be reduced into scientific order. Which, after becoming in a manner extinct, shone again with its pristine splendor, among the philosophers of the Alexandrian school; was learnedly illustrated, with Asiatic luxuriancy of style by Proclus; was divinely explained by Iamblichus; and profoundly delivered in the writings of Plotinus.[16]

Dupuis, a brilliant scientist who invented semaphor, was concerned with science, not philosophy. He decoded the classical myths, which he took to be Egypto-Greek, to find their astronomical bases. More threateningly than Taylor, Dupuis combined his contempt for Christianity with political radicalism. He was director of cultural affairs under the Directory from 1795 to 1799 and became president of the legislative body under the Consulate that followed. Thus, Dupuis seems to have represented a cultural and theological aspect to the political and military threat of the French Revolution and Napoleon. As such, he seems to have inspired a terror among the politically and religiously orthodox during the years of reaction after 1815 (BA I: 250–251). The historian of science Giorgio de Santillana has suggested that this and his discomforting emphasis on Egypt are the reasons why Dupuis is so little known today.[17] Taylor too was cast into oblivion except among the mid-nineteenth-century American Transcendentalists.[18]

Even though Taylor was a powerless eccentric, Mill thought it worthwhile to devote two articles to attacking him. Mill's animus came from the fact that Taylor had produced the only contemporary translation of Plato into English. The first of the articles appeared in 1804 in Mill's own *Literary Journal*. The second was published in 1809 in the *Edinburgh Review*.[19] The English poet and historian Kathleen Raine, who read the second article without identifying its author, saw the controversy as one between eighteenth-century Augustans and nineteenth-century Utilitarian materialists on the one hand and Romantic Hellenists on the other.[20] This dichotomy is thoroughly misleading, and in fact the opposition between Romanticism and the Enlightenment, always imprecise, breaks down completely at this point. It is true that eighteenth-century Augustans were very wary of the Greeks. It is also the case that the pagan Taylor had declared war on "the inductive philosophy of Modern times," and Mill, then under the influence of the Christian champion of common sense and induction Thomas Reid, felt obliged to defend inductive reasoning.[21] Furthermore, William Blake—to the extent he can be considered a Romantic—was profoundly influenced by Taylor.[22] Percy Bysshe Shelley and Samuel Taylor Coleridge too were impressed by the Neoplatonists as presented by Taylor.

The fact that Taylor influenced Romantics and Philhellenes does not make him either. There are many reasons why it is difficult to categorize Taylor as a Romantic. First, he stayed firmly in the hermetic and Masonic traditions in his suspicion of language. He argued that language can conceal truths as well as reveal them and "that words, indeed, are in no otherwise valuable than as subservient to things."[23] Like the hermeticists and Masons, Taylor was much more concerned with consciously constructed allegories and visual symbols than he was with the unconscious expressions of language and song, so loved by the Romantics. Second, dealing in absolute and universal truth, Taylor completely lacked the Romantic geographic determinism and love of local peculiarity and ethnicity. The nineteenth-century Romantic image of Greece, as epitomized by Shelley in his *Hellas*, was as the pure source of European culture. This was far from the cosmopolitan view of the Neoplatonic Taylor but close to that of James Mill.

If Raine's classification of the two sides as Augustans and Utilitarians against Romantic Philhellenes breaks down, why did Mill need to attack Taylor so violently? Raine pinpoints a major difference between Taylor and Mill: the dichotomy between Mill's common sense and practicality and Taylor's idealist mysticism. Another distinction between the two was that between the traditional view (maintained by Taylor) of Greece as the preserver and transmitter of Ancient Egyptian and Oriental wisdom and the new Eurocentric image (proposed by Shelley and Mill) of Greece as the pure self-created childhood of Europe from which sprang all of the continent's art and philosophy (BA I: 281–307).

Thus, the chief flaw in Raine's classification lies in her interpretation of the nineteenth-century Utilitarians. Bentham was a man of the eighteenth century, intellectually formed by Locke, Hume, and other modern writers, unable to read Greek and skeptical about the Ancient Greeks. By contrast, his chief exponent in the early nineteenth century, Mill, was a passionate Philhellene, as was his best-known disciple George Grote.[24]

In fact, one of Mill's main charges against Taylor was that he had revived the contamination and "Orientalizing" of the Hellenic Plato by the decadent Alexandrian Neoplatonists: "Those men were in fact the *charlatans* of antient philosophy; and we have nothing in modern times to compare either with the phrensy of their writings, or the infamy of their lives. A gross mixture of the allegorical genius of Oriental theology, with the quibbling genius of the worst kind of Grecian metaphysics."[25] Mill accused Taylor of following the Hermetic tradition of Massilio Ficino, the fifteenth-century reviver of Neoplatonism and Ficino's Latin translation, rather than reading Plato in the original.[26] This was a weapon in his struggle to show that Taylor did not know Greek. The well trained Mill scored a number of technical—but not very important—points against the autodidact Taylor, who outraged the Romantic professionals in a number of ways, the most notorious of which was his complete neglect of Greek accent.[27] This neglect was obviously linked to his concern with the "truths" revealed and concealed by language rather than the medium itself. He made his priorities clear in a statement about himself, according to which he "ha[d] often been heard to say, that he learned Greek rather through the Greek philosophy, than the Greek philosophy through Greek."[28]

MILL AND PLATO

In his attacks on Taylor and his efforts to detach a purely Hellenic Plato from the "Oriental" Neoplatonists, Mill was attempting something quite new in Britain—although Schleiermacher, following the Neo-Hellenist and Romantic traditions established by the end of the eighteenth century, was doing the same in Germany.[29] In the middle of the eighteenth century, scholars such as Bishop William Warburton and the historian of philosophy Jacob Brucker and thinkers such as the historian and statesman Anne-Robert Turgot had all placed Plato among the late, decadent Egyptians, and not with the modern philosophers, who, according to them, began with Francis Bacon or the latter's projection into the past, Aristotle (BA I: 197–200). Well into the nineteenth century, Plato was widely seen as a seductive poet rather than a philosopher (BA I: 475 n. 35). Mill's "Utilitarian" Plato was not at all like this:

> [His] business is to give specimens of investigation, to let in rays of light, to analyze particular points, and, by throwing out queries or hypotheses, to encourage speculation, rather than lay down and establish any system of opinions. . . . nothing under heaven can be more different, both as to matter

and manner, than the writings of Plato and those of the *soi disant* Platonists. The business of the Platonists is all in supernaturals; of Plato, as far as we have yet gone, is all in moral or political, or at most metaphysical subjects. The language of the one is as wild, and mystical, and obscure, as their ideas; that of the other is always elegant, often highly figurative; and eloquent; and unless when he is puzzling himself with abortive attempts to explain the nature of abstract ideas, highly clear and appropriate.[30]

This view, which still predominates, obviously has a good deal of evidence to back it.[31] But as a pioneer, Mill had to face problems that many of his successors have been able to avoid. Mill had to qualify, as we can see above, the mysteriousness of Plato's writing. He also had to confess that "there are a few [of his writings] which are to be regarded, in some sort as *jeux d'esprit*, and in which the principal object of the writer seems to have been, to afford a specimen or a display of his genius." [32] Mill portrayed other writings of Plato that he disliked merely as statements the philosopher had "thrown out in a manner between jest and earnest . . . he did not regard them in a serious light." [33]

Mill's bête noire was the *Timaeus*, which had been the primary text read by the Alexandrian and later Neoplatonists. Interestingly, Friedrich Schleiermacher did not publish *Timaius* or *Kritias* in his otherwise complete translation of the Platonic dialogues.[34] Mill tried to deal with this dialogue in the following way:

It was not merely the orators whom Plato was ambitious of rivaling; he desired to contend too with the philosophers, at their own weapons. As explanations of the origin and economy of the universe was that on which the Sophists chiefly plumed themselves, and which was often, indeed, most available to their reputation, Plato seems to have been desirous of showing them how easy even here, it would be to excel them. Accordingly, in the Timæus, he puts into the mouth of a philosopher of that name a discourse, in which a cosmogony, far more ingenious than any before invented by the philosophers, is laid down. But it is merely presented as a mode, according to which any one may conceive that the universe originated and was composed; not as a delineation on which any one is called upon to rely as a relation of the fact. It is accordingly not presented to us in the person of Socrates, in which form, any thing that Plato designed should be considered as an opinion of his own, is always given; but in that of Timæus, a philosopher of a different country, and a different school. This discourse, however, afforded a plausible, and an unlucky plea for the Alexandrian sages to claim the illustrious Grecian for the founder of that wild plan of mystic conjecture which they pursued in the name of philosophy.[35]

It was at this stage, and in this atmosphere, that the cardinal Platonic text changed from the metaphysical *Timaeus* to the—mainly—political *Republic*.

THE MILLS AND INDIA

This chapter is, however, concerned with a particular aspect of Mill's attempts to whitewash Plato: that is, his efforts to extricate a rational European philosopher from what he saw as his wild and irrational Egyptian and Asiatic followers. While Schleiermacher seems to have been Europeanizing Plato to purge Christianity of its Oriental and Semitic elements (BA I: 321, 48), Mill was pushing back from Aristotle to establish Plato and Socrates as the European founders of philosophy.[36] As I try to show below, Mill saw an exclusive and unbreakable link between Europe and reason.

This leads us to Mill's concern with India, which was to dominate his life and that of his son. The economic reasons for his wanting to write some "permanent works" are quite plain. Friends of his had secured adequate incomes with such works and, when his first son, John Stuart—named after his patron—was born in 1806, this problem became acute for him.[37] In the event, James Mill's *History of British India* brilliantly secured his career, but we do not know whether his choice was crudely calculating. It is difficult to believe that he did not have some specific interest in the subject. In his introduction to the project Mill stated convincingly that he saw an absence and hence the need for a single book containing "the material part of the requisite information" on India.[38] But what led him to the subject in the first place? Clearly, what attracted him was not India itself but the British activities on the subcontinent. In this regard it is interesting to note that in May 1804 his *Literary Journal* contained a review of two volumes entitled *Indian Recreations . . .* by William Tennant, a chaplain who had spent many years in India. Both the author and the reviewer were thoroughly disparaging about Indians, who, according to them, "had no history" and for whom British rule was a liberation.[39] The newly established dogma, that only Europeans were capable of having "histories," alone necessitated Mill's title *History of British India*. The reviewer praised Tennant's attitude and the mass of information the volumes contained, but he complained of their disorganization in very much the same way that Mill was to complain in the introduction to his *History* that "what was useful lay embedded in a large mass of what was trifling and insignificant." [40] Mill almost certainly read (and probably wrote the review of) Tennant. This is not only because he edited the *Literary Journal* but because it contained a passage describing the Indian *Jangernauts*, religious pilgrimages and festivals at which the natives "consume their time in idle and expensive ceremonies." [41] The term "jug," derived from Juggernaut, became the Utilitarians' standard contemptuous term for Christianity and religion in general. Indeed, their religiosity was yet another reason why Mill, who lost his faith soon after meeting Bentham in 1808, despised Indians in general and Hindus in particular.

Mill's interest, however, was chiefly in the importance of India to Britain's commerce. In 1807 he wrote a long tract with the resounding title *Commerce Defended: An Answer to the Arguments by which Mr. Spence, Mr. Cobbet, and others, have attempted to prove that Commerce is not a Source of National Wealth.*[42] For Mill, as for imperialists for the next 140 years, India was seen as an indispensable support for British wealth and progress.

Mill had anticipated taking three years to write his history; it took him twelve. The ten volumes finally appeared in 1818. Pinpointing exactly when any section of the work was started or completed is, thus, very difficult. However, the outline of the ideas set forth in his preface probably existed from the beginning, that is to say, about the time he was attacking Taylor and before he became a friend and disciple of Bentham in 1808.

From the outset, Mill made it clear that he believed the historian should be a "judge" — *kritēs* in Greek — and that his was going to be a "critical history." He would "discriminate between real causes and false causes; real effects and false effects." [43] Although this approach was not old, Mill was here following a line established by Gibbon. Also, in the decades before Mill was writing, German scholars, particularly from Göttingen, were developing *Quellenkritik*, which has been outlined elsewhere in this volume.[44] In both Germany and Britain it was used almost exclusively to dismiss evidence that could be construed as diminishing European civilization or favoring that of other continents.[45] We shall soon see how clearly this was the case in Mill's *History*.

The next point Mill made in his preface was an attempt to preempt an objection he foresaw: "This writer, it will be said, has never been in India; and, if he has any, has a very slight and elementary acquaintance with any of the languages of the East." [46] He had a plausible defense: many good historians from Tacitus on had not known the languages of the countries with which they were concerned. However, Mill went on to write: "The mental habits which are acquired in mere observing, and in the acquisition of languages, are almost as different as any mental habits can be, from the powers of combination, discrimination, classification, judgement, comparison, weighing, inferring, inducting, philosophizing in short: which are the powers of most importance for extracting the precious ore from a great mine of rude historical materials."[47] In this context it is interesting to recall the great play Mill made of Taylor's linguistic incompetence when Mill attacked him. Mill's argument against going to the country concerned was more straightforwardly ideological:

> I will not go so far as to deny, that a man would possess advantages, who, to all the qualifications for writing a history of India which it is possible to acquire in Europe, should add those qualifications which can be acquired only by seeing the country and conversing with its people. Yet I have no doubt of being able to make out, to the satisfaction of all reflecting minds, that the man who should bring to the composition of a history of India, *the qualifications alone which can be acquired in Europe*, would come, in an almost infinite degree, better fitted for the task, than the man who should bring to it the qualifications alone which can be acquired in India; and that the business of acquiring the one set of qualifications is almost wholly incompatible with that of acquiring the other [my emphasis].[48]

Having made clear that reason was the unique possession of Europe and that critical thinking could take place only on that continent, Mill went on to state that a case like that of the history of India, which covers so much time and space, must necessarily rely on secondary sources, and nearly all of these were reports on India by Europeans. The "best man" (Mill, unlike his son but like most of his contemporaries, did not consider the possibility of a woman historian) to sift the variegated evidence from India was the historian in Europe, who was impartial, like a judge, precisely because he had never visited the subcontinent.[49] The idea that a European or British vantage point could skew the vision was not raised. He did not consider the possibility that belonging to the conquerors might make him partial. For him as for many others, then and now, the upper classes of northern Europe were the universal men.

Not surprisingly, Mill had an unfavorable view of Hindu "civilization." According to him, the Hindus' government was "despotic"; their law, always inferior, had degenerated; their customs were "degraded"; and their religion "detestable." They had no philosophy worthy of the name and, though extremely cruel, their military skills were negligible. Their medicine was primitive and their so-called arts produced only trinkets. Above all, they had none of that mysterious substance "history," only a succession of events. In the eyes of most nineteenth- and many twentieth-century thinkers, this unique possession placed Europe on a categorically higher level than that of other continents.[50]

Many nineteenth-century writers, including Karl Marx, saw such overall inferiority as an indication that on the scale of world history non-European cultures were simply less advanced than Europe itself. At times, Mill toyed with this idea, though he saw the danger of its application: "It is to be lamented that philosophers have not as yet laid down any very distinct canons for ascertaining the principal stages of civilization. . . . All they do, is to fix on one or two of the principal nations of Europe as at the highest point of civilization; and wherever, in any country, a few of the first appearances strike them as bearing a resemblance to some of the most obvious appearances in these standards of comparison, such countries are at once held to be civilized."[51] In the *History of British India*, however, Mill denied the principle altogether:

> Should we say that the civilization of the people of Hindustan, and that of the people of Europe, during the feudal ages, are not far from equal, we shall find upon a close inspection, that the Europeans were superior, in the first place, notwithstanding the vices of the papacy in religion; and notwithstanding the defects of the schoolmen in philosophy. . . . In point of manners and character, the manliness and courage of our ancestors, compared with the slavish and dastardly spirit of the Hindus, place them in an elevated rank. But they were inferior to that effeminate people in gentleness, and the winning arts of address. Our ancestors, however, though rough were sincere.[52]

This quotation raises a theme that goes back to Cleopatra and her literary reflex, Virgil's Dido in the first century B.C.E., and which became standard in the nineteenth and twentieth centuries. It was that Europe or the Aryans were essentially "male," and that their absolute dominance over lesser eastern and southern "female" races was as "natural" as men's dominance over women.

Mill was not prejudiced exclusively against India; according to him, they were merely typical Asiatics: "This gives a peculiar interest and importance to the inquiry respecting the Hindus. There can be no doubt that they are in a state of civilization very nearly the same with that of the Chinese, the Persians, and the Arabians."[53]

Mill devoted a number of pages to recent Western reports on the evils of

Chinese government and society. In fact, these reports were the forerunners of the wave of Sinophobia that by 1840 had swept away the extremely positive attitudes toward China held by the enlightened in the seventeenth and eighteenth centuries.[54] Mill is scathing about previous praise of China:

> In these conclusions, *distance* appears to have been an agent of great potency and the title to civilization has always been admitted on slighter grounds to those who were farthest removed from us. The Turks for example, we have always denominated barbarians. The Hindus and Chinese we have regarded as civilized; and for that civilization [the Chinese], many of us have contended and continue to contend. . . . A critical examination of the state of these people demonstrates, that, in every particular . . . the Turks are their superiors.[55]

MILL'S ATTACK ON SIR WILLIAM JONES (1746–1794)

China, however, was not a major problem for Mill's scheme because he was able to cite recent, much more hostile material about that country.[56] On India itself, however, he had more difficulties. These did not come from the huge enthusiasm for India and Sanskrit that was raging in Germany at the time, from which Indo-European linguistics and the concept of "Aryan" both emerged (BA I: 227–234). Mill, like nearly every Briton of his generation, did not read German and never cited German sources. He was concerned with the Germans' inspiration, Sir William Jones, the founder of modern Indian studies who had once and for all established the close relationship between Sanskrit and Greek and Latin. According to Mill, Jones was hopelessly infatuated with all the nations of the East. Mill gave the following example: "So crude were his ideas on the subject, that the rhapsodies of Rousseau, on the virtue and happiness of the savage life, surpass not the panegyrics of Sir William on the wild, comfortless, predatory, and ferocious state of the wandering Arabs. . . . We need not wonder if the man who wrote . . . this, found the Hindus arrived at the highest civilization.[57]

Jones was not, in fact, an uncritical admirer of Asia, and as a judge employed by his government, he did all he could to promote British power in the East. He had no doubts about the innate superiority of Europeans over Asians:

> Whoever travels in *Asia*, especially if he be conversant with the literature of the countries through which he passes, must naturally remark on the superi-

ority of *European* talents: the observation, indeed is at least as old as Alexander; and, though we can not agree with the sage preceptor of that ambitious prince [Aristotle], "the *Asiatics* are born to be slaves," yet the *Athenian* poet seems perfectly in the right, when he represents *Europe* as a *Sovereign Princess,* and *Asia* as *her Handmaid:* but, if the mistress be transcendently majestick, it cannot be denied that the attendant has many beauties, and some advantages peculiar to herself . . . although we must be conscious of our superior advancement in all kinds of useful knowledge, yet we ought not therefore to contemn the people of Asia, from whose researches into nature, works of art and inventions of fancy, many valuable hints may be derived for our own improvement and advantage.[58]

Even such qualified admiration for Indians and other Asians was intolerable to Mill and nineteenth-century imperialism. Though Mill never stated it, Jones was also inconvenient to him because Jones combined a stay in India and knowledge of Indian languages with what, for the cultivated world of the day, passed for critical judgment. Mill had two ways with which to overthrow Jones. One was apparently trivial:

The nations of Europe became acquainted nearly about the same period, with the people of America and the people of Hindustan. . . . The Hindus were compared with the savages of America [in a footnote, he attacks early reports of the high level of the Mexican civilization]; the circumstances in which they differed from that barbarous people, were the circumstances in which they corresponded with the most cultivated nations; other circumstances were overlooked; and it seems to have been little suspected that conclusions too favourable could possibly be drawn.[59]

Mill made a more interesting point when he relegated Jones to a qualitatively past age: "Notwithstanding all that modern philosophy had performed for the elucidation of history, very little had been attempted in this great department at the time when the notions of Sir William Jones were formed."[60]

Jones was born only twenty-seven years before Mill, but he died in his forties in 1794. Thus, Mill is right to see a qualitative break, or what Michel Foucault saw as a *coupure,* at this point. The French Revolution and the reactions to it had transformed not only the sentiments but the thinking of northern Europe. A return to Christianity and the Romantic promotion of the image of young, dynamic Europe overthrowing old, stagnant Asia were included among these new sentiments. These, in turn, were linked to increasing support for colonial expansion. Mill neatly combined the ideological with the political and economic transformations.

It is difficult not to see a connection between Mill's harsh attitude toward Asia and its European sympathizers and his success in the East India Company. As Leslie Stephen put it, Mill's History "produced a remarkable change in Mill's position." [61] In 1819, within a year of the book's publication, he received an important position in the company, and by 1830 he was appointed the Examiner of India Correspondence, the second-highest position in the company. This impressive rise is all the more extraordinary for a leader of the atheist Utilitarians with outspoken advanced and radical opinions on most of the political issues of the time. His successful career can only indicate that apart from his great abilities and extraordinary capacity for hard work he was considered "sound" on India and the company's policies there.

Mill's History remained the standard work on the subject through much of the nineteenth century, and its consistent denigration of Indian culture played an important role in justifying the Company's ruthless exploitation of the subcontinent. An indication of this comes from Horace Hayman Wilson, who brought out the third edition of Mill's work in 1840. Wilson combined being a distinguished scientist with a career as a Sanskritist. Unlike Mill, he had a great deal of firsthand experience of India and was a fervent admirer of Sir William Jones. Wilson's footnotes to the History of British India devastatingly expose the crude superficiality and inaccuracy of most of Mill's attacks on Indian culture. In his preface Wilson wrote:

> Considered merely in a literary capacity, the description of the Hindus in the History of British India, is open to censure for its obvious unfairness and injustice; but in the effects that it is likely to exercise upon the connexion between the people of India, it is chargeable with more than literary demerit: its tendency is evil; it is calculated to destroy all sympathy between rulers and the ruled; to preoccupy the minds of those who issue annually from Great Britain, to monopolize the posts of honour and power in Hindustan, with an unfounded aversion towards those over whom they excercize that power . . . and to substitute for those generous and benevolent feelings, which the situation of the younger servants of the Company in India naturally suggests, sentiments of disdain, suspicion and dislike, uncongenial to their age and character, and wholly incompatible with the full and faithful discharge of their obligations to the Government and to the people. There is reason to fear that these consequences are not imaginary, and that a harsh and illiberal spirit has of late years prevailed in the conduct and councils of

the rising service in India, which owes its origin to impressions imbibed in early life from the History of Mr. Mill.[62]

Today few historians would place so much significance on the effects of a single work, even if it was required reading for the company's trainees. Nevertheless, Mill's attitudes were undoubtedly congenial to the East India Company, and they helped provide ideological justification for its most exploitative phase, from 1820 to the "Indian Mutiny" of 1857, provoked by the company's exploitation and cultural insensitivity. The "Mutiny" in turn led to the company's liquidation—against the strenuous opposition of John Stuart Mill—in the interests of direct as opposed to corporate imperialism.[63]

Neither of the Mills saw any contradiction between their liberalism or radicalism in Western Europe and their devotion to imperialism in the East. Europe represented freedom, civilization, and progress, whereas Asia was opposite in every respect. James Mill ended the second book of his History with an approving reference to the passage from Adam Smith cited above: "The opinion by which he [Smith] supports his disbelief of the ancient civilization of Asia is at once philanthropic and profound; That 'despotism is more destructive of leisure and security, and more adverse to the progress of the human mind, than anarchy itself.'"[64] Such ideas were in the European air. For instance, the ancient historian Barthold Niebuhr is reported to have said in the 1820s: "European dominion naturally supports science and literature, together with the rights of humanity, and to prevent the destruction of a barbarous power would be an act of high treason against intellectual culture and humanity."[65]

Mill appears to have felt similarly about Sir William Jones and Jones's fellow sympathizers with Asian "civilizations." In his eyes, they were traitors to Europe, freedom, and progress, in a way remarkably similar to the Neoplatonists, whom he saw as having corrupted Greece with Eastern influences and their absurd praise of the Orient. Mill was quite explicit about the parallel: "The admiration which the Greeks, no very accurate observers of foreign manners, expressed of the Egyptians, and which other nations have so implicitly borrowed at their hands, not a little resembles the admiration among Europeans which has so long prevailed with regard to the Hindus."[66]

Mill's view repeats a paradox, still heard today, that the peoples who had achieved the highest civilizations—the Ancient Greeks and the modern Europeans—should not be trusted in their observations of other nations.

Fortunately, Mill and his contemporaries could transcend this "error." He continued: "The penetrating force of modern intelligence has pierced the cloud: and while it has displayed to us the state of Egyptian civilization in its true colours, exhibits a people who, standing on a level with so many celebrated nations of antiquity . . . correspond, in all the distinctive marks of a particular state of society, with the people of Hindustan."[67]

For Mill, what he saw as Europe's monopoly of civilization was clearly related to the necessity for Plato and Greek culture as a whole to have been uncontaminated by Oriental influences. Mill's attack on Thomas Taylor and his desire for a purely Hellenic Plato is congruent with his justification of European colonization, and the fact that this radical in British politics devoted the later part of his life to the East India Company.

Part 2: George Grote (1794–1871)

George Grote came from a rich banking family. He was sent to Charterhouse, which had become the chief public school for the London upper-middle class. By 1800, Charterhouse had a very high level of Greek studies, though not of the new style which came in later in the century with the German Altertumswissenschaft. Greek studies in England at this time showed the traditional lack of concern with history or philosophy but emphasized composition, which provided the clearest status marker. This was particularly important in a school of this marginal class, close in wealth to but far in status from the aristocracy. Classical studies provided one of the very few avenues to the top of British society. In any event, it is striking that Charterhouse of the first decades of the nineteenth century produced not only Grote but Connop Thirlwall, the other great English historian of Greece, and H. G. Liddell, the famous lexicographer who compiled Liddell and Scott's *Greek-English Lexicon*, which is still standard today. (Liddell was also the father of Alice, the inspiration for Lewis Carroll's *Alice in Wonderland*.)

Thirlwall and other contemporaries went on to Oxbridge and the Church and became respectable reformers working within the establishment (BA I: 320–323). To his enormous intellectual benefit, Grote was saved from this by his father, who made him go straight into the bank. George Grote read widely in Classics, history, and modern political economy and, what was very rare for someone of his generation, he learned German.[68] In 1819 he met James Mill. The meeting was, as Grote's biographer puts it, "momentous for Grote's further development . . . he fell completely under Mill's spell and became his most thoroughgoing and loyal pupil."[69] From then on, Grote was at the heart of the Utilitarian and radical movement pushing for electoral reform and the establishment of London University, which he insisted was to be free of Christian religious superstition. After the first Reform Bill in 1832, he became a member of Parliament while carrying on his work at the bank. He loved France and became a friend and supporter of Auguste Comte and helped promote the latter's positivism in England.

Today, however, Grote is remembered less for these activities and achievements than as a great historian of Greece. The earliest traces of Grote's interest in Greek history came in 1815, although the idea of writing a history of Greece seems to have emerged only in 1823.[70] His brilliant but not altogether reliable wife, Harriet Grote, claimed credit for the idea.[71] On the other hand, as Grote's biographer pointed out, "It is probably true to say that Grote found his main inspiration in the circle of James Mill and that the historian of British India was more his master than the historian of Republican Rome [Bartholdt Niebuhr, for whom see below]."[72]

Grote's first publication on Greek history, which came in 1826, was a review of a minor work in the *Westminster Review*. He used this as the pretext for an all-out onslaught on William Mitford's *The History of Greece*, which had dominated the field since its publication between 1784 and 1804. The power and eloquence of Grote's radical attack on Mitford's conservatism and fetish of royalty can be seen as a precursor to his own *History of Greece*, which started to appear in 1846. This has been well described and analyzed by Arnaldo Momigliano and Frank Turner.[73] I should like, however, to underline the explicitness of Grote's awareness that his quarrel with Mitford was simultaneously scholarly and political. As he concluded his article in 1826:

> And should Grecian history ever be re-written with care and fidelity, we venture to predict that Mr. Mitford's reputation . . . will be prodigiously lowered. That it should have remained so long exalted, is a striking proof how much more apparent than real is the attention paid to Greek literature in this country. . . . It is not surprising, indeed, that the general views of Mr. Mitford should be eminently agreeable to the reigning interests in England; nor that instructors devoted to those interests should carefully discourage those mental qualities which might enable their pupils to look into evidence for themselves.[74]

The outline of Grote's political case was already clearly worked out by 1826. He took it as self-evident, as did all progressives of the time, that there had been a "Greek miracle" (BA I: 209–233, 281–292) — something not at all evident to Mitford and his contemporaries (BA I: 173–188).[75] Grote also believed that this extraordinary phenomenon needed rational explanation, and he attributed it to the excellent mixed and democratic institutions of Ancient Greece as a whole and Athens in particular. The small scale of Greek states in turn caused by the broken geography of Greece allowed these institutions to emerge.[76] He emphasized his indebtedness to the historical approach of Barthold Niebuhr, whose name was one to conjure with in advanced circles of the time (BA I: 320–321). No doubt Grote was influenced by the institutional approach to history developed in the late eighteenth century at Göttingen and epitomized later by Niebuhr, but it is difficult to distinguish this from the institutional and economic approaches of the Scottish Enlightenment and the Utilitarians. Grote's biographer, Martin Lowther Clarke, is convincing when he claims that the British modes of thought were the major influences on Grote.[77]

Niebuhr's skepticism and Grote's requirement of proof are strikingly similar. Momigliano, however, convincingly derived Grote's principle from the Utilitarians' concern with jurisprudence and the careful examination of evidence: "His [Grote's] voice became particularly solemn when he spoke of the 'law respecting sufficiency of evidence.'"[78]

Momigliano saw Niebuhr's time spent as a student in Edinburgh as a connection between the German new historians and later Utilitarians, including John Stuart Mill. Momigliano deduced a further connection in the person of George Lewis, the Victorian man of letters and long-time companion of George Eliot. Lewis combined, among many other things, translations from the German and publications on the influence of institutions and laws on society and national character.[79] Momigliano saw Lewis's central concern as "his passion for rigorous examination of evidence."[80] Grote's introduction to the first volume of his History bears Momigliano out on this. After referring respectfully to his schoolfellow Thirlwall's History, Grote then added:

> The liberal spirit of criticism, in which Dr. Thirlwall stands so much distinguished from Mitford, is his own: there are other features of superiority which belong to him conjointly with his age. For during the generation since Mitford's work, philological studies have been prosecuted in Germany with remarkable success: the stock of facts and documents, comparatively scanty, handed down from the ancient world, has been combined and illustrated in a thousand different ways. . . . Some of the best writers in this department —

Boekh, Niebuhr, O. Müller—have been translated into our language so that the English public has been enabled to form some idea of the new lights thrown upon many subjects of antiquity by the inestimable aid of German erudition. The poets, historians, orators and philosophers of Greece, have thus been all rendered both more intelligible and more instructive than they were to a student in the last century.

He ended on a smug note that did not jibe well with the caution toward the evidence that he advocated: "The general picture of the Greek world may now be conceived with a degree of fidelity, which considering our imperfect materials, it is curious to contemplate." [81]

I have discussed Karl Otfried Müller's attitude toward mythology in this book and elsewhere.[82] I shall come to its influence on Grote a little later. Meanwhile, I think it worth considering the possibility that Grote was using the new German scholarship to justify his radical departure from eighteenth-century historiography, a departure he had in fact made before he read any of this work, except possibly Niebuhr's *Römische Geschicht*. Even this is unlikely, as Niebuhr's Roman history is far too long and badly written for anyone other than Germans and Thirlwall to have read it in its entirety.

James Mill's views on the writing of history can be found in the preface to his *History of British India*. He maintains that history should be critical, that it should judge. . . . Thus the historian exercises his judgement in two respects; he judges the evidence and he judges the facts which he deduces from the evidence. In both of these respects Grote is a follower of Mill; he has a strict regard for evidence. . . . Judgement includes moral judgement, and Grote himself said that what he regarded as of special value in his historical work was "earnestness [note the key German and Victorian word, lampooned by Oscar Wilde] [83] of moral interest combined with the laborious study of the evidence." Like Mill again, Grote was not averse from giving . . . the reasons for his judgements, and like Mill he thought it no disadvantage not to have visited the country whose history he wrote. Finally, it was from Mill and his circle that he derived his lively democratic sympathies. Though his *History* as we have it belongs to the middle of the nineteenth century, we should not forget that the general conception and much of the detailed work date from the eighteen-twenties when the influence of James Mill was strong. Grote's *History* may justly be considered the most distinguished example of Benthamite historiography.[84]

GROTE AND GREEK MYTHOLOGY

There was one crucial area where Grote could draw on both the Göttingen and the Utilitarian schools of historiography. James Mill's distrust and dislike of Greek respect for Ancient Egypt was powerfully reinforced by K. O. Müller's treatment of myth to attack and destroy the Ancient model. Müller established the requirement of proof and shifted the onus of such proof from those who wanted to attack the Ancient model onto those who defended it. His conclusion was that there was no early evidence of Egyptian or Phoenician settlements in Greece and that the widespread attestation to these and to other Greek cultural borrowings from the Near East were concocted by later Orientalizers.[85] The boldness of Müller's approach can be seen in Thirlwall's remarks near the beginning of his *History*:

> In a comparatively late period—that which followed the rise of historical literature among the Greeks—we find a belief generally prevalent, both in the people and among the learned, that in ages of very remote antiquity, before the name and dominion of the Pelasgians had given way to that of the Hellenic race, foreigners had been led by various causes to the shores of Greece and there had planted colonies, founded dynasties, built cities, and introduced useful arts and social institutions, before unknown to the ruder natives. The same belief has been almost universally adopted by the learned of modern times. . . . *It required no little boldness to venture even to throw out a doubt as to the truth of an opinion sanctioned by such authority, and by prescription of such a long and undisputed possession of the public mind* [my emphasis].[86]

Müller first directly challenged the Ancient model in 1820 with the publication of *Orchomenos und die Minyer*, the first volume of his trilogy *Geschichte hellenischer Stämme und Städte*. This volume has never been translated into English, and Grote probably did not read it before writing his first article in 1826. Nevertheless, in a second review, published in the *Westminster Review* in 1843, Grote was writing entirely in the spirit of Müller:

> The increase of communication . . . familiarised the traveled man with legends for which he had acquired no early reverence . . . mystic rites, and expiatory ceremonies, such as the Orphic and Pythagorean, acquired footing: Egypt, with its ancient civilization and its many wonders and peculiarities, first became largely visited by curious Greeks in the sixth century before the

Christian era, and the effect which it produced upon their religious belief was evidently considerable; it not only displaced old legends and superadded new, but it seems also to have degraded their own native antiquities in their own eyes, and to have brought the Egyptian priests into higher estimation than their own poets. An influence of this kind pervades especially a large portion of the narrative of Herodotus.[87]

Momigliano maintained that, by making a sharp distinction between legendary and historical Greece, Grote "broke with K. O. Müller and his English admirers."[88] Müller, however, began his *Introduction to a Scientific System of Mythology* with the statement that there was "a tolerably distinct boundary between legend and history."[89] Both Müller and Grote followed Wolf in believing that writing had not existed in Greece before the eighth century B.C.E. and that there had been no priestly instruction, as there had been in the East. Thus, the links with earlier times were extremely tenuous.[90] Furthermore, Müller and Grote agreed that, though myth could contain historical elements, it was not useful to think of a nucleus of pure reality on which mythical elements had been imposed. Rather, they thought the two elements should be seen as having been integrated from the beginning.[91] Thus, here the distinction between Grote and the Romantic historians, like Thirlwall, who were directly influenced by the Germans does not seem to be as great as Momigliano supposed.

Grote, however, was unlike most of the German Romantics, who were concerned with Greece as the infancy of Europe. As a radical and not a conservative, he did not regret the passing of the mythopaeic age. Grote was interested in Homer and the early ages, but his passion was for the late and sudden flowering of democracy, particularly in Athens. As we have seen, his main concern was to refute Mitford's Tory skepticism about Greek democratic institutions.[92]

Momigliano argued that Grote was strictly neutral on the question of the historicity of Greek myths. He simply demanded "collateral evidence" before accepting them.[93] However, Grote's neutrality on this issue is in serious doubt, because the tone of his discussion of historicity of myths is skeptical, if not scoffing. He cited the late-eighteenth-century historian and mythographer Jacob Bryant with approval when he argued that it was impossible to take seriously the accounts of people who believed in centaurs, satyrs, nymphs, and horses that could speak.[94]

This argument seems plausible, but it should be remembered that every period has general beliefs that later ages consider absurd. I maintain that in this case, what we now consider to be the mistaken beliefs in centaurs and the rest are less misleading on the issues with which we are concerned, than are nineteenth-century myths on race, unchanging national characteristics, the productiveness of purity and the deleterious effects of racial mixture, and, above all, the semidivine status of the Greeks that made them transcend the laws of history and language. Thus, though we should be wary of the ancient reports, we should have a still greater suspicion of nineteenth- and early-twentieth-century interpretations of them. Later generations will certainly be equally shocked or condescending about our concerns and beliefs at the turn of the third millennium.

Momigliano claims that because of Grote's "neutrality," his views on mythology have not been invalidated by later archaeological discoveries that have confirmed legendary accounts.[95] This excuse does not apply if, as I maintain, his views were skeptical. Grote's skepticism, however, seems more justifiable than does that of his twentieth-century successors. Having been bitten over Troy, Mycenae, Knossos, and so on, one would expect contemporary ancient historians to give the benefit of the doubt at least to those traditions that were uncontested in antiquity. It would have seemed prudent, for instance, to have considered as working hypotheses the ideas that Boiotia had a special relationship with Phoenicia or that Sesōstris and Memnōn-Senwosret and Amenemḥet had made widespread expeditions around the Eastern Mediterranean in the twentieth century B.C.E. rather than denying them as absurd, only to be humiliated when archaeological or inscriptional evidence is found to strengthen them.[96]

To return to Müller's influence on Grote's ideas on mythology: there is no doubt that between 1826 and 1843 Grote had read Müller with approval. One reason for this approval was that neither scholar had any time for the pro-Indian passion of the Romantics of Heidelberg. (Such sentiments were, of course, anathema to the Mills.) Müller was interested in myths throughout the world, but as myths, not history. His skepticism about the historicity of myths was greatest when it came to traditions concerning Near Eastern settlements in or cultural influence on Greece. Grote too had a particular distaste for these myths, but his position was more consistent than Müller's. Grote's Comtean positivism allowed him to demand "proof" from ancient history with more consistency than could either Niebuhr or Müller with their frequent use of "inference." Grote specifically deplored what he saw as the "German license to conjecture."[97] As stated above, Grote's dislike of these particular legends and traditions can equally be associated with James Mill's hatred of Greek credulity about

Egyptian civilization and its influence on Greece, and Mill's parallels between this credulity and what he saw as contemporary overestimations of non-European "civilizations."

Grote was closer to his British traditions in his lack of explicitness about "race" or the "ethnic principle of history." Niebuhr pioneered these concepts and they were taken up with enthusiasm by his English popularizers, the historians Dr. Thomas Arnold and H. H. Vaughan and the novelists Charles Kingsley and Benjamin Disraeli (*BA* I: 303–305). Unlike Niebuhr or James Mill, Grote was not consistently in favor of European expansion. In particular, he led opposition to Britain's joining with Austria and Russia in checking Mohamed Ali's Egyptian empire in 1840, though his motives in this seem to have been essentially pro-French and anti-Turkish.[98] Implicitly, however, the belief in the categorical cultural superiority of Europe over Asia and Africa was as clear in George Grote as it had been in James Mill.

Grote made a sharp distinction in his *History* between the purely Hellenic Greece and "later" Asiatic and Egyptian influences on the Hellenistic world. Furthermore, he shared the prevailing Romantic preference for northern or Alpine small communities over the decadent, large, and wealthy societies of warmer climates. He wanted to place Ancient Greece in the former category. Grote's admiration for the Greek polis seems in many ways similar to that of Rousseau. Indeed, as Momigliano pointed out, Grote had a "sympathy for small states . . . [which] led him later to make a close study of the politics of Switzerland."[99]

Conclusion

Robert Fenn, who has written on James Mill's political thought, points out what he sees as the "treacherousness" of Mill's position. Fenn sees a contradiction between the elitism implicit in Mill's theories of mind and "Platonic" education on the one hand and the democratic radicalism of his politics on the other.[100] At the political level, Mill's radicalism in British politics was even more inconsistent with his exploitative and repressive attitudes and actions toward the outside world in general and India in particular.

Ancient Greece played a pivotal role in Mill's thought. Despite the nonparticipation of the majority, who were women and slaves, Greece and Athens in particular represented democracy. Ancient Greece also represented Europe in opposition to Asia. Thus, for Mill, as for many of his generation and more of the next, Greece epitomized youth, progress, and freedom against the decadence, despotism, and savagery of Asia and the other non-European continents. Mill's position was clearly articulated before 1821 and the outbreak of the Greek War of Independence, which made such views almost universal among Northern Europeans. For Mill it was essential to have an Ancient Greece that was purely European and untainted by despotic Near Eastern Influences. This purification could be achieved in the same way that he had dismissed earlier favorable references to India and China. Mill required that any testimony to that effect should be considered false unless it could be proven by outside corroborative evidence.

Karl Otfried Müller confronted the same problem of the purity or hybridity of Ancient Greece with the same historical method and the same devastating results. Müller too formulated his denial of any southern influences on the Aegean before 1820 in the absence of any new sources of evidence. Grote appears to have followed both Mill and Müller in using what all three saw as the method of "detached critical historiography" to deny that non-European civilizations could have had any significant impact on Greece. To do this both Müller and Grote had to discredit the large quantity of Ancient Greek writing that emphasized the importance of the East and especially Egypt in forming Greek culture at all levels.

Grote's contempt for tradition's failure to satisfy the requirements of "proof" has been immensely influential. His insistence, added to that of Müller, that Greece must be assumed to have been isolated from the Middle East until proven otherwise, has been useful as a tool to expel from the academic fold heretics who doubt the Aryan model (BA I: 495). Similarly, by making a complete divorce between the legendary and historical periods and starting Greek history with the first Olympiad in 776 B.C.E., Grote powerfully reinforced the impression that Classical Greece was an island in both space and time. Thus, Greek civilization was seen to have come from nothing, springing up almost fully armed in a way that was more than human.

Grote's *History* immediately became standard for scholars, not only in England but also in Germany and elsewhere on the continent.[101] Nevertheless, however exhilarating Grote's drastic procedure on myth might have been, it did not satisfy other historians, who still felt obliged to present some opinion on early legendary Greek history. For the next half century, they seem to have followed Thirlwall's compromise position that although Greek legends maintained that there had been both Egyptian and Phoenician invasions, the former was impossible and the latter was open to doubt.

Such a compromise position could not be ruled out even though the "scientific" evidence of linguistics now seen to "demonstrate" that the Greek language was autochthonous and pure (BA I: 329–366). From the 1890s, however, Müller's and Grote's radical denial of the traditions of Middle Eastern influences on Greece became increasingly accepted (BA I: 366–389). Thus, from the 1920s to the 1970s, Ancient Greece was seen by scholars as Romantic Hellenists since Winckelmann had always wanted it to be: as the pure, white, northern epitome and model of European civilization.

V

Science

ROBERT PALTER HAS WRITTEN approximately a quarter of *Black Athena Revisited*. His two long articles, one on historiography and one on science, are the most substantial in the book and contain many trenchant criticisms. That is not to say that I accept them all or that they have forced me to alter the fundamentals of my case. Nevertheless, our arguments have stimulated me—and I believe him too—into new and interesting lines of thought.

No doubt, Palter knows far more than I do about ancient science—and for that matter, science itself. This fact, however, does not make him right. In the first place, there are others, such as professors Lumpkin and Pappademos, whose articles appear in DBA, who possess the same skills as he and have devoted even more time to relations between Egyptian and Greek science. They disagree with him on the issues of whether it is useful to claim that there was "science" in Ancient Egypt and whether that "science" fundamentally affected the development of Greek "science." The word is enclosed in quotation marks because none of the ancient languages had a word similar to the modern European "science." Therefore, a certain arbitrariness inevitably enters these questions.

On the surface, Palter appears to accept the now conventional work of Otto Neugebauer and his school that holds that something that can usefully be called "science" existed in Ancient Mesopotamia and that this something significantly affected the development of Greek "science." Passages in Palter's essay, however, indicate that he still hankers after the notion of a "Greek miracle" and after the idea of "science" as an exclusively European product. Palter also challenges the general view that Egyptian medicine was the major source of Greek medicine and takes an unusually narrow view of the achievements of Egyptian astronomy. On the other hand, he is willing to accept both that the Egyptians had not merely the concept of but also a sign for zero and recent scholars' assessment that "*there are depths in Egyptian geometry that have sometimes gone unrecognized.*" For my part, I am willing to concede that some of the astronomy and mathematics Greeks attributed to Egypt may originally have been developed in Mesopotamia but had been taken into Greece *through* Egypt.

At a methodological level, my debate with Palter is the same as with most of the other contributors: Is *proof* required to justify seeing cultural loans from Egypt and the Levant to Greece? Here, as elsewhere, my argument is twofold. First, I contend that the demand for proof is inappropriate in academic debate on such distant periods. Second, I believe that given the closeness in space and the overlap in time, it would be astonishing if substantial cultural exchange had not occurred around the Eastern Mediterranean. Furthermore, given the greater age, wealth, and elaboration of Egyptian and Levantine civilizations, it would be surprising if the predominant cultural flow during the Bronze and Early Iron Ages had not been from southeast to northwest rather than the other way around. Thus, I believe that all that is required to hypothesize Greek borrowings in science as well as other subjects from Egypt and Syro-Palestine is, once again, not *proof* but *competitive plausibility.*

10 Was There a Greek Scientific Miracle?

A REPLY TO ROBERT PALTER

Robert Palter may not be delighted to read these words, but to judge from the interesting, learned, and long article to which I am now responding, I think that we share much common ground.[1] For instance, on the essential question of my credentials to venture into the field of ancient science at all, he describes my rhetoric as "predicated . . . on ignorance and superficial understanding." In the first paragraph of "Animadversions on the Origins of Western Science"—the original article that provoked his learned critique, which is included as the next chapter of this volume—I described my conviction that I was inadequately prepared for the task.[2] Nevertheless, I agreed to write the essay partly because I was invited by the editor of *Isis* to do so, but also because I maintain that there are times when outsiders can usefully participate in specialist debates. Although they lack expertise, outsiders can sometimes bring a perspective on larger topics that those working within the disciplines concerned may not have.

In the case of ancient studies generally, I find the *presumption of cultural isolation* around the Eastern Mediterranean held by most Hellenists, ancient historians, and archaeologists of the Aegean extremely implausible. The four basic reasons for maintaining the opposite position of openness to the possibility of fundamental cultural contacts are geographical proximity, temporal overlap, material evidence of contact, and substantial Greek traditions of cultural borrowings from Egypt and the Levant. Furthermore, nineteenth- and twentieth-century historians had clear historical and ideological reasons for creating a cultural barrier between "East" and "West." Given all of these factors, a lack of substantial Greek cultural as well as material borrowings from the older adjacent civilizations would be surprising. Thus, unlike scholars in the tradition represented by Palter, I do not require *proof* of any particular contact, merely a strong plausibility of one.

For example, Palter refers to the disagreement between the Egyptologist J. H. Breasted and the medical historian Henry Sigerist on whether the clear similarity between the Egyptian and the Greek methods of treating dislocated jaws was the result of diffusion from Egypt or independent invention (p. 212). Sigerist argued for the latter, as he saw "really only one anatomically possible way to do this." Therefore, as Palter puts it, "Egyptians and Greeks *may well* have independently discovered the procedure" (p. 212; emphasis added).

No doubt, the arbitrary nature of a correspondence between cultural phenomena in different societies substantially increases the probability of diffusion. Such arbitrariness is clearly lacking in this case. If the treatment had been used in ancient Peru, for example, we should undoubtedly see it as an independent invention. In this instance, however, substantial cultural contact between Egypt and Greece not only took place during the relevant millennia but, as Sigerist himself maintained, these contacts were particularly close in medicine (p. 256 n. 5).

Reports of the high reputation of Egyptian doctors abroad throughout the millennia do not come merely from what Palter calls "secondary sources" but from primary ones as well. It should also be remembered that healers are not able to treat dislocated jaws in all cultures. Furthermore, according to Herodotus, the Greek doctors of the sixth century B.C.E. were, in general, less inclined than the Egyptians to treat dislocation violently.[3] Thus, jerking the jaw would seem more anomalous in Greek medicine. In the light of all this, Palter's innuendo might be more plausibly reversed: Greek doctors *may well* have learned how to treat dislocated jaws from Egyptians. Naturally, however, one cannot be certain. I offer other examples of this type of probability elsewhere in my response.

Much of the appearance of disagreement between us comes from Palter's tone and his attacks on other writers. Black Athena gets top billing, in the sense that these words appear in the article's title, but most of the specific charges are against Cheikh Anta Diop, John Pappademos, and Beatrice Lumpkin. Unfortunately, the first is no longer able to reply, but the latter two have now joined in the discussion (see DBA, forthcoming). Palter tries to associate me with them with references to what he sees as my enthusiasm for their works. The fact that I have learned from them and am impressed by their boldness does not mean that I agree with every position they have taken, nor they with mine. I insist, however, that their works contain both general and specific ideas that can be very helpful to historians of ancient Western science. The most important of the general ideas is their insistence on the profound influence of racism within conventional scholarship. I completely agree with them that this influence is something that scholars working within traditions established in the nineteenth and early twentieth centuries should never forget.

Though I insist that the work of the Afrocentrists should not be dismissed out of hand, this is not at issue here, because I do not consider myself to be an Afrocentrist. Therefore, I shall devote the rest of this essay to responses to Palter's criticisms of my work, not of theirs.

Palter restates a division I made in "Animadversions" between two distinct claims: "first, that there were scientific elements in Egyptian medicine, mathematics and astronomy long before there was any Greek science at all; and second, that Egyptian medicine, mathematics and astronomy critically influenced the corresponding Greek disciplines" (p. 210).[4] Interestingly, Palter's answers to these claims are not clear-cut, but the implications of his criticisms of both are clearly negative. As I argued in my article, the meaning of the word "science" contains many ambiguities. With that proviso, however, I accept his restatement of my two claims and stand by both of them.

Palter begins his criticism by hitting out in two directions. On the one hand, he argues that both the Afrocentrists and I are out of touch with modern scholarship, and, on the other, he disparages the "newer historiographic approaches" (p. 210) because they would not help this debate. I agree with the last point and am glad that he agrees to engage both the Afrocentrists and me on what he calls our "own ground" of "old-fashioned intellectual history." I can see no other way to debate the issues with which we are concerned.[5]

Palter goes on to use the distinction between what he calls "primary" and "secondary" sources made by the great historian of ancient science and mathematics Otto Neugebauer. The former come from the culture and time of the "science" concerned, and the latter are digests and reports made at other times or in other cultures. The example given to illustrate the supposed inferiority of the secondary sources is that of Greek and Latin writers who misled the nineteenth-century scholar Gustav Bilfinger, who concluded that the Babylonian day began at sunrise and the Egyptian at sunset. In fact, according to Palter, "all the classical authors had it backwards! That a consensus of error among the classical authors can obtain on such a straightforward factual matter suggests that we should exercise extreme caution when we rely solely on secondary texts" (p. 211).

I have a number of comments to make on this passage. In the first place, use of another and much more obvious set of "secondary" texts—the Jewish tradition—would have led to the correct conclusion that the Mesopotamian day started at sunset. Second, the beginning of the Egyptian day is far from "a straightforward factual matter." Scholars still debate it with passion.[6] Third, as I am sure Palter would agree, we should *always* use extreme caution with any text, not merely "secondary" ones.

Obviously, we should also always use as many sources as possible. Though I am unable to make sense of "primary" sources on the history of science in the original Akkadian and Egyptian, I do not rely merely on "secondary texts" but also on "tertiary" ones. By tertiary sources I mean both translations of Egyptian and Mesopotamian writings and modern scholarship itself. Neugebauer and Palter's binary classification indicates that for them, nineteenth- and twentieth-century scholarship transcends the realm of "texts." I strenuously deny this. I am convinced that we should treat tertiary sources too with "extreme caution." On such ideologically sensitive issues as the origins of Greek science, we should pay particular attention *both* to the level of the scholarship, as far as it can be objectively determined, and to the scholar's social and individual circumstances. For instance, it is significant that in searching for the beginnings of the Mesopotamian day, Bilfinger paid more attention to the classical than to the Semitic evidence.

Ancient Astronomy

The second section of Palter's article is entitled "Ancient Astronomy." (From now on, I shall try to divide this response according to Palter's sections.) Not surprisingly, much of this section is concerned with Otto

Neugebauer. Palter begins with a quibble by contesting my statement that "Neugebauer's range is astounding." He points out correctly that Neugebauer did not consider the social and historical background of science.[7] On the other hand, I believe that I am quite right to be astounded by the range of a scientist and mathematician who dealt as an expert with Greek, Roman, Babylonian, Byzantine, Ethiopic, Indian, Egyptian, Islamic, medieval Latin, and early modern European science. Furthermore, Neugebauer's mathematical reviews made him one of the most influential mathematicians of his own century.

In general, Palter and I agree that Neugebauer both admired many of the qualities of Egyptian civilization and denied that the Ancient Egyptians had produced any science.[8] Palter claims that in "Bernal's haste to impugn Neugebauer's objectivity he barely notices Neugebauer's down grading of the scientific originality of the Greeks" (p. 216). I find both aspects of this interpretation difficult to accept. In "Animadversions" I refer to Neugebauer as "a magnificent champion of liberalism and foe to racism."[9] I might add that I have been told that his tolerance even extended to BA I.[10] I refer in BA and many times in "Animadversions" to Neugebauer's demonstration not only of the existence of a Mesopotamian science but also of its significance in the development of Greek science. See, for instance, the statement: "The work of Neugebauer and his school has made it impossible to deny that some Mesopotamian mathematicians and astronomers were 'scientific' in the positivist sense and that Mesopotamian 'science' in these areas was crucial to the creation of Greek mathematics and astronomy." I continue, "However, I should like to challenge these scholars' dismissal of claims that there was an Egyptian mathematics that could have had a significant influence on Greek thinkers."[11] I have never desired to question Neugebauer's superb and, I insist, wide-ranging scholarship or his general broadmindedness and generosity. I merely want to challenge his dismissal of Egyptian science.

Palter rightly faults me for maintaining in BA that Neugebauer "does not take on the Pyramid school, he simply denounces them" (p. 215). However, in "Animadversions," where, as Palter has observed, I make my first focused attempt at the history of science, I restricted this claim to Neugebauer's Exact Sciences in Antiquity. I went on to refer to, and tentatively accept, Neugebauer's note "On the Orientation of Pyramids" in which he claimed that pyramids could have been exactly oriented purely on the basis of solar shadows and without stellar observations.[12] It seems that I was too timid and conventional in this acceptance. The engineer and historian of dynamics James Williams has demonstrated serious problems with Neugebauer's conjecture that the extraordinarily precise orientation was achieved merely by casting shadows of a pyramidion or similar object. As Williams sees it, the most formidable difficulty with Neugebauer's claim is the near impossibility of measuring a shadow sharply enough to provide the basis for such accuracy. To have done so, the planners of the pyramid would have had to know, among other things, Fresnel diffraction fringes. Thus, if the orientation of the pyramid is as accurate as is generally supposed, it would seem simpler to accept that astronomical measures were used.[13]

Palter follows Neugebauer in dismissing any significant Egyptian astronomy. Neugebauer maintained that the only Ancient Egyptian decans or constellations that can be correlated with modern ones are Sirius, Orion, and the Big Dipper. On the other hand, the Egyptologist Jean Vercoutter, the historian of Greek mathematics Thomas Heath, and the historian of early astronomy Willy Hartner all believed that the Egyptians knew much more astronomy than this limitation suggests. These scholars have, in fact, maintained that the Egyptians had identified many more "modern" constellations.[14] Recently, Arielle Kozloff and Betsy Bryan strongly reinforced the views of these scholars by re-creating the sky of the third millennium B.C.E. in a planetarium—something not done by Neugebauer and Parker. Kozloff and Bryan have shown that the goddess Nut can plausibly be seen as representing the Milky Way. Their re-creation also made sense of the positions of many other constellations represented by Ancient Egyptians.[15] How to strike a balance between the two contrasting views of Ancient Egyptian astronomy? On the one side, Neugebauer's great expertise coupled with the Egyptological skills of his collaborator, R. A. Parker; on the other, three eminent scholars, mentioned above, who were themselves generally skeptical of Egyptian intellectual abilities. The three have been reinforced by recent information based on technology.[16] Given other Egyptian achievements, competitive plausibility leads me to side with the latter, but here again there is no *proof* in the positivist sense.

The presence or absence of sophisticated astronomy in the Ancient Egyptian tradition is not of critical importance to my second claim, that Egyptian science, as Palter puts it, "critically influenced the corresponding Greek disciplines" (p. 210). Although Palter denies that there "was any Egyptian mathematical astronomy," he immediately qualifies this denial by stating "at least not until the so-called Late Egyptian Period (670–332 B.C.E.) when there was demonstrable influence of Babylonian and Greek mathematical astronomy" (p. 215). I do not know to what "demonstrable" Greek mathematical influence on Egypt before 332 B.C.E. he is referring, but I quite agree that Mesopotamian science influenced Egyptian astronomy and mathematics during these centuries. Indeed, I wrote in the conclusion to my article in *Isis* that there is "a very strong case indeed that there were rich mathematical—particularly geometrical—and astronomical traditions in Egypt by the time Greek scholars came in contact with Egyptian learned priests. After the first Persian conquest of Egypt in the 6th century B.C. Egyptian mathematics and astronomy were substantially influenced by Mesopotamian 'scientific' thought."[17]

I should now, with Palter, like to push this Egyptian cultural opening to the east, back to the Assyrian raids and hegemony over Lower Egypt in the mid–seventh century B.C.E. I do not claim any originality for my view of Egyptian transmission of Mesopotamian mathematics and astronomy. Thomas Heath, for instance, claimed that Thales' prediction of a solar eclipse on May 25, 585 B.C.E.—in which Heath believed—was probably made possible by Babylonian observations "known to Thales, either directly or through the Egyptians as intermediaries (my italics).[18]

Having said this, I do not wish to deny that Egyptian and Mesopotamian astronomy may well have had still earlier influences on Greece. As far as can be seen, however, these elements did not constitute mathematical astronomy in the sense that it appeared in Egypt and Greece after the fifth century B.C.E.

Toward the end of this section, Palter reiterates the charge that "Bernal's political goal which requires the 'useful' image of black or 'essentially' African, Egyptians undermines his scholarly goal 'to open up new areas of research'" (p. 217). Palter's characterization of my stated political purpose is mistaken. What I wrote *and what I meant* (on the page he cites) was something very different: "The political purpose of *Black Athena* is, of course, to lessen European cultural arrogance" (BA I: 73).

The idea that scholars can be completely detached from politics is peculiar to North America. Furthermore, within the humanities and social sciences on this continent, it is largely restricted to ancient history and Classics. In most other countries and disciplines it is assumed that a scholar has a political position that has a greater or lesser bearing on her or his scholarship. Without wanting to raise the status of my work to their level, there is no doubt that many great and useful histories, such as those of George Grote and H. G. Wells, have been written with clear and passionate political missions.[19]

Nearly all of the historiography of Ancient Greece in the past 180 years has been written to glorify Hellas and, by extension, Northwestern Europe, and to diminish the significance of outside influences; Neugebauer and his school are great exceptions here. Given this background, I believe that a revival of emphasis on the Egyptian and Levantine contributions to Greek civilization serves a double purpose. On the one hand, it solves some historical puzzles and poses interesting new questions. On the other, it removes the spurious notion that only "white men" can be culturally creative. Not that many ancient historians today hold such views, but they do tend to be working within scholarly frameworks established by men of previous generations who were convinced of it.

Egyptian Astronomy and Afrocentrism

As its title suggests, most of Palter's third section, "Egyptian Astronomy and Afrocentrism," does not concern me directly, for in Black Athena and elsewhere I have little to say on these subjects. Thus, I should like to take up only a couple of the issues raised in it.

The first item is Palter's taking me to task for having stated that the Greeks adopted an Egyptian rather than a Mesopotamian calendar and that "this adoption is indicative of what seems to have been a wider Greek tendency to draw from nearby Egypt rather than more distant Mesopotamia."[20] He then goes on to mention the chaos of Greek calendrical systems and to suggest the possibility of a "universal" "Metonic" lunar calendar of nineteen years, which he plausibly sees as deriving from Mesopotamia (p. 258 n. 19). He is right on both counts; I should have specified that the Egyptian calendar began to be used in Ptolemaic territories (not merely Egypt) only in the third century B.C.E., the period of the beginning of Greek science.[21] The Ptolemaic territories made up the region where nearly all of Greek science developed. On the Metonic Cycle and its direct or indirect derivation from Mesopotamia, I would go even further than Palter and accept the argument of the classicist Gilbert Murray that the nineteen-year cycle was known to the writer of the Odyssey in the ninth century B.C.E.[22]

Palter is contemptuous of the notion that the extant record of Egyptian mathematics and astronomy is incomplete. He cannot understand "why it should have been precisely the advanced texts which were damaged or lost" (p. 217). Other scholars have not found this possibility to be a problem. For example, J. F. Lauer wrote: "Even though up to now, no esoteric Egyptian mathematical document has been discovered, we know, if we can believe the Greeks, that the Egyptian priests were very jealous of the secrets of their science and that they occupied themselves, Aristotle tells us, in mathematics. It seems then reasonably probable that they had been in possession of an esoteric science." [23] In "Animadversions" I referred to the analogous Ptolemaic papyrological record, from which it would be possible to reconstruct much of the first book of Euclid but virtually nothing of the later ones.[24] As happened with the huge number of papyrological fragments from the Homeric epics and commentaries on them (which almost equals the remains of the rest of Greek literature), elementary texts—and magical spells to accompany the dead—were far more widely produced than advanced mathematical writings.[25] The existence of other, more technical and theoretical works is strongly suggested by the sprinkling of advanced problems among the practical ones in the Rhind and Moscow papyri.

The second issue between Palter and me in this section is the reputation of Giorgio de Santillana. Palter describes him as "at best a minor figure," whose book *The Crime of Galileo* was "provocative and passionately anti-clerical" (p. 223). I know that since antiscientism has overtaken anticlericalism, modern scholars tend to assign most of the blame for his trials on Galileo himself. Although I would not claim that Galileo's social behavior or scientific honesty were perfect, anticlericalism still seems to be a reasonably good standpoint from which to view this history.

Palter is quite right to say that de Santillana's reputation is low today, but this was not always the case. Thirty years ago, Stillman Drake, whom Palter sees as the greatest expert in the field of Galilean studies, was not as contemptuous of de Santillana's translations as Palter is today. Drake included an abridgment of Santillana's version of *Letters on Sunspots* in his own *Discoveries and Opinions of Galileo.*[26] In the debate over a crucial point regarding the events of February 26, 1616, Drake was extremely respectful toward de Santillana's position. Furthermore, he was perfectly willing to concede that both of their conflicting interpretations of the evidence required "conjecture." [27]

I too am skeptical about some of de Santillana's later work, especially when it goes beyond Charles François Dupuis, but, as with the Afrocentrists, I do not think that I should be held to account for every position held by men and women whose other work I admire. I know that scholars' reputations often fluctuate and I am convinced that de Santillana's will not always remain at its present low ebb.

Newton and Egypt

In his section "Newton and Egypt," Palter accuses me of going beyond the "unexceptionable" claim that Newton "certainly believed in an Egyptian *prisca sapientia*, which he saw it as his mission to retrieve," to claiming that Newton "actually *depended* on Egyptian ideas in his own scientific work" (p. 226). In fact, I make no claim that Newton used or even knew Egyptian units of measurement or that they would have in any way helped him had he possessed them. All I maintain is that *he wanted* to discover them and that *he thought* they could help him in his calculations of gravity.

After the apple fell in 1666 and Newton's calculations of the gravitational pull of the earth on the moon answered the problem "pretty nearly" but not quite, Palter claims that Newton set the problem aside and did not take it up again "until he was compelled to by a dispute with Robert Hooke in 1679." Palter goes on to say: "*In a totally different context*" (his italics), Newton became concerned with the length units of ancient peoples (p. 227). Although the fall of the apple was important, the situation was not so simple. As Richard S. Westfall puts it in his latest biography of Newton: "Universal gravitation did not yield to Newton at his first effort. He hesitated and floundered. . . . Some idea floated at the border of his consciousness not fully formulated, not perfectly focused, but solid enough not to disappear." [28]

During this interim in the 1670s, Newton began his study of the sacred cubit. Therefore, I am not convinced by Palter's description of this as having taken place in "*a totally different context.*" The work of James McGuire, Piyo Rattansi, and Betty Jo Dobbs has made it impossible to make categorical distinctions between Newton's "science" and his alchemy, theology, and concern with ancient measurements of time and space. [29] Given his belief in an Egyptian *prisca sapientia*, I, following Professor Dobbs, find it implausible to maintain that Newton cleanly separated his searches for ancient units of measurement and a precise knowledge of the earth's circumference. [30]

Ancient Mathematics

In his section on ancient mathematics, Palter states that the two experts on Egyptian mathematics he most respects, B. L. van der Waerden and Richard Gillings, "do not significantly disagree (especially since . . . Gillings has brought van der Waerden around to his own interpretation of one of the high points of the Egyptian achievement" (p. 228). In his original article, Palter followed these two scholars in restricting his assessment of Egyptian mathematics to the so-called mathematical papyri. These papyri, however, do not exhaust our information on Egyptian mathematics; other sources can provide important information. For instance, where Gillings accepts that Egyptians had a "zero concept," he goes on to say that they had no sign for it.[31] However, in the revised version of his article published in BAR, Palter now agrees, thanks to a communication from Frank Yurco, that by 1740 B.C.E. the Egyptians used a sign for zero in accounting texts (p. 260 n. 36). This fact has been known to Egyptologists—though not to historians of Egyptian mathematics—for many generations. Furthermore, this sign ⌡, nfr ("beautiful") was also used to indicate zero on leveling lines in the foundations of the Pyramid of Mycerenus at Giza that Egyptian engineers used for "above" and "below" the zero line.[32]

Palter accepts that Egyptians surpassed Babylonians in computing areas and volumes (p. 230). He also writes, "If Gillings is correct [on problem 48 of the Rhind Mathematical Papyrus, squaring the circle] *there are depths in Egyptian geometry that have sometimes gone unrecognized*" (p. 231; my italics).[33] This conclusion corresponds with the position I took in "Animadversions" that, although Mesopotamian arithmetic and astronomy appear to have been superior, "the Egyptians were the better geometers."[34] Furthermore, the Greek writers of the "secondary" texts Palter distrusts had a particular respect for Egyptian geometry and insisted that Greeks learned much of their geometry from Egyptians.[35]

Palter cannot accept such assertions. For instance, he maintains, against the ancient sources, that Eudoxos did not learn mathematics in Egypt, where he spent at least one year, maybe more, and learned Egyptian, but from Archytas of Tarantun. I find no reason to see these two influences as mutually exclusive. A very plausible case has been made that much of Plato's enthusiasm for and knowledge about Egypt came from Eudoxos when the latter visited the Academy in 368 B.C.E.[36] No doubt this knowledge included a deep respect for Egyptian mathematics.[37] At the very least, the ancient sources indicate that Eudoxos gave the impression that he had learned mathematics in Egypt. Palter's refusal to accept the ancient testimony about such a relatively well-recorded figure as Eudoxos indicates to me an unreasonable commitment to the nineteenth- and twentieth-century scholarly tradition of Greek cultural isolation. De Santillana is not the only modern historian to have accepted that there were Egyptian intellectual influences on Eudoxos; Thomas Heath also followed the ancient tradition on this.[38]

Palter concedes that Archytas, as a Pythagorean, could be said to have derived some of his knowledge indirectly from Egypt. He hastens to add that, though Pythagoras probably did have contact with Egypt, this contact had no significance for later Pythagorean mathematics. Palter follows the eminent classicist Walter Burkert in distrusting the tradition that Pythagoras knew or transmitted any Egyptian mathematics (p. 233). Burkert pointed out that the earliest references to Pythagoras, those of Herodotus and Isocrates, do not specifically link him to mathematics. Isocrates did, however, associate Pythagoras with Egyptian "philosophy," and it is hard to restrict this term to politics, as some scholars have attempted to do.[39]

Palter rightly argues (p. 233) that one should not dismiss Burkert "out of hand, as an unregenerate Hellenophile" because of his recent book on Mesopotamian and Phoenician influence on Greece. Burkert is indeed a distinguished and extremely broadminded scholar.[40] Even he, however, suffers from that besetting vice of Classics, misplaced precision. Most commonly, this takes the form of attempts to discredit ancient sources on the basis of "the argument from silence" and to claim that a phenomenon was not present until first attested in the extremely fragmentary evidence. I should like to cite two related examples of this in Burkert's work.

In a paper given in 1981, Burkert argued that the "folded tablet" was associated with alphabetic writing, and that therefore, the *pinax ptuktos* ("folding tablet") referred to in the *Iliad* must date to the eighth century B.C.E., when he believed the alphabet to have been transmitted to the Aegean.[41] This assertion was safe, because at that point the earliest folding tablets known were those from Nimrud in Assyria from the seventh century B.C.E. In 1986, however, fragments of a wax-covered tablet were found in the Ulu Burun shipwreck off the southern coast of Turkey and were dated to the fourteenth century B.C.E.[42] Thus, Burkert has been forced to choose between breaking the association of *pinakes* with alphabetic scripts or redating their introduction to the Aegean. For reasons that will become clear, he chose the former.

This choice leads to a major instance of Burkert's misplaced precision. In chapter 13, I praise Burkert's wonderful book *The Orientalizing Revolution*, but I criticize the minimalism to his periodization. Lacking any direct evidence from texts that he believes antedate the second half of the eighth century B.C.E., he tries to cram all the "Semitic" influence he sees as saturating Greek culture to the century 750–650 B.C.E. This not only runs counter to the evidence, which he accepts, pointing to Semitic loan words in Linear B texts, but it also forces him to date the introduction of the Semitic alphabet to Greece to the second half of the eighth century, a position that few, if any, scholars hold today.[43]

As a young man, Burkert used the same principles and Besserwisserei to deny the widespread ancient traditions that Pythagoras had been concerned with numbers. Even if he did not have the intention, Burkert's proposal that Greek mathematics developed not through a religious sect but solely through "public" figures like Thales and Anaxamander has the effect of creating what, to my mind, is an unjustifiably sharp contrast between "rational" Greece and "irrational" Oriental mysteries. I am convinced that given the scarcity of sources, the "argument from silence" is far from sufficient evidence to overthrow the widely attested ancient tradition that Pythagoras was deeply concerned with geometry and numerology. This tradition contains nothing that is inherently improbable.

As for the question of the Pythagorean theorem, Palter argues that, although the famous Plimpton 322 tablet shows that Babylonians were able to generate "Pythagorean triples" by 1700 B.C.E. and, therefore, comprehended the principle behind it, no Egyptian understood the theorem even though they used 3:4:5 triangles in practice (pp. 238–239). Here again we come up against the issue of whether one should require *proof* or merely *competitive plausibility*. Gay Robins and Charles Shute maintain that the Old Kingdom builders of the later pyramids changed the inclination or slope from 14/11 to 4/3 not only because they knew of the 3:4:5 triangle but because they believed that the ratio had a special significance. Otherwise, why would they have made a change of proportions that was "barely perceptible"?[44]

Elsewhere, Robins and Shute have found it helpful to explain the "remarkable result" of an accurate squaring of the circle in problems in the Rhind Mathematical Papyrus by supposing that these Egyptian mathematicians of the Middle Kingdom had used Pythagoras' theorem.[45] In Egypt, no smoking gun like Plimpton 322 has been found. However, given the generally high standard of Egyptian geometry, these pieces of evidence strongly suggest that Egyptian mathematicians since the later Old Kingdom did not merely use 3:4:5 triangles but were attracted to their numerical qualities.

Such early knowledge is not necessary to explain the tradition of Pythagoras' having learned "his" theorem from Egyptians. His supposed stay in Egypt was during the sixth century B.C.E., in the Egyptian Late Period, when there was already Mesopotamian influence on Egyptian science. This would seem to be confirmed by the three Pythagorean triples found on an Egyptian papyrus dating to c. 300 B.C.E. Palter argues that this "late" papyrus shows "therefore, obvious Babylonian or Greek influence" (p. 239).[46] The former may well be the case, but the latter claim would seem very unlikely for a text so early in the Ptolemaic Period.

Euclid, Archimedes, and Egyptian Mathematics

Palter devotes a section of his chapter to Euclid, Archimedes, and Egypt and largely directs these pages against Diop, so I have little to respond to. I should merely like to add something to the debate over levers. The balance with cursors was used by Egyptians by the Middle Kingdom, which suggests that, at least by this period, a relatively sophisticated notion of centers of gravity existed. The earliest representation of scales in the Aegean is a gold leaf model discovered in a tomb at Mycenae, which dated from the middle of the second millennium B.C.E. This find in a funerary context clearly links it to the familiar Egyptian scene of the weighing of the souls of the dead.[47] Another indication of an early Greek derivation of levers from Egypt is the plausible origin of the Greek word mokhlos ("lever") attested in Homer. This word, which has no satisfactory Indo-European etymology, could well be from the Egyptian mḫ3t ("balance").[48]

Pyramidology

In his section titled "Pyramidology," Palter does not deny, though he remains skeptical of, Robins and Shute's inclination to accept that some pyramid builders used 3:4:5 triangles "as a convenient basis for set-squares used by the stone masons" (p. 242).[49] On the other hand, he is unconvinced by claims that the golden section ϕ or π could have been built into them. He goes on to argue that even if the two could be found in the measurements of the pyramids, this would be the result of chance. This, he argues, is because "with no prior constraints on just what is to constitute a fit, almost any large set of measurements can be shown to contain 'interesting' numerical relationships" (p. 243). No doubt this is the case, but Palter's reductio ad absurdum of this argument illustrates the fact that the problem is rather more complicated than he supposes. He cites the discovery by the mathematician and puzzle setter Martin Gardner of "a plethora of allusions to the number 5 in the dimensions of the Washington Monument" (p. 243). Both he and Gardner see this construction purely as the result of chance, seized on as significant only by amateurs with fevered imaginations.

I am not convinced. There is no doubt that the Washington Monument is an Egypto-Masonic construction. It commemorates a high-ranking Freemason; it is carefully set in the geometrical pattern of Washington, D.C.; and it takes the form of an Egyptian obelisk. A Masonic grand master laid its foundation stone in a largely Masonic ceremony. Whether or not the Egyptians built numbers or mathematical ratios into their monuments, Freemasons following the "secondary sources" are convinced that the Egyptian priests—whom they see as their spiritual forefathers—did. As Masons, they also believe that buildings represent cosmic order and, therefore, that their proportions are extremely significant. Palter points out (p. 243) that they also see "fiveness" as critically important. Thus, though I do not, of course, attach any significance to the number of letters in the name Washington or any relation it may have to the speed of light, I can with no trouble see that the 5s in the English unit measurements of the monument were deliberately built into it.[50]

If the pyramids do contain measurements suggesting a knowledge of ϕ or π, we cannot be certain either that they were built in or that they are the result of chance. Indications that some of the problems in the Rhind Papyrus date back to the Old Kingdom provide independent evidence suggesting that the builders of the pyramids had a reasonable approximation of π.[51] As far as I know, no such evidence exists for ϕ. Nevertheless, a majority of historians of Egyptian art and architecture believe that it was employed in pharaonic times.[52] Given Plato's interest in ϕ and his respect for Egyptian sources, it would seem likely that it was used.[53] The fact that a number of "secondary sources" report that Egyptian priests saw mathematical significance in the measurements of the pyramids does not clinch the argument that sophisticated mathematics went into creating these proportions, but it does give it increased plausibility. The fact that such ratios can occur by chance does not necessarily mean that they did; we need to weigh the probabilities.

Egyptian and Greek Medicine

In his discussion of medicine, Palter has a problem in that the authorities in this field—R. O. Steuer, J. B. de C. M. Saunders, Paul Ghalioungui, and

Henry Sigerist—all agree that Egyptian medicine had a major if not central influence on the formation of that of Greece.[54] Palter relies instead on the classicist Heinrich von Staden, and writes, "Here we are in the fortunate position of possessing as a guide Heinrich von Staden's recent systematic and balanced analysis" (p. 246).

Elsewhere in his chapter, Palter rightly points out the broadmindedness and lack of Eurocentricity of Otto Neugebauer and Walter Burkert. Heinrich von Staden might appear to be of that ilk, but it is not so simple. In his interesting essay published in the *Isis* symposium on "The Cultures of Ancient Science," von Staden states: "Like some ancient Greeks, I believe that the permeability of their cultural boundaries permitted a rich productive two-way flow. Moreover, I believe that during much of the history of Greek science, the 'non-Greek' and the distinctively Greek coexist in inextricably intertwined, creative but often opaque relations." Nevertheless, von Staden insists convincingly that the search for origins "can be misleading, since the original semantic, structural, theoretical, or functional context of the borrowed often is usurped and transformed by new cultural contexts in science as in art and myth." [55]

Von Staden also argues against Jack Goody's revival, in a modified form, of Eric Havelock's thesis that one can think rationally only with the help of a vocalized alphabet. He opposes any suggestion that Greek science can be associated with Greek democracy. Von Staden then points out that no one "paramount causal factor," be it a "non-Greek fountainhead," alphabetic literacy, or democracy, can explain "the distinctiveness of Greek science or . . . its—or 'our' [European]—origins." [56] The truth of the general claim that there is no one "paramount causal factor" is undeniable, but the implication of the statement could be misleading, in that it appears to put the three factors on an equal plane. In fact, at least one "non-Greek fountainhead" was of great importance, alphabetic literacy was of some significance, and democracy was not a factor.

Von Staden rightly puts "our" in quotation marks. I am not sure where Palter stands on this, but I am not prepared to accept that the seventeenth-century "scientific revolution" can usefully be said to have derived solely or even principally from Hellenistic science. Rather, it arose from a particular political social and economic conjuncture and the accumulated "science" of many different cultures.[57]

Von Staden's earlier views on Greek isolation and qualitative superiority over other cultures are discussed later; he has undoubtedly come a long way from these. Nevertheless, his continuing loyalty to his discipline is shown by his use of the argument that Classics has always been open to the idea that there had been substantial contributions to Greek culture from the "Near East."[58] For the implausibility of this argument, see chapter 13.

From the above it is clear that von Staden now sees Greek culture in its Mediterranean context. However, although his major work, *Herophilus: The Art of Medicine in Early Alexandria*, was published in 1989, it was conceived and written in an earlier and less self-conscious period. Palter admires and cites the old von Staden, not the new one. For instance, Palter points out that more than 800 different drugs are named in Egyptian medical texts, whereas the Hippocratic corpus contains only 130. He continues, "From Homer on, the idea of Egypt as a fertile source of drugs is a constant refrain among Greek authors so that: [quoting von Staden] '[A]n influx of Egyptian ingredients into pre-Alexandrian Greek pharmacology is . . . solidly attested. *It probably reflects an interest in exotica* whose use would enhance the physician's prestige'" (p. 252; my italics).

Only firm commitment to the presumption of isolation allows one to explain the introduction of so many Egyptian drugs into Greek pharmacology by "an interest in exotica." Evidence from both primary and secondary sources shows that Egyptian medicine was considered more effective than the Greek until the Ptolemaic or even the Roman period. To his credit, however, Palter follows von Staden in admitting that the Herophilan pharmacology was "further enriched by Egyptian drugs . . . such as castor oil leaves, plantain juice . . ." (p. 252). Palter continues, "One precaution is in order, however, as Ann Hanson explains: 'The fact that broadly similar drugs, techniques and remedies can be documented widely among societies at similar stages of development, makes arguments for a direct line less convincing'" (p. 252).

To anyone outside the traditions of Eurocentrism and modern Classics, such statements merely show the lengths that people will go to avoid the unpleasant but obvious. At the beginning of this chapter, I argued that whereas many cultural similarities could reasonably be attributed to independent invention when they occur in distant communities, similarities like these should not be so explained when they are found between societies as close in time and place as Egypt and Greece. Certainly, this is true when there is considerable evidence of contact in the particular field concerned. Hanson's attempt—supported by Palter—to claim that the Greeks living in Egypt did not derive their use of particular drugs and treatments from Egyptian healers is still more preposterous.[59]

Palter accepts and uses some of von Staden's most Graecocentric claims.

For example, the old von Staden wrote and Palter quotes, "*It is conceivable* that Herophilus' careful study of reproductive physiology and obstetrics . . . convinced him of *the absurdity and uselessness* of these Egyptian intrusions into Greek medicine" (p. 253; my italics). What is of even further interest is that by 1992, von Staden had moved beyond these isolationist claims, while Palter has been left behind. Because of this he now disagrees with the post-1989 von Staden. For instance, Palter refers to the "numerous texts, in which the physician is admonished to eschew supernatural or magical explanations such as the Hippocratic treatise on epilepsy entitled 'The Sacred Disease'" (p. 268). Showing awareness of the unreliability of tertiary sources, von Staden writes very differently in his *Isis* article:

> There has been inadequate reflection on the cultural conditions that have shaped modern historians' selections and elisions. These cultural conditions include, centrally, two mutually reinforcing collective experiences: the modern reception of Ancient Greece as the fountainhead of our culture and, second, modern western scientific culture as our lodestar. These long-lived collective constructions of fountainhead and lodestar have led to concrete entrenched consequences in the modern history of science. Thus the Hippocratic treatise on sacred disease, with its criticisms of magic and with its overt questioning of etiologies that resort to the divine, is known to practically all historians of ancient science, having been translated often (and anthologized even more often), whereas there is no English translation of the Hippocratic gynecological treatises, which are replete with the "otherness" of Greek science—and which constitute a far larger part of the Hippocratic corpus.[60]

In his refusal to draw a clear distinction between "irrational" Egyptian medicine and a "rational" Hippocratic tradition, the new von Staden appears to have removed the chief barrier between his earlier work and the majority view of the profound connections between Egyptian and Greek medicine.

Conclusion

In concluding his BAR chapter on ancient science, Robert Palter takes up Geoffrey Lloyd's argument that public oral debate in Greece was a critical factor in the development of a qualitatively new and superior Greek science. He then disparages as "hardly an adequate response" my reference to the

Dispute between a Man and His Ba of the Egyptian Middle Kingdom. He argues that this dispute was a purely private affair. He does not mention that this text was only one of the three examples I gave to show the great importance of oral debate to Egyptian culture. One of the other two was the equally ancient popular story *The Eloquent Peasant*, in which the upper-class listeners gained esthetic pleasure from the peasant's oratory. The third consisted of two of the central scenes of Egyptian myth: the public trials, first between Seth and Osiris and later between Seth and Horus, in which the winner was acclaimed to be m3ꜥ ḥrw ("True of Voice").[61] The centrality of this image of a legal victory through speech is illustrated by the fact that m3ꜥ ḥrw was used as the standard term for the blessed dead.

Thus, as I noted in my original *Isis* article, it is clear that, as in Greece and most other cultures in the world, there was an Egyptian tradition of public debate, rhetoric, and persuasion centered around legal disputes. What I did not mention there was that some Greek etymologies indicate that the scene of the legal battles between the Egyptian gods and Egyptian courts in general had a direct impact on Mycenaean Greece. The Egyptian connotations of the appearance of scales in a Mycenaean tomb was referred to above. Closely associated with this is the fact that the derivation of the Greek *makarios* ("the blessed dead") from m3ꜥ ḥrw is one of the few Egyptian etymologies in Greek to have been widely accepted.[62]

As stated in chapter 6 (n. 137), I maintain that derivation of the Greek stem *timē* or *timā* ("justify, honor") from the Egyptian dỉ(t) m3ꜥt. (Coptic *tmaio*) ("justify, praise") and *martyros* ("witness") from the Egyptian *mtrw* with the same meaning would seem equally likely, especially as they have no Indo-European etymologies. If these legal terms have such Egyptian origins, they must have been introduced to the Aegean during the Bronze Age. They were, therefore, thoroughly Hellenized by the Archaic, Classical, and Hellenistic periods in which Greek science developed. Nevertheless, they suggest that here, as in so many other aspects of Greek culture, it is futile to draw a hard and fast boundary across the Eastern Mediterranean and to explain developments in any one of its civilizations without frequent reference to the others.

Now, at the conclusion of my response to Professor Palter, I should like to return to the two claims noted at the outset. Clearly, Palter and I differ considerably on my first, "that there were scientific elements in Egyptian medicine, mathematics, and astronomy long before there was any Greek science at all." As noted above, however, Palter agrees that there may have been "depths in Egyptian geometry that have sometimes gone unrecognized." We are even closer in our assessment of the levels of Egyptian mathematics and astronomy in the Late Period after the seventh century B.C.E. This, of course, was the period in which ancient tradition maintained that Greeks had learned mathematics, astronomy, and medicine in Egypt.

The second claim is that Egyptian medicine, mathematics, and astronomy critically influenced the corresponding Greek disciplines. Here, as I see it, the essential difference between us lies in Palter's isolationism and my modified diffusionism. When Palter confronts apparent parallels between Egyptian and Greek "science," he asks why the one should be derived from the other when there is no proof. My answer is Burkert's in reference to borrowings from the Semitic-speaking Levant: "In any case, the kind of minimalism that rejects all connections . . . which are not crystal clear remains, on the whole, the most unlikely of hypotheses."[63]

Palter concludes his essay by claiming that I have achieved precisely the opposite of what I intended to do. He maintains that I have "strengthen[ed] the case for recognizing a revolutionary approach to the study of nature in Classical Greece. Whether in this connection, one wishes to talk about a 'Greek miracle' is perhaps just a matter of taste. (I myself abhor the phrase and would be quite pleased never to hear it again)" (p. 255).

Any trace of ambiguity in these sentences has been removed by the end of a footnote added to the revised text of his article. In this, Palter quotes from a review by Jonathan Barnes, who wrote in 1988: "It is unfashionable to speak of a 'Greek miracle' . . . but let the pendulum of fashion swing as it may, the Greeks invented science and philosophy" (p. 266 n. 88). The obvious relish with which Palter ends the last footnote of his article indicates his sharp differences not only with me but also with Neugebauer, Pingree, and their school as well as with most contemporary historians of ancient science.

11 Animadversions on the Origins of Western Science

I spent the first fifty years of my life trying to escape from the shadow of my father, John Desmond Bernal, and hence, among other things, from his major fields of science and the history of science. Therefore, the trepidation that is proper for anyone who is neither a scientist nor a historian of science writing on this subject, and particularly in the first published version of this chapter for the distinguished journal Isis, is multiplied manifold here. Nevertheless, I remain grateful for the original invitation by Isis's editor, Ronald Numbers, to put forward my views on the origins of Western science and I am glad to offer a revised version of these views here.[1]

Any approach to the origins of Western science immediately stumbles over the definition of "science." As no ancient society possessed the modern concept of "science," or a word for it, its application to Mesopotamia, Egypt, China, India, or Greece is bound to be arbitrary. This lack of clarity is exacerbated by the clash among historians. Some, like David Pingree, are concerned with "sciences" as "functioning systems of thought" within a particular society. Other scholars apply transhistorical standards and see "science" as "the orderly and systematic comprehension, description and/

or explanation of natural phenomena . . . [and] the tools necessary for the undertaking including, especially, mathematics and logic."[2] I should add the words "real or imagined" after "natural phenomena."

Egyptian Wisdom, Greek Science?

Pingree denounces the claim of what he calls "Hellenophilia" that "science" was an exclusively Greek invention owing little or nothing to earlier civilizations and passed down without interference to the Western European makers of the "scientific revolution." Puzzlingly, the authoritative work of Otto Neugebauer and his school, including Pingree himself, on the extent and sophistication of Mesopotamian astronomy and mathematics and Greek indebtedness to it, as well as Martin West's demonstration of the Near Eastern influences on Pre-Socratic cosmologies, appear to have left this Graecocentric thinking unscathed.[3]

The claim is still made that Thales (seen as a Greek) was "the first philosopher scientist," the word "scientist" being used here in the positivist sense. According to G. E. R. Lloyd, the Greeks were the first to "discover nature," "practice debate," and introduce such specifics as the study of irrational numbers and geometrical modeling for astronomy. Lloyd sees the discovery of nature as "the appreciation of the distinction between 'natural' and 'supernatural,' that is, the recognition that natural phenomena are not the products of random or arbitrary influences but regular and governed by determinable sequences of cause and effect."[4] At least by the early second millennium B.C.E., however, Mesopotamian astronomy and Egyptian medicine, to take just two examples, were clearly concerned with regular and, if possible, predictable phenomena with relatively little supernatural involvement.[5]

Egyptian medicine did contain some religion and magic. At one point, even the "scientific" Edwin Smith Papyrus on surgery turns to magical charms. E. R. Dodds and others, however, have shown that the natural philosophers' skepticism of the supernatural was isolated in the context of the widespread Greek belief in the efficacy of magic.[6] Even Hippocratic medicine, which is generally regarded as highly rational, was institutionally centered on the religious cult of Asclepius and his serpents, which laid great emphasis on the religious practice of incubation. Both the cult and the practice, incidentally, had clear Egyptian roots.[7]

As for the alleged uniqueness of Greek "scientific debate," the Mesopotamian historical epic of *Gilgamesh and Agga* contains records of "debates" that are almost as old as literature itself. Some ancient debates, such as the *Dispute between a Man and His Ba*, which dates back to Middle Kingdom Egypt, contain profound philosophy.⁸ It is also clear that different Mesopotamian, Syrian, and Egyptian cities had not merely different gods but distinct cosmogonies, most involving abstract elements or forces without cults. Attempted and actual syncretizations of such cosmologies suggest that debates and contests between them took place.⁹ Such situations resemble those plausibly reconstructed for the cosmological disputes of the Greek Pre-Socratics.

Later Greek philosophical and scientific debates clearly owed a great deal to the Sophists, who came from the Greek tradition of "persuasion," which was closely associated with legal disputes. Oratory and persuasion are highly valued in nearly all cultures but received particular emphasis in Ancient Egypt.¹⁰ The central scene in Egyptian religious iconography is the judicial weighing of the soul of the dead person. This is a mystic repetition of the legal battles between Osiris/Horus and Seth with their climaxes, in which the victor, having persuaded the court, is declared *m3ꜥ ḥrw* ("true of voice"), and which form central episodes in Egyptian mythology. One of the most popular Egyptian texts was that of *The Eloquent Peasant*, which its most recent translator into English, Miriam Lichtheim, describes as "both a serious disquisition on the need for justice and a parable on the utility of fine speech."¹¹

In chapter 15 of this volume, I discuss the centrality of the image of Egyptian justice to both Mycenaean and Iron Age Greece, and there is little doubt that Greeks of the Classical and Hellenistic periods saw Egyptian law as the ultimate basis of their own.¹² As Aristotle wrote at the end of his *Politics*: "The History of Egypt attests the antiquity of all political institutions. The Egyptians are generally accounted the oldest people on earth; and they have always had a body of law and a system of politics. We ought to take over and use what has already been adequately expressed before us and confine ourselves to attempting to discover what has already been omitted."¹³

Although the first attestation of written law in Egypt comes from the tomb of Rekhmire only in the fifteenth century B.C.E., there is no reason to doubt that it existed much earlier.¹⁴ In any event, the Egyptian New Kingdom is old by Greek standards. It is clear that what Aristotle was recommending had not hitherto been carried out. Nevertheless, given the conventionality of his political views on other matters, Aristotle was probably also conventional in his belief that the true foundation of Greek law and justice lay in Egypt, even though Egyptian and Greek laws were very different in his day, the fourth century B.C.E.

The emphasis on law is important for the history of science both because of its promotion of argument and dialectic and because of the projections of social law into nature in the establishment of regularities.[15] There is no doubt that the Egyptian (M3ʿt) Ma'at ("truth, accuracy, justice") was central to both social and natural spheres in the same way as the Greek Moira (generally translated "Fate"), which derived from it etymologically.[16] Similarly, it is clear that the Egyptians applied the "justice" of scales to social and legal life at least as early as the Middle Kingdom.[17]

Some of the specific claims made for the originality of Greek science also fall short. Babylonian scholars were concerned with $\sqrt{2}$ and "Pythagorean" triples, and it is equally clear that they had a good approximation of π.[18] The Egyptian estimate for π was even more accurate.[19] Modern scholars have poured scorn on the widespread ancient tradition that Egyptians knew of the "Pythagorean" triangle.[20] The very cautious Gay Robins and Charles Shute, however, have accepted the argument that knowledge of the "Pythagorean" triangle can be found in Late Old Kingdom pyramids. The pyramids of a *seked* of 5¼ palms imposed "a half-base width to height of 3:4 and so could have been modeled on a 3:4:5 right-angled triangle."[21]

I discuss below the strong possibility that geometry, thought to be typically Greek, came from Egypt. Indeed, it is difficult today to argue that —with the possible exception of axiomatic mathematics—any aspect of Greek "science" was more advanced than the sciences of Mesopotamia or Egypt before the second half of the fourth century B.C.E.[22]

Was Neugebauer Right to Dismiss Ancient Traditions of Egyptian Science?

In this section, I should like to take it as a given that Steuer, Saunders, and Ghalioungui have established not merely that Egyptian medicine contained considerable "scientific" elements long before the emergence of Greek medicine, but also that Egyptian medicine played a central causative role in the development of the Greek.[23] Similarly, the work of Neugebauer—and his school—has made it impossible to deny that some Mesopotamian mathematicians and astronomers were "scientific" in the positivist sense or that Mesopotamian "science" in these areas was crucial in the creation of Greek mathematics and astronomy. I should like to go further and challenge these scholars' dismissal of claims that an Egyptian mathematics existed that could have significantly influenced Greek thinkers.

Despite his early passion for Ancient Egypt and his considerable work on Egyptian astronomy, Neugebauer insisted throughout his long life that the Egyptians had no original or abstract ideas and that they were not on the same mathematical or scientific level as Mesopotamians.[24] According to him, the accurate astronomical alignments of the pyramids and temples in Egypt, and the use of π and ϕ, "the golden section," could all be explained as the results of practical knacks rather than of profound thought.[25] An example of this approach is the following: "It has even been claimed that the area of a hemisphere was correctly found in an example of the Moscow papyrus, but the text admits also of a much more primitive interpretation *which is preferable*" (my italics).[26] For an opposing interpretation, see below.

In *The Exact Sciences in Antiquity*, Neugebauer did not argue with the Pyramidological school; he simply denounced it. He recommended that those interested in "the very complex historical and archaeological problems connected with the pyramids" read Edwards and Lauer on the subject.[27]

I. E. S. Edwards did not involve himself with the Pyramidologists and their calculations, but the surveyor and archaeologist J.-P. Lauer did, despite opposition from Egyptologists, who were "astonished that we should give so much importance to the discussion of theories which have never had any credit in the Egyptological world."[28]

Lauer's work had a certain contradictory quality. He admitted that the measurements of the pyramids do possess some remarkable properties: that one can find such relations as π, ϕ, and Pythagoras' triangle from them, and that some of these relations correspond to what Herodotus and other ancient writers claimed for them. On the other hand, he denounced the "fantasies" of Pyramidologists and claimed that the formulae and the extraordinary degree of sidereal accuracy with which the pyramids were aligned were purely the result of "intuitive and utilitarian empiricism."[29]

A tension between the acceptance of the extraordinary mathematical precision of the Great Pyramid and a "certainty" that the Greeks were the first "true" mathematicians runs throughout Lauer's many writings on the subject. The strain is intensified by the facts that some Greeks had been told about many of this pyramid's extraordinary features and that they believed the Egyptians to have been the first mathematicians and astronomers. In addition, many of the Greek mathematicians and astronomers were supposed to have studied in Egypt.[30] Lauer's honest attempt to deal with these difficulties was as follows:

Even though up to now, no esoteric Egyptian mathematical document has been discovered, we know, if we can believe the Greeks, that the Egyptian priests were very jealous of the secrets of their science and that they occupied themselves, Aristotle tells us, in mathematics. It seems then reasonably probable that they had been in possession of an esoteric science erected, little by little in the secrecy of the temples during the long centuries that separate the construction of the pyramids, towards the year 2800 [I should put it 200 years earlier], to the eve of Greek mathematical thought in the 6th century B.C. As far as geometry is concerned, the analysis of buildings as famous as the Great Pyramid would take a notable place in the researches of these priests; and it is perfectly conceivable that they could have succeeded in discovering in it, perhaps long after their erection, chance qualities that had remained totally unsuspected to the constructors.[31]

Unless it was after the fourth century B.C.E., and hence was the result of Greek influence, the question of exactly when Egyptians developed this sophisticated mathematical knowledge is not directly relevant to the topic of this chapter. Nevertheless, the precision and intricacy of Old Kingdom architectural constructions is not the only argument for the existence of relatively "advanced" mathematics in the first half of the third millennium. The two great mathematical texts that have survived, the Moscow and the Rhind Papyri, come from the Middle Kingdom in the twentieth and nineteenth centuries B.C.E. Some of the problems set in them, however, use long-discarded measures belonging to the Old Kingdom.[32]

Lauer's solution still allowed some later Egyptians to have been capable of some relatively advanced thought. He continued: "For the whole length of the three thousand years of her history, Egypt thus little by little, prepared the way for the Greek scholars who, like Thales, Pythagoras and Plato came to study and then even to teach like Euclid at the school in Alexandria. But it was in their philosophic spirit which knew how to draw from the treasure amassed by the technical positivism of the Egyptians that geometry came to the stage of a genuine science."[33] Even this degree of recognition was too much for Neugebauer. As he put it: "Ancient science was the product of a very few men and these few happened not to be Egyptians."[34] In his note "On the Orientation of Pyramids," published in 1980, he argued that accurate alignments could be made simply by measuring and turning the shadow of a model pyramid or the capstone over a period of some weeks "without sophisticated astronomical theory whatsoever beyond the primitive experience of symmetry of the shadows in the course of one day." (The implausibility of this view was considered in the previous chapter.)[35] Neugebauer's choice of the word "primitive" to describe the alignment seems inappropriate, but, as we shall see below, it indicates his general opinion of the Ancient Egyptians.

This modern view of the Egyptians' lack of mathematics and science has undoubtedly been influenced both by a distaste for the theology and metaphysics in which much of Egyptian (and Platonic) knowledge was embedded and by progressivist views that no one who lived so early could have been so sophisticated. Assumptions, almost universal from the nineteenth to the mid–twentieth centuries, that Africans of any sort could not have been capable of great intellectual achievements may also have influenced this view.

Even such a champion of liberalism and foe of racism as Neugebauer may have been touched by these attitudes. In one of the bibliographical notes to *The Exact Sciences in Antiquity* he recommended that "a deeper understanding of the background that determined the character of Egyptian arithmetic" was Levy-Bruhl's *Fonctions mentales dans les sociétés inférieures*.[36] Levy-Bruhl was far from the worst of his generation in the early twentieth century. Nevertheless, he belonged to it; it was appropriate that his work was translated into English as *How Natives Think*.

Despite this, Neugebauer had some substantial arguments to back his case. The strongest was his claim that none of the surviving mathematical papyri from pharaonic Egypt contained what he believed to be sophisticated calculations and that the Egyptians' systems of numbers and fractions were too crude for the profound mathematical and astronomical thought attributed to them by Greeks and Romans. Nonetheless, there are seven major arguments against this position of Neugebauer.

1. The strong possibility that scholars such as V. V. Struve, Richard Gillings, Gay Robins and Charles Shute, Beatrice Lumpkin, and John Pappademos are right—and Neugebauer wrong—when they claim that the surviving Egyptian papyri do contain "advanced" mathematics.[37]

2. Parallels from Mesopotamia and Ptolemaic Egypt that show that one cannot rely on the papyrological record to gauge the full range of Pharaonic Egyptian "science."

3. The agreement that Egyptian geometry was equal to or better than that of Mesopotamia, combined with the conventional belief that one of the chief Greek additions to Mesopotamian "arithmetic" was geometric modeling, suggesting that the geometrical input may well have come from Egypt.

4. A sophisticated geometry and computation that would tally well with the extraordinary Egyptian practical achievements.

5. The Greeks' insistence that they learned mathematics — and medicine — not from Mesopotamia but from Egypt.

6. The later Greek adoption of an Egyptian rather than a Mesopotamian calendar.

7. That much of Hellenistic and Roman science took place in Egypt, not Greece, and that, although they wrote in Greek, several of its practitioners were Egyptian, including the astronomers Sosigenes and Ptolemy as well as the physicist and inventor Heron of Alexandria.[38]

The first argument is buttressed by the fact that, as we have seen, Neugebauer preferred "more primitive interpretations." Thus, his impartiality on the issue is suspect. Therefore, we should not use his justifiably great authority to contradict the later scholars who have argued that Ancient Egyptians used sophisticated mathematics. For instance, there is no reason to doubt Robins and Shute when they see the use of arithmetical and geometrical progressions in the Rhind Papyrus problems 40 and 79.[39]

The Soviet scholar V. V. Struve, who was the first to study the Moscow Mathematical Papyrus, was much more respectful than Neugebauer. He wrote, for instance, "We must admit that in mechanics the Egyptians had more knowledge than we wanted to believe." [40] He was convinced that both the Moscow and the Rhind Mathematical Papyri demonstrated a theoretical knowledge of the volume of a truncated pyramid. Struve has been followed in this interpretation by later scholars.[41] Given the many pyramids successfully constructed during the Old and Middle Kingdoms, this would not in itself seem unlikely. Nevertheless, Archimedes maintained that the volumes of pyramids were first measured in the fourth century B.C.E. by Eudoxos of Knidos.[42]

Here, as in other instances, Archimedes was knowingly or unknowingly mistaken. Even so, it is possible that Eudoxos was the first man to transmit the formulae to Greece. Eudoxos spent considerable time in Egypt and was reported to have learned Egyptian and made translations into Greek. Some of the translations may have come from the Egyptian *Book of the Dead*. As the historian of science Giorgio de Santillana pointed out, it is unlikely that Eudoxos translated them merely for their entertainment value; it is much more probable that he believed that they contained esoteric astronomical information.[43] Thus, we come to the important issue of the possibility that esoteric mathematical and astronomical wisdom was contained in Egyptian religious and mystical writings and drawings.

We must return to earth with the particular case of the measurement of the surface areas of either a semicylinder or a hemisphere in the Moscow Papyrus. The historian of Egyptian mathematics Richard Gillings, who believed that it was a hemisphere, described the Egyptian operations:

> If this interpretation . . . is the correct one, then the scribe who derived the formula anticipated Archimedes by 1,500 years! Let us, however, be perfectly clear [that] in neither case has any *proof* that either $A_{cylinder} = \frac{1}{2}\ pdh$ or $A_{hemisphere} = 2\ pr^2$ been established by the Egyptian scribe that is at all comparable with the clarity of the demonstrations of the Greeks Dinostratos and Archimedes. All we can say is that, in the specific case at hand, the mechanical operations performed are consistent with those operations which would be made by someone applying these formulas even though the order and notation might be different.[44]

In general, it is clear that the specifically mathematical papyri give considerable indications of sophisticated operations. As Struve put it in concluding his study of the Moscow Papyrus: "These new facts through which the Edwin Smith and Moscow Papyri have enriched our knowledge, oblige us to make a radical revision of the evaluation made up to now of Egyptian 'science' [Wissenschaft]. Problems such as the research into the functions of the brain or the surface area of a sphere do not belong to the range of practical 'scientific' questions of a primitive culture. They are purely theoretical problems."[45] Earlier in the same article Struve had written, "The Moscow Papyrus . . . confirms in a striking way the mathematical knowledge of the Egyptian scholars and we no longer have any reason to reject the claims of the Greek writers that the Egyptians were the teachers of the Greeks in geometry."[46]

Objections by Neugebauer and others to Struve's specific interpretation of the surface area of a hemisphere have now been removed.[47] Similarly, as mentioned above, the use of "Pythagorean" triangles and the sophistication of the measurement of the volume of the truncated pyramid have both survived earlier skepticism. If these bases of Struve's case still stand, should one accept Neugebauer's dismissal of it?

Even if one were to concede Neugebauer's argument that the mathematics contained in the papyri is merely practical and primitive, more sophisticated work may well have been recorded on others that have not been preserved. As mentioned earlier in this chapter, J.P. Lauer pointed to the many reports indicating that the Egyptian priests were secretive about their writings and argued that because of this few copies would have been made and their chances of survival would have been slim. Relatively few papyri of any kind have survived. Even in Mesopotamia, where there are thousands of baked clay tablets, there are very few mathematical or "scientific" ones. Neugebauer himself points out that the "great majority" of these mathematical tablets come from one of two periods: the Old Babylonian Period—of two hundred years—in the first half of the second millennium B.C.E. and, approximately 1,500 years later, in the Seleucid Period after Alexander's conquest. Continuities between the two sets of texts make it clear that sophisticated mathematics was carried out in the intervening twelve or more centuries, but no record of this survives.[48]

In Egypt it seems that most of the mathematical papyri written and all of those that have survived certainly were texts used for teaching scribes techniques that were useful for practical accounting rather than "state-of-the-art" advanced mathematics.[49] An instructive parallel comes from Ptolemaic Egypt. Many more mathematical papyri have been found from these three centuries than from the whole pharaonic period, yet none of these go beyond Book 1 of Euclid, or give any indications of the extraordinary sophistication that textual transmission shows was taking place in Hellenistic Egypt.[50] Thus, the argument from silence, which should always be applied sparingly, should be used with particular caution when looking for textual *proof* of advanced Egyptian mathematics.

One can argue that the few existing texts show a consistency of techniques and notation that make it impossible for Egyptians to have produced sophisticated mathematics. This raises the third argument against skepticism. Although Egyptian numerical notation may not have been as flexible and helpful as the Mesopotamian, it was, if anything, better than the Greek notation for its sophisticated formulae. No doubt, Egyptian mathematics was based on quite simple principles, but the surviving papyri show that extraordinarily elaborate mathematical structures were erected on them.

Neugebauer admits that although Egyptian arithmetic was not up to Babylonian standards, Egyptian geometry was equally good. If we are to believe other scholars' interpretation of the Moscow Papyrus, Egyptians were able to carry out geometrical operations beyond those of the Mesopotamians. The notion that the Egyptians were the better geometers fits both with their unparalleled architectural achievements and with their reputation among the Greeks as the founders of geometry and their teachers in it.[51]

Given this concern with geometry, it is not surprising that many direct and indirect proofs indicate that Egyptians relied on plans for their architectural constructions. Struve may have been exaggerating when he wrote: "The Egyptian plans are as correct as those of modern engineers."[52] Nevertheless, they were not inferior to Greek and Roman plans.

According to the Egyptians, the tradition of making plans went back to Imhotep, at the beginning of the Third Dynasty, c. 3000 B.C.E. Most modern scholars see this merely as a projection onto the deified prototype of all architects. It is now known, however, that architectural plans were used during the Old Kingdom and that Imhotep did design the Step Pyramid and the elaborate complex of buildings around it. Furthermore, an ostrakon found at the Step Pyramid contains measurements for a vault.[53]

This coordination of geometry and computation with architecture constitutes the fourth argument against the modern denial that the Egyptians possessed a superior mathematics. Textual evidence for such knowledge may be ambiguous, but the architectural evidence greatly strengthens it. Pyramids, temples, granaries, and huge irrigation networks required extraordinary planning and the ability to visualize these in advance on writing or drawing surfaces.

The fifth reason for supposing that the Egyptians had sophisticated mathematics is that the Greeks said so. Greek writers on the subject were unanimous that Egyptian mathematics and astronomy were superior to their own. They also agreed that, whereas only two Greek mathematicians were supposed to have studied in Mesopotamia, the majority of Greek scientists, astronomers, and mathematicians were reported to have studied or spent time in Egypt.

Modern historians of science treat these reports with skepticism because they *know* that there was no Egyptian science or mathematics worth studying. However, as Giorgio de Santillana wrote about Eudoxos, who undoubtedly studied in Egypt: "We are asked to admit, then, that the greatest mathematician of Greece learned Egyptian and tried to work on astronomy in Egypt without realizing that he was wasting his time."[54]

After the Persian conquests, the mathematics and astronomy available in Egypt drew from both Egyptian and Mesopotamian sources. The Greek belief that it was an Egyptian tradition, however, strengthens the case that the native component was significant.

The sixth argument against the skeptics is the fact that later Greeks adopted an Egyptian rather than a Mesopotamian calendar. The Egyptian solar calendar was more convenient, but this adoption also indicates a Greek tendency to draw from nearby Egypt rather than from more distant Mesopotamia.

The final argument is that in Hellenistic times, although Athens remained the center of Greek philosophy, nearly all "Greek" science took place in Egypt. Ptolemaic patronage was responsible for part of this but, if we are to believe Greek and Roman sources, the Alexandrian scientists also drew on and built on Egyptian wisdom. Euclid worked in Egypt at the very *beginning* of the Ptolemaic Period, a mere fifty years after Eudoxos had felt the need to learn Egyptian to study mathematics and astronomy. Thus, Euclid's work should be viewed as a synthesis of Greek and Egyptian geometry rather than as an imposition of the Greek rational mind on Oriental muddled thinking. It is true that Babylonian mathematics and astronomy flourished under the Seleucids, as stated above, but most of the great "Greek" scientists wrote in Greek but lived in Egypt, and some may indeed have been Egyptian.[55]

The great Greek contribution to mathematics and astronomy is generally held to be the introduction of geometric modeling and, in particular, the transposition of Mesopotamian arithmetical astronomical cycles into rotating spheres.[56] As discussed above, however, Greeks generally agreed that geometry developed in Egypt, and this belief is strengthened by what we know of Egyptian architectural sophistication and the mathematical papyri. Furthermore, the men most responsible for the Greek view of the heavens as spinning spheres, Plato and Eudoxos, were widely reported to have spent time in Egypt and were known for their deep admiration of Egyptian wisdom.[57] We have seen that Eudoxos was particularly closely associated with Egyptian priests and that he established the new astronomy of complex concentric spheres.

These seven arguments provide a strong case that rich mathematical, particularly geometrical, and astronomical traditions existed in Egypt by the time Greek scholars came into contact with Egyptian learned priests. After the Assyrian incursions into Egypt in the seventh century B.C.E., Mesopotamian "scientific" thought substantially influenced Egyptian mathematics and astronomy and continued to influence Ptolemaic and Roman Egypt.[58] The Egyptian medical tradition appears to have been less affected by Mesopotamia. In general, however, the "scientific" triumphs of Hellenistic Egypt would seem to be the result of propitious social, economic, and political conditions and the meeting of three "scientific" traditions: those of Egypt, Mesopotamia, and Greece. It should be remembered that Egypt and Mesopotamia were much more substantial and older civilizations, reaching back to the third millennium or beyond. In addition, the point at which Greeks "plugged into" Near Eastern "science" was Egypt, and for this reason the Greeks always emphasized the depth and extent of Egyptian wisdom.

I mentioned the arbitrariness of applying the word "science" to ancient civilizations at the beginning of this essay. Like Lewis Carroll's Humpty Dumpty, who employed words to follow his whim, we can apply the word "science" more or less as we please, but the only way to claim that Greeks were the first Western scientists is to define "science" as "Greek science." If less circular definitions are used, the practice and theory of much earlier Mesopotamians *and Egyptians* cannot be excluded.

VI

Recent Broadening
Scholarship

IN BA I, I DISTINGUISHED between what I call the "Broad" and the "Extreme" Aryan models. The Extreme model insists on the separation of Greece from the rest of the Eastern Mediterranean and welcomes any evidence of northern influences. The Broad Aryan model, by contrast, accepts certain Southwest Asian, including Semitic, influences on the formation of Greece, while it denies any significant ones from Egypt or the rest of Africa. The Broad Aryan model was predominant from 1840 to 1890 and was in competition with its rival from 1890 to 1920. After that, it was eclipsed by the Extreme model. Since the 1980s, however, a relatively rapid turnaround has brought the Broad Aryan model once again to the ascendant.

To consider this important new—or revived—trend in Classics, I have included in this volume reviews of works by three of its most distinguished proponents: Walter Burkert, Martin West, and Sarah Morris. This section also contains a previously published paper of mine dealing with Egyptian and Phoenician influences of Greece and the differences between them.

Only one of these scholars, Sarah Morris, has contributed to BAR. I have not written a response to her chapter. Instead, I have included a review of her much more substantial work, *Daidalos and the Origins of Greek Art*. Morris, whose work was written in the 1980s, fits the schematic chronology set out above, but the other two writers whose work I review here do not. Burkert and West have been propounding the Broad Aryan model since the 1970s. Both scholars have worked with Reinhold Merkelbach, a specialist in the mystery religions in Greco-Roman antiquity. In the light of this subject, it is not altogether surprising that Merkelbach should have been ahead of his contemporaries in his openness to Oriental influences on Greek religion.

The fact that this group does not fit the pattern of scholarship I set up in BA I shows, yet again, that my picture of the discipline was oversimplified. Burkert's and West's situations within Classics, however, also demonstrate the overall utility of the scheme. This is because, in their attitude to Asiatic influences on Greece, these scholars were perceived as deviants until the late 1980s. Their linguistic and historical credentials were impeccable, but their conclusions on "Oriental" influences were ignored or dismissed. As Burkert put it in 1992, "My thesis about the indebtedness of Greek civilization to eastern stimuli may seem less provocative today than it did eight years ago." [1] Burkert, West, and Morris are now not merely welcomed by the orthodox but portrayed as true representatives of the discipline of Classics "as it always was," or at least of how it would have developed smoothly if it had not been for outside interference from *Black Athena* and Afrocentrism.

This image of Classics opening up to ideas of Near Eastern influence has some slight substance to the extent that dissident voices have called out during the period of the dominance of the Extreme Aryan model. What is more, a number of the orthodox have paid lip service to the idea of Oriental influences on Greece, although they have always preferred what they called "Asianic" to Asiatic influences. By "Asianic" they meant Anatolian. The most welcome of the Anatolian peoples were those like the Hittites and the Phrygians, who spoke Indo-European or Indo-Hittite languages. Any other Anatolian group was acceptable, however, because the important barrier was that excluding Semitic speakers. Among them, Mesopotamians were preferable to West Semites (i.e., Phoenicians and Jews, although Jewish influence was accepted in the Hellenistic Period). West tactfully indicates the superficiality of these concessions when, in his latest book, *The East Face of Helicon*, he writes, "Since then [the 1930s] they [the Hellenists] have shown themselves increasingly tolerant of oriental comparisons, *if not particularly active* in investigating the oriental literatures for themselves" (my italics).²

I greatly admire Merkelbach, Burkert, and West as well as such other pioneers of this openness to the East as Peter Walcot and Joseph Fontenrose. They had to work constantly against the grain of their discipline. On the other hand, possibly through loyalty to their profession, they have signally failed to support such Semitists as Cyrus Gordon, Michael Astour, Saul Levin, and John Pairman Brown or even classicists from peripheral universities such as Ruth Edwards, working in Aberdeen and Reading. All these have, for many years, made similar claims of contact between the Levant and the Aegean with equal scholarship and linguistic competence. Burkert and West do sometimes list such "outside works" in their bibliographies and cite them very occasionally. They prefer, however, to quote each other or go to experts who have restricted themselves to the discrete fields of Assyriology or Hittitology rather than rely on scholars who transcend disciplinary frameworks, especially those whose work is based on West Semitic but who are interested in Aegean connections.

Even as late as the 1980s, this kind of selectivity may have been necessary to persuade their traditional colleagues. However, this is no longer the case. Burkert and West, ably supported by the younger Morris, have seen the Broad Aryan model triumphant. The vast majority of classicists now accept—in principle at least—that Southwest Asia had a major impact on Greek religion, literature (especially poetry), and art. The danger in recognizing that Gordon, Astour, and the others have been saying this for a long time is now less because it challenges the isolationist tradition—to which fewer and fewer classicists admit to belonging—than because it could be damaging to the authority of the discipline of Classics itself.

Significant differences still occur between those like Burkert and Edith Hall, who see Greek civilization as beginning in the Archaic Period, after the Dark Ages, and West, Morris, and others with a wider and deeper perspective. The latter believe that many of the characteristics of that civilization and the Semitic influences on it came much earlier, in the Late Bronze Age.

Nevertheless, the principal division in the historiography of the Ancient Eastern Mediterranean is no longer between the Broad and Extreme Aryan models but between the Broad Aryan model and the Revised Ancient model. As I see it, this conflict involves three major areas. First, the role of Egypt: The champions of the Broad Aryan model are, if anything, more hostile to the idea of Egyptian influences on Greece than many more traditional scholars. For instance, Morris denies the central role generally granted to Egypt in the development of Greek sculpture in the seventh and sixth centuries B.C.E. West describes the extent of Egyptian influence on Greek civilization as "vanishingly small in comparison to that of Western Asia."[3] Clearly, Burkert, West, and Morris, having made heroic efforts to follow arguments that require knowledge of Semitic languages, are daunted at the thought of having to enter Egyptology. I suspect, however, that they may also believe that, though their colleagues might tolerate one heresy (that of Southwest Asian influences), to add Egypt, especially now that it has become entangled with Afrocentrism, would be going too far.

The second area of conflict is language. Although Burkert, West, and Morris demonstrate conclusively the many detailed Greek borrowings of artistic motifs, literary forms, and tropes from Southwest Asia, they produce only a handful of Semitic loan words, nearly all of which have been acknowledged previously. The loans they propose are also largely restricted to the permitted semantic field of trade goods. Thus, for all their radicalism, these scholars do not threaten the sacred cow of Classics, the linguistic purity of Greek.

The last chapter in this section is a slightly revised version of an article of mine published in 1993, "Phoenician Politics and Egyptian Justice in Ancient Greece." I have included this article because it outlines my views on the different aspects of Greek civilization affected by Egypt and the Levant. Egyptian influence, though often transmitted by way of the Levant, was preeminent in the Bronze Age. The Greek polis, however, had no resemblance to any Egyptian political or economic entity, but was very similar both politically and economically to the Phoenician city states of the Early Iron Age. Given the closeness in space and time, and archaeological evidence of contact in these centuries, it is inconceivable that Phoenician models did not heavily influence the structures of the polis. Such institutional influences fit chronologically with the literary borrowings from Southwest Asia, as West has demonstrated during the same period, the tenth to the eighth centuries B.C.E. Most of the relevant "political" and literary vocabulary, however, cannot be derived from any Semitic language. I maintain that the simplest explanation is that this vocabulary was already in place, much of it of Egyptian origin, and had entered Greek during the Mycenaean Period or earlier.

The situation is complicated by the fact that from the late seventh century

B.C.E., Phoenician influence declined in the Eastern Mediterranean and Greeks were once more in close contact with Egypt. It was then that Greek art, philosophy, mathematics, and "science" drew on and developed from Egyptian models and more Egyptian words found their way into Greek. Greeks then intensified their admiration for the depth and subtlety of Egyptian civilization, in which they recognized some deep roots of their own.

12   Greek Art Without Egypt, *Hamlet* Without

the Prince: A Review of Sarah Morris's *Daidalos and*

the Origins of Greek Art

Daidalos and the Origins of Greek Art is a tour de force. Sarah Morris is both a trained archaeologist with interests in the Levant and a professor of Classics who has passed its most stringent linguistic and literary requirements. Her book consists of a string of studies mostly focused on the elusive figure of Daidalos and stretching in time from the Bronze Age to Alexander and in space from Ugarit to Ithaca and beyond.

   Daidalos and the Origins of Greek Art is really four books in one. Each of the parts or sections contains several chapters and a massive apparatus that more than qualifies it to stand on its own as a monograph. The first half of this chapter is an outline of the book's parts; the second contains my criticisms of Morris's work.

   In the first section, Morris thoroughly studies the name Daidalos and all the references to the root *daidal*, both as an adjective and as a noun, in epic,

Archaic, and Classical poetry and ritual. Morris begins by admitting that she can find no Indo-European or Semitic etymology for the root. Even without such an aid, however, she reconstructs a semantic field for *daidal*: of "elaborate" or "decorated," especially focused on descriptions of metalwork. In the earlier literature the term is used concretely, but by the fifth century, it is also employed as a metaphor.

Much of Morris's early chapters is concerned with adjectival uses of *daidal*. Indeed, Morris appears to prefer to date the personage of Daidalos himself to a later period, but she is unable to get around this passage from the *Iliad* (18.590–592):

ἐν δὲ χορὸν ποίκιλλε περικλυτὸς ἀμφιγυήεις
τῷ ἴκελον, οἷον ποτ' ἐνὶ Κνωσῷ εὐρείῃ
Δαίδαλος ἤσκησε καλλιπλοκάμῳ Ἀριάδνῃ

[And on it the renowned, ambidextrous artist inlayed a dance,
like the one which once in broad Knossos
Daidalos crafted for Ariadne of the lovely hair.]

As she points out, this passage not only establishes the existence of Daidalos before the composition of the epic but also locates him in Crete and appears to portray him as an architect.

These associations reappear in her second section, "Daidalos and Kadmos," concerned with parallels and connections between the civilizations of the Levant and the Aegean. She begins this section with a discussion of the toponym Da-da-re-jo found on a Linear B tablet from Knossos. She considers the arguments of Killen and others for linking it to Daidalos as something like the later Δαιδάλειον. She prefers, however, an agnostic position and links it to other places called Δαιδάλα. Still, she is reluctant to associate it with decoration or artifice, let alone with Daidalos himself. She makes the good point that if δαιδάλεος had been current in the Mycenaean Aegean, one would expect to find it in the Linear B corpus which is so devoted to descriptions of luxury goods. Even so, she is well aware that one uses the argument from silence at one's peril.

Sarah Morris is in no way as restrictive as Walter Burkert, who in his *Orientalizing Revolution* maintains that Greek religion and literature became permeated with Levantine influences almost exclusively in the single century from 750 to 650 B.C.E.[1] This claim is a development of a strand of scholarship first apparent early this century in the art historical work of

Frederick Poulsen, and it is extremely improbable on at least two levels.[2] First, one finds admitted Semitic loan words in Linear B and many other indications of Levantine influence both before and after Burkert's century of the "Orientalizing revolution." Second, theoretically the idea that a society should be wide open to outside influences for one century and essentially closed for the three thousand years around it is implausible. As Morris puts it, "The case of the Phoenicians helps illustrate how the period called 'Orientalizing' extends from the Bronze Age to late antiquity and remains better understood as *a dimension of Greek culture rather than a phase* (p. 130; my italics).

Morris is only relatively even-handed in allocating "Orientalisms" in Greek culture to Bronze and Early Iron Age influences, and she tends to focus on the latter. Nevertheless, she is convinced that the Greek Hephaistos closely parallels the artificer god Kothar wa Ḥasis, known from fourteenth- and thirteenth-century B.C.E. texts from Ugarit. She also presents a powerful case, based on archaeological finds, for cultic connections between the Levant and the Aegean in the Late Bronze Age (pp. 105–116). On the other hand, she suggests that the "Orientalism" in the ninth-century Cretan decorative style known as Protogeometric B, which, as she points out, is in fact "most ungeometric and ornamental," did not derive from Bronze Age cosmopolitanism of the past, as most scholars see it, but from contemporary Phoenicia (p. 151). I see no reason to doubt that both sources combined with local traditions to form the new style. Similarly, Morris sees Southwest Asian influences on the earliest surviving Greek law codes from Archaic Crete and sees these as indications of the origin of law in the Aegean (pp. 164–166). I try to show below that this too is a very unlikely proposition.

Turning to the one uncontested Levantine influence on Greece, the introduction of the alphabet, Morris is uncertain when this took place. In one treatment of the issue, she clearly favors a Bronze Age transmission (pp. 106–108). Later (pp. 159–161), however, she suggests that the true Greek alphabet emerged only as a result of Oriental influences on Crete after 1000 B.C.E. I find her earlier argument more convincing. As with her argument on the transmission of law, I believe that she mistakes the clear evidence of contemporary Phoenician influence on the alphabets of Early Iron Age Crete for the script's first introduction to the Aegean.[3]

Thus, despite her admission of earlier and later East-West contacts, the period in which she maintains that the most substantial Oriental cultural influence reached Greece is the Early Iron Age, beginning in the eleventh century. It is three hundred years before Burkert places it, but to my mind even this is still far too late.

Indeed, by using parallels and analogies from Bronze Age texts from Ugarit, Morris makes some of her most interesting and useful hypotheses about Daidalos. She notes two Levantine practices: making divine epithets into independent deities, and turning deities into sages or culture heroes— reverse Euhemerism. Even more precisely, she points to the fact that the Ugaritic Kothar wa Ḥasis reappears in the writings of Philo of Byblos (of the late first and early second centuries C.E.) as Khousōr. Philo saw Khousōr and his brother as the original human metalworkers and he explicitly equated Khousōr with Hephaistos. On these bases, she is able to postulate plausibly that Daidalos, the "decorator," began as an epithet for Hephaistos—with whom he was always closely associated in the Greek tradition— but became a deity in his own right and finally ended up a culture hero.

Using the same principles of comparison and possible cultural diffusion, Morris points out that Kothar wa Ḥasis and Khousōr were most concerned with the craft of shipbuilding. Using Greek traditions, she shows at least a poetic equivalence between sails and wings (pp. 192–194). This equivalence, she argues, following Plutarch in a plausible though rather Euhemerist fashion, would explain the myth of Daidalos' most famous and tragic invention: the wings with which he and Ikaros tried to escape from Crete.[4]

Morris emphasizes the early identification of Daidalos with the island. She points out that both the Linear B Da-da-re-jo and the Homeric Daidalos were associated with Knossos. On the basis of the increasing number of archaeological finds and epic and Archaic literary references and inscriptions, she also argues for a special connection between Phoenicians and Crete between 1000 and 600 B.C.E. This is one of the ways she attempts to link the great engineer with the Levant. On the other hand, Morris does not deny Phoenician penetration of the Aegean itself. She writes on this topic:

> The modern tendency to identify "Euboians" in Syria, Cyprus, Crete, Ischia, and even Euboia itself may be a mistake. Euboians saw rich iron ores in Etruria and North Africa west of Utica, as Phoenicians from Crete and Thera migrated to Libya. . . . Those who initiated this network of trade and settlement were not Greek but Levantine, and the culture they helped sponsor was too mixed to call Greek. The presence of Phoenician pottery in the Aegean *before* Greek (Euboian) pottery appears in Cyprus or the Levant means that traffic may have flowed from the East, before it did in the other direction. . . .

Lefkandi's wealth of Levantine material has inspired philologists to revive the Oriental origins of Greek epic. (p. 141)

Her concerns with Euboia and metallurgy naturally make Morris turn to the place-name of its largest city, Khalkis, and its associations with bronze. She prefers, however, to point out the island's iron deposits and the substantial archaeological evidence of Phoenician presence on the island in the Early Iron Age (pp. 139–140). Interestingly, the toponym Khalkis, also found elsewhere in Greece, comes from a stem attested in Linear B as Ka-ke-. Furthermore, Khalk- has no Indo-European etymology and a plausible Semitic one in the consonantal root ḫlq, which softened to ḥlq in later Canaanite. Ḥlq means "smooth pebble," "make smooth" in Hebrew. The Arabic ḫalaqa is "make smooth, lie, forge, fabricate." The consonantal fit of Khalkis from the earlier form ḫlq is perfect. Such an etymology would help Professor Morris's case for Semitic influences on Greek metallurgy— but given the form Ka-ke- it would push them back into the Bronze Age.

In general, Morris is reluctant to use etymologies. She follows the modern scholar Bruno Dombrowski's emphasis on calques as opposed to loans as indicators of cultural contact (p. 98). Calques are translations of a foreign term into a native one, as, for instance, turning the German Übermensch into the English "superman." Here, as elsewhere, Morris displays her tendency toward monism, the belief that a phenomenon must be one thing or another but not both. In fact, the presence of calques in no way lessens the likelihood of loans. Quite the contrary: calquing indicates cultural contacts of such an intensity that one would expect loans as well. Dombrowski's demonstration of similarities between the characters of the Ugaritic ʿAnat and Europa in no way weakens the widely accepted case that the Greek mythological figure derived her name from the Semitic ʿereb ("sunset" or "evening").[5] To take another example, it is virtually certain that γνώμων ("gnomon") is a calque from the Egyptian sb3 ("gnomon" or "triangular apparatus for observing the angle of the sun"). This is because gnōmon is derived from the Greek root gno ("to know") and the Egyptian word comes from sb3 ("wisdom"). The likelihood remains strong, however, that a loan was made from the Egyptian sb3 ("teach, teaching, school") to the Greek sophos ("wise man") and sophia ("wisdom").[6] On the other hand, given its early associations with Egypt, the Greek word philosophos ("lover of wisdom") is probably a calque from Late Egyptian. The term mai sbō ("loving instruction") is attested in Coptic. Thus, in this, as in many other cases, loaning and calquing are often intertwined.

Morris also maintains that calquing is a better indicator of cultural contact than loaning because calquing shows that the alien phenomenon is understood, whereas simply accepting a foreign word does not. In fact, the borrowing of a word necessitates some knowledge of its meaning. True, the receiving culture does not need to understand proper names. In Greece, however, the high status of West Semitic and Egyptian and the repeated contacts around the Eastern Mediterranean allowed the elite to understand and popularize their significance of foreign names. They did this by combining the names on the principle that Victor Bérard called "doublets," with an alternative or epithet for the mysterious place-name. This was precisely a calque for the borrowing. Morris herself refers to the derivation of the name of Kythera from the Semitic *keter* ("crown") (p. 135 n. 142). She does not go on to mention the point made by Bérard that this borrowing matches the island's capital Skandaia, meaning the same thing in Greek.[7]

At this point, we should return to Daidalos and his association with Crete. Morris gives good descriptions of the rises and falls of the modern scholarly term "Daedalic" as applied to the island in the Early Iron Age (pp. 252–256). She underlines the island's great prosperity during this period, which she plausibly links to the intensity of its relations with Phoenicia. She sees its decline after the seventh century as the result of the dramatic fall of the Assyrian Empire in 612 B.C.E.

This last argument is much less convincing than her others. It assumes that Phoenicia experienced a boom under the Assyrians, whereas historians of Phoenicia see its greatest period of prosperity as the centuries c. 950–750 B.C.E., when the great land powers in Egypt, Anatolia, and Mesopotamia were at their weakest. Indeed, the Phoenician decline, which began in the late eighth century, can best be attributed to Assyrian sieges of their cities and sustained Assyrian pressure from that period.[8] Morris quotes a passage from the *Lament for Tyre* contained in the Book of Ezekiel as if it were from the sixth century and referred to the fall of Assyria (p. 171). In fact, the style and a number of references in the *Lament* indicate that its original version was probably composed in the ninth century and certainly before 700 B.C.E. and that it refers to a humiliation of the city by the Assyrians.[9] The relative decline of the Phoenicians in the later eighth century provided the opportunity for the huge contemporary expansion of Greek and Etruscan trade, colonization, and naval power.

True, Phoenician and particularly Tyrian power did fall still further under Neo-Babylonian rule in the middle of the sixth century, but this relatively short period was followed by a renaissance of Sidon under the Persians, and it cannot explain the decline of Crete. The island may have fallen behind, its cities unwilling or unable to take part in the Greek expansion of trade and colonization of the late eighth century. Another factor could have been the increasing production of metals by Greeks in the Aegean and on the Greek Mainland. Morris's views of the Cretan recession as sudden rather than gradual and as linked to the startling collapse of the Assyrian Empire rather than to the changing patterns of production and trade that began in the late eighth century are extremely implausible.

Morris's mistaken linking of Phoenician prosperity to the Assyrians is disturbing because it shows that, in this instance, she has accepted the views of the scholars who have desired to diminish the significance of Phoenician influence on Greece and against whom she usually struggles so valiantly.[10] In the twentieth century classicists have consistently tried to confine "Oriental" influences on Greece to the seventh century B.C.E. or at most to the period 750–600 B.C.E., the period of greatest Neo-Assyrian power. The internalist reason for this periodization has been Fredrik Poulsen's establishment of the so-called Orientalizing ceramic period in which Orientalizing motifs and artistic styles pointing to northern Syria were blatantly apparent on Greek pottery.[11]

Relating all cultural influences to ceramic design and restricting such influence to the seventh century has also had a number of ideological advantages. First, it enabled the establishment of the Olympic Games and the formation of the polis in the early eighth century to be seen as purely Hellenic developments. Second, it located in Assyria the first "Orient" encountered by Greeks. The Assyrian Empire fits remarkably well with the stereotype of Oriental despotism and, thus, diverts attention from the Phoenicians, the foreigners with whom Greece had had most contact in the tenth, ninth, and eighth centuries, and whose city states looked disconcertingly similar to those developing in Greece toward the end of that period.

The third reason for emphasizing the seventh century is the most sinister, because denial of earlier contact allows the image of the Phoenician "Semites" to remain essentially passive. They were supposed to have needed stimulus from the only "semi-Semitic" Assyrians to reach the Aegean. As Rhys Carpenter put it: "Not until the eighth century does the awakening come, with a great onset of oriental, predominantly Assyrian, influence, presumably carried by the Phoenician vassals (and vessels) tributary to the Assyrian conquerors." [12]

The third part of Morris's *Daidalos* is devoted to what she sees as the Athenian appropriation of the Cretan hero in the fifth century B.C.E. Here, as in the first part of her book, she exhaustively treats references to Daidalos in the literature of the period, in drama, poetry, Herodotus, and the Platonic dialogues. She shows how Daidalos came to be seen as the Athenian culture hero of technology. He now became a magical sculptor whose statues were so realistic that their legs had to be tied together to stop them from running away. As the inventor ($\epsilon \dot{v} \rho \epsilon \tau \dot{\eta} s$) of sculpture and the other arts, however, he was later associated with "primitive" sculpture. Diodorus Siculus made the notable statement: "The style of old statues in Egypt is the same as those made by Daidalos among the Hellenes." [13] Pausanias suggested something similar: "As many statues as Daidalos made, they are somewhat odd in appearance, but something divine stands out in them." [14]

This was one reason modern scholars identified Archaic sculpture as "Daedalic." The other was Pausanias' association of Daidalos with $\xi \acute{o} a v a$ ("wooden images") and the descriptions of the Boiotian rituals of $\varDelta a \acute{\iota}-\delta a \lambda a$ described by Plutarch. In the latter, tree trunks were carved into the shape of women, dressed, and then ritually burned (pp. 53–58). Morris points out that these associations contradict the view of Daidalos as the liberator of Classical styles from the rigidity of what we now call Archaic art. She ends the third part by noting the continued view of Daidalos as a craftsman with Eastern connections. She discusses Pausanias' paradoxical attribution to the ancestral figure of Greek craftsmanship of a royal Persian $\delta \acute{\iota} \phi \rho o s$ $\dot{o} \kappa \lambda a \delta \acute{\iota} a s$ ("folding throne") found in the Athenian treasury (p. 264).

Politics and the Myth of Athens
MORRIS'S CRITICISM OF BLACK ATHENA

In the fourth part, Morris shifts the focus of her book from Daidalos and craftsmanship to myth making and, in particular, to the myth of Athens. This part is linked to the rest of the book by a concern with the iconography of what she sees as the new patriotism and "antibarbarianism," and the paradoxical fact that many of the motifs and styles used for this had Oriental precedents.

Morris blames fifth-century Athenians for having created the Aryan model. She sees the creation of the "Athenian Empire" and the "treacherous" or equivocal roles of other cities in the Persian Wars as important in the creation of a myth of Athenian autochthony. Furthermore, she suggests in the introduction to Daidalos that these points substantially weaken the case I make in BA. She claims that the beginnings of "Bernal's 'Aryan Model' were in the fifth century after the Persian Wars," as opposed to my contention that the Aryan model was "fabricated" only in the early nineteenth century (p. xxii).

I do not see our positions as that far apart. In BA I (p. 90), referring to Aeschylus, whose work is central to my case, I wrote: "His play *The Persians* directly expressed the xenophobic passions of his generation. In *The Suppliants* they are only thinly disguised. . . . In such a passionately chauvinist atmosphere, it would seem more plausible to suppose that Aischylos wanted to diminish rather than exaggerate the Egyptian components in the myth cycle."

Nowhere did I deny the general hatred of and contempt for "barbarians" among fifth- and fourth-century Greeks in general and Athenians in particular. Neither did I question their desire to lessen any perceptions of cultural or other dependence on them. I quoted—in boldface—William Mitford's lines: "Some of the best supported Ancient Grecian traditions relate to the establishment of Egyptian colonies in Greece; traditions so little accommodating to national prejudice."[15]

I follow Mitford in believing that the "national prejudice" among fifth-century and later Greeks was such that one should expect them to diminish their cultural debts to "barbarians." I also agree with him that the survival of stories of Oriental and Egyptian colonization provides testimony to the strength of the traditions despite such passions.

It could be argued that the stories of foreign settlements and rule in Boiotia and the Peloponnese were Athenian fabrications designed to elevate themselves as the only "true" Greeks. Indeed, I refer to this tradition and the supplementary one that all Greek culture derived from Athens, hence all Greek culture was pure. In BA I, I traced this tradition only back to Lucretius, though I had no doubt that it originated earlier. It is, of course, in Plato's dialogue *Menexenus*.[16] What Plutarch saw as the denigration of Boiotian and Argive Hellenism led him to attack Herodotus' "barbarophilia." Nevertheless, Thebans were clearly conscious and proud of their associations with the Phoenician Kadmos, as the Argives were proud of Danaos' coming from Egypt.

In BA III, I shall argue along the principles set out by Morris that fifth-century Athenians had good political reasons for trying to expunge traditions of barbarians in their foundation. Thus, we should question myths of Athenian autochthony rather than challenge the traditions of foreign influences on Boiotia and the Peloponnese. What I call the Ancient model

portrays the extent to which fifth-century Greeks accepted that foreign influence was part of the formation of their culture even *after* the traditions
had been modified by Hellenic chauvinism. I quite agree with Morris that
the extent of foreign influences on the formation of Greek civilization were
in fact greater than they later admitted.

My Criticisms of *Daidalos and the Origins of Greek Art*

In some ways, Morris's fourth section, with its shifts both in time from
the seventh to the fifth century and in topic from myth and craftsmanship
to legends and politics, can be seen as a bonus added to the main structure and first three sections of her work. In other ways, however, the final
section is flawed, and interestingly it reveals flaws in the work as a whole.
What is more, it is precisely these flaws that, for all its radicalism, make
Daidalos and the Origins of Greek Art acceptable to the Classical establishment.

Let me explain. Although Morris touches on the question of Phoenician
influences on the early Cretan laws, her concentration on technology and
art in the early sections of the book enables her to avoid the area with the
greatest Levantine impact on the Aegean from the tenth to the eighth centuries: political organization. She fails to investigate the startling similarities between the economic, social, and political orders of the city states
of Syro-Palestine and the manufacturing and trading poleis that emerged
in Greece some centuries later. Such a lacuna would be acceptable if the
book were entirely devoted to art and technology, but the fourth section is
concerned with political ideology and political institutions.

Morris has set out the substantial archaeological evidence for contact between the two regions from the tenth to the eighth centuries. She argues
persuasively that the trade in this period was initiated by the Phoenicians.
Thus, it becomes virtually inconceivable that such a similar complicated
cluster of institutions could have developed independently in the nearby
Aegean.[17] However, the idea that the polis could have been substantially
derived from the East is still unacceptable to most classicists.

The second major sensitive subject for Morris is Egypt. She manages to
avoid this subject by eliding the sixth century B.C.E. that falls between the
first three parts of *Daidalos* and the fourth. Morris follows the school of
classicists who see the Persian Wars as formative in most, if not all, aspects of Athenian and, hence, Greek culture, art, literature, and politics.
She focuses on what she sees as "the invention of Theseus" as both a king

and a champion of democracy and the founder of *synoikismos:* Attic unity. She insists that the Theseus myth "must have developed no earlier than the Kleisthenic reforms" for which they were used as a precedent (pp. 338–339). The political use of a mythical precedent, however, does not necessarily negate its historicity. The fact that Sir Edward Coke dug up and altered the sense of the *Magna Carta* for his own political purposes in the early seventeenth century C.E. does not mean that the document had not, in fact, been drawn up four centuries earlier and had been available, though little used, in the interim. Quite possibly, the Attic synoikismos or unity had existed in earlier times and some of the legendary kings of Athens before the Trojan War had controlled more than the city itself. Even in the Bronze Age, the state's power was probably linked to the extraordinary mineral wealth of Laurion, from where we now know metals were exported in that period.

Morris is convincing when she shows the effect of the Persian Wars on the development of Panhellenism and contempt for barbarians and the concomitant beliefs that Greeks were or should be free, whereas barbarians, especially those from Asia, were portrayed by Greeks as naturally slavish in their dispositions. However, even here clear precedents can be found. A reasonable case can be made that, although Homer did not use the terms "Hellene" and "Barbarian" (except the latter in one restricted case), the later interpretations of the Trojan War as one between Greeks and barbarians were not misplaced. The term "panhellene" is attested from the middle of the seventh century B.C.E.[18] The statement that epitomizes the sense of the Greeks as a culturally united free people as opposed to Oriental despotism is Phokylides' famous fragment: "Better a small city perched on a rock, than all the splendour of senseless Nineveh." Probably this verse was not written before the fall of Nineveh in 612 B.C.E. and it may refer obliquely to the growing Persian menace to Ionia in the 540s. Nevertheless, the lines show that a Greek image of themselves as a poor but free and superior people was not the result of the Greek triumphs in the Persian Wars in the fifth century but was current at their start.

Egypt and the Sixth Century B.C.E.

In general, it is misplaced minimalism to date the formation of Classical Athens to the fifth century. I see no reason to deny the credit given to the men whom fifth-century Athenians saw as having created the city they knew and loved: Solon, Peisistratos, and Kleisthenes. The first two were born and raised before there was any thought of Persia, and the Persian menace probably had little impact on Kleisthenes' democratic reforms. Indeed, Aristotle saw the Persian Wars as having halted democracy and given power to the more elitist assembly, the Areopagus.[19] The late seventh and early sixth centuries, in which two of the three men flourished, was a period of intense Egyptian cultural influence. Morris is wary of accepting Diodorus' claim that Solon's *seisachtheia* ("shaking off burdens or debts") was influenced by the legal reforms on indebtedness of the pharaoh Bocchoris (717–711 B.C.E.) (p. 168). Given the similarities between the two reforms, the high reputation of Egypt among Greeks of the sixth century, and the associations with Egypt attributed to all of the Greek "Seven Sages" of that century, such influence is very likely.[20]

Peisistratos, too, was sometimes included among the Seven Sages. His self-serving promotion of the cult of Athena used strikingly Libyan symbols. He placed on a chariot a tall and splendidly armored young woman impersonating Athena, and Herodotus described a very similar ceremony in Libya.[21] That Peisistratos' enthusiasm for the goddess came at the same time that Pharaoh Amasis was promoting the cult of Athena's Egyptian counterpart Neith and the cults of Athena and Hera in the Aegean seems more than coincidence.[22] Amasis' friendship with Polykrates of Samos, the prototype of "tyrants," was well-known. The quadriga, a four-horse chariot, that was later used as a symbol of tyrannical power was thought to be Libyan. Herodotus specified that it had been introduced to Greece from Libya.[23] It should be noted that Amasis' capital, Sais, was on the Libyan border of Egypt. Unlike the reforms of Solon and Peisistratos, Kleisthenes' reforms in the last quarter of the sixth century show no sign of Egyptian influence or symbolism. They can be explained relatively easily in terms of local Athenian developments.

The late seventh century and the first three quarters of the sixth saw not only the formation of the Athenian political structure but also what are conventionally seen as the beginnings of Classical art, sculpture in particular. Unlike the political developments, the artistic shift is widely acknowledged to have been heavily influenced by Egypt. Morris admits that this is the general view, but she attempts to undermine both the ancient and modern understandings of the connections. She tries hard to dismiss Diodorus' statement quoted above, that "the style of the old statues in Egypt is the same as those made by Daidalos among the Hellenes."[24] In the first place,

she translates Diodorus' word *ruthmos* as "style" when it is conventionally rendered as "proportion." It is precisely the proportions of Greek *kou-*
roi ("naked young men") and *korai* ("clothed young women") that Eleanor
Guralnick had fruitfully compared to Egyptian canons.[25] Morris then cites
various authors whom she sees as preferring Levantine origins for Greek
sculpture.[26] These sources are used to refute Diodorus, Guralnick, Martin
Robertson, John Boardman, and conventional wisdom, because according
to Morris:

> These recent trends in scholarship discourage the use of archaeological evi-
> dence to interpret the passage in Diodorus which must be understood within
> its historical and literary context. Nor should this passage be invoked to
> defend the *superficial* similarity in statue types as a historical phenomenon.
> Rather than comparing Egyptian statues with Greek *kouroi*, Diodorus *could be*
> expressing (or merely transmitting) the judgement that the works of Daida-
> los occupy the same venerated position in the history of Greek art that an-
> cient Egyptian ones do. (pp. 240–241; my italics)

It is extraordinary that Morris wants to reject not only the use of the archaeological evidence that the proportions of Egyptian and early Greek
sculptures often match but also their *superficial* similarities and Diodorus'
explicit statement. All this largely on the basis of her own speculation.
On the modern scholarship she writes with some skepticism, "It has been
argued that the Saite canon in sculpture was known and copied by Greek
sculptors. But kinship between Egyptian and Greek sculpture seems more
manifest in the sixth century than the seventh, when the first statues and
reliefs were made" (p. 240; my italics). In fact, though nothing is certain,
Guralnick's computerized studies of the generally "Egyptian" proportions
of kouroi are as close to a scientific demonstration as one could hope to
find in Classical archaeology.[27]

Very seldom is there a complete *coupure* in the artistic tradition of a
single culture, and clearly there were visual arts in Greece between the
tenth and the seventh centuries B.C.E. As Morris also claims, these arts
were heavily influenced from the Levant and elsewhere in Southwest Asia.
Martin Robertson, John Boardman, and the others, however, are not merely
being arbitrary when they see the kouroi, with their dependence on contemporary Egyptian forms, as the beginning of something altogether new.[28]
Toward the end of the seventh century B.C.E., Greek sculpture and other
arts really did make a qualitative leap.

The Role of Egypt in the Bronze Age

The artistic break at the end of the seventh century B.C.E. is somewhat obscured by the fact that Egypt heavily influenced the art of Bronze Age Crete, Greece, and that of the Levantine coast. The pattern is confusing, for characteristic styles in all three regions had come together and diverged again many times before the late seventh century.

Morris has achieved so much with so much effort in combining primary and secondary material on both the Levant and the Aegean that it seems hard to ask her to master yet another discipline, Egyptology, but it is necessary if one is to make sense of her topic. She does not neglect Egypt entirely. Morris is open, for instance, to the possibility that the mythical Minos and Rhadamanthus and the Labyrinth derived their names from Egypt (pp. 181–183). In general, however, as with the origins of Greek sculpture, she is skeptical of claims of Egyptian influence. Even more often, she simply ignores Egyptian parallels. For instance, in her extensive treatment of Pandora she does not mention Peter Walcot's demonstration of the extraordinary similarities between the creation and divine endowment of Pandora and those of the Egyptian woman pharaoh Hatshepsut, five hundred years before Hesiod.[29]

Morris's emphasis on influence from Southwest Asia as opposed to Egypt is intertwined with two other predilections that I have previously noted: her preference for the Early Iron Age, when the Phoenicians were dominant in the Eastern Mediterranean, and skipping the century 625–525 B.C.E., when the Egyptians had the greater cultural influence on Greece both directly and indirectly. For example, she extends her accurate observation of "Semitic" influences on Cretan law codes in the Archaic Period to the extremely dubious argument that Greek law originated from this quarter. In the mythological realm, she finds it "tempting to seek" the sources of the image of Minos as a king, a lawgiver, and a judge of the dead in "the archaeological record of Early Iron Age Crete" (p. 175). Therefore, she looks to parallels with the Levant and to Moses as a lawgiver.

As I noted above, Morris admits that the name Minos may have come from the Egyptian Min/Mēnēs, and there is no doubt that the judge of the dead par excellence was Osiris. The finding of gold leaf scales in the funerary context of a Shaft Grave provides archaeological evidence strongly suggesting that Mycenaean Greeks knew of the Egyptian tradition of weighing the souls of the dead.[30] Furthermore, a significant number of Greek terms concerning justice and law have plausible Egyptian etymologies. Homer and Herodotus saw Egypt as a seat of justice, and Aristotle believed it to be the source of Greek law.[31] This tradition and the firm establishment of law, under Semitic influence, in the Aegean by the early seventh century make it impossible for the Egyptian connections with Greek justice to have been first established during the Saite Period.

In some cases, a more serious consideration of Egyptian culture would have helped Morris's arguments. Her interesting discussion of the close relations among metalwork, carpentry, magic, and poetry demonstrates striking parallels between the Levantine and Aegean traditions. She is skeptical of the Indo-European etymology for Homer of ὁμοῦ plus ἀραρίσκω ("fitting together") (p. 85). Indeed, a much more plausible one comes from the Egyptian. The word ḥmt means "craft." The term ḥm(w)t r or ḥm(-w) r3 means "art of the mouth." It is also a magical formula used at the end of an incatantion. Ḥm(w)t r appears as hmhr in Coptic. With the Egyptian personal suffix -w, *hmhrw is close to Ὅμηρος, "the wordsmith."

Morris points out that classical scholars since Joseph Scaliger in the sixteenth century have known that the name of the Kabeiroi derives from the Semitic Kabir ("great") and that their cults at two centers of Semitic influence in the Aegean, Thebes and Samothrace, strongly suggest Phoenician influence (p. 143). The representations of the Kabeiroi as dwarfish and with caricatured "negroid" features suggest an African involvement in the cult. Herodotus pointed out similarities between the appearance of the Kabeiroi and the Egyptian statue of Hephaistos at Memphis: "This statue closely resembles the Pataikoi which the Phoenicians carry about on the prows of their warships—but I should make it clearer to anyone who has not seen these, if I said it was like a pygmy. He [the Persian King Kambyses] also entered the temple of the Kabeiroi, which no-one but the priest is allowed to do, made fun of the images there (they resemble those of Hephaistos and are supposed to be his sons)."[32] This passage, to which Morris does not refer, is almost too rich in the themes with which she is concerned. Herodotus seems to have been somewhat confused in describing the statue, because representations of Hephaistos' usual Egyptian counterpart Ptah do not resemble pygmies or the Kabeiroi. On the other hand, images of Bes, the god of physical and spiritual birth, initiation, and music, do, and Bes had many small helpers. Kothar was also a god of music, dancing, and merrymaking and had cheerful companions.[33] Thus, representations of Bes would fit the magical aspects of the cluster with which Morris is concerned. The Phoenician Pataikoi bring out Morris's excellent discussion of the craft of shipbuilding in the Ugaritic tradition, Philo of Byblos, and Daidalos, maker of wings (pp. 87, 191–194). The name Pataikoi points back to Ptah. Morris herself brings out the relationship between the Levantine divinity and the Egyptian god of craftsmanship when she quotes the lines from Ugaritic (p. 93):

> Kaphtor is the home of his dwelling
> Memphis is the land of his inheritance.

Kaphtor, Crete, was an ideal home for a Levantine god of craftsmanship. The island was high, far away, and in the Bronze Age admired for its fine workmanship. The name translated as "Memphis" was Ḥkpt, from the Egyptian Ḥt k3 Ptḥ ("House of the ka, spirit of Ptah"), the religious name of the city, from which, by extension to the whole country, the Greek Aigyptos and our "Egypt" are derived. Kothar wa Ḥasis was also given the epithet Bʿl Ḥkpt ("Lord of Memphis"), linking him even more tightly to Ptaḥ.

Morris admits to this Egyptian connection but tries to mitigate it: "It *may have been* through the Levant in the Bronze Age that speakers of Greek, from the Aegean learnt the name of Egypt, just as their experience of Egypt was channelled through the Levant" (p. 94; my italics). Here again, Morris is tripped up by her two greatest weaknesses: monism and an exclusive focus on the Levant. Much Egyptian trade and some cultural influences were transmitted to the Aegean in a counterclockwise direction around the Levant and Anatolia, but this was not the sole route by which Egyptian culture was transmitted to the Aegean. Many aspects of Cretan and Aegean art and archaeology can best be explained as coming directly from the south.[34]

If Morris had looked toward Egypt she would have found many parallels for topics that interest her. For instance, she discusses Daidalos' connection with statues so realistic their legs had to be tied together to prevent their running away (pp. 221–226). No source for this idea can be found in the generally aniconic Levant, but the notion of living statues was central to Egyptian thought.[35] Morris stresses what she sees as a Greek tradition of the various parts of the body having their own independent voices and the power of the voice to animate matter (pp. 220–221). These tally with the Egyptian beliefs of independent deities for different body parts as set

out at the beginning of the *Memphite Theology*. In this, Ptah "gave life to all
the gods and their *kas* through his heart and his tongue." [36]

Etymologies

Although Morris provides evidence of contacts between the Aegean and the
Levant and points out the mythological parallels between them, she has
been unable to establish many etymological connections between Greek
and West Semitic. Here too she would have profited by considering Egypt.
Some of the vocabulary of metalworking associated with Daidalos lacks
Indo-European or Semitic etymologies but has plausible Egyptian ones.
These include the following:

Greek	Meaning	Egyptian	Meaning
ἀσκέω	fashion, cloth, or metal	sqr	strike, work metal
δίφρος	litter, chariot, vehicle of the sun throne	dpt	ship, ship of state
ἔντεα	armor, equipment	nd̠	save, protect
οἶμος	route, band, stripe	wmt(t) 🗍	wall, circumvallation
'Iκμάλιος	the craftsman	qm3	produce, hammer out

The city name Κάμ(ε)ιρος, which, with the other Rhodian cities, was
closely associated with craftsmanship, also has a plausible etymology from
qm3.
    The most striking possible Egyptian etymology is that of δαιδαλ—itself.
Morris states on her opening page, "The etymology of its root remains
unknown: Indo-European sources (*del-) and Semitic *dal (as in δέλτος,
"writing tablet") have been proposed but neither demonstrates an independent connection with its epic manifestations" (p. 3).
    The Egyptian cluster of words around the consonants d̠ȝd̠ȝ is rich and
confusing. In Middle Egyptian, one finds d̠ȝd̠ȝ ("head") and, possibly derived from this, d̠ȝd̠ȝ ("magistrates and assessors"). It is interesting that the
latter was written with the determinative ⊢⊣⊢ ("irrigation runnels"), which
Gardiner tentatively equates with the more elaborate form ≣≣≣ . [37] This could
be explained in terms of the Asiatic mode of production and the centrality
of the allocation of water to Egyptian administration. Something else also

appears to be going on, and the pattern of segmented horizontal bands could have had a significance of its own.

The derivation of Daidalos from ḏ3ḏ3(w) presents a phonetic problem. A partial merger of ḏ with d began in the Middle Kingdom. Substitution of d for ḏ in Late Egyptian is frequent and is found in Greek transcriptions; for instance, the city name 3bḏw was rendered as Abydos. In Coptic, which lacked a ḏ, many words deriving from earlier forms with ḏ were rendered with the other dental stop, t.[38] The difficulty lies in the fact that at least in writing, the ḏs in the word ḏ3ḏ3 appear to have retained their distinction from d very late.[39] Because we do not know the vocalizations, it could well be that this was not the case with the ḏs in ḏ3ḏ3w. As set out in chapter 6, the "double aleph" was originally pronounced as a liquid r or l.[40] The process through which 3 lost these consonantal values was not complete until the middle of the New Kingdom. A loss of the first 3 in ḏ3ḏ3w with this value would suggest, however, that the process had already begun. This and the fact that the semantic parallels are closest to Late Egyptian point to an introduction of the term to the Aegean during the Eighteenth Dynasty (c. 1570–1300 B.C.E.), a period of intense contact between Egypt and the Mycenaean kingdoms.

In his *Dictionary of Late Egyptian*, the lexicographer Leonard Lesko tentatively suggests that another common word, ḏ3ḏ3wt, meant "courses." [41] With commendable caution, Lesko used an English word that is thoroughly ambiguous. In one instance, the determinative of ḏ3ḏ3wt is the 𓉘 also found in wmt(t), which was proposed above as the etymon of οἶμος. In this and another instance, it is found with 𓈗 ("irrigation canal"), which brings us back to the determinatives 𓈖 and 𓈘. The use of 𓉘 suggests that Lesko was quite right not to restrict the meaning of ḏ3ḏ3wt to *water* courses and that, although this was the original sense, ḏ3ḏ3(wt) was also extended to mean segmented horizontal band. In Coptic there is the word *tote*, meaning "border, fringe." [42]

This process seems to be present on a larger scale in the Late Egyptian architectural term ḏ3ḏ3w ("pavilion, kiosk, landing stage," and possibly "collonade"). In Middle Egyptian, ḏ3dw written with the determinative 𓉐𓉐 meant "audience hall." Ḏ3ḏ3w in this sense would provide a plausible origin for the Linear B locality Da-da-re-jo. A strong ancient tradition maintained that the *khoros* Daidalos built for Ariadne was a "dancing floor," a "place (topos) complete with columns and statues arranged in a circle" (Morris, p. 14). This would be appropriate for the builder of a ḏ3ḏ3w ("pavilion, kiosk, landing stage, or collonade") and would confirm the hypothesis that linked the Linear B Da-da-re-jo to the later $\Delta\alpha\iota\delta\alpha\lambda\epsilon\hat{\iota}o\nu$, interpreted by Morris as "place of Daidalos" (see p. 75). In Ptolemaic inscriptions of the last three centuries B.C.E., ḏꜣḏꜣ appears as a verb meaning "to erect part of a temple" and "to set up or place a divine statue."[43]

So much for Daidalos as an architect. What about his role as a decorator of luxury objects? In Middle Egyptian one finds the special term ḏꜣḏꜣw ("pot"), and ḏꜣḏꜣt is attested for "harp" and "lyre" in both Middle and Late Egyptian. Although these are special terms, there is no clear evidence that they mean "decorated." Nevertheless, it is interesting to note that Homer had Achilles play on a lyre that was described as kalē daidadaleē.[44] In Egyptian, Levantine, and Aegean art, "decoration" was generally the addition of bands, often segmented, to frame or divide the central representations. Such motifs can be seen in virtually all of Morris's plates at the end of her volume. This pattern also emerges from the epic use of the adjectives daidaleos and polydaidaleos ("with bands or panels"). In the absence of any Indo-European or Semitic competitor ḏꜣḏꜣ(w) would seem a plausible etymon for daidal-. It should be remembered at this point that though extant Greek writings never linked Daidalos or the Labyrinth with the Levant, the architect and his edifice were associated with Egypt.[45] The etymology is uncertain. Nevertheless, such an Egyptian derivation would be a good basis for Morris's convincing sequence that Daidalos, the "decorator," began as an epithet for Hephaistos, became an independent deity, and ended up a culture hero, all within the Greek tradition.

Morris's rich and thoughtful book has greatly widened and deepened our knowledge of many aspects of Greek civilization, and it will be difficult to go beyond her study of the elusive and important figure of Daidalos. Unfortunately, the second half of her title, The Origins of Greek Art, is less well served. The civilization of the Ancient Eastern Mediterranean was not merely a meeting of the Levant with the Aegean or of Semitic speakers with Greeks. The mix was more complicated, with three main elements: Egypt, Syro-Palestine, and the Aegean. In the visual arts, despite its many glories, the Levant played a lesser role, possibly because of its aniconic traditions. The Nile Valley was, therefore, the most significant single source of both Levantine and Aegean art. To do as Morris has done and consider technical and artistic development anywhere around the Eastern Mediterranean between 3500 and 500 B.C.E. without giving a central role to Egypt is to have staged Hamlet without the prince.

13   One or Several Revolutions? A Review of

Walter Burkert's *The Orientalizing Revolution: Near Eastern*

Influence on Greek Culture in the Early Archaic Age

Walter Burkert's compact classic has had, and will continue to have, a revolutionary impact on the historiography of Ancient Greece and even more on the discipline of Classics. Burkert, though the professor of classics at Zürich, is a German trained in the great tradition and internationally recognized as the leading authority on Greek religion. If the English version had appeared at the same time as the German, 1984, it would have shaken the profession to the core and would probably have been publicly ignored as unworthy of a great scholar. The English translation of *The Orientalizing Revolution*, however, appeared only in 1992, when the situation had been transformed. Burkert's book is now hailed as a model of how to study "Oriental" influences on Greece in a professional manner. It is contrasted with irresponsible works by outsiders to the discipline.[1] Despite his professional credentials, however, Burkert, like Martin West, whose book *The East Face of*

Helicon is reviewed in the next chapter, was tainted with heresy because he took as his mentor and collaborated with Professor Reinhold Merkelbach at Cologne. Merkelbach's work on Greek mystery religions led him to see the impossibility of understanding such cults without paying full attention to their "Oriental" features.[2]

Originally published in German in 1984 as *Die orientalisierende Epoche in der griechischen Religion und Literatur*, the work was much more radical than this innocuous title suggests. Burkert claimed that Semitic influence on Greek culture had been massive during the "Orientalizing period," conventionally seen as c. 750–650 B.C.E. Burkert forcefully maintained that the chief Oriental influence on Greece came from the Levant and Mesopotamia, not Anatolia, and was not restricted, as orthodox scholars have held, to artistic styles and the alphabet. He saw major Semitic influences on the Homeric epics and the poems of Hesiod, as well as on Greek myth and religion as a whole.

In the preface to the English translation, which appeared in 1992, he writes: "My thesis about the indebtedness of Greek civilization to eastern stimuli may appear less provocative than it did eight years ago. This change may be partly an effect of the original publication, but mainly it reflects the fact that classics has been losing more and more its status as a solitary model in our modern world" (p. ix).

No doubt these claims are true and significant, and to some extent the author has moved with the times. The title has indeed become more dramatic, changing from *The Orientalizing Epoch* to *The Orientalizing Revolution*. The content too has been expanded. The tone, however, has not changed significantly, as the original was already very radical, at least by the gentlemanly standards of Classics. Burkert begins the introduction with a stinging indictment of such men as Julius Beloch, "a scholar of genius flawed by his idiosyncrasies and overt anti-Semitism." However, he also describes the hostility and "irascibility" toward "Semites and Egyptians" found among nineteenth-century founding fathers of Classics such as Ulrich von Wilamowitz-Moellendorff (pp. 2–3).

Burkert points out, acutely, that one reason for the anti-Oriental passion was "a certain insecurity" caused by the sensational discoveries of ancient civilizations around the Eastern Mediterranean. These discoveries threatened "the image of [a] pure self-contained Hellenism which makes its miraculous appearance with Homer." It also necessitated the neutralization of "foreign elements" by "policies of containment." Some of these were adventitious, though they were leaped on with enthusiasm by Hellenists. Burkert mentions (p. 4) the "hermeneutic approach" fashionable between the World Wars that "promoted concentration on the individual internal form and style in the interpretation of cultural achievements to the detriment of outward [outside?] influence."

He further describes what he senses to be "a new line of defense" of Greek purity: "It is generally and freely accepted that in the Bronze Age there were close contacts between Anatolia, the Semitic East, Egypt and the Mycenaean World, and that some 'Aegean koinē' can be found to characterize the thirteenth century B.C. . . . what is much less in focus is the 'orientalizing period' . . . between approximately 750 and 650 B.C." I think that both claims are overstated, though most conventional scholars would accept the first position. For all his radicalism, however, Burkert appears to share the Graecocentric view that the Mycenaeans dominated the Eastern Mediterranean at the end of the Bronze Age. More important, he believes that the Greek "Dark Ages" provide a significant barrier between the cosmopolitan society of the palaces and the "repurified" Greek society that emerged in the early eighth century B.C.E. I shall return later to these dubious propositions.

At the end of his introduction, Burkert launches a wonderful plea for modified diffusionism and a passionate and powerful attack on what he sees as the

> final and perhaps insuperable line of defense, the tendency of modern cultural theories to approach culture as a system evolving through its own processes of internal economic and social dynamics, which reduces all . . . [outside] influences to negligible parameters. There is no denying the intellectual acumen and achievement of such theories. But they still represent just one side of the coin. *It is equally valid to see culture as a complex of communication with continuing opportunities for learning afresh, with conventional yet penetrable frontiers in a world open to change and expansion.* (p. 7; my italics)

I would put it only slightly differently: To defend the purity of Ancient Greece, classicists have preserved broad developments in anthropology and other social sciences that took place in the early and mid–twentieth century. Earlier anthropologists' desires to reconstruct a pristine model of the society studied, untouched by colonialism or other outside influences; the use of structural functionalism; and a preference for synchronic rather than diachronic analysis were some of these developments and are linked to a reluctance to consider origins. The last is rather strange among Hellenists, who are essentially historians and for whom at least one reason for their choice of field is the attraction of Ancient Greece as the "origin" of European civilization. From 1950 until only very recently, such tendencies have been reinforced in Classics by the triumph of historical isolationism and a visceral hatred of even modified diffusionism. Literary criticism and the reluctance to see a text as anything more than an expression of the author's confused present and personal thoughts and feelings have also contributed. Thus, Greek writings about the past or other cultures are interpreted solely as "projections" of their own concerns, which can provide no information about their ostensible subjects.

Like Burkert, I do not deny "the intellectual acumen and achievement of such theories." I also agree with him completely that such theories are hopelessly one-sided and that much additional knowledge can be gained from other approaches. In short, Classical Greece cannot be fully or even interestingly analyzed or understood in geographical and temporal isolation.

The first chapter of *The Orientalizing Revolution* is concerned with migrant craftsmen, or *demioergoi*. Burkert points out that Orientalists have been unwilling to accept the importance of this group because of the frequent references in Mesopotamian and Syrian texts to royal craftsmen attached to the throne. Classical archaeologists, with their requirements of method, are equally "reluctant to consider opportunities for personal, almost anecdotal coincidence" (p. 23). Burkert is not discouraged by these attitudes, and he makes a strong argument for the presence of Levantine and even Mesopotamian migrant craftsmen around the Aegean in the Orientalizing period. Clearly, traveling craftsmen were found in Greece in Classical times and some of them must have come from regions to the east and south. Assembling many scraps of archaeological evidence, Burkert makes a plausible case for projecting this situation back to the Archaic Period, 700–500 B.C.E.

He goes on to suggest that there "is a clear distinction between western and eastern traditions" (p. 23). This proposition is much more debatable than his previous claim. Much more likely, the emergence of migrant craftsmen came not with some ineffable atmosphere of freedom in Europe but with the weakening and destruction of the palaces and the advent of a commercial "slave society," which was not a purely Greek phenomenon.[3] Burkert admits that by Hellenistic times traveling craftsmen were taken for granted in the Semitic world, and I see no reason why this realization too should not be projected back into the early first millennium. The example Burkert cites is of archaeological evidence from Crete pointing to Phoenician craftsmen on the island in the ninth and eighth centuries B.C.E., and there is no reason to suppose that they were not working at home in a similar way.[4]

Burkert provides massive evidence of Southwest Asian material culture in Greece in the period of his concern. He also points out a definite tendency among nineteenth- and twentieth-century scholars to play down its importance. Thus, "many of the oriental finds of the great Greek sanctuaries have long remained—and some still remain—unpublished" (p. 4). This assertion is irrefutable, but Burkert's claim that migrant craftsmen were largely, if not solely, responsible for the introduction of "Oriental" objects is less secure. Although the migrant craftsmen were clearly important in the transmission of both objects and skills, Burkert exaggerates their role in this process. Some objects clearly came directly from Phoenicia and provided models for Greek craftsmen to imitate. We also know from Herodotus that between 750 and 550 B.C.E., Egyptian and Anatolian monarchs sent rich gifts to Greek oracles and sanctuaries. Thus, though traveling craftsmen were obviously important, transmission in this period through trade and diplomatic exchanges was also significant.

Burkert's later discussions of subsets of his migrant craftsmen—the seers, healers, and singers—present different problems. Basing his claims on the splendid pioneering work of such scholars as Martin West and Peter Walcot, he shows the saturation of Greek epic and religion with Oriental motifs. Although these scholars, too, tend to see the main period of transmission as the Archaic Age, they are more open to the idea of earlier influences than Burkert, who wants to squeeze all of these influences into the single century 750–650 B.C.E. The implausibility of Burkert's compression is increased because he can achieve it only by taking extremely low dates for Homer and Hesiod and the introduction of the alphabet. I return to this topic below.

One of the strongest and most passionately argued sections of the book is that on the sociology of knowledge concerning the extent of Semitic influences on the Greek language. He attacks Indo-Europeanists for their single-minded concern with Indo-European languages and subsequent playing down of the significance of—or dismissal of—non-Indo-European etymologies for Greek words. He also faults the Indo-Europeanists for requiring that loans follow the rigid phonetic standards for loans that are really suitable only for relations among cognate words within the same language family. Burkert goes on to condemn the attitudes of such Indo-Europeanists as Debrunner and Meillet and the "highly restrictive critical work" of Emilie Masson. On the other hand, he praises the bold but sound etymologies of Oswald Szemerenyi and John Pairman Brown, who have expanded the number of Semitic loan words in Greek. He ends with a flourish: "Thus there can be no method to discover borrowed words: they imitate and go into hiding, adapting themselves to the roots and suffixes of native Greek . . . popular etymology plays its role in this metamorphosis; no rules for phonetic evolution can be established" (p. 35).[5]

I am in general agreement with this, but my own position is not identical with Burkert's. In the first place, some foreign loans did remain unassimilated. Take, for instance, the letter names *alpha, beta, and so on,* or *onar* ("vision, dream"), all of which were indeclinable. This in itself gives a strong indication that they were borrowings. The source of the letter names from West Semitic is obvious, whereas that of *onar* from Egyptian is only a little less so. It almost certainly derived from *wn ḥr* ("clear vision, reveal") in that language. Another borrowing from the same source that has been largely assimilated, although the gender varies, is *oneiros* (masculine), *oneiron* (neuter), meaning "dream." Nevertheless, Burkert is quite right to claim that the vast majority of foreign loans became thoroughly absorbed into the structures of Greek phonetics and morphology.

He exaggerates slightly when he states that "no rules for phonetic evolution" of borrowings can be established. I argue that, although the range of phonetic metamorphoses in loans is far greater and looser than those of "genetic" relationships, there are limits to the transformations that are possible.[6] Nevertheless, Burkert is absolutely right when he concludes this section: "In any case, the kind of minimalism that rejects all connections with Semitic that are not crystal clear remains, on the whole, the most unlikely of possible hypotheses" (p. 40).

Such a bold, clear, broad-ranging and plausible work as The Orientalizing Revolution cannot be perfect. Indeed, it suffers from two fundamental weaknesses: the attempt to cram all Oriental influence on Greece into the single century 750–650 B.C.E., and the exclusive focus on Semitic-speaking Southwest Asia and the consequent omission of Egyptian influences.

Burkert's restricted temporal scheme requires him to date the introduction of the West Semitic alphabet to Greece to the second half of the eighth century. This date is lower than virtually any scholar would go today. Among classicists the consensus is "the earlier part of the eighth century," but many believe it to be still higher.[7] Burkert himself concedes (p. 171 n. 12) that it is impossible to find a Semitist who would go later than the ninth century B.C.E.

Burkert is also aware of the work of Joseph Naveh, who has argued powerfully for an eleventh-century transmission, but he tries to isolate it by
claiming that Naveh is contradicted not only by specialists in Greek, but
also by some Semitists (p. 171 n. 12). Burkert has been disingenuous here.
The Semitist B. J. Isserlin, whom he cites as being opposed, has in fact
given Naveh qualified backing.[8] Another Semitist, P. K. McCarter, hesitated
between 1100 and 800 B.C.E.[9] Burkert completely fails to mention the cautious acceptance of De Hoz and the strong support given to Naveh by F. M.
Cross, the leading Semitic epigraphist in the United States.[10] He also omits
any mention of writers who have argued at some length, largely on the basis
of letter forms, for an earlier date than Naveh and a return to the conventional wisdom of transmission during the Bronze Age that existed before
1933, when Rhys Carpenter drastically lowered the date to the later eighth
century.[11]

Burkert is in even more trouble when it comes to language. He concedes
that a number of the Semitic loan words he lists in Greek are attested on
tablets in Linear B (pp. 36–37). The discovery of Semitic words in the Greek
used in the thirteenth century B.C.E. overthrew the previous conventional
wisdom that these words began to be introduced only in the eighth century,
at the same time as the alphabet. Only a dozen or so examples of such words
are conventionally accepted today, partly because of the relative small size
of the corpus of tablets and the repetitiveness of the texts. Other words
may be missed because, as Burkert points out, the assimilation of foreign
words to fit Greek phonetic and morphological patterns makes them hard
to detect. The thoroughly "Greek" forms of words admitted to be of foreign
origin in the works of Hesiod and Homer strongly suggest that these borrowings had been in use in Greek for some considerable time. Thus, there
is every reason to suppose that there were many other loans from Semitic
into Greek in the Bronze Age.

The same argument can be made for many of the parallels between
Greece and the Middle East in myth and cult that seem deeply rooted in
Greek religion. For example, the striking Semitisms that Victor Bérard
demonstrated in the cults of Arkadia could hardly have been introduced into that remote and conservative region during the "Orientalizing
period." [12]

This chronology leads to another issue on which Burkert has sadly followed conventional wisdom: the belief that the "Dark Ages" provide a substantial barrier between the Bronze and the Archaic Ages. The decipherment of Linear B as Greek and the prefigurations of later periods found

in the contents of the tablets have confirmed the theories of Nilsson and others who long ago saw an essential continuity from the Mycenaean to later Greek religion and culture as a whole. The presence of Semitic loan words on the tablets forced a shift in conventional wisdom. Over the past thirty years archaeology has increasingly indicated that there were contacts between the Levant and Greece, not merely in the thirteenth century but for most of the five centuries from 1700 to 1200 B.C.E. Even earlier than that, there is substantial evidence of Southwest Asian influence on Minoan Crete, much of which was transmitted to Mycenaean Greece. Thus, the ancient bedrock of Archaic Greece was already permeated with Semitic influences.

Burkert agrees (p. 15) that during the Dark Ages, long before the "Orientalizing period," there was considerable contact between the Levant and the Aegean. It is also virtually certain that this had a cultural impact. The admittedly "Orientalizing" decoration found on Cretan Proto-Geometric B pottery of the ninth century can be explained either as a continuation of Bronze Age "Orientalism" or as a result of contemporary Levantine contacts. We know from the excavations of Joseph Shaw and his colleagues at Kommos that such contacts were significant on Crete in the tenth and ninth centuries.[13] These explanations are not mutually exclusive, and the "Oriental" influences apparent in the decorations of the pots could very well have come both from the past *and* from the contemporary Near East.[14] Thus, although there clearly was an economic boom around the Mediterranean in the eighth century B.C.E., the intensification of contacts at that time were in no sense the *beginning* of "Oriental" influence.

Aside from the author's overemphasis on the single century 750–650 B.C.E., a second problem with *The Orientalizing Revolution* is the virtual absence of Egypt. Although they are not exactly congruent, the prejudices among nineteenth- and twentieth-century scholars against Egyptian influences on Greece were equally strong or stronger than those against the "Semites" described so powerfully by Walter Burkert. Because the idea of cultural influence from either sphere blasphemed the cult of Greek purity, we should no more blindly accept the modern scholars' denial or minimization of Egyptian influence on Greece than Burkert does their treatment of the Levantine influence.

I should like to provide a single, though centrally important, example of this prejudice at work. During his long life, Arthur Evans created the modern archaeology of Minoan Crete. Among many other accomplishments, he built up a massively documented case for Egyptian influences on the island. Other scholars resented this work during Evans's old age and it was played down after his death. Over the past thirty years, the tendency has been to limit the irrefutable visual influence to iconography and to resist the notion of any religious or other cultural baggage having accompanied it. Recent research is now showing the untenability of this inherently implausible idea.[15]

Close contact between Egypt and the Aegean during the Late Bronze Age is now impossible to deny. The pictorial, documentary, and archaeological evidence is so overwhelming that the leading Egyptologist Donald B. Redford has written recently: "There is no reason to doubt that the Egyptian court was at all times during the Mycenaean age in correspondence with the court at Mycenae, although the letters have not as yet been recovered."[16]

Although the Mycenaean kingdoms played significant roles in the Late Bronze Age concert of powers, between 1500 and 1250 B.C.E., the political, economic, and cultural hegemony in the Eastern Mediterranean lay with Egypt. The area was not, as Burkert appears to believe, an "Aegean koinē." Joined with the explanation of previous isolationism provided by sociology of knowledge, such relationships and contacts should lead one to reassess the modern denials of the claims by Herodotus and other Greeks of the Classical Period that Egypt fundamentally influenced the formation of Greek religion and culture as a whole.

During the Geometric and early Archaic Ages, with which Burkert is concerned, Greece appears to have received more cultural influences from Southwest Asia than from Egypt. We also know that after the seventh century, Egypt was central to the development of Greek sculpture and that the leading painter of pots in sixth-century Athens had the Egyptian name Amasis.

Furthermore, Greek lawgivers, philosophers, and mathematicians of these centuries and later believed that they could learn a great deal from Egypt and may well have done so.[17] If this was the case in periods of relative Egyptian weakness, Greeks were likely to be even more impressed and influenced by the splendors of the Eighteenth Dynasty.

Given these contacts over a long period and the large number of Greek words for which neither Indo-European nor Semitic etymologies can be found, a substantial Egyptian component in the Greek vocabulary would seem very likely. In the case of the Semitic loans, considerable scholarship had been carried out before the Romantic view of "pure" Greece and Greek took hold. This scholarship left a residue of plausible Semitic etymologies for Greek names and words that could not be covered for long by the

Aryanist tide. For instance, Burkert (p. 2) approves of the sixteenth-century scholar Scaliger's well-known derivation of the name Kabeiroi from the Semitic *kab(b)ir* ("great"), which Romantic scholars after Karl Otfried Müller had tried to deny.[18] Ancient Egyptian was deciphered too late for there to have been parallel earlier scholarship. Thus, apart from the names of some exotic trade goods, Indo-Europeanists have been even more unwilling to consider the possibility of significant loans into Greek from Egyptian than from Semitic.[19]

Burkert does not *deny* Egyptian influence on Greece—he simply does not consider it and thus leaves the structure of his book unbalanced. Though severe, this problem is not as serious as that of his periodization. Burkert attacks the scholars who want to preserve a "pure" Hellas. He himself, however, appears to maintain a version of this Romantic dream, when he insists on the importance of the century 750–650 B.C.E. and, therefore, implies an earlier autochthonous Greece, which only later incorporated massive and pervasive Semitic influence. In fact, however, there is no reason why his excellent description, quoted above, of *"culture as a complex of communication with continuing opportunities for learning afresh, with conventional yet penetrable frontiers"* should be restricted to this short period.

No Orientalizing revolution took place in this or any other century. Greece was always Oriental. Although the intensity of contact differed, at no stage was there a "pure" Greece, just as at no stage has there been a "pure" Levant or a "pure" Egypt. Dating the beginnings of the Semitic and the Egyptian influences on native Greek culture is as impossible as deciding *when* Rome was influenced by Greece. The essence of Hellenism or "Greekness" cannot be located in any particular time or space—it can be discerned only as a succession of styles or modes in which local developments and foreign introductions were intertwined or amalgamated.

Despite these misgivings, *The Orientalizing Revolution* is a superb work and I do not intend to travel far without it.[20] What is more, its radical and scathing analysis of conventional ancient history has been written by the world's leading authority on Ancient Greek religion. Something seismic is happening in Classics and surrounding disciplines. The shift is both welcome and timely.

14 There's a Mountain in the Way:

A Review of Martin West's *The East Face of Helicon:*

West Asiatic Elements in Greek Poetry and Myth

Martin West is a classicists' classicist. He trained at Oxford and thereby received the best possible English Classical education. He has edited and commentated on several Greek texts and has published works on many different Greek poets. Between 1964 and 1991 he taught at Oxford and London, until he was given a senior research fellowship at All Souls College in Oxford. West has employed his privileged leisure to the best possible advantage. Although now just over sixty, he has used the time to train himself in Assyriology and to increase his already prodigious rate of publication, which has culminated in his massive, 662-page *The East Face of Helicon.*

His desire to learn Akkadian and acquaint himself with Semitic studies in general has been long-standing. Like his mentor and collaborator Reinhold Merkelbach and Walter Burkert, another scholar close to Merkelbach, West has for many decades maintained that Greek culture was substantially influenced from Western Asia. His chief concerns have been with myth and poetry, with a focus on Hesiod, the most ancient Greek poet whose works are extant. West also wrote an important book, *Early Greek Philosophy and the Orient*, published in 1971. Although his editing and commentaries have been welcomed and used by his colleagues, until recently his general ideas have been dismissed or, at least, disregarded. His hypotheses on Western Asiatic influences on early Greek literature certainly did not reach the mainstream of the discipline.

At this point, I must apologize to West for having neglected his work in the first volume of *Black Athena*. My excuse is that, whereas my work focused on the Bronze Age, his work has generally been on the Iron Age. Nevertheless, I should have referred to him and the "Cologne school" in my survey of contemporary Classics. Furthermore, I could have learned specific points from him. For instance, for many years West has defied the conventional classicists' reversal of the predominant ancient belief that Hesiod was earlier than Homer (p. 276). If I had referred to his writings I would not have had to work the idea out for myself (BA I: 86–88). From this preamble, then, I turn to reviewing his most recent book.

The East Face of Helicon

The East Face of Helicon is an enormous and wide-ranging work essentially concerned with literature. It begins, however, with a short survey of the archaeological evidence of contacts between Southwest Asia and the Aegean during the Bronze Age and a sketch of parallel social, political, and intellectual structures in the two regions. For instance, West demonstrates conclusively that Greek astronomy was derived from Mesopotamia (p. 29) and, with rather less plausibility, that phrases used in oaths and treaties in the two regions match each other.

West continues with long sections in which he educates his classicist colleagues about the extant literatures in Sumerian, Akkadian, Ugaritic, Hebrew, and Phoenician.[1] He shows the striking parallels to be found between Southwest Asian and Greek concepts of heaven and earth, divine panthea, cosmology and mythical geography, eschatology, the social and sexual mixing of gods and mortals, as well as relations among mortals. He then does the same for literary tropes, styles, words, and idioms.

Some of West's parallels are intricate. For instance, he (pp. 109–110) follows Burkert in pointing to parallel passages found in the *Iliad* (15.187–

193) and the Akkadian epic *Atrahasis* (verses I.11–16), which dates back to the seventeenth century B.C.E. In these, the cosmos was divided among the leading gods into three provinces: Anu and Zeus were given heaven, Enlil and Hades the underworld, and Enki and Poseidon the sea. Remarkably, in both theologies, the allocation was by lot!

Other parallels are simpler, but also convincing. West cites the work of the Semitist and classicist John Pairman Brown, who has shown that in both the Hebrew Bible and the Greek epics (though not later Greek poetry) heaven or the firmament is thought of as beaten metal, bronze or iron (pp. 139–140). Other parallels are not quite so impressive. For example, though Southwest Asians and Greeks both saw kings as godlike or equal to god (pp. 132–133), the concept is not unusual; similar descriptions occur in many widely scattered and unrelated cultures. West's citing this case, however, illustrates an important implicit principle that occurs throughout his work, one I believe to be correct: The fact that a particular cultural artifact occurs worldwide does not, in itself, falsify the hypothesis of borrowing between neighboring civilizations that share that artifact.

The second half of *The East Face of Helicon* approaches the same cross-cultural topic by looking for examples of Eastern influences in the works of Greek poets. West is clearly afraid that this part will be thought to be redundant. He reassures his readers that this section "will by no means be merely a matter of redistributing material that has already been presented. There is much more to come" (p. 275). He is right. There are, of course, many duplications, but these are well cross-referenced. By focusing on particular literary works he is able to demonstrate sustained parallels.

He starts with Hesiod not only because he is the earliest poet whose writings are extant but also because Eastern influences are most evident in his work. For example, the parallels between Hesiod's "Origin of the gods" and the Hurrian history of the gods, named after the god Kumarbi, are striking. Modern scholars realized these parallels as soon as the text was deciphered, read, and published in the 1930s and 1940s (p. 279).[2] As West puts it, this discovery "finally forced Hellenists to accept the reality of Near Eastern influence on early Greek literature." He continues delicately, but not altogether accurately: "Since then they have shown themselves increasingly tolerant of oriental comparisons, if not particularly active in investigating the oriental literatures for themselves" (p. x). My interpretation of this sentence is that conventional classicists have paid lip service to the idea, while continuing their isolationist business as usual.

West shows that there are also striking similarities between *Kumarbi* and the *Theogony* on the one hand and the *Enūma Eliš* on the other. The *Enūma Eliš* was the annual Babylonian liturgy for their patron god Marduk. All of these have parallels with the cosmogony or origin of the gods set down by Philo of Byblos in the second century C.E., though Philo attributed it, with some plausibility, to the priest Sanchuniaton from before the Trojan War. West's comparisons between Hesiod's inspiration by the Muses to write the *Theogony* and biblical and Mesopotamian divine poetic inspiration are less tight and convincing, although here too Hesiod is clearly part of a wider Near Eastern tradition. I shall come back to this later.

West then turns to Hesiod's other most famous long poem, *Works and Days*. This poem is both a farmer's calendar and a litany of complaints against the modern age, the corrupt rulers of the day, and the poet's brother Perses. Scholars have long seen similarities between *Works and Days* and the biblical prophetic tradition of complaint and denunciation. Parallels are particularly close between Hesiod and the earliest attested Hebrew prophet, Amos, who lived in the eighth century B.C.E.[3] For West, Hesiod and Amos were contemporaries, though I should put the Greek poet a century earlier. Beyond similarities in the substance of their poetry, both Hesiod and Amos described themselves as simple workers on the land who had been inspired to sing or write by divine powers.

West has worked on Hesiod all of his scholarly life and his work here is of the highest order. His chapters on Homer, however, are equally impressive. The tightest and most convincing parallel he draws here is between Achilles and the Mesopotamian hero, Gilgamesh. The historical prototype of Gilgamesh lived in the first half of the third millennium B.C.E., and his myth was already well established by the end of that millennium. As West points out, the central theme of the *Iliad* is not the Trojan War but the anger (*mēnis*) of Achilles. The similar character of the two heroes leads West into a rare but very welcome flash of humor. Gilgamesh is described as *hadi-ū ˀa amēlu* ("rejoice/alas man"). West sees this as "the best possible Akkadian rendering of 'manic-depressive'" (p. 337).

The *Iliad* and the Gilgamesh epic also feature the close attachment of the two heroes to their sidekicks, Patroklos and Enkidu. The killing of these characters provokes both heroes into passionate and raging mourning.[4] Encounters with their ghosts also follow. To clinch the case for a Greek borrowing, West points out that the Gilgamesh legend was not restricted to a particular place or time but had been known throughout the Near East for over two millennia.

West's claim that Gilgamesh in his wide travels was the prototype for

Odysseus is less convincing. People in virtually all cultures have been fascinated by real or imagined descriptions of voyages to remote places. Visits to
the world of the dead, which both Gilgamesh and Odysseus undertook, are
less common but these too occur in many traditions. Nevertheless, on the
principle mentioned above that worldwide occurrence does not rule out the
possibility of neighborly transmission, West may well be right in following a long scholarly tradition among the unorthodox that has held that the
adventures of Odysseus were in some ways shaped by those of Gilgamesh.[5]

West then goes on to provide dozens of possible "Oriental," largely
Southwest Asian, prototypes for passages, literary tropes, and images
found not only in the Homeric epics but also among later Greek poets and
playwrights, notably Aeschylus.[6] Individually, the parallels are of varying
quality, but cumulatively, they make his case for massive Southwest Asian
influence on Greek literature overwhelming. Some of West's examples have
been pointed out by earlier scholars, notably Cyrus Gordon and Michael
Astour, as well as by the open-minded and perceptive classicists Peter Walcot and John Pairman Brown.[7] West has found other parallels that had been
suggested as far back as the seventeenth century. He makes splendid use
of Z. Bogan's Homerus Ἑβραΐζων, a comparison of Greek epics with the
Bible, published in the 1650s, during the extraordinary intellectual ferment
of the English Commonwealth. However, many of the parallels West raises
are new and the product of his profound knowledge of Greek texts and
long-term interest in the literatures of Southwest Asia.

The Dynamics of Transmission

What West has done overall in The East Face of Helicon is to bring together
scattered earlier research and put a capstone of his own upon it. The case
he has made for massive "Oriental" influence on Greek literature from its
beginnings is irrefutable. After the publication of this book, classicists cannot maintain their traditional isolationism.

The least satisfactory chapter of the book is the final one, "The Dynamics of Transmission." He proposes two major periods of contact, the later
Mycenaean Period from 1450 to 1200, and the eighth and seventh centuries B.C.E. (p. 586). For the second period he plausibly envisages intercourse of many different types and the possibility of both written and oral
transmission among literate societies. West's recognition of contacts in the
Late Bronze Age comes from archaeological evidence as well as through

the presence of Semitic loan words and names on the tablets in Linear B. West, however, does not see significant transmission of literature during the earlier period. He rightly emphasizes that Hesiod's "Age of Iron" cannot derive from the Bronze Age. When he suggests, however, that the image of the simple man's being granted the divine art of poetry found in Hesiod and Amos cannot belong to the second millennium because Babylonian parallels only date to the eighth century, his argument is less compelling. I shall return below to West's belief that the Muses who inspired Hesiod are purely Greek and restricted to the Archaic Age.

West cannot pinpoint the agency or agencies of transmission in the Late Mycenaean Period (1450–1200 B.C.E.). He specifically denounces Cyrus Gordon's suggestion that "the Gilgamesh epic may well have reached the Aegean both in Akkadian and in translations (perhaps including Mycenaean Greek) during the Amarna Age" (p. 592).

West argues that, although the sphere in which Akkadian was the lingua franca was large, it was not limitless. He points out that the tablet from the state of Arzawa in Western Anatolia, found at the Egyptian capital of Amarna, was written in Hittite and required an answer in that language. Therefore, he argues that Mycenaean Greece was beyond the Akkadian sphere and legends of Gilgamesh could not have been transmitted through writing at this stage (p. 592).

This approach illustrates one way in which, for all his boldness and originality, West is still hobbled by his discipline. The lack of tablets from Mycenaean kingdoms in the Egyptian archives does indeed suggest that there was little or no communication in cuneiform between them and other states. However, other forms of writing existed around the Eastern Mediterranean in the Late Bronze Age. We know that the chief writing material used by Egyptians and Phoenicians was papyrus, which was sometimes preserved in the dry climate of Egypt but scarcely ever in the humidity of the Levant and the Aegean. Thus, even though no traces of it exist today, written communication on papyrus was possible in Egyptian Hieratic and in the linear alphabets used for Canaanite (and very probably Ugaritic too) found in Syro-Palestine during the Late Bronze Age.

Writing on papyrus was presumably the medium envisaged by the Egyptologist Donald Redford when he wrote: "There is no reason to doubt that the Egyptian court was at all times during the Mycenaean age in correspondence with the court at Mycenae, although the letters have not as yet been recovered."[8] In 1950 the Semitist William Albright pointed out that the city of Byblos provided a specific link between this form of writing material and the Aegean through the Greek word βύβλος or βίβλος (papyrus, scroll, or writings). Albright also showed that because the ancient Semitic name of Byblos was Gubla, Greeks must have first heard the city name before 1500 B.C.E. The only explanation for the difference between the two names is that βύβλος was taken into Greek as *Gʷubla. It became Byblos following the general breakdown of labiovelars in Greek in the middle of the second millennium.[9] Although βύβλος does not appear in Homer, its derivative βύβλινος ("papyrus cordage") does (*Odyssey*, 21.391). I see no reason to doubt Albright's conclusion that "the historical and linguistic evidence . . . makes it hard to believe that the Greek word for papyrus and book roll came into use after the Mycenaean Age."[10]

Albright was writing before the decipherment of Linear B. However, this source does not contradict his conclusions. βύβλος does not appear written phonetically in Linear B. On the other hand, ideogram 124, which has no fixed interpretation, could have had this meaning and been pronounced in this way because of its similarity to the Egyptian determinative ⌇ (papyrus rolled up and tied).[11]

Leaving aside questions of papyrus, a lesser but still significant medium of written communication was the folded wax tablet *pinax ptuktos* mentioned in Homer's telling of the Bellerophon story. West refers with approval to Walter Burkert's study of this medium in the early 1980s (p. 366). At that time, Burkert linked such tablets to alphabetic writing and argued on this basis that the *Iliad* must date to the eighth century, because it was only then, he believed, that the alphabet was transmitted to the Aegean.[12]

Like Burkert, West knows of the fourteenth century B.C.E. wax tablet from Ulu Burun but he does not seem aware of its implications for the date of alphabetic transmission. He is, in fact, conservative in maintaining that the Greek alphabet developed only in the eighth century. The leading classicist authority on the Greek alphabet, the late Lillian Jeffery, noted in her last publication that the arguments put forward by Joseph Naveh suggesting that the date of transmission should be put back to "the tenth or even eleventh cent. B.C. . . . deserv[ed] serious attention by Greek epigraphists."[13] It is sad that a champion of East-West contacts such as West should have completely ignored Naveh's seminal article on the subject.[14] From an epigraphic point of view, the key assessment of the date of transmission should focus on which stage of Semitic alphabets come closest to those of the earliest Greek letters. Therefore, the judgment of students of Semitic alphabets should be taken more seriously than that of the epigraphers of Greek. In fact, even those Semitist epigraphers who do not accept Naveh's views have moved back to the tenth century. None of them follow Rhys Carpenter's ultralow, late-eighth-century dating.[15]

I have proposed a date in the middle of the second millennium for the Semitic-to-Greek transmission. The proposal is based both on letter forms and on the striking semiotic and phonetic similarities between letters that disappeared from Canaanite scripts in the fourteenth century B.C.E. and the so-called new letters of the Greek alphabet: Φ, X, Ψ, and Ω.[16] Now, I am sure that Dr. West does not agree with these hypotheses, but he ought to consider them before asserting an eighth-century date of transmission and pouring scorn on Cyrus Gordon's suggestion that channels of written as well as oral communication crossed the Eastern Mediterranean in the Late Bronze Age.[17] In arguing this I do not wish to deny the virtual certainty that both oral and written communication between East and West took place not merely in the Archaic Age (750–500 B.C.E.) but also in the preceding "Dark" and Geometric Ages.

Martin West is not as restrictive as Walter Burkert, who tries to cram all Semitic influence on Greece into the single century 750–650 B.C.E. West is more open to both earlier and later influences. At the same time, however, Burkert is bolder and less loyal to his discipline than West. Unlike Burkert, West does not openly consider the sociology of knowledge or the influence of anti-Semitism on earlier scholars. West's main contact with Semitists is with Assyriologists, a link that fits with his belief in the importance of Mesopotamian literature for that of Greece and also with a whole body of scholarship resembling in miniature the tightly defined and meticulous work of classicists.[18] He is also reasonably at home with biblical studies, although his acceptance of minimalist orthodoxy over the dating of Ecclesiastes and Job causes him some difficulty. The Book of Job clearly contains much second millennium material, which fits West's argument that it belongs to an ancient tradition. Ecclesiastes, conventionally dated between 500 and 300 B.C.E., has been well described as having its "deepest roots . . . in the skeptical, pessimistic side of Egyptian and Mesopotamian wisdom on the one hand; on the other in certain basic tenets of Hebrew thought." [19] A major reason for the late datings attributed by conventional scholars to both books is that they appear to have Greek resonances. Given the prevalence of the Aryan model, it has been assumed that the Greek ideas influenced the biblical ones rather than the other way around. This attitude is what West is attacking.

West is noticeably less at ease with broad-ranging scholars like Victor Bérard, Cyrus Gordon, and Michael Astour, who have pioneered the study of Semitic-Greek relations. Unlike Burkert, he does refer to them, but only sparingly.[20] This circumspection may come from a desire to bring his classicist colleagues along by not giving offense unnecessarily with names that are anathema to them. It may also be because he himself believes such heterodox work to be unsound. For an instance of his slighting of this minority tradition, note that he includes Bérard's *Les Phéniciens et l'Odyssée* in his bibliography, but not his more impressive *De l'origine des cultes arcadiens*.[21] The latter work is important because it shows the deep penetration of Semitic cult practices and myth in Arkadia, the most conservative region in southern Greece. This in turn shows that Semitic influence in Greece cannot all be dated to the Archaic Period but must be put earlier to the Bronze Age.

West occasionally refers to Astour's *Hellenosemitica*, from which he could have gained a great deal more. For instance, when looking at the Semitic origin of the Laconian cult of Apollo Amuklai and the Cypriot Phoenician cult of Ršp Mukal, he refers (p. 55) to Burkert's article on the subject published in 1975. Astour had established all this eight years earlier in his *Hellenosemitica*, and he had traced Amuklai back to the Eme-sal or women's dialect of Sumerian and the divine name ^{d}mu-gal-la ("Great Tree").[22]

Similarly, West could have referred to Bérard's *Les Phéniciens et l'Odyssée* and Astour's *Hellenosemitica*, thereby improving his discussion (pp. 299–300) of the images of night and day or dawn and dusk as two siblings who cross each other's paths but never come together. In these works, the two scholars discuss the mythological aspect of Kadmos' (the East, dawn) fruitless pursuit of Europa (the West, dusk). Astour relates this to the Ugaritic divine siblings Šḥr and Šlm mentioned by West.[23]

West's greatest animus is against Cyrus Gordon, whose *Homer and the Bible*, first published in 1955, opened up the modern field of Semito-Hellenic relations. The hostility can be seen in West's listing (p. 86 n. 81) of the five scholars who in his view have produced the "soundest translations" from Ugaritic. West does not include Gordon, who was the author of the first Ugaritic grammar and one of the founders of Ugaritic studies.[24] Later, when writing about the epic of King Keret, West notes (p. 483 n. 134): "Gordon mistakenly supposes that Keret is recovering a wife who has gone away: his error is refuted by M. Maroth." The idea that a specialist scholar's interpretation of an Ugaritic text can be *refuted* is puzzling, because as West himself had previously and rightly emphasized, these texts are extremely ambiguous, and very varied translations can be made of them (pp. 84–85). Gordon wrote about Keret's siege of the city where his wife was living. West's eagerness to discredit Gordon is shown by the strange sentence with which he continues the note: "We should also remember that the Trojan War did not, strictly speaking, involve a siege."

It is common for conventional scholars to attack those who were right too soon; indeed, it is probably necessary for disciplinary authority that they should do so. However, it is sad to see such a distinguished pioneer in this field as Martin West join the pack in this instance.

Some Details

Before going on to the contentious issues of the role of Egypt and etymology, I should like to raise some detailed problems within West's general subject of the Southwest Asian influences on the formation of Greek religion and literature.

West discusses music, among other topics, and argues, "Most of the musical instruments used by the Greeks came from the Near East at one period or another" (p. 31). If one includes Egypt in the Near East, the claim is unexceptional. West points out that the *gingros* ("a small flute") and the *nabla*, a Phoenician type of harp, both have Semitic etymologies, and he later discusses the Hellenistic Greek *kinúra* from the Canaanite *kinnor* ("a form of lyre"). The very cautious Egyptologist and Semitist James Hoch maintains that the Greek *kithára* "is almost certainly a loan word from the Semitic."[25] Furthermore, I am convinced that *psállō* ("to play a stringed instrument"), which has no Indo-European etymology, derives from the Semitic root z/ṣll or z/ṣlṣl ("tingle, quiver"). In Hebrew, ṣe|ṣə|îm are musical instruments.[26]

Whereas the conventional view derives the Greek *temenos* ("sacred precinct") from the Greek *temnō* ("cut off"), West (p. 36) convincingly supports the derivation of *temenos* from the Akkadian *tem(m)en(n)u* and Sumerian *temen* ("boundary marker, foundation deposit"; later, platform for a temple). West continues: "The word does not occur in West Semitic, so that the middle-men appear to be lacking. It seems that we must postulate a direct borrowing from Akkadian-speakers in this case, or else reject the parallel as a mirage." In fact, a West Semitic form is found in the place-name Timnah found in Joshua 19:50 and 24:30 and again in Judges 2:9: "They buried him [Joshua] within the border of his own patrimony at Timnath Ḥeres [in one case] or Serah [in two others]."[27]

Discussing the Greek word *leskhē* and the Hebrew word *liškāh*, both meaning "social centers attached to places of religious ceremonial," West (p. 38

n. 148) dismisses Gordon's suggestion that the Hebrew word, which has no Semitic cognates, was borrowed from Greek.[28] He argues first that there are no similar borrowings from Greek into early Hebrew, and second that the Philistines, whom John Pairman Brown believes may have introduced the word, were not Greek. On the first objection, although Gordon may be wrong here, other words in early biblical texts have plausible Greek etymologies. The most famous of these is the word *makerrâ*, a *hapax legomenon*, meaning "weapon," found in Genesis (49:5), and the Greek *makhaira* ("dagger"). Similarly, there is *'âgar* ("gather together"), which appears in some of the so-called Israelian or northern biblical texts (Deuteronomy 28:23 and Proverbs 6:4, 8, and 10:5). *'âgar* has no Semitic cognates and would seem to come from the Greek root found in *ageírō* ("assemble, gather together") and *agorá*. On West's second objection, I felt very daring when I wrote an appendix to BA I giving the textual and archaeological reasons for believing that Mycenaean Greeks provided the biggest linguistic grouping among the Philistines. It is now a commonplace.[29] It is strange that West should, in this instance, be *plus royaliste que le roi* in denying the possibility of a two-way cultural traffic from Greek to Canaanite as well as from Canaanite to Greek.

West (p. 58) restates the etymology of the Kabeiroi, the seven dwarves of Greek cult and mythology, and rightly finds it from the Semitic *kabbir* ("great"). The etymology is hard to resist, especially when they were also known in Greek as Megaloi Theoi ("Great Gods"). West might have cited Astour's examination of this question and mentioned that the etymology goes back at least to Scaliger in the sixteenth century.[30] The credit for the refusal to see this obvious connection goes to Karl Otfried Müller, a refusal that remained for many years a staple of German scholarship.[31]

West writes (p. 194) that "in what survives of 'historical' epics we cannot identify any formal assemblies." In fact, the Sumerian "historical" epic *Gilgamesh and Agga*, not normally included in the mythical Gilgamesh cycle, refers to a bicameral constitution with a senate and an assembly of the people, both of which had considerable power. The distinguished Assyriologist Thorkild Jacobsen used this text and the *election* of Marduk as king of the gods in the *Enuma Elish* to argue that there was a primitive democracy in Ancient Mesopotamia.[32]

West (p. 303) appears to approve of the identification of the Canaanite Ṣapôn with the Greek Typhōn. The former is a holy mountain to the north; the latter is the monstrous opponent of Zeus. The two might seem very different, but most of the incongruities can be resolved. Phonetically, there is no serious difficulty, especially if the initial phoneme was originally ḍ or ẓ. Semantically, as West points out, Baʿal Ṣapôn was a storm god in the Ugaritic pantheon. In Hellenistic and Roman times, Typhōn was considered the equivalent of the Egyptian god Seth, the divinity of tumult, the desert, the sea, and earthquakes.³³ There is uncertainty as to where Ṣapôn/Typhōn is situated. In Ugaritic he is to the north, and in Proverbs (25:23) rûaḥ ṣapônâh is the north wind holding back the rain. By contrast, a Canaanite/Akkadian tablet from Amarna refers to ṣapânu as the setting of the sun. In any event, the image is clearly of wild winds. Given the earlier initials ḍ or ẓ and the easy slippage between the liquids "n" and "r," *ẓpn would provide a good etymology for ζέφυρος (west or northwest wind), often associated with βορέας (north wind).³⁴ We tend to think of zephyrs as gentle breezes, but for Homer ζέφυρος was a violent wind. Chantraine associates ζέφυρος with ζόφος ("darkness obscure, the west"). Two other words with the same meanings are ψέφας and δνόφος. The different initials would be explained by a borrowing from a Semitic phoneme ḍ or ẓ by Indo-European speakers, whose phonetic inventory did not contain such sounds.³⁵

After this long list of specifics, let us turn to a much larger issue.

Egypt

For me, the central problem of *The East Face of Helicon* is West's dismissal of Egyptian influences. He faces the difficulty on the first page of his preface, where he writes:

> In my subtitle I have used the expression "West Asiatic" rather than "Near Eastern." This is to signal the fact that I have drawn my material almost wholly from Mesopotamian, Anatolian, Syrian, and biblical sources, and deliberately left Egypt more or less out of the picture. I have occasionally cited Egyptian material when it demanded to be cited, but in general my view is that the influence of Egypt on Greek poetry and myth was vanishingly small in comparison with that of western Asia. This may to some extent reflect my own ignorance. But it may be felt that Egypt has had more than its due from others in recent years. (p. vii)

I assume that the last passive and oblique sentence refers to the storms around *Black Athena* and Afrocentric claims, which seem to be the determining factors in his present reluctance to draw on Egyptian sources. Previously, West had looked favorably on evidence of Egyptian cultural influences on Greece. He had even argued for the very unorthodox case that one should not dismiss the possibility that metempsychosis existed in Egypt.[36] Nevertheless, West's present desire to play down the significance of Egyptian influence on Greece is underlined by the fact that he does not list Egyptian passages cited in the index devoted to passages from ancient languages.

His strange formulation that he only "cited Egyptian material when it *demanded* to be cited" (my italics) hardly indicates balanced scholarship. The statement suggests that he admits Egyptian examples only where no better or even equally good Southwest Asian parallel to the Greek passage can be found.

Grudgingly as they are admitted into his book, the number of Egyptian passages cited is not "vanishingly small." First is the Egyptian priority in wisdom literature and proverbs. West cites Egyptian examples of these on pages 325, 328, and 511. He uses an Egyptian poem on the battle of Qadesh to parallel Greek references to divine intervention on a battlefield (p. 361). As a precedent to Odysseus' being the only one able to string his great bow and shoot through twelve iron axes, West cites (p. 432) Amenophis II's shooting through copper targets. He sees the story of Zeus' impersonating King Amphitryon to engender Herakles, thus giving the hero both royal and divine ancestry, as clearly deriving from Egypt (p. 458). (I missed this and Herakles' being suckled by Hera, when giving other Egyptianisms surrounding the birth of the hero [BA II: 79–81].) West refers (p. 424) to the image of the divine and disappearing island found in both the Egyptian *Tale of the Shipwrecked Sailor* and the island of Skhēria in the *Odyssey;* Gordon first pointed out this parallel. Even more strikingly, West recognizes:

The story of the Wooden Horse has no close parallel in Near Eastern literature, but it has often been compared with an Egyptian account of how Thuti, an eminent general under Tuthmosis III (c. 1479–1427) took Joppa in Palestine. He had apparently been besieging it without success. He pretended to be giving up. The prince of Joppa came out to discuss terms. Thuti got him drunk, and mellowed him further with talk of surrender. The prince asked if he might be allowed to see the pharaoh's splendid mace, which Thuti had in his camp. Thuti brought it in, displayed it, and then knocked him out with it and tied him up. After making further preparations, he sent a message into the city to the effect that he had capitulated, and that they were to expect his tribute. Five hundred men followed behind, bearing two hundred bulky sealed baskets. The gates of Joppa were opened for them. Once they were in, soldiers equipped with bonds and fetters leapt out of the baskets and seized all the able bodied men in sight. (pp. 487–488)

Thus West concedes the single most important theme in Greek legend to Egypt. Here, in fact, he underestimates the contribution of Southwest Asian themes. Although he is right to state that there is "no close parallel in Near Eastern literature" to the story of the wooden horse, Sarah Morris has recently demonstrated that siege engines or "rams" containing men pictured on Assyrian reliefs look remarkably like animals. Nevertheless, West is right to indicate the Egyptian literary precedent.[37]

To choose another example, West's book offers two solar references to Egyptian precedents for Greek conceits: the sun's progress underground (p. 470) and the toiling of the sun across the sky (p. 508).[38] When describing Herakles' labors, he states, "The [Egyptian] sun-god's and the soul's adventures show little correspondence in detail with those of Herakles and cannot be their source." He continues: "But the overall scheme is curiously similar." He then reverses his earlier statement by providing a couple of detailed parallels: "As the Egyptian soul travels in the sun god's boat along the stream that connects sunset and sunrise, so Heracles embarks on the sun's bowl-shaped vessel at sunset. . . . In his final labor he masters Cerberus. . . . Cerberus may be compared to the monster in the Egyptian underworld . . . [who] . . . squats by the scales on which the soul is weighed and devours all those that are burdened with guilt. . . . Heracles' victory over Cerberus, therefore, might be seen as analogous to the Egyptian soul's aquittal and admission to eternal life" (p. 471).

West gives the Egyptian *Harper's Song* as the best ancient instance of the cynical view of life and death found in Greek thought and the recognition that "you can't take it with you" (pp. 512, 534). Then he cites the romantic desire found in both Egyptian and Greek literature to become a piece of the beloved's jewelry (p. 534). Finally, he cites the well-known precedent for Hebrew monotheism found in the hymns of Akhenaton (p. 576).

As if this were not enough, the inventory of Egyptian origins for Greek literary forms should be enlarged in two other ways. The first are those West omits and the second are those he attributes to West Asiatic sources that could equally well have been derived from Egypt. I spend the next two sections of this review on these two issues.

Egyptian Themes Missing from *The East Face of Helicon*
MUSES AND NYMPHS

A central theme of this review is my belief that many of the Egyptian influences on Greek religion, myth, literature, and language arrived during
the Bronze Age. Thus, they are older and hence more fundamental than
those from Southwest Asia, which generally arrived in the early Iron Age.
The "lateness" of this Southwest Asian influence makes traces of it more
evident. For instance, whereas Egyptian religion contained swallowing and
regurgitating deities and divine castration, the structure of Hesiod's *Theogony* is closer to Hurrian and Mesopotamian precedents than it is to any
known Egyptian ones.[39]

Still, Egyptian influence would seem to be evident in the prelude to *Theogony*, in which the poet was inspired by the Muses. West writes about the
Muses that they "are, as far as we know, purely Greek creatures, and have no
counterpart in the orient" (p. 170). However, though it is clear that Muses,
like nymphs and Furies, have many purely Hellenic features, they all have
plausible and very ancient origins from Egypt. In the first chapter of his
book, West refers to a "hippopotamus-headed demon" imported to Greece
from Egypt by way of Crete (p. 10). These demons were miniature versions
of the hippopotamus goddess of childbirth, Tawaret or Thueris. The function of the Egyptian "demons," who later developed lion heads, in Egypt,
was to protect women in childbirth. They were also concerned with pouring water and purification, especially after childbirth, and acted as armed
guards to the portals of the realm of the dead.

Recent work by Judith Weingarten has shown that the introduction of
these demons to Crete was not merely iconographic, as had previously
been supposed, but that some of the Egyptian cultic associations were also
transmitted to the Aegean. Iconography in Minoan Crete and Mycenaean
Greece shows that these demons or "genii" were groups of young creatures whose white coloring revealed them to be female, following the Egyptian artistic convention adopted in the Aegean.[40] They were concerned with
lustration and watering plants, hunting, and serving a goddess very similar
to the goddess of childbirth, Eileithya or Artemis, to whom Eileithya was
later assimilated.

The Aegean images of the genii hunting parallel the ferocity of the hippopotamus- or lion-headed demons in Egypt. Both seem to have been related to the pain and trauma not only of childbirth, but also of later transformations. That is to say, the associations of a goddess and her helpers were not restricted to physical childbirth but included rebirth or initiation into immortality, usually, but not always, after death.[41]

In what seems to have been a purely Aegean development, the Minoan genii developed bee- or wasplike characteristics. There was a long-standing association of honey with immortality in Egypt, which was expressed practically in medicine and mummification. West shows striking parallels between the fears of Gilgamesh and Achilles' that their beloved's body would decay before the funeral (p. 343). He does not mention, however, that the method used to preserve Patroklos' corpse by Achilles' mother Thetis — the introduction of ambrosia/honey through the nose — was one used in Egyptian mummification.[42] However, the spiritual use of honey to nourish the dead immortal was also important.[43] In Late Egyptian times Tawaret was the partner of Bes, the god of initiation and music, later assimilated with Horus, whose Greek counterpart was Apollo. Mus- ic was often used in initiation.[44]

Such features appear in the introduction to the *Theogony* in the verse "They [the Muses] dance around the darkly bubbling spring" and later, when the poem continues:

> And when the daughters of great Zeus would bring
> Honour upon a heaven favoured lord
> And when they watch him being born, they pour
> Sweet dew upon his tongue, and from his lips
> Flow honeyed words, all people look up to him
> When he is giving judgement uprightly,
> . . . .
> Advising with soft words. And when a lord
> Comes into the assembly, he is wooed
> With honeyed reverence just like a god,
> And is conspicuous above the crowd,
> Such is the Muses' holy gift to men.[45]

Hesiod's graceful figures seem worlds away from the genii of Minoan and Mycenaean art as well as from Thueris and her fierce helpers in Middle Kingdom Egypt. Nevertheless, many of the earlier characteristics persist:

flowing water, dew, washing; making plants grow; sweetness and honey; gentle daughters; using dance, song, and mus(e)ic; being in the dark; being present at birth; raising status, giving godlike powers or initiation.[46]

The simplest etymology for Musai is from the Egyptian *m^{w}es ("child"). The excellent phonetic fit is made even stronger by the form Moisa, used by the poet Sappho of Lesbos writing in the Aeolic dialect, which was generally archaic. Semantically, the case for deriving Musai or Moisai from *m^{w}es is almost equally good. The early poets laid great stress on the Muses being daughters or children of Zeus.

A further and deeper reason why they were called Musai may be because of a connection not merely with ms, 𓀔𓏤, "child," but with msi, 𓀔𓈖𓏤, "childbirth," and the Demotic ms ꜥ3 (t), "midwife." [47]

Muses are often confused with nymphs, who share many of the same characteristics. I believe that both groups derive from Minoan genii and Tawaret's helpers. Some scholars have tried to link nymphē to the Latin nubo ("marry"), and West sees these too as "Indo-European or at least European" (p. 111). Chantraine, however, is not satisfied with the name and states that the etymology is "obscure." I believe that nymphē ("bride") should be derived from the Egyptian n3 n(y) nfr(w)t ("the beautiful young women"). The Egyptian nfr meant "youth" as well as "beauty." In fact, the Greek root nymph-, like the Egyptian nfr, could be used for young people of either sex.

In Greek, however, nymph had a number of other meanings. For instance, nymphaia was a Greek name for water lilies and lotuses, including species called nenuphar, a term derived from the Arabic ninufar that in turn appears to come from the Egyptian n3n(y) nfrt. Aristotle used nymphē as a term for "young bee or wasp in the pupa stage," a scientific usage that persists today. In these species the form of the "pupa," or penultimate stage of metamorphosis, resembles that of the adult and could, in fact, be called an "adolescent." This is remarkable, in view of the bee- or wasplike appearances of the young genii. The association survived iconographically into the Archaic Period; an Archaic metal plaque from Rhodes has figures that are half-nymph and half-bee.[48]

PANDORA AND OTHER EGYPTIAN THEMES IN HESIOD

Having discussed the plausible Egyptian origins of Muses and nymphs, let me now turn to a second important Egyptian theme found in the Greek tradition, that of Pandora. Hesiod considered the story of Pandora significant enough to include in both of his major works. In his discussion of the legendary woman, West provides some loose parallels between Pandora, whose name simply means "All gifts," and Mesopotamia. He finds examples of men having been made out of clay and kings having been given specialized gifts by the relevant gods and goddesses (pp. 310–311). More than thirty years ago, however, Peter Walcot demonstrated the far closer parallels between Pandora and the birth and divine endowments lavished on the female pharaoh Hatshepsut, as illustrated in a frieze at her temple at Deir el Bahri.[49] The misbehavior of the legendary Pandora should be seen in the light of the hostile propaganda about Hatshepsut put out by her stepson and heir, Tuthmosis III.[50]

Further, *Works and Days* is clearly in the instructional tradition earliest and most richly attested in Egypt, though here too it could well have come through the Levant. The other central theme of *Works and Days* is the quarrel between the poet and his brother Perses ("destroyer"?). Walcot derives this from a Hittite text of two brothers, one good and one bad. However, the best-known fraternal conflict of the Ancient Near East, with clear-cut moral values, is that between Osiris and Seth.[51] The Egyptologist Edmund Meltzer sees a still closer parallel to Hesiod and Perses in the Late Egyptian tale "The Binding of Truth by Falsehood." He quotes W. K. Simpson, who saw it as "a text circulating in the Near East before Hesiod's own times which incorporated . . . a pair of brothers, one good and one bad, and a dispute between them over their father's property which culminates in a redress to law." [52]

OEDIPUS AND AKHENATEN

West provides a relatively loose but still interesting prototype for the *Oresteia*, with the killings of Agamemon, his wife, and her lover, in a series of murders carried out in the Hittite royal family in the sixteenth century B.C.E. (pp. 473–475). In 1960, Immanuel Velikovsky published his view of the much closer parallels between that other great sequence in Greek tragedy, that of Oedipus his and family, and the story of the "heretic" pharaoh Akhenaten and his successors.[53] Velikovsky's wild astronomy and drastic chronology, by which he attempted to eliminate many centuries, have rightly been completely discredited. The plausibility, however, of some of the proposed parallels between legendary events in the Greek Thebes and the closing decades of the Egyptian Eighteenth Dynasty in the fourteenth century B.C.E. should not be affected by his other claims. Indeed, the longer chronology provided by conventional scholarship makes the parallels more convincing by allowing time for the stories to become "Hellenized" and diffused into the different versions found in Hesiod and the fifth-century tragedians.

Velikovsky pointed out many similarities between the stories: Oedipus' "swollen foot/leg" and the grossly enlarged legs in all representations of Akhenaten; Oedipus' incest with his mother and the complex patterns of incest in the court of Akhenaten; the oracular roles of the blind seers Amenhope, son of Hapi, and Teireisias, both of whom were associated with serpents; the "fratricidal" conflicts between Oedipus' sons Eteokles and Polyneikes and Akhenaten's heirs Smenkhare and Tutankhamun; and the "brothers'" tight relations with their sisters. The royal uncle, Ay in Egypt and Kreon in Boiotia, played remarkably parallel roles. Furthermore, the Greek legends have other Egyptian associations, such as the name Thebes and the Theban sphinx, whose riddle has striking solar associations that fit the role of the great Egyptian sphinx.[54]

It is not difficult to trace possible modes of transmission. Egyptian records show that men from W3ḏ wr ("the Aegean") delivered tribute to the court of Akhenaten, and a drawing shows others making obeisance to one of his successors, either Tutankhamun or Ay, from a tomb in Memphis.[55] We know that Greek mercenaries were employed in Egypt at this time.[56] Mycenaean pottery has been found at Akhenaten's capitol at Amarna and also at Memphis, one of the capitols after Amarna. The wreck at Ulu Burun shows that there was intensive trade between Egypt and the Aegean at the end of the Eighteenth Dynasty.[57] Thus, even without the regular correspondence postulated by Donald Redford, the interesting doings at the Egyptian Court in the fifteenth and fourteenth centuries B.C.E. would have been known in contemporary Greece.

This is not to say that the stories of Oedipus were merely rehashes of Eighteenth Dynasty scandals, any more than West claims that the *Oresteia* is simply Hittite history. The Boiotian Thebes was a rich and powerful city that really was destroyed in the late thirteenth century B.C.E., quite possibly by Argives or Mycenaeans, as the legends claim. Furthermore, the fifth-century tragedians added their own political, social, and personal concerns to make their dramas the rich and fascinating works they are. Nevertheless, in the case of Oedipus, the basic structure for these elaborations came from Eighteenth Dynasty Egypt.

Themes Attributed to West Asia That
Could Equally Well Have Come from Egypt

I have argued that the female inspirations of Greek poetry and music have fundamental origins in Egypt and that two of the central stories in Greek legend, those of Pandora and Oedipus, can be derived from actual events in the Egyptian Eighteenth Dynasty. It is for these reasons that West has been unable to find Southwest Asian precedents for them. On the other hand, there are many aspects of Greek culture for which plausible origins can be found in both Egypt and Mesopotamia. In such cases, I believe that the benefit of the doubt should be given to Egypt or the Levant either as the originator of the cultural feature or as the transmitter of Mesopotamian forms.

I justify this preference on the following grounds: One of the great difficulties with West's scheme is that Greek references to Mesopotamia can scarcely be found before the fifth century B.C.E.; on the other hand, references to Egypt and Phoenicia are abundant. This Greek emphasis is altogether to be expected given both the greater geographical proximity of Egypt and Syro-Palestine to Greece and the archaeological records of Egyptian and Levantine objects in the Aegean and Aegean objects in Egypt and Syro-Palestine. By contrast, Anatolian and Mesopotamian finds are rare in Greece. The Sumerian, East Semitic, and Hurrian names of the gods appear to have been completely unknown to Greeks of the Archaic and Classical Periods, whereas they were aware of those of Egypt. The fifth-century poet Pindar did not write "Hail to Teššub or Marduk, Lord of Olympus," but "Hail to Ammon, Lord of Olympus."[58]

Thus, if parallels or precedents for Greek literary forms or conceits can be found in both Mesopotamia and Egypt, one should not simply reverse West's dictum and require that Mesopotamian examples should be used only "when they demanded to be cited." If the parallels are equally tight, I would prefer the Egyptian precedent but would refer to the Mesopotamian one, pointing out that it may also have had a direct or indirect impact. Ancient Greek civilization, like any other, could absorb influences from many different quarters, either in sequence or simultaneously, and weave them into its own fabric.

I should now like to consider Egyptian and Southwest Asian influences on two critically important aspects of Greek civilization: royalty and death.

ROYALTY

The region stretching from Persia to Greece and from Greece to the Sudan shared many similarities in the treatment and presentation of royalty. West cites a number of features of kingship in Western Asia and Greece: the king as leader in war or as judge, having a mace or scepter as symbol of authority, kingship as hereditary, and the dead king as the object of a cult (pp. 16–18). All these features are also abundantly testified in relation to pharaohs. West also cites the religious significance and activities of kings in Mesopotamia and biblical records, and these were even more salient for pharaohs. West (p. 227) relates Greek descriptions of the king as shepherd of his people to Mesopotamian and biblical descriptions, but this natural image was equally strong in Egypt, where pharaohs and the god Osiris held shepherds' crooks as a symbol of royal office and ḥqȝ ("crook/scepter") meant "rule" or "ruler." West (p. 189) draws parallels from Western Asia to Zeus as king of the gods, but the Egyptian Amon, who was explicitly identified with Zeus in antiquity, was also portrayed as king of the gods. Furthermore, like Zeus, Amon was associated with rams and thunder. West points out (p. 114) that Zeus was unlike the hypothetical Indo-European term *dy-ēu, with its associations with the bright sky. The image of the king as a god found in both Southwest Asia and Greece (pp. 242–243) is stronger and more widespread in Egypt. The same is true of comparisons between kings and bulls and between heroes and lions.

West (p. 116) points out that Babylonian, Hebrew, and Greek mythology agree that gods once mingled more easily with mortals. Egyptians held a long-standing belief that before the human dynasties, first gods and then demigods had directly ruled the country.

DEATH

The idea that no one returns from death is common in many societies, not just those of Mesopotamia and Greece, as West suggests (p. 154). In fact, at another point (p. 512), West quotes lines from the Egyptian "Harper's Song" of the Middle Kingdom, including, "Lo, none who departs comes back again." He cites (pp. 155–156) the image of the dead person having to cross a river as coming from Southwest Asia. Emily Vermeule, however, sees this, like so many other aspects of Greek images of death, as having Egyptian precedents.[59] In this case, she is backed by the fact that Egyptian funerals often involved and still involve crossing the Nile. West believes the argument for Southwest Asian influence is strengthened by the fact that, in Greece, the river was often called Akherōn, for which he provides a very plausible Semitic etymology (p. 156).[60] The more common name for the river of death is Styx, from the root found in στυγέω ("hate, abhor") and στυγνός ("hateful, gloomy"). The lexicographers' suggestion that this root is related to Slav words for "cold" is much less likely than that it derives from the Egyptian *stkn* ("cause to approach," "induct," and "bring on doom"). Clearly, in this instance, both Southwest Asian and Egyptian influences should be taken into account.

West has some difficulty (p. 162) finding an Oriental precedent for the Greek image of the dead as shadows. In Egyptian the *šwt* ("shadow") was one of the souls, usually of the dead.[61] On the other hand, West finds Mesopotamian and biblical examples of the notion of the dead soul as a bird (p. 163). This image too Vermeule sees as coming from Egypt, and she is backed by strong iconographic evidence of Egyptianizing soul-birds from Mycenaean Greece.[62] West sees the Homeric phrase "speaking to one's *thumos*" as close to a Mesopotamian and Hebrew idiom of "speaking to one's heart" (p. 199), but *thumos* is not "heart" but a form of soul. Here too the Egyptian parallel is closer. In Egypt, souls were always to some extent detachable; there is, for example, the famous *Dispute Between a Man and His* Ba (a form of soul).[63]

A long scholarly tradition links the *psykhostasia* or *Kērostasia*, the weighing against each other of the souls of two heroes, as found in Homer and Aeschylus, to the centrally important Egyptian image of weighing a dead man's heart against the feather of Maat (m3ʿt).[64] West prefers some Hittite parallels that he admits "are far from exact" (p. 394). Vermeule and others have also insisted that the Greek Elysion closely resembles the Egyptian Field of Reeds, the habitation of blessed souls. Nothing like it is found in the gloomy Ugaritic or Canaanite views of the afterlife.[65] West's Mesopotamian example is much more far-fetched (pp. 166–167).

MISCELLANEA

A number of other points offer Egyptian precedents that seem closer than those West proposes from Southwest Asia. For instance, West discusses two Homeric terms, "black earth" and "broad earth," and he cites Hittite and Mesopotamian parallels to them (pp. 220–221). The color black is not generally appropriate for Greek soils; the term is much more likely to have come from Egypt. The classicist R. Drew Griffiths has pointed out that Kmt ("black") was the Egyptian name for Egypt and that one of the reasons for this name was the black soil of the Nile Valley.[66]

West (p. 226) plausibly sees the Homeric formula υἷες Ἀχαιῶν ("sons of the Achaeans") as a calque from the common Semitic formula bənê X "sons of X"). The standard Greek way of expressing "children of," however, was with the patronymic suffix -id or -ad, which has no Indo-European etymology and would seem to come from the Egyptian id ("child").

West writes about the "unflattering Homeric epithet βοῶπις" ("cow face") applied to Hera and other goddesses and further refers (pp. 443–444) to Southwest Asian stories in which gods copulate with cows, but Hathor, the Egyptian goddess of beauty and sexual attractiveness, was also represented as a cow. This relationship in turn may be related to the continuing love of cows and their beauty among the Nuer, Shilluk, and other peoples of the Upper Nile.

Many other examples of "Oriental" parallels with Greek myth and literature brought out by West have equal or better precedents from Egypt. For reasons given above, in such cases, it is preferable to choose the Egyptian precedent. This stand does not deny the many other cases where the Mesopotamian, Ugaritic, or biblical parallels are much stronger or where there are no Egyptian examples. Most striking of these are the epic form itself, the parallels between Kumarbi and the Enūma Eliš with the Theogony, and those between Gilgamesh and Achilles.

My first major quarrel with West is his attempt to dismiss or minimize the significance of Egypt in the formation of Greece. My second objection is to his failure to make full use of one of the most useful tools available for tracing cultural interconnections around the Eastern Mediterranean: etymology.

Etymology

West does not share the widespread disdain for etymology held among classicists.[67] Nevertheless, he is extremely cautious on the subject. Although he praises and uses the work of the seventeenth-century scholar Z. Bogan, who showed so many striking parallels between Greek and Hebrew literary forms and tropes, he is much less enthusiastic about Bogan's contemporary Samuel Bochart, who proposed many Semitic etymologies. He writes that Bochart "went much too far in his attempts to identify them [Semitic loan words], as did most of those before the present century" (p. 12). In a footnote, he timidly challenges the classicist orthodoxy: "Lewy (1895) remains a valuable repertoire of the results formulated by that time." Other surveys, not cited by West, are equally valuable, notably the excellent and very scholarly articles by W. Muss-Arnolt.[68] West mentions the book on Semitic loans by Emilie Masson, published in 1967, but goes on to say that since then "a fair number of the old Semitic etymologies have been brought back into favor and some new ones found" (pp. 12–13). It is not quite clear why West should praise Masson's extraordinarily restrictive work. Possibly, he wants to use it to draw a line between his own views and earlier, "prescientific" work. In practice, however, his own position is almost identical to that of Lewy and Muss-Arnolt. I believe he should go back further still.

I have no doubt that there are more Egyptian than Semitic loan words in Classical and Hellenistic Greek and that this is the case both in general and in the spheres with which West is concerned. To give some examples, he shows many intricate parallels between Southwest Asian and Greek oaths and treaties. However, the Greek word for "oath," horkos, has no Semitic derivation but a very strong one from the Egyptian ʿrq and the Coptic ôrk ("swear"). The etymology was pointed out by the Abbé Barthélemy in 1763.[69] Similarly, when writing about Semitic and Greek divination, West rightly begins with the interpretation of dreams (p. 46). However, oneiros ("dream") has no clear Indo-European etymology. The fact that there is a parallel form, onar, which cannot be declined suggests a loan. However, no Semitic or other Southwest Asian etymology has been found. A plausible Egyptian one exists in wn ḥr ("open the sight of, clear vision").[70]

When writing about the Greek and Semitic oracles, West mentions prediction through the rustling of leaves at Shechem in Israel and at Zeus at Dodōna in northwest Greece (p. 34). Rustling of leaves was also seen as a sign at the oracle Siwah in the Western Desert, which Herodotus explicitly linked to both Thebes in Egypt and Dodōna in Greece.[71] The patron god at Siwah was Zeus' Egypto-Libyan counterpart, Am(m)on, who was merged there with the Nubian god Ddwn. Dodōna has no Indo-European or Semitic etymology.

When considering the names of the gods, West writes about Apollo that "according to the prevailing opinion, his name is Greek, from the apellai or annual gatherings of tribes or clans" (p. 55). The Egyptian name for the god of the "young" sun in the morning, however, was Ḫprr. This etymology is much more plausible. The semantic fit with Apollo, the young god of the sun, is perfect. Phonetically, the derivation might be better seen as having come through Canaanite, in which ḫ merged with ḥ. * Ḫprr. would provide an excellent fit with Apollo.[72] This, like many other examples, shows the advantage of seeing Southwest Asian and Egyptian influences on Greece as complementary, not in competition with each other.

West conventionally and rightly sees Adonis as deriving from the West Semitic Adônî ("my Lord") (p. 57). However, he is unable to provide Semitic, Sumerian, Hurrian, Hittite, or—with the possible exceptions of Zeus and Hestia—any other Indo-Hittite etymologies for other divinities. In the absence of competition, it is reasonable to follow Herodotus' statement that the names come from Egypt, which I believe can be confirmed.[73]

As mentioned above, West provides Semitic etymologies for some Greek musical instruments. Others have mixed or Egyptian origins. For an instance of the former, *salpinx* ("trumpet") has parallels in the Ugaritic *ṭlb* and Akkadian *šulpu* ("flute"), but there is also the Egyptian word *šnb* ("reed"), which can be found in the most ancient *Pyramid Texts*. The Egyptian aspect of the etymology is strengthened by the Greek *salpingion* ("reed").[74] A word with a more clear-cut Egyptian etymology is *tereitēs* ("an Egyptian flute") from the Egyptian *twrit* ("wood, bone, or reed pipe"). However, there is a related word, *teretizō* ("hum, chirp, chatter"). There is also Tyrtaios, the name of a Laconian poet of the seventh century B.C.E. who composed elegies for the pipe!

The *iambos* was a satyrical song, festivity, or entertainment with frequent sexual and scatological references. West sees it as ancient and, because of its non-Greek name, as having "roots in the pre-Hellenic culture of the Aegean" (p. 495). This too has a reasonable Egyptian etymology in *ib(3)* ("dance, rejoice").

West has an interesting discussion on the use of days to symbolize time in Greek. He writes that the origin of the idea of well- and ill-omened days may have come originally from Egypt, where these were scattered throughout the year. He holds, however, that the simpler form found in Greece and set out by Hesiod, in which they occurred regularly each month, must have come from Southwest Asia where this was the pattern (p. 329). The Greek word for "day," *(h)ēmar/(h)ēmera*, appears to have originated not as a stretch of time but as the animated good or bad spirit or the guardian of the day.[75] Thus, *(h)ēmar* can be plausibly derived from the attested Egyptian term, *imy hrw.f* ("who is on duty for the day").[76]

Periods of Borrowing

In prior sections of this chapter, I provided examples of what I am convinced is a widespread pattern in Archaic and Classical Greece: a discrepancy between Semitic institutions and literary tropes on the one hand and words and names derived from Egyptian on the other. Such a pattern can be explained by postulating different periods in which one or other of the external stimuli predominated in the Aegean. That is to say, the earlier borrowings came from Egypt but the later organization from Southwest Asia. In crude terms, one could claim that Egyptian influence predominated during the New Kingdom/Late Bronze Age and Southwest Asian influence in the Dark and Early Archaic Ages. Such a chronology would fit with the archaeological evidence with the fact that the Greek poleis were constituted in the ninth and eighth centuries B.C.E. more or less according to the Phoenician model.[77]

The situation, however, is more complicated than that. In the first place, there has been sporadic Southwest Asian influence on the Aegean since the Neolithic. It was significant on Mainland Greece in the middle of the third millennium and crucial in the foundation of the palaces in Crete around 2000 B.C.E. From this period iconographic evidence indicates that Egyptian cults such as those of Neith and Tawaret entered the island. Names such as "Athena," "Muse," and "nymph" probably arrived in Crete then, before being transmitted to the Greek Mainland.

Archaeological and legendary evidence suggests that both Southwest Asian and Egyptian civilizations influenced the Aegean during the Hyksos period. This would be a plausible period for the entry of most of the Semitic words found in Linear B. The period when most Egyptian culture entered Greece would indeed seem to be that from 1575 to 1200 B.C.E., when the Eighteenth and Nineteenth Dynasties dominated the Eastern Mediterranean. Much of this influence must have come by way of Phoenicia, and thereby simultaneously introduced West Semitic and, indirectly, Mesopotamian influences. At this time, Phoenicia itself was much more heavily Egyptianized than either Israel or Ugarit, our two major sources of information on the Bronze Age Levant.

By 1100 B.C.E. the power of Egypt was in eclipse, and by the beginning of the new millennium, Phoenician cities dominated the Eastern Mediterranean. It is striking that when Southwest Asia had palaces, the Aegean had palaces and when cities, cities. Although they clearly drew from Bronze Age sources, *Theogony, Works and Days*, and the Homeric epics were written under this Southwest Asian influence in the tenth and ninth centuries B.C.E.

Another complication to the simple scheme outlined above comes from the foundation in the mid–seventh century of the Egyptian Twenty-sixth Dynasty, which often allied with Greeks. During the sixth century B.C.E. the two civilizations had close cultural contact. In that period, to be a "wise man" in Greece it was necessary to have been to Egypt. Greek sculpture, medicine, mathematics, science, and philosophy were all heavily influenced by Egypt in this period. I believe that a number of Greek linguistic borrowings from Egyptian, notably that of the word *sophia* from the Egyptian *sb3* ("wisdom, learning"), took place at this time.[78]

Conclusion

West has conclusively shown the central importance of Southwest Asian civilizations on the formation of Greek literature and other aspects of Hellenic culture. In this case, however, I believe we should follow the dictum of Mao Zedong and "walk on two legs." One should not restrict one's vision to either Southwest Asia or Egypt; both have to be taken into account.

The East Face of Helicon is not merely a wonderful culmination to Martin West's life work, it is also a vindication of his point of view. Although no one has ever been able to challenge his scholarly credentials, until recently West's ideas on Semitic influence have been seen as eccentric. Today, his writings on this topic are being received as orthodox. His work, like that of his colleague Walter Burkert, is now welcomed as proof that the discipline of Classics has always been open to the idea of outside influences on Greece.[79] This fabrication underestimates the loneliness and bravery of these two scholars' persistent championship of an unpopular cause. It is altogether justified that West and Burkert should now be hailed as saviors of their profession.

As a final vignette, I should like to point out that standing on the east face of Helicon, one does not, of course, see Asia, let alone Mesopotamia. The view is of Mount Ptōon, a mountain that plays a significant role in the stories of Oedipus. The toponym clearly comes from the Egyptian P3 ḏw, in Coptic, Ptou, "the Mountain."

15   Phoenician Politics and

Egyptian Justice in Ancient Greece

This chapter is a revised version of an article written for the conference on "The Beginnings of Political Thought in Antiquity," held in Munich in June 1990.[1] It begins with a consideration of scholarship on questions of diffusion in general and Southwest Asian and Egyptian influences on Greece in particular. I then consider the utility of Marx's distinction between what he saw as the two historic stages of the Asiatic mode of production (AMP) and Slave Society. I conclude that the distinction remains useful, despite the important flaws in his analysis of the AMP, which have been revealed by archaeological and textual research in the twentieth century. I also argue that Marx was mistaken when he saw Slave Society as a peculiarly European form of social organization beginning in Ancient Greece. I think it is more revealing to draw a line between land-based or riverine societies on the one hand and maritime ones on the other. Therefore, I argue that one should place the origins of Slave Society in Phoenicia on the coastal Levant rather than in Greece.

The first of the two main sections of this chapter is concerned with summarizing what we know about the political economy of the Phoenician cities of the Early Iron Age, c. 1100–800 B.C.E. I then look at the similarities and differences between these Phoenician cities and the Greek cities or poleis that emerged at the end of this period, in the ninth century. I conclude that there were fundamental similarities between them. In light of the clear evidence of contacts between the Levant and the Aegean during this time, I argue that most of the similarities are best explained as results of diffusion. The differences come from the fact that the Greek society that received these influences was not a tabula rasa. Some of the Greek peculiarities can be explained as remnants of the preexisting warlike tribal society portrayed so vividly by Homer. Even beyond this I argue that in the ninth century B.C.E. there were not merely memories of but also institutional survivals from the palatial society of the Late Bronze Age, which had largely collapsed three hundred years before. This earlier society had itself been heavily influenced from Southwest Asia but even more from Egypt.

In the second section of the chapter, therefore, I examine what I see as the Egyptian influences on some aspects of Mycenaean society, particularly religion and law, as well as on the vocabulary with which they were excercised. I see such practices and words as having survived through the so-called Greek Dark Ages, c. 1150–800 B.C.E.

The last part of the second section is a consideration of another phase of Egyptian influence on Greece in the late seventh and sixth centuries B.C.E. This came about as a result of the weakening of the Phoenician cities by the Assyrian Empire and a revival of Egyptian prosperity. In this period, Egyptian art, mathematics, philosophy, and science all had major effects on Greece. Although some Greek conservatives, notably Plato, admired the stability and stratification of Egyptian society, with its unified monarchy and agricultural economic basis, Egypt could not provide a feasible model for the minuscule Greek city states (with the possible exception of Sparta). As the Greek poleis were small, with a limited land base, they often emphasized manufacture and commerce. Phoenician—rather than Egyptian—politico-economic models were, therefore, much more appropriate for them. In their political structures, both Phoenicians and Greeks as well as others, such as the Etruscans, moved unsteadily among the forms earlier provided by Phoenicians' wide political repertoire: monarchy/tyranny, aristocracy/plutocracy, and democracy/ochlocracy.

Ex Oriente Lux?

This chapter contains an attempt to revive two approaches that have been distinctly unfashionable since the 1950s, especially in English-speaking countries. In the early part of the twentieth century, scholars such as Oscar Montelius, John Myres, Arthur Evans, and Gordon Childe maintained the two principles of modified diffusion and *ex oriente lux* ("Light from the East"). They rejected the beliefs of the extreme diffusionists, who maintained that "master races" simply transposed their superior civilization to other places and "less developed" peoples. They argued instead that, unless there was a rapid genocide, diffusion was a complicated process of interaction between the outside influences and the indigenous culture and that this process itself produced something qualitatively new.[2] They also noted that such interactions are reported throughout history and argued that there was no reason to suppose that the situation had been different in prehistory. Furthermore, they believed that they saw archaeological evidence for similar processes in the earlier period.

The theory of ex oriente lux has had more recent champions. The Austrian archaeologist and prehistorian Fritz Schachermeyr continued to see not merely Neolithic agriculture but also Bronze Age culture of the Aegean as deriving largely from Southwest Asia but also from Egypt.[3] In a way similar to the young Gordon Childe, Schachermeyr combined this diffusionist view with a tendency to play down the fundamental nature of "Oriental" influences after the arrival of Indo-European speakers in Greece between 2500 and 1650 B.C.E.[4] Both Childe and Schachermeyr stressed Indo-European expansion in general and that of Mycenaean Greece in particular.[5]

The scholars' belief in ex oriente lux came from a number of simple observations. First, there was the fact that the cluster of cultural artifacts conventionally called "civilization" had existed in the Near East long before it developed in Europe. Second, there was no doubt that the first European region to acquire "civilization" was the one closest to the Near East. Third, there was the fact that many of the specific features of Aegean civilization were remarkably similar to those of Egypt and Southwest Asia.

Even though classicists were aware that there was archaeological evidence of early contacts between the Near East and the Aegean, they were not too concerned, because the Greece they studied and loved began with

Homer and the first Olympiad in the early eighth century. For instance, the immensely popular book *The Greeks*, published in 1951 by the classicist H. D. F Kitto, moved straight from brief chapters on "The Formation of the Greek People" (entirely in northern and indigenous terms) to one on Homer.

Working against such a view, however, were the discoveries made by Martin Nilsson and other scholars demonstrating clearly from iconography that there was a direct line of cultural succession from Minoan Crete to Mycenaean Greece and on to the Dark, Geometric, Archaic, and Classical Ages.[6] This perception, combined with the desire to keep Greece at arm's length from the Near East, explains why Nilsson and many scholars of the mid–twentieth century were much less ready than the generation of Arthur Evans to accept Egyptian, Libyan, and Levantine influences on Minoan Crete and the Aegean in the third millennium.

The sharpest attack on the idea of ex oriente lux was that of Colin Renfrew, later to become Lord Renfrew, Master of Jesus College, Disney Professor of Archaeology, and director of the McDonald Archaeological Institute. Renfrew argued that despite appearances to the contrary, early Aegean culture had not been influenced from the Near East. He specifically linked this claim to his conviction that Minoan, Mycenaean, and later Greek civilizations were all "determined" in the third millennium.[7]

Renfrew clearly felt and feels a need to establish a fundamental, "original," and authentic Greece unaffected from the outside or at least from the southeast. He believes that with this early and pure essence, any later external influences can and should be considered superficial. I think this view is utterly mistaken. Renfrew's image of an essentially pure Greece is illusory. There have been fruitful contacts between Greece and the Near East since the Neolithic. These have been more or less intense at different periods, and at certain times the cultural flow was from the Aegean to Egypt and the Levant. In general, however, in the three thousand years from 3400 to 400 B.C.E., the predominant flow of influence has been from the Near East to the Aegean.

As is abundantly clear from the previous chapters, I am not the first to argue against the isolationism represented by Renfrew. The works of Cyrus Gordon, Michael Astour, Martin West, Walter Burkert, and Sarah Morris have all been discussed in earlier chapters.[8] Nevertheless, isolationism remains a powerful force in these scholarly fields and it needs to be contested. The idea that Greek civilization should have been massively affected by those of Egypt and the Levant is exactly what one should expect. In earlier chapters, I referred to the Northeast Asian analogy of the relationships among China, Korea, and Japan. This time I use a Southeast Asian parallel, that between India and Indonesia. There is a far greater geographical distance between the subcontinent and the archipelago than there is between Egypt, the Levant, and Greece. Yet East Javanese and Balinese civilization, though distinctively Indonesian, is saturated with Hindu myths, artistic motifs, and cultic practices. Furthermore, even though Old Javanese is undoubtedly a Malayo-Polynesian language, unrelated to Indo-European, the bulk of its vocabulary derives from Sanskrit or Pali. There are also traditions of visits to the islands by Hindu and Buddhist holy men. In these circumstances it would be absurd to attempt to understand aspects of Javanese and Balinese culture that are not explicable in local terms without reference to possible Indian prototypes.

I find the analogy between Greece and Java plausible for a number of reasons. First, there are the consistent Greek traditions of substantial cultural borrowings from Egypt and the Levant; second, there is the fact that so much of the Greek language and nomenclature is inexplicable in terms of Indo-European; finally, as I have argued at length in many previous publications, I believe that one can explain in terms of the sociology of knowledge why nineteenth- and twentieth-century scholars should generally have failed to acknowledge such massive borrowings.

THE PHOENICIAN ORIGINS OF THE POLIS

It is with this model in mind that I should like to look at some Greek developments in the ninth and eighth centuries B.C.E., and in particular to consider the origins of what we think of as Greek politics. To do this it is necessary to have a cursory look at the economic and social background of the polis in which such politics took place. In doing so I will need to discuss a range of views, from Marx to M. I. Finley, over the developments and changes in broad-scale social systems in the ancient world.

Ancient Greek writers maintained that most of their cities had been founded during the Bronze Age, and archaeology and toponymy confirm these legends. Therefore, one should not expect to find any Greek tradition of Near Eastern colonization in the Aegean between the ninth and seventh centuries B.C.E., when the poleis were established. Ancient historians plausibly asserted that the new civic constitutions introduced during this period were created by Greeks. However, as I discuss below, some of the key constitution makers were supposed to have gone to Egypt and/or Phoenicia to study legal and constitutional forms.

Lacking a clear definition of their own economic system, the Greeks and Romans had no explicit traditions about the origins of what Marx called Slave Society. There are, however, indications that at least the latter believed that it came from Phoenicia. As Cicero put it: "The Phoenicians with their traffic in merchandise were the first to introduce into Greece greed, luxurious living and insatiable desires of all sorts."[9] This statement fits the pattern found in the Homeric epics and later writers, in which Phoenicians were especially active in trade in general and slaving in particular.[10] Thus, the idea prevalent among Marxists and non-Marxists alike, that Slave Society—or something like it—originated in Greece, would seem to conflict with ancient views.

Marx and Engels were products of the peak of Philhellenism in German-educated circles between 1820 and 1840. Marx had a lifelong love for Greece and completely accepted the prevailing view that in every aspect of her civilization Greece was categorically different from and superior to all that had gone before. According to him it was only in Greece that the individual had cut the umbilical cord from his community to become a zôon politikon' ("political being").[11] Marx's concept of "Asiatic Society" or "the Asiatic Mode of Production" as a historical stage was one in which, although society was technically advanced, it had not broken free from the primitive tribal community. Thus, it was characterized by self-sufficient village communities whose surplus production was taken directly by the state, which meant that there was no distinction between rent and tax. This mode of production, according to Marx, was typically "Asiatic" and essentially static.[12]

By contrast, Marx's next historical stage, Slave Society, was dynamic and European. In it there was private property in land. Landowners thus mediated between the state and the lower classes, and its cities were typically ruled by them. Marx denied that in the initial stages of Slave Society, trade and specialized manufacture were dominant. Nevertheless, he and Engels saw them as leading to the growth of commodities and private ownership of land and people, that is, the commercial or chattel slaves on whose labor the economy grew to depend.[13]

We now know that all recorded ancient societies in Southwest Asia had family land as distinct from that of the community, palace, or temple. They also had considerable trade in both luxuries and staples. Thus, it was only in some peripheral regions of Ancient Mesopotamia and Syria that there was any village autarky.[14] Some slavery, especially of women, existed from the earliest times, and at least in later Mesopotamian society there was a pattern of servitude that the Soviet ancient historian Mohamed Dandamaev has shown to have been in every way as complex as those in Greece and Rome.[15]

As Moses Finley, Ferenc Tökei, Carlo Zaccagnini, and Perry Anderson hasten to assure us, such anomalies in no way invalidate Marx's scheme, which does not refer to the whole society but only to a given epoch's dominant mode of production.[16] Dandamaev and others have demonstrated that most land in Mesopotamia was cultivated by people whom it is not helpful to call slaves.[17] Within these limits, we may usefully distinguish the social and economic systems of Egypt, Mesopotamia, and the other territorial or riverine societies from those of the Classical world of the Mediterranean.[18]

However, is the distinction best drawn, as it was in the 1820s during the Greek War of Independence, between what was seen as old, static "Turkey/Asia" and young, dynamic "Greece/Europe"? Against such a division we now know that Mycenaean Greece had a palatial economy and society of the bureaucratic "Asiatic" type.[19] Even more striking is the fact that there were Slave Societies on the Levantine coast; that is, in the ancient world there were "Eastern" societies in the West and "Western" ones in the East. It would, therefore, seem better to take up Max Weber's argument that Slave Society was overwhelmingly *coastal* and distinguish not between Asia and Europe but—from the beginning of the Iron Age, c. 1100 B.C.E.—between land- and water-born societies.[20] The association of both ancient and more recent Slave Societies with the sea is not accidental. Without the ease of bulk shipping of staples, food-deficient, specialized manufacturing economies could not develop. To some extent this is possible in riverine societies, but the sea provides much wider scope. Chattel slavery, however, requires the sea.[21] This is because in both ancient Slave Society and early capitalism, the rich and powerful monopolized the sea passage; therefore, the slave could not run home.

In ancient territorial or riverine societies, women could be effectively enslaved in a patriarchal social structure that made them unsafe anywhere. Male slaves, on the other hand, were both dangerous to the slave owner and capable of running away. Thus, in ancient Southwest Asia and Egypt—and, for that matter, China—male slaves were blinded, castrated, otherwise mutilated or branded, both to incapacitate them and to distinguish them from the free population.[22]

In maritime societies with slaves being shipped across the sea, the slave's

choices were restricted to accepting slavery, suicide, suicidal revolt, or trying to join suspicious barbarians beyond the pale. Most resigned themselves to their fate, thus making it possible for slave owners to make use not
only of women and incapacitated men but also of whole men more capable
of short bursts of heavy labor. It also made it economically feasible to employ slaves outside confined workshops or mines in relatively unguarded,
extensive, and long-term agriculture and extraction. The slave owners also
secured themselves by a conscious policy of mixing slaves from the very
different cultures reachable by sea. Such possibilities were not open to territorial empires.

Marx had considerable difficulty explaining the rise of slave society in
what he saw as noncomercialized Greece, and twentieth-century scholars have been unable to do much better.[23] The German Marxist Gabriele
Bockische was equally unable to understand it. Moses Finley promised to
explain the process in *The Ancient Economy*, but failed to do so.[24] Later, in
Ancient Slavery and Modern Ideology, Finley was disarmingly modest on the
question: "Little as we may understand the processes by which [the necessary conditions for slavery] arose . . . That is the critical and most difficult
question. I do not pretend that I can answer it satisfactorily." [25]

The linguist and ancient historian Michel Lejeune has tried to show that
the slave system existed in embryo in the presence of slaves in the Mycenaean *damoi* ("village communities").[26] However, the Marxist historian of
Africa Jean Suret-Canale pointed out that, as in other "Asiatic" societies,
Mycenaean slaves did not form "l'essentiel de la production." [27] In any
event, the survival of a social system as delicate as chattel slavery, after the
twelfth-century destruction of the palaces and three hundred to four hundred years of "Dark Ages," is almost impossible. Thus, although the geography of the Aegean lends itself to trade, it is hard, using ordinary views of
the ancient world, to trace the steps by which Greek tribal society, even with
a memory of the Mycenaean bureaucracy, could have become commercial
in the eighth and seventh centuries B.C.E.

Let us turn for a moment from the new economic system to the corresponding new political one, the polis. Respectable classicists today still
cannot explain its emergence in a rational way. Oswyn Murray, Fellow of
Balliol College at Oxford, wrote about the new institutional forms in the
introduction to his popular work, *Early Greece*: "Discontinuity with the past
was virtually complete." He fleshes this scheme out: ". . . the origins and development of Greek political institutions, the continuing process of change
and reform towards a political rationality which seems unique in world his-

tory. A society with little or no previous history emerged from the Dark Age and was able to create a community based on justice and reason . . . in this sense the *polis* is a conceptual entity, a specific type of political and social organisation." [28] Murray's reluctance to see Phoenician influence in the formation of the polis is all the more remarkable because he has accepted Burkert's and West's demonstrations of a massive Southwest Asian cultural impact on Greece in the eighth and seventh centuries B.C.E.[29] Thus, according to Murray, the polis was a conscious creation by men of extraordinary ability. In short, he sees the creation of the new society as a Greek miracle; there is no rational explanation for its emergence.[30]

In my opinion, the difficulties classicists have had in tracing the origins of Slave Society and the polis come from having asked the wrong question. The place to investigate these is not Greece but Phoenicia. This, however, is not easy because of the lack of source materials. Phoenicians made great use of writing and papyrus. It is no coincidence that Byblos, the Greek name for the great Levantine city of Gu/ebal, was used as the Greek word for "papyrus" or "scroll." As Josephus and Pliny both noted, Phoenicians were renowned for their records and archives.[31]

However, because the Phoenicians were defeated by the Greeks and Romans, wrote principally on a fragile medium, and lived in a rainfall climate, virtually nothing of their literature survives except for that preserved in the Bible. Thus, paradoxically, we know much less about the Phoenician society of the first millennium B.C.E. than we do about those of much older Bronze Age Mesopotamia and Syria, where records were kept on clay in drier climates. The patterns of Phoenician economy and politics have to be gleaned from fragmentary and disparate scraps of evidence, mostly found in the writings of their enemies.

Trade and manufacture had been important on the Levantine coast since at least the fourth millennium. Family ownership of land was well established there, as in the rest of the Middle East, by the middle of the second millennium, and from this period there was a gradual "laicization" of landed property until "land became a commodity like any other." [32] By the early first millennium B.C.E., this was certainly true on the coast. The model, urban, and quite possibly Phoenician "capable wife" described in Proverbs 31:16–17 "buys a field and plants a vineyard out of her earnings." However, in up-country Israel, the sale of land was clearly subordinated to the legality of ancestral land. The story of Naboth's vineyard can be seen in the early-ninth-century conflict between the traditional Israelite Naboth and the Phoenicianized King Ahab, husband of the original Jezebel of Tyre.

Naboth refused to sell his ancestral land to Ahab, who offered him a good price for it.[33] Along the Phoenician coast, there was an absolute shortage of cultivable land. Many coastal cities seem to have been agriculturally deficient and dependent on exchanging their timber and finished goods for grain and other agricultural products (BA II: 482–489).

In the thirteenth and twelfth centuries B.C.E. the Eastern Mediterranean was devastated by the "Peoples of the Sea." Egypt managed to preserve its traditional social structures with difficulty, but qualitative changes occurred elsewhere. In Greece, the breakdown was followed by three hundred to four hundred years of depopulation and very little urban life. Phoenicia, by contrast, recovered quickly, but with new economic and political structures. Until the continuous Assyrian pressure of the late eighth century there were no sustained threats to the coast from land-based states. Thus, from c. 1100 to 750 B.C.E., Phoenician cities, notably Tyre, maintained political independence and generated enormous wealth. The Tyrian Lament quoted in Ezekiel, which seems to refer to the early ninth century, contains an astounding description of the city's trading network, which stretched from Tarshish (probably Tartessos) in Spain to Persia and the southern Red Sea to Greece.[34]

By 850 B.C.E. Tyre was a major entrepôt for staples and luxuries transported by both land and sea. Much was reexported, but as the historian of Tyre Jacob Katzenstein has plausibly argued, much must also have been consumed in the city itself.[35] As early as the tenth century B.C.E., King Hiram of Tyre, in return for help in building the temple at Jerusalem, asked Solomon for corn "which we stand in need of because we inhabit an island." [36] Solomon sent twenty thousand kor of wheat annually, which appears to have been more than 60 percent of the amount consumed by his own court.[37]

None of the goods mentioned on the list from Ezekiel appears to have come from a Tyrian colony. There is nevertheless little doubt that overseas colonization too was initiated by Phoenicians. Groups of merchants from one city living corporately in another had existed in the Near East at least since the Early Bronze Age, and the establishment by cities of villages around their periphery was also very ancient. The biblical metaphor is of a city as the "mother," or metropolis, and the villages as "daughters" over which she has authority.[38] By the ninth century at the very latest, Phoenicians were establishing "daughter cities" overseas.[39]

Great efforts have been made to distinguish such daughter cities from Greek colonies, but the Phoenician ones seem to have been founded and maintained for many of the same varied reasons as the Greek: as markets for specialized manufactures, to increase supplies of staples and metals, for the export of population to ease social problems, and to provide protection and refuge in time of trouble. Furthermore, in both cultures, even those colonies that had achieved political and economic autonomy tended to retain religious ties with the mother city.[40]

The broad-scale historical shift to predominantly commercial and manufacturing societies with food deficits seems to have been reflected in a change of emphasis in the pattern of labor. The Bible offers some guidance to the different kinds of labor in Israel, which presumably resembled those of similar Canaanite-speaking tribal federations or kingdoms, such as Moab, Ammon, and Edom. In these, the most widespread form of servitude was the *mas*. This term was used to describe both permanent helotry for subjugated peoples and temporary levies of the Israelites themselves.[41] Despite the preponderance of these kinds of helotry, commercial slavery played an important role in Israelite society in particular and Canaanite society in general. This can be seen in the references to Yahweh as a slave dealer who "sells" and "redeems" his people.[42] Typically, slaves were foreigners captured or bought abroad. However, there were also temporary or bond slaves from the nation itself, who sold themselves or were sold as children because of debts or poverty. Distinctions between these and foreign slaves were often blurred, as can be seen from repeated attempts to have Israelite slaves released at regular intervals.[43] In addition to helots and slaves, there were also wage laborers and independent craftsmen.

The same types of labor also existed in Phoenicia. Hiram, King of Tyre, sent ʿabâdîm ("servants" or "slaves"), to cut timber and build the temple at Jerusalem. But Solomon raised a *mas* ("levy") to work with them.[44] Some of these men came from a corvée; others appear to have been state or personal slaves. In contrast, Solomon appears to have dealt directly with another Hiram, a craftsman and major contractor, who was clearly free.[45]

There is scattered evidence to strengthen the plausible hypothesis that chattel slavery was more important in Phoenicia, with its urban manufacture and commerce, than it was inland. The *Tyrian Lament* mentions buying slaves from Greece, and the two major references to Phoenicians in the *Odyssey* are concerned with slaving.[46] Odysseus' story of having been kidnapped by a Phoenician is particularly significant because it was untrue and therefore had to be plausible. In the eighth century, Amos condemned Tyre for "forgetting the ties of kinship" and selling Israelite refugees to Edom.[47] Two centuries later, Joel denounced Tyrians and Sidonians for selling Judaeans to the Greeks.[48] Herodotus opened his History with a reference to Phoenician slaving.[49] It should be noted that in all the cases except one, the slaves were taken overseas. Thus, the evidence, though scanty, indicates that commercial slavery dominated relations of production in Phoenicia from the tenth if not the eleventh century, well before it was prevalent in Greece.

Phoenicians, incidentally, seem to have been the first people to eat lying on couches. This practice became a marker of freedom as opposed to slavery, expressing slave-owning indolence. It was taken up by Greeks and Etruscans, who were also heavily influenced by Phoenician culture, and from the Etruscans the custom spread to Rome.[50] If Phoenicia had chattel slavery, it also had its opposite, free citizens, but freedom was not, as is sometimes suggested, the creation of slave society.[51] All that is necessary for a consciousness of freedom is the existence of some servitude. The contrast between servility and freedom—amargi ("to the mother") in Sumerian—existed in Mesopotamia at least since the third millennium.[52] There were a number of different Ancient Egyptian words for freedom. One of them, wstnw, came from the verb wstn ("stride," "travel freely"). Another, t3w, has the basic meaning of "wind," which, apart from its general sense of free movement, was generally associated with the breath of life and cool refreshing breezes. In Canaanite, the terms baʿal and ḥôr mean both "noble" and "free," and dᵉror ("free") combines images of "free-flowing water" and "swallows," which never touch the ground. Such poetic images show the extraordinary value placed on freedom in the ancient world. It is simply European cultural arrogance to claim that the Greeks invented the concept.[53]

In the ancient world of the Near East, freedom was also associated with the concept of common access to law. One should not exaggerate the extent of illiteracy in societies using nonalphabetic scripts, the Mesopotamian practice of inscribing laws on publicly visible stone stelae or tablets. Nevertheless, it became something very different in Canaan, with its alphabet and widespread literacy.[54] The classical archaeologist Anthony Snodgrass has plausibly suggested that the early Greek law code inscriptions derived from Phoenician ones.[55] Such influences on Greek law from unattested Phoenician codes would parallel the striking influences of Middle Eastern law codes on the Roman law code the Twelve Tables. These appear to have been transmitted to Rome in the early fifth century B.C.E. through West Phoenician cities, especially Carthage.[56]

During the fourteenth century B.C.E. we have the first reference to the people, as opposed to a monarch, as sovereign in a Levantine city, Arwad.[57] Michael Astour points out that "this situation was not unique." The ease of the transition from personal to collective rule demonstrates that even under royal regimes, the city states of Canaan possessed the necessary institutions for such transformations.[58] In the Late Bronze Age, however, republics were unusual. The normal pattern in the Levant was that of a constitutional monarch ruling with the elders and backed by a major foreign land power, the Egyptian or Hittite Empires. An example of this can be seen in the city of Ugarit, whose "king" has been convincingly compared to a Venetian doge. However, as Astour put it: "Social relations in Ugarit . . . [lacked] . . . the rigidity and exclusiveness of the Venetian mercantile oligarchy." [59]

Most Phoenician cities had walls to protect the whole people and were dominated by the hêkāl. This word, deriving from the Sumerian e-gal ("big house"), changed its meaning approximately with the crisis of the twelfth century from "palace" to "temple." The temple was usually dedicated to the city or tribal divinity, representing the people as a whole. Many Jews and Tyrians chose to die rather than have this symbol of their corporate identity profaned. We should also note the biblical insistence that Solomon built the Temple before and on a grander scale than his own palace.[60]

Free citizens participated widely in the running of Phoenician cities. Ancient Mesopotamia and Syria had long traditions of mixed democratic and aristocratic rule.[61] Thus, the Phoenician constitutions drew on patterns already available through general historical precedent in Southwest Asia and the specific institutions of Bronze Age Canaan mentioned above. Unlike the situation in earlier periods, during the heyday of Phoenician wealth and power, the local councils and assemblies were not subject to outside territorial monarchs.

As among the Greek city states that developed subsequently, the Phoenician cities and the inland Canaanite-speaking kingdoms of Israel, Moab, and Ammon shared a common language, literary culture, and religious practices, though they each had their own gods. Politically, they were often bitterly divided. In this respect too Phoenicia in the ninth and eighth centuries strikingly resembled Greece of later times. The ancient historian Boustanay Oded has described Phoenicia as having had an "absence of any attempt to unite, even temporarily, in order to confront the enemy from without. The history of the coastal cities is replete with internal strife arising from commercial competition and territorial disputes." [62] Furthermore, like the later Greeks, the Phoenicians had varied and changing political forms: monarchies, plutocracies, aristocracies, democracies, and mixed constitutions. They seem to have preferred constitutional monarchies, though, as mentioned above, Canaanite republics existed at most periods between the Late Bronze Age and the fall of Carthage.⁶³

In Carthage there were two "kings"—called *sufetes* in Latin, from the Canaanite *šōpᵉṭîm* ("judges")—and a council of elders. Aristotle's description of the city's constitution was written in the fourth century B.C.E. but probably referred to earlier periods. According to this, issues to be discussed by the *dēmos* were selected by the two kings and the elders. However, in theory at least, ultimate power rested with the people. Aristotle saw the Carthaginian kings and elders as the counterparts of the Spartan double kingship and *gerousia* or "senate." ⁶⁴ Another striking parallel between the Spartan and Carthaginian constitutions was that in Carthage there were mess halls of companions, *sussitia tōn hetairōn*, very like the Spartan *phiditia*. The title of the Spartan mess halls would seem to have come from the Egyptian *pḏt(y)* ("bowmen, troop"). Functionally, there is a Canaanite equivalent in the root *ḥbr* ("association"). This institution was found in the report of the Egyptian traveler Wen Amun in the eleventh century B.C.E., in a Carthaginian inscription, and frequently in the Bible.⁶⁵ Institutionally, traces of this community hall have been seen in the *curiae* or voting colleges within the assemblies found in cities of North Africa in the Roman period, which preserved much of their "Carthaginian heritage." ⁶⁶

Most Canaanite states seem, like Carthage, to have had councils or senates of elders or notables. In general, both elders and people met at the town gate, but in larger cities they may have met in a special building.⁶⁷ Decisions were often by acclamation. The question of whether there were votes or elections is basically semantic, for a fine line separates these from casting lots to discover God's wishes, which, in Israel at least, was done by casting pebbles. This process usually took place at great assemblies and often involved large numbers of people, as is evident from the phrase "both the small and the great" sometimes used with it.⁶⁸ In Greece "casting lots" had what would now be seen as the two meanings of casting lots and voting, frequently with *psephoi* ("pebbles"), often placed in a *ketharion* or *kêthis* ("voting urns"), which, like the Greek *kados* ("jar") come from the Canaanite *kad* ("jar").⁶⁹

Despite the six centuries that separate Davidic from late Carthaginian institutions, and the undoubted changes that both Israel and Carthage went through during the course of their existence, it would seem reasonable to see parallels between such practices. Aristotle insisted on the antiquity of the Carthaginian constitution, comparing it with the oldest—and best—in Greece, those of Crete and Sparta. At no point did he suggest that Carthage had borrowed from Greek political patterns.[70] Even if appointment by lot in Archaic Greece did not derive from Canaan, it is clear that conventional wisdom has been misled by Eurocentrism and anti-Semitism into the belief that Greek cities differed categorically from Phoenician ones in being "free," whereas the latter were authoritarian if not despotic.[71]

In this regard, what later Western scholars termed Assyrian "Oriental despotism" became dominant on the Levantine coast only in the late eighth century. Even then, Tyre and the other Phoenician cities maintained considerable autonomy. Thus, from 850 to 700 B.C.E., when the polis emerged, the Phoenicians, the Middle Easterners with whom the Greeks had most contact, were living in very similar city states.

The Swiss classicist Kurt Raaflaub has listed five preconditions for the emergence of Greek political thought in the Archaic Period.[72] Only one of these, the uncertain, that is, the sometimes positive relationship between lower aristocrats and the independent farmers he sees in Greece, is not apparent on the Levant. The four others—the lack of centralized absolute monarchies, the disunity and small size of independent states, the commercial economic development, and the double sense of unity and independence especially as engendered by colonization—all existed in eleventh, tenth, and ninth century Phoenicia. What is more, it is extremely unlikely that Greece should have developed such similar institutions and ideas independently, as the presence of Phoenicians in the Aegean before the late eighth century is attested both in Homer and the archeological record.[73] All in all, there is today no justification for statements such as that made by Victor Ehrenberg in 1961: "There is no direct road leading from the [Oriental] territorial state under its kings to the Greek community of free citizens." [74]

In short, whereas in Greece it is necessary to postulate the emergence of Slave Society ex nihilo, in Phoenicia it can plausibly be seen to have arisen from early Levantine patterns of trade and manufacture, the economic, social, and political developments of the Late Bronze Age, the shock of the invasions of the Peoples of the Sea, and three hundred years of freedom from interference from land empires. This plausible origin, together with the appearance of an economy based on chattel slavery and the city state in Phoenicia centuries before those of Greece, and the literary and archeological evidence for the presence of Phoenicians in the Aegean in the intervening period, make a plausible case for a connection between the two developments. Thus, it is virtually certain that slave society and the city state of the type conventionally seen as originally and autochthonously Greek started in Phoenicia in the eleventh century B.C.E. and spread to Greece some centuries later.

Egyptian Justice
THE BRONZE AGE LEGACY

The fact that many of the political institutions of Archaic Greece and hence much political thought came from Phoenicia does not mean that Greek politics and political thought were mere reproductions of Levantine proto-types. Geometric Greece was not a blank sheet on which anything could be written. There were inevitably many complex interactions between the new externally derived economic, social, and political forms and the indigenous society. Some of the most profound differences between Phoenician and Greek cities, such as the Hellenic emphasis on the citizen army, the gym-nasium, and the canonization of the Homeric epics, seem to have come from the desire of the tribal chiefs to preserve martial spirit while civilian-izing or civilizing city life and manners. Raaflaub has shown in detail how some political concepts in use in Archaic and Classical times were already apparent in Homer, whom I, following the eminent classicist Denys Page, would place around 900 B.C.E.[75]

I am convinced that one must go still further back in time and consider the possibility that Greece of the Dark and Geometric Ages was still heavily influenced by the Mycenaean past. Most scholars today agree that the Dark Ages did not create a hermetic seal between Bronze and Iron Age Greece. Virtually no one now doubts that a form of Greek that in some ways was less Archaic than that of Homeric poetry was in use in the Mycenaean palaces. The work on Greek religion by Martin Nilsson and others has shown defini-tively the religious and cultic continuities from before and after the Dark Ages.[76] Archaeologically, there is now considerable evidence to show that the devastation of the twelfth and eleventh centuries was much more un-even than had been supposed.[77] It was always clear that although some cities never recovered after the Bronze Age and some new ones came to prominence in Archaic times, there was an essential continuity of urban settlement. There are even indications of some family continuity.[78] Further-more, evidence from Linear B and Egyptian texts show that most major place-names remained the same.

There is to my mind no doubt that although literacy declined during the Dark Ages, as in the period after the fall of the Western Roman Empire, it did not break down completely. Most scholars do not accept the claims of Herodotus, the Semitist Robert Stieglitz, and me that there was alphabetic writing in Greece before the Trojan War, c. 1200 B.C.E.[79] More and more Semitists, however, are inclined to believe Naveh's more cautious contention that the transmission took place in the eleventh century.[80] Equally, few classicists today would go down with Rhys Carpenter to the end of the eighth century; the majority now appear to have shifted back to the first decades of that century.[81] In any of these cases, it is inconceivable that there was a period in which neither Linear B nor an alphabet were in use in the Aegean. The survival of syllabic writing in the one island of Cyprus or of Linear A of over a thousand years on Crete makes it very unlikely that all knowledge of Linear B disappeared everywhere within one or two centuries of the destruction of the palaces, despite the lack of attestation.

If Egyptian institutions, language, and thought were adopted and adapted in Mycenaean Greece, could any of them have been transmitted through the Dark Ages to the Archaic Period? Let us now consider some possible survivals specifically concerned with political thought.

The first of these is the tradition of the *psychostasia* or *kērostasia*, the weighing of souls. The image of the souls of two heroes being weighed against each other to determine which shall win a mortal combat is described explicitly in the final battle between Hector and Achilles.[82] This theme was used elsewhere for the Greeks and Trojans collectively.[83] Homer's other allusions to weighing souls are even more interesting and significant. The classicist B. C. Dietrich has plausibly argued that the abbreviation of the reference to it in the *Iliad* shows that the concept was of long standing and familiar to Homer and his readers.[84] Early in the twentieth century, the classicist G. E. Lung mentioned in this connection, but with some skepticism, the find of scales made of gold leaf in one of the tombs at Mycenae.[85] The presence of scales in a funerary context strongly suggests some knowledge in Mycenaean Greece of the Egyptian weighing of souls and the trial of the dead in which it took place.

The similarity of the Egyptian iconography to the scene described by Homer is so striking that it has been seen even by scholars who were otherwise very wary of postulating any Egyptian influences on Greece. Otto Gruppe drew a parallel between the two, pointing out that in the Greek representations, Hermes has a central role in the weighing, just as his counterpart Thoth is always shown recording the balance in the Egyptian scenes.[86] Lung put this potentially dangerous idea into proportion: "In this form [Gruppe's theory] is untenable because it is not possible to detect any Egyptian influence in the Greek psychostasia; one should rather say that Hermes conforms somewhat to Thoth."[87]

This confusion is an excellent example of what happens when a paradigm—in this case, the blanket denial of Near Eastern influences on early Greece—is unable to cope with the evidence. There is, of course, an important difference between the two scenes, in that in Egypt it is not a competition between two souls, but the weighing of a single soul against a feather representing m3ʿt ("truth" or "fate" or communal values).[88] On the other hand, Gruppe's case can be strengthened by noting that the Greek Hermes is the counterpart not merely of the Egyptian Thoth but also of Anubis, and that in *The Book of Coming Forth by Day* (commonly known as *The Book of the Dead*) Anubis is also always present at the weighing. Indeed, I believe that a good argument can be made that the fusion of the two gods in Late Egyptian and Greek religion comes from their close cooperation in this key scene (BA I: 141). Twentieth-century scholars have also made a strong case for there having been a *psychostasia* between Achilles and the Trojan ally Memnōn. This hero's provenance is uncertain, but there is no doubt that he had an ultimately Egyptian name and was black, though not necessarily African (BA II: 257–269). In the case of Memnōn, Hermes is sometimes represented in Anubis' chief role of passing between life and death and guiding the soul to immortality.[89]

One should also take into account the traditions reported by Homer, and later writers that Minos and Rhadamanthys acted as judges of the dead.[90] Aeschylus described the "underground" Zeus who tried the dead in a context very much concerned with Egypt.[91] Thus, here there seems to be a case in which the Egyptian idea of the scales of justice used in the trial of the dead was present in Mycenaean Greece and preserved in the Homeric epics and elsewhere.[92] Furthermore, in the Egyptian funerary trial par excellence, that between the gods Horus and his wicked uncle Seth, the victor was acclaimed as m3ʿ ḫrw ("true of voice") by the judges and the crowd. This was both a reflection of an Egyptian legal process and a model for it, and, given the circumstantial evidence cited above, there are good reasons to suppose that the same was true in Mycenaean Greece.

I believe that there is etymological evidence that both confirms and broadens this pattern. Here, I am aware that I am going far beyond the bounds of conventional Classics—though staying well within those of linguistics. As stated many times elsewhere in this book, notably in the reply to Jasanoff and Nussbaum, I maintain that in cases where there is no plausible Indo-European etymology for a Greek word, it is perfectly permissible to look to neighboring languages for loans, especially those of Egypt and the Levant for which there is strong archaeological, documentary, and traditional evidence of close contact with Greece.

To start with one central to the legal and funerary theme I have been considering, the term mḫ3t, the standard Egyptian word for a balance and the beam across it, appears in the Greek mochlos ("lever or beam"). It is an ancient term in Greek, occurring in Homer.[93] Another relevant Homeric word is aisimos ("destined"). Its root, aisa, already present in Mycenaean, means "part accorded" and, by extension, "destiny." It is supposed to have an Indo-European cognate in the Oscan aetis ("portion"). The Greek root would seem more likely to come from the Egyptian isw-, Coptic asou and esou- ("fair reward, compensation to which one is entitled").[94] >Isw is almost certainly the etymon of the Greek isos, with the archaic feminine form eisē ("equal in share, number, or right"). Compounds of iso- such as isonomia ("equality") and isēgoria ("equal right of speech" or simply "political equality") were critical in the formation of Greek democratic theory.[95]

As mentioned above in connection with the feather weighed against the heart/soul of the dead man, the Egyptian word for "righteousness and justice" was m3ʿt.[96] This root and its compounds appear to have been very productive in Greek. The earliest loan, made when the m was still a rounded mʷ and the 3 was pronounced as a liquid r or l, was that to the Greek moira ("fate" or "the permanent moral and physical state of the universe").[97] Moira may well have been influenced by the Semitic root mwr, which is very probably related to m3ʿ . . , meaning "recompense or property acquired through exchange or inheritance." However, the Egyptian connection is indicated by the two m3ʿty, the dual or doubled form of m3ʿt. These two played key roles in the weighing of the dead souls and were sometimes represented as the scales themselves. These functions are strikingly close to those of the Greek Moirai or Fates. It should be remembered that there were not always three Fates, and at Delphi there were only two.[98]

In the Late New Kingdom, the 3 lost its consonantal quality, and by its end, the m in m3ʿt. ceased to be rounded. Pronounced as *ma, m3ʿ(t.) appears to have been borrowed again into Greek as ma as a particle used in asseverations and oaths. With the preposition m, m m3ʿt. ("in truth") was also used, though not in the same syntactical position, as a marker of oaths—which were used in Egyptian law courts.[99] The strength of the etymology of ma from m3ʿ(t.) is weakened both by the word's simplicity and the existence of a Hittite suffix, -ma, meaning "but." The plausibility of the Egyptian etymology is strengthened, however, by other Greek stems that can be derived from m3ʿ.

The derivation of the Greek stem timā, found in timh, meaning "honor" but also "assess," from an Egyptian *dit m3ʿ was discussed in chapter 6.[100] M3ʿ ḥrw ("true of voice"), the title given to the virtuous dead, who, as mentioned above, have stood their trial in judgment, is widely accepted as the origin of the Greek makar, makaria, usually translated "blessed or happy." [101] Already in Hesiod, hoi makares were "the blessed dead," and the makarōn nēsōn were the "Isles of the Dead"; the Egyptian dead also lived in the West. In Homer the adjective makar- was generally applied to gods and immortals rather than mortal men and women. In the fifth century C.E. makarites meant one recently dead, as makarios does in Demotic Greek today. In Greek hagiology St. Makarios is involved in the judgment of souls.

The derivations from isw and m3ʿt. are not the only Egyptian terms associated with law and justice to be found in Greek. There is, for example, the Greek martyros, martys or maityrs, and maitys ("witness"); the variations alone lead one to expect a loan here. This would seem to come from Egyptian mtr ("testify") and mtrw ("witness") and the Coptic mate ("correct, accurate") and mto ("be present"). Another plausible etymology, Greek horkos and horkon ("oath") from the Egyptian ʿrk and Coptic ōrk ("swear"), was considered in the previous chapter.[102]

Other terms of political significance, lacking convincing Indo-European roots and with plausible Egyptian origins, include the key official term basileus ("high official, priest, king").[103] In Egyptian, ḥrp means "baton of office, govern, control." The Greek khalepos fits phonetically with ḥrp and is unexplained in terms of Indo-European. However, in Greek, khalepos has the interestingly different meanings of "severe, painful, difficult." If ḥrp and khalepos are related, it would reflect different views of the same situation by speakers of Egyptian and Proto-Greek. There are also a number of words for "people" or "subjects." One example is dēmos, originally "territory," from the Egyptian dmi ("township") and dmiw ("townsmen"); a second is ethnos from ṯnw> *iṯnw, Coptic ato ("census, multitude"); a third is ochlos ("crowd, rabble") from ʿš3 ("many, multitude").[104] None of these have Indo-European etymologies.

THE IRON AGE IMAGE

Even if one accepts only a few of these etymologies, they indicate that Mycenaean culture was fundamentally influenced by Egypt in its language and presumably in its concepts of politics in general and courts and justice in particular. However, by the period with which we are principally concerned, the ninth and eighth centuries B.C.E., these words had been largely assimilated into Greek and the concepts Hellenized. This was the cultural basis onto which the new Phoenician economic, social, and political structures were grafted.

Nevertheless, I believe that some of the earlier cultural imports, such as weighing the dead, retained a sense of their Egyptian origins and that Greeks never lost their sense that Egypt was the prime source not only of wealth, wisdom, and magic but also of justice. This is particularly remarkable in light of the general contempt Greeks had for all foreigners, including Egyptians. The earliest evidence of this respect is the report of the generous treatment given to the Pseudo-Cretan by the Egyptian king in the *Odyssey*. The Egyptian's mercy was especially striking as the Greek describes the devastation he and his men caused in Egypt.[105]

The next indirect references to a Greek view of Egyptian justice come from the stories surrounding the Spartan Lykurgos around 800 B.C.E. Both Diodorus and Plutarch reported that Egyptians believed the legislator to have studied in Egypt—among other places—and to have borrowed social and political institutions from there. Plutarch did not commit himself on this, but he noted that some Greek historians also shared this opinion.[106]

There is nothing inherently implausible about the idea of Lykurgos, or other Spartans with whom the legendary figure may have been conflated, having been in Egypt at this time. There were no navigational difficulties in sailing from the Peloponnese to Egypt. Even in its disunity at the end of the Twenty-second and the beginning of the Twenty-third Dynasties, Egypt was—by contemporary Greek standards—immensely rich. Furthermore, Egypt possessed the cultural prestige of two and a half millennia of civilization. There is archaeological evidence of contact between Egypt and Sparta at around this period from Egyptian objects of the earliest strata (mid–eighth century) of the temple of Artemis Orthia.[107] It is also striking to find that a number of specifically Spartan names for Dorian institutions, *lochos* and *ōba* as well as *phitidia* mentioned above, have plausible Late

Egyptian etymologies.[108] Even more significantly, there is the later commonplace that the Spartan customs and constitution somehow resembled those of the Egyptians.[109] All these possible Egyptian influences must be seen in light of the fact that the Spartan kings believed themselves to be of Egyptian descent or at least as having come from Egypt.[110] This would explain why, in the sixth century, the second Meneleion or shrine to Spartan royalty was built as a pyramid, and why in the second century B.C.E. the last Spartan king should have had the non-Greek—probably either Semitic or Egyptian—name of Nabis.[111] This is not to deny either that Sparta was essentially a Dorian tribal state or that it received substantial Phoenician influences directly or through Crete. It is interesting that Aristotle classed the Spartan, Cretan, and Cathaginian constitutions together with the highest approval.[112] Nevertheless, it would seem likely that Spartan rulers turned to Egypt as a model of a stable agrarian polity rather than the specialized manufacturing commercial society of the Phoenician type that Corinth and other Greek cities were adopting.

However, Sparta was not the only Greek state that may have borrowed institutions and legal ideas from Egypt. Egyptians told Diodorus that the three social orders of Athens were the result of Egyptian influence.[113] Plutarch believed that these orders were established by Theseus in what we now call the Bronze Age.[114] Given the abundant archaeological and documentary evidence for contact between Egypt and the Aegean in the fifteenth and fourteenth centuries and the arguments on Egyptian terminology and imagery in Pre-Homeric Greece made above, I see nothing inherently implausible in the claims of Egyptian influence on the Athenian forms during this period.[115] They are made more probable in the light of Athenian pride in their city's survival of the upheavals of the twelfth century. A modified diffusionist would not be distressed by the fact that the Athenian social orders or castes did not mirror exactly what we know of their supposed Egyptian prototypes. This is both because of the many centuries that would have intervened between the hypothetical introduction of the system in the Bronze Age and its first description over a thousand years later and, even more important, because one would expect modification of Egyptian institutions in a Greek context.

Whether or not the orders were inherited from the Bronze Age, there seems no reason to doubt Aristotle's claim that they antedated Solon's reforms in the early sixth century.[116] A number of modern scholars, most recently Alan Lloyd, have denied that Solon ever went to Egypt.[117] They demand proof for what they consider to be an extremely unlikely event.

This requirement seems to me absurd, as other evidence makes it clear that it was not difficult to make the crossing in the sixth century and that there was frequent contact between Egypt and the Aegean in this period. As archaeological evidence for this, Richard Brown lists over fifteen hundred Egyptian objects found in Geometric and Archaic Greek contexts.[118] Furthermore, there were clearly great gains in both wealth and prestige for a Greek traveling to Egypt. Thus, despite the impossibility of one of the best-known stories of Solon's voyages, the visit to Croesus of Lydia as the king came to the throne in 560 B.C.E., the year the Athenian died, I see no reason to doubt the many and circumstantial reports that Solon visited Egypt and other places.[119] The verisimilitude of these reports is increased by a line from one of Solon's poems referring to the Canopic mouth of the Nile.[120] There is also no chronological objection to Solon's having talked with the pharaoh Amasis, who came to power in 570 B.C.E.

Only Plutarch refers to Solon's having traveled as a young man.[121] Other authors write of his visits to Egypt and elsewhere after his reforms in 594–593 B.C.E. This would make it impossible for him to have drawn up his laws in general, or that on idleness in particular, on the basis of *his own experiences* in Egypt,[122] even though Herodotus, Diogenes Laertius, and Plutarch all maintained that he did so.

Arguments that Solon was influenced by Egyptian precedents have been given above.[123] It is even more significant, however, that, at least by the time of Herodotus and possibly much earlier, Greek writers worked to establish connections between legislators of whom they approved and Egypt. An Egyptian precedent was felt to increase the legitimacy of any Greek regulation. I would go on to argue that if Greek writers in the fifth century held Egypt in such respect at a time when it was in decline, it is likely that Greek statesmen in the sixth century, when Egypt was independent and prosperous, borrowed and adapted Egyptian institutions.

As an example of Greek respect for Egyptian justice in the sixth century, there is Herodotus' report that an embassy from the city of Elis, which had just gained control of the Olympic Games, visited the pharaoh Psammis (Psammiētichus II) to gain approval from the "wisest" Egyptians for regulations of the Games.[124] The pharaoh told them that their regulations were not perfect because they allowed men of Elis to compete. Here, there is an anachronism in that Psammitechos II reigned from 595 to 589 B.C.E. and the Eleans gained control of the Games only c. 570 B.C.E. However, Diodorus rectified this by attributing the advice to Amasis.[125] Both the embassy and its discomfort illustrate the notion that Egypt was seen by Greeks as the fount of justice that could bestow legitimacy on Greek institutions.[126] The high reputation of Egyptian justice was not restricted to Greece. At the end of the sixth century, the Persian ruler Darius I appears to have had an Egyptian judicial code translated not merely into Demotic for use in Egypt, but into Aramaic for use elsewhere in the empire.[127]

Plato, particularly in his later dialogues, maintained that Egypt was the source of most aspects of civilization. In *Philebus* Plato went into considerable detail on Theuth or Thoth as the creator of writing, even language and all sciences.[128] Elsewhere, he praised Egyptian art and music and argued for their adoption in Greece.[129] The only reason for doubting that *The Republic* was based on Egypt is the fact that Plato does not say so in the text. This omission, however, has an ancient explanation. As his earliest commentator, Krantor, wrote within a few generations of Plato: "Plato's contemporaries mocked him, saying that he was not the inventor of his republic, but that he had copied Egyptian institutions. He attached so much importance to the mockers that he attributed to the Egyptians the story of the Athenians and the Atlantines to make them say that the Athenians had really lived under this régime at a certain moment in the past."[130] Faced with this evidence in favor of an Egyptian derivation for Plato's political thought, even in the nineteenth century scholars continued to associate Plato's republic with Egypt. As Marx put it in *Capital*: "Plato's Republic, in so far as division of labor is treated in it, as the formative principle of the state, is merely an Athenian idealization of the Egyptian system of castes."[131] More recently, scholars sympathetic toward Plato have forcefully denounced the idea that he favored an Egyptian type of caste system.[132] The majority simply omit any mention of Egypt in connection with *The Republic* (BA I: 106–107).

One also finds Egyptian connections for another, though lesser Greek thinker, Archytas of Tarentuon. In addition to indications from the extant fragments of his work, the facts that he was a Pythagorean and the teacher of the Egyptophile Eudoxos suggest that Archytas was influenced by the image of Egypt. Aristotle appears to have derived from Archytas his concepts of proportional equality as the basis of distributive justice and of equity and the mean, as well as the distinction between monarchy as lawful rule and tyranny as unlawful. Fragments of Archytas' *On Law and Wisdom* also contain the image of the king as animate *empsychos* ("law") and the distinction between the written law necessary for republics and the unwritten law in the virtue of monarchies, a distinction that is also found both in Plato's *Laws* and Aristotle's *Politics*.[133]

No one doubts the Platonic roots of the notion of the just king as the living embodiment of law, the court of the last instance and the source of equity, a notion that later became central in Hellenistic and Roman times. Although it is certain that the Persian model also played a role in the formation of such an image, I find the case that the idea comes through the Greek thinkers from Egypt very persuasive. In Pharaonic Egypt there are frequent references to the pharaoh as the constant expression of the general will.[134] In the Nineteenth Dynasty there are statements alluding to the pharaoh as the lawgiver and renderer of justice. Thus, the explicit titles of this kind that were applied to Ptolemaic rulers fit well with the Egyptian tradition.[135] It appears, then, that here, as in so much else, Plato and the Platonists drew from Egypt.

Despite the emphasis on the animate unwritten law of the virtuous monarch, written case law flourished under the Hellenistic and Roman divine rulers, and this too was seen as having originated in Egypt. Aristotle recommended that Greeks return to Egyptian law as a basis for their own.[136] The clear implication of the passage from Aristotle is that what he was recommending had not hitherto been carried out. Nevertheless, it would seem likely that Aristotle was conventional in his beliefs in the greater antiquity and the superiority of Egyptian law. Thus, even though Egyptian law and the varied laws of the Greek cities were very different in his own day, the true foundation of Greek law and justice was in Egypt.

Conclusion

In this chapter I have slipped easily from politics and political theory to law and justice and to etymology. I believe that such slippage is inevitable given the integral links that bind them and the spotty nature of the evidence, which is not sufficient to follow a single line on its own. Nevertheless, the distinction made in the title of this chapter between Phoenician politics and Egyptian justice seems to me to be helpful. I have argued that the polis and other social institutions of Geometric and Archaic Greece were essentially local modifications of those of the contemporary Levantine city states and that therefore it is useful to refer to "Phoenician politics." On the other hand, I maintain that the local Greek culture with which the Phoenician influences interacted was itself thoroughly mixed. It contained not merely the tribal culture of nobility, valor, and violence of the Dark Ages and the end of the Mycenaean Period but also many aspects of earlier Mycenaean civilization, language, religion, and historical traditions, all of which had been massively influenced by Egypt and the West Semitic cultures of the Levant.

I maintain that there is enough evidence to indicate that the traditions passed down through the Dark Ages contained such elements as the Egyptian judgment of the dead and hence the notions of a balanced justice and court procedure. I further argue that although such notions became substantially Hellenized, their Egyptian origins were never entirely lost from view, and that this sense, and the continued wealth and power of Egypt, led Greeks of the Archaic and Classical Periods to maintain an idealized picture of Egypt as the source of justice to which Greeks could and should still refer.

VII

A Popularizing Effort

THIS FINAL SECTION has only one chapter, "All Not Quiet on the Welles-ley Front." It is a review of Mary Lefkowitz's popular book *Not Out of Africa* (NOA). My chapter was originally published in the *Bryn Mawr Classical Review* and enlarged during an e-mail debate between Lefkowitz and me in May 1997. NOA is relatively short and Lefkowitz states that it is not self-sufficient but relies on the scholarship contained in *Black Athena Revisited.* Nevertheless, NOA raises some issues not touched on in BAR and it is these to which I reply.

Ostensibly her argument is with "Afrocentrists" as a collectivity. In fact, however, her prime targets are a single Afrocentrist, George G. M. James, and me. The reason for this is that Lefkowitz is more tolerant of the idea of Egypt's Africanity than most of her colleagues. Classicists, like many others in "Western" society, see West and Central Africans as the polar opposites of Hellenic/European civilization. Potentially at least, Ancient Egypt could confuse this dichotomy. The most frequent way to keep the two apart is the double claim that Ancient Egypt was neither truly African nor truly civilized and that it had only a marginal impact on Greek civilization. Lefkowitz, by contrast, has taken an extreme position, beyond that of most of her colleagues. She maintains that Egypt had no significant impact on the formation of any aspect of Greek civilization. Thus, she is more willing than most of her colleagues to accept the "Africanity" of Egypt. This issue is the major concern of most Afrocentrists. Although they belong to the African and diasporic intellectual tradition that accepts the Ancient model of Greek origins, they do not consider the origination of European culture as either good or particularly important. For them as for Lefkowitz, "North is North and South is South and never the twain shall meet." Civilizations on the two continents can have mutual respect but not mutual kinship.

What Lefkowitz finds intolerable is the proposal that an African Egypt had a central and formative influence on Greek civilization. This was what George G. M. James claimed in the 1950s and I have argued since the 1980s. In short, she is less worried by Afrocentric chauvinism than she is by notions of Greek hybridity.

Most of the review is taken up with contesting Lefkowitz's sharp denials of any Egyptian impact on Greek religion, philosophy, mysteries, and other aspects of Hellenic civilization. I end the review by claiming that in many ways the Afrocentric views of Egypt and the formation of Greece is traditional and that the true radicals were Lefkowitz's academic ancestors, the destroyers of the Ancient model and creators of the Aryan model: the men who established the discipline of Classics.

16   All Not Quiet on the Wellesley Front:

A Review of Not Out of Africa

It is curious withal, that the earliest known civilization was, we have the strongest reason to believe, a negro civilization. The original Egyptians are inferred, from the evidence of their sculptures, to have been a negro race: it was from negroes, therefore, that the Greeks learnt their first lessons in civilization; and to the records and traditions of these negroes did the Greek philosophers to the very end of their career resort (I do not say with much fruit) as a treasury of mysterious wisdom. — JOHN STUART MILL, "The Negro Question"[1]

This chapter is concerned with Not Out of Africa (NOA), a popular book by Mary Lefkowitz that appeared at the same time as Black Athena Revisited (BAR), 1996. The two books are not merely linked by their editor/author and their simultaneous appearance but also by a fact pointed out by Lefkowitz in the second (paperback) edition. She explains that NOA is "not long" because it draws on the "detailed research" to be found in BAR (NOA, p. 185).[2] It is interesting to note, however, that the blurbs on the cover of NOA continue to describe it in such terms as "a learned demolition" and "the definitive statement." Even though I agree with Professor Lefkowitz that it is nothing of the kind, I believe that NOA deserves attention both because it discusses some issues not covered in BAR and because it reveals aspects of Lefkowitz's thinking that are somewhat obscured in the larger book.

Mary Lefkowitz Discovers Afrocentrism

In 1991, when Lefkowitz first encountered Afrocentrism through reading *Black Athena*, she was appalled. She discovered that there were people writing books and teaching that Greek civilization had derived from, or had even been "stolen" from, Egypt. They were making claims that the Ancient Egyptians were black, as were Socrates, Cleopatra, and other important cultural figures in the ancient world. They maintained that Greece had been invaded from Africa in the middle of the second millennium B.C.E., that Greek religion and mystery systems were based on Egyptian prototypes, and that what was called "Greek" philosophy was in fact the secret wisdom of Egyptian lodges of a Masonic type. She also discovered that these arguments were being supported by gross errors of fact, such as the idea that Aristotle had plundered the Egyptian library at Alexandria as a basis for his own massive philosophical and scientific writings. In fact, of course, the library at Alexandria was founded by Macedonian Greeks at least thirty years after Aristotle's death.

If Lefkowitz *knew* that this was all *fantasy* and did not conform to the *facts* as painstakingly assembled by modern classicists and ancient historians, why did she bother to confront it at all? She explains that it was because Afrocentric literature was widely read and that it was being taught not merely in a number of school districts but also in some universities. Furthermore, when she had attempted to question Afrocentric speakers on her own campus (Wellesley) she had been rudely rebuffed. Even worse, when she appealed to colleagues for help they had often failed to support her. The ostensible grounds for this reluctance was the relativist position that, as all history is fiction, there is room for many different stories. Thus, for these colleagues, Afrocentric history was no less true than the classicists' version of the roots of Greek civilization. However, Lefkowitz believes that another and more significant reason her colleagues let her down was their fear of being labeled racist (NOA, pp. 2–6).

She sees the Afrocentrists as living in a sealed-off intellectual ghetto, impervious to outside information, where they pay no attention to the truth of their propositions but are purely concerned with the "feel-good" factor and boosting the sympathy of African Americans. Though she has some respect for these motives, she denies that they have any place in the writing and teaching of history, which should always remain objective. Thus, she has felt obliged to stand up and be counted against what she sees as the Afrocentrist assault on the basic principles of education, respect for the facts, logical argument, and open debate. As mentioned above, her first and primary concern has been with their treatment of Ancient Greece. She writes about this: "Afrocentrists are not content with establishing a special relationship to the ancient Greeks. Instead they seek to remove the ancient Greeks from the important role they have previously [been seen to have?] played in history, and to assign to the African civilization of Egypt the credit for the Greeks' achievements" (NOA, p. 6). Thus, her defense of reason and truth in general is integrally linked to what she sees as the particular truth about the civilization of Ancient Greece.

For this reason, she wrote a series of overlapping articles on Afrocentric "myths" concerning Ancient Greece. NOA is a compilation from these with added material and argument. Its purpose is to expose Afrocentric *absurdities* once and for all, but its final length of almost three hundred pages is required because their demolition has turned out to be rather more complicated than she had first supposed.

Afrocentrism-Nilocentrism

Before going any further, I should like to look at what is commonly meant by "Afrocentrism." Lefkowitz sees the term as having been invented by Professor Molefi Asante of Temple University.[3] Asante views Afrocentrism as a way to escape Eurocentrism and its extensions by looking at the world from an African standpoint. Since then, the label "Afrocentrist" has been attached to a number of intellectual positions, ranging from "All good things come from Africa" (or, as Leonard Jeffries puts it, "Africa creates, Europe imitates") to merely maintaining that Africans and peoples of African descent have made many significant contributions to world civilization and that for the past two centuries, these have been systematically played down by European and North American historians.

Lefkowitz's dislike is focused on those who have argued that African Americans share a common African heritage with Ancient Egypt and further, that through Egypt, Africa played a significant role in the formation of Ancient Greece and hence "Western civilization." Thus, she criticizes Frederick Douglass, Edward Blyden, and W. E. B. Du Bois for maintaining this belief (NOA, pp. 126–130). For much of the nineteenth century, however, the view that Egypt had played a central role in the formation of Ancient Greece was still acceptable in cultivated lay circles. The quotation from John Stuart Mill that heads this chapter is exceptional in its emphasis on the Egyptians' Africanity, but many others were happy to believe that a white or indeterminate Egypt had been the cradle of Western civilization.[4] Lefkowitz's principal objection is to the modern Afrocentrists who have continued to hold to these beliefs after they had become outmoded both among professionals and the white public at large. The modern Afrocentrists are sometimes referred to as "Nilocentric" by other African American intellectuals because of their relative neglect of other African regions and civilizations and their focus on the Nile Valley and Egypt. Her rogues' gallery of Nilocentrists consists of John Henrik Clark, Cheikh Anta Diop, Yosef Ben-Jochannan, Joel Rogers, George G. M. James, and me.[5]

At this point, I should like to examine two related questions: first, my perception of my relationship with Afrocentrists, and second, Professor Lefkowitz's view of the same question. As stated above, I do not believe that all good things come from any one continent. Furthermore, I do not join with those Afrocentrists whose ideal of African purity is a mirror image of European and Euro-American desires for white separation and purity. I also do not accept the many mistakes and exaggerations made by Afrocentrist writers and spokespersons. On the other hand, I admire their courage in sticking to their beliefs in the face of hostility and ridicule, not only from the white academic establishment but also from black intellectuals who have accommodated themselves to that establishment. Far more important than this, however, is the fact that I am intellectually convinced that the Afrocentrists are right on two essentials: first, that it is useful to see Ancient Egypt as an African civilization, and second, that Egypt played a central role in the formation of Ancient Greece.

Lefkowitz's basic view of my relationship to Afrocentrism is summed up in the questionnaire on the extent of Afrocentric teaching in schools, sent out on her behalf: "While Bernal does not consider himself an Afrocentrist and [is] far more sophisticated in his use of ancient evidence . . . his work can be fairly listed with Afrocentric literature." [6]

NOA is ostensibly an attack on Afrocentrists as a group, of which I am considered as, at most, a peripheral member. Nevertheless, George James and I receive more hostile attention than the others.[7] The explanation for this emphasis is that although Lefkowitz deplores their inaccuracies and what she sees as their refusal to enter debates, on substantial matters, the gap between her and the mainstream Afrocentrists is not unbridgeable. This is because their chief aim is to establish the Africanity of Egypt. They accept the ancient view that Greek civilization was largely derived from Egypt but it is not of critical importance to them. Equally, Lefkowitz is less concerned about the nature of the population or culture of Ancient Egypt than she is about the integrity and essential autochthony of Ancient Greece. Unlike the others she criticizes, James and I have focused precisely on the issue of Egypto-Greek relations. We see Egypt (and, in my case, Southwest Asia as well) as having had a massive cultural influence on Greece. It is this view of Greek hybridity and dependence on older, non-European civilizations that Lefkowitz finds disturbing.

That some Afrocentrists should have made so many mistakes is overdetermined. They have the sense of being embattled in a hostile world and of possessing an absolute and general truth, which can make one have less concern about details. More important than these reasons, however, are the extraordinary material difficulties they have faced in acquiring training in the requisite languages, in finding time and space to carry on research, money to buy books or even gain access to libraries, let alone finding publishers who could provide academic checks and competent proofreaders. None of these difficulties has encumbered Lefkowitz, who has been thoroughly educated in Latin and Greek (though not in Ancient Egyptian) and has for many years been tenured at a rich college. That Lefkowitz, who champions "warranted facts" and claims to base her case on them, should make so many factual errors is much more intriguing.

Why Lefkowitz Has Made So Many Mistakes

Some of the mistakes in the first edition have been corrected in the paperback edition of NOA in the light of criticisms made by me and others. For example, Lefkowitz has adjusted her mistaken claim that Pelops "was the founder of Argos" to "Pelops the founder of the dynasty at Argos" (NOA,

p. 13). Even this is misleading, because although descendents of Pelops are supposed to have ruled Argos at the time of the Trojan War, there was also a legendary earlier dynasty of the descendents of Danaus. After the return of the Heraklids, sometimes known as the Dorian invasion, another dynasty claiming its origins in this earlier dynasty and divine and Egyptian or Syrian descent ruled Argos.[8] Thus, the Pelopid dynasty was not "the" dynasty of Argos.

By contrast, she has not corrected her statement that the theory that the Nile flood is the result of snow melted by south winds "was not far from the truth" (NOA, p. 77). In fact, it is false and, as Greek geographers in the Hellenistic Period realized, the flood was the result of rains in Ethiopia.[9]

We are all capable of this kind of sloppiness and such errors are relatively trivial and harmless. Other mistakes are less innocent. For instance, she claims that "recent archaeological discoveries suggest that the Hyksos came to Egypt from Greece rather than vice versa" (NOA, p. 23). By "recent archaeological discoveries" she can only be referring to murals of Minoan style originally thought to be of the Hyksos period, from the Hyksos capital at Tel ed Daba'a in the Nile Delta and floors from Tel Kabri in Israel. It now seems that they come from the early Eighteenth Dynasty. Even when they were thought to be painted in a Hyksos building, no scholar made the extraordinary suggestion that the Hyksos themselves had arrived in Egypt from Greece.[10] Lefkowitz's claim reveals not merely a profound ignorance of the Mediterranean in the Bronze Age but also the strength of her desire to give Greeks (or at least peoples of the Aegean) a greater dynamism than Southwest Asians and Egyptians.

Lefkowitz made an equally substantial and significant error when she wrote: "Since the founding of this country [the United States], ancient Greece has been intimately connected with the ideals of democracy" (NOA, p. 6). In fact, the source she cited states something very different: "In 1787 and 1788 the Anti-Federalists did not have a classical leg to stand on. There was no tradition of representative democracy to which they could appeal, and direct democracies like Athens bore the stigma of instability, violence, corruption and injustice . . . [such] that even many friends of democracy in America avoided using the word. Like the advocates of mixed government, they used the word 'republic.'"[11] When confronted by me with this distortion of the text, Lefkowitz responded in the paperback edition: "But I am talking about *ideals*, not actual Athenian democracy (which the founding fathers rejected). The founding fathers had read Plato and Aristotle, as well as Plutarch on Solon and Lycurgus. The purpose of this brief discussion was to remind readers why ancient Greek history has been the subject of proportionately more attention than the history of other ancient civilizations" (NOA, p. 241). In fact, of course, she had claimed a good deal more. Problems remain, even in the reduced and abstracted version of her claims. Plato and Aristotle were generally hostile to Athenian democracy and Lykurgos was the founder of the Spartan constitution, the polar opposite of the Athenian one established by Solon.

AFROCENTRISTS AS THE ENEMIES OF FREEDOM?

Lefkowitz's sloppiness here might seem inconsequential, but in fact, it serves a very important purpose in her general argument. The link she sees between reason and truth on the one hand and her view of the origins of Ancient Greece on the other has been mentioned above. Her mistake about the attitudes of the Founding Fathers seems to have come from the same intuition that not merely is it impossible to have freedom or democracy without a respectful awareness of Ancient Greece, but also that there has been a continuous flame of such reverence. This would explain the inclusion of the Founding Fathers, which would otherwise have been unnecessary.

It was in this context that I wrote in my first criticism of NOA, "She implies—the Afrocentrists are enemies of freedom." In the paperback edition she vehemently denies that this was what she had intended (NOA, p. 242). The bases of what I called her "implication" were, first, the need to explain why she should have misrepresented the text on the Founding Fathers she had in front of her, and second, because the theme that the Afrocentrists are the enemies of democracy is found in many of her articles. In one of these her conclusion begins: "Afrocentrist historians appear to have discarded this important rationalist tradition. Instead they appeal to emotions and deny opportunity for debate." [12]

In an interview in the Greek journal *To Vima* in which Lefkowitz described the compilation of BAR, she was still more apocalyptic and unselfconscious:

> (Interviewer): Were there many students who rejected your views?
> M.L.: Enough. But if there are 50 or 500 today, tomorrow there will be 50,000 and up to millions, brainwashed . . . and something more basic concerning teaching, if we do not push our children to reflect, to love dialogue, to discover, but we prevent them from opening their ears to opposing ideas—

as the Afrocentrists do—what sort of democratic citizens shall we send out into society? [13]

To return to the claim that Athenian democracy formed the basis of modern democracy, such a claim is untenable even in the Western tradition. The English "Revolution" of the seventeenth century relied on the anti-royalist aspects of the Hebrew Bible and myths of Saxon freedom, whereas the American and French Revolutions of the eighteenth century took Republican Rome as their ancient model. Nevertheless, there is no doubt that since the 1820s, the images of Ancient Greece, and Athens in particular, have usually served a positive function in Europe and North America. This has not been universally true; antebellum Southern writers used Ancient Greece and Athens to demonstrate what they saw as the political and cultural benefits of slavery.[14] And today, conservatives are still using images of Ancient Greece for their own political agendas.

In my reviews of the first edition of NOA I mentioned a number of slips contained in it, most of which I omit here.[15] However, in addition to those mentioned above, I should like to take up again one more. This is Lefkowitz's defiance of nineteenth- and twentieth-century Classical scholarship when she wrote: "Every English translation (of Herodotus II.43.2) that I know of says that Heracles was descended distantly 'from Egypt.' But the translation is incorrect. Herodotos is talking about Aegyptus the man rather than *Aigyptos* the country" (NOA, p. 25).

In my review of the first edition of NOA I argued that, in this case, one should trust conventional scholarship rather than her contention that all the earlier scholars had mistranslated the preposition *apo*. According to Lefkowitz, in this context it could only mean "descent from." She continued: "If he [Herodotus] had meant Egypt the country he would have written *ek*" (NOA, p. 181). I pointed out that there was no point in making any distinction, because Danaos' twin brother and rival, the earliest legendary Aegyptus, was supposed to have come directly from Egypt. I also argued that Lefkowitz had exaggerated the difference between *apo* and *ek* and that was the reason the earlier scholars had not been concerned by Herodotus' use of *apo* here. Thus, there are scores if not hundreds of instances of Herodotus' having used *apo* in its original sense of "motion from or out of." The phrase *ap' Aigyptou* itself appears twice, a few sections after the contested use, in the lines "Melampos brought into Greece things that he had learned *in Egypt*" and "The names of nearly all the gods came to Greece *from Egypt*." [16]

In a supplementary note in the paperback, Professor Lefkowitz has refined her argument to say that *apo* when associated with the verb *genesthai* "'to originate from' does mean 'descend from' in *nearly all cases*" (my italics). I certainly accept that this is usually so. However, that does not remove the problem of why all previous English translations have rendered it "from Egypt." In addition to the reasons for this that I have given above, one should consider the context in which the claim is made. In the Penguin edition, Aubrey de Sélincourt translates the passage as follows: "Nevertheless, it was not the Egyptians who took the name of Heracles from the Greeks. The opposite is true: it was the Greeks who took it from the Egyptians—those Greeks who gave the name to the son of Amphitryon. There is plenty of evidence to prove the truth of this, in particular the fact that both the parents of Heracles—Amphitryon and Alcmene—were *of Egyptian origin*. Again the Egyptians say . . ." (my italics).[17] Given the repeated references to Egyptians in this passage, it is, to say the least, unreasonable to suggest that Herodotus suddenly switched the sense away from Aigyptos the country to the hero Aigyptos and then back to Egypt.

Lefkowitz's far-fetched claim here can easily be explained in terms of her eagerness to detach Greece from Egypt. It does not cast doubt on her knowledge of Greek and Latin. She undoubtedly knows these languages, but she does not know much about linguistics and she has virtually no understanding of language contact, which is the relevant field when looking at the relations between Ancient Egyptian and Greek. For instance, speaking of European scholars, she writes: "Once they were able to read real Egyptian . . . it became clear to them that the relation of Egyptian to Greek culture was less close than they had imagined. Egyptian belonged to the Afro-Asiatic family, while Greek was an Indo-European language, akin to Sanskrit and European languages like Latin" (NOA, pp. 57–58). The family relationships are correct, but, to my knowledge, no Afrocentrist has ever argued that there was a genetic relationship between Egyptian and Greek. What they and I maintain is that Ancient Egyptian culture had a massive impact on that of Greece and that this is reflected in a substantial number of Egyptian loan words in Greek.[18] Lefkowitz does not seem to realize that lexical loans primarily reflect contemporary contacts, not past genetic relationships. For example, Arabic is even more distant genetically from the Bantu languages than Egyptian and Semitic are from Greek, yet much of the vocabulary of Swahili, including such well-known words as *safari* and *uhuru* ("freedom") comes from Arabic.[19]

At another point she writes: "Vague similarities do not prove any connection between words. The sound qualities of vowels and consonants alike change when words are assimilated from one language to another, and even loanwords are transformed: for example, the Latinized Greek word *episcopus* becomes *bishop* in the mouths of Saxon converts in the 9th century A.D." (NOA, pp. 23–24).[20] The second long sentence actually undermines her basic argument. If words as apparently dissimilar as *episcopus* and *bishop* can be related, it shows that given semantic parallels, "vague [phonetic] similarities" may be taken into account. Furthermore, the net must be cast still more widely when, as is the case with Egypt, the Levant, and Greece, contact among the three cultures has been carried on for many thousands of years and sound shifts in all of them have brought about many different phonetic correspondences.[21]

Professor Lefkowitz goes on to say: "Linguists have long since noted the relatively few words of Egyptian origin that have made their way into Greek" (NOA, p. 24). She does not mention that 60 percent of the Greek vocabulary cannot be explained in terms of other Indo-European languages.[22] Nor does she consider the arguments I have made at length in *Black Athena* I: first, that lexicographers of Greek did not know Ancient Egyptian, and second, that since the 1820s, when hieroglyphics were first deciphered, there have been ideological reasons why they should not have not wanted to find Egyptian etymologies for significant or fundamental Greek words.[23] It should also be pointed out that it is precisely this historiographical or ideological aspect of my work that has been most widely accepted.[24] Nevertheless, Lefkowitz argues strongly against any idea of substantial contact between Egypt and Greece before the African country's conquest by Alexander the Great, and her faith in this general truth sustains her in all the twists and turns of her argument.

POLITICAL BIASES OR POLITICAL AGENDAS

Before turning to her major attacks on Afrocentrist claims, it is necessary to consider two important issues of approach and method. The first of these is raised by Lefkowitz when she admits that she may have biases but that this is very different from "consciously setting out to achieve a particular political goal" (NOA, p. 161). Furthermore, she claims that it was not her intention to pursue right-wing aims and that it is not her fault that the right wing should praise her book (NOA, pp. 182–183).

Professor Lefkowitz does not say what her biases are, but two of the most important come out loud and clear throughout her latest books. They are that Europe owes little or nothing to Africa, or Greece to Egypt, and that untrained outsiders should not question the conclusions of trained and "competent" professionals. Ten years ago, she would have been able to avoid the charge of "consciously setting out to achieve a political goal" because she and those who think like her then held complete academic power in Classics and surrounding disciplines. This had been achieved during the nineteenth century by Northern European scholars, who did have the explicit ideological and political aims of denying European or Aryan indebtedness to Africans and "Semites." [25] Since 1991, however, Lefkowitz has been "consciously setting out to achieve a particular political goal," that is, the discrediting of those who propose considerable Greek cultural indebtedness to Egypt and Phoenicia. The basis for this goal is because she sees our work as a threat not merely to Classics but to American education and society as a whole.

In the second edition of *NOA* Lefkowitz counters her critics by asking of them "What are *their* hidden agendas?" (p. 186). Speaking for myself, even though I have joined far fewer left-wing or liberal organizations than she has joined conservative ones, I deny that my political agenda is hidden.[26] On the first page of the preface to volume 1 of *Black Athena* I wrote of my active opposition to the war in Indo-China, thus situating myself on the left of the political spectrum. I concluded the introduction with the statement: "The political purpose of *Black Athena* is, of course to lessen European arrogance" (BA I: 73).

I felt it important to indicate my political attitudes to my readers. What I object to in Lefkowitz's position on this issue is not her association with the right wing but her refusal to acknowledge that it could have any impact on her writings. I also deny her claim that, unlike her opponents, she and those who think like her are alone in possessing scholarly neutrality and objectivity.[27]

PROOF AND COMPETITIVE PLAUSIBILITY

For Lefkowitz, there is a natural and intimate connection between objectivity and respect for "facts." Throughout *NOA* she insists on a sharp distinction between what she calls "warranted facts" and "acceptable claims" (p. 51). This antinomy appears to be similar to what I have called "proof" and "competitive plausibility." I agree that there are certainties, as, for instance, that there was the Holocaust in which over six million Jews and others were murdered by Nazis. However, for Lefkowitz (NOA, p. 161) to put this massively documented event, which took place in her and my life time, on the same plane as the reconstruction of the murky origins of Greek civilization over thirty-five hundred years ago is absurd. When treating this distant period we are not dealing with proof or "warranted facts" but with "competitive plausibility." Furthermore, Lefkowitz herself appeals to plausibility and acceptability from her audience as often, if not more often, than the Afrocentrists do from their constituency.

As she follows the modern Classical establishment in its denial of the many Greek and Roman writers who believed in the massive Greek cultural debt to Egypt, she is forced to overcome this ancient testimony by frequently using such words and phrases as "apparently," "evidently," "do not seem," "what if . . . ?" and "why not . . . ?" An extreme example of this is her treatment of an ancient tradition that Plato had based his *Republic* on an idealized image of Egypt.[28] She writes: "Bernal would take the story . . . at face value. But the *true* origin was *probably* a joke in *some* comedy, which was later taken seriously" (NOA, p. 82; my italics). Is this a "warranted fact" or an "acceptable claim"? We are both operating on the plane of competitive plausibility.

Stolen Legacy

I shall now turn to the nub of Lefkowitz's attack and what Glenn Bowersock, the eminent classicist at the Princeton Institute, has described as her "impassioned polemic . . . through which rage boils" against the Afrocentric charge that Greeks *stole* Egyptian religion, philosophy, and science.[29] In the epilogue to the revised edition in a subsection entitled "*Not Out of Africa* and Its Critics," she writes: "It is not surprising that so far none of my reviewers or critics has been able to offer a persuasive challenge to the central thesis of this book: that the Greeks did not steal or even borrow their philosophy from Egypt, that Egyptian influence on Greek philosophy was not extensive and the idea that scholars have ignored the Greeks' Egyptian origins has its foundation in Masonic myth rather than in historical fact" (NOA, p. 179).[30] The word "persuasive" allows Lefkowitz the freedom of subjectivity. By any other criterion one could say that "the central thesis" of her book has been seriously challenged. The challenges set out in the following sections of this chapter were all available to her, either in my reviews in the *Journal of Blacks in Higher Education* or the *Bryn Mawr Classical Review* or from our Internet debate. In these her denials of Greek "stealing" or cultural borrowing were contested in some detail.

The first issue to be confronted in this debate is that of the *Hermetic Corpus*. These mystical and philosophical dialogues, many of them concerned with spiritual initiation and centered on the mysterious figure of the sage or divine Hermes Trismegistos, were circulating in Egypt at least from the first century B.C.E. Though written in Greek and containing many features and ideas that resemble those in Platonic and Neoplatonic writings, the characters described are Egyptian. On this issue, Lefkowitz follows the standard interpretation of the early twentieth century, which is that, in the early seventeenth century C.E., the Hermetic texts had been exposed as forgeries and that they are essentially Greek writings in which the authors portray themselves as Egyptians to enhance their reputation and as a literary conceit. She pays no attention to the reversal of scholarly opinion since the publication in the 1970s of the library of Coptic Gnostic texts at Nag Hammadi in Upper Egypt, originally found in 1945. The result of the evident parallels between these and the *Hermetic Corpus* has been to see that, as the modern scholar Garth Fowden puts it, "the intellectual context and origins of Hermeticism, viewed in ever closer relationship to traditional Egyptian thought and to gnosticism, are the subject of a fast-increasing number of scholarly studies." [31]

According to the Ancients, a major Egyptian equivalent of Hermes was the Egyptian god of wisdom, Thoth. The name Hermes Trismegistos has a clear Egyptian prototype in the attested title "Thoth Thrice Great." [32] Nevertheless, Lefkowitz is adamant: "There is no record of any Egyptian-language original from which they [the Hermetic texts] were derived" (NOA, p. 101). Apart from the close parallels in Coptic texts, there are, in fact, a number of Demotic (that is, Late Egyptian) papyri containing substantial sections of a dialogue of thoroughly Hermetic type between Thoth and a disciple. [33] Furthermore, Lefkowitz does not engage the argument put forward by the Egyptologist Sir William Flinders Petrie that some texts in the *Hermetic Corpus* date back to the Persian Period in the sixth century B.C.E. [34] Thus, there is a real possibility that at least some of the similarities between the Hermetic texts and Platonic and Neoplatonic philosophy could be the result of Plato and his followers' having drawn on Egyptian sources. [35]

This brings us back to the central issue of the "stolen legacy." Lefkowitz lays great stress on George James and other Afrocentrist writers' having taken their ideas from the Masonic tradition, which in turn was based on eighteenth-century novels, notably *Sethos* by the Abbé Terrasson.[36] This argument neatly supports her distinction between the "facts" taught by orthodox classicists and the "fiction" propounded by the Afrocentrists. There is no doubt that, as I made clear in *Black Athena*, many of the details and particulars of Masonic ranks and initiations put forward in *Stolen Legacy* and other Afrocentrist writings do derive from this fictional origin. Nevertheless, as Lefkowitz herself agrees, the novels had a scholarly apparatus and were based on Ancient Greek and Latin sources, which stressed the Egyptian origin of the Greek mysteries and wisdom. However, she feels able to dismiss Herodotus as idiosyncratic, and Diodorus, Strabo, and the other authors of the Hellenistic and Roman periods as "late," which is somewhat startling coming from someone writing at the end of the twentieth century C.E. She writes: "There never was such a thing as an Egyptian Mystery System. The notion of mysteries, or rituals of initiation is fundamentally Greek, and such information as we have about Egyptian mysteries dates from a period when Egypt had been occupied and influenced by both Greeks and Romans" (NOA, p. 157).

Now, let us turn to these mysteries.

MYSTERIES

Mysteries are by their nature mysterious and are seldom if ever described directly. It is also true that the only two detailed descriptions of Egyptian initiations available to contemporary scholars come from the Roman period. The first is contained in a description in the Latin novel *The Golden Ass*, written by the North African author Apuleius. It is of the initiation of his hero Lucius to the goddess Isis that took place in Greece. In one of her supplementary notes to the paperback edition Lefkowitz agrees that there were "Egyptian elements in Apuleius's ritual." However, she continues: "But there is a characteristic difference in timing: Lucius is initiated while alive; the Egyptian reciter of the scroll will be allowed to cross the threshold after his death" (NOA, p. 248).

She refers here to an article by the German Egyptologist Jan Assman entitled "Death and Initiation in the Funerary Religion of Ancient Egypt." Here, once again, Lefkowitz has cited a source that states something very different from what she claims. After a survey of Pharaonic texts and Apu-

leius' description of Lucius' initiation as an initiate of Isis, Assman begins
the conclusion of this essay:

> No one doubts that the initiation rites of the Isis Mysteries as Apuleius de-
> scribes them, are deeply rooted in the elaborated rituals and conceptions of
> Egyptian funerary religion. The same holds true for other initiation rituals.
> Seen from this aspect, a relationship between death and initiation is not dis-
> puted. A number of clues listed in this survey, however, have given us reason
> to look in the opposite direction. Let us attempt to formulate our results into
> a hypothesis: the funerary rites take the form of an "initiation into the mys-
> teries of the underworld" . . . because they reflect the corresponding rites and
> conceptions of cultic rituals in "this" world, of which, for obvious reasons,
> we know next to nothing.[37]

I would not go as far as Assman in claiming that funerary rites were based
on initiations of the living. However, it is clear that Ancient Egyptian initiations and funerary directions were very closely related and that therefore
the sharp distinction Lefkowitz wants to make between the living initiate
and the dead soul is meaningless.[38]

The other detailed ancient report of a mysterious initiation comes in a
papyrus in the cursive Egyptian script of Hieratic describing the initiations
of a priest named Horsiesis, which took place in the ancient cult centers
of Abydos, Busiris and Karnak.[39] There are three striking features of the
rituals described by Apuleius and Horsiesis. The first is that they appear
to be based entirely on Egyptian tradition. The second is that many of the
passages resemble those found in the *Book of the Dead* or, to use its original
title, *The Book of Coming Forth by Day.* The third is that they resemble descriptions of many of the rituals practiced in the most famous Greek mysteries,
those at Eleusis, northwest of Athens.

The very skeptical scholar Gwyn Griffiths has attempted to reconcile the
three parallels. He maintains that the essential theme of spiritual regenera-
tion in the present life was specifically Greek and Eleusinian. Nevertheless,
he adds: "Yet this may have developed in the Hellenistic era in Egypt as
a development and projection of a very ancient funerary tradition."[40] His
position seems to be that the Greeks and Late Egyptians both independently invented spiritual initiations for the living resembling the journeys
of the souls of the dead. The situation was then confused by a widespread
"Egyptomaniac" fantasy that the Greek mysteries had been developed from
Egyptian ones, which were fleshed out by the introduction of some Egyp-

tian ritual. This seems much more cumbersome than simply accepting the view of the Ancients, that the Greek mysterious initiations were derived from Egypt.

At least at a superficial level, the mystery and initiations in the cult of Demeter at Eleusis resembled those of Osiris at Abydos and other holy centers in Egypt. Furthermore, Egyptian scarabs and a symbol of Isis—Demeter was her Greek counterpart—were found in a tomb at Eleusis of the ninth or eighth century B.C.E.[41] It is for these reasons that although the majority of classicists deny it, a number of the most distinguished specialists of the twentieth century C.E. have followed the predominant ancient tradition that the cult of Demeter was imported to Eleusis from Egypt before the Trojan War or during what we now call the Late Bronze Age. Most notable of these was the French classicist Paul Foucart, who dominated Eleusinian studies in the early part of the twentieth century and whose detailed work is still respected, even by the most conventional.[42] A later French ancient historian, Charles Picard, is generally supposed to have refuted Foucart. However, even Picard admitted that "well before" the eighth century, the Eleusinian mysteries had received substantial influence from Egypt.[43] In 1971, the British scholar A. A. Barb also saw fundamental connections.[44] The firm isolationist Jean Hani admitted when referring to Isis and Demeter: "It seems that there has always been a type of 'understanding' between Greece and Egypt since prehistory."[45]

Beyond the evidence from Apuleius and Horsiesis, there is the mysterious underground "Cenotaph of Seti the 1st" (c. 1309–1291 B.C.E.) or *Oseirion*. This structure contains complex passages inscribed with broken hieroglyphs and sections of the *Book of the Dead*, a strange underground island and a hall decorated with the text of a mysterious religious play.[46] It is very plausible to suggest that this was used for initiations.

In addition to this, there are references going back to the seventeenth century B.C.E. to men who, though alive, were called m3ꜥ ḥrw or "true of voice," the title generally applied to the immortal dead.[47] There is even one from a man who claimed to have taken part in a ritual described in *The Book of Coming Forth by Day*.[48] Thus, a substantial body of evidence backs Assman's contention that funerary instructions closely resembled initiations of the living and specifically that the *Book of the Dead* was sometimes used for such initiations. It also supports the Ancient view that the Greek mysteries and the initiations associated with them derived from Egypt. I admit that these arguments are based not on certainty but on competitive plausibility. Lefkowitz's contention is that there are no "warranted facts" backing a derivation of the Eleusinian mysteries from Egypt. I claim against her that there is a mass of circumstantial evidence to suggest precisely this. Even more important, however, I do not accept a "presumption of isolation." If anything, the onus of proof should be on those who deny both the significance of these striking similarities between the Egyptian and Greek mysteries and the widespread Ancient testimony that the latter had come from Egypt, rather than on those who are inclined to support these traditions.

ANCIENT EGYPTIAN UNIVERSITIES?

Lefkowitz raises another interesting question when she is scornful of the claims made by Terrasson and the Afrocentrists that there were universities in Ancient Egypt (NOA, pp. 112–113). The issue of whether there were "colleges" or "universities" at Memphis and other Egyptian cities depends on definition. Clearly, they were not the same as the Medieval or modern universities, the first of which, Al Azhar, was founded in Cairo only in the tenth century C.E. Nevertheless, it is known that at least since the Old Kingdom, c. 3000 B.C.E., there was an elaborate bureaucracy of specialized scribes, doctors, and magicians. It is also known that from the Middle Kingdom, c. 2000 B.C.E., there was an institution called pr ʿnḫ "House of Life." Alan Gardiner described it merely as a "scriptorium," a place of restricted entry where some papyri were kept.[49] The consensus today is that it was "a kind of university." For instance, the Egyptologist P. Derchain maintained that by the first period of Persian rule, 525–404 B.C.E., these institutions contained papyri on subjects ranging across medicine, astronomy, mathematics, myths, embalming, geography, and more: "In a word one ought to find there the complete totality of all the philosophical and scientific knowledge of the Egyptians."[50] The subject is not altogether clear, but equally clearly, Lefkowitz is wrong to claim that the Ancient, eighteenth-century, and Afrocentrists' descriptions of "Egyptian colleges" are based *solely* on fiction.

ANCIENT EGYPTIAN SCIENCE AND PHILOSOPHY?

Did the Ancient Egyptians possess a "science"? And if they did, did it have a significant impact on the Greeks? For some years now, I have argued in favor of both claims. When I presented my arguments to the departments of the History and Philosophy of Science at both Harvard and Cambridge, some of the audience agreed, others did not, but the claims were clearly accepted as legitimate topics of scholarly discussion. The debate on science between me and Robert Palter has been published earlier.[51] It is not for me to say which argument has prevailed, but Victor Katz, the historian of Greek mathematics, has written: "As far as mathematics goes, although Palter argues with Bernal on many specific points and seems to deny both of Bernal's claims, he does not give a clear and definitive response to them." [52] Here again, Lefkowitz is wrong to dismiss Afrocentric claims as absurd.

This is not to say that Hellenistic science, geographically based in Greek-dominated Egypt after 300 B.C.E., did not add to what had been received from Pharaonic Egypt. The same is true of philosophy. The term "philosophy" is extraordinarily slippery. It is certain that in the sense of "wonder, or speculation on truth and reality," it was present in Ancient Egypt. However, one can go further and argue plausibly that such points as Plato's theory of ideas and moral dialectic were anticipated in Egypt by over a thousand years.[53] The Egyptologist John Ray recently has written:

> The range and quality of Egyptian technical achievements presupposes a degree of theoretical knowledge, some of which has survived and some of which can be reconstructed from Egyptian texts themselves or from commentaries in the classical authors, but modern scholars are increasingly inclined to agree with the high value which Greek commentators place placed on Egyptian thinking. . . . Iamblichus . . . was convinced that it [Egyptian religion] foreshadowed the Platonic Theory of Forms. Most Egyptologists have been dismissive of these ideas although they have begun to gain credibility over time.[54]

Assmann, Bilolo, Karenga, and Löwstedt have all argued that on some important issues Greek thinkers did not reach the levels achieved in Egypt and that we still have much to learn from Egyptian philosophy.[55] Other points on this topic are raised in Professor Flory's chapter in the forthcoming companion volume to this book, Debating Black Athena. Despite some disclaimers from Greeks who disliked the idea for chauvinist reasons, it was conventional wisdom among Greeks and Romans that philosophy had derived from "barbarians" in general and Egyptians in particular.[56]

Furthermore, an Afrocentric perspective can sometimes add to our understanding of some details of Greek philosophy. For instance, Lefkowitz (NOA, p. 149) describes as "purely fanciful" the proposal by James in his Stolen Legacy that Democritus's use of the word "atom" derived principally not from *a-tom* ("indivisibility") but from the Egyptian god Atum.[57] The name of this divinity appears to have meant both "fullness" or "being" and "nonbeing." The Egyptologist Erik Hornung, after describing the difficulties of translating such a concept, concludes: "Atum is the god who 'in the beginning was everything,' complete in the sense of being an undifferentiated unity and at the same time nonexistent because existence is impossible before his work of creation."[58]

The philosopher Anthony Preus has argued: "If we put that statement beside the notoriously difficult fragment DK 156 — '$\mu\grave{\eta}$ $\mu\hat{\alpha}\lambda\lambda o\nu$ $\tau\grave{o}$ $\delta\grave{\epsilon}\nu$ $\mathring{\mathring{\eta}}$ $\tau\grave{o}$ $\mu\eta\delta\grave{\epsilon}\nu$ $\epsilon\hat{\iota}\nu\alpha\iota$' [Being should be no better than not-Being] — we might come to the conclusion that Democritus is aware of the ambiguity of the Egyptian 'Atom' and has imported it into Greek."[59]

Lefkowitz tries to avoid this in a note in the second edition. First, she argues that "we cannot be sure that the Greeks actually knew about Atum" (NOA, p. 253). However, the cult of Atum, though often fused with that of Re, retained its independence in the Late and Ptolemaic Periods. It was particularly important in Sais and Heliopolis, two of the Egyptian cities most frequently visited by Greeks.[60] There was also a strong and widespread Ancient tradition that Demokritos spent several years in Egypt, Babylonia, and further east.[61] Thus, the chances that the Greek mathematician knew of the Egyptian god and his double characteristic are very high.

Lefkowitz then admits that the Egyptian concept of nonexistence in primeval chaos and existence and nonexistence intermixed in the present world is "complex," although naturally she does not use the word "philosophical." Paradoxically, she contrasts this with what she describes as the Greek "Democritus's simple concept of nothingness" (NOA, p. 253). No one has previously suggested that Demokritos was simple-minded; the trouble his statement on nothingness has caused later commentators strongly indicates the difficulty and subtlety of his thinking here.

On a more general level, the classicist Geoffrey Kirk and others have seen the Pre-Socratics as a group as having been significantly influenced by Egyptians and Mesopotamians.[62] There is no doubt that Plato was deeply impressed by Egypt, and for more than two thousand years his followers saw Plato's thought as a glorious link in a chain leading back to Egypt.[63]

Lefkowitz's conviction that there is a categorical distinction between a rational Greece and an irrational Egypt holds only if one believes that reason began only with Aristotle's formal syllogistic logic and Euclid's axiomatic geometry, neither of which existed—as far as we know—in Ancient Egypt. However, this claim should be tempered by the works of some scholars who have thought profoundly about the issue. The first of these is the classicist E. R. Dodds, whose *Greeks and the Irrational* showed the centrality of madness and shamanism to Greek life and thought.[64] The second is the classicist and historian of science Heinrich von Staden, who has written recently on the exaggeration and distortion brought about by modern scholars' emphasis on the few "rational" Greek texts and neglect of the many more "irrational" ones.[65]

In Egypt too, there were areas of "rationality" — sophisticated and rigorous mathematics, superb geometry, wonderfully observed medical symptoms, precise surgery, and more — amidst what we now consider to be magic and superstition. Thus, Lefkowitz's categorical distinction between these two cultures on this criterion is much less hard and fast than she supposes.

STOLEN LEGACY AGAIN: THEFT OR PLAGIARISM

Now, once again, I turn to Lefkowitz's ultimate bugbear, the Afrocentrists' claims of a "stolen legacy." As stated above, there is no doubt that some Afrocentrists have been wrong on many particulars. Furthermore, there is little chance that Greeks could have stolen ideas that Egyptians of the Pharaonic Period do not appear to have possessed, such as Aristotelian syllogistic logic and Euclidian geometry. Nevertheless, on the issue of "stealing" too the Afrocentrists are tapping into a tradition of great antiquity and, at least in the areas of religion and science, of some validity.

In the first century C.E., the Neo-Pythagorean sage Apollonios of Tyana visited India. According to his biographer, Philostratos, the Indians were surprised to find Apollonios virtuous because Egyptians had told them that they, the Egyptians, had established "all the sacrifices and rites on initiation that are in vogue among the Greeks," who were ruffians.[66] The idea that Greeks were taking aspects of Egyptian religion also comes in a passage in the *Hermetic Corpus*.[67] Philo of Byblos, writing around 100 C.E., claimed that Greeks had appropriated Phoenician and Egyptian ancient myths and had then imposed their versions or fictions on other peoples.[68] In the second century C.E., the Assyrian Christian Tatian argued that the Greeks had taken their culture from "barbarians," including Phoenician letters and Egyptian geometry and historical writing.[69] The church father Clement of Alexandria went all the way and called the Greeks "thieves." [70]

Despite the obvious biases of Christian and other non-Greek writers and the openness with which Herodotus, Plato, Aristotle, and other Greeks accepted the central importance of the Egyptian contribution to their culture, such arguments are not altogether implausible. We know, for instance, that "Pythagorean" triangles were used in the Near East more than a thousand years before Pythagoras.[71] The volumes of pyramids were measured almost equally early, long before the time of Eudoxos, who, according to Archimedes, was the first person to do so.[72] Furthermore, Archimedes' balanced scales and screw were in use in Egypt centuries before the Greek scientist was born.[73]

In everyday conversation one often hears of ideas being "stolen." In this sense then, the Afrocentrists are right to refer to a "stolen legacy." In more careful speech, however, theft is usually restricted to tangibles, so that after the event, x possesses it and y no longer has it. With intangibles this is generally not the case, because y has not lost it. In this historical instance, however, the military, political, and cultural power of Greeks after Alexander's conquests did, in fact, allow Greeks to deprive Egyptians of many of their traditions, because, as Philo of Byblos put it, they had "imposed their versions or fictions on other peoples." [74]

Even so, strictly speaking, it is inaccurate to refer to the relationship between Ancient Egypt and Ancient Greece as one of cultural theft. Probably the best description of the relationship is as "appropriation." The Ancient Greeks as a whole were only partially guilty of the more severe charge of plagiarism, as they often cited their Egyptian and Oriental antecedents. It was the classicists of the nineteenth and twentieth centuries who completed the denial of the earlier sources, giving all the credit to the European Greeks. Nevertheless, I prefer the fashionable word "appropriation" because it implies further developments by the new owners.

Afrocentrism as a Preservation of the Ancient Model

At this point, I should like to set the positions of both parties in a wider historical context. Though there have been a number of deformations, the Afrocentrists have maintained a particular branch of the Ancient model taken up by their predecessors, the Vindicationalists, which was prominent at the turn of the nineteenth century. This was partly based on Masonic traditions and novels, but also on the works of scholars such as Charles François Dupuis, Constantine de Volney, and A. H. L. Heeren. These three maintained that the Ancient Egyptians were black or nearly so, and that hence Europeans had derived their civilizations from Africans.[75] In the first half of the nineteenth century, this argument was used by abolitionists in their attacks on race-based slavery. See, for instance, the passage from an article by John Stuart Mill quoted at the beginning of this chapter.[76] This late-eighteenth-century shift of emphasis in the Ancient model, however, was not a drastic *coupure* of the order of the destruction of the Ancient model in the 1820s and 1830s and the establishment of the Aryan model in the 1840s and 1850s.

There is no reason why the fact that Greek is a fundamentally Indo-European language should not be combined with the Ancient model's multiple reports of Egyptian and Semitic influences. However, such cultural and linguistic mixture was intolerable to the Romantic racists who established the Aryan model and who, like Mary Lefkowitz today, insisted that there had been no significant Egyptian influence on Greece.

"FEEL GOOD" EDUCATION: AFRICAN AND EUROPEAN

The European abandonment of the Ancient model and the emergence of the Aryan model in the face of the new image of a black Egypt raises an amusing irony. Lefkowitz reiterates Arthur J. Schlesinger's charge that Afrocentric history is purely an attempt to promote group self-esteem. "Real" history, he argues, should consist of "dispassionate analysis, judgment and perspective." [77] In fact, however, this is far from the way history is taught in schools anywhere in the world. In virtually every case, the nation or locality is always emphasized and placed above others. For instance, when I was sent to France at the age of seventeen, my French companion and I knew completely different sets of battles between the English and French. We had been told of our country's victories, not of the defeats. Thus, for African American children to be taught about African and diasporic triumphs is not unusual, and is particularly useful given the constant psychological battering they receive in a racist society.

On the other hand, I agree with Schlesinger and Lefkowitz that historical researchers should try to transcend their own environments and achieve objectivity as far as it is possible to do so. However, the Aryan model, with its denial of Ancient tradition and its insistence on a purely white, purely European Greece, is a supreme example of "feel-good" scholarship and education for whites, who have far less need of it than blacks.

Lefkowitz ends her last chapter with an appeal to George Orwell's description in his novel 1984 of the systematic destruction of the world's old culture, which was due to be completed by 2050, by which time the old culture would be obliterated. She continues: "What Orwell predicted for 2050 actually happened a century earlier, with the publication of *Stolen Legacy* in 1954. For in that book George G. M. James rewrote Ancient History so drastically that it became both different from and contradictory to what it had previously been" (NOA, p. 154). She is mistaken by more than a century. For all his errors, James was maintaining the Ancient historical tradition. It was the founders of the Aryan model, to which Lefkowitz adheres, who made the categorical break with all the previous history of the formation of Ancient Greece.

Conclusion

A new scientific truth does not triumph by convincing its opponents and making them see the light but rather because its opponents eventually die and a new generation grows up that is familiar with it. —MAX PLANCK, *Scientific Autobiography and Other Papers*, 1949[1]

In the later chapters of this book that have focused on recent transcultural interest in classical studies, I may have given the impression that the Broad Aryan model has triumphed completely. It is true that the eminent Hellenist Oswyn Murray in his almost canonical *Early Greece* has accepted the work of Martin West and Walter Burkert. However, it is still the case that, as West wrote about an earlier stage, "they [the Hellenists] have shown themselves increasingly tolerant of oriental comparisons, if not particularly active in investigating the oriental literatures for themselves."[2]

A superficial survey I made of the five hundred–odd books on Greece reviewed over the past ten years in the widely read electronic *Bryn Mawr Classical Review* indicated that slightly more than half of the books on Greece were concerned with the traditional twin staples of Homer and the Classical Period, 500–300 B.C.E. The surprise is that the proportion should be so low, which makes it worth considering some of the topics of the remainder. One increasingly common theme is historiography of the discipline of Classics. These works tend to be less hagiographic than earlier histories and the new authors often level severe criticisms at individual practitioners. None of these books, however, is fundamentally critical of the discipline as a whole.

In the 1960s and 1970s a good number of works were published on Marxist historical interpretations and studies of class conflict in the Greco-Roman world. Times have changed and such works no longer appear. In the 1990s, reflecting the intellectual mood of the day, feminism and the varieties of sexual orientation have often become the new lenses through which to view ancient history.

There have been fewer such works, however, than relatively conventional studies of the Hellenistic Period after the conquests of Alexander the Great. Some of these new works are on Hellenistic treatments of earlier authors or on developments in the Greek-speaking Hellenistic world. But others have broader horizons and are concerned with interactions between Greeks and "Barbarians." As these describe relations between the two groupings when Greeks were politically and culturally dominant, they do not disturb the idea of Hellenic or, in modern terms, European superiority over peoples of other continents.

The increase of books on these various topics and the move away from the traditional core of Classics show that the traditional discipline is fraying at the edges. The title of a book edited by two classicists in 1989, *Classics: A Discipline and Profession in Crisis*, may be unduly alarmist, but there is something to be said for their assessment.[3] The "crisis" and the writings of Burkert, West, and Morris, however, still have not led to a fundamental reassessment of Ancient Greece as a culture not only *in* but *of* the Eastern Mediterranean. A handful of books concerned with Asian topics unrelated to Greece appears on the list of the *Bryn Mawr Classical Review* as well as one or two on *parallels* between the Near East and Greece. Only five, or approximately 1 percent, of the total treat possible Near Eastern *influences* on Greek civilization.[4]

Clearly, classicists are reluctant to venture into areas that require new language skills and lack the detailed documentation that later periods possess. Morris, Burkert, and West have shown, however, that many problems of Greek literature, philosophy, and art—I would add Greek institutional forms—become knowable, or at least more satisfactorily addressable, if one extends the range of inquiry to Southwest Asia. I maintain that the boundary can be expanded still further if one brings linguistic contact and Egypt into the picture. I do not claim that such expansions will enlighten all aspects of Ancient Greek history and culture. In many cases, they will merely pose new questions along these lines: If Greece obtained and adapted cultural artifact x from region y, from where or how did people in y receive or develop it? Nevertheless, the aims of scholarship should be dynamic, not static. We should be satisfied with an ability to ask more questions and illuminate some of them, and not hope to provide definitive conclusions.

Notes

Abbreviations Used in Notes

BA I *Black Athena*, vol. 1 (Bernal, 1987a)
BA II *Black Athena*, vol. 2 (Bernal, 1991b)
BA III *Black Athena*, vol. 3 (Bernal, forthcoming)
BAR *Black Athena Revisited* (Lefkowitz and Rogers, 1996)
DBA *Debating Black Athena* (Bernal and Moore, forthcoming)
NOA *Not Out of Africa* (Lefkowitz, 1997a)
Cross-references are given by note number. These are usually indicators of position in the text; sometimes, however, they refer to the note itself.

Introduction

1 For a discussion of this, see ch. 6 n. 51.
2 For a discussion of this, see ch. 6 nn. 50–57.
3 For this, see *BA* I, ch. 1.
4 For more discussion of this, see n. 8 below.
5 Elias, 1978, pp. 3–10.
6 This was the title of the famous *Skizze* (Sketch) on the subject. See *BA* I: 284.

7 For a discussion, see BA I: 284–288.

8 Thirlwall, 1835–1844, 1: p. 63.

9 See BA I: 308–316. For more on Müller, see ch. 7 nn. 70–86.

10 See BA II: 367–399.

11 Lakatos, 1970.

12 See, for instance, BA II: xvi–xx, and Bernal, 1997g, pp. 66–76.

13 See, for instance, "Review of the 2nd Volume of 'Black Athena,'" 1991;
Turner, 1989, p. 109; Weinstein, 1992, p. 383.

14 Berlinerblau (1999, p. 6) estimates a ratio of seven hostile to three favorable.

15 Rendsburg, 1989; Ray, 1990.

16 Jasanoff and Nussbaum. For their chapter in BAR, see ch. 6 below. All references to BAR (Lefkowitz and Rogers, 1996) are cited in the text throughout this volume.

17 See Vermeule, BAR, p. 271. The quotation is also discussed in ch. 4, n. 8 below.

18 See Astour, 1967, pp. 347–361; Bunnens, 1979, pp. 6–7; Burkert, 1992/1984, pp. 4–6; Schmitz, 1999, pp. 55–60. Even his champion Josine Blok agrees that K. O. Müller was strongly prejudiced against the Egyptians. See Blok, 1996, pp. 718–719.

19 T. Martin, 1993, p. 58.

20 Martel, 1997, p. 6, section N.

21 See BA I: 436–437, and Carruthers's contribution to DBA.

22 For the difficulties of travel through Anatolia before the seventh century B.C.E., see M. L. West, 1998, pp. 3–4.

23 Konstan, 1997, p. 262.

24 Peter Daniels makes the same point in his electronic review of BAR (1996). For my many previous replies to John Coleman, see the bibliography.

25 I also include a section on an important criticism of my historiography published by Josine Blok in the *Journal of the History of Ideas*.

I Egyptology

1 Sarah Morris's short and idiosyncratic "thought piece" does not warrant its section heading "The Near East."

2 John Desmond Bernal (1901–1971) was born in County Tipperary. His father was half Jewish and half Irish and his mother was American. He studied and carried out research at Cambridge and London. For thirty years he held a professorial chair in physics at Birkbeck College in London. As a student, he became a crystallographer and later was a founder of biophysics. He also trained a number of Nobel Prize winners. In 1939 he published *The Social Function of Science*, the first book on the sociology of science. Initially attracted to Sinn Fein and Irish independence, he turned to communism in the 1920s and Marxism in the 1930s. He was a founda-

tional organizer of the Association of Scientific Workers. During the Second World War he was a senior scientific advisor to Louis Mountbatten's team, Combined Operations, in which, among other things, he played a key role in the D-Day landings. After the war, he continued teaching and research, combining them with political activity in the World Peace Council, of which he became president. He also found time to write a four-volume history of science, *Science in History*. For more on him, see Goldsmith, 1980, and Swann and Aprahemian, 1999.

3 Poe, 1997, pp. 482–494.
4 See ch. 7 n. 60; ch. 8 nn. 9–10; and ch. 16 nn. 1, 76.

1. Can We Be Fair? A Reply to John Baines

1 Baines, 1991, pp. 12–13.
2 They offered to take Loprieno's own essay, but he decided that "it would not be proper" for his piece to be included. See Loprieno, 1994.
3 See ch. 7 n. 12.
4 See ch. 9 nn. 67–98.
5 Baines and Málek, 1980, p. 24.
6 Dawson and Uphill, 1995.
7 See, for instance, Edith Hall, in BAR, pp. 340–342; Cartledge, 1991.
8 Stubbings, 1973.
9 Bernal, 1990b, pp. 118–119.
10 See ch. 6 nn. 210–216 for the argument that Nēith had blue eyes *and* was African.
11 Russman, 1989, p. 50.
12 For an instance of the former, see the summary by the distinguished Egyptologist Francis Llewellyn Griffith in the eleventh edition of *Encyclopedia Britannica* (1910–1911, 9: 43): "According to the evidence of the mummies, the Egyptians were of slender build, dark hair and of Caucasian type. Dr Elliot Smith, who has examined thousands of skeletons and mummies of all periods, finds that the prehistoric population of Upper Egypt, a branch of the North African–Mediterranean–Arabian race, changed with the advent of the dynasties to a stronger type, better developed than before in skull and muscle. This was apparently due to admixture with Lower Egyptians, who themselves had been affected by Syrian immigration."
13 Harris and O'Connor, 1982.
14 This is not quite accurate because my thesis was on the introduction and adaptation of European socialism to China. Thus, in its concern with cultural hybridity it was similar to my present work on *Black Athena*.
15 See ch. 4 n. 15; ch. 8 nn. 30–32. See also Bass and Bikai, 1989, pp. 111–114; Bass, 1997, pp. 75–77.
16 Young, 1953; C. H. Gordon, 1957; Rendsburg 1981. For the reverse, see Hoch, 1994.

17 Helck, 1989.
18 Lichtheim, 1975–1980, 1:211.
19 I am grateful to Professor T. A. Schmitz (1999, p. 24) for having demonstrated that my previous use of the infinitive *Besserwissen* in a nominal sense was incorrect.
20 P. James et al., 1991.
21 "Review of the 2nd Volume of 'Black Athena,'" 1991.
22 Baines suggests (p. 36) that I had accepted Kemp and Weinstein's criticisms of Mellaart's high chronology. I merely stated that they had "the effect of discrediting" it. I went on to discuss how the work of Haas and his team had reopened the issue (BA II: 209–11).
23 Saghieh, 1983, p. 131.
24 Ch. 3 n. 42; ch. 4 nn. 22–24.
25 See ch. 3 nn. 21–22.
26 See ch. 15 nn. 9–74.
27 Bernal, 1990a.
28 David Moore rightly points out that my example is somewhat weakened by the fact that many of the "cultural records and memories" were safely in Arab and Byzantine hands for much of this period. However, there is no doubt that though it degenerated, writing and some literature was preserved in Western Europe during these centuries.
29 See ch. 3 n. 5; ch. 7 nn. 86–87.
30 See Bernal, 1990a, pp. 7–15.
31 See ch. 3 n. 20.
32 Burkert, 1992/1984, p. ix.
33 See, for instance, the collective cry of rage by Mesoamericanists against Ivan van Sertima's argument for African influences on their territory, and the comments that followed it, in Haslip-Viera, Ortiz de Montellana, and Barbour, 1997.
34 Renfrew, 1972.
35 See, in particular, my response to Edith Hall in ch. 5.
36 Bacon, 1863/1620, p. 210.
37 Ludendorf, 1936, p. 85.
38 Rehak, 1997, p. 402.

2. Greece Is Not Nubia: A Reply to David O'Connor

1 Farag, 1980; Giveon, 1985, p. 16 n. 34; Helck, 1989; Posener 1982; Ward, 1986. Ward scrupulously admitted that he had been wrong about this (personal communication at Brown University, October 1992).
2 For the Kültepe, see E. N. Davis, 1977, pp. 69–78, esp. 72. For the Aegean parallels, see Warren and Hankey, 1989, pp. 131–134, pll. 5–11; and Warren, 1995, p. 5.
3 Two other possible archaeological indications of Egyptian contacts with

the north and east coasts of the Black Sea, not mentioned in BA II: The first is the finding of a tray-stand on the banks of the Dniester on the Ukrainian border with Moldavia, resembling a Twelfth Dynasty "soul house" (M. Murray, 1941; Griffiths, 1964). Flinders Petrie wanted to derive Egyptian civilization from the Caucasus or further north. Unfortunately for his hypothesis, the stylistic parallels pointed to the Twelfth Dynasty, not earlier. The second indication is a basalt sculpture of a pharaoh—of unknown period—found at the village of Chaisubani in the Adzharia autonomous region of Georgia (*Interfax* [Moscow]; *Agence France Presse*, 8 Feb. 1998).

4 Schaeffer, 1948, pp. 544–545.

5 Porada, 1984.

6 E. Meyer, 1928–1936, vol. 2, pt. 1, pp. 40–58, 162–175; Stubbings, 1973, pp. 634–637. See also ch. 1 n. 8 and ch. 4 n. 22.

7 See Dessenne, 1957, pp. 35–43, 178–179; Bisi, 1965, pp. 21–42. For further discussion of this, see ch. 4 nn. 23–24.

8 Pollinger Foster, 1987; N. Marinatos, 1984, esp. p. 32; Morgan, 1988, esp. p. 171.

9 A. H. Gardiner, 1947, I *207; Vercoutter, 1956, pp. 16–17; A. H. Gardiner, 1957, p. 573.

10 T. G. H. James, 1973, pp. 303–307.

11 Sethe and Steindorff, 1906–1958, 4: 21,9–16.

12 Bietak, 1995, p. 26, and 1999. See also Cline, 1998.

13 Sethe and Steindorff, 1906–1958, 4: 17,12–13.

14 Cline, 1987.

15 Vercoutter, 1956, pp. 132–133.

3. Who Is Qualified to Write Greek History?
A Reply to Lawrence A. Tritle

1 Bernal, 1993c. Somehow, the reference to my response to Tritle was, as Molly Myerowitz Levine put it (1998, p. 354 n. 35), "lost in transit" from the excellent bibliography she prepared for *Black Athena Revisited*.

2 I discuss all of these quotations later in the chapter.

3 In 1976, the latter two wrote such powerful letters on my behalf that I received the quite exceptional honor and opportunity of a year's study leave at the Cornell Society for the Humanities to pursue my interests in the Ancient Eastern Mediterranean. This was despite the fact that I had been trained in Chinese history and culture.

4 For examples of these, see Pembroke, 1967, and E. Hall, 1989.

5 Turner, 1989, pp. 108–109.

6 Manning, 1990, p. 269.

7 For my previous mistaken use of the form *Besserwissen*, see ch. 1 n. 19. Like other authors in BAR, Tritle made no objection to it.

8 For more on these issues, see ch. 7 nn. 17, 19–20; ch. 9 n. 44.

9 There is a discussion of Meiners below, in ch. 7 nn. 19–21.

10 See also Momigliano, 1966, pp. 3–23.

11 See, for instance, Bernal, 1992g, pp. 209–210; ch. 1 n. 7; ch. 5 nn. 1–2, 9; ch. 6 n. 5.

12 Lorimer, 1950, p. 93; Wace and Stubbings, 1962, p. 308; and Stella, 1965, pp. 41–45.

13 Bernal, 1990a.

14 Ibid., pp. 89–128.

15 Thucydides did not mention his remote Thracian ancestry in the section cited by Tritle (IV:105). It is clear that he belonged to a Greek elite in the region. Indeed, it could be argued that in the previous section, Thucydides' mentioning that Thasos—where he was at the time—was "a Parian colony" was to make sure that he not be mistaken for a Thracian.

16 Frazer, 1898, 5: 165–166; Schwartz, 1950.

17 This statement, of course, flatly contradicts Lefkowitz's insistence on proof and "warranted facts." See, for instance, 1996e, p. 51.

18 A. H. Gardiner, 1961; see, for example, pp. 88, 120. For another example, see Hoffman, 1991.

19 Tritle, 1992, p. 85.

20 Bass, 1989. Bass returned to this issue in 1997 (p. 84), where he insists that his *Cape Gelidonya* "was found unacceptable by classical and preclassical scholars who reviewed the book," and cites many examples. See also ch. 4 n. 15.

21 Renfrew, 1972, pp. 110, 288.

22 Van Andel and Zangger, 1990, pp. 145–148; 1992, pp. 383–386.

23 In his footnote 5, Tritle writes that I attribute "the origins of the modern idea of progress to Turgot and the French Enlightenment without a single word of reference to Adam Smith and the Scottish Enlightenment which developed the idea of progress independently and at the same time. . . . Admitting that something like this could happen, however, would seriously undermine the whole concept of diffusionism." In the first place, admission of instances of independent invention does not undermine "the whole concept of diffusionism." No one in her or his senses would deny that both processes take place. Second, Tritle's example is a peculiarly bad choice for his case. To begin with, the section in BA I immediately before that on Turgot is headed "Europe as the 'Progressive' Continent." It is concerned with the optimism and general sense of progress felt among intellectuals after the 1680s in Western Europe, which naturally included both France and Scotland. I focused on Turgot and his speech "On the Successive Progress of the Human Spirit" given in 1750 because he was among the earliest to articulate this previously inchoate pattern of thought. Without wanting to offend the segment of the political spectrum that believes that Adam Smith should be included in everything, I should point out that his *Theory of Moral Sentiments* appeared in 1759, nine years after Turgot's speech, and *The Wealth of Nations* not until 1776. Smith started the

latter during an eighteen-month stay in Toulouse, after which he went to Geneva, where he met Voltaire, and on to Paris, where Hume introduced him to the *économistes* or Physiocrats, with whom Turgot was associated. There is some debate as to the precise degree of influence they had on his thinking, but Smith thought sufficiently highly of the leading Physiocrat, François Quesnay, that he wanted to dedicate *The Wealth of Nations* to him. I do not want to portray the Scottish Enlightenment as a mere projection of the French one; on the other hand, they shared a common background and had considerable social and intellectual intercourse. The case Tritle cites provides an excellent example of modified diffusion.

24 Schoffeleers, 1992, p. 160.

25 Snowden, 1989, pp. 84–86.

26 Snowden, 1970, p. 12.

27 Keita, 1993a.

28 Yurco, 1989.

29 The only possible exception to this is that it could strengthen "white" prejudices that "blacks" are irrational.

30 See ch. 8 n. 50.

31 For more on the dangers of Eurocentric classical scholarship, see ch. 16 n. 77.

32 For a discussion of earlier precedents for Greek "freedom," see ch. 15 nn. 51–53.

33 Herodotus II:123; A. B. Lloyd, 1975–1988, 3: 59.

34 Burkert, 1977/1985, p. 37.

35 See, for instance, ch. 6. nn. 96–99.

36 Rendsburg, 1989; Ray, 1990.

37 This interpretation is also followed by Zangger, 1992, p. 47.

38 See Pang, 1985, 1987; Pang and Chou, 1984, 1985.

39 See, for instance, Gong, 1982, pp. 44–46; Public Security Bureau, 1989, p. 53. I am grateful to Scott Wilson for these references.

40 This is the objection of Jasanoff and Nussbaum; see ch. 6 n. 175.

41 See Astour, 1967b, p. 293.

42 See Spyropoulos, 1972, 1973a, 1973b, 1981; Symeonoglou, 1985, p. 25.

43 Unless, that is, one accepts the controversial proposal that pyramids in the Argolid should be dated to EHII. See Lazos, 1995, pp. 171–180.

44 Foucart, 1914, p. 2.

45 See Bernal, 1993b. See also chs. 14 n. 79; 15 nn. 9–75.

46 Molly Levine in DBA has a long footnote on this problem, in which she argues that I have been "sloppy" in my notes (BA II: 444 nn. 156–157) on Aithiops and *simo/simian*. I think my sloppiness is less than she supposes. John Chadwick made no connection between the Mycenaean names *sima/simo* and the Latin "monkey." On the other hand, Pierre Chantraine did not, as Levine suggests, dismiss or even query M. Leumann's hypothesis that a Greek form, *simias*, was loaned into Latin as *simia*. This is accepted as a matter of course by Ernout and Meillet (1985). Levine also fol-

lows Kenneth Dover in claiming that it is uncertain that calling someone a monkey was a racial slur. She quotes my reference to the connotations of the usual Greek word for "ape" (*pithekos*): "jackanapes, tricksters and dwarves." Ernout and Meillet, more convincingly, refer to *simia* simply as a "term of insult."

47 See St. Clair Drake, 1987–1990, 1: 260–272.
48 L. Thompson, 1989.
49 See also the references in Mudimbe, 1988, pp. 69–71.
50 Jordan, 1969, pp. 28–32. St. Clair Drake praised this section as "a brilliant discussion" (1987–1990, 1:24).

4. How Did the Egyptian Way of Death Reach Greece?
A Reply to Emily Vermeule

1   Vermeule, 1979, p. 69.
2   Bury, 1900, p. 62; as quoted in BA I: 293.
3   For this general view, see Rawson, 1969, pp. 308 n. 2; p. 351; Cartledge, 1979, pp. 116, 119.
4   Bury, 1900, p. 77.
5   Personal communication from E. M. Forster, Cambridge, England, 1968.
6   Shelmerdine, 1995, p. 99; Vermeule, 1964.
7   For a general survey of these, see Davies and Schofield, 1995.
8   *Paradise Lost*, II:113–115. This is also quoted in the introduction n. 17.
9   Dachslager, 1992.
10 "Review of the 2nd Volume of 'Black Athena,'" 1991.
11 For evidence that the denial lasted much longer than that, see Renfrew, 1998; ch. 1 n. 15; ch. 8 nn. 30–32.
12 Renfrew, 1972, p. xxv.
13 Ventris and Chadwick, 1973.
14 Stubbings, 1973, p. 637.
15 See ch. 3 n. 20.
16 For an example of this sequence, see the bold, original, and broad-minded work of Peter Walcot, 1966.
17 See, for instance, Ellenbogen, 1962; Hoch, 1994.
18 See ch. 15 nn. 9–75.
19 See ch. 3 nn. 42–43.
20 Vermeule and Vermeule, 1970, pp. 36–37.
21 Watrous, 1987, pp. 65–66, 70.
22 Stubbings, 1973; ch. 1 n. 8; ch. 2 n. 6.
23 See, for instance, Pollinger Foster, 1987; Morgan, 1988; and the articles collected in, Hardy, Doumas, Sakellarakis, and Warren, 1989.
24 See ch. 2 nn. 10–12.

5. Just Smoke and Mirrors? A Reply to Edith Hall

Edith Hall's original review of Black Athena appeared in Arethusa 25 (1992): 181–201, to which I replied in the same issue. Hall's essay was very slightly revised for BAR. This response is also a revision of my original reply.

1 In her note 2, Professor Hall writes, "Bernal singularly overlooks Pelops" because he was supposed to have come to Greece from Anatolia. In fact, I do refer to Pelops and the Pelopids four times in BA I (pp. 21, 84, 365, 491), and I discuss him in his Anatolian context in BA II (pp. 452–458).

2 S. Marinatos, 1969, pp. 374–375; 1973b, pp. 199–200.

3 Karageorghis, 1988, esp. p. 10 n. 2.

4 Ventris and Chadwick, 1973, p. 537.

5 Ibid. p. 582; Chantraine. For simos/simian, see ch. 3 nn. 46–47.

6 Xenophanes, 1901, 16.

7 Bernal, 1990b, pp. 131–132.

8 See, for instance, Morris, 1992, pp. 124–149.

9 Odyssey XIX.246–248. For a discussion of interpretations of this description, see St. Clair Drake, 1987–1990, 2: 318–319, n. 75. Hesiod cited in Strabo, 7.3.7, in Snowden, 1970, p. 103.

10 I discussed this in earlier in Bernal, 1989g, p. 22.

11 Timaeus, 21E–22A.

12 Herodotus I, 60; II,182; IV,180.

13 See Astour, 1967, esp. pp. 212–217.

14 Hekataios of Miletos in Scholiast on Euripides, Orestes 872.

15 Pausanias, II.16.1; 19, 3; 30.6; 38.4; IV.35.2.

16 For the Spartan pyramid, see Pendlebury, 1930, p. 47. Cartledge does not refer to the form in his description of the sanctuary (1979, p. 121).

17 For a discussion of Areios' letter, see BA I: 109–110, 460 n. 168. See also Cartledge and Spawforth, 1989, p. 37. Cartledge is inclined to believe the letter to be genuine though absurd.

18 For the first possible etymology, see Cartledge and Spawforth, 1989, pp. 67–68; P. Green, 1990, p. 301.

19 See Fakhry, 1973, pp. 82–83; Pausanias III.18.3.

20 For these, see ch. 15 nn. 107–112.

21 Herodotus, VI.55.

22 Ventris and Chadwick, 1973, pp. 127, 411.

23 Caskey, 1980.

6. Ausnahmslosigkeit über Alles:
A Reply to Jay H. Jasanoff and Alan Nussbaum

1 For a discussion of the relationship between perceived similarities of words and historical linguistics, see Ruhlen, 1994, pp. 284–285.

2 Ray, 1997.

3 Daniels, 1996. Jasanoff and Nussbaum wish to disqualify Gary Rendsburg's (1989) favorable review of my work because he declared himself to
be a "dear friend of Bernal." The tone of their article makes the authors'
position at the other end of the spectrum equally clear.

4 Jasanoff and Nussbaum state that they are "traditional" in not using the
widely accepted term "Indo-Hittite" (p. 203 n. 2). The term's usefulness
has now been confirmed by computerized studies (Trask, 1996, p. 369).
Over the years, I have asked Indo-Europeanists to explain their dislike of
the term "Indo-Hittite" and I have never received a satisfactory answer. I
can only assume that they are reluctant to drop the element "-European"
from the name of the language family. Jasanoff and Nussbaum are also
traditional in their continuing to use the Neogrammarian reconstruction of Proto-Indo-European consonants that most contemporary Indo-
Europeanists are now abandoning. See Collinge, 1985, p. 265.

5 Notably in chapters 1 and 5, the responses to John Baines and Edith Hall.
In a later talk, Jasanoff made still more extraordinary exaggerations. For
instance, he said that I claimed that "Black African pharaohs established
the first organized governments on the Greek mainland" (1997, p. 59).
This is wrong in every particular; the only invasion of the Greek mainland from Egypt, discussed in BA I and II, is that of the Hyksos princes,
who were fundamentally Southwest Asian (BA II: 320–360). I also maintain that there were organized states in Greece in the ceramic period EHII,
a thousand years before the possible Hyksos invasions (BA II: 123–153).

6 For the influence of nineteenth-century geology on the Neogrammarians,
see Christy, 1983.

7 Although the term is generally associated with the Neogrammarians, the
latter took this concept from their predecessor, August Schleicher. See
Jankowsky, 1968, p. 98.

8 See van Coetsem, 1994, pp. 20–22.

9 Bolinger, 1968; Jacobson, Waugh, and Mouville-Burston, 1990; Malkiel,
1990; Blench, 1997, p. 170.

10 Chantraine rejects this but is still less satisfied with the only other explanation offered. We know that in the fifth century B.C.E. the process by
which oi merged with i in Byzantine Greek had already begun and specifically that loimós and līmós were very close. See Thucydides II, 54. All
references to Chantraine's dictionary (1968–1975) can be found under the
entry discussed.

11 For a description of this major modification of Neogrammarian principles
and the posthumous vindication of their contemporary Hugo Schuchardt,
who was savagely condemned by the Neogrammarians for having seen this
difficulty, see Trask, 1996, pp. 227–228, 285–290. See also van Coetsem,
1994, pp. 32–33; Lass, 1997, pp. 139–143. Lass reassures his readers that
"independent pathways" can in "their own way be regular."

12 The only exception to this is that Holger Pedersen of a later generation of Neogrammarians wrote a final chapter on Semitic languages in his *Linguistic Science in the Nineteenth Century* (1931). Pedersen's own publications were entirely devoted to Indo-European languages.

13 Koerner, 1989, p. 94.

14 Burkert, 1992/1984, p. 34.

15 This tendency in conventional historical linguistics is discussed by Thomason and Kaufman, 1988, pp. 1–2. For a general account of the use and misuse of uniracinated trees, see Gould, 1989, esp. ch. 1, "The Iconography of an Expectation." For an argument in favor of the "mangrove" model, see Moore, 1994.

16 Jasanoff, 1978; Nussbaum, 1986.

17 Saul Levin argues that *qarn* is a loan from Indo-European, on the grounds that it is unattested elsewhere in Afroasiatic (for a bibliography on this, see Levin, 1995 p. 29). However, Orel and Stolbova (1995) see cognates in Late Egyptian and Omotic. Even if Levin is right, the significance of Nussbaum's omission is not lessened. For vivid descriptions of the state of siege in Indo-European studies, see R. Wright, 1991, pp. 39–68, esp. pp. 41–48; P. Ross, 1991, pp. 139–147. For the pain these articles have caused conventional Indo-Europeanists, see Lass, 1997, p. 162.

18 See Pope, 1952, §1151, pp. 441–442.

19 Lexicographers agree that "cant" derives from *cantare*, as can be seen in the sense of "singsong" or "whining." It is more likely that in the sense of "jargon" or "secret language" it comes from the Irish *caint*, pronounced ka:nt ("talking" or "idiom"). This is a good example of a mixed etymology or "contamination." Other examples of Irish words in English slang or cant included "twig" in the sense of "understand" from the Irish *tuig* ("understand") and "gob" (mouth) from the Irish *gob* ("beak").

20 Both conditions are necessary. See, for instance, Dutch borrowings made within the short time span between 1900 and 1950 of the English football term "goal." In the northern Netherlands, it is pronounced *kol*, in the South and Flanders as *γol*, and by purists as *gol*. In this case, the variation was caused by dialect differences in the borrowing language. A striking example of this factor can also be seen in two Italian borrowings from the Arabic: *dār aṣ ṣinā'a* ("factory"): *darsena* ("internal part of a port where ships are disarmed or repaired"; probably through Genoese), and *arsenale* ("naval shipyard, arsenal") through Venetian. See Aboul Nasr, 1993, p. 43. I am also grateful to Lori Repetti for this example.

   For drastic changes brought about over short periods, see the difference between the Japanese treatment of Chinese words introduced before and those borrowed after 630 C.E., discussed below.

21 This usage is a slight anachronism because the city name Changan was not adopted until the early Tang.

22 See Pulleyblank, 1984, p. 3.

23 It is probable that in both cases most of the transmission was through Chinese scholars, skilled craftsmen, and concubines at the Japanese Court in addition to Japanese students sent to study in China.

24 Pulleyblank, 1984, pp. 154–155.

25 See Karlgren, 1957, pp. 211–367; Pulleyblank, 1984, p. 155.

26 Jasanoff and Nussbaum rightly emphasize the huge number of Chinese words introduced into Japanese (p. 184). I argue that only 40+ percent of the Greek vocabulary came from Egyptian and Semitic, but equally I accept the conventional estimates that fewer than 40 percent have clear Indo-European etymologies. Thus, even assuming that the latter figure is an underestimate, it would seem reasonable to assume that over 50 percent derived from Afroasiatic and other loans.

27 Though the wider terms *science* and *Wissenschaft* are still sometimes used in this context in French and German. "Scientific" is not found in such English-language works as T. Bynon, 1977, or Thomason and Kaufman, 1988.

28 For a bibliography of the nineteenth-century literature on this word, see Muss-Arnolt, 1892, pp. 56–57. For a more recent survey of the two traditions, see West, 1997, p. 154. Still more recently, J. P. Brown has written about this and two other examples of words with strong Indo-European *and* Semitic etymologies, "The perfect parallelism of the Greek and Hebrew forms implies contamination." However, he is inclined to view "the Greek word as having traveled" (2000, p. 303).

29 E. Meyer, 1928–1936, vol. 2, pt. 1, p. 547 n. 4.

30 R. D. Griffith (1997a) has pointed out that Jasanoff and Nussbaum's acceptance of the derivation of Aíguptos from Ḥt k3 Ptḥ violates their own criteria for loaning.

31 Loprieno, 1995, p. 38.

32 Burkert, 1992/1984, p. 35.

33 To return to a Japanese parallel, there is the vivid statement: "The English word looted by the Japanese can expect to be systematically stripped of its national identity after a series of cruel and little known initiation rites" (*The Guardian* [Manchester (England)], 20 March 1976, quoted in Loveday, 1996, p. 138).

34 Liddell and Scott, 1968, pp. 2009–2012.

35 See Masson, 1967, pp. 42–44. This in turn derives from the Egyptian qd ("pot").

36 For kētharion and kēthis as "voting urns," see ch. 15 n. 69. The cluster around kēd- ("to trouble or mourn") is much more likely to derive from the Egyptian qdd ("watch over the dead") and/or the Semitic kdr ("mourn") than from a putative Indo-European root found in the Gothic hatis ("hate"). However, kēd- may also have been "contaminated" by kad in the sense of "funerary urn."

37 Burkert, 1992/1984, p. 40.

38 See, for instance, Chadwick, 1975, pp. 805–818.

39 Humboldt, 1988/1856, p. 216; Aarsleff, 1988, pp. x, lxi–lxiv.

40 Humboldt, 1903–1935/1793, 1: 255–281, 266. See also R. L. Brown, 1967, p. 80.

41 Humboldt, 1903–1935/1793, 3:188.

42 Thomason and Kaufman, 1988; Jasanoff, 1989.

43 Thomason and Kaufman, 1988, pp. 74–146.

44 As stated above, this sequence is schematic and should not be taken literally. The actual pattern must have been very irregular both historically and geographically and probably many more generations were involved.

45 For three of the few borrowings into English, see n. 19. This line from "Road to the Isles" is actually from Scottish Gaelic, which in this case has the same construction as the Irish. Irish, in contrast to Irish English, is a good example of a contact language. While retaining its phonology, morphology, and syntax, it is full of English and other foreign words.

46 Jasanoff and Nussbaum, discussing this phenomenon, cite the English and East Asian examples and add Iranian loans in Armenian and Arabic ones in modern Persian (p. 184).

47 Humboldt, 1988/1836.

48 Because the semantic areas occupied by Greek in Coptic overlap with the non-Indo-European areas found in Greek, I believe that a high proportion of the Greek loans into Coptic themselves had Egyptian or Semitic origins.

49 Gamkriledze and Ivanov, 1995, pp. 55–56.

50 Thomason and Kaufman, 1988, pp. 74–75.

51 Morpurgo-Davies, 1986, p. 105. The closeness of her relationship with the authors can be seen in the thanks they offer her in their first note.

52 For the linguistic mosaic of the Pre-Indo-European languages of North India, see Witzel, 1999.

53 See Thomason and Kaufman, 1988, pp. 39–40, 85–86.

54 See Trask, 1996, pp. 327–328.

55 Quoted in Thomason and Kaufman, 1988, p. 65; see also pp. 215–222.

56 For the list, see Swadesh, 1971, pp. 271–284. The complete list of these words in Greek will be provided in BA III.

57 These are *ear, haima* ("blood"), *osse, ophthalmos* ("eye[s]"), and *neos, kainos* ("new").

58 See Thomason and Kaufman, 1988, p. 365 n. 22.

59 In the summer of 1997, Colin Renfrew generously invited me to lunch at his college in Cambridge. There, I argued that Greek was not a shift but a contact language. Though conventionally unorthodox, this view fit well with the "model of autochthonous origin" that Renfrew has promoted for many years. Thus, with typical daring and energy, he plunged into the field, and that November, he presented a paper arguing that the bulk of the non-Indo-European vocabulary in Greek derived from an adstrate "or even a superstrate" rather than from a substrate. He published this the following year (Renfrew, 1998).

Unfortunately, he was unable to remove his Aegean blinkers or consult

anyone who knew West Semitic or Egyptian. Thus, he insists that the "adstrate" was "Minoan." Also, surrounded by conventional Graecocentric
scholars, Renfrew not only failed to note the considerable work carried
out on Semitic loans into Greek by W. Muss-Arnold, Heinrich Lewy, Cyrus
Gordon, Michael Astour, Saul Levin, and John Pairman Brown, but also
that by the classicists Walter Burkert and Martin West and the Indo-Europeanist Oswald Szemerényi. The only specialist in this area to whom he referred was Emilia Masson, whose extraordinarily restrictive list of Semitic
loans into Greek has made her work acceptable to the Classical establishment. Had he consulted the others, Renfrew would have realized that many
of the words on which he based his case—*asaminthos, kados, kithara, xiphos,
pallakis, plinthos, sak(k)kos, salpinx, sidē, sitos, syrinx, phorminx*, and khitōn—
all have well-established Semitic or Egypto-Semitic etymologies. I should
add more, as well as an equal number of purely Egyptian ones. Renfrew's
determination to retain a purely European identity for Greece is shown in
his strange proposal that his hypothetical Minoan language, about which
the only thing known is its non-Indo-European vocabulary, may have belonged to the Indo-Hittite family (pp. 259–260). His desire to exclude
southeastern influences also appears in his preference for an unknown
language over two, Egyptian and West Semitic, that we know relatively
well. I am convinced that it is only when these sources are exhausted that
we should turn to unknown ones. It may well be that some of the Afroasiatic words came into Greek through Crete, as many reflect the sophistication that archaeology indicates came to the island from Egypt and Southwest Asia.

60 Morpurgo-Davies, 1986, p. 105.

61 See Bonfante and Bonfante, 1983, p. 60. This statement uses "Indo-Euro-
    pean" in the narrow sense (see n. 4 above). Quite possibly, Etruscan was
    an Anatolian language and, therefore, belonged to the Indo-Hittite family.
    For arguments in favor of this hypothesis, see Georgiev, 1979, pp. 84–100;
    Adrados, 1989; Bomhard and Kerns, 1994, pp. 33–34. For skepticism of
    the Anatolian connection, see Pallotino, 1956, pp. 53–56; Bonfante and
    Bonfante, 1983, pp. 41–43. Etruscan appears to have had a very mixed
    vocabulary from many different sources.

62 Their selection of Semitic as opposed to Ancient Egyptian examples was
    probably influenced by their unfamiliarity with the latter language.

63 C. W. Haley and Blegen, 1927.

64 Kretschmer, 1924.

65 Szemerényi, 1958, p. 159. For other criticisms of linking these place-
    name elements to a hypothetical Pre-Hellenic substratum, see E. Laroche,
    1977?, p. 213; Wyatt, 1968; Hooker, 1976, p. 23.

66 Szemerényi, 1974, p. 152.

67 Ibid. pp. 145, 149.

68 Ventris and Chadwick, 1973, p. 387.

69 See Gelb, 1977, pp. 3–27; Cagni, 1980.

70 For a description and bibliography of C. H. Gordon's articles on the subject, see his 1968, pp. 157–171.

71 See Ventris and Chadwick, 1973, p. 106.

72 For parallels, see the alternations Didyma/Dindymon and Athedon/ Anthedon.

73 Pokorny, 1959, 1: 40–41.

74 Chantraine, 1968–1975, 1: 90.

75 Antonio Loprieno thinks the change took place between Middle and Late Egyptian (1995, p. 38). However, earlier instability is indicated by the alternations ptr/pty ("who, what") and mtr/mty ("fame, renown") in Middle Egyptian.

76 See A. H. Gardiner, 1957, §272, p. 209.

77 The idea that there was a prothetic ỉ in early Egyptian is strengthened by the possibility that nṯr is related to the Cushitic enkera, inkira ("soul, life demon"). See Calice, 1936, p. 167, cited in Hornung, 1982/1971, p. 35. Thus, nṯr could be a cognate of k3.

78 Brugsch, 1885–1888, 1: 93.

79 See, for instance, Hornung, 1982, p. 41.

80 Bonnet, 1952, pp. 120–121.

81 See Parke, 1977, pp. 106–124.

82 A shift from long stressed ā to a long stressed ō took place in Egyptian near the end of the second millennium B.C.E. See Loprieno, 1995, p. 38.

83 See Loret, 1949.

84 See Trask, 1996, p. 349.

85 G. Bass, 1991, 1997, p. 87.

86 Lejeune, 1987/1972, pp. 54, 72–73; Levin, 1995, p. 235.

87 For this uncertainty in Egyptian, see Loprieno, 1995, p. 34. For the confusion in Semitic, see Moscati et al., 1969, pp. 35–37; Steiner, 1977.

88 See Gauthier, 1925–1931, 2: 50. Nonnos, the Egypto-Greek poet of the fifth century C.E., maintained that the city of Byzantium had been founded by the hero Byzas, who, like Danaos, had come from Egypt. See Nonnos, Dionysiaka, III.365–369.

89 See, for instance, Sesōstris from S n Wsrt.

90 Lejeune, 1987/1972, §143, pp. 146–147.

91 Szemerényi, 1974, p. 148.

92 The roots are from W3g, a major religious festival associated with Osiris and the beginning of the growing season after the Nile flood, and d3b ("fig tree"). Grounds for these etymologies will be given in BA III. Jasanoff and Nussbaum merely view terébinthos as coming from the Pre-Hellenic "substrate" (p. 186).

93 Loret, 1945; Hodge, 1992, 1997.

94 Loprieno, 1995, pp. 31, 38; Kammerzell, 1994, p. 31. The value of 3 as a liquid is now accepted by informed classicists; see M. L. West, 1997, p. xxiii.

95 See, for instance, Jean Vergote, 1971, p. 44. For a bibliography of earlier

recognition that *ꜣ* was originally a liquid, see Vercoutter, 1956, p. 20, n. 4. Vercoutter himself also accepted it as possible. Nevertheless, it was not known by Otto Rössler in 1964 (p. 213) or Carleton Hodge in 1971 (pp. 13–14), 1977, and 1992, when they independently published the same results. See Hodge, 1997.

96 Lee, 1961, pp. 191–193.

97 *Iliad*, 23.78.

98 Parke, 1977, pp. 116–117. The link between *nṯr* and *ánthos* is discussed above.

99 See Kaplony, 1980.

100 See n. 28 above.

101 Clackson, 1994, p. 33. This is also the view of Lejeune; see 1987/1972, §146, pp. 148–149.

102 Pokorny, 1959, 1: 334.

103 Bomhard and Kerns, 1994, pp. 523–524.

104 Levin (1995, p. 288) comes to the same conclusion on the different grounds that the *ǵ* in the Arabic form *ǵrb* cannot be derived from Indo-European. However, a number of Semitists cited by Bomhard (Bomhard and Kerns, 1994, p. 523) have maintained that the *ǵ* in this case came from an ʿ*ayin* in contact with an *r*.

105 J. P. Brown, 1995, pp. 57–58.

106 Astour, 1967, p. 130. Actually, Astour uses the form *erēbu*. Gelb et al. (1956–, 4: 258) distinguish *erēbu* with the general sense "enter" from the specific *erebu*, "setting sun." They do, however, see "conflation" of both with *erēpu*, "dusky, dark."

107 The conventional view is that there is no Indo-European root for "black." See Ernout and Meillet, 1985, p. 441. For the Semitic, see J. P. Brown, 1995, pp. 57–58. For the Egyptian influence on this semantic field, see Vermeule, 1979, pp. 69–82.

108 Chantraine says it is certainly a loan. Neither Pokorny, 1959, nor Van Windekins, 1986, claims an Indo-European etymology for it. Pokorny accepts the conventional link between *deilós* and *deídō* and ultimately *duo* ("two").

109 Liddell and Scott refer to the second sense as being employed "more commonly."

110 Diakonoff, 1970, p. 456.

111 For an outline of this, see BA I: 56–57. BA III, forthcoming, will give more detail.

112 Hodge also reconstructed rounded dentals unconditionally in Proto-Chaddic (1987, p. 16).

113 That is to say, Amharic has letters to represent dwa, twa, and t'wa. See "A New Proto-Semitic," my paper given to NACAL 1981.

114 For instance, the root *mwr* ("border, limit, share") is *mʷärä*, and *mwt* ("death") is *mʷätä* in most Gurage languages.

115 Chantraine is not convinced by an etymology for this from an Indo-Euro-

pean root *g^wel ("swallow"), which Pokorny (1959, p. 365) only finds attested the Greek *délear*. It is also possible that the sense of *dólos* ("trick") was influenced by a West Semitic form found in the Arabic *dal* ("coquetry"). The semantic puzzle provided by the Latin words *doleo* ("suffer"), *dōlium* ("pottery vessel"), and *dolus* ("trickery") can be explained by borrowings from the Canaanite *dl* in the senses "depend, suspend, and entangle," either through Greek and South Italic languages or directly.

116 See Edel, 1978, pp. 120–121. As Akkadian *š* was a rendition of the Egyptian *s*, I have used the form Pasiyara. See n. 131 below.

117 For interchange between *b* and *p* in Middle and Late Egyptian, see n. 30 above and Ward, 1978. There are also the extremely plausible derivations of *bárbax* ("Libyan falcon") from *p3 ḥr bîk ("the falcon") and the Greek name for the king of Libya, Battos, from the Egyptian *p3îty* ("the sovereign"). Also see *p3qt* ("fine linen"), *brákos* ("luxurious robe"), *pr* ("house, household, estate"), and *báris* ("domain, fortified great house").

118 Ventris and Chadwick, 1973, p. 399.

119 Szemerényi, 1966, p. 29.

120 For examples of these, see Lejeune, 1987/1972, §33, pp. 46–47.

121 See Arapoyanni, 1996.

122 See Ventris and Chadwick, 1973, p. 38; Dow, 1973, p. 601.

123 In modern Hebrew, foreign words are transcribed with *quf* and *tet* rather than by the more frequent *kaf* and *tav* (though this may be to avoid spirantization when the latter are preceded by a vowel). In any event, the rarer letter indicates that the word is of foreign origin. The Japanese use of *katakana* syllabary to represent foreign words, rather than the far more common *hiragana*, is not at all ambiguous.

124 Schindler, 1976.

125 Szemerényi, 1958, p. 178; Perpillou, 1973.

126 See A. H. Gardiner, 1957, §353–361, pp. 270–278. See also Hoch, 1995, §§117–125, pp. 168–178. Callender believed that -*w* originally came from a nominative marker *u*; see Callender, 1975, p. 51. Similar forms are found throughout Afroasiatic (personal communication, Bender and Jungraithmayr, Mar. 1997).

127 For a bibliography on this, see Edel, 1978, pp. 120–121.

128 Albright, 1923, p. 66. See also Loprieno, 1995, pp. 38–39.

129 Loprieno, 1995, p. 38.

130 The existence of such words as *hippeús* ("horseman") based on the Greek word of Indo-European origin *híppos* shows that the suffix was active during the Mycenaean period.

131 Because the pronunciation of the letter transcribed as *š* in Hebrew is uncertain before 1000 B.C.E., I prefer to transcribe it simply as *s*. See n. 116 above. For arguments on this, see Bernal, 1990a, pp. 102–107.

132 Rendsburg, 1989, p. 77.

133 Nussbaum, 1976.

134 This is the opinion of Collinge, 1985, p. 25.

135 This alternation could have already existed in the plausible Egyptian etyma wš, Coptic *ouoš* ("fall out, of hair, be destroyed, shame, deformity, lacking") and wšr ("dry up, be despoiled, barren"). For the Late Egyptian shift u >*e*, see n. 128 above and Loprieno, 1995, p. 46.

136 Because of the precision possible in tracing phonetic developments within language families, a much higher degree of accuracy is required of etymologies establishing "genetic" relationships than for loans between languages.

137 The alternatives include "offering," sʿr; "bringing," in; and "giving," m3ʿt (Karenga, 1994, pp. 570–578).

138 The final w in inw would seem to be reflected in the -u in the Greek root, and the uncertainty in the length of the i in tinō could come from the contrast between the Demotic ty inw and the Coptic *tnnou*.

139 inw itself means "booty, dues, tribute."

140 See Hemmerdinger, 1968, p. 239.

141 The quotation comes from A. H. Gardiner, 1957, p. 428.

142 Ibid., p. 28.

143 Ibid., p. 644.

144 Loprieno, 1995, pp. 61–62. Though I am happy to accept the quotation as it stands, I suspect the author means "less" rather than "more" diversified.

145 Szemerényi, 1966, p. 36. His parallel with *kapnós* ("smoke, smell of cooking") is even more unreliable than he supposes, in that *kapnós* has a plausible Egyptian etymology in qfn ("bake").

146 See Hemmerdinger, 1968, p. 239.

147 Burkert, 1992/1984, p. 40.

148 Loprieno, 1995, p. 41.

149 For the former, see ibid., pp. 44–45.

150 This is putting it mildly. Frisk describes the root as isolated and Chantraine admits his ignorance. Even the bold Windekens does not attempt to find Indo-European etymologies for *neós* and *naíō*.

151 Exodus 15:13; Rendsburg, 1989, pp. 77–78.

152 Fick, 1905, pp. 83, 105. Loewe, 1980/1936 is more limited as a listing of toponyms containing divine names.

153 In my discussion in BA II (pp. 98–99) of the two cataracts in Boiotia and Arkadia, I referred to the mysterious name Athena Ong/ka, whom I linked to the Egyptian goddess ʿnqt Anukis associated with the Egyptian first cataract. I have since found that at Thelpousa in Arkadia, Apollo was known as Onkeatas (Pausanias, VIII.25.11).

154 2 Kings 5: 10–14; Pausanias V.5.7–11; Frazer, 1898, 3: 478–479.

155 The initial a- could come from the Late Canaanite definite article ha-. This too would indicate an origin after 1300 B.C.E. For ngr, see Bernal, 1997a.

156 Qbbt was the name of one of the legendary caverns at the first cataract at Elephantine from which, according to some mysterious texts, the Nile was supposed to originate. The Arkadian town and rock named Kaphúai were both associated with sacred springs; see Pausanias, VIII.13.6, 23.4.

For the association of a river Kēphis(s)ós with purification, see Pausanias I.37.3.

157 Chantraine describes the etymology of these words as "doubtful."

158 Imhoof-Blumer and Gardner, 1885–1887, p. 68, pl. p. vii, cited in Frazer, 1898, 3:453.

159 Pausanias, II.24.

160 Strabo XIII.3.4. The passage was quoted by K. O. Müller, 1820, p. 126. This information was in front of Jasanoff and Nusbaum in BA I: 76.

161 Xenophon, Hellenika, III.7.

162 Pausanias, VI.609.

163 Cited in the Scholia on Apollodorus Rhodius I.40.

164 This Greek word would seem to come from the Canaanite dmh ("resemble"), specifically the form dimyon found in the Bible (Psalms 17:2) meaning "likeness, manifestation." Given the calque with the Egyptian k3, this etymology is considerably more plausible than the conventional derivation of daimōn from daíō ("I share out").

165 A. H. Gardiner, 1947, II. *155.

166 See Smyth, 1956, §897, p. 253.

167 Lakōn itself could plausibly be explained as a participial form of laskō and/or Lakízō or both.

168 Szemerényi, 1960, p. 15.

169 Plutarch, Lykurgos, 18.1.

170 Pausanias, III.11.11; Imhoof-Blumer and Gardner, 1885–1887, p. 55, pll. 5–7. For an Egyptian prototype of this motif, see Faulkner, 1972, p. 167, spell 168. The idea that the Egyptian god was known in the Southern Peloponnese during the Bronze Age is strengthened by Astour's tentative but plausible identification of the Mycenaean personal name from Pylos, Anopo as Inpw/Anubis (1967, p. 340).

171 See Lazos, 1995, p. 114, pl. 91.

172 For example, see the names Kynoura, given to a Lakedaimonian people, and Kynosoura ("dog tail"), a ward of the city of Sparta, and kynosouris, a type of Lakedaimonian hound.

173 A. H. Gardiner, 1947, II.*127–128. The other Spa(r)tas around the Aegean would seem to have the same origin. See BA III, forthcoming.

174 For example, Tritle, BAR, p. 319.

175 See Smyth, 1956, §1005, p. 270.

176 The "construct" is a bound form of a nominal used only in conjunction with another in which the stress is modified; its use often leads to different forms from free or absolute nominals.

177 C. H. Gordon, 1962b, pp. 137–139.

178 See A. H. Gardiner, 1947, II.*6; Gauthier, 1925–1931, 6: 126–128; Brugsch, 1855–1888, p. 922.

179 Astour, 1967, pp. 157–158.

180 Jasanoff is still more peremptory in his later talk, simply dismissing the etymology as "absurd" (1997, p. 67).

181 Many other cities, apart from the capital of Attica, were named Athēnai. See BA II: 100–106; Loewe, 1980/1936, pp. 43–50.

182 Egbert, 1997, pp. 157–158 provides a list of fourteen Coptic or Greek renderings of ḥt. Of these, six had lost the initial aspirate and three of these retained the final -t.

183 See Hodge, 1991. Shifts from ʿayin to ʾaleph occur in both Egyptian and some Semitic languages. See Loprieno, 1995, p. 44; Moscati et al., 1969, p. 41.

184 See Collinge, 1985, pp. 238–239. This interpretation would require Ḥt Nt to have been seen as a compound.

185 Genesis 41:50; see Vergote, 1959, p. 148.

186 The idea that the form Athēnaíe comes from "she of the city Athēnai" is made less likely by the fact that most historians of Greek religion believe that the city gained its name from the goddess, not vice versa. See Nilsson, 1941, p. 407; Burkert, 1985/1977, pp. 139–140.

187 Such an early transmission for the toponym Athens is by no means improbable, as the city names Byblos and Tyre must have entered Greek before sound changes that took place around the middle of the second millennium. See Friedrich, 1923, p. 4; Albright, 1950, p. 165.

188 This is not to deny the possibility that Adana itself came from Ḥt Nt, although there are many difficulties with the Anatolian toponym; see BA II: 418–420.

189 The form Sathan does not exist. This is another example of their use of ponderous humor to defend the status quo.

190 Herodotus, II, 28, 49–50; Plato, Timaeus, 21E.

191 Sauneron, 1959–1970, 2: 188.91.

192 See A. H. Gardiner, 1947, II, p. *56.

193 See Otto, 1975.

194 In C. Müller, 1841–1870, 3: 639.

195 See Newberry, 1906, pp. 71–73 and A. Evans, 1921–35, 2, pp. 51–53. The African sign seems to have originated as a cockroach on a stick; see Keimer, 1931, pp. 145–182.

196 A. Evans, 1921–1935, II.1, p. 52.

197 See E. Gardiner, 1893. See also Nilsson, 1941, p. 407.

198 Warren, 1980, pp. 82–85; 1981, pp. 155–167.

199 A. Evans, 1921–1935, II.1, pp. 53–55.

200 Herodotus IV. 188; A. B. Lloyd, 1975–1988, 2: 88–89.

201 A. Evans, 1921–1935, II.1, pp. 53–55.

202 For the influential work on the "white" Libyans, see Bates, 1914.

203 A. H. Gardiner, 1947, II, pp. *116–119. This view has been strongly reinforced by Claude Vandersleyen, 1995.

204 Inscription in the Solar Temple of the Fifth Dynasty pharaoh Niuserre; see El Sayed, 1982, pp. 261–262, doc. 182. See also A. H. Gardiner, 1947, II, p. *118.

205 Gauthier, 1925–1931, 2: 139.
206 An early association between the goddess and ṯḥnt ("brilliant greenness") can be seen in the *Pyramid Texts*, Utterance 317. See Faulkner, 1969, p. 99.
207 See Erman and Grapow, 1982/1926–1935, 5: 391. This indicates that at least the Egyptians among the ancients saw the sky as blue; *pace* J. P. Brown, 1968, pp. 37–38.
208 There was also a goddess called G3g3wt. It is impossible to tell whether she was a form of Nt.
209 See n. 199 above.
210 See n. 207 above.
211 El Sayed, 1982, p. 262.
212 Plato, *Hippias Major* 290 C; Cicero, 1985–1989, *De natura deorum*, I.30.83.
213 Diodorus, I.12.8; Diodorus Siculus I Books I–II,34; Oldfather, 1968, p. 45.
214 For the uncanniness of blue eyes in Greece, see Chantraine, 1966, pp. 195–196; Maxwell-Stewart, 1981. For opposition to the notion, see Watson-Williams, 1954. I am indebted to R. Drew Griffith for these references.
215 For her veiling, which seems to have indicated both her virginity and the upper blue sky, see Plutarch, *De Iside* . . . , 354.C; Proclus, *In Platonis Timaeum Commentarii*, 30. For the Egyptian theological reality behind their reports. See Hani, 1976, p. 244. See also Assmann, 1997, p. 119, for the possibility that the concept of veiling may have derived from a mistranslation of the term *wp ḥr.*
216 Pausanias, I.14.6.

IV Historiography

1 Marchand and Grafton, 1997, p. 3. They accuse me of not writing history because I fail to consult all the primary and secondary sources. For instance, on these grounds, they condemn my failure to treat all the seventeenth-century debates on Isaac Casaubon's attack on the antiquity of the Hermetic Texts (pp. 3–6). They do not, however, contest my conclusion that the attack had considerably less impact on contemporary scholars than twentieth-century historians, notably Frances Yates, supposed. I based my conclusion on the fact that Athanasius Kircher in the middle of the century and the Cambridge Platonists in its second half still saw the Texts as containing ancient Egyptian material, while fully aware of Casaubon's work. It is interesting to note that Marchand and Grafton do not apply the same insistence on exhaustive research to themselves. They frequently refer to criticisms of my work in BAR without any reference to my responses to them. These were not hard to find as, with one exception, they were all listed in Molly Levine's bibliography of that volume.

7. Accuracy and/or Coherence?
A Reply to Robert Palter, Robert Norton, and Josine Blok

1 Quoted by van Coetsem, 1988, p. xv. I have changed the translation of the Dutch *"terwijl"* from "while" to "when," as it makes for more idiomatic English.

2 Berlin, 1976, p. 146.

3 More recently, it has been brought to my attention that despite Herder's principled cultural relativism in regard to Africans, he shared much of the contempt toward them held by his contemporaries, notably Kant. See Henningsen, 1992, pp. 840–841. For Kant, see n. 32 below.

4 Herm, 1975, p. 118.

5 Lindquist, 1996, p. 10.

6 Rose, 1990, pp. 97–109.

7 Kuhn, 1970, p. 10.

8 Marchand and Grafton (1997, p. 6) cite the classical historian of philosophy Diogenes Laertius as having stated that the Greeks were the first philosophers. He also wrote that Greeks began the human race (1.3) and backed his claims with the vaguest myths. On the other hand, Diogenes' work is full of references to Greek philosophers' having studied in Egypt. It appears to have been for these reasons that later historians discounted his initial statement. Diogenes' motives are discussed by Preus, 1997. See also ch. 16, n. 56 below.

   For an instance of seventeenth-century attitudes, Susan James has pointed out to me that Thomas Stanley in his *History of Philosophy*, the earliest such work in English (published in 1656), was convinced that Greek philosophy came from Egypt and Phoenicia. See his preface and chs. 1, 3, and 4. For the passions for and against Egypt of Stanley's younger contemporary John Spencer, see Assmann, 1997, pp. 55–79.

   Palter does not cite either Diogenes, or the two counterexamples I give (BA I: 216) of the well-known statement in *Epinomis* that the Greeks "make everything finer," or the claim that only Greeks could philosophize, attributed to Epicurus by Clement of Alexandria. Possibly, failure to mention the last was because Palter is aware of Epicurus' interest in denigrating his Stoic rival, the Phoenician Zeno of Kition.

9 In at least one case, the denial of Egyptian *genius* was explicitly linked to racism. Edward Long in his violently racist *History of Jamaica*, published in 1774, insisted on the mediocrity of the Ancient Egyptians in all things (2: 355, 371, and elsewhere). On a trivial issue, Palter is mistaken both in fact and in his reading of my book, when he describes the French scholar J.-J. Barthélemy as an opponent of the Ancient model. I make it clear that even in his last major work, the historical novel *Anacharsis*, Barthélemy still accepted the traditions of colonizations of Greece from Egypt and Phoenicia (BA I: 186–187).

10 Palter denies categorically (p. 365) that Newton's concern with ancient measurements had anything to do with his desire to know the earth's circumference. For my response on this issue, see ch. 10 nn. 28–30 below.

11 Westfall, 1982, p. 30.

12 For further evidence on the centrality of respect for Egypt as the ancestral culture of Europe in seventeenth- and eighteenth-century Britain and Germany, see the excellent assessment in Assmann, 1997, esp. pp. 91–143.

13 The first Aberdonian I referred to was Thomas Blackwell, who taught MacPherson, the creator of Ossian. This northeastern Philhellenic tradition continued in the nineteenth century in the writings of James Mill. See ch. 9 nn. 4–19 below. The title of this article disappeared from M. M. Levine's bibliography when it was published in BAR.

14 Gibbon, 1796/1761, 2: 449–495, 483 (my translation from the original French). He also wrote: "The ancient republics of Greece did not know the first principle of good government. The people assembled in tumult to decide rather than to deliberate. Their factions were furious and undying. . . . The calm administration of laws derived from the cabinet of one or a small council to benefit the whole people only excited the poet to admiration, the coldest of all the passions."

15 Gibbon, 1815, 3: 502.

16 For the defense of slavery, see ibid., 3:503. For the letter, see Gibbon, 1796/1761, 1: 241–242.

17 Blok, 1996, p. 709; 1997, p. 181.

18 Bernal, 1989b, p. 7. There is some confusion over the reference, which Palter refers to as Bernal, 1989d, p. 7.

19 Palter, with characteristic scrupulousness, cites the respectable scholar Paolo Casini as making "a closely related complaint" to mine in his readings of Newton (p. 401 n. 71).

20 For a good treatment of the mistakes that can occur by following the method advocated by the source critics and Palter, see Ahl and Roisman, 1996, esp. pp. 17–23.

21 Thomas Beddoes, "A Memorial concerning the state of the Bodleian Library . . . by the Chemical Reader," cited and quoted by Schaffer, 1975, pp. 29–30.

22 Snowden, 1983, p. 70.

23 For the first racial classification, see Bernier, 1684.

24 Elias, 1978, pp. 3–4. A considerable literature has recently appeared on the rise of the concept of "civilization" and its inextricable ties to the upper classes of Europe. See, for instance, Caffentzis, 1995, pp. 13–36; T. C. Patterson, 1997; Mendelsohn, 1995; and Ambjörnson, 1995. I have comments on the last two in Bernal, 1995b.

25 Pagliaro, 1973, p. ix.

26 "Symposium: Racism in the Eighteenth Century," 1973, pp. 239–243.

27 Popkin, 1973, p. 245.

28 Hume, 1994/1772, p. 86.

29 Palter, 1995. In his eagerness to defend Hume, Palter also tries (p. 7) to excuse Hume's claim that there were no "eminent" Africans by arguing that the best-known of these only became significant in the 1780s. In fact, Hume wrote this after the death of the theologian Jacobus Capitein (1718?–1747) and during the meteoric career of Abraham Petrov Hannibal (1697 [1704?]–1781), who rose to become first personal secretary to Peter the Great, studied mathematics in Paris, and was finally in charge of all military engineering in Russia; he was also a great-grandfather of the poet Alexander Pushkin. See Debrunner, 1979, pp. 80–81, 115–117.

30 There is debate on the question of whether Hume's racism was in accord with his overall philosophy. For the argument that it was, see Bracken, 1973, 1978. Popkin argues that it was not (1992, esp. pp. 72–75). Neither doubts that Hume "was facilitating a racist ideology." I concede that Hume's thinking on race was to some extent consistent with his philosophic system, but I certainly do not agree with Bracken that one should throw the baby out with the bath water and abandon empiricism because of its early close association with racism. Rationalists could be racist too.

31 Grégoire, 1997/1808, p. 15. For this reason, if no other, Grégoire did not mention Hume in his long list of champions of emancipation (pp. xxv–xxvi). For the uses made of Hume's footnote, see Popkin, 1992, p. 75.

32 Kant, "Lectures on Ethics of the Years 1765–66," cited in Eze, 1997/1994, p. 214.

33 Kant, 1831, p. 353, quoted in Eze, 1997/1994, p. 215.

34 Quoted in C. Neugebauer, 1990, p. 264.

35 St. Clair Drake, 1987–1990; Jordan, 1969.

36 The Writings of Benjamin Franklin 6: 222, quoted in Jordan, 1969, p. 282.

37 The Papers of Franklin 4: 225–234, quoted in Jordan, 1969, p. 143. For others who have found it useful to classify Franklin as racist, see Popkin, 1973, p. 245; Takaki, 1993, p. 79.

38 Jordan, 1969, p. 283.

39 For the consensus, see Popkin, 1973, p. 245.

40 For Chiflet's accuracy, see Dumas, 1976, pp. 5, 23, pl. 5. For scarabs in northern France, see Podvin 1988.

41 Blumenbach, 1795, quoted by Curtin, 1964, p. 38.

42 Blumenbach, 1817, pp. 401–402.

43 Palter writes: "It is not true (as Bernal says) that he supposed Caucasians to be 'more talented' either morally or intellectually than other races" (p. 378).

44 See Debrunner, 1979, p. 142.

45 Some modern scholars think that the painting was by Rubens, with whom Van Dyck was collaborating closely around 1620. See Debrunner, 1979, p. 142.

46 Blumenbach, 1787, I, pt. 4, p. 2; 1799, p. 142. Her name, which was not given by Blumenbach, was Pauline Hyppolite Buisson.

47 Blumenbach, 1799, p. 142. The original text says, "the Italian part of Switzerland," but Debrunner is certainly right to alter this to "the French-speaking part of Switzerland."

48 Palter describes this incident on p. 381. Elsewhere, he quotes another of Forster's letters, this time to Herder, which begins: "I also have Mr. Meiners work. It is Göttinge-ish erudition in support an untenable hypothesis." Interestingly, I quote this at the head of my article, "Black Athena Denied: The Tyranny of Germany over Greece" (Bernal, 1986, pp. 3, 54 n. 1). This article too is missing from the final version of the bibliography of BAR.

49 See Coleridge, 1907, 1: 138–141.

50 "... ('solitary') ('Gregarious') Coleridge manuscripts," quoted by Haeger, 1974, p. 335. With his general hostility to materialism, Coleridge differed from Blumenbach in stressing the moral as opposed to the environmental or physical causes for degeneration. In his view, Judeo-Christianity had saved the white races from degeneracy. See Haeger, pp. 340–341.

51 "'The Historic Race,' Coleridge manuscripts," quoted by Haeger, 1974, p. 342. How much of this is Blumenbach and how much Coleridge is difficult to say, but the cumbersome term "Circumstantial Nature" looks more like the German Umwelt than the Romance-English word "environment."

52 Ibid., p. 343.

53 See Haeger, 1974, pp. 343–345.

54 See, for instance, the entry on Blumenbach in the 11th edition of the Encyclopedia Britannica: "He is best known for his work in connection with anthropology, of which science he has been justly called the founder. He was the first to show the value of comparative anatomy in the study of man's history, and his craniometrical researches justified his division of the human race into several great varieties or families."

55 Momigliano, 1982, p. 10.

56 Although I think the Roman proverb overestimated the dependence of Egypt on Mesopotamia, I have no doubt that the two great civilizations influenced each other. I wrote, "After the ... 6th century B.C.E., Egyptian mathematics and astronomy were substantially influenced by Mesopotamian 'scientific thought.'" See ch. 11 n. 57 below. In my response I agree with Palter that the date should be raised to the seventh century (see ch. 10 n. 18).

57 See Bernal, 1988a, p. 100, reprinted below, ch. 9 n. 8. I associate Smith's dislike of Egyptians with his distrust of the state and with the widespread pro-Greek attitude in eastern Scotland. Possibly, Smith's having been stolen by Gypsies as a child was also a factor!

58 Iversen, 1993/1961, pp. 143–144.

59 Lindquist has written a book on the antiracist tradition, and incidentally criticizing my work, but he insists that racism was "the mainstream" (1997, p. 5).

60 See the passage from John Stuart Mill quoted below, ch. 16 nn. 1, 76.

61 See, for instance, the statement by the great abolitionist the Abbé Raynal: "Negro blood is perhaps mingled in all the ferments which transform, corrupt and destroy our people" (quoted in Poliakov, 1974, p. 169).

Abolitionism cannot be explained in purely economic terms, but its success required the support of important political and economic interests. I tend toward the view rejected by Palter and summarized in a hostile manner by Drescher (1977, p. 61) "that abolition was hardly more than a dramatic, quite anomalous interlude in a pattern of general hostility [of whites toward blacks]" (see also Drescher 1992, p. 388). Drescher and his fellow historical revisionists have weakened Eric Williams's claims that the cotton manufacturers opposed slavery as a tool of the sugar planters. On the other hand, they have not damaged Williams's suggestions that proponents of free trade wanted to remove the monopoly of the West Indian planters, and that the East India Company and trading partners, who relied significantly less on chattel slavery, were eager to remove the privileges of their West Indian rivals (E. Williams, 1964/1944, pp. 179–196; 1970, pp. 244–245). Blackburn (1988, p. 26) criticizes Williams for claiming that early capitalism required slavery but later capitalism required its abolition. However, Blackburn himself, in The Making of New World Slavery (1997, p. 572), compromises on the issue of the centrality of New World slavery to the formation of capitalism though he recognized its great importance. In his earlier work, he makes many significant points not made by Marx or Williams, notably the importance of slave resistance. He does not, however, challenge their view that even in the United States, nineteenth-century capitalism tended to prefer the flexibility of wage labor. For further remarks on the East India Company's hostility to West Indian slavery and the positions on this issue of James and John Stuart Mill, see ch. 8 nn. 8–10.

There was also a far smaller number of nonracist advocates of slavery. See Palter, 1995, pp. 8–9.

62 In his "Hume and Prejudice," Palter (1995) chips away at the extent of Hume's anti-Semitism and anti-Catholicism and at Hume's influence on eighteenth-century racism. However, he strengthens the centrality of racism to Hume's thought by quoting the following passage from the latter's essay "Of National Characters" (1994/1772): "There is some reason to think, that all the nations, which live beyond the polar circles or between the tropics, are inferior to the species, and are incapable of all the higher attainments of the human mind" (in E. F. Miller, 1987, p. 207).

63 See Trefousse, 1969, pp. 29–31; Aptheker, 1989, p. 147.

64 Harold Pagliaro has written a very good study of the racism involved in two of the best-known examples of this sentimentality, Dr. Johnson's relationship with his servant Francis Barber and Blake's poem "The Little Black Boy." See Pagliaro, 1973, pp. xv–xviii.

65 See nn. 24–26 above; Popkin, 1973; Faull, 1994; esp. Eze, 1997/1994.

66 Turner, 1989, pp. 108–109.

67 The trend is strikingly revealed in the entry "negro" in successive editions of the *Encyclopedia Britannica*. As mentioned above, these showed some uncertainty about racial equality in the late eighteenth and nineteenth centuries. However, the entry in the 10th edition of 1911 clearly asserted the anatomical and physiological inferiority of "negroes" according to the tenets of "scientific" racism.

68 Turner, 1989, p. 108.

69 Blok, 1996; references are cited in the text. A slightly different and longer version of this section has appeared as Bernal, 1997a.

70 See her belief, mentioned in n.17 above, that I had selected Meiners as the inventor of source criticism in order to link the historical method to the Nazis.

71 See K. O. Müller, 1820, p. 113.

72 For more, see Blok, 1998, p. 81; K. O. Müller, 1848, pp. 523–527.

73 See Momigliano, 1994b, pp. 115–116.

74 Letter by M. H. E. Meier, quoted by Blok, 1998, p. 82.

75 Pfeiffer, 1976, p. 187; Finley, 1980, p. 21.

76 Blok, 1998, pp. 82–85.

77 For Müller's shifting and ambivalent attitudes toward Kantian thought, see Blok, 1998, esp. pp. 89–91.

78 See the essays in Calder and Schlesier, 1998. The blurb on the back of the book calls Müller *einflußreichen* (rich in influence).

79 For the complex direct and indirect relationships between Wolf and Müller, see BA I: 308.

80 Thirlwall, 1835–1844, 1: 63.

81 Marchand and Grafton, 1997, p. 1. For evidence that the *Journal of the History of Ideas*, in which the articles by Blok, Marchuand, and Grafton have appeared, has itself not always been above "politics," see Stonor Saunders, 1999, pp. 333, 338. For the general issue, see Howard Becker's classic article in *Social Problems*, "Whose Side Are We On?" (1967).

82 Edward Gibbon, *The Decline and Fall of the Roman Empire*; William Mitford, *History of Greece*; James Mill, *History of British India*; George Grote, *A History of Greece*; John Motley, *The Rise of the Dutch Republic: A History*; Julius Beloch, *Griechische Geschichte*; Connop Thirlwall, *A History of Greece*; and John Bury, *A History of Greece*.

83 Marchand, 1996, p. 44. She lays similar charges against me and Edward Said in the introduction, p. xxii. Blok thanks Marchand at the beginning of her paper.

84 I go on to refer to his "anti-Semitism," a charge I now withdraw; see above.

85 See Blok, 1998, p. 96 n. 136.

86 An example of this approach can be seen in the criticism made in Marchand and Grafton (see the introduction to part 4, n. 1 above). A minor example of this can be seen in Blok's criticism of my statement that Arnaldo Momigliano had not written on K. O. Müller, whereas in fact he published an article on him while I was writing BA I. Despite this omission, Blok

agrees with my general conclusion reached on the basis of Momigliano's other writings, and states that this "is an excellent example of Momigliano's tendency to stress the rational aspects of his discipline" (1996, p. 720 n.45).

It is interesting to note that although there is considerable intersection between Blok's two papers, the earlier one, "Proof and Persuasion in *Black Athena*," is not cited in her text of 1998. Whatever the editors' intention, this has the effect of keeping my name and that of *Black Athena* out of the whole of Calder and Schlesier, 1998. This, of course, weakens my claim that there is a temporal sequence of ignore, dismiss, attack, absorb.

87 Ch. 3 n. 5.
88 See ch. 1 n. 15; ch. 4 n. 15; ch. 8 n. 32.

8. Passion and Politics: A Reply to Guy Rogers

1 B. Lewis, 1993/1982, p. 99.
2 Bernal, 1995c, p. 3.
3 See ch. 4 n. 16; BA I: 415–433; Bernal, 1992k. See also Bass and Bikai, 1989; Bass, 1997, pp. 77–93; Burkert, 1992/1984, p. ix.
4 A few examples suffice. The leading Indo-Europeanist, Georges Dumézil, was a supporter of the fascist *Action Française*; see Momigliano, 1982, p. 1. Although he was famous as a racist politician, the late Enoch Powell was also recognized as a brilliant and distinguished classicist. For the influence of such political views on their scholarship, see Burkert (1992/1984, p. 34), quoted in ch. 6 nn. 14, 32 and referred to in ch. 13 n. 5.
5 Momigliano, 1994b, p. 20.
6 These are the seventh and eighth printings (12/91) and (4/94); in the ninth printing (7/99), I have returned to the original formulation.
7 Bernal, 1988a. Republished as chapter 9 in this volume.
8 See the epigraph to ch. 16 and n. 76 in that chapter.
9 See ch. 7 n. 61; ch. 16. n. 76.
10 Robson, 1986, p. xxxiv; J. S. Mill, 1986/1823, pp. 25–30. Similarly, James Cropper, the Liverpool businessman and philanthropist and a friend of Wilberforce, agitated against the West Indian slave owners and for the East India Company in this respect. He was the largest importer of East Indian sugar into Liverpool and also traded in American slave-produced cotton (E. Williams, 1964/1944, pp. 186–187; see also Fletcher, 1822). Blackburn (1988, p. 434) describes the shift in the balance of British exports between 1804–1806 and 1824–1826 from the West Indies to Asia, thus increasing the economic clout of the East India Company. See ch. 7 n. 60.
11 Rogers supposes that I have claimed that Thebes was conquered by Egyptians in the second millennium (p. 435). In fact, my discussion refers to the traditions of Phoenician settlement which I link to the Hyksos, not to Egyptians (BA II: 497–504).

12 See ch. 7 n. 71; Marchand, 1996, p. 44; Blok, 1996, p. 718; 1997, p. 199.

13 See, for instance, John Ray in the film *Black Athena* (1991) made by Bandung File for British Channel 4.

14 Stubbings, 1973, pp. 627–658.

15 To take a few examples: J. B. Bury's *History of Greece* (though first published in 1900, it remained in print and respected until the 1970s), makes no reference to influences from Southwest Asia, though he does refer briefly to contact with Egypt. For examples of the "brief, vague and general" references, see M. I. Finley, 1970, pp. 9–11; Hopper, 1976, pp. 7–8; see also Kitto, 1951, pp. 12–28. Kitto's attitude toward the "Orient" is well illustrated by the following passage about Homer's epics (p. 23): "The interesting inaccuracy is that the art and articles which Homer describes are attributed to the Phoenicians. The *fact* that they were of native workmanship is completely forgotten" (my italics). Martin Nilsson wrote: "Traces of Semitic and Babylonian influence upon Minoan-Mycenaean culture are vague and difficult to detect." He then goes on to say that the evident signs of Egyptian influence are deceptive and "the evidence points to the independence and originality of Minoan-Mycenaean religion" (1964, pp. 10–11). The most extreme isolationist text is Colin Renfrew (1972). The topic of Mesopotamian as opposed to Egyptian and Levantine influence on Greece is taken up in detail in ch. 15.

16 Bernal, 1989b, 1993b.

17 See the second to last paragraph in ch. 11 below, and Bernal, 1992a, p. 607.

18 The land route through Anatolia was far more difficult than any sea passage. This fact is strikingly brought out by the passionate cry of *thalatta!* shouted by Xenophon's men when, having crossed the mountains with great difficulty, they saw the sea and their salvation.

19 I also accept Kretchmer's derivation of Hebe, the name of Herakles' wife, from Teššub's divine partner Ḫepât (BA II: 119–120).

20 See Cline, 1991a, pp. 133–144.

21 For a much more penetrating and sometimes painfully perceptive study of my psychology and motivation for starting *Black Athena*, see van Binsbergen, 1997, pp. 16–64. See also Berlinerblau, 1999, pp. 13–15.

22 Momigliano, 1952, reprinted in Bowersock and Cornell, 1994, pp. 15–31. The parallel with my work was also mentioned by Turner, 1989, p. 100.

23 See Humboldt, 1903–1935/1793, 4: 35–56; 1967, pp. 57–71. This is discussed in BA I: 286–287.

24 See Keita, 1990, 1992, 1996b; Keita and Kittles, 1997. David Moore argues in DBA that the continent of Africa contains so many different and distinct populations that the word "African" is so vague as to be almost meaningless, except as a sociopolitical term in the present intensely racist age. For my mild reservations on this, see the entry on "Africa" in this volume's glossary.

25 Bernal, 1989g, p. 31.

26 See ch. 1 nn. 11–14.

27 Hassan, 1988.

28 The Africanist Roger Blench puts the *Urheimat* in the Upper Nile (1993, pp. 130–131). The linguist Christopher Ehret sees it on the Red Sea coast (1996, pp. 25–27). I have suggested the Ethiopian Rift Valley. See Bernal 1980 BA I: map 1.

29 See Bernal, 1992d, 1992h, 1992i.

30 Burkert, 1992/1984, p. ix.

31 Lefkowitz and others still justify this hostility by making vague claims that Gordon and Astour had (unspecified) "methodological problems." See her speech in the debate with me at George Washington University, 1996f.

32 See ch. 1 n. 15; ch. 4 nn. 11–12; Bass and Bikai, 1989, pp. 111–114; Bass, 1997, pp. 75–77.

33 The editors did invite a contribution from the archaeologist Eric Cline, who specializes in relations around the Eastern Mediterranean in the late Bronze Age. However, they then rejected it, telling him that there was no room for it. The piece is short. Mary Lefkowitz told me at the debate in Washington in March 1996 that Cline had sent it in too late. Cline vehemently denied this and Lefkowitz has since apologized to him privately. See Cline 1996; personal communication, 1996. The simplest explanation for the rejection is that although it contains criticisms it is generally favorable to my project. It is included in DBA. The contribution by Sarah Morris would seem to be a partial exception to this exclusion; however, her contribution was deemed satisfactory possibly because of her extreme hostility to any suggestion of Egyptian influence: "The mirage of Egypt has distorted views (both ancient and modern) of the Western relationship with the Near East" (BAR, p. 169).

34 Redford, 1992, pp. 242–243.

35 See Bleiberg, 1984, pp. 155–167.

36 Redford, 1992, pp. 241, 243.

37 Vermeule, 1979, pp. 69–81. See ch. 7 n. 1.

38 Pausanias, X.9. Since then, of course, Greeks have followed a Palestinian religion for two thousand years.

39 Ch. 16 nn. 37–48.

40 Bérard, 1894.

41 Rendsburg, 1989; Ray, 1990. S. Levin and J. P. Brown, who know both Hebrew and Greek take some of my Semitic etymologies very seriously. Levin, 1995, pp. 120, 354, and Brown, 1995, pp. 24, 58, and 2000, pp. 8, 43, 195.

42 See Morris, 1992.

43 Trolle Larsen, 1987, pp. 104–110.

44 The question did not originate with Rogers; it was first posed by Edith Hall (see BAR, p. 335). For my answer, see ch. 5 n. 2.

45 Ch. 5 nn. 10–21; Bernal, 1995f, p. 122.

46 See, for instance, Pausanias IX.12.1, II.19.3.

47 See ch. 7 n. 84.

48 See ch. 3 n. 3.

49 For Cline's position, see his chapter in DBA. For George Bass, see his intervention referred to in n. 32 above.

50 See ch. 7 n. 26. I find the critics' particular dislike of my use of the word "useful"—in a heuristic and not political sense—interesting, because the term derives directly from the all-American philosopher John Dewey, but then he is pretty unpopular with conservatives because of his emphasis on democracy.

51 Poe, 1997, pp. 493–494, 499.

9. The British Utilitarians, Imperialism, and
the Fall of the Ancient Model

1   This chapter is based on an article published in the Danish journal *Culture and History* (Bernal, 1988a), which derived in turn from a paper presented to the conference on "The Canonization of Greece in the Human and Social Sciences" given by the Department of Modern Greek Studies and the Center for Literary Studies, Harvard University, in November 1987. I am indebted to Uday Mehta for having led me to James Mill and for having pointed out the significance of his attitudes for the historiography of ancient Greece.

   The obscurity of the original article is underlined by the fact that none of the five authors of a symposium on Grote, held in 1994, appear to have seen it (Calder and Trzaskoma, 1996). This is particularly remarkable in the case of John Vaio's contribution on "Grote and Mill." Vaio's reference to me (p. 64) is based on impressions of *Black Athena*.

2   J. S. Mill, 1924, p. 2.

3   Mazlish, 1975, p. 1.

4   J. S. Mill, 1924, p. 4.

5   The Scottish parliament established schools in every parish in the seventeenth century more than 200 years before there was universal education in England.

6   J. Mill, 1809b, p. 188.

7   Bain, 1882, p. 7.

8   Smith, 1795, pp. 26–27. Smith's distaste for the Egyptians and other dark peoples may have started with direct or related memories of his kidnapping by Gypsies at the age of three.

9   Duff, 1976/1767, pp. 27–29.

10 Stephen, 1900, 2: 12–13.

11 Bain, 1882, p. 15.

12 Ibid., pp. 18–19.

13 Pappé, 1979, pp. 296.

14 T. Taylor, 1969/1801, pp. 105–113.

15 Ibid., 1801, pp. 113–117; Raine, 1969, pp. 15–17.

16 Quoted in Raine and Harper, 1969, p. 139.

17 de Santillana, 1963, p. 819.

18 Harper, 1969, pp. 49–104.

19 J. Mill, 1804, 1809b.

20 Raine, 1969, pp. 29–43.

21 Fenn, 1987, pp. 7–15.

22 Glenn, 1983, pp. 339–347; Harper, 1961.

23 Quoted in Raine and Harper, 1969, p. 137.

24 Pappé, 1979, pp. 297–307.

25 J. Mill, 1809b, p. 193.

26 Ibid., pp. 202–207.

27 J. Mill, 1804, pp. 580–590, 1809b, pp. 202–209.

28 Taylor, 1969/1798, p. 111.

29 Sandys, 1908, 3: 82–83; BA I: 348.

30 J. Mill, 1809b, pp. 199–200.

31 Pappé, 1979, pp. 296–297.

32 J. Mill, 1809b, p. 200.

33 J. Mill, 1804, p. 453.

34 Sandys, 1908, 3:82.

35 J. Mill, 1809b, p. 200.

36 For much more on this, see DBA.

37 Bain, 1882, p. 61.

38 J. Mill, 1840, p. xi.

39 "Review of William Tennant's *Indian Recreations*," 1804, p. 327.

40 Ibid., p. 333; J. Mill, 1840, p. xi.

41 "Review," 1804, p. 330.

42 See Bain, 1882, p. 62. For the land nationalist Spence, see Bernal, 1976,
    p. 42.

43 J. Mill, 1840, p. xiv.

44 See ch. 3 nn. 6, 7; ch. 7 nn. 17–18.

45 See ch 3; BA I: 216–219.

46 J. Mill, 1840, p. xviii.

47 Ibid., p. xxi.

48 Ibid., pp. xix–xx.

49 Ibid., p. xxiv. It is interesting that Mill cited as an exemplar of a "critical"
    historian whose views had not been confused by visiting the country of his
    study his fellow Scot, William Robertson, who in his 1777 *History of America*,
    denounced the descriptions by Bernal Diaz and other sixteenth-century
    Spaniards of Mexican stone buildings and pyramids, claiming that, in fact,
    they had only been earthen mounds!

50 J. Mill, 1840, 2: 162–210. For a thorough refutation of these views, see
    Goonatilake, 1999.

51 J. Mill, 1809a, p. 413.

52 J. Mill, 1840, 2: 210–211.

53 Ibid., 2: 213.

54 Ibid., 2: 217–224. For the earlier views, see BA I: 237–238; Blue, 1999, pp. 70–78.
55 J. Mill, 1809a, p. 413.
56 J. Mill, 1840, 2: 217–254.
57 Ibid., 2: 157.
58 W. Jones, 1807, pp. 12–13.
59 J. Mill, 1840, 2: 161. The footnote was based on the work of William Robertson, mentioned in n. 49 above. For Robertson's views on Meso-american civilizations that would be considered absurd today, see Poe, 1997, p. 51.
60 J. Mill, 1840, p. 156.
61 Stephen, 1900, p. 24. See also Bain, 1882, pp. 184–185.
62 This wonderful example of a subversive footnote comes under J. Mill, 1840, pp. viii–ix.
63 For the strenuous opposition, see J. S. Mill, 1924, p. 169.
64 J. Mill, 1840, 2: 232.
65 Niebuhr, 1852, 1: 98–99.
66 J. Mill, 1840, 2: 228.
67 Ibid.
68 M. L. Clarke, 1962, pp. 16–19.
69 Ibid., p. 20.
70 Ibid., p. 33.
71 H. L. Grote, 1873, p. 20.
72 M. L. Clarke, 1962, p. 105.
73 Momigliano, 1994a/1966, pp. 60–61; Turner, 1981, pp. 205–234. For the alleged differences between me and Momigliano on the interpretation of Mitford, see ch. 7 nn. 35–36.
74 G. Grote, 1826, pp. 330–331.
75 See also Vaio, 1996, p. 64.
76 G. Grote, 1826, pp. 271–282.
77 M. L. Clarke, 1962, pp. 104–106.
78 Momigliano, 1952, pp. 10–11, 1994a/1966, pp. 62–63.
79 Momigliano, 1982, p. 7.
80 Momigliano, 1994a/1966, p. 63.
81 G. Grote, 1846–1856, 1: vii.
82 See BA I: 308–316. See also Blok, 1996, 1997, and my response ch. 7 n. 85 above.
83 For Wilde's use of "e(a)rnest" in its slang meaning of homosexual, see Annan, 1990, p. 143.
84 M. L. Clarke, 1962, pp. 105–106.
85 See n. 82 above.
86 Thirlwall, 1834–1844, 1: 63. This passage is also discussed in ch. 7 n. 80 above.
87 G. Grote, 1843, p. 302.
88 Momigliano, 1994a/1966, p. 63.

89 K. O. Müller, 1825, p. 59, 1844, p. 1. Turner (1981, p. 87) writes that Grote drew on Müller to sever the connection between myth and history.

90 K. O. Müller, 1825, pp. 249–251; 1844, pp. 189–190; G. Grote 1846–1856, 2: 157–159, 182–204.

91 K. O. Müller, 1825, p. 108; 1844, p. 49; G. Grote 1846–1856, 2: 157–159, 182–204.

92 Momigliano, 1994a/1966, pp. 56–74; Turner, 1981, pp. 90–91.

93 Momigliano, 1994a/1966, p. 6; Turner, 1981, pp. 87–88.

94 G. Grote, 1846–1856, 1: 440.

95 Momigliano, 1994a/1966, pp. 63–64.

96 Edwards, 1979, p. 132; Porada, 1981; Farag, 1980, pp. 75–81.

97 Momigliano, 1994a/1966, p. 62.

98 M. L. Clarke, 1962, pp. 62–63.

99 Momigliano, 1994a/1966, p. 61.

100 Fenn, 1987, pp. 47–55.

101 M. L. Clarke, 1962, pp. 125–128; Momigliano 1994a/1966, pp. 64–67.

10. Was There a Greek Scientific Miracle? A Reply to Robert Palter

1 Palter, 1993, reprinted in BAR, 1996, pp. 209–266.

2 This article, Bernal, 1992a, is reprinted with revisions as ch. 11 below. See 1992a, p. 596.

3 Herodotus, III:130.3.

4 For my statement, see Bernal, 1992a, p. 599, and ch. 11 nn. 3–7.

5 For an extended discussion of what I mean by Afrocentrist, see ch. 16.

6 See Luft, 1987, pp. 3–11; Leitz, 1989, pp. 1–5; Krauss, 1990, pp. 55–56.

7 To illustrate the importance of social factors, Palter (p. 214) follows Hetherington (1987, p. 22) in speculating that astronomy developed in Mesopotamia and not in Egypt because the uncertainty of life in the former encouraged astrology. The idea is interesting, but not convincing. It is undoubtedly true that the anxieties of Mesopotamian rulers played an important role in the development of astrology and astronomy; I would argue further that Egyptian pharaohs had similar concerns. Egyptians of the New and possibly of the Middle Kingdom also had complicated calendars of good and bad days controlled by particular gods and goddesses, linked at least indirectly through the calendar to astronomy and astrology. See Spalinger, 1991. The idea of a divinity of the day is also found in the earliest uses of the Greek ἦμαρ; see Onians, 1988/1951, pp. 411–415. An Egyptian derivation for this concept is suggested by a plausible etymon for ἦμαρ in the attested Egyptian term ỉmy ḥrw.f ("who is on duty for the day").

8 Bernal, 1992a, pp. 600–602; ch 11, nn. 22–26; Palter, pp. 214–216. The intention of my reference to Neugebauer's "early passion for Egypt" was

to indicate that it predated his interest in Mesopotamia, not that his sympathy toward it changed later.

9   See ch. 11, n. 36.

10 Personal communication, M. Alexiou, Harvard University, November 1987.

11 Bernal, 1992a, p. 599.

12 Ch. 11 n. 34.

13 J. H. Williams, 1996, pp. 43–44.

14 Vercoutter, 1963, pp. 35–37; Heath, 1932; Hartner, 1963, pp. 868–876.

15 Kozloff and Bryan, 1992, pp. 336–338.

16 With typical scrupulousness, Palter himself points out (p. 213) that not all modern historians agree with Neugebauer's dismal assessment of Egyptian astronomical observations. He cites Kurt Locher's description of a "high level of observational astronomy" in Egypt in the twenty-first century B.C.E. (1983, p. 141). The historian of Egyptian mathematics and science Anthony Spalinger is also convinced that Neugebauer's views of ancient Egyptian scientific capacities were sometimes much too harsh (personal communication, March 1992).

17 Bernal, 1992a, pp. 606–607, ch. 11, n. 58.

18 Heath, 1981/1921, pp. 137–138.

19 Turner (1989, p. 100) makes this point very clearly.

20 Bernal, 1992a, p. 606, ch. 11, n. 58.

21 See Bickerman, 1980, pp. 38–39.

22 G. Murray, 1934, pp. 210–212. Murray pointed out that the nineteen years of Odysseus' voyage ended precisely at the Feast of Apollo at the winter solstice. The Metonic Cycle was named for Metôn, the Athenian astronomer of the fifth century B.C.E. The cycle brings the lunar months into synchronism with the solar year after nineteen years.

23 Lauer, 1960, pp. 1–2.

24 I am grateful for this idea, which was suggested to me by the learned Henry Mendell. In a letter to me (4 May 1990) he wrote: "So it seems that Greek mathematics is profoundly more sophisticated than our papyrological evidence. Given that the total of Egyptian papyri is less than a dozen from a much broader period, it might seem reasonable to suppose mathematics was more sophisticated than it appears." He then went on to make "three counter points": (1) that the paucity of Egyptian mathematical papyri might not be completely accidental; (2) that there is no evidence of qualitative Euclidian Egyptian mathematics; and (3) that there is no reason to suppose that that the Democratean work on pyramids and cones is likely to have come from Egypt. I accept the possibility of 1 and 3 and I have never claimed 2.

25 For the frequency of Homeric papyri, see M. I. Finley, 1978, p. 21.

26 Stillman Drake, 1957.

27 Stillman Drake, 1965.

28 Westfall, 1993, pp. 51–52.
29 McGuire and Rattansi, 1966; B. J. T. Dobbs, 1975; see also ch. 7 n. 10.
30 B. J. T. Dobbs, 1991, pp. 193–212. Palter does not accept Dobbs on this: "My critique of Bernal does not depend on the validity of . . . Dobbs' interpretation" (p. 226).
31 Gillings, 1982/1972, p. 228. For more on this see the chapters by Lumpkin and Pappademos, DBA.
32 Reisner, 1931, pp. 76–77; cited by Lumpkin, DBA.
33 In his n. 44 (p. 261), Palter dismisses the views of two extremely knowledgeable and very skeptical specialists on Egyptian science, Gay Robins and Charles Shute (1987, pp. 44–45). They argue that the circle area formula was derived from the Pythagoras theorem, which, on axiomatic grounds, Palter believes the "Egyptians almost certainly did not know."
34 Bernal, 1992a, p. 605, ch. 11, n. 50.
35 For collections of references on Egyptian science, mathematics, and geometry and their transmission to Greece by Plato and Aristotle, see Froidefond, 1971, pp. 309–323, 350–353.
36 Ibid., pp. 268–269.
37 Plato, Phaedrus, 274d, and elsewhere.
38 Heath, 1981/1921, p. 322, n. 21.
39 Isokrates, 1928–1944, Busiris, 22; Froidefond, 1971, p. 239.
40 For my view of Burkert's work, see ch. 13.
41 Burkert, 1983, p. 52.
42 See Bass, Pulak, Collon, and Weinstein, 1989, pp. 10–11.
43 For a survey of modern views on the subject, see Bernal 1990a, pp. 7–26. For more on Burkert's arguments, see Bernal, 1996g, reprinted as ch. 13 below.
44 Lumpkin, 1980; Robins and Shute, 1985, p. 112.
45 Robins and Shute, 1987, p. 44.
46 The circularity of this argument is evident from the "therefore." Though I see no reason to doubt Palter here, his reference to Gillings (1982, p. 690) is wrong as Gillings's 1982 has only 286 pages. He seems to be referring to Gillings, 1978, p. 696.
47 Tomb 3, published in Schliemann, 1878, pp. 196–198. See BA II: 262–263.
48 See ch. 15 n. 85.
49 Robins and Shute, 1985, p. 112.
50 Palter's appendix (1994, pp. 466–468) shows that the numbers 5, 55, and 555 all appear in plans for the construction of the Washington Monument and that "the alleged ancient Egyptian proportion of ten to one for the ratio of height to base" was followed. He asks in conclusion whether I really believe that "the group of army officers, diplomats, and politicians involved in the construction of the Washington Monument over a period of forty years was engaged in some sort of Masonic conspiracy." "Conspiracy" is not the word I should choose, and neither Palter nor I know

how many Freemasons were involved. However, I remain convinced that all of the planners were directly or indirectly influenced by the masonic image of ancient Egypt in making their decisions.

51 See Robins and Shute, 1987, p. 58.

52 For a discussion and bibliography on this, see W. Davis, 1989, pp. 48–50.

53 For Plato and Egyptian art, see W. Davis, 1979, pp. 121–127. For Plato and Egyptian philosophy, see Preus, 1992–1993, pp. 9–11. For Plato and Egyptian politics, see BA I: 105–108; Stephens, 1993. Relying on the essay by Markowsky (1992), Palter (p. 244) plays down the significance of the "golden section" even in the Renaissance. To do this, he joins the Young Turks who attack the plausible conventional wisdom as set out in Panofsky (1955). Panofsky claimed that architecture and painting were significantly influenced by this measurement.

54 For the first three, see the bibliographical n. 15 in Bernal 1992a ch. 11 n. 22, to which Palter adds Ghalioungui (1968). In a later work, Thierry Bardinet states that "some passages in the Carlsberg and Kahun papyri even would appear almost word for word in the Hippocratic corpus." However, writing when the subject has become extremely contentious, Bardinet reasserts his orthodoxy and continues: "We shall see that if the transmission is undeniable, the correspondence with the Egyptian texts is not always as exact as one might believe at least for the basic ideas" (1995, p. 19). See also Iversen, 1939, 1953. For Sigerist, see 1967/1951, pp. 357–358. See also Westendorf, 1992, pp. 10, 14–18, 129.

Palter pays special attention to the liver, arguing plausibly (p. 246) that this was first described anatomically in Hellenistic times. He suggests that earlier Greek interest in the organ derived from the practice of hepatoscopy: "Unlike the Mesopotamians, Etruscans and Romans, the Egyptians did not practice hepatoscopy (divination through examination of the livers of animals)" (p. 264 n. 70). In fact, in stark contrast to the Etruscans, there is no evidence of hepatoscopy among the Greeks before Hellenistic times. The earliest reference to it comes in the Septuagint! This omission provides yet another Greek cultic parallel with the Egyptians and difference from the Mesopotamians.

55 von Staden, 1992, pp. 587–588.

56 Ibid., pp. 589–593.

57 I am convinced by Joseph Needham's arguments on this (1972, pp. 41–54). For an excellent general survey of "civilizational" and "conjunctural" explanations for the rise of capitalism and modern science, see Wallerstein, 1999, pp. 34–56.

58 von Staden, 1992, pp. 581–582.

59 Palter's strange conviction (p. 259 n. 31) that Greek and Egyptian cultures coexisted in Ptolemaic, Roman, and Byzantine Egypt but "did not coalesce or blend" leads him to quote with approval a long statement by N. Lewis including the claim that, "except for some local designations of places, measures, and so on, no native Egyptian word made its way into Greek

usage" (1986, pp. 154–155). This is ludicrous; even Jasanoff and Nussbaum admit that there were some (p. 188). A survey of Chantraine would
show that there were many more.

60 von Staden, 1992, p. 584. Without our being aware of each other's papers,
I made the same general point in my contribution to the symposium.
See Bernal, 1992a, p. 597, and ch. 11. Palter quotes with approval Guido
Majno's statement that Egyptian medical texts are limited and "read on the
whole like catalogs" (1975, p. 247) without mentioning the very similar
aphoristic nature of the Hippocratic corpus.

61 Bernal, 1992a, p. 598, ch. 11, nn. 8–11. I had missed an even better example of an Egyptian dialectic in the "philosophical" debate between the
scribe Any and his son Khonshotep in the epilogue to "The Instructions
of Any," translated in Lichtheim, 1975–1980, 2: 144–145.

62 For pros and cons on this, see Bernal, 1993b, p. 257 nn. 78, 79. See also
Rendsburg, 1989, pp. 78–79, who suggests a Semitic etymology for $\mu\alpha\kappa\acute{\alpha}$-
$\rho\iota o\varsigma$ but accepts the derivation of the Greek $\mu\acute{\alpha}\rho\tau\upsilon\rho o\varsigma$ from the Egyptian mtrw.

63 See ch. 7 n. 37; ch. 13 n. 6.

11. Animadversions on the Origins of Western Science

1   I could not have begun, let alone completed, the paper on which this chapter is based without many years of patient help and encouragement from
Jamil Ragep, who, it should be pointed out, is far from accepting all my
conclusions.

2   For Pingree, see 1990, p. 2. For Clagett and Lloyd, see G. E. R. Lloyd, 1970,
p. 1; Clagett, 1962, p. 15. The quotation is from Lloyd.

3   O. Neugebauer, 1969; M. L. West, 1971; pace John Vallance, 1990, p. 715.
See also Kirk, 1960, pp. 327–328; 1961, pp. 105–106.

4   G. E. R. Lloyd, 1970, p. 8. Vallance, 1990, holds the same opinions.

5   O. Neugebauer, 1969, pp. 29–52; Ghalioungui, 1973, 1983.

6   Dodds, 1951; G. E. R. Lloyd, 1979, pp. 10–58, 263–264; Fowden, 1986,
pp. 81–82; von Staden, 1992, p. 584. See also ch. 10 n. 60.

7   Saunders, 1963, p. 12.

8   For Gilgamesh and Agga, see the translation from the Sumerian by S. N.
Kramer in J. B. Pritchard, 1969, pp. 44–47. For The Dispute between a Man
and his Ba, see Lichtheim, 1975–1980, 1: 163–169.

9   See Budge, 1904, 1: 282–287; Clagett, 1989, vol. 1, pt. 2, pp. 263–372.

10 For the sophistication of oratory and rhetoric in Ancient China, see Lu,
1998.

11 Lichtheim, 1975–1980, p. 169.

12 Bernal, 1993b, reprinted in this volume as ch. 15.

13 Aristotle, Politics, 7.10, in Barker, 1958, p. 304.

14 Théodoridès, 1971, pp. 291–313; Burton, 1972, pp. 219–225.

15 Needham et al., 1954–1994, 2: 518–583.

16 For this etymology, see ch. 15 n. 97. Clagett (1989, pp. xi–xii) subtitles his first volume *Knowledge and Order.* These are translations of the Egyptian r̲ẖt and m3ꜥt, which he sees as the Egyptian "rudimentary" science.

17 See the constant references to balances and plumb lines as symbols of justice in *The Eloquent Peasant,* in Lichtheim, 1975–1980, 1: 170–182.

18 For the triples, see the bibliography in Schmidt, 1980, p. 13.

19 Gillings, 1982/1972, pp. 142–143; Robins and Shute, 1987, pp. 44–46.

20 For a list of these, see Gillings, 1982/1972, appendix 5.

21 Robins and Shute, 1985, p. 112; Lumpkin, 1980. See ch. 10 n. 44.

22 I use the word "possible" here because it has been suggested that axiomatic geometry was first practiced in Greece by Eudoxos, who had studied in Egypt. As G. S. Huxley put it, "The 'Euclidean' presentation of axioms and propositions may well have been systematized by him [Eudoxos]." (1970, p. 466)

23 See Ghalioungui, 1973, 1983; Saunders, 1963; Steuer and Saunders, 1959. Pace J. A. Wilson, 1962, 1964a; G. E. R. Lloyd, 1983, p. 13n.

Even von Staden in his skeptical phase, when he was very reluctant to concede Egyptian influences on Hellenistic medicine, admits that study of pulses and their timing by water clocks, for which his subject Herophilus of Alexandria was famous, probably came from Egyptian tradition (1989, p. 10).

24 For his early passion for Egypt, see Shore, 1979, p. 16.

25 For more on the golden section, see ch. 10 nn. 52–53.

26 O. Neugebauer, 1969, p. 78.

27 Ibid., p. 96.

28 Lauer, 1960, p. 11.

29 Ibid., pp. 10, 4–24. The translations here are my own unless otherwise indicated.

30 See Sarton, 1936, pp. 429–430; Pappademos, in DBA.

31 Lauer, 1960, pp. 1–3. For a more skeptical view of this, see Robins and Shute, 1985, p. 109.

32 Robins and Shute, 1987, p. 58.

33 Lauer, 1960, p. 10.

34 O. Neugebauer, 1969, p. 91.

35 O. Neugebauer, 1983b/1980, p. 2; 1983a, p. 212. For the implausibility, see ch. 10 n. 13.

36 O. Neugebauer, 1969, p. 92.

37 Struve, 1930; Gillings, 1982/1972; Robins and Shute, 1987; Lumpkin, in DBA; Pappademos, in DBA.

38 For their Egyptian origins, see Pappademos, in DBA.

39 Robins and Shute, 1987, pp. 42–43, 56.

40 Struve, 1930, p. 184.

41 Ibid., pp. 174–176; Gillings, 1982/1972, pp. 187–194; Robins and Shute, 1987, p. 48.

42 Ver Eecke, 1960, p. xxxi.

43 de Santillana, 1962, p. 814.

44 Gillings, 1982/1972, p. 200.

45 Struve, 1930, p. 185; my translation from the German.

46 Ibid., p. 183; my translation from the German.

47 Gillings, 1982/1972, pp. 194–201.

48 O. Neugebauer, 1969, p. 29.

49 Robins and Shute, 1987, p. 58.

50 This point, along with many others, was made by Henry Mendell, personal communication, 5 Apr. 1990.

51 See Herodotus, II: 109; Diodorus Siculus I: 69.5, 81.3, 94.3; Aristotle, *Metaphysics* I: 1(981b); Hero, *Geometria* II; Strabo, 16: 2, 24, 17: 1, 3; Clement of Alexandria, 1869, *Stromateis*, I: 74.2. See also Diop, 1991/1981, pp. 257–258.

52 Struve, 1930, pp. 163–165.

53 Donadoni, 1982, cols. 1058–1060. See also Kemp, 1989, p. 106.

54 de Santillana, 1962, p. 814.

55 See n. 37 above.

56 Pingree, 1990, p. 7.

57 See the bibliographies in W. Davis, 1979, p. 122 n. 3; Preus, 1992–1993, p. 9.

58 A clear example can be seen in the fragment discussed by O. Neugebauer in his exquisite swan song: "A Babylonian Lunar Ephemeris from Roman Egypt" (1988).

VI Recent Broadening Scholarship

1 Burkert, 1992, p. ix.

2 West, 1997, p. x.

3 Ibid., p. vii.

12. Greek Art Without Egypt, *Hamlet* Without the Prince:
A Review of Sarah Morris's *Daidalos and the Origins of Greek Art*

An earlier version of this appeared as Bernal, 1995f. References to Morris, 1992, are cited in the text.

1 Burkert, 1992/1984.

2 See Poulsen, 1912.

3 For arguments against this, see Bernal, 1990a, esp. pp. 126–127.

4 Plutarch, *Theseus*, 19.

5 Dombrowski, 1984. For more on this, see ch. 6 nn. 100–107.

6 Bernal, 1985, p. 76; Rendsburg 1989, p. 75.

7 See Bérard, 1927, 1: 207. Strictly speaking, Skandeia is an Egypto-Greek

name, as the Greek word can be plausibly derived from the Egyptian *shmty* ("double crown of Egypt"); see *BA* I: 501 n. 37.

8 See, for example, the standard works of Harden, 1963, pp. 53–54, and Massa, 1977, pp. 47–48.

9 Katzenstein, 1973, pp. 323–324.

10 Carpenter, 1933, p. 18; Starr, 1977, p. 26.

11 See Burkert, 1992/1984, p. 4.

12 Carpenter, 1933, p. 18. For the degree to which the Assyrians were viewed as only partially Semitic, see Bernal, 1990a, p. 10.

13 Diodorus Siculus, 1935, I.97.6.

14 Pausanias, II.4.5.

15 Quoted in *BA* I: 187.

16 *BA* I: 195–196; Plato, *Menexenus*, 245.D. These sentiments are reported sarcastically as part of Plato's attack on Perikles' Athenian chauvinism.

17 See ch. 15.

18 Starr (1977, p. 28) points out it was used by the poet Archilochus in that century.

19 Aristotle, *Athenion Politeia*, 23.

20 See Théodorides, 1971, p. 319.

21 For the Attic young woman, Phye, see Herodotus I: 60. For his descriptions of the Libyan worship of Athena, see IV: 188.

22 For Amasis' presents to Greek temples of Athena at Lindos and Hera at Samos, see Herodotus II: 182.

23 For the Libyan origin of the Greek quadriga, see Herodotus IV: 188.

24 Diodorus Siculus, 1935, I:93.

25 Guralnick, 1973, 1978, 1981, 1997.

26 Morris cites the work of R. M. Cook (1967), who wrote before Guralnick published her computer studies of proportions. Two of Morris's other sources were writing about Cypriot, not Greek, sculpture. Cyprus remained under considerable Levantine influence in the seventh and sixth centuries B.C.E., and the same naturally applies to Punic Sicily, on which she also cites work. Thus, for Greece itself, she is left only with the forthcoming work *The Beginning of Greek Sculpture* by Jane Carter.

27 Guralnick, 1973, 1978, 1981, 1997.

28 W. Robertson, 1977, 1: 41–44; Boardman, 1978, pp. 18–24. Stephanie Böhm has shown that the figures of the "naked goddess," whose origin is clearly Levantine, were widespread in Greece in the late eighth and most of the seventh centuries B.C.E. However, she has also demonstrated that this orientalizing theme par excellence disappeared without trace in the last quarter of the seventh century (1990, p. 143 and elsewhere).

29 Walcot, 1966, pp. 65–72. See also ch. 14 nn. 52–53.

30 See Johansen and Whittle, 1980, pp. 71–72. For more on this, see ch. 15 nn.84–87; *BA* II: 262–263.

31 *Odyssey*, XIV: 279–282; Herodotus, II: 160; and Aristotle, *Politics*, 1329b. See also ch. 11 n.13; ch.15 nn. 105–136.

32 Herodotus, 1974, III: 37, trans. de Selincourt, 1974, p. 219.
33 See C. H. Gordon, 1965, pp. 421, 425.
34 For a discussion of this, see Watrous, 1992, pp. 172–173. See also Cline, 1987, 1990.
35 See Derchain, 1962.
36 For the limbs, see, for instance, Iversen, 1984, pp. 59–60. For the "Memphite Theology," see Lichtheim, 1975–1980, pp. 51–57. For the creative power of speech in Egyptian thought, see Karenga, 1994, pp. 334–352.
37 A. H. Gardiner, 1957, p. 540.
38 See, for instance, *taibe* from *ḏbȝt* ("chest, coffin"); *tēēbe* from *ḏbʿ* ("finger"); *tōōre* from *ḏrt* ("hand"); and many others.
39 See the LXX form σισόη ("roll of hair") from the Egyptian "of the head" (ḏȝḏȝy) and the Coptic ϫⲱϫⲱⲓ.
40 Ch. 6 nn. 93–95.
41 Lesko, 1982–1990, 4: 151–152.
42 Crum 439b in Cerny (1976) lists it among Coptic words without etymologies. Vycichl 1983 does not mention it. Nevertheless, an origin from ḏ3ḏ3 is very plausible.
43 Erman and Grapow, 1982/1926–1935, 5: 532.
44 *Illiad*, 9.187.
45 Herodotus II: 147; Diodoros Siculus, 1935, 1: 96.

13. One or Several Revolutions?
A Review of Walter Burkert's *The Orientalizing Revolution*

This chapter first appeared as Bernal 1996g. References to Burkert (1992/1984) are cited in the text.
1 See, for instance, O. Murray, 1993, p. 326.
2 I use the word "Oriental" because it is central to Burkert's work and thinking. I have placed the word in quotation marks because it is not a word that I would employ myself.
3 See Bernal, 1993a, and 1993b, and ch. 15 below.
4 See ch. 15 nn. 9–27, 44.
5 The full quotation is given and discussed in ch. 6 nn. 14, 32.
6 For a discussion of this, see ch. 6 nn. 32–33.
7 See Johnston, 1990, p. 426. For a recent higher dating to the eleventh or tenth centuries, see Lloyd-Jones, 1992, p. 56.
8 Isserlin, 1983.
9 See McCarter, 1975, p. 126.
10 See De Hoz, 1983; Cross, 1979.
11 See Stieglitz, 1971, 1981; Bernal, 1987b, 1990a, pp. 8–. For the earlier views, see Bernal, 1990a, p. 7; McCarter, 1975, p. 7.
12 Bérard, 1894.
13 See J. W. Shaw, 1977, 1979, 1980, 1981, 1982, 1984, 1986.

14 See ch. 12 nn. 2–3.

15 See ch. 14 n. 40.

16 Redford, 1992, pp. 242–243. For the archaeological evidence of these contacts, see Cline, 1987, 1994.

17 For the artistic influences, see Guralnick, 1973, 1978, 1981, 1997.

18 See ch. 14 n. 30.

19 See ch. 6.

20 My admiration for Burkert's work was not immediately reciprocated, as he wrote in one article, "Bernal's scandalous book is completely lamentable" (1991, p. 172). Personal contacts since then suggest that he is less hostile today.

14. There's a Mountain in the Way:
A Review of Martin West's *The East Face of Helicon*

References to M. L. West (1998) are cited in the text.

1 West's work on Mesopotamian literature has been greatly aided by *Before the Muses* (1993), a massive and wonderful anthology of Akkadian literature compiled and translated by Benjamin R. Foster.

2 For bibliographies, see M. L. West, 1997, p. 279 n. 5; Penglase, 1994, p. 2.

3 For a bibliography, see M. L. West, 1997, p. 307 n. 87.

4 West does not consider the strong possibility that the name "Achilles" Akhil(l)eus/lêos may itself be Semitic. Aḫi ("my brother is" is one of the most common Canaanite initial segments of personal names. The -leus/lêos is less clear, but the hero's many leonine characteristics suggest that this element is related to *leôn* (lion). Achilles' father was named Peleus, a name that could well come from Late Egyptian *P3rw* ("the lion"). The Greek *leôn* almost certainly derives from the Egyptian *rw*. West also fails to mention the fact that Herakles, the hero par excellence in Greek mythology, also had a sidekick or minion, Abderos. This name is clearly Semitic Abd- ("slave or servant" of) -heros (i.e., the hero Herakles).

5 See C. H. Gordon, 1962a, pp. 20, 68, 74–75, 87, 223; Astour, 1967, p. 212. See also the bibliography on the topic in Santo Mazzarino, 1989/1947, p. 24. More recently, classicists have developed the idea; see E. Cook, 1992; Alford, 1992.

6 His arguments could have been further strengthened by references to Westbrook's fascinating and sound work on legal parallels between Mesopotamia and early Greece. See, for instance, "The Trial Scene in the *Iliad*," 1992.

7 For a recent summary of those in Gordon, see C. H. Gordon and Rendsburg, 1997, pp. 95–108.

8 Redford, 1992, pp. 242–243.

9 See ch. 6 n. 49.

10 See also Lewy, 1895, p. 172. Given Masson's (1967, pp. 101–107) ex-

treme minimalism it is not surprising that she should have disregarded Albright's plausible explanation.

11 Ventris and Chadwick, 1973, p. 50.

12 Burkert, 1983, p. 52. See above ch. 10 nn. 41–42.

13 Jeffery, 1982, p. 823 n. 8. Sadly, though not surprisingly, younger epigraphists of Greek have not followed Jeffery's advice. See, for instance, the failure to confront Naveh's arguments in Powell (1991) and Woodard (1997).

14 Naveh, 1973.

15 Bernal, 1990a, pp. 23–26.

16 Ibid., pp. 89–122.

17 For an example of classicists who do take these arguments seriously, see Ahl and Roisman, 1996, p. 4.

18 West also makes good use of the excellent and meticulous comparative work of John Pairman Brown.

19 For Job, see M. H. Pope, 1965, pp. xxxii–xl. See also Hurvitz, 1968, who explains the alleged Aramaisms used to downdate Job as coming from much earlier Israelian or other northern influences. I am grateful to Chen Yiyi for this reference. For Ecclesiastes, see R. B. Y. Scott, 1965, p. 198. Albright dated the latter book on stylistic grounds to around 500 B.C.E. (1978/1968, p. 226).

20 The same pattern of Burkert's complete failure to mention this type of scholarship and West's cautious references to details and apparent reluctance to discuss the general arguments can be seen in their treatment or lack of treatment of *Black Athena*.

21 Bérard, 1894; 1902–1903.

22 Astour, 1967, pp. 311–312.

23 Ibid., pp. 152–155.

24 West does not appear to be aware of C. H. Gordon's (1978) latest translations of Ugaritic literature.

25 Hoch (1994, p. 324 n. 45) maintains that it is from *kinnor*. I believe that it was at least contaminated by Kothar or Kuthar, the West Semitic god of the smithy and probably, like his late Egyptian counterpart Bes, also a god of music and merriment.

26 For a discussion of the rendering of Semitic *ṣade* and *zayin* by a Greek *psi*, see Bernal, 1990a, p. 119.

27 Gesenius's (1953) dictionary suggests that the inversion is because of idolatrous association of Ḥeres, possibly connected with an Egyptian word *hirati* for "sun." I cannot identify this, unless Heres is merely a form of Ḥr, Horus. This does not affect the West Semitic word *timnah* ("sacred precinct").

28 My own belief is that both the Hebrew and the Greek words derive from a regular but unattested Egyptian form, *r-ski* ("place for passing time").

29 Bernal, 1987a, pp. 445–450. For the common opinion, see, for instance, Dothan and Dothan, 1992.

30 Astour, 1967, p. 155; Bernal, 1991b, p. 629 n. 20. See ch. 13 n. 18.

31 Kern, 1926, pp. 235–241; Hemberg, 1950. Other scholars were less impressed, as Santo Mazzarino wrote in 1947: "Kabeiroi è il massimo nome della mitologia 'Greca' di cui sia sicuro l'etimo fenicio" (Kabeiroi is the greatest name in Greek mythology with the most secure Phoenician etymology) (1989, p. 259).

32 T. Jacobsen, 1943.

33 I maintain that the earlier counterpart of Seth was Yam in the Ugaritic pantheon and Poseidon in the Greek. It is somewhat surprising that West does not refer to Fontenrose's extensive and learned treatment of this subject (1980/1959, pp. 239–147 and elsewhere). Although not as focused as West, Fontenrose anticipated West's arguments on many different issues.

34 βορέας has no Indo-European etymology and would seem much more likely to come from the Egyptian b3ḥw ("direction to the north and west of Egypt") and the Canaanite brḥ ("wind") found in Job 26:13.

35 West (p. 370) shows the parallels between the Greek rivers named Iardanos and the Hebrew Yardên (Jordan). In a note (n. 38), he does not deny the connection, but he states, "The name is easily but perhaps falsely derived from the W. Semitic yrd 'descend'; it may rather be pre-Semitic." Few if any pre-Semitic place-names are found in Palestine, and the sense of "descend" would fit well with a river flowing to the Dead Sea, the lowest spot on the earth's land surface. See also ch. 6 n. 154.

36 M. L. West, 1971, pp. 62–63.

37 See Morris, 1995, pp. 233–235. For the "Taking of Joppa," see ch. 1 n. 18.

38 He treated the former Egyptian parallel in detail in M. L. West, 1971, pp. 46–47.

39 Meltzer, 1974, pp. 154–157.

40 Weingarten, 1990.

41 The concept of achieving immortality before death is still very much alive among the "born again."

42 Nectar was also used. West (p. 39) accepts Saul Levin's (1971) "persuasive" derivation of the word "nectar" from the West Semitic passive niqtar ("smoked" or "perfumed" wine). Levin does not make the suggestion, but I think that niqtar may even refer to distilled, hence immortal liquor, even though no record exists of distillation in Classical times. Nevertheless, the Arabic qatr means "infuse, filter, refine" and istaqtara, also from the same root qtr, means "distill."

43 See, for instance, Pyramid Texts, Utterance 444, in Faulkner, 1969, p. 148.

44 Altenmüller, 1975.

45 Lines 81–91, in Wender, 1973, pp. 25–26.

46 I provide a longer treatment of this topic in a popularization of my project with the tentative title Moses and Muses (forthcoming). Much of the ferocity of the Egyptian demons and Minoan genii seems to have been largely taken on by another group of their "descendents," the Erinyes or Furies.

47 The Indo-European etymologies suggested for "Muse" are derived from a hypothetical *Mont-ya, which could mean "nymph of the mons (mountain)." It is true that the Muses or Musai were often associated with mountains but mons montis is a Latin and not a Greek word, which makes the semantic case as weak as the phonetic one. Another possibility is that *Mont-ya was connected to men ("mind") and manthanô ("learn"). As the Muses were patrons of the arts and their mother was called Mnemosyne or "memory," this connection would be possible semantically. Phonetic problems include the fact that men is a long way from Musai.

48 Hampe and Simon, 1981, p. 212 pl. 325.

49 Walcot, 1966, pp. 67–70. See also ch. 12 n. 29.

50 This criticism and defacing of her monuments did not occur for some twenty years after the beginning of her reign. See Tyldesley, 1998, pp. 210–215.

51 Walcot, 1966, pp. 98–99.

52 Simpson, 1966, p. xv, quoted in Meltzer, 1974, p. 154 n. 7.

53 Velikovsky, 1960.

54 I provide a longer treatment of this topic in Moses and Muses (forthcoming).

55 G. T. Martin, 1992, p. 48.

56 Parkinson and Schofield, 1993, 1995.

57 See Bernal, 1991b, pp. 428, 472–473.

58 Quoted in commentary to the Pythian Ode, 9.81.

59 Vermeule, 1979, p. 71.

60 This etymology has been proposed many times and was included in Lewy, 1895, p. 229, and Astour, 1967, p. 314. It should be noted that the loan almost certainly took place in the Bronze Age, as Akherôn is far more easily derived from *ʾaḥărôn than from ʾaḥărôn before the two hs merged in the middle of the second millennium B.C.E.

61 A. H. Gardiner, 1957, p. 173.

62 Vermeule, 1979, pp. 75–76. Egyptian influences on Mycenaean funerary practices can be seen in other instances.

63 See Lichtheim, 1973, pp. 75–80, 83.

64 This is discussed in more detail in ch. 15 nn. 83–87. See also Vermeule, 1979, p. 76.

65 Vermeule, 1979, p. 72; Alford, 1992. Alford derives the name Elysion from the Egyptian i3rw ("rushes"). I find the -s- difficult to explain. On the other hand, I do find sḫt i3rw ("Field of Rushes") a plausible etymology for the heavenly and toil-free island of Σχερίη visited by Odysseus.

66 R. D. Griffith, 1996.

67 The reason for the disdain is clearly that, operating within the Aryan model and insisting on Indo-European derivations, they cannot get etymology to work for them.

68 Muss-Arnolt, 1892.

69 Barthélemy, 1763, p. 222.

70 For a discussion of the relationship between onar and its counterpart hupar

from the Egyptian ḥpr "become," see *BA III*, forthcoming. For the lack of an Indo-European root for *onar*, see Chantraine 1968.

71 Herodotus, II: 54.

72 West (p. 44) refers to the divinity "Paiawon" found in Linear B as "having no Greek etymology." Paiawon is commonly seen as an ancient name for Apollo. It is interesting to note that Apollo's counterpart the young Horus was known, among many other names, as *iwn mut.f* ("Pillar of his mother"). *P3 iwn* ("The pillar") provides a perfect phonetic and a reasonable semantic origin for Paiawon, later Paian.

73 Herodotus, II: 50. He listed seven exceptions that did not include Apollo. For a discussion on Athena, see ch. 6 nn. 180–216.

74 See Hoch, 1994, pp. 281–282.

75 Onians, 1988/1951, pp. 411–415. See also above ch. 10 n. 7.

76 The only Indo-European cognate proposed is the Armenian *awr* ("day"), with links to a hypothetical *amor* analogous to *tekmor*. The latter is, however, probably Semitic.

77 See ch. 15.

78 I first published this etymology in Bernal, 1985, p. 76.

79 See, for example, *BAR*, pp. ix, 168.

15. Phoenician Politics and Egyptian Justice in Ancient Greece

1 Bernal, 1993b.

2 Trigger, 1980, pp. 24–31, 44–49.

3 Schachermeyr, esp. 1967, 1984, pp. 22–44.

4 Childe, the champion of modified diffusionism and ex oriente lux, also wrote a book on *The Aryans* (1926) that emphasized "Aryan" vigor and creativity.

5 Schachermeyr, 1984, pp. 55–66.

6 Nilsson, 1972/1932.

7 For the full quotation, see ch. 4 n. 12.

8 See C. H. Gordon, esp. 1962a; Astour, esp. 1967; chs. 12–14 above.

9 Cicero, *De Republica*, fr. 3.3.

10 See Homer, *Odyssey*, 14.292, 15.403; Herodotus, 1,1.

11 Marx, 1973/1939, 1953, pp. 375–413.

12 See Bailey and Llobera, 1981; Dunn, 1982; Friedman, 1979; Krader, 1975; Suret-Canale, 1974; Tökei, 1979. For the best bibliography on the Asiatic mode of production in the Near East, see Zaccagnini, 1981, pp. 3–65.

13 M. I. Finley, 1968, 1973, 1980; Anderson, 1974, pp. 18–28.

14 Diakonoff, 1969, pp. 173–202; Zaccagnini, 1981, pp. 22–36; Van de Mieroop, 1997, pp. 145–146, 203–213.

15 Dandamaev, 1984, pp. 67–101.

16 M. I. Finley, 1973, pp. 28–29; Tökei, 1979, pp. 21–24; Zaccagnini, 1981, p. 16; Anderson, 1974, p. 21.

17 Dandamaev, 1984, pp. 646–654; Postgate, 1992, pp. 183–188; Van de Mieroop, 1997, p. 147.
18 *Pace* Diakonoff, 1974, pp. 45–78; Komoroczy, 1978, pp. 9–26.
19 See Stella, 1965. This, like the critically important work of Cyrus Gordon on Linear A, is omitted from Ventris and Chadwick's extensive bibliography (1973, pp. 595–605). For the "Oriental" aspects of the society, see also Suret-Canale, 1974, pp. 178–182. M. I. Finley points out these anomalies (1973, p. 182 n. 39).
20 Weber, 1976, pp. 40–41, 155–163.
21 Moses Finley rightly drew a categorical distinction between helots, with their attachment to land and intact families, and deracinated chattel slaves, who were generally not self-reproducing. Finley does not, however, make an explicit link between this and maritime society (1980, pp. 70–71).
22 In early capitalism this distinction was achieved by the institution of caste- or race-based slavery.
23 Bockische, writing in the German Democratic Republic, was unable to do any better (1982, pp. 314–325). I am grateful to Barry Strauss for this reference.
24 M. I. Finley, 1973, p. 71.
25 M. I. Finley, 1980, p. 87.
26 Lejeune, 1965.
27 Suret-Canale, 1974, p. 179 n. 2.
28 O. Murray, 1993, pp. 8, 63.
29 Ibid., pp. 81–101.
30 O. Murray toys with the idea that the formation of the polis was the result of the introduction of alphabetic literacy. However, he has great doubts "whether it [literacy] was so important as to constitute a sufficient cause or even a major factor in these changes" (1993, p. 100). His hesitation is praiseworthy given the probability that the alphabet was introduced much earlier.
31 Josephus, 1.17; Pliny, 18.22.
32 Zaccagnini, 1981, p. 28. Van de Mieroop does not accept this view of progress, arguing that even in early Mesopotamia, although temples and palaces held great areas of land, there were private landowners and tenants (1997, p. 147). Postgate, however, while accepting the existence of some private land in third millennium Mesopotamia, downplays its significance at that stage (1992, pp. 94–96, 183–184).
33 1 Kings 21:1–8. See also Leviticus 27:20; Ruth 4:1–6.
34 Ezekiel 27:12–24. For convincing arguments in favor of dating this Phoenician *Vorlage* to the early ninth century, long before the time of Ezekiel, see Katzenstein, 1973, p. 154.
35 Katzenstein, 1973, p. 158.
36 Josephus, *Antiquities of the Jews*, 8.54.
37 1 Kings 5: 2. He also sent twenty *kor* of olive oil. See also Katzenstein, 1973, p. 99.

38 2 Samuel 8:1, 20:19; Ezekiel 16: 46–49.

39 See the bibliography in Bunnens, 1979, pp. 281–282. H. G. Niemayer (1984, pp. 1–94; 1988, pp. 201–204) argues for a late eighth century date. Such minimalism is attacked by Sabatino Moscati (1985, pp. 179–187), who argues for Canaanite activities in the Western Mediterranean in the fourteenth and thirteenth centuries and Phoenician ones in the tenth. Cross (1979), basing his dating on epigraphical evidence, goes still higher to the eleventh century. Boardman sees Phoenician expansion in the Mediterranean as having taken place in the tenth or ninth centuries (1990, p. 178).

40 *Pace* Bunnens, 1979, pp. 280–284. For an analysis of the story of the foundation of Carthage in the late ninth century to avoid social conflict, see Decret, 1977, pp. 46–53; Katzenstein, 1973, pp. 186–191. Five hundred years later, Aristotle described a system by which social discontent was avoided at Carthage by sending some of the poor to outlying districts to turn them into men of property (*Politics*, 6,5). See also Sallust, *Jugurtha*, 19. 1–2. Arguments among scholars as to which was the *essential* motive for colonization seem futile. See Graham, 1964, 1971, pp. 35–47; Coldstream, 1977, pp. 231–233; R. M. Cook, 1962. It is clear that economic, political, and social motives were all involved in varying proportions. For the political autonomy granted to the cities dependent on Carthage, see Sznycer, 1975, p. 51.

41 For the Israelite *mas*, see Judges 1:28–35; 1 Kings 5:13 and elsewhere. *Mas* has no Semitic cognates. Klein (1987, p. 358) argued that it was borrowed from the Egyptian *ms* ("bring, offer"). I believe that it can be more plausibly derived from the Egyptian *mšꜥ*, Coptic *mēēše* ("troop, work gang"). For a short survey of Israelite slavery, see Wolff, 1974, pp. 192–205. M. I. Finley (1973, p. 65) has quite rightly pointed out that to squeeze the many and varied forms of servile labor in the ancient world into the three categories slavery, helotry, and wage labor does violence to the complexities of the actual society. See also Dandamaev, 1984, p. 77. Though accepting this, I still maintain that this categorization, however crude, has heuristic value.

42 Judges 2:14, 3:8, 6:2, 9, 10:7; 1 Samuel 12:9.

43 Leviticus 25:41–46; Deuteronomy 15:12–19.

44 1 Kings 5:9–14 (23–26).

45 1 Kings 7:13–14.

46 Ezekiel 27:13; Homer, *Odyssey*, 14.292, 15.403.

47 Amos, 1:9.

48 Joel, 3:6.

49 Herodotus, 1.1.

50 See Amos 6:4. The Egyptians and Mesopotamians feasted sitting on chairs. See also Dentzer, 1971. The idea that eating from couches symbolizes freedom has been preserved in the Jewish tradition. Throughout the Passover, the celebration of liberation, there is a repeated insistence

that the rituals should be carried out while reclining. See the *Haggadah šel Pesaḥ*.

51 See, for instance, Raaflaub, 1985, pp. 40–41; O. Patterson, 1991, pp. 48–63.

52 Saggs, 1962, pp. 170–173; Kramer, 1963, pp. 78–80.

53 *Pace* M. I. Finley, 1963–1964, pp. 236–239; Anderson, 1974, pp. 21–23; O. Patterson, 1991, esp. pp. 9–63. See Bernal, 1993b, p. 249. Another Semitic word for "freedom" is *ḥurr.* from the same Semitic root *ḥrr* as the Hebrew *ḥôr*. Bernard Lewis is eager to demonstrate that "liberty" is a uniquely European concept. He concedes, however, that the Arabic term *ḥurr* had existed earlier and that although *ḥurr* was usually a legal term, "it did at certain times and in certain places also have a social content, being applied to social groups enjoying privileges and exemptions." He cites an Arabic-Spanish word list published in Granada in 1505 that translates *ḥurr* as "*franco, privilegiado*" (1988, p. 111). See also ch. 3 n. 32 above.

54 Widespread literacy in ancient Israel is suggested by the poverty of the material remains associated with the abecedary found at Izbet Sartah. See Kochavi, 1977, pp. 1–13, esp. 1–2. See also Judges 8:14, where a young man captured at random in a remote village was able to write down the names of village elders.

55 Snodgrass, 1980, p. 120; see also Pound, 1984; *pace* Gagarin, 1986, p. 128.

56 Westbrook, 1988.

57 *Amarna Letters*, Moran, 1992, p. 236.

58 Astour, 1964, p. 14.

59 See ch. 4 n. 18.

60 1 Kings 6: 38–7:2; 2 Chronicles 2–3.

61 Jacobsen, 1943; Kramer, 1963, pp. 73–75; Saggs, 1962, pp. 160–163; Dandamaev, 1984, pp. 42–45; Pettinato, 1981, pp. 69–154; Van de Mieroop, 1997, pp. 118–139; Schmeil 2000.

62 Oded, 1974, p. 40.

63 See Astour, 1964. There are some striking cases of this in the Bible. See, for instance, the idyllic description of "free" Laish in Judges 18:7.

64 For constitutions in Phoenicia, see Moscati, 1968, pp. 51, 169–175. For the Carthaginian constitution in the fourth century B.C.E., see Aristotle, *Politics*, 2.11. For its later developments in a democratic direction, see Polybius, 6.51–53. The most complete study of the literary sources on the Carthaginian constitution is still that of Gsell, 1918, pp. 183–244. For parallels between Phoenician and Spartan constitutions, see Drews, 1979.

65 A vocalization *piḍity is suggested by the Demotic form *ptyt* and the Coptic *pite* for the related word "bow." The probable Egyptian origins of *phiditia* and other peculiarly Spartan terms will be discussed in BA III. For a discussion of *ḥbr*, see Katzenstein, 1983; Aristotle, *Politics*, 2.11. It should be pointed out that Aristotle was not always consistent in his description of the Carthaginian constitution and was probably drawing on information from different periods. See Sznycer, 1975, p. 48.

66 Slousch, 1913. These and the Roman *curiae* themselves would seem to derive their titles from the Canaanite qir‘yat ("town") or q‘ri›ê ("summoned").

67 For the role of the "elders" and the é-am ("house of the people") in Ebla in the twenty-fifth century B.C.E., see Pettinato, 1981, pp. 92–95, 144. For the biblical evidence, see, for instance, Job, 29:7–10; Proverbs, 21:3. I hope to set out elsewhere my arguments for believing that the Bêt millô at Shechem (Judges 9:6) and the Millô in Jerusalem were senate houses or at least walled spaces for assemblies near the gates.

68 1 Samuel 10:20–25; Micah 2:5; 1 Chronicles 24:31, 25:8, 26:15.

69 *Kad* in turn derived from the Egyptian qd ("jar"). See ch. 6 nn. 35–36.

70 Drews, 1979.

71 *Pace* O. Patterson, 1991, pp. 48–63; Hammond, 1972, pp. 172–173. Interestingly, Hammond contradicts this view when he refers to the antiquity of Canaanite councils (p. 87).

72 Raaflaub, 1989, pp. 28–31. This article is headed with a quotation stating: "There were no Greeks before the Greeks" (p. 1). This is doubly Eurocentric; on the one hand, there is the denial of precedents, and on the other, the belief that only "Greeks" could have preceded Greeks.

73 Sznycer, 1979; Helm, 1980, pp. 75, 95–96, 126, Bikai, 1990; Morris, 1992, pp. 124–129. More evidence of Phoenician contact with the Aegean during the Geometric Period, 900–700 B.C.E., is being discovered every season. See Sapouna-Sakellarati, 1998.

74 Ehrenberg, 1961, p. 9.

75 Raaflaub, 1989. For the arguments for an early dating, see BA I: 86–88.

76 For a bibliography of Nilsson's works on this, see Nilsson, 1964, pp. 2–6. Burkert (1985/1977, pp. 47–53, 366 n. 22) tends to deny the continuity of cultic tradition in Mainland Greece while accepting it for Crete and Cyprus. However, for anyone outside the minimalist tradition it would seem that he has provided sufficient evidence to contradict his case.

77 Snodgrass, 1971.

78 Vermeule, 1986, p. 81.

79 Herodotus, V. 57–61. Stieglitz, 1981; Bernal, 1990a.

80 See ch. 13 nn. 3–6.

81 *Pace* Burkert, 1992/1984, pp. 29–32. See ch. 13 nn. 7–11 above.

82 Homer, *Iliad*, 22.208–213.

83 Ibid., 8.60–70.

84 Dietrich, 1964, p. 108; Clark and Coulson, 1978, p. 67.

85 Lung, 1912, pp. 20–21. See also Schliemann, 1878, pp. 196–198, pl. 301–302.

86 Gruppe, 1897–1906, 2: 681 n. 7.

87 Lung, 1912, p. 20.

88 For m3‘t and communal values, see Karenga, 1994, pp. 508–514.

89 Clark and Coulson, 1978, p. 71.

90 Homer, *Odyssey*, IV, 564; Diodorus Siculus, 1935, V.79; Nonnos, XIX.190.

91 Aeschylus, *Suppl.* 130–31; BA I: 90–98.
92 Clark and Coulson, 1978.
93 See ch. 10 n. 48; BA III.
94 For a discussion of this, see Posener, 1960, p. 40.
95 Kagan, 1965, pp. 76–77.
96 See Assmann, 1984, p. 106; Karenga, 1994.
97 For the value of 3 as a liquid, see ch. 6 nn. 93–97.
98 Pausanias, X. 24.4.
99 J. A. Wilson, 1949.
100 See BA I: 61.
101 Krappe, 1940, p. 245; Vermeule, 1964, p. 72; Hemmerdinger, 1968, p. 240. Chantraine described the proposal as "improbable" without stating any reasons for his objections. Similarly, Pierce attacked the etymology for its "fundamental arbitrariness" (1971, p. 105). Gary Rendsburg (1989, p. 80) prefers an etymology of *makar* from the West Semitic *brk* ("bless"). This derivation seems to me inferior on both phonetic and semantic grounds to that from M3ʿḥrw.
102 See ch. 14 n. 69.
103 See ch. 6.
104 This loan would seem to be very old, as the value of the sign ⸗ later represented as š seems to have shifted from ḫ by the Middle Kingdom. There is a possible calque from Egyptian in *hoi polloi* ("the many") in the sense of the multitude of poor.
105 Homer, *Odyssey*, xiv, 275–280.
106 Diodorus Siculus, 1935, 1.98.1; Plutarch, *Lyk.*, 4.5.
107 Pendlebury, 1930, pp. 45, 109.
108 *Lochos* ("a company") from *rḥyt* ("plebeians, subjects"), *ōba*, a Spartan tribe, from *ip*, Coptic *ōp* ("assess, detail for work") and the related words *wpi* ("open, divide") and *wpwt* ("household"). The origin of *phitidia* is given above n. 65.
109 Herodotus, II.80; Isokrates, *Busiris*, 17.
110 Herodotus, VI.55; 1 Maccabees 14:21.
111 For the Menelaion, see Pendlebury, 1930, p. 46. For a discussion of Nabis, see ch. 5 n. 18.
112 Aristotle, *Politics*, II. 9–12; Drews, 1979.
113 Diodorus Siculus, 1935, 1.28.5.
114 Plutarch, *Theseus*, 25.
115 See Cline, 1994; Bass, 1997; Redford, 1992, pp. 241–243; BA II: 409–494.
116 Aristotle, *Athenian Politics*, 13.2.
117 A. B. Lloyd, 1975–1988, 1:56–57.
118 R. B. Brown, 1975; Skon-Jedele (1994) lists even more.
119 Herodotus, 1.30; 2.177; Plato, *Timaeus and Critias*; Aristotle, *Athenian Politics*, 11; Diodorus Siculus, 1935, 1.69,96,98; Plutarch, *Solon* 26, 31, 32; Diogenes Laertius, 1980, 1.50.
120 Solon, frag. 28, in Bergk, 1882, 4:110.

121 Plutarch, *Solon*, 2.4.
122 Herodotus, II.177; Diogenes Laertius, 1980, I.55; Plutarch, *Solon*, 32.
123 For a discussion of a possible Egyptian for Solon's *seisachtheia*, see ch. 12
     n. 20. For the issue in general, see Théodoridès, 1971, p. 319.
124 Herodotus, II. 150.
125 Diodorus Siculus, 1935, I.95.
126 *Pace* Froidefond, 1971, pp. 137–151; A. B. Lloyd, 1988, pp. 166–167.
127 Burton, 1972, pp. 274–275; Théodoridès, 1971, p. 319.
128 Plato, *Philebus*, 16C. See also the Platonic author of *Epinomis*, 986E–987A.
129 W. Davis, 1979.
130 Krantor, quoted in Proclus, *In Platonis Timaeum Commentarii*, 76. See also BA
     I: 106–107. For Lefkowitz's interpretation of this, see 1996a, p. 82. For
     my response to this, see ch. 16 n. 28. See also Stephens, 1993.
131 Marx, I.4.
132 See, for example, Taylor, 1929, pp. 275–286.
133 Springborg, 1984, 1990, pp. 234–235, 1992, p. 47.
134 Assmann, 1984, pp. 103–104.
135 Springborg 1990, pp. 246–248.
136 For a discussion of this and the passage itself, see ch. 11 nn. 12–13; Aris-
     totle, *Politics*, VII.10; Barker, 1958, p. 304.

16. All *Not* Quiet on the Wellesley Front: A Review of *Not Out of Africa*

 1 For more on the situation of this quotation, see n. 76 below and ch. 8 n. 8.
 2 Lefkowitz, 1997a, p. 185. Page references are to the second paperback
    edition and are cited in the text. Lefkowitz and Rogers, 1996.
 3 In fact, the term was used by W. E. B. Du Bois in 1962; see Moses, 1998,
    p. 2.
 4 See, for instance, Florence Nightingale, 1987, pp. 73–74.
 5 For a good survey of black and Afrocentrist historical scholarship, see the
    bibliographic essay in St. Clair Drake, 1987–1990, pp. 309–332. Lefkowitz
    does not consider the younger scholars who have combined their Afrocen-
    tric approach with conventional scholarship, obtaining extremely inter-
    esting results. See, for instance, T. M. Scott, 1991; Karenga, 1994.
 6 Martel, 1997, p. 6, item N.
 7 To use the crude measure of entries in the index of *NOA*: the mainstream
    Afrocentrists with the exception of Molefi Asante received a total of 39,
    and Asante as the founder of Afrocentrism had 11. But George James re-
    ceived 33 and I was awarded 23.
 8 Herodotus, VI.55.
 9 See Strabo, 17.1.2. The words "not far from the truth" indicate the source
    of Lefkowitz's error. They occur in the section dealing with the Nile in
    A. B. Lloyd, 1976, p. 110. However, Lloyd and his ancient and modern
    sources are mistaken when they say that the Nile received water from the

snows of the Mountains of the Moon. Although the peaks of these mountains (the Ruwenzori) are snow-covered, snowmelt from them forms an insignificant proportion of the flow of the White Nile. The lakes in Uganda from which the river originates, all derive from rainfall. Lefkowitz compounds the error by attributing the Nile flood to this snowmelt. Whereas the White Nile is more or less constant, the Nile flood is caused by the dramatic rise in the Blue Nile and the Atbara during and following heavy summer rains in Ethiopia.

10   See Bietak, 1995; Morgan, 1995. For the murals coming from the Eighteenth Dynasty, see Cline, 1998.

11   Richard, 1994, p. 234. Radicals continued using the Roman term for several decades. From the late 1790s it became possible to use "democracy" but only in conjunction with the modifiers "republican" or "representative." It was only in the late 1820s that, with the election of Andrew Jackson and in the fervor of Philhellenism, the words "democracy" and "democrat" began to be used on their own.

12   Lefkowitz, 1992a.

13   Lefkowitz, 1995.

14   Richard, 1994, p. 241. The historian of education F. Rudolph put it this way: "In the South the classics were regarded with special favor because in ancient Rome and Greece the South found justification for itself and slavery" (1977, p. 57, quoted in Purdy, 1997, p. 296).

15   Bernal, 1996a, 1996f.

16   Herodotus II.49.2, 50.1.

17   Herodotus, 1974, II.43, p. 146.

18   I estimate that about 25 percent of the basic Greek vocabulary comes from Egyptian and a further 15 to 20 percent from West Semitic.

19   Incidentally, neither Korean nor Japanese has been significantly influenced by Chinese in its morphology and phonetics. It is normal for speakers of any language to give up their vocabulary long before abandoning more fundamental linguistic structures. For a discussion of this phenomenon see ch. 6 nn. 45–46.

20   To be pedantic, the English were converted to Christianity in the seventh century C.E. and *bisceop* (not *bishop*) is attested from the beginning of the eighth, though no doubt it was in use much earlier.

21   See ch. 6 n. 20.

22   For the figure of 60 percent, see Morpurgo-Davies, 1986, p. 105, cited in ch. 6 n. 51.

23   See BA I: 281–399.

24   Anderson, 1987; Leach, 1987; Vickers, 1987; Malamud, 1989; Assmann, 1997, pp. 13, 143; and many others. Three more recent and trenchant criticisms of my historiography are discussed in ch. 7.

25   See BA I: 281–399.

26   For the conservative organizations, see Bernal, 1996f.

27   For an enlightening discussion of the general tendency of conservatives to

describe the work of any challenger to the status quo as "political" while the objectivity of their own writing in its defense is taken for granted, see Becker, 1967; and ch. 7 n. 86 above.

28 For more on this, see ch. 15 nn. 130–131.

29 Bowersock, 1996, p. 490.

30 There is a slight confusion in the argument here in that "the idea that scholars have ignored the Greeks' Egyptian origins" could not have arisen from Masonic myth.

31 Fowden, 1986, p. xv. Copenhaver describes the same scholarly shift in more detail (1992, pp. lvi–lviii). See also Assmann, 1997, pp. 84–85. For still more on this, see Stanley Burstein's assessment of the situation in DBA.

32 For references to this, see BA I: 465 n. 53.

33 See Jasnow and Zausich, 1995.

34 Petrie, 1908a, pp. 224–225; 1908b, pp. 196–197; 1909a, pp. 85–91.

35 See my assessment of this in BA I: 465 n. 48. In the paperback edition, Lefkowitz adds a reference to another modern scholar, David Potter, who saw "very real" influences on the Hermetica from the Egyptian past (1994, p. 193).

36 In BA I: 178–181, I treat these novels in some detail, stressing their importance. Therefore, it is puzzling that Lefkowitz should thank "the late F. W. Sternfeld" who "alerted me to the work of the Abbé Jean Terrasson" (p. xvii).

37 Assmann, 1989, pp. 154–155. For his belief that there were multiple layers of restricted religious knowledge, see Assmann, 1970. For further evidence of these links, see Merkelbach, 1987; Baines, 1990, p. 14; Delia, 1992, pp. 181–190; Derchain, 1962, pp. 175–198.

38 My views in this respect are very orthodox. Marvin Meyer, the editor of a standard book on ancient mysteries, sees the obvious connection between the Book of the Dead and Egyptian and Hellenistic initiations (1987, p. 158).

39 Stricker, 1950, 1953; Guilmot, 1977, pp. 95–175.

40 Griffiths, 1975, p. 31.

41 See Snodgrass, 1971, pp. 116–117. In her note to the second edition (p. 246), Lefkowitz relies on the work of the archaeologist Mylonas to suggest that it was just by chance that the scarabs and symbol of Isis were found in the tomb associated with the cult of Isis' Greek counterpart Demeter. This is certainly possible, but the argument is hopelessly cumbersome compared to one based on the ancient conviction that the Eleusinian cult derived from Egypt. Lefkowitz admits the argument made by Emily Vermeule that Greek conceptions of death were heavily influenced by Egypt between the fifteenth and the fifth centuries B.C.E. Thus, once again, Lefkowitz tries to make a categorical distinction between (Eleusinian) initiations of the living and Egyptian funerary religion.

42 See Foucart, 1914; for the respect, Kevin Clinton, personal communication, 1988. Lefkowitz relies on Clinton to claim that the Hellenistic Isis

mysteries were formed on Greek models (*NOA*, p. 249). Unlike Paul Foucart, whose son Georges was an Egyptologist who had a considerable knowledge of Ancient Egypt, Clinton has virtually no knowledge of that civilization.

43 Picard, 1927, p. 324.

44 Barb, 1971, p. 152.

45 Hani, 1976, p. 9.

46 See Frankfort, 1933; Guilmot, 1977, pp. 100–103. It appears that a similar Late Egyptian underground complex has been found under the Giza Plateau, but this has not yet been published.

47 Montet, 1946, pp. 298–300; Guilmot, 1977, pp. 124–125.

48 Varille, 1954, pp. 131–132.

49 A. H. Gardiner, 1938.

50 Derchain, 1965, p. 57. Lichtheim tends to agree with Derchain about the pr ʿnḫ and writes that Gardiner "defined its function too narrowly" (1975–1980 3:36 n. 10). See also Clagett, 1989, pp. 1–46.

51 See Bernal, 1992a, reprinted as ch. 11; Palter, 1993, reprinted in BAR, 1996; Bernal, 1994c, reprinted as ch. 10; Palter, 1994. See also DBA chapters by Pappademos and Lumpkin.

52 Katz, 1995.

53 See D. James, 1995, pp. 7–10; Assmann, 1997, p. 115. The striking parallels between the Egyptian qd and the Greek *idea* will be discussed in BA III.

54 Ray, 1998, p. 250.

55 Assmann, 1975, 1993b, 1995b, 1996; Bilolo, 1986; Karenga, 1994; Löwstedt, 1995, 1997. Löwstedt writes: "The Greeks never brought together regress and progress (reversible development), they never formulated evolutionary ethics (like the Egyptian anti-selectionist one), they never conceived of an epistomology like the Shabaka (and Kantian) ones (beyond empiricism and rationalism), they never made tolerance and solidarity a part of the foundations of philosophy and they never conceived an ontological or semantic primacy of relations" (1998, pp. 38–39). On the latter sections, see also Karenga, 1994, esp. pp. 751–756.

56 The prime example of the denial is Diogenes Laertius, 1980, I,1. For a discussion of his motives, see Preus, 1997; ch. 7 n. 8 above. For the conventional view which Diogenes contested, see Isocrates, *Bousiris*, 28. See also DBA; BA I: 104; Preus, 1992–1993; Evangeliou, 1994. Evangeliou brings out the sharp contrast on this issue between the Ancients, notably Plato and Aristotle, and modern Classical scholars and concludes firmly on the side of the former (pp. 26–29).

57 G. G. M. James, 1973, p. 75; Preus, 1992–1993, p. 8.

58 Hornung, 1982/1971, pp. 66–67.

59 Preus, 1992–1993, p. 8. My tentative translation of the fragment.

60 See A. B. Lloyd, 1976–1988, 2:14, 3:204.

61 For a survey of the ancient sources on this, see Preus, 1992–1993, p. 7.

62 Kirk, 1960, pp. 326–327. See also M. L. West, 1971.

63 See BA I: 130–134, 164–172.

64 Dodds, 1951.

65 von Staden, 1992, p. 584.

66 Philostratos, 1969, 3.32.

67 *Hermetica* 16,1–2, in Copenhaver, 1992, p. 58. This in itself suggests that the authors were Egyptian, not Greek.

68 See Philo, "Phoenician History," in Jacoby, 1963–1969, 3.C, 813.10. See also Baumgarten, 1981, p. 19.

69 Tatian I.1, 40ed., in Marcovitch, 1995, pp. 7–75.

70 Clement, 1869, *Stromateis*, I.87.2, and elsewhere. See also Ridings, 1995, p. 223.

71 For a discussion of this, see below and Bernal, 1994c, p. 11.

72 See Gillings, 1982/1972, pp. 185–193.

73 See J. H. Williams, 1996, p. 30.

74 Philo, in Jacoby, 1923–1969, 3C.2, pp. 805, ll.18–19, 813.

75 Howe discusses Volney though not Dupuis in his *Afrocentrism: Mythical Past and Imagined Homes* (1998). His treatment of Afrocentrism largely in terms of sociopathology leads him away from serious evaluation of any objective value in the Afrocentrist claims.

76 J. S. Mill, 1850, pp. 29–30. This was a response to Thomas Carlyle's notorious "On the Negro Question," published in *Fraser's Magazine* and later issued as a pamphlet under the title "On the Nigger Question." See Levy, 1999, p. 41. I am grateful to Professor Levy for the references. See also BA I: 173–188, 294–307. It is interesting to note the stark contrast between John Stuart Mill and his father on both "race" and Ancient Greece. The fact that John Stuart Mill, the leading English philosopher and logician of the nineteenth century, upheld the Ancient model in its most African form refutes John Coleman's claim that "higher standards of rational analysis in the eighteenth-century were surely important factors [in the abandonment of the Ancient model]" (BAR, p. 289). See also Bernal, 1992e. For other examples of the use of this argument in abolitionist rhetoric, see Grégoire, 1997/1808, pp. 4–5; Schoelcher, 1977/1840, pp. 74–85. For questions about J. S. Mill's motivation on this issue, see ch. 7 n. 61, ch. 8 n. 9.

77 Quoted by Lefkowitz, NOA, p. 4.

Conclusion

1 Quoted in Kuhn, 1970, p. 151.

2 M. L. West, 1997, p. x.

3 Culham and Edmunds, 1989.

4 Carter and Morris, 1995; Drews, 1993; Lefkowitz, 1997a; Merkelbach, 1995; Penglase, 1994: Reyes, 1994. Interestingly, the works by Burkert, Morris, and West on the subject have so far not been reviewed.

Glossary

Abkhaz   A living language belonging to the Northwest Caucasian linguistic family and ethnic group living in Abkhazia on the east coast of the Black Sea to the northwest of Georgia.

Africa   Africa fits the conventional definition of a continent as a large body of land surrounded by water. Like the concept of "continent" itself, the definition of "Africa" is problematic. Africa contains a range of climates, from desert to rainforest, and is divided by many natural boundaries: deserts, mountains, and rainforests. Furthermore, as the continent in which modern humans have lived for the longest period, the inhabitants of Africa have a wider genetic variety than the rest of the world put together. There is, however, a surprising degree of linguistic uniformity. The conventional view is that all African languages can be classified as belonging to one or other of the Khoisan, Niger-Congo, Afroasiatic, or Nilo-Saharan language families, although it may be that the Nilo-Saharan family is an unjustifiably cohesive grouping. Nevertheless, the linguistic clustering indicates widespread interaction across the continent, often when geographical barriers were less formidable than they have been during the past few millennia. In particular, during the warm/wet period after the last Ice Age, there were significant cultural connections across what is now the Sahara desert. For these reasons, despite the continent's very real diversity, "Africa" remains too useful a concept to be completely deconstructed. (On this last point, I differ from David Chioni Moore.

Afroasiatic   Otherwise known as Afrasian and formerly called Hamito-Semitic, a linguistic superfamily consisting of a number of language families including Berber, Chadic, Egyptian, Semitic, Omotic and East, South, and Central Cushitic.

Akkadian   The Semitic language of Ancient Mesopotamia, heavily influenced by Sumerian. It was replaced by Aramaic around the middle of the first millennium B.C.E.

Alphabet   A particular form of script in which signs uniquely represent single phonemes. Nearly all known alphabets derive from a single form developed in Egypt or the Levant, in the third millennium B.C.E. The only exceptions to this pattern are a very few alphabets, created by analogy to others descended from the original alphabet. The outstanding examples of this latter type are the Irish Ogham and Korean alphabets.

Anatolia   Ancient region, more or less coextensive with modern Turkey.

Anatolian   The extinct Indo-Hittite but non-Indo-European languages of Anatolia. They include Hittite, Palaic, Luvian, Lycian, Lydian, and probably Carian and Etruscan.

Aramaic   A West Semitic language, originally spoken in parts of what is now Syria, that became the lingua franca of the Assyrian, Neo-Babylonian, and the Persian Empires. It replaced the Canaanite dialects of Phoenician and Hebrew in the Eastern Mediterranean around the middle of the first millennium B.C.E. It was in its turn replaced as the dominant language in the Levant by Greek and then by Arabic.

Archaic Greece   Greek historical period, which was conventionally dated from the First Olympic Games in 776 B.C.E. to the beginning of the Classical Age around 500 B.C.E.

Armenian   Indo-European language of an ancient people in eastern Anatolia. It is sometimes supposed to be especially close to Greek. However, as the earliest surviving texts go back only to the fourth century C.E., the similarities may be the result of Greek influence or common contacts with Semitic languages.

Aryan   Term derived through the Semitic ʾary from the Ancient Egyptian, iri ("companion"). The people later called Persians described themselves as "Arya." Nineteenth- and twentieth-century scholars used the term to describe the speakers of the Indo-Aryan or Indo-Iranian branch of the Indo-European language family. These appear to have invaded Iran and India from the northwest in the first half of the second millennium B.C.E. In the late nineteenth century C.E., the term came to be used for the Indo-European or "white race," specifically excluding Jews.

Asia   A name derived from the Anatolian state of Assuwa of the second millennium B.C.E. Among the Greeks of the first millennium B.C.E., Asia was used as a name both for Anatolia (Asia Minor) and for the whole continent to the east across the sea from Greece, the other two continents being Libya (later Africa) across the sea to the south and Europe, the west.

In modern terms, neither Asia nor Europe qualifies as a continent because they share the same land mass with a very uncertain boundary between them. Furthermore, Asia is broken up by permanent geographical barriers and is populated by peoples with very distinct languages and cultures.

Assyria   An ancient city state and kingdom dating back to the third millennium B.C.E. Its greatest periods were at the end of the second millennium and between 900 and 600 B.C.E. Its language was a dialect of Akkadian.

Autochthonous   Native or aboriginal.

Babylon   Ancient city in south-central Mesopotamia. Seat of several important kingdoms and of the Neo-Babylonian Empire between 600 and 538 B.C.E.

B.C.E.   Before the Common Era.

Berber   The Afroasiatic languages spoken by the original inhabitants of northwest Africa. They are still spoken in territorial pockets from the Western Desert of Egypt to Morocco.

Besserwisserei   The German for "knowing better," a scholarly approach based on the belief that the "science" and alleged "historical method" of nineteenth- and twentieth-century historians make their conclusions categorically superior to those of ancient writers.

Book of Coming Forth by Day   Commonly known as the Book of the Dead. A compilation of prayers, spells, and instructions to guide the soul of the dead person through the journey of the afterlife.

Bronze Age   The historical period in which bronze, an alloy usually of copper and tin, was used for making tools and weapons, before it was largely replaced in these uses by iron. In Southwest Asia and around the Eastern Mediterranean this period lasted from approximately 3500 to 1100 B.C.E. In Eastern Asia and Western Europe it started and ended later. Most of Africa went straight from a stone age to an iron age.

Byblos   Ancient port city in what is now southern Lebanon. In close touch with Egypt, it was the most important Levantine city until it was eclipsed by Sidon at the end of the second millennium B.C.E.

calque   A literal translation of a word, expression, or idiom from another language. "Superman" from the German Übermensch is an example of this. As a counterexample, "flirt" from the French fleureter (originally "garland with flowers") is not a calque, it is a loan.

Canaanite   A Semitic language influenced by Ancient Egyptian, spoken in southern Syro-Palestine between 2000 and 500 B.C.E., when it was displaced by Aramaic. Phoenician and Hebrew are the best-known later Canaanite dialects. "Canaanite" is also used by archaeologists to describe the material culture of southern Syro-Palestine in the Late Bronze Age, c. 1500–1100 B.C.E.

Caria   Region in southwest Anatolia. Its language was probably Anatolian but may have been non-Indo-Hittite. Alphabetic inscriptions in Carian date from the sixth century B.C.E.

C.E. Common Era. Term used by non-Christians in general and Jews in particular to avoid the sectarianism of the letters A.D., Anno Domini.

ceramic period A time period reconstructed by archaeologists on the basis of pottery styles.

Chinese dynasties Xia (Hsia) c. 1900–1600 B.C.E.; Shang c. 1600–1100 B.C.E.; Zhou (Chou) c. 1100–221 B.C.E. The Zhou dynasty lost political power in the eighth century B.C.E. but survived with the title of "emperor" until finally overthrown by Qinshihuangdi, first emperor of the shortlived Qin (Ch'in) Dynasty, who unified China. The Western name "China" is probably derived from Qin.

Classical Greece Greece in the fifth and fourth centuries B.C.E., which is generally held to have seen the greatest and "purest" products of Greek genius.

Colchis Ancient country at the eastern end of the Black Sea in the present Georgia and Abkhazia.

Coptic The language and culture of Christian Egypt. Spoken until the fifteenth or sixteenth centuries C.E., Coptic remains the liturgical language of Egyptian Christians. It is written in the Greek alphabet with some additional letters derived from Demotic, the latest form of Ancient Egyptian script.

cuneiform A script developed in Mesopotamia using nail-shaped reed ends pressed into wet clay. It was employed over much of Southwest Asia from the fourth millennium B.C.E. It survived in Mesopotamia into the Common Era.

Dark Ages (Christian) Name conventionally given to the period after the fall of the Western Roman Empire in the fifth century C.E. and before the Middle Ages, which are generally considered to have begun in the ninth or tenth centuries.

Dark Ages (Greek) Name given to the period of Greek history after the fall of the Mycenaean palaces in the twelfth century B.C.E. and before the rise of Archaic Greece in the eighth.

Demotic Strictly speaking, Demotic is the script derived from Hieroglyphic and Hieratic used in Egypt after the seventh century B.C.E. The word is also used to describe the Egyptian language of this period.

demotic The language of the ordinary people, regardless of time and place.

dendrochronology The method of determining the age of wood and its archaeological context by counting and examining the nature of tree rings.

dentals Consonants formed with the tongue against the teeth, as, for example, d and t.

determinative Element in hieroglyphic representation signifying the meaning of a word as opposed to its sound.

diffusionism The belief that cultural characteristics can be transmitted from one culture to another; the opposite of isolationism. See also modified diffusionism.

Diodorus Siculus Greek historian from Sicily c. 80–20 B.C.E., known for his *Library of History.*

Dorians A Greek tribe originating from northwestern Greece who overran much of southern Greece in the twelfth century B.C.E.

Dravidian   Independent language family that extended in ancient times from southern India to eastern Mesopotamia. It was possibly the language of the civilization of Harappa. The best-known contemporary Dravidian languages are Tamil and Telegu, which still flourish in southern India. Elamite, the extinct language of the ancient Elamite civilization, was possibly Dravidian.

Early Helladic   A ceramic period, the name was applied to Mainland Greece in the Early Bronze Age, c. 3300–2000 B.C.E. It was derived from Early Minoan.

Early Minoan   A ceramic period, the name applied to Crete in the Early Bronze Age c. 3300–2000 B.C.E. This was seen to correspond to the Egyptian Old Kingdom.

Ebla   An ancient Syrian city first excavated in the 1970s. It had an extensive trading network in Syro-Palestine and Mesopotamia around 2500 B.C.E.

Eblaite   The language of Ebla, a distinct Semitic language that can usefully be seen as a predecessor of Canaanite.

Egyptian   This is generally used in this book to refer not to the Arabic spoken in Egypt today but to the language of Ancient Egypt, which was an independent Afroasiatic language. It is subdivided into a number of phases. The first two are Old Egyptian, spoken in the Old Kingdom c. 3400–2400 B.C.E., and Middle Egyptian, spoken during the Middle Kingdom 2200–1750 B.C.E. Middle Egyptian remained the official written language for the next 1,500 years. Therefore, when "Egyptian" is not qualified it usually refers to this. Late Egyptian was spoken by the sixteenth century B.C.E. but was not commonly used in writing until 200 years later. For the later stages of the language's development, see Demotic and Coptic.

Elam   Ancient civilization in the east of Mesoptamia from the fourth millennium to c. 300 B.C.E.

Elamite   The language of Elam, probably belonging to the Dravidian language family.

Eratosthenes (c. 275–195 B.C.E.)   Hellenistic scholar and librarian of the great library at Alexandria. The first Greek to calculate the circumference and tilt of the earth.

Ethiopia   Name given by the Ancient Greeks to two regions inhabited by black people. One approximated to Elam, and the other, much better known, was the territory to the south of Egypt.

Ethiopic   Name of the very varied Semitic languages spoken in the modern Ethiopia and Eritrea. These include Ge'ez, the ancient language of the Ethiopian Christian Church; Amharic, the national language of Ethiopia today; and the still extant Gurage languages, some of which retain extremely archaic forms of Proto-Semitic.

Etruscan   Civilization in Ancient Central Italy. Greek and Roman writers generally maintained that the Etruscans came from Lydia in northwest Anatolia. The Etruscan language, which is not well understood, could well be Anatolian. A very closely related language and script has been found on an inscription from the island of Lemnos near the Turkish coast. Etruscan culture seems to have been heavily influenced by Phoenician and Greek civilizations from the ninth to the sixth centuries B.C.E. Etruscan was a central influence on the formation of Latin culture.

Eudoxos   Greek astronomer and mathematician from Knidos on the west Anatolian coast who studied in Egypt. Born c. 400, died c. 350 B.C.E.

euhemerism   Doctrine attributed to Euhemeros, according to which figures commonly worshipped as divinities were actually deified heroes. By extension, the word has been used in modern times to mean the explanation or reduction of religious beliefs in pseudo-rational terms.

Euhemeros   Greek philosopher c. 300 B.C.E.

Europe   One of the three continents visualized by Greek geographers, deriving its name from some form of the West Semitic root ʿereb ("sunset" or "west"). As the largest surviving fragment of the Christian world after it had been fractured by the Islamic conquests, the name "Europe" became a synonym of "Christendom," even though Christianity did not arise in Europe and many ancient Christian communities existed in the past and exist today in Asia and Africa. Furthermore, a significant number of Europeans are Moslems or Jews. With European expansion and the emergence of full-blown racism, Europe was portrayed as the continent of the "white race." Here again many people with similar features and complexions have lived in other continents since long before the advent of colonialism. As a collection of complex promontories on the edge of the Euro-Asiatic land mass, Europe does not fit the normal definition of a continent as a large land mass surrounded by water.

Ge'ez   The most anciently attested Ethiopian Semitic language. It is still used in Ethiopian Church liturgy.

genetic   A genetic relationship between languages is one in which they are supposed to come from a single ancestor. For example, French and Romanian have a genetic relationship because for all their differences, they both derive from the Vulgar Latin spoken in the Roman army.

Georgian   People who have inhabited the Central Caucasus since the earliest times. The Georgian language belongs to the Kartvelian language family.

Harappa   The names of this site and another, Mohenjo Daro, are used for the ancient civilization that flourished in northwest India from c. 2500 to 1700 B.C.E., when it was destroyed, probably by invading Aryans from the north. The writing of this civilization has not been deciphered.

Hatti   Ancient name for Central Anatolia, the homeland of the Hittites.

Hattic   A non-Indo-European language spoken in Hatti.

Hebrew   Canaanite dialect spoken in the kingdoms of Israel, Judah, and Moab in the first millennium B.C.E. For religious regions, it is often treated as a distinct language. Modern Hebrew stems from a nineteenth-century C.E. revival of the language that had largely been restricted to religious use for two millennia.

Helladic   Name given to three ceramic periods on Mainland Greece roughly approximating to the three Minoan ceramic periods in Crete, which in turn are based on the Old, Middle, and New Kingdoms of Egypt.

Hellenic   Greek or Greek-speaking, but particularly associated with Thessaly in northern Greece. Since the late eighteenth century C.E., the word has gained many associations of nobility and of northern and Aryan "blood."

Hellenistic   The pejorative name given to the mixed Greek and "Oriental" culture found around the Eastern Mediterranean and beyond after the conquests of Alexander the Great in the late fourth century B.C.E., until the incorporation of the region into the Roman Empire in the first century B.C.E.

Hellespont   Strait linking the Black Sea to the Mediterranean and dividing Europe from Asia.

Herodotus (c. 485–425 B.C.E.)   Writer of the earliest extant Greek history, from Halikarnassos in Asia Minor.

Hesiod   Greek poet of the tenth century B.C.E. from Boiotia, most famous for his *Theogony*.

Hieratic   Egyptian cursive script based on the same principles as Hieroglyphics; used for writing on papyrus.

Hieroglyphic   Egyptian partially pictorial script first attested in the second half of the fourth millennium B.C.E.; used for formal writing, especially inscriptions.

Hittite   Empire in Central Anatolia during the second millennium B.C.E. Its language was an Anatolian one. It was first written in a form of cuneiform and later in its own hieroglyphic system.

Homer   Legendary epic poet. Modern conventional wisdom tends to place him in the eighth or seventh centuries B.C.E., whereas the ancient tradition and a minority of contemporary scholars (to which I belong) see him as having lived more than a century earlier. There is equally sharp division over whether or not the Homeric poems were composed orally. On this issue too I side with the minority, who see the *Iliad* and the *Odyssey* as sophisticated written compositions.

Hurrian   Name of a people who lived in Syria and Eastern Anatolia in the third and second millennia B.C.E. Their extinct language, like that of Urartu, belongs to the linguistic family now represented by the Northeast Caucasian languages, the best-known member of which is Chechen. It was neither Afroasiatic nor Indo-Hittite. The most important Hurrian-speaking states were Mitanni, which flourished in western Mesopotamia and northern Syria in the second half of the second millennium B.C.E., and Urartu, which was a powerful adversary to Assyria in the early first millennium.

Hyksos   Invaders from the northeast who dominated much of Egypt between 1725 and 1575 B.C.E. The bulk of the Hyksos seem to have spoken a West Semitic language, but they also seem to have contained Hurrian and possibly Indo-Aryan speakers.

Indo-Aryan   Branch of Indo-European spoken for many millennia in Iran and most of northern India.

Indo-European   A subset of the Indo-Hittite language family. Indo-European includes nearly all European languages, the Indo-Aryan, and the Tokharian linguistic families. Although Phrygian and Armenian were situated in Anatolia they are Indo-European languages and do not belong to the Anatolian branch of Indo-Hittite.

Indo-Hittite   A language family that includes both the Anatolian and the Indo-European branches.

inflected languages   Languages such as Greek, Latin, and German that rely to a great extent on inflection or changing word shapes or morphology, rather than syntax or word order, to convey meaning.

interdentals   Consonants formed by putting the tongue between the teeth, as in th.

Ionians   Central Greek tribal grouping who survived the Dorian conquest. Some Ionians migrated to the west coast of Anatolia.

Iron Age   Period following the Bronze Age in which most tools and weapons were made of Iron. The term tends to be restricted to the first few centuries following the shift. Later periods are given names known from written history.

isolating languages   Languages such as Chinese and English that have little or no inflection but rely heavily on syntax or the order of words.

isolationism   The belief that cultures cannot be fundamentally affected by cultures from elsewhere, in contrast to diffusionism.

Kassites   A people from the mountains to the east of Mesopotamia, who conquered the region in the late eighteenth century B.C.E. and held it until the second half of the thirteenth century.

Kekrops   Legendary founder and king of Athens. He was generally portrayed as autochthonous, although a minority tradition saw him as coming from Egypt.

labials   Consonants formed with the lips, such as b, p, m.

labiovelars   Velars completed with a rounding of the lips such as the English qu.

laryngeals   Sounds made in the larynx or throat as a whole; more precisely, they can be divided into velar fricatives (ẖ and ǵ), pharyngeals (ḥ and ʿ), and the laryngeals in the narrow sense (ʾ and h). All of these except ǵ exist throughout Semitic as well as in Ancient Egyptian. Some survived in Anatolian languages, but all, with the very occasional exception of h, have disappeared from Indo-European in the narrow sense.

Late Helladic or Mycenaean   Ceramic period in Mainland Greece c. 1675–1100 B.C.E.

Late Minoan   Ceramic period in Crete c. 1675–1450 B.C.E., when the island became dominated by Mycenaean Greeks.

lead isotope   The measurement of the proportion of radioactive isotopes in lead, from which it is possible to determine the geological age of a particular lead deposit and hence the place of origin of objects containing lead.

Lemnos   Island in the northeast Aegean where a non-Indo-European language related to Etruscan was spoken in Classical times.

Levant   Term used for the east in general but generally restricted to Syro-Palestine.

Linear A   Syllabary with determinatives used on Crete and elsewhere in the second millennium B.C.E. before the establishment of Greek on the island. It may have survived considerably longer in eastern Crete.

Linear B   Syllabary with determinatives derived from a prototype of Linear A, used for writing Greek. It is attested from the seventeenth century B.C.E. but may have originated earlier. It was deciphered by the architect Michael Ventris in 1952.

liquids   Consonants such as l and r that flow.

loan   A word in which both the sense and the sound has been adopted from another. For example, the English "catch" came from the Old North French cachier. The impermanence suggested by the word "loan" and the similar term "borrowing" is misleading; they merely indicate the early-nineteenth-century linguists' disapproval of what they felt to be an unnatural process, sullying the purity of the original language.

Lycia   Region in southern Anatolia. The Lycian language was Anatolian and an indirect descendant of Hittite. Alphabetic inscriptions in Lycian date from the fifth century B.C.E.

Lydia   Region in northwestern Anatolia. The Lydian language belonged to the Anatolian family. Most traditions maintained that the Etruscans came from Lydia. Alphabetic inscriptions in Lydian date from the fifth century B.C.E.

Mandate of Heaven   Tianming in Chinese, an ancient political theory according to which a dynasty ruled only as long as it held the Mandate of Heaven. The mandate was eventually removed and handed over to the dynasty's successors.

Mesopotamia   The basin of the two rivers, the Tigris and the Euphrates, more or less corresponding to modern Iraq. It was the site of the emergence of one of the world's earliest civilizations.

metathesis   Alternation or switching of consonantal orvocalic position in language. Examples of this can be heard in the alternation "ask" and "aks."

Middle Helladic   Ceramic period in Mainland Greece c. 2000–1675 B.C.E.

Middle Kingdom   Egyptian historical period containing the Eleventh, Twelfth, and Thirteenth Dynasties c. 2150–1750 B.C.E. The Middle Minoan and Middle Helladic ceramic periods were loosely based on this.

Middle Minoan   Ceramic period on Crete c. 2000–1675 B.C.E.

Minoan   Modern name derived by Arthur Evans from Minos, the legendary king of Crete; applied to the Bronze Age cultures of Crete before the arrival there of Greek speakers and to the three ceramic periods, early, middle, and late, also established by Evans.

modified diffusionism   The belief that cultures can be modified or transformed by outside forces but that in most cases the changes take place only after considerable interaction with the local culture. See diffusionism and isolationism.

monism   In this book "monism" is used to indicate the notion that all things or processes have single fundamental causes.

monogenesis   The belief in single origins, largely restricted in this book to humanity and language. It is the opposite of polygenesis.

morphology   Modifications of words to indicate such things as number, case, tense, or temporal aspect.

Mycenae   City near Argos in the northeastern Peloponnese, famous as the leading city of Greece in the Late Bronze Age.

Mycenaean   Name of Late Bronze Age material culture first discovered at Mycenae. By extension, "Mycenaean" is used to describe Greek culture as a whole in that period.

nasals   Consonants such as m and n formed in the nasal passage.

Neo-Babylonian   An empire ruled from Babylon that dominated much of Mesopotamia between the fall of the Assyrian Empire c. 600 B.C.E. and the rise of the Persian Empire some sixty years later.

Old Kingdom   Period of Egyptian strength and prosperity from the Third to the Sixth Dynasties, c. 3000–2500 B.C.E.

Olympic Games   Religious festival and games held at Olympia in the northwest Peloponnese every four years from 776 B.C.E. until they were discontinued by the Roman emperor Theodosius at the end of the fourth century C.E. They were revived in the late nineteenth century in the same spirit of European ethnicity and elitism from which the Aryan model had emerged.

Orphics   Followers of the divine Orpheus, from the sixth century to the second century C.E. Very much like the Pythagoreans, the Orphics promoted Egyptian religious beliefs and were especially concerned with personal immortality.

Pantheism   Belief that God is in all things and all things are God. This worldview, which closely resembled that of Egyptian and Greek religion, became significant in the seventeenth century C.E., especially after the publication of the works of Spinoza.

Pausanias   Greek writer of an extensive *Guide to Greece*, who lived in the second century C.E.

Pelasgians   According to Classical traditions, the Pelasgians were the earliest inhabitants of Greece.

Pericles   Ruler of Athens during its apogee in the fifth century B.C.E.

Persian Empire   Founded by Cyrus the Great in the mid–sixth century B.C.E., it dominated Southwest Asia, Egypt, and much of the Aegean, until pushed back by an alliance of Greeks. It was destroyed by Alexander the Great in the late fourth century B.C.E.

Philistines   One of the peoples coming from the Aegean and Anatolia who invaded the Levant and attacked Egypt in the thirteenth and twelfth centuries B.C.E.

Phoenicia   Cities along a strip of coast stretching from Lebanon to northern Palestine/Israel. The most famous of these were Byblos, Tyre, and Sidon. The name "Phoenicia" refers to this region throughout antiquity; however, it is generally used to refer to the period of the cities' greatest power and prosperity between 1100 and 750 B.C.E. The Phoenician language, like Hebrew, was a Canaanite dialect. The alphabet is often referred to as a Phoenician invention. It may well have originated in this region but it was developed long before the "Phoenician" period.

phoneme   The minimal unit of sound within a language.

phonetic correspondences   Sounds that are actually or etymologically similar.

Phrygia   Region in northern Anatolia. It was a powerful state in the first half of the first millennium B.C.E. The Phrygian language, which was written alphabetically, was not Anatolian but Indo-European and closely related to Greek.

pictogram   Writing in which the object signified is pictured or directly represented. Hieroglyphics and Chinese characters contain pictograms, though they also have abstract ideographic and phonetic symbols.

polygenesis   The belief in multiple origins, in particular of humanity or language. The opposite of monogenesis.

prothetic or prosthetic   Vowels placed at the beginnings of words to avoid certain initial consonants. It is particularly common before double consonants.

Proto-Greek   The unattested language or people reconstructed as having been the origin of Greek or Greeks.

Ptolemaic   Name given to Egyptian culture under the Ptolemies.

Ptolemy   Name of a succession of descendents of Ptolemy, a general of Alexander who seized power in Egypt after Alexander's death. The last ruler of this dynasty was Cleopatra VII, loved by both Caesar and Mark Anthony, who died dramatically in 30 B.C.E.

Pythagoras (c. 582–500 B.C.E.)   Greek philosopher and mathematician. He studied in Egypt and brought back Egyptian mathematical and religious principles and founded the Pythagorean brotherhood.

Pythagoreans   Followers of Pythagoras organized into a "brotherhood" along what were generally seen to be the principles used by Egyptian priesthoods. The Pythagoreans played important political, religious, and scientific roles in the Greek society of Sicily and southern Italy in the fifth and fourth centuries B.C.E.

race   A concept that is meaningless biologically but is of immense social importance in the world today. "Races" are divided by the arbitrary focus on particular superficial characteristics, notably complexion and facial physiognomy. Sometimes, these coincide with particular geographical regions and peoples' residence in them for many millennia. However, given the relatively recent development of the human species, the genetic differentiation among these populations is extremely slight. Nevertheless, a "racism" or sense of their intellectual or moral superiority has arisen among Europeans and their descendents in other continents to justify and is used to perpetuate their dominance over other peoples with different appearances.

root   Essential part of a word that remains after all the others have been removed.

Seleucid   Name of the dynasty established in Syria and Mesopotamia by Alexander's general Seleukos from 322 to 64 B.C.E.

semantic   Relating to signification or meaning.

Semitic   A language family containing Akkadian, Arabic, Aramaic, Canaanite, Ge'ez, and other Ethiopian languages. Semitic itself belongs to the Afroasiatic language family and probably originated in East Africa.

sibilants   Consonants with hissing sounds such as s, š, ṣ, and z.

Sidon   Ancient Phoenician city dedicated to the sea god Sid. Its apogee was in the very early Iron Age. Therefore, "Sidonian" was often used to designate Phoenician in Homer and in the early historical books of the Bible. Sidon's dominance was replaced by that of its rival, Tyre, during the ninth century B.C.E.

stele   Upright stone slab with sculptured designs and/or inscriptions.

stem   Verbal form derived from the root by special vocalization or the addition of various prefixes or suffixes.

stop   A complete consonantal explosion of breath, as in the sounds represented by the letters b, p, d, t, g, and k.

Strabo   Greek geographer of the first centuries B.C.E. and C.E.

Sumerian   People inhabiting regions of Mesopotamia in the fifth and fourth millennia B.C.E. Their language, Sumerian, which is neither Afroasiatic nor Indo-Hittite, served as a literary language and status marker for millennia after it died out as a spoken language.

syllabary   A script that represents syllables, usually of the pattern consonant + vowel rather than with single letters.

syntax   The order of words.

theogony   Ancestry or birth of the gods. It was the name and subject of a number of poems, the most famous being that of Hesiod.

Thera   Volcanic island seventy miles north of Crete. It suffered a major eruption during the second millennium B.C.E., which is now dated to 1628 B.C.E.

Thucydides (c. 460–c. 400 B.C.E.)   Greek historian of the Peloponnesian War.

Tokharian   Indo-European language spoken in the first millennium C.E. in the still largely Turkic-speaking "autonomous region" of Xinjiang (Sinkiang) in China. Tokharian shares several features with Western Indo-European languages that are not present in the Indo-Aryan ones. It therefore provides critical information on the nature of early Indo-European.

Toponym   Place-name.

Tyre   Ancient Phoenician city; its period of greatest glory was from the tenth to the eighth centuries B.C.E. It remained an important economic, political, and cultural center for many centuries, even after its destruction by Alexander the Great in 333 B.C.E.

Ugarit   Major port on the Syrian coast that flourished particularly in the second half of the second millennium B.C.E.

Ugaritic   The West Semitic language spoken at Ugarit and recorded in an alphabetic form of cuneiform on many of the tablets found in the city.

Urartu   Kingdom in the Southern Caucasus in the first half of the first millennium B.C.E. Its language was related to Hurrian and the present Northeast Caucasian languages.

velars   Stops formed with the tongue at the back of the mouth, as, for example, k and g.

vocalization   Infusing a consonantal structure with vowels.

Zoroaster   Iranian religious reformer who lived in the second millennium B.C.E.

Zoroastrianism   Religion founded by Zoroaster, which became the state religion of the Persian Empire. It maintained that the universe was the scene of a perpetual and finely balanced struggle between light good and dark evil. It was largely destroyed in Iran after the Muslim conquest, but it is still flourishing elsewhere in the world among the Parsees.

Bibliography

Aarsleff, H. (1988). Introduction to *On Language: The Diversity of Human Language-Structure and Its Influence on the Mental Developments of Mankind*, by W. von Humboldt. Trans. Peter Heath. Cambridge, England: Cambridge University Press.

Aboul Nasr, I. (1993). *Les substrats Arabes dans les mots Français et Latin: Essai de linguistique comparée*. Cairo, Egypt: Librairie Franco-Egyptienne.

Adrados, F. R. (1989). "Etruscan as an IE-Anatolian but Not Hittite Language." *Journal of Indo-European Studies* 173.4: 363–383.

Aeschylus. *The Suppliants.*

Ahl, F., and H. Roisman. (1996). *The Odyssey Re-Formed.* Ithaca, NY: Cornell University Press.

Albright, W. (1923). "The Principles of Egyptian Phonological Development." *Recueils de Travaux* 40: 64–70.

———. (1950). "Some Oriental Glosses on the Homeric Problem." *American Journal of Archaeology* 54: 162–176.

———. (1978 [1968]). *Yahweh and the Gods of Canaan.* Repr. Winona Lake, IN: Eisenbraun.

Alford, G. (1992). "Ἐλύσιον: A Foreign Eschatological Concept in Homer's *Odyssey*." *Journal of Indo-European Studies* 20: 151–162.

Allen, N. (1990). "Black Athena: An Interview with Martin Bernal." *Free Inquiry* 10: 18–22.

Allen, P. S. (1992). "Black Athena." Film review. *American Anthropologist* 94.4: 1024–1026.

Allen, R. E., ed. (1985). *Greek Philosophy: Thales to Aristotle.* 2d ed. New York: Free Press.

Altenmüller, H. (1975). "Bes." In Helck and Otto (1975–1984). I. cols. 721–724.

Ambjörnson, R. (1995). "East and West of a European Identity." *VEST* 4: 97–112.

Ammerman, A., and L. L. Cavalli-Sforza. (1984). *The Neolithic Transition and the Genetics of Populations in Europe.* Princeton, NJ: Princeton University Press.

Anderson, P. (1974). *Passages from Antiquity to Feudalism.* London: New Left Books.

———. (1987). "The Myth of Hellenism." *The Guardian* (Manchester) 13 Mar.: 14.

Annan, N. (1990) *Our Age: The Generation That Made Post-war Britain.* London: Fontana.

Apollodorus. *The Library.*

Appiah, K. A. (1992). *My Father's House: Africa in the Philosophy of Culture.* New York: Oxford University Press.

———. (1993a). "African-American Philosophy." *Philosophical Forum* 24.34: 40.

———. (1993b). "Europe Upside Down: Fallacies of the New Afrocentrism." *Times Literary Supplement* (London) 12 Feb.: 24–25.

Aptheker, H. (1989). *Abolitionism.* Boston: Twaine.

Arapoyanni, K. (1996). "A New Linear B Text from Olympia." *Ethnos* 3.27: 6.

Aristotle. *Atheneion Politeia.*

———. *Metaphysics.*

———. *The Politics.*

Arnold, D. (1991). *Building in Egypt: Pharaonic Stone Masonry.* New York: Oxford University Press.

Asante, M. K. (1990). *Kemet, Afrocentricity, and Knowledge.* Trenton, NJ: Africa World Press.

———. (1991a). "Multiculturalism: An Exchange." *American Scholar* 60.2: 267–272.

———. (1991b). *Response. Challenging Tradition: Cultural Interaction in Antiquity and Bernal's Black Athena.* Tape 5B. Departments of African American Studies and Classics, Temple University, Philadelphia, PA.

———. (1993). "Social Studies." *African–Puerto Rican Centric Curriculum Guide,* vol. 1 (grades 1 and 2). Camden, NJ: Camden City Public Schools.

Ascher, Maria. (1991). *Ethnomathematics A Multicultural View of Mathematical Ideas.* New York: Chapman and Hall.

Ashmore, Malcolm. (1989). *The Reflexive Thesis: Wrighting Sociology of Scientific Knowledge.* Chicago: Chicago University Press.

Assmann, J. (1970). *Der König als Sonnenpriester: Ein kosmographischer Begleittext* zur kultischen Sonnenhymnik in thebanischen Tempeln und Gräbern. *Abhandlungen des Deutschen Akademie der Wissenschaften zu Berlin*, 7.

————. (1975). *Zeit und Ewigkeit im alten Ägypten*. Heidelberg, Germany: Winter.

————. (1984). "Politik zwischen Rituel und Dogma: Spielräume politischen Handelns in pharaonischen Ägypten." *Saeculum* 35: 97–114.

————. (1989). "Death and Initiation in the Funerary Religion of Ancient Egypt." In *Religion and Philosophy in Ancient Egypt*, ed. J. P. Allen. New Haven: Yale Egyptological Series 3, pp. 135–159.

————. (1992a) *Das kulturelle Gedächtnis: Schrift, Erinnerung und politische Identität in frühen Hochkulturen*. Munich: C. H. Beck.

————. (1992b). "Sentimental Journey zu den Wurzeln Europas, zu Bernals Black Athena." *Merkur: Deutsche Zeitschrift für Europäisches Denken* 46: 921–931.

————. (1993a). "Diskussionen." In *Anfänge politischen Denkens in der Antike: Die nah-östlichen Kulturen und die Griechen*, ed. K. Raaflaub. Munich: R. Oldenbourg, p. 400.

————. (1993b). *Monotheismus und Kosmotheismus: Ägyptische Formen eines Denkens des Einen und ihre europäische Rezeptionsgeschichte*. Heidelberg, Germany: Winter.

————. (1995a). "Jehova-Isis: The Mysteries of Egypt and the Quest for Natural Religion in the Age of the Enlightenment." In *Egypt and the Fabrication of European Identity*, ed. I. A. Bierman. Los Angeles: UCLA Near East Center Colloquium Series, pp. 35–84.

————. (1995b). *Ma'at, Gerechtigkeit und Unsterblichkeit im Alten Ägypten*. Munich: Beck.

————. (1996). *Ägypten: Eine Sinnesgeschichte*. Munich: Hanser.

————. (1997). *Moses the Egyptian: The Memory of Egypt in Western Monotheism*. Cambridge, MA: Harvard University Press.

Astour, M. C. (1964). "The Amarna Age Forerunners of Biblical Anti-Royalism." In *For Max Weinreich on His Seventieth Birthday*, ed. L. Davidowitz. The Hague: Mouton, pp. 6–17.

————. (1967a). *Hellenosemitica: An Ethnic and Cultural Study in West Semitic Impact on Mycenean Greece*. 2d ed., with additions and corrections. Leiden: Brill.

————. (1967b) "The Problem of Semitic in Ancient Crete." *Journal of the American Oriental Society* 87, 3: 290–295.

August, E. R., ed. (1971). *The Negro Question*. New York: Appleton Century Crofts.

Aune, J. (1993). "Review of Black Athena 2." *Quarterly Journal of Speech* 79: 119–122.

Austin, N. (1975). *Archery at the Dark of Moon*. Berkeley: University of California Press.

Bacon, F. (1863 [1620]). *Novum Organum*. Vol. 8 of *The Works of Francis Bacon*, ed. J. Spedding, R. L. Ellis, and D. D. Heath. Boston: Brown and Taggard.

Bailey, A. M., and J. R. Llobera. (1981). *The Asiatic Mode of Production: Science and Politics*. London: Routledge and Kegan Paul.

Bain, A. (1882). *James Mill: A Biography*. London: Longmans.

Baines, J. (1990). "Restricted Knowledge, Hierarchy, and Decorum: Modern Perceptions and Ancient Institutions." *Journal of the American Research Center in Egypt* 27: 1–23.

———. (1991). "Was Civilisation Made in Africa?" *New York Times Book Review* 11 Aug.: 12–13.

———. (1996). "The Aims and Methods of *Black Athena*." In *Black Athena Revisited*, ed. M. R. Lefkowitz and G. MacLean Rogers. Chapel Hill: University of North Carolina Press, pp. 27–48.

Baines, J., and J. Málek. (1980). *Atlas of Ancient Egypt*. Oxford: Phaidon.

Barb, A. A. (1971). "Mystery, Myth and Magic." In *The Legacy of Egypt*, ed. John Harris. 2d ed. Oxford: Oxford University Press, pp. 138–169.

Bard, K. (1992). "Ancient Egyptians and the Issue of Race." *Bostonian* 2: 41–43, 69. Repr. Lefkowitz and Rogers, (1996), pp. 103–111.

Bardinet, T. (1995). *Les papyrus médicaux de l'Égypte pharaonique: traduction intégrale et commentaire*. Paris: Fayard.

Barker, E., trans. (1958). *The Politics of Aristotle*. London: Oxford University Press.

Barnes, J. (1987). *Early Greek Philosophy*. Harmondsworth, England: Penguin.

———. (1988). "Review of G. E. R. Lloyd 1987." *Times Literary Supplement* (London) 16–22 Dec.: 1392.

———. (1991). "The Hellenistic Platos." *Apeiron* 24.2: 115–128.

Barthélemy, J.-J. (1763). "Réflexions générales sur les rapports des langues égyptienne, phénicienne et grecque." *Recueils des Mémoires de l'Académie des Inscriptions* 32: 212–233.

———. (1790). *Voyage du jeune Anacharsis en Grèce dans le milieu du quatrième siècle avant l'ère vulgaire*. Paris: de Bure.

Bass, G. (1967). *Cape Gelidonya: A Bronze Age Shipwreck*. Transactions of the American Philosophical Society 57, part 8. Philadelphia: American Philosophical Society.

———. (1986). "A Bronze Age Shipwreck at Ulu Burun (Kas): 1984 Campaign." *American Journal of Archaeology* 90: 269–296.

———. (1987). "Oldest Known Shipwreck Reveals Splendors of the Bronze Age." *National Geographic* 172: 692–733.

———. (1991). "Evidence of Trade from Bronze Age Shipwrecks." In *Bronze Age Trade in the Mediterranean*, ed. N. Gale. Jonsered: P. Åströms förlag, pp. 69–82.

———. (1997). "Beneath the Wine Dark Sea: Nautical Archaeology and the Phoenicians of the *Odyssey*." In *Greeks and Barbarians*, ed. J. Coleman and C. Walz. Bethesda, MD: CDL Press, pp. 71–101.

Bass, G., and P. Bikai. (1989). "Responses." In Levine and Peradotto: 111–112.

Bass, G. F., C. Pulak, D. Collon, and J. Weinstein. (1989). "The Bronze Age Shipwreck at Ulu Burun: 1986 Campaign." *American Journal of Archaeology* 93: 1–29.

Bates, O. (1914). *The Eastern Libyans: An Essay*. London: Macmillan.

Baumgarten, A. I. (1981). *The Phoenician History of Philo of Byblos: A Commentary*. Leiden, Netherlands: Brill.

Becker, H. (1967). "Whose Side Are We On?" *Social Problems* 14: 239–247.

Begley, S. F. Chideya, and L. Wilson. (1991). "Out of Egypt, Greece." *Newsweek* 23 Sept.: 49–50.

Beider, R. E. (1986). *Science Encounters the Indian, 1820–1880: The Early Years of American Ethnology*. Norman: University of Oklahoma Press.

Beloch, Julius. (1893–1904). *Griechische Geschichte*. 3 vols in 4. Strasbourg: Trübner.

Bendall, C. (1922). "H. H. Wilson." *Dictionary of National Biography*, 21: 568–570.

Bender, L. (1975). *Omotic: A New Afroasiatic Family*. Carbondale: Southern Illinois University Press.

———. (1997). *Upside-Down Afrasian*. Paper given at the 25th annual meeting of the North American Conference on Afroasiatic Languages. Miami 22–25 Mar.

Ben-Jochanan, Y. A. A. (1970). *Black Man of the Nile*. New York: Alkebu-lan Books.

———. (1988 [1971]). *Africa, Mother of Western Civilization*. Baltimore: Alkebu-lan Books/Black Classic Press.

———. (1989). *Black Man of the Nile and His Family*. Baltimore: Alkebu-lan Books.

Bérard, V. (1894). *De l'origine des cultes arcadiens: Essai de méthode en mythologie grecque*. Paris: Bibliothèque des Écoles Françaises d'Athènes et de Rome.

———. (1902–1903; 2d ed. 1927). *Les Phéniciens et l'Odyssée*. 2 vols. Paris: Armand Colin.

Bergk, T. (1882). *Poetae Lirici Graeci*. 4 vols. Leipzig, Germany: Teubner.

Berkhofer, Robert F. (1978). *The White Man's Indian: Images of the American Indian from Columbus to the Present*. New York: Vintage.

Berlin, I. (1976). *Vico and Herder: Two Studies in the History of Ideas*. London: Viking.

Berlinerblau, J. (1996). "Black Athena Redux." *Nation* 28 Oct.: 42–46.

———. (1999). *Heresy in the University: The Black Athena Controversy and the Responsibilities of American Intellectuals*. New Brunswick, NJ: Rutgers University Press.

Bernal, M. (1976). *Chinese Socialism to 1907*. Ithaca, NY: Cornell University Press.

———. (1980). "Speculations on the Disintegration of Afroasiatic." Paper given at the 8th annual North American Conference of Afroasiatic Linguistics, and presented in absentia to the 1st International Congress of Somali Studies, Mogadishu.

———. (1981). "A New Proto-Semitic." Paper given at the 9th annual North American Conference of Afroasiatic Linguistics, Boston.

————. (1985). "Black Athena: The African and Levantine Roots of Greece." In *African Presence in Early Europe*, ed. I. Van Sertima. New Brunswick, NJ: Transaction Books, pp. 66–82.

————. (1986). "Black Athena Denied: The Tyranny of Germany over Greece and the Rejection of the Afroasiatic Roots of Europe: 1780–1980." *Comparative Criticism* 8: 3–69.

————. (1987a). *Black Athena: The Afroasiatic Roots of Classical Civilization*. Vol. 1. *The Fabrication of Ancient Greece 1785–1985*. London: Free Association Books.

————. (1987b). "The British Utilitarians, Imperialism and the Fall of the Ancient Model." Paper presented to the conference on "The Canonization of Greece in the Human and Social Sciences." Given by the Department of Modern Greek Studies, Harvard University, November, 1987.

————. (1987c). "On the Transmission of the Alphabet into the Aegean before 1400 B.C." *Bulletin of the American School of Oriental Research* 267: 1–19.

————. (1988a). "The British Utilitarians, Imperialism and the Fall of the Ancient Model." *Culture and History* 3: 98–127.

————. (1988b). "Ελλάδα άρια ή μεσογειακή." *Αρχαιολογία* 27: 6–10.

————. (1989a). "Black Athena and the APA." In Levine and Peradotto: 17–38.

————. (1989b). "First by Land, Then by Sea: Thoughts about the Social Formation of the Mediterranean and Greece." In *Geography in Historical Perspective*, ed. E. Genovese and L. Hochberg. Oxford: Blackwell, pp. 3–33.

————. (1989c). "Classics in Crisis: An Outsider's View In." In *Classics: A Discipline and Profession in Crisis?*, ed. P. Culham and L. Edmunds. New York: University Press of America, pp. 67–76.

————. (1989d). "Response to Professor Morris." In Levine and Peradotto: 20–23.

————. (1989e). "Response to Professor Rendsburg." In Levine and Peradotto: 32–37.

————. (1989f). "Response to Professor Snowden." In Levine and Peradotto: 30–32.

————. (1989g). "Response to Professor Turner." In Levine and Peradotto: 26–30.

————. (1990a). *Cadmean Letters: The Transmission of the Alphabet to the Aegean and Further West before 1400 B.C.* Winona Lake, IN: Eisenbrauns.

————. (1990b). "Responses to Critical Reviews of *Black Athena*, Volume 1." *Journal of Mediterranean Archaeology* 3.1: 111–137.

————. (1991a). *Black Athena*. Video. London: Bandung File; San Francisco: Californian Newsreels. Christopher Spencer, director; Tariq Ali, producer.

————. (1991b). *Black Athena: The Afroasiatic Roots of Classical Civilization*. Vol. 2. *The Archaeological and Documentary Evidence*. London: Free Association Books.

————. (1991c). Response to *Challenging Tradition: Cultural Interaction in Antiquity and Bernal's Black Athena*, tape 7A. Departments of African American Studies and Classico, Temple University, Philadelphia, PA.

———. (1992a). "Animadversions on the Origins of Western Science." Special section, "The Cultures of Ancient Science," *Isis* 83.4: 596–607.

———. (1992b). "Becoming Homer: An Exchange." Letter. *New York Review of Books* 14 May: 52.

———. (1992c). "Bernal Replies to *New York Review* Attack." *The Bookpress* Apr.: 2, 4, 9, 13–14.

———. (1992d). "Book Review, *Freedom in the Making of Western Culture* by Orlando Patterson." *American Journal of Sociology* 97. 5: 1471–1473.

———. (1992e). "The Case for Massive Egyptian Influence in the Aegean." *Archaeology* 45.5: 53–55, 82–86.

———. (1992f). "An Exchange on 'Black Athena.'" Letter. *New York Review of Books* 14 May: 52–53.

———. (1992g). "Response to Edith Hall." *Arethusa* 25: 203–214.

———. (1992h). "A Response to John Coleman I." *The Bookpress* 2.1: 2, 4, 16.

———. (1992i). "A Response to John Coleman II." *The Bookpress* 2.2: 2, 13.

———. (1992j). "A Response to John Coleman III." *The Bookpress* 2.4: 2, 12–13.

———. (1992k). "Response to Mary Lefkowitz, 'Not Out of Africa.'" *New Republic* 9 Mar.: 4–5.

———. (1993a). "Diskussionen." In *Anfänge politischen Denkens in der Antike: Die nah-östlichen Kulturen und die Griechen.* Munich: R. Oldenbourg, ed. Raaflaub, pp. 365–367, 379, 390, 395–400, 403–404.

———. (1993b). "Phoenician Politics and Egyptian Justice in Ancient Greece." In *Anfänge politischen Denkens in der Antike: Die nah-östlichen Kulturen und die Griechen,* ed. K. Raaflaub. Munich: R. Oldenbourg, pp. 241–261.

———. (1993c). "Reply to L. A. Tritle." *Liverpool Classical Monthly* 18.2: 18–32.

———. (1993d). "Response, The Debate over Black Athena." *Journal of Women's History* 4.3: 119–135.

———. (1993e). "Response to S. O. Y. Keita." *Arethusa* 26: 315–319.

———. (1994a). "The Image of Ancient Greece as a Tool for Colonialism and European Hegemony." In *Social Construction of the Past: Representation as Power. One World Archaeology* 24, ed. George C. Bond and Angela Gilliam. London: Routledge, pp. 119–128.

———. (1994b). Letter. *Academic Questions* summer: 7.

———. (1994c). "Response to Robert Palter." *History of Science* 32.4: 445–464.

———. (1995a). "Black Athena: The Historical Construction of Europe." *VEST: Tidskrift för Vetenskapsstudier,* 8.4: 25–34.

———. (1995b). "Comments on the Proceedings of the 2nd Day." *VEST: Tidskrift för Vetenskapsstudier* 8.4: 113–121.

———. (1995c). "Greece: Aryan or Mediterranean? Two Contending Historiographical Models." in Federici, pp. 3–11.

———. (1995d). "Race, Class and Gender in the Formation of the Aryan Model of Greek Origins." *South Atlantic Quarterly* 94.4: 987–1008.

———. (1995e). "Responses to Comments." *VEST: Tidskrift för Vetenskapsstudier* 8.4: 53–58.

———. (1995f). "Review of Sarah P. Morris: *Daidalos and the Origins of Greek Art*." *Arethusa* 28.1: 113–135.

———. (1996a). "The Afrocentric Interpretation of History: Bernal Replies to Lefkowitz." *Journal of Blacks in Higher Education* 11: 86–94.

———. (1996b). "Black Athena Revisited." Letter. *New York Review of Books* 7 Nov.: 60.

———. (1996c). Debate with Mary Lefkowitz on May 9, 1996. Available through HarperCollins online forum electronic debate archive: (http://www.HarperCollins.com/basic/lefko2.htm).

———. (1996d). "Reply to Mary Lefkowitz's Response to My Review." Debate, HarperCollins online, May.

———. (1996e). "Reply to ML's Reply to My Reply to Her Response to My Review." Debate, HarperCollins online, May.

———. (1996f). "Review of Mary Lefkowitz *Not Out of Africa*." *Bryn Mawr Classical Review* Apr. (electronic).

———. (1996g). "Review of *The Orientalizing Revolution: Near Eastern Influence on Greek Culture in the Early Archaic Age*, by Walter Burkert." *Arion* 3.4.2:137–147.

———. (1996h). "Rocking the Cradle: Review of Mary Lefkowitz *Not Out of Africa* and *Black Athena Revisited*." *The Bookpress* Nov.: 11–12.

———. (1996i). "Whose Greece? Review of Mary Lefkowitz *Not Out of Africa* and *Black Athena Revisited*." *London Review of Books* 12 Dec.: 17–18.

———. (1997a). "Black from the Oases." pp. 149–171. In *Crossing Boundaries and Linking Horizons: Studies in Honor of Michael C. Astour*, ed. G. D. Young, M. W. Chavalas, and R. E. Averbeck. Bethesda: CDL Press, pp. 149–171.

———. (1997b). "Η Μαύρη Αθηνά και η υποδοχή της." *ΣΥΓΧΡΟΝΑ ΘΕΜΑΤΑ* 19.64: 24–26.

———. (1997c). "Politically Correct: Mythologies of Neo-Conservatism in the American Academy." *New Political Science* 38.9: 17–28.

———. (1997d). "Race in History." In *Global Convulsions: Race, Ethnicity and Nationalism at the End of the 20th Century*, ed. W. Van Horne. University of Wisconsin, Institute of Race Relations Monograph Series, pp. 75–92.

———. (1997e). "Response to Arno Egberts." *Talanta* 27: 149–155.

———. (1997f). "Response to Josine Blok." *Talanta* 27: 193–202.

———. (1997g). "Responses to Black Athena: General and Linguistic Issues." *Talanta* 27: 53–86.

———. (1998a). "'Civilized Discourse' in Academe." Letter. *Chronicle of Higher Education* 3.4:B11.

———. (1998b). "On 'Robbing Native American Cultures.'" *Current Anthropology* Aug.–Oct.: 512–514.

———. (forthcoming). *Black Athena: The Afroasiatic Roots of Classical Civilization: III: The Linguistic Evidence*. London: Free Association Books; Brunswick, NJ: Rutgers University Press.

———. (forthcoming). *Moses and Muses*. London: Polity Press.

Bernal, M., and D. C. Moore (forthcoming). *Debating Black Athena*. Durham, NC: Duke University Press.

Bernier, François. (1684). "Nouvelle division de la terre, par les différentes espèces ou races d'hommes qui l'habitent, envoyée par un fameux voyageur à Monsieur_____." *Journal des Scavants* 24 Apr.

Bianchi, B. (1992). *Who Was Cleopatra?* Film.

Bickerman, E. J. (1952). "Origines Gentium." *Classical Philology* 47: 65–81.

———. (1980). *Chronology of the Ancient World.* 2d ed. Ithaca, NY: Cornell University Press.

Bieder, R. E. (1986). *Science Encounters the Indian, 1820–1880.* Norman: University of Oklahoma Press.

Bietak, M. (1992). "Minoan Wall-Paintings Unearthed at Ancient Avaris." *Egyptian Archaeology: Bulletin of the Egyptian Archaeological Society* 2: 26–28.

———. (1995). "Connections between Egypt and the Minoan World: New Results from Tell el-Daba'a/Avaris." In *Egypt, the Aegean and the Levant: Interconnections in the Second Millennium B.C.,* ed. W. V. Davies and L. Schofield. London: British Museum, pp. 19–28.

———. (1999). Lecture. Cornell University, Ithaca, NY, 29 Jan.

Bikai, P. (1990). "Black Athena and the Phoenicians." *Journal of Mediterranean Archaeology* 3.1: 67–75.

Bilfinger, G. (1888). *Der bürgerliche Tag.* Stuttgart, Germany: W. Kohlhammer.

Bilolo, M. (1986). *Les Cosmo-Theologies Philosophiques de l'Égypte antique.* Academie de la Pensée Africaine, section 1, vol. 1. Kinshasa, Zaire: Publications Universitaires Africaines.

Bisi, A. M. (1965). *Il Grifone: Storia di un motivo iconografico nell'antico oriente Mediterraneo.* Rome: Centro di studi semitici, Istituto di studi del vicino oriente.

Blackburn, R. (1988). *The Overthrow of Colonial Slavery 1776–1848.* London: Verso.

———. (1997). *The Making of New World Slavery: From the Baroque to the Modern 1492–1800.* London: Verso.

Bleiberg, E. (1984). "The King's Privy Purse during the New Kingdom: An Examination of INW." *Journal of the American Research Center in Egypt* 31: 155–167.

Blench, R. (1993). "Recent Developments in African Language Classification and Their Implications for Prehistory." In *The Archaeology of Africa,* ed. T. Shaw, P. Sinclair, B. Andah, and A. Okpoko. New York: Routledge, pp. 126–137.

———. (1997). "Crabs, Turtles and Frogs: Linguistic Keys to Early African Subsistence Systems." In *Archaeology and Language I: Theoretical and Methodological Orientations,* ed. R. Blench and M. Spriggs. London: Routledge, pp. 166–183.

Blok, J. (1996). "Proof and Persuasion in *Black Athena*: The Case of K. O. Müller." *Journal of the History of Ideas* 57.2: 705–724.

———. (1997). "Proof and Persuasion in *Black Athena*: The Case of K. O. Müller." *Talanta* 27: 173–208.

———. (1998). "Romantische Poesie, Naturphilosophie, Construktion der

Geschichte: K. O. Müller's Understanding of History and Myth." In Calder and Schleisier, pp. 55–97.

Blue, G. (1999). "China and Western Social Thought in the Modern Period." In *China and Historical Capitalism: Genealogies of Sinological Knowledge*, ed. G. Blue and T. Brook. Cambridge, England: Cambridge University Press, pp. 57–109.

Blumenbach, J. F. (1787). "Einige naturalhistorische Bemerkungen bey Gelegenheit einer Schweizer Reise von den negern." *Magazine für das Neuste aus den Physik und Naturgeschichte* 1.4: 1–12.

———. (1795). *De Generis Humani Varietate Nativa*. Göttingen, Germany: Vandenhoeck & Ruprecht.

———. (1799). "The Bodily Conformation and Mental Capacity of the Negro." *Philosophical Magazine* 3: 141–147.

———. (1817). *The Institutions of Physiology*. Trans. John Elliotson. Philadelphia: Warner.

Boardman, J. (1978). *Greek Sculpture: The Archaic Period*. London: Oxford University Press.

———. (1990). "Al Mina and History." *Oxford Journal of Archaeology* 9: 169–190.

Bockische, G. (1982). "Zur Entstehung der Produktionssklaverei im alter Griechenland." In *Produktivkräfte und Gesellschaftsformationen in vorkapitalistischer Zeit*, ed. Joachim Herrmann. Berlin: Akademie Verlag.

Bogan, Z. (1658). *Homerus Ἑβραΐζων sive comparatio Homeri cum scriptoribus sacris quoad normam loquendi*. Oxford: Hall and Robinson.

Böhm, S. (1990). *Die "Nakt Göttin": Ikonographie und Deutung unbekleiditer weiblicher Figuren in der frühgriechischer Kunst*. Mainz, Germany: Ph. von Zabern.

Bolinger, D. L. (1968 [1950]). "Ryme, Assonance and Morpheme Analysis." *Word* 6: 117–136. Repr. *Forms of English: Accent, Morpheme, Order*, ed. I. Abe and T. Kanekiyo. Cambridge MA: Harvard University Press, pp. 203–226.

Bomhard, A. R. (1984). *Toward Proto-Nostratic: A New Approach*. Amsterdam: Benjamins.

Bomhard, A. R., and J. C. Kerns. (1994). *The Nostratic Macrofamily: A Study of Distant Family Relationship*. Berlin: Mouton de Gruyter.

Bonfante, G., and L. Bonfante. (1983). *The Etruscan Language*. Manchester, England: Manchester University Press.

Bonnet, H. (1952). *Reallexikon der Ägyptischen Religionsgeschichte*. Berlin: Walter de Gruyter.

Boswell, J. (1965 [1791]). *Life of Johnson*. London: Oxford University Press.

Bower, B. (1991). "Race Falls from Grace: Report from the Annual Meeting of the American Anthropological Association." *Science News* 140: 380.

Bowersock, G. (1989). "Review of *Black Athena I*." *Journal of Interdisciplinary History* 19: 490–491.

———. (1996). "Review of *Not Out of Africa* and *Black Athena Revisited*." *New York Times Book Review* 25 Feb.: 6.

Bowersock, G. W., and T. J. Cornell, eds. (1994). *A. D. Momigliano: Studies on Modern Scholarship.* Berkeley: University of California Press.

Bracken, H. M. (1973). "Essence, Accident and Race." *Hermathena* 116: 81–96.

———. (1978). "Philosophy and Racism." *Philosophia* 8: 241–260.

Branham, B. (1989). "Hellenomania." *Liverpool Classical Monthly* 14: 56–60.

Braun, L. (1973). *Histoire de l'histoire de la philosophie.* Paris: Editions Ophrys.

Breasted, J. H. (1906). *Ancient Records of Egypt: Historical Documents from the Earliest Times.* Vol. 1. Chicago: University of Chicago Press.

Brodhead, F. (1987). "The African Origins of Western Civ." *Radical America* 21.5: 29–37.

Brown, J. P. (1968). "Cosmological Myth and the Tuna of Gibraltar." *Transactions of the American Philological Asociation* 99: 37–82.

———. (1995). *Israel and Hellas.* Vol. 1. Berlin: de Gruyter.

———. (2000). *Israel and Hellas.* Vol. 2. Berlin: de Gruyter.

Brown, R. B. (1975). *A Provisional Catalogue of and Commentary on Egyptian and Egyptianizing Artifacts Found on Greek Sites.* Ph.D. thesis, University of Minnesota.

Brown, R. L. (1967). *Wilhelm von Humboldt's Conception of Linguistic Relativity.* The Hague: Mouton.

Brugsch, H. (1879–1880). *Dictionnaire géographique de l'ancienne Égypte.* 2 vols. Leipzig, Germany: Hinrichs.

———. (1885–1888). *Religion und Mythologie der alter Ägypter.* Leipzig, Germany: Hinrichs.

Budge, E. A. W. (1904). *The Gods of the Egyptians: Studies in Egyptian Mythology.* 2 vols. London: Methuen.

Bulmer-Thomas, I. (1980). "Conon of Samos." *Dictionary of Scientific Biography,* vol 3. New York: Scribner, pp. 70–85.

———. (1970–1985). "Euclid." In *Dictionary of Scientific Biography,* ed. C. C. Gillispie, vol. 4. New York: Scribner, pp. 414–437.

Bunnens, G. (1979). *L'expansion Phénicienne en Méditerrané: Essay d'interprétation fondé sur une analyse des traditions littéraires.* Brussels: Institut historique Belge de Rome.

Burkert, W. (1972 [1962]). *Lore and Science in Ancient Pythagoreanism.* Cambridge, MA: Harvard University Press.

———. (1983). "Oriental Myth and Literature in the Iliad." In *The Greek Renaissance of the 8th century B.C.: Tradition and Innovation. Proceedings of the Second International Symposium of the Swedish Institute in Athens,* 1–5 June 1981, ed. R. Hägg. Stockholm: Svenska Institutet i Athens, Paul Åströms, pp. 51–56.

———. (1984). *Die orientaliserende Epoche in der griechischen Religion und Literatur.* Heidelberg, Germany: Winter Verlag.

———. (1985 [1977]). *Greek Religion: Archaic and Classical.* English translation of *Griechische Religion der archaischen und klassischen Epoche.* Cambridge, MA: Harvard University Press.

———. (1987). *Ancient Mystery Cults.* Cambridge, MA: Harvard University Press.

————. (1991). "Homerstudien und Orient." In *Zweihundert Jahre Homer-forschung*, ed. J. Latacz. Stuttgart, Germany: Colloqium Rauricum, 2.

————. (1992 [1984]). *The Orientalizing Revolution: Near Eastern Influence on Greek Culture in the Early Archaic Age.* English translation of *Die orientaliserende Epoche in der griechischen Religion und Literatur*, trans. M. E. Pinder and W. Burkert. Cambridge, MA: Harvard University Press.

Burn, A. R. (1966). *A Pelican History of Greece: From the Neolithic Pioneers to the Closing of Athens's Philosophic Schools.* Harmondsworth, England: Penguin.

Burnet, J. (1968 [1914]). *Greek Philosophy: Thales to Plato.* New York: St. Martin's Press.

————. (1968 [1929]). *Essays and Addresses.* Freeport, NY: Books for Libraries Press.

Burstein, S. (1993). "Review of Black Athena, Volume 2." *Classical Philology* 88.2: 157–162.

Burton, A. (1972). *Diodorus Siculus Book I: A Commentary.* Leiden, Netherlands: Brill.

Bury, J. B. (1900). *A History of Greece to the Death of Alexander the Great.* London: Macmillan.

————. (1950). *A History of Greece to the Death of Alexander the Great*, ed. R. Meiggs. 3d ed. rev. London: Macmillan.

Butterfield, H. (1960). *Man on His Past: The Study of the History of Historical Scholarship.* Boston: Beacon.

Bynon, J., ed. (1984). *Current Progress in Afro-Asiatic Languages: Papers of the 3rd International Congress of Hamito-Semitic Linguistics in London.* Philadelphia: Benjamins.

Bynon, J., & T. Bynon, eds. (1975). *Hamito-Semitica: Proceedings of a Colloquium Held by the Historical Section of the Linguistic Association at the School of Oriental and African Studies, University of London the 18th, 19th, and 20th of March 1970.* The Hague: Mouton.

Bynon, T. (1977). *Historical Linguistics.* Cambridge, England: Cambridge University Press.

Cadogan, G. (1969). "Review of *Cape Gelidonya: A Bronze Age Shipwreck*, by G. Bass." *Journal of Hellenic Studies* 89: 187–189.

Caffentzis, G. M. (1995). "On the Scottish Origin of Civilization." In Federici, pp. 13–36.

Cagni, L., ed. (1980). *La Lingua di Ebla: Atti del Convegno Internazionale*, vol. 14. Naples: Istituto Universitario orientale.

Calder, W. M., and R. Schlesier, eds. (1998). *Zwischen Rationalismus und Romantik: Karl Ottfried Müller und die Antike Kultur.* Hildesheim, Germany: Weidmann.

Calder, W. M., and S. Trzaskoma, eds. (1996). *George Grote Reconsidered: A 200th Birthday Celebration with a First Edition of his Essay "Of the Athenian Government."* Hildesheim, Germany: Weidmann.

Caldwell, R. S. (1989). *The Origin of the Gods: A Psychoanalytical Study of Greek Theogonic Myth.* New York: Oxford University Press.

Calice, F. (1936). *Grundlagen der ägyptisch-semitischen Wortvergleichen. Wiener Zeitschrift für die Kunde des Morgenlands*. Beiheft I. Vienna: Selbstverlag des orientalischen Institutes der Universität Wien.

Callender, J. B. (1975). *Middle Egyptian*. Malibu, CA: Undena.

Capella, Martianus. (1975). *De Nuptiis Philologiae et Mercurii, Liber Secundus*. Introduction and Commentary by Luciano Lenaz. Padu, Italy: Liviana.

Carlson, J. B. (1984). "The Nature of Mesoamerican Astronomy: A Look at the Native Texts." In *Archeoastronomy and the Roots of Science*, ed. E. C. Krupp. Boulder, CO: Westview Press, pp. 211–252.

Carpenter, R. (1933). "The Antiquity of the Greek Alphabet." *American Journal of Archaeology* 37: 8–29.

———. (1966). *Discontinuity in Greek Civilization*. Cambridge, England: Cambridge University Press.

Carruthers, J. (1990). "The Defenders of Western Civilization and the Battle over the Multicultural Curriculum." Lecture, Malcolm X College, Chicago, October.

———. (1992). "Outside of Academia: Bernal's Critique of the Black Champions of Ancient Egypt." *Journal of Black Studies* 22.4: 459–476. First presented as *Challenging Tradition: Cultural Interaction in Antiquity and Bernal's Black Athena*, tape IB. Departments of African American Studies and Classics, Temple University, Philadelphia, PA.

Carter, J. (forthcoming). *The Beginning of Greek Sculpture*. New Haven, CT: Yale University Press.

Carter, J., and S. Morris. (1995). *The Ages of Homer: A Tribute to Emily Townsend Vermeule*. Austin: University of Texas Press.

Cartledge, P. (1979). *Sparta and Laconia: A Regional History 1300–362 B.C.* London: Routledge and Kegan Paul.

———. (1991). "Out of Africa?" *New Statesman* 16 Oct.: 5–36.

Cartledge, P., and A. Spawforth. (1989). *Hellenistic and Roman Sparta: A Tale of Two Cities*. London. Routledge.

Casini, P. (1984). "Newton: The Classical Scholia." *History of Science* 22: 1–58.

Caskey, M. E. (1980). "Dionysos in the Temple of Agia Irini, Keos." *American Journal of Archaeology* 84: 200.

Celenko, T., ed. (1996). *Egypt in Africa*. Bloomington: Indiana University Press.

Černy, J. (1937). "Restitution of, and Penalty Attaching to, Stolen Property in Ramesside Times." *Journal of Egyptian Archaeology* 23: 186–189.

———. (1976). *Coptic Etymological Dictionary*. Cambridge, England: Cambridge University Press.

Chace, A. B. et al. (1979 [1927]). *The Rhind Mathematical Papyrus*. Vol. I. Reston, VA: Mathematical Association of America.

Chadwick, J. (1975). "The Prehistory of the Greek Language." in *The Cambridge Ancient History II, part 2, The Middle East and the Aegean Region c. 1380–1000 B.C.* Cambridge, England: Cambridge University Press, pp. 805–819.

———. (1976). *The Mycenaean World*. Cambridge, England: Cambridge University Press.

Challenging Tradition: Cultural Interaction in Antiquity and Bernal's Black Athena.
(1991). Proceedings of a conference held at Temple University, 19–20 Oct.
Audio and videotape. Temple University Classics Department, Philadelphia.

Chantraine, P. (1961). *Morphologie historique du grec.* Paris: Klincksieck.

———. (1968). *Dictionnaire étymologique de la langue grecque: histoire des mots.*
2 Vols. Paris: Klincksiek.

———. (1966). "Grec γλαυκός Γλαῦκος et mycénien 'karauko." In *Mélanges
d'archéologie, d'épigraphie et d'histoire offerts à Jérome Carcopino.* Paris: Hachette,
pp. 193–203.

———. (1968–1975). *Dictionnaire etymologique de la langue grecque.* 4 vols. Paris:
Klincksieck.

Childe, G. (1926). *The Aryans.* London: Kegan Paul.

Christy, C. (1983). *Uniformitarianism in Linguistics.* Vol. 31. *Studies in the History
of Linguistics.* Amsterdam: Benjamins.

Cicero. (1929). *De Divinatione.* Trans. W. A. Falconer. In *Selections* (Loeb Classical Library). Cambridge, MA: Harvard University Press.

———. *De Republica.*

———. (1985–1989). *De natura deorum.* Ed. and trans. A. E. Douglas. Warminster, England: Aris and Phillips.

Clackson, J. (1994). *The Linguistic Relationship between Armenian and Greek.*
Oxford: Blackwell.

Clagett, M. (1962). *Greek Science in Antiquity: How Human Reason and Ingenuity
First Ordered and Mastered the Experience of Natural Phenomena.* New corrected
ed. New York: Collier, Macmillan.

———, ed. (1989). *Ancient Egyptian Science: A Source Book,* Vol. 1 (in two parts).
Knowledge and Order. Philadelphia: American Philosophical Society.

Clark, M. E., and W. D. E. Coulson. (1978). "Memnon and Sarpedon."
Museum Helveticum 35: 65–73.

Clarke, M. L. (1962). *George Grote: A Biography.* London: Althone Press.

Clarke, S., and R. Engelbach. (1990 [1930]). *Ancient Egyptian Construction and
Architecture.* New York: Dover.

Clayton, P. A. (1982). *The Rediscovery of Ancient Egypt: Artists and Travellers in the
19th Century.* London: Thames and Hudson.

Clement of Alexandria. (1869). *Stromateis.* In *Elementis Alexandrini Opera,* ed.
W. Dindorf. Oxford: Oxford University Press.

Clifford, J. (1992). "Travelling Cultures." In *Cultural Studies,* ed. Lawrence
Grossberg, Cary Nelson, and Paula A. Treichler. New York: Routledge, pp.
96–116.

Cline, E. (1987). "Amenhotep III and the Aegean: A Reassessment of Egypt-
Cretan Relations in the 14th Century B.C." *Orientalia* 56: 1–36.

———. (1990). "An Unpublished Amenhotep Faience Plaque from Mycenae." *Journal of the American Oriental Society* 110: 200–212.

———. (1991a). "Hittite Objects in the Bronze Age Aegean." *Anatolian Studies*
41: 133–144.

———. (1991b). "A Possible Hittite Embargo against Mycenae." *Historia* 41.1: 1–9.

———. (1994). *Sailing the Wine Dark Sea: Foreign Trade and Contact in the Late Bronze Age Aegean.* BAR International Series 591. Oxford: Tempus Reparatum, Archaeological and Historical Associates Ltd.

———. (1996). "Review of *Black Athena Revisited.*" *American Journal of Archaeology* Oct.: 781–782.

———. (1998). "Rich beyond the Dreams of Avaris: Tel El-Dabaʿa and the Aegean World—A Guide for the Perplexed." *Annual of the British School at Athens* 93: 199–219.

Coldstream, J. N. (1977). *Geometric Greece.* New York: St. Martin's.

Coleman, J. E. (1992a). "Did Egypt Shape the Glory That Was Greece? The Case against Martin Bernal's *Black Athena.*" *Archaeology* 45.5: 48–52, 77–81.

———. (1992b). "Greece and the Eastern Mediterranean." *Bostonian* summer: 44–46.

Coleman, J. E., and C. A. Walz, eds. (1997). *Greeks and Barbarians: Essays on the Interactions between Greeks and Non-Greeks in Antiquity and the Consequences for Eurocentrism.* Ithaca, NY: Cornell University Press.

Coleridge, S. T. (1907). *Biographia Literaria.* 2 vols. Ed. with his *Aesthetical Essays* by J. Shawcross. Oxford: Clarendon Press.

Collinge, N. E. (1985). *The Laws of Indo-European.* Philadelphia: Benjamins.

Connor, W. R. (1970). "Review of *Blacks in Antiquity: Ethiopians in the Greco-Roman Experience,* by F. M. Snowden, Jr." *Good Reading: Review of Books Recommended by the Princeton Faculty* 21.3: 3–4.

Cook, E. (1992). "Ferrymen of Elysium and the Homeric Phaeacians." *Journal of Indo-European Studies* 20.3: 239–267.

Cook, R. M. (1962). "Reasons for the Foundation of Ischia and Cumae." *Historia* 9: 113–114.

———. (1967). "Origins of Greek Sculpture." *Journal of Hellenic Studies* 87: 25–32.

Coon, C. (1962). *The Origin of Races.* New York: Knopf.

———. (1965). *The Living Races of Man.* New York: Knopf.

Coon, C., S. M. Garn, and J. Birdsell. (1950). *Races: A Study of Race Formation in Man.* Springfield: Thomas.

Copenhaver, B. (1992). *Hermetica.* Cambridge, England: Cambridge University Press.

Copernicus. *De Revolutionibus.*

Coughlin, E. K. (1991). "In Multiculturalism Debate, Scholarly Book on Ancient Greece Plays Controversial Part: Afrocentric Scholars and Classicists at Odds over *Black Athena.*" *Chronicle of Higher Education* 31 July: A5–A6.

Critchley, Simon. (1995). "Black Socrates? Questioning the Philosophical Tradition." *Radical Philosophy* 69: 18–20.

Crombie, A. C., ed. (1963). *Scientific Change: Historical Studies in the Intellectual, Social and Technical Conditions for Scientific Discovery and Technical Invention from*

Antiquity to the Present. Symposium on the History of Science Held at the University of Oxford 9–15 July 1961. London: Heinemann.

Cross, F. (1979). "The Early Alphabetic Scripts." In *Symposia: Celebrating the Seventy-fifth Anniversary of the American Schools of Oriental Research (1900–1975)*, ed. F. Cross. Cambridge, MA: American Schools of Oriental Research, pp. 97–123.

Culham, P., and L. Edmunds. (1989). *Classics: A Discipline and Profession in Crisis.* Lanham, MD: University Press of America.

Cuny, A. (1910). "Les mots du fonds préhellenique en grec, latin et sémitique occidental." *Revue des Études Anciennes* 12: 154–164.

Curtin, P. D. (1964). *The Image of Africa: British Ideas and Action, 1780–1850.* Madison: University of Wisconsin Press.

Dandamaev, M.A.-K. (1984). *Slavery in Babylonia: From Nabopolassar to Alexander the Great (626–331 B.C.)* Trans. Victoria A. Powell. Rev. ed. De Kalb: Northern Illinois University Press.

Daniels, P. (1996). "Review of *Black Athena Revisited.*" *Athena List* (http://www.harpercollins.com/basic/lefko2.htm) 20–26 May.

Daschslager, E. L. (1992). "Letter." *New York Review of Books* 5.14: 53.

David, R. (1993). *Discovering Ancient Egypt.* London: Facts on File.

Davies, W. V., and L. Schofield. (1995). *Egypt, the Aegean and the Levant: Interconnections in the Second Millennium B.C.* London: British Museum Press.

Davis, D. B. (1984). *Slavery and Human Progress.* New York: Oxford University Press.

Davis, E. N. (1977). *The Vapheio Cups and Aegean Gold and Silver Ware.* New York: Garland.

Davis, W. (1979). "Plato and Egyptian Art." *Journal of Egyptian Archaeology* 65: 121–127.

———. (1989). *The Canonical Tradition in Ancient Egyptian Art.* Cambridge, England: Cambridge University Press.

Dawson, W. R., and E. P. Uphill. (1995). *Who Was Who in Egyptology.* London: Egypt Exploration Society.

Debrunner, H. W. (1979). "Presence and Prestige: Africans in Europe. A History of Africans in Europe before 1918." *Afrika Bibliographen* 22: 80–81, 115–117.

Decret, F. (1977). *Carthage ou l'empire de la mer.* Paris: Editions de Seuil.

Defoe, D. (1708). *The True-Born Englishman: A Satyr.* London (Black-Fryars): H. Hills.

De Hoz, J. (1983). "Algunas concideraciones sobre los orígines del alfabeto griego." In *Estudios metodológicos sobre la lengua griega*, ed. J. A. Fernández Delgado. Cáceres: Instituto de ciencias de la educación de la Universidad de l'Extremadura, pp. 1–48.

Delia, D. (1992). "The Refreshing Water of Osiris." *Journal of the American Research Center in Egypt* 29: 181–190.

Dentzer, J.-M. (1971). "Aux origines de l'iconographie du banquet couché." *Revue Archéologique* 13: 215–268.

Derchain, P. (1962). "L'authenticité de l'inspiration égyptienne dans le 'Corpus Hermeticum.'" *Revue de l'histoire des religions* 161: 175–198.

———. (1965). "Le Papyrus Salt 825 (B.M. 10051) rituel pour la conservation de la vie en Égypte." *Académie Royale de Belgique, Classe des Lettres Mémoires* 58: 57.

de Santillana, G. (1961). *Origins of Scientific Thought from Anaximander to Proclus: 600 B.C. to 300 A.D.* Chicago: Chicago University Press.

———. (1963). "On Forgotten Sources in the History of Science." In Crombie, pp. 813–828.

———. (1964). Preface to *The Dawn of Astronomy.* Cambridge, MA: MIT Press.

de Santillana, G., and H. von Dechend. (1969). *Hamlet's Mill: An Essay on Myth and the Frame of Time.* Boston: Gambit.

Dessenne, A. (1957). *Le Sphinx: Étude iconographique.* Paris: Bibliothèque des Écoles françaises d'Athènes et de Rome.

Diakonoff, I. M. (1965). *Semito-Hamitic Languages: An Essay in Classification.* Moscow: Nauka.

———. (1969). "The Rise of the Despotic State in Ancient Mesopotamia." Trans. G. M. Sergheyev. In *Ancient Mesopotamia Socio-Economic History: A Collection of Studies by Soviet Scholars,* ed. I. M. Diakonoff. Moscow: Nauka.

———. (1970). "Problems of Root Structure in Proto-Semitic." *Archiv Orientalni* 38: 453–477.

———. (1974). "Slaves, Helots, and Serfs in Early Antiquity." *Acta Antiqua* 22: 45–78.

———. (1981). "The Earliest Semites in Asia." *Altorientalische Forschungen* 8: 23–74.

"Dialogue: Martin Bernal's *Black Athena.*" (1993). *Journal of Women's History* 4.3: 6–8, 84–135.

Dietrich, B. C. (1964). "The Judgement of Zeus." *Rheinische Museum* 107: 97–125.

Diodorus Siculus. (1935). *The Library of History.* Vol. 1. Trans. C. H. Oldfather (Loeb Classical Library). Cambridge, MA: Harvard University Press.

Diogenes Laertius. (1980). *Lives of Eminent Philosophers.* 2 vols. Trans. R. D. Hicks (Loeb Classical Library). Cambridge, MA: Harvard University Press.

Diop, C. A. (1974). *The African Origin of Civilization: Myth or Reality.* Westport, CT: Lawrence Hill.

———. (1978). *The Cultural Unity of Black Africa: The Domains of Patriarchy and Matriarchy in Classical Antiquity.* Chicago: Third World Press.

———. (1987). *Precolonial Black Africa: A Comparative Study of the Political and Social Systems of Europe and Black Africa, from Antiquity to the Formation of Modern States.* Trans. H. J. Salemson. Westport, CT: Lawrence Hill.

———. (1991 [1981]). *Civilization or Barbarism? An Authentic Anthropology.* Trans. Yaa-Lengi Meema Ngemi. Chicago: Laurence Hill.

———. (1990). "Discussion and Debate: Special Review Section on M. Bernal, *Black Athena: The Afroasiatic Roots of Classical Civilization.*" *Journal of Mediterranean Archaeology* 3.1: 53–137; 3.2: 247–274.

Dobbs, B. J. T. (1975). *The Foundations of Newton's Alchemy: The Hunting of the Greene Lyon*. Cambridge, England: Cambridge University Press.

————. (1991). *The Janus Faces of Genius: The Role of Alchemy in Newton's Thought*. Cambridge, England: Cambridge University Press.

Dodds, E. R. (1928). "The *Parmenides* of Plato and the Origins of the Neoplatonic One." *Classical Quarterly* 22: 129–130.

————. (1951). *The Greeks and the Irrational*. Berkeley: University of California Press.

Dombrowski, B. (1984). *Name Europa auf seinem griechischen und altsyrischen Hintergrund ein Beitrag zur ostmediterranen [sic] Kultur-und Religionsgeschichte in frügriechischer Zeit*. Amsterdam: Hakkert.

Donadoni, S. (1982). "Plan." In Helck and Otto (1975–1984), vol. 4, cols. 1058–1060.

Dörrie, H. (1990). *Der Platonismus in der Antike: II der hellenistische rahmen des kaiserzeitlichen Platonismus*. Stuttgart, Germany: Frommann-Holzboog.

Dothan, T., and M. Dothan. (1992). *People of the Sea*. New York: Macmillan.

Dover, K. J. (1993). "Simia." *Liverpool Classical Monthly* 18.3: 46.

Dow, S. (1973). "The Linear Scripts and the Tablets as Historical Documents: Literacy in Minoan and Mycenaean Lands." In *Cambridge Ancient History*, 3d ed. vol. 2, part 1. Cambridge: Cambridge University Press, pp. 582–608.

Drake, St. Clair. (1987–1990). *Black Folk Here and There: An Essay in History and Anthropology*. 2 vols. Los Angeles: Center for Afro-American Studies, University of California.

Drake, Stillman. (1957). *Discoveries and Opinions of Galileo*. Garden City, NY: Doubleday.

————. (1965). "The Galileo-Bellarmine Meeting: A Historical Speculation." In *Galileo Galilei: A Biography and Inquiry into His Philosophy of Science*, by L. Geymonat. Trans. S. Drake, with a foreword by Georgio de Santillana. New York: McGraw-Hill, appendix A.

Drescher, S. (1977). *Econocide: British Slavery in the Era of Abolition*. Pittsburgh: University of Pittsburgh Press.

————. (1992). "The Ending of the Slave Trade and the Evolution of European Scientific Racism." In *The Atlantic Slave Trade: Effects on Economies, Societies, and Peoples in Africa, the Americas, and Europe*, ed. J. E. Inikori and S. L. Engerman. Durham, NC: Duke University Press, pp. 361–396.

Drews, R. (1979). "Phoenicians, Carthage, and the Spartan Eunomia." *American Journal of Philology* 100: 45–59.

————. (1993). *The End of the Bronze Age: Changes in Warfare and the Catastrophe ca 1200 B.C.* Princeton, NJ: Princeton University Press.

Du Bois, W. E. B. (1946). *The World and Africa*. New York: Viking.

————. (1965). *The World And Africa: An Inquiry into the Part Which Africa Has Played in World History*. New York: International Publishers.

Duff, W. (1976 [1767]). *An Essay on Original Genius: and its various modes of Exertion in Philosophy and the Fine Arts, Particularly in Poetry*. Repr. New York: Garland.

Dumas, F. (1976). *Le tombeau de Childeric*. Paris: Bibliothèque Nationale, Départements Médailles et Antiques.

Dunn, S. P. (1982). *The Fall and Rise of the Asiatic Mode of Production*. London: New Left Books.

Dupuis, C. (1984 [1795]). *Origin of All Religious Worship*. English trans. of *Origine de tous les cultes*. Introduction by R. Richardson. New York: Garland.

Dyson, M. E. (1992). "On *Black Athena*." Interview with Martin Bernal. *Z* 5.1: 56.

Eckstein, A. (1992). "Greece and the Mediterranean World." Lecture. Prince George's Community College Forum, Cheltenham, MD, 29 Oct.

Edel, E. (1966). *Die Ortsnamenlisten aus dem Totentempel Amenhopis III. Bonner biblische Beiträge* 25. Bonn: Hanstein.

————. (1978). "Der Brief des ägyptischen Wesirs Pasiyara an den Hethiterkönig Ḫattusili und verwandte Keilschriftbriefe." *Nachrichten der Akademie der Wissenschaften in Göttingen, I Philologisch-historisch Klasse* no. 4: 117–158.

Eder, W. (1993). Epilog. In *Anfänge politischen Denkens in der Antike: Die nahöstlichen Kulturen und die Griechen*, ed. K. Raaflaub. Munich: R. Oldenbourg, pp. 427–449.

Editor. (1845). "A Sketch of the Progress of Archaeological Science in America." *Southern Literary Messenger* 11: 427.

Edwards, R. (1979). *Kadmos the Phoenician: A Study in Greek Legend and the Mycenaean Age*. Amsterdam: Adolf M. Hakkert.

Egbert, A. (1997). "Consonants in Collision: Neith and Athena Reconsidered." In *Black Athena: Ten Years After*, ed. W. M. J. van Binsbergen. Special ed. of *Talanta* 28–29: 149–162.

"Egypt Says Ramses II Wasn't Black." (1989). *Washington Post*, 23 Mar.: D8.

Ehrenberg, V. (1961). *The Greek State*. Rev. ed. London: Methuen.

Ehret, C. (1996). "Ancient Egyptian as an African Language, Egypt as an African Culture." In *Egypt in Africa*, ed. Theodore Celenko. Bloomington: Indiana University Press, pp. 25–27.

El Sayed, R. (1982). *La Déesse Neith de Sais*. 2 vols. Cairo: Institut Français d'archéologie oriental du Caire.

Elias, N. (1978). *The History of Manners: Vol. 1. The Civilising Process*. New York: Urizen Books.

Ellenbogen, M. (1962). *Foreign Words in the Old Testament: Their Origin and Etymology*. London: Luzac.

Elliot-Smith, G. (1970 [1923]). *The Ancient Egyptians and the Origin of Civilization*. Freeport, NY: Books for Libraries Press.

Erman, A., and H. Grapow (1982 [1926–1935]). *Wörterbuch der ägyptischen Sprache*. 7 vols. Berlin: Akademie Verlag.

Ernout, A., and A. Meillet. (1985). *Dictionnaire étymologique de la langue latine*. 4th ed. by Jacques André. Paris: C. Klincksieck.

Evangeliou, C. (1994). *When Greece Met Africa: The Genesis of Hellenic Philosophy*. Binghamton, NY: Institute of Global Studies.

Evans, A. (1921–1935). *The Palace of Minos*. 4 vols. in 6. London: Macmillan.

Eyre, C. J. (1995). *Proceedings of the Seventh International Congress of Egyptologists: Cambridge 3–9 Sept. 1995.* Leuven, Belgium: Peeters.

Eze, E. C. (1997 [1994]). "The Color of Reason: The Idea of Race in Kant's Anthropology." In *Anthropology and the German Enlightenment,* ed. Katherine Faull. London: Bucknell University Press, pp. 214–251. Repr. "The Color of Reason: The Idea of 'Race' in Kant's Anthropology." In *Postcolonial African Philosophy: A Critical Reader,* ed. Emmanuel Eze. Cambridge, MA: Blackwell, pp. 103–140.

———. (1998). *The Color of Reason: The Racial Economy of Modern Philosophy.* Cambridge, MA: Blackwell.

Fagan, Brian. (1975). *The Rape of the Nile: Tomb Robbers, Tourists, and Archaeologists in Egypt.* New York: Scribner's.

Fakhry, A. (1973). *Siwa Oasis.* Cairo: American University of Cairo Press.

Farag, S. (1980). "Une inscription memphite de la XIIe dynastie." *Revue d'Égyptologie* 32: 75–82.

Faulkner, R. O., trans. (1969). *The Ancient Egyptian Pyramid Texts.* Warminster, England: Aris and Phillips.

———, trans. (1972). *The Ancient Egyptian Book of the Dead.* London: British Museum.

Faull, K., ed. (1994). *Anthropology and the German Enlightenment.* London: Bucknell University Press.

Federici, Silvia, ed. (1995). *Enduring Western Civilization: The Construction of the Concept of Western and Its "Others."* Westport, CT: Praeger.

Fenn, R. A. (1987). *James Mill's Political Thought.* London: Garland.

Fick, A. (1905). *Vorgriechischer Ortsnamen als Quelle für die Vorgeschichte Griechenlands.* Göttingen, Germany: Vandenhoeck & Ruprecht.

Finley, J. H. (1978). *Homer's Odyssey.* London: Harvard University Press.

Finley, M. I. (1963–1964). "Between Slavery and Freedom." *Comparative Studies in Society and History* 6: 236–239.

———. (1968). *Slavery in Classical Antiquity.* Cambridge, England: Cambridge University Press.

———. (1970). *Early Greece: The Bronze and Archaic Ages.* New York: Norton.

———. (1973). *The Ancient Economy.* London: University of California Press.

———. (1978). *The World of Odysseus.* Rev. ed. New York: Viking.

———. (1980). *Ancient Slavery and Modern Ideology.* New York: Viking.

———. (1987 [1975]). *The Use and Abuse of History.* New York: Viking. Repr. New York: Penguin.

Flegg, G. (1989). *Numbers through the Ages.* Houndsmills, England: Macmillan Education.

Fletcher, T. (1822). *Letters in vindication of the rights of the British West India colonies, originally addressed to the editors of the Liverpool Mercury, in answer to Mr. James Cropper's letters to W. Wilberforce, Esq. M.P.* Liverpool: West India Association.

Fontenrose, J. (1980 [1959]). *Python: A Study of Delphic Myth and Its Origins.* Berkeley: University of California Press.

Forster, G. (1958–1990). *Georg Forsters Werke.* Various eds. 18 vols. Berlin: Akademie-Verlag.

Foster, B. R. (1993). *Before the Muses: An Anthology of Akkadian Literature.* 2 vols. Bethesda, MD: CDL Press.

Foucart, P. (1914). *Les mystères d'Eleusis.* Paris: A. Picard.

Fournet, J.-L. (1989). "Les emprunts du grec a l'égyptien." *Bulletin de la Société de Linguistique de Paris* 84: 55–80.

Fowden, G. (1986). *The Egyptian Hermes: A Historical Approach to the Late Antique Pagan Mind.* Cambridge, England: Cambridge University Press.

———. (1993). *Empire to Commonwealth: Consequences of Monotheism in Late Antiquity.* Princeton, NJ: Princeton University Press.

Francis, E. D. (1986). "The Impact of Non-Indo-European Languages on Greek and Mycenaean." Paper given at the IREX Conference on Comparative Linguistics, Austin, TX, Nov.

Frankfort, H. (1933). *The Cenotaph of Seti I at Abydos.* London: Egypt Exploration Society no. 39.

———. (1956 [1951]). *The Birth of Civilization in the Near East.* Bloomington: Indiana University Press.

Frazer, J., trans. and commentary. (1898). *Pausanias's Description of Greece.* 6 vols. London: Macmillan.

Frey, H. (1892). *L'annamite, mère des langues: communauté d'origine des races celtiques, sémitiques, soudanaises et de l'Indochine.* Paris: Hachette.

———. (1905). *Les Egyptiens préhistoriques identifiés avec les Annamites d'après les inscriptions hiéroglyphiques.* Paris: Hachette.

Friedman, J. (1979). *System, Structure, and Contradiction in the Evolution of Asiatic Social Formations.* Copenhagen: National Museum of Denmark.

———. (1992). "The Past in the Future: History and the Politics of Identity." *American Anthropologist* 94.4: 837–859.

Friedrich, J. (1923). "Zum Phonizisch-Punischen." *Zeitschrift für Semistik* 2: 1–10.

Frisk, H. (1955–1972). *Griechisches etymologisches Wörterbuch.* Heidelberg, Germany: Carl Winter.

Froidefond, C. (1971). *Le mirage Égyptien dans la littérature Grecque d'Homère à Aristote.* Aix en Provence, France: Publications universitaires des lettres et sciences humaines.

Gagarin, M. (1986). *Early Greek Law.* Berkeley: University of California Press.

Gamkriledze, T. V., and V. V. Ivanov. (1995). *Indo-European and the Indo-Europeans: A Reconstruction and Historical Analysis of a Proto-Language and a Proto-Culture.* Part 1. Trends in Linguistics: Studies and Monographs 80. English version by Johanna Nichols. Berlin: Mouton/de Gruyter.

Garbini, G. (1980). *I Fenici: Storia e religione.* Naples: Istituto Universitario Orientale.

Gardiner, A. H. (1932). *Late Egyptian Stories.* Brussels: Fondation Égyptologique.

———. (1938). "The House of Life." *Journal of Egyptian Archaeology* 24: 157–179.

———. (1941). "Writing and Literature." In *The Legacy of Egypt*, ed. S. Glanville. Oxford: Clarendon Press, pp. 53–79.

———. (1947). *Ancient Egyptian Onomastica.* 2 vols. Oxford: Oxford University Press.

———. (1957). *Egyptian Grammar.* 3d ed. Oxford: Oxford University Press.

———. (1961). *Egypt of the Pharaohs.* Oxford: Oxford University Press.

Gardiner, E. (1893). "Palladia from Mycenae." *Journal of Hellenic Studies* 13: 21–28.

Gardner, J. F. (1991). "The Debate on *Black Athena*." *Classical Review* 41.1:67.

Gauthier, Henri. (1925–1931). *Dictionnaire des noms geographiques contenus dans les textes hieroglyphiques.* 7 vols. Cairo: Societé royale de géographie d'Égypte.

Gelb, I. J. (1977). "Thoughts about Ibla: A Preliminary Evaluation: March 1977." *Syro-Mesopotamian Studies* 1.1: 3–27.

Gelb, I. J., T. Jacobsen, B. Landsberger, and A. L. Oppenheimer (1956–) *The Assyrian Dictionary of the Oriental Institute of Chicago.* Glückstadt, Germany: J. J. Augustin.

Georgakas, D. (1993). "Black Athena: Aryans, Semites, Egyptians, and Hellenes." *Cineaste* 19.2–3: 55–56.

———. (1994). "Defending Greek Athena." *Odyssey* summer: 34–38.

Georgiev, V. (1979). *La Lingua e le origini degli Etruschi.* Rome: Nagard.

Gesenius, W. (1953). *A Hebrew and English Lexicon of the Old Testament.* Trans. E. Robinson, rev. F. Brown, S. R. Driver, and C. A. Briggs. Oxford: Clarendon.

Ghalioungui, P. (1968). "The Relation of Pharaonic to Greek and Later Medicine." *Bulletin of the Cleveland Medical Library* 15.3: 96–107.

———. (1973). *The House of Life: Per Ankh. Magic and Medical Science in Ancient Egypt.* 2d ed. Amsterdam: B. M. Israel.

———. (1983). *The Physicians of Ancient Egypt.* Cairo: Al. Ahram Center for Scientific Translation.

Giannaris, C. (1987). "Rocking the Cradle." *New Statesman* 10 July: 31.

Gibbon, E. (1796 [1761]). "Essai sur l'Étude de la litterature." In *Miscelaneous Works of Edward Gibbon Esquire, with Memoires of his Life and Writings, Composed by himself and Illustrated by his own Letters and Occasional Notes and Narrative by Lord John Sheffield*, Vols. 1–2. London: Strahan, Cadell and Davies, pp. 455–495.

———. (1796). "Letter to Lord Sheffield, 5/3/1792." In *Miscelaneous Works* 1: 238–241.

———. (1815). "On the Position of the Meridional Line and an Inquiry into the Supposed navigation of Africa by the Ancients." In *Miscelaneous Works.* Vol. 3. London: John Murray, pp. 482–504.

———. (1984). *Memoirs of My Life.* Ed. B. Radice. New York: Penguin.

———. (1932). *The Decline and Fall of the Roman Empire.* New York: Modern Library.

Gillings, R. J. (1982 [1972]). *Mathematics in the Time of the Pharaohs*. New York: Dover.

———. (1978). "The Mathematics of Ancient Egypt." In *Dictionary of Scientific Biography*, ed. C. C. Gillispie. Vol. 15, Supplement 1. New York: Scribner, p. 696.

Gilroy, P. (1993). *The Black Atlantic: Modernity and Double Consciousness*. Cambridge, MA: Harvard University Press.

Giveon, R. (1985). *Egyptian Scarabs from Western Asia, from the Collection of the British Museum*. Freiburg, Germany: Universitäts Verlag.

Glauser, W. (1990). "Three Approaches to Locke and the Slave Trade." *Journal of the History of Ideas* 51: 199–216.

Glenn, H. (1983). *Vision and Disenchantment: Blake's Songs and Wordsworth's Lyrical Ballads*. Cambridge, England: Cambridge University Press.

Gliddon, G. R. (1948 [1850]). *Ancient Egypt: A Series of Chapters on Early Egyptian History, Archaeology, and Other Subjects*. 12th ed. Philadelphia: T. B. Peterson.

Goldsmith, M. (1980). *Sage: A Life of J. D. Bernal*. London: Hutchinson.

Goldstein, L. J. (1989). "Review of Black Athena I." *International Studies in Philosophy* 21: 98–99.

Gomme, A. W. (1913). "The Legend of Cadmus and the Logographoi." *Journal of Hellenic Studies* 33: 53–72, 223–245.

Gong, J. L. (1982). "Weishenmo mixin huodong you taitouliao? Shanghai shi chuanshi xian nongcun mixin huodong di diaocha." *Shehui* 3: 44–46.

Goodhart, S. (1991). "Review of Black Athena I." *Philosophy and Literature* 15: 145–147.

Goonatilake, S. (1989). "The Son, the Father, and the Holy Ghosts." *Economic and Political Weekly* 5 Aug.: 1768–1769.

———. (1999). *Toward a Global Science: Mining Civilizational Knowledge*. Bloomington: Indiana University Press.

Gordis, R. (1968). *Koheleth: The Man and His World. A Study of Ecclesiastes*. New York: Schocken.

Gordon, C. H. (1955). "Homer and Bible," *Hebrew Union Annual* 26: 1–66.

———. (1957). "Egypto-Semitica." *Rivista degli studi orientali (Scritti in onore di Giussepe Furlani)* 32: 269–277.

———. (1962a). *Before the Bible: The Common Background of Greek and Hebrew Civilizations*. New York: Harper and Row.

———. (1962b). "Eteocretan." *Journal of Near Eastern Studies* 21: 211–214.

———. (1965a). *Ugaritic Textbook*. Rome: Pontificium Institutum Biblicum.

———. (1965b). *The Common Background of Greek and Hebrew Civilizations*. New York: Norton.

———. (1968). *Forgotten Scripts: The Story of Their Decipherment*. London: Pelican.

———. (1978). "Poetic Legends and Myths from Ugarit." *Berytus* 25: 5–133.

Gordon, C. H., and G. A. Rendsburg. (1997). *The Bible and the Ancient Near East*. New York: Norton.

Gordon, P. (1993). "On *Black Athena*: Ancient Critiques of the 'Ancient Model' of Greek History." *Classical World* 87.1: 71–72.

Gossett, Thomas. (1963). *Race: The History of an Idea in America*. Dallas: Southern Methodist University Press.

Gould, S. J. (1978). "Morton's Ranking of Races by Cranial Capacity." *Science* 200: 503–509.

———. (1981). *The Mismeasure of Man*. New York: Norton.

———. (1987). *Time's Arrow, Time's Cycle: Myth and Metaphor in the Discovery of Geological Time*. Cambridge, MA: Harvard University Press.

———. (1989). *Wonderful Life*. New York: Norton.

Gow, J. (1968 [1884]). *A Short History of Greek Mathematics*. New York: Chelsea Publishing Company.

Graham, A. J. (1964). *Colony and Mother City in Ancient Greece*. Manchester, England: Manchester University Press.

———. (1971). "Patterns in Early Greek Colonization." *Journal of Hellenic Studies* 91: 35–47.

Green, P. (1990). *Alexander to Actium: The Historical Evolution of the Hellenistic Age*. Berkeley: University of California Press.

———. (1994). " 'By Klepht and Styx': The Glory That Was Greece." *Times Literary Supplement* (London) 29 July: 3.

Green, T. (1989). "*Black Athena* and Classical Historiography: Other Approaches, Other Views." In Levine and Peradotto, pp. 55–65.

Greenberg, J. H. (1955). *Studies in African Linguistic Classification* New Haven: Compass.

———. (1963). *The Languages of Africa*. Bloomington: Indiana University Press.

Greene, M. (1992). *Natural Knowledge in Preclassical Antiquity*. Baltimore: Johns Hopkins University Press.

Greener, L. (1967). *The Discovery of Egypt*. New York: Viking.

Gregoire, H. (1997 [1808]). *An Enquiry Concerning the Intellectual and Moral Faculties, and Literature of Negroes*. Trans. D. B. Warden. New ed. Ed. G. R. Hodges. Brooklyn: Thomas Kirk.

Gress, D. (1989). "The Case against Martin Bernal." *New Criterion* 8.4: 36–43.

Griffin, J. (1989). "Who Are These Coming to the Sacrifice?" *New York Review of Books* 15 June: 25–27.

———. (1996). "Anxieties of Influence." *New York Review of Books* 20 June: 67–73.

Griffith, F. L. (1890 [1887]). "Note." In *The Mound of the Jew and the City of Onias*, by E. N. Naville. Egyptian Exploration Fund.

———. (1892). "Notes on Egyptian Weights and Measures." *Proceedings Society of Biblical Archaeology*, 14 June, pp. 403–450.

———. (1910–1911). *Encyclopaedia Britannica 1910–1911*. 11th ed. 9:43.

———. (Undated). "The Hieratic Papyri." In *Ilahun, Kahun and Gurov*, by Sir W. M. Flinders Petrie. Warminster, England: Aris and Phillips and Joel L. Malter, p. 48.

Griffith, R. D. (1996). "Homer's Black Earth and the Land of Egypt." *Athenaeum: Studi di letteratura e Storia dell' Antichità* NS 84.1: 251–254.

———. (1997a). "Criteria for Evaluating Hypothetical Egyptian Loanwords in Greek: The Case of Αἴγυπτος." *Illinois Classical Studies* 22: 1–6.

———. (1997b). "Homeric διπετέος ποταμοῖο and the Celestial Nile." *American Journal of Philology* 118.3: 353–362.

Griffiths, J. G. (1964). "Siberian Links with Egypt?" *Antiquity* 38.151: 222–224.

———. (1975). *The Isis Book (Metamorphoses, Book XI)*. Leiden, Netherlands: Brill.

Grimal, N. (1992). *A History of Ancient Egypt*. Trans. I. Shaw. Oxford: Blackwell.

Grote, G. (1826). "Review of Mitford's History of Greece." *Westminster Review* Apr.: 269–331.

———. (1843). "Review, *Griechischen Heroen Geschichten, von B.G. Niebuhr an seinen Sohn erzält*." *Westminster Review* 39: 285–328.

———. (1846–1856). *A History of Greece*. 12 vols. London: John Murray.

Grote, H. L. (1873). *The Personal Life of George Grote*. 2d ed. London: John Murray.

Gruen, E. S. (1993). "Cultural Fictions and Cultural Identity." Presidential Address, 1992. *Transactions of the American Philological Association* 123: 1–14.

Gruppe, O. (1897–1907). *Griechische Mythologie und Religionsgeschichte*. 2 vols. Munich: Beck.

Gsell, S. (1914–1928). *Histoire ancienne de l'Afrique du Nord*. 8 vols. Paris: Hachette.

Guilmot, M. (1977). *Les initiés et les rites initiatiques en Égypte ancienne*. Paris: Lafont.

Guralnick, E. (1973). "Kouroi, Canon and Men: A Computer Study of Proportions." *Computer Studies* 42:77–80.

———. (1978). "Proportions of Kouroi." *American Journal of Archaeology* 82: 461–472.

———. (1981). "Proportions of Korai." *American Journal of Archaeology* 85: 269–280.

———. (1997). "The Egyptian Connection." In Coleman and Walz, pp. 127–154.

Guthrie, W. K. C. (1962). *A History of Greek Philosophy I: The Earlier Presocratics and the Pythagorians*. Cambridge, England: Cambridge University Press.

Haeger, J. H. (1974). "Coleridge's Speculations on Race." *Studies in Romanticism* 14: 333–357.

Haider, P. W. (1988). *Griechenland-Nordafrika: Ihre Beziehungen zwischen 1500 und 600 v. Chr.* Darmstadt, Germany: Wissenschaft Buchsgesellschaft.

Haley, C. W., and C. Blegen. (1927). "The Coming of the Greeks: The Geographical Distribution of Prehistoric Remains in Greece." *American Journal of Archaeology* 32: 141–152.

Haley, S. P. (1993). "Black Feminist Thought and Classics: Re-membering,

Re-claiming, Re-empowering." In *Feminist Theory and the Classics*, ed. N. S. Rabinowitz and A. Richlin. New York: Routledge, pp. 23–43.

Hall, E. (1989). *Inventing the Barbarian: Greek Self-Definition through Tragedy.* Oxford: Clarendon Press.

———. (1991). "Myths Missing That Black Magic." *Times Higher Education Supplement* (London) 13 Sept.: 15, 18.

———. (1996 [1992]). "When Is a Myth Not a Myth?" *Arethusa* 25: 181–201. Repr. Lefkowitz and Rogers.

Hall, J. (1990). "Black Athena: A Sheep in Wolf's Clothing?" *Journal of Mediterranean Archaeology* 3.2: 247–254.

Hamilton, E. (1942). *The Greek Way.* New York: Norton.

Hamlyn, D. W. (1987). *A History of Western Philosophy.* London: Penguin.

Hammond, M. (1972). *The City in the Ancient World.* Cambridge MA.: Harvard University Press.

Hampe, R., and E. Simon. (1981). *The Birth of Greek Art from the Mycenaean to Archaic Period.* New York: Oxford University Press.

Hamza, M. (1930). "Excavations of the Department of Antiquities at Qantir, 1928." *Annales du Service des Antiquités de l'Egypte* 30 (Cairo).

Hani, J. (1976). *La Religion Égyptienne dans la pensée de Plutarque.* Paris: Belles Lettres.

Hankey, V. (1993). "Egypt, the Aegean and the Levant." *Egyptian Archaeology* 3: 27–29.

Haraway, D. (1991). *Simians, Cyborgs, and Women: The Reinvention of Nature.* New York: Routledge.

Harden, D. (1963). *The Phoenicians.* London: Penguin.

Harding, S., ed. (1993). *The "Racial" Economy of Science: Toward a Democratic Future.* Bloomington: Indiana University Press.

Hardy, D. A., C. G. Doumas, J. A. Sakellarakis, and P. M. Warren. (1989). *Thera and the Aegean World III: Vol. 1. Archaeology.* London: Thera Foundation.

Harris, J. R. (1971). *The Legacy of Egypt.* Oxford: Oxford University Press.

Harper, G. M. (1961). *The Neoplatonism of William Blake.* Chapel Hill: University of North Carolina Press.

———. (1969). "Thomas Taylor in America." In *Thomas Taylor the Platonist: Selected Writings,* ed. Kathleen Raine and George Mill Harper. London: Routledge and Kegan Paul, pp. 3–48.

Harris, G., and D. O'Connor. (1982). *Gods and Pharaohs from Egyptian Mythology.* London: Collins.

Harten, S. (1995). "Archaeology and the Unconscious: Hegel, Egyptomania and the Legitimation of Orientalism." In *Egypt and the Fabrication of European Identity,* ed. I. A. Bierman. Los Angeles: UCLA Near East Center Colloquium Series, pp. 1–33.

Hartner, W. (1963). "Comments on G. de Santillana's 'On Forgotten Sources in the History of Science.'" In Crombie, pp. 868–875.

Haslip-Viera, G., B. Ortiz de Montellana, and W. Barbour. (1997). "Robbing

Native American Cultures: Van Sertima's Afrocentricity and the Olmecs,"
and the comments that followed it. *Current Anthropology* 38.3: 419–444.

Hassan, F. A. (1988). "The Predynastic of Egypt." *Journal of World Prehistory* 2: 135–185.

Hawkins, G. S. (1973). *Beyond Stonehenge*. New York: Harper and Row.

Heath, T. L. (1913). *Aristarchus of Samos: The Ancient Copernicus*. Oxford: Clarendon Press.

———. (1932). *Greek Astronomy*. New York: E. P. Dutton.

———, ed. (1981 [1921]). *History of Greek Mathematics I: From Thales to Euclid*. New York: Dover.

Hegel, G. W. F. (1837). *Lectures on the Philosophy of World History*. Trans. H. B. Nisbet. Cambridge, England: Cambridge University Press.

Heidegger, M. (1975). *Early Greek Thinking*. Trans. David Farrell Krell and Frank A. Capuzzi. New York: Harper and Row.

Helck, W. (1962). *Die Beziehungen Aegyptens zu Vorderasien im 3. und 2. Jahrtausend v. Chr.* Wiesbaden, Germany: Harrasowitz.

———. (1989). "Ein Ausgreifen des Mittleren Reiches in den Zypriotischen Raum?" *Göttinger Miszellen: Beiträge zur ägyptische Diskussion* 109: 27–30.

Helck, W., and E. Otto. (1975–1984). *Lexikon der Ägyptologie*. 5 vols. Wiesbaden, Germany: Harrassowitz.

Heliodorus. (1957). *An Ethiopian Romance*. Trans. with an introduction by Moses Hadas. Ann Arbor: University of Michigan Press.

Helm, R. P. (1980). *Greeks in the Neo-Assyrian Levant and "Assyria" in the Early Greek Writers*. Ph.D. thesis, University of Pennsylvania.

Hemberg, B. (1950). *Die Kabiren*. Uppsala, Sweden: Almqvist and Wiksells Boktryckeri.

Hemmerdinger, B. (1968). "Noms communs grecs d'origine égyptienne." *Glotta* 46: 238–247.

Henningsen, M. (1992). "Der heilige Mauritius und der Streit um die multikulturelle Identität des Westens." *Merkur* 46.9–10: 834–845.

Herm, G. (1975). *The Phoenicians: The Purple Empire of the Ancient World*. Trans. C. Hillier. New York: Morrow.

Hero. *Geometria*.

Herodotus. (1924). *The Egypt of Herodotus: Being the Second Book, Entitled Euterpe, of the History*. Trans. G. Rawlinson, preface and notes by E. H. Blakeney. London: Martin Hopkinson.

———. (1974). *The Histories*. Trans. Aubrey de Selincourt. Harmondsworth, England: Penguin.

———. (1985). *The History*. Trans. David Grene. Chicago: University of Chicago Press.

Herrnstein, R., and Murray, C. (1994). *The Bell Curve: Intelligence and Class Structure in American Life*. New York: Free Press.

Hesiod. See Wender.

Hetherington, N. S. (1987). *Ancient Astronomy and Civilization*. Tucson, AZ: Pachart.

Hiernaux, J. (1968). *La Diversitè Humaine en Afrique Subsahariènne: Recherches Biologiques*. Brussels: Institut de Sociologie del l'Universitè libre de Bruxelles.

―――. (1975). *The People of Africa*. New York: Charles Scribner.

Hobsbawm, E., and T. Ranger, eds. (1983). *The Invention of Tradition*. Cambridge, England: Cambridge University Press.

Hoch, J. (1994). *Semitic Words in Egyptian Texts of the New Kingdom and Third Intermediate Period*. Princeton, NJ: Princeton University Press.

―――. (1995). *Middle Egyptian Grammar*. Mississauga, Canada: Benben.

Hock, H. (1991). *Principles of Historical Linguistics*. 2d ed. Berlin: Mouton de Gruyter.

Hodge, C. T. (1971). "Afroasiatic: An Overview." In *Afroasiatic a Survey*, ed. C. T. Hodge. The Hague: Mouton, pp. 9–26.

―――. (1977). "Review of J. B. Callender, *Middle Egyptian*. Malibu: Undena 1975." *Language* 53.4: 930–940.

―――. (1987). "The Status of Lisramic (Hamito-Semitic) Sound Correspondences." In *Proceedings of the Fourth International Hamito-Semitic Congress Hamburg 20–22 September 1983*, ed. H. Jungraithmayr and W. W. Müller. Amsterdam: Benjamins, pp. 11–24.

―――. (1991). "Prothetic Alif in Egypto-Coptic." In *Ägypten im Afro-orientalischen Kontext: Aufsätze zur Archäologie, Geschichte und Sprache Eines unbegrenzten Raumes, Gedenkschrift Peter Behrens*, ed. D. Mendel and U. Claudi. *Afrikanistiche Arbeitspapiere*. Köln, Germany: Universität zu Köln, pp. 171–176.

―――. (1992). "Tooth and Claw." *Anthropological Linguistics* 34: 202–234.

―――. (1997). "Egyptian Vulture, Reedleaf and Now." Included as looseleaf with *Mother Tongue* 28.

Hodson, F. R., ed. (1974). "The Place of Astronomy in the Ancient World." Article on "Astronomical Alignments in Britain, Egypt, and Peru." *Philosophical Transactions of the Royal Society of London* 1257: 276.

Hoffman, M. A. (1988). "Prelude to Civilization in Egypt: The Predynastic Period in Egypt." in *The First Egyptians*, ed. K. L. Willoughby and E. B. Stanton. Columbia: McKissick Museum, University of South Carolina, pp. 33–46.

―――. (1991). *Egypt before the Pharaohs*. Rev. and updated ed. Austin: University of Texas Press.

Hogben, Lancelot. (1960). *Mathematics in the Making*. New York: Doubleday.

Holmes, R. (1989). *Coleridge: Early Visions*. London: Hodder and Stoughton.

Hood, S. (1978). *The Arts in Prehistoric Greece*. London: Penguin.

Hooker, J. T. (1976). *Mycenaean Greece*. London: Routledge and Kegan Paul.

Hopfner, T. (1925). *Orient und griechische Philosophie*. Leipzig, Germany: Hinrichs.

Hopper, R. J. (1976). *The Early Greeks*. New York: Harper and Row.

Horace. (1934). *Horace: Odes and Epodes*. Ed. C. E. Bennet. New York: Allyn and Bacon.

Hornung, E. (1982 [1971]). *Conceptions of God in Ancient Egypt: The One and the Many.* Trans. John Baines. Ithaca, NY: Cornell University Press.

Hotz, R. L. (1996). "Scientists: Race a Superficial Characteristic." *Los Angeles Times*, repr. *Chicago Sun Times*, October.

Howe, S. (1998). *Afrocentrism: Mythical Pasts and Imagined Homes.* London: Verso.

Hugh of St. Victor. (1961 [c. 1128]). *The Didascalicon: A Medieval Guide to the Arts.* Trans. and introduction by Jerome Taylor. New York: Columbia University Press.

Humboldt, W. von. (1903–1935 [1793]) "Über das Studium des Altertums und des Griechischen insbesondre." In *W. v. Humboldt Gesammelte Schriften.* 17 vols. Berlin: Leitzmann and Gebhardt, 1: 255–281.

———. (1967). "Ueber die aufagbe des Geschichtsschriebers." In *Wilhelm von Humboldts gesammelte Schriften,* 4: 35–56. Trans. G. I. Iggers as "The Task of a Historian," *History and Theory* 6.

———. (1988 [1836]) *On Language: The Diversity of Human Language-Structure and Its Influence on the Mental Developments of Mankind.* Trans. Peter Heath. Cambridge, England: Cambridge University Press.

Hume, D. (1994 [1772]). "Of National Characters." In *Political Essays: Hume,* ed. Knud Haakonsen. *Cambridge Texts in the History of Thought.* Cambridge, England: Cambridge University Press.

Humphreys, S. (1978). *Anthropology and the Greeks.* London: Routledge and Kegan Paul.

———. (1993). *The Family, Women and Death: Comparative Studies.* Ann Arbor: University of Michigan Press.

Hurst, B. C. (1981). "The Myth of Historical Evidence." *History and Theory* 20: 278–290.

Hurvitz, A. (1968). "The Chronological Significance of 'Aramaisms' in Biblical Hebrew." *Israel Exploration Journal* 18: 234–240.

Hussey, Edward. (1972). *The Presocratics.* New York: Scribner's.

Huxley, G. S. (1970–1985). "Eudoxus of Cnidus." In *Dictionary of Scientific Biography,* ed. C. C. Gillispie. Vol. 4. New York: Scribner's, pp. 465–467.

Ifrah, G. (1985). *From One to Zero: A Universal History of Number.* New York: Viking.

Imhoof-Blumer, F., and P. Gardiner. (1885–1887). *A Numismatic Commentary on Pausanias. Journal of Hellenic Studies* 6: 50–101, 7: 57–113, 8: 6–63.

Immerwahr, John. (1992). "Hume's Revised Racism." *Journal of the History of Ideas* 53: 481–486.

Immerwahr, J., and Michael Burke. (1993). "Race and the Modern Philosophy Course." *Teaching Philosophy* 16: 21–34.

Ingpen, R., and W. E. Beck, eds. (1965). *The Complete Works of Percy Bysshe Shelley.* New York: Gordian Press.

Inikori, J. E., and S. L. Engerman, eds. (1992). *The Ending of the Slave Trade and the Evolution of European Scientific Racism. The Atlantic Slave Trade: Effects on Econo-*

mies, *Societies and Peoples of Africa, the Americas and Europe*. Durham, NC: Duke University Press.

Ishmael, T. (1971). *The UAR in Africa: Egypt's Policy under Nasser*. Evanston, IL: Northwestern University Press.

Isocrates. *Busiris*.

———. (1928–1944). *Works*. 3 vols. Vol. 1–2 trans. G. Norlin; Vol. 3 trans L. Van Hook. Cambridge, MA: Harvard University Press.

Isserlin, B. J. (1983). "The Antiquity of the Greek Alphabet." *Kadmos* 22: 151–163.

Iversen, E. (1939). "Papyrus Carlsberg No. VIII with Some Remarks on the Egyptian Origin of Some Popular Birth Prognoses." *Det Kgl. Danske Videnskabernes Selskab Historisk-filologiske Meddelser* 28: 5.

———. (1953). *Studia Orientali Ioanni Pedersen Septuagenario* A.D. *VII id nov. anno a collegis discipulis amicis Dicata*. Copenhagen, Denmark: Munksgaard.

———. (1953). "Wounds on the Head in Egyptian and Hippocratic Medicine." In *Studia Orientalia Ioanni Pedersen Dicata*. Copenhagen, Denmark: Munksgaard, pp. 165–171.

———. (1957). "The Egyptian Origin of the Archaic Greek Canon." *Mitteilungen des deutschen archaeologischen Instituts Abt. Kairo* 15: 134–147.

———. (1984). "Egyptian and Hermetic Doctrine." *Opuscula Graecolatina, Supplementa Musei Tusculani* 27.

———. (1993 [1961]). *The Myth of Egypt and Its Hieroglyphs in European Tradition*. New ed. Princeton, NJ: Princeton University Press.

Jacobsen, T. (1943). "Primitive Democracy in Ancient Mesopotamia." *Journal of Near Eastern Studies* 2: 159–172.

Jakobson, R., L. R. Waugh, and M. Monville-Burston, eds. (1990). *On Language*. Cambridge, MA: Harvard University Press.

Jacobson, V. A. (1971). "Some Problems Connected with the Rise of Landed Property (Old Babylonian Period)." In *Beiträge zur sozialen Struktur des alten Vorderasiens*, ed. Horst Klengel. Berlin: Akademie Verlag, pp. 33–37.

Jacoby, F. (1923–1969). *Die Fragmente der griechischen Historiker*. Leiden, Netherlands: Brill.

James, D. (1995). "The Instruction of Any and Moral Philosophy." In *African Philosophy: Selected Readings*, ed. A. G. Mosley. Englewood Cliffs, NJ: Prentice Hall, pp. 147–155.

James, G. G. M. (1973 [1954]). *Stolen Legacy: The Greeks Were Not the Authors of Greek Philosophy, but the People of North Africa, Commonly Called the Egyptians*. New York: Philosophical Library. Repr. San Francisco: Julian Richardson Associates.

James, P., et al. (1991). *Centuries of Darkness: A Challenge to the Conventional Chronology of Old World Archaeology*. London: Cape.

James, T. G. H. (1973). "Egypt from the Expulsion of the Hyksos to Amenophis I." In *Cambridge Ancient History*, 2d ed. Cambridge, England: Cambridge University Press, vol. 2, part 2, pp. 289–312.

Jankowsky, K. R. (1968). *The Neogrammarians: A Re-evaluation of Their Place in the Development of Linguistic Science.* Washington, DC: Georgetown University Press.

Jasanoff, J. (1978). *Stative and Middle in Indo-European.* Innsbruck, Austria: Institut für Sprachwissenschaft der Universität Innsbruck.

———. (1989). "Review." *Language* 65: 623–628.

———. (1997). "Stolen Legacy? The Evidence from Language." In Ross and Lea, pp. 57–68.

Jasnow, R., and K.-T. Zauzitch. (1995). "A Book of Thoth," in *Proceedings of the Seventh International Congress of Egyptologists: Cambridge, England, 3–9 September 1995.* Ed. C. J. Eyre, pp. 607–619.

Jefferson, T. (1982). "Query XIV." In *Notes on the State of Virginia,* ed. William Peden. Chapel Hill: University of North Carolina Press.

Jeffery, L. H. (1982). "Greek Alphabetic Writing." In *Cambridge Ancient History,* 2d ed. Cambridge, England: Cambridge University Press, vol. 3, part 1, pp. 819–833.

———. (1990). *The Local Scripts of Archaic Greece: A Study of the Origin of the Greek Alphabet and Its Development from the Eighth to the Fifth Centuries B.C.* Rev. with supplement by A. W. Johnston. Oxford: Clarendon.

Jenkins, W. S. (1935). *Pro-Slavery Thought in the Old South.* Chapel Hill: University of North Carolina Press.

Jenkyns, R. (1980). *The Victorians and Ancient Greece.* Oxford: Blackwell.

Johansen, H. F., and E. W. Whittle. (1980). *Aeschylus: The Suppliants.* 3 vols. Arhus, Denmark: Nordisk Forlag.

Johnson, E. M. (1978). "Who Homer Really Was." *College Language Association Journal* 22: 54–62.

Johnson-Odim, C. (1993). "Comment: The Debate over *Black Athena.*" *Journal of Women's History* 4.3: 84–89.

Johnston, A. W. (1990). "Supplement." In Jeffery, pp. 425–481.

Jones, H. L., trans. (1967). *The Geography of Strabo.* London: William Heinemann.

Jones, William. (1807). "The Second Anniversary Discourse. Delivered 24th of February 1785." In *The Works of Sir William Jones with the Life of the Author by Lord Teignmouth.* 13 vols. London: John Stockdale, 1: 10–23.

Jordan, W. D. (1969). *White over Black: American Attitudes toward the Negro, 1550–1812.* Baltimore: Penguin.

Joseph, G. G. (2000 [1992]). *The Crest of the Peacock: Non-European Roots of Mathematics.* New ed. Princeton: Princeton University Press.

Josephus. *Against Apion.*

———. *Antiquities of the Jews.*

Joyau, A. (1977). *Panorama de la littérature à la Martinique: XIXe siècle.* Morne-Rouge-Martinique: Éditions des horizons caraibes.

Jungraithmayr, H., and W. W. Müller, eds. (1987). *Proceedings of the Fourth International Hamito-Semitic Congress, Hamburg 20–22 September 1983.* Amsterdam: Benjamins.

Kadish, G. (1993). "Some Egyptian Concepts of Space and Time." Paper given at the 12th Annual Conference of the Society for the Study of Islamic Philosophy and Science and the Society for Ancient Greek Philosophy etc., Binghamton, NY, Oct.

Kagan, D. (1965). *The Great Dialogue: History of Greek Political Thought from Homer to Polybius*. New York: Free Press.

Kaiser, J., ed. (1996). "Were Cattle Domesticated in Africa?" *Science* 5.24. 272: 1105.

Kammerzell, F. (1994). *Zur Umschreibung und Lautung des Ägyptischen*. Göttingen, Germany: Seminar für Ägyptologie und Koptologie.

Kant, I. (1831). *Immanuel Kants Menschenkunde: Oder philosophische Anthropologie*. Ed. F. C. Starke. Leipzig, Germany: Die expedition des europaischen Aufsehers.

Kaplony, P. (1980). "ka (k3)." In Helck and Otto, vol. 3, cols. 275–281.

Karageorghis, V. (1988). *Blacks in Ancient Cypriote Art*. Houston, TX: Menil Foundation.

Karenga, M. (1991). "The Contested Terrain of Ancient Egypt: Diop, Bernal and Paradigms in Africana Studies." *Challenging Tradition: Cultural Interaction in Antiquity and Bernal's Black Athena*, tape 5A. Departments of African American Studies and Classics, Temple University, Philadelphia, PA.

———. (1994). *Maat: The Moral Ideal in Ancient Egypt. A Study in Classical African Ethics*. Ph.D. thesis, University of Southern California. (U.M.I. 1994. 9601000).

Karlgren, B. (1958). *Grammata Serica Recensa. Bulletin of the Museum of Far Eastern Antiquities* 29: (1957):211–367.

Katz, V. (1993). *A History of Mathematics*. New York: Harper Collins.

———. (1995). *Newsletter of the International Study Group on the Relations between the History and the Pedagogy of Mathematics* 35: 10.

Katzenstein, H. J. (1973). *The History of Tyre: From the Beginning of the Second Millennium B.C.E. until the Fall of the Neo-Babylonian Empire in 538 B.C.E.* Jerusalem: Schocken Institute.

———. (1983). "The Phoenician Term Hubur in the Report of Wen Amon." *Atti del I Congresso Internazionale di Studi Fenici e Punici* 2: 599–602.

Kaufman, M., et al., eds. (1984). *Dictionary of American Medical Biography*. Westport, CT: Greenwood Press.

Keimer, L. (1931). "Pendeloques en forme d'insecte." *Annales de Service* 31: 145–182.

Keita, S. O. Y. (1990). "Studies of Ancient Crania from Northern Africa." *American Journal of Physical Anthropology* 85: 35–48.

———. (1992). "Further Studies of Ancient Northern African Crania." *American Journal of Physical Anthropology* 87: 445–454.

———. (1993a). "Black Athena: 'Race,' Bernal, and Snowdon." *Arethusa* 2G: 295–314.

———. (1993b). "Response to Bernal and Snowden." *Arethusa* 2G: 329–334.

———. (1996). "Analysis of Naqada Predynastic Crania: A Brief Report." In *Interregional Contacts in the Later Prehistory of Northeastern Africa*, ed. L. Krzyzaniak, K. Kroeper, and M. Kobusiewicz. Poznan: Poznan Archaeological Museum, pp. 203–213.

Keita, S., and R. A. Kittles. (1997). "The Persistence of Racial Thinking and the Myth of Racial Divergence." *American Anthropologist* 99.3: 534–544.

Kelly, D. H. (1991). "Egyptians and Ethiopians: Color, Race, and Racism." *Classical Outlook* G8: 77–82.

Kemp, B. J. (1989). *Ancient Egypt: Anatomy of a Civilization.* London: Routledge.

Kendall, T. (1991). In "Nubian Treasures Reflect Black Influence on Egypt," by J. N. Wilford. *New York Times*, 11 Feb.: C1, C10.

Kern, O. (1926). *Die Religion der Griechen.* Berlin: Weidmann.

Kirk, G. S. (1960). "Popper on Science and the Presocratics." *Mind* 69: 318–339.

———. (1961). "Sense and Common Sense in the Development of Greek Philosophy." *Journal of Hellenic Studies* 821: 105–117.

———. (1974). *The Nature of Greek Myth.* London: Penguin.

Kirk, G. S., J. E. Raven, and M. Schofield, eds. (1983). *The Presocratic Philosophers.* 2d ed. Cambridge, England: Cambridge University Press.

Kitto, H. D. F. (1951). *The Greeks.* London: Penguin.

Klein, E. (1987). *A Comprehensive Etymological Dictionary of the Hebrew Language for Readers of English.* New York: Macmillan.

Kline, M. (1962). *Mathematics: A Cultural Approach.* Reading, MA: Addison-Wesley.

Knox, T. M., trans. (1948). *Early Theological Writings.* Philadelphia: University of Pennsylvania Press.

———, trans. (1978). *Hegel's Philosophy of Right.* New York: Oxford University Press.

Kochavi, M. (1977). "An Ostracon of the Period of the Judges from Izbet Sartah." *Tel Aviv* 4: 1–13.

Koerner, K. (1989). *Practicing Linguistic Historiography.* Studies in the History of Language Sciences 50. Amsterdam: Benjamins.

Komoroczy, G. (1978). "Landed Property in Ancient Mesopotamia and the Theory of the so called Asiatic Mode of Production." *Oikumene* 2: 9–26.

Konstan, D. (1997). "*Not Out of Africa: How Afrocentrism Became an Excuse to Teach Myth as History*" and "*Black Athena Revisited*" (reviews). *History and Theory* 36.2: 223–235.

Kosso, P. (1993). "Historical Evidence and Epistemic Justification: Thucydides as a Case Study." *History and Theory* 32: 1–13.

Kosso, P., and C. Kosso. (1995). "Central Place Theory and the Reciprocity between Theory and Evidence." *Philosophy of Science* 62: 581–598.

Kozloff, A. P., and M. B. Bryan, with L. M. Berman. (1992). *Egypt's Dazzling Sun: Amenhotep III and His World.* Bloomington: Cleveland Museum of Art, Indiana University Press.

Krader, L. (1975). *The Asiatic Mode of Production: Sources, Development and Critique in the Writings of Karl Marx.* Assen, Netherlands: Van Gorcum.

Kramer, S. N. (1963). *The Sumerians: Their History, Culture and Character.* Chicago: University of Chicago Press.

Krappe, A. H. (1940). "MAKAP." *Revue de Philologie* 66: 245–246.

Krauss, R. (1990). "Vorläufige Bemerkungen zu Seth und Horus/Horusauge im kairener Tagewählkalendar nebst notizen zum Anfang des Kalendartages." *Bulletin de la société d'égyptologie* 14: 32–61.

Kretchmer, P. (1924). "Das nt- suffix." *Glotta* 13: 84–106.

Kristeller, P. (1995). "Comment on *Black Athena.*" *Journal of the History of Ideas* 56.1: 125–127.

Krupp, E. C. (1977). "Astronomers, Pyramids, and Priests." In *In Search of Ancient Astronomies*, ed. E. C. Krupp. Garden City, NJ: Doubleday, pp. 186–218.

———. (1980). "Egyptian Astronomy: The Roots of Modern Timekeeping." *New Scientist* 85.3: 24–29.

———. (1984). "Egyptian Astronomy: A Tale of Temples, Tradition, and Tombs." In *Archeoastronomy and the Roots of Science*, ed. E. C. Krupp. AAAS Selected Symposia Series No. 71. Boulder, CO: Westview.

Kuhn, T. S. (1970). *The structure of scientific revolutions.* In *International Encyclopaedia of Unified Science*, 2d ed. Chicago: Chicago University Press.

Kyriazopoulos, N., trans. (1997). *Η ΜΑΥΡΗ ΑΘΗΝΑ Μύθοι και πραγματικότητα ή οι παραποιήσει" του ((αφροκεεντρισμου))* [Not Out of Africa]. Athens: Kaktos.

Lakatos, I. (1970). "Falsification and the Methodology of Scientific Research Programmes." In *Criticism and the Growth of Knowledge*, ed. I. Lakatos and A. Musgrave. Cambridge, England: Cambridge University Press, pp. 106–117.

Lamdin, T. O. (1983). *Introduction to Sahidic Coptic.* Macon, GA: Mercer University Press.

Laroche, E. (1977?). "Toponymes et frontières linguistiques en Asie Mineur." In *La Toponymie Antique: Actes du Colloque de Strasbourg 12–14 juin 1975*, ed. T. Fahd et al. Leiden, Netherlands: Brill, pp. 205–213.

Laroche, J. (1949). *Histoire de la racine *nem- en grec ancien: nemo, Nemesis, nomos, nomizo.* Paris: Klincksieck.

Lass, R. (1997). *Historical Linguistics and Language Change.* Cambridge Studies in Linguistics 81. Cambridge, England: Cambridge University Press.

Lateiner, D. (1989). *The Historical Method of Herodotus.* Toronto: University of Toronto Press.

Latour, B. (1987). *The Pasteurization of France and Science in Action: How to Follow Scientists and Engineers through Society.* Trans. Alan Sheridan and John Law. Cambridge, MA: Harvard University Press.

Lauer, J.-P. (1948). *Le Problème des Pyramides d'Égypte.* Paris: Payot.

———. (1960). *Observations sur les pyramides.* Cairo: Institut français d'archéologie orientale.

———. (1976). *Saqqara, the Royal Cemetery of Memphis: Excavations and Discoveries since 1850.* New York: Scribner's.

Lazos, C. D. (1995). *Pyramides Stin Hellada.* Athens: Aiolos.

Leach, E. (1987). "Aryan Warlords in Their Chariots." *London Review of Books* 2 Apr.: 11–12.

Lee, D. (1961). "Homeric kér and Others." *Glotta* 39: 191–207.

Lefkowitz, M. R. (1981). "Princess Ida, the Amazons and a Women's College Curriculum." *Times Literary Supplement* 27 Nov.: 1399–1401.

———. (1983). "Feminism in the American University." *Salisbury Review* 18: 18–20.

———. (1990 [1986]). *Women in Greek Mythology*. Baltimore: Johns Hopkins University Press.

———. (1992a). "Afrocentrism Poses a Threat to the Rationalist Tradition." *Chronicle of Higher Education* 6 May: A52.

———. (1992b [1996]). "Not Out of Africa." *New Republic*, 10 Feb.: 29–36. Repr. in Lefkowitz and Rogers.

———. (1992c). "Reply to Martin Bernal." *New Republic* 9 Mar.: 5.

———. (1993a). "Afrocentrists Wage War on Ancient Greeks." *Wall Street Journal* 7 Apr.: A14.

———. (1993b). "Ethnocentric History from Aristobulus to Bernal." *Academic Questions* 62: 12–20.

———. (1994). "The Myth of a 'Stolen Legacy'." *Society* 31.3: 27–33. Abridged version in *Alternatives to Afrocentrism*. Washington, DC: Manhattan Institute, pp. 27–31.

———. (1995). "I afrokentristes kai i arkhaia Ellada." Interview with Amalia Magapanou. *To Vima* 28 May.

———. (1996a). "The Afrocentric Interpretation of Western History: Lefkowitz Replies to Bernal." *Journal of Blacks in Higher Education* 12: 88–91.

———. (1996b). CBS Interview. "60 Minutes." 24 Nov.

———. (1996c). Interview. "All Things Considered." NPR. 6 Feb.

———. (1996d). Interview. "Newsmaker Luncheon." PBS. May.

———. (1996e). *Not Out of Africa: How Afrocentrism Became an Excuse to Treat Myth as History*. New York: New Republic and Basic Books.

———. (1996f). Speech in the debate with Bernal at George Washington University, 9 Mar.

———. (1997a). *Not Out of Africa: How Afrocentrism Became an Excuse to Treat Myth as History*, 2d paperback ed. New York: New Republic and Basic Books.

———. (1997b). Preface. In Ross and Lea.

———. (1997c). η ΜΑΥΡΗ ΑΘΗΝΑ: Μύθοι και πραγματικότητα: ήοι παραποιήσει" του ((αφροκεεντρισμου)) [*Not Out of Africa*]. Trans. N. Kyriazopoulos. Athens: Kaktos.

———. (1998). "Point of View." *Chronicle of Higher Education* A64.

Lefkowitz, Mary, and G. M. Rogers, eds. (1996). *Black Athena Revisited*. Chapel Hill: University of North Carolina.

Leitz. C. (1989). *Studien für ägyptischen Astronomie*. Wiesbaden, Germany: Harrassowitz.

Lejeune, M. (1965). "Le Δᾶμος dans la societé mycenéene." *Revue des Études Grecques* 78: 1–22.

———. (1987 [1972]). *Phonétique Historique du Mycénien et du Grec Ancien*. Paris: Klincksieck.

Lerner, G. (1993). "Comment: The Debate over Black Athena." *Journal of Women's History* 4.3: 90–94.

Lesko, L. H. (1982–1990). *A Dictionary of Late Egyptian*. 5 vols. Berkeley, CA: Scribe Publications.

Levi, P. (1979). *Pausanias Guide to Greece*. 2 vols. Harmondsworth, England: Penguin.

Levin, S. (1971). "The Etymology of νέκταρ Exotic Scents in Early Greece." *Studi micinei ed anatolici* 13: 31–50.

———. (1995). *Semitic and Indo-European: The Principal Etymologies. With Observations on Afro-Asiatic*. Amsterdam: Benjamins.

Levine, M. M. (1989). "The Challenge of Black Athena to Classics Today." In Levine and Peradotto, pp. 7–15.

———. (1990). "Classical Scholarship: Anti-Black and Anti-Semitic?" *Bible Review* 6.3: 32–36, 40–41.

———. (1992a). "Multiculturalism and the Classics." *Arethusa* 25: 215–220.

———. (1992b). "The Use and Abuse of *Black Athena*." *American Historical Review* 97.2: 440–464.

———. (1998). "The Marginalization of Martin Bernal: Review Essay on *Black Athena Revisited* by M. Lefkowitz and G. Rogers." *Classical Philology* 98: 345–363.

Levine, M. M., and J. Peradotto, eds. (1989). *The Challenge of Black Athena*. Special issue, *Arethusa* 22.1.

Levy, D. M. (1999). "How the Dismal Science Got Its name: Debating Racial Quackery." Unpublished paper, Center for the Study of Public Choice, George Mason University.

Lewis, B. (1988). *The Political Language of Islam*. Chicago: Chicago University Press.

———. (1993 [1982]). "The Question of Orientalism." *New York Review of Books* 24 June. Repr. *Islam and the West*, ed. B. Lewis. New York: Oxford University Press, pp. 99–113.

Lewis, N. (1986). *Greeks in Ptolemaic Egypt: Case Studies in the Social History of the Hellenic World*. Oxford: Clarendon.

Lewy, H. (1895). *Die semitischen Fremdwörter im Griechischen*. Berlin: Gaertner.

Lichtheim, M. (1975–1980). *Ancient Egyptian Literature*, vols. 1–3. Berkeley: University of California Press.

———. (1983). *Late Egyptian Wisdom Literature in the International Context: A Study of Demotic Instructions*. Göttingen, Germany: Vandehoek and Ruprecht.

Liddell, H. G., and R. Scott. (1968) [1925–1940]. *A Greek-English Lexicon*. 9th ed., with supplement. Rev. by H. Stuart Jones and R. McKenzie. Oxford: Clarendon.

Lindquist, S. (1996). *Exterminate All the Brutes: One Man's Odyssey into the Heart of*

Darkness and the Origins of European Genocide. Trans. Joan Tate. New York: New Press.

———. (1997). *The Skull Measurer's Mistake and Other Portraits of Men and Women Who Spoke Out against Racism.* New York: New Press.

Lloyd, A. B. (1975–1976, 1988). *Herodotus Book II.* 3 vols. Leiden, Netherlands: Brill.

Lloyd, G. E. R. (1970). *Early Greek Science: Thales to Aristotle.* New York: Norton.

———. (1979). *Magic, Reason and Experience.* Cambridge, England: Cambridge University Press.

———. (1983). Introduction to *The Hippocratic Writings.* London: Penguin.

Lloyd, R. B. (1988). "Review of Black Athena, Vol. I." *Choice* 25: 1547.

Lloyd-Jones, H. (1992). "Becoming Homer." *New York Review of Books* 5 Mar.: 52–57.

Locher, K. (1983). "A Further Coffin-Lid with a Diagonal Star-Clock from the Egyptian Middle Kingdom." *Journal for the History of Astronomy* 14: 141–44.

Lockyer, J. N. (1964 [1894]). *The Dawn of Astronomy.* Repr. Cambridge, MA: MIT Press.

Loewe, B. (1980 [1936]). *Griechische Theophore Ortsnamen.* Repr. Chicago: Ares.

Long, E. (1774). *The History of Jamaica: General survey of the antient and modern state of that island.* London: Lowndes.

Loprieno, A. (1994). "Circular to the panelists of the ARCE Meeting, Berkeley, 1990, Re: M. Bernal, Black Athena." 6 Mar.

———. (1995). *Ancient Egyptian: A Linguistic Introduction.* Cambridge, England: Cambridge University Press.

———. (1996). "Defining Egyptian Literature: Ancient Texts and Modern Literary Theory." In *The Study of the Ancient Near East in the 21st Century: William Foxwell Albright Centennial Conference,* ed. J. S. Cooper and G. M. Schwartz. Winona Lake, IN: Eisenbrauns, pp. 209–232.

Loraux, N. (1986). *The Invention of Athens: The Funeral Oration in the Classical City.* Trans. Allan Sheridan. Cambridge, MA: Harvard University Press.

Loret, V. (1945). "La Lettre dans l'alphabet hiéroglyphique." In *Academie des Inscriptions et Belles Lettres,* comptes rendus. Paris: Henri Didier.

———. (1949). *Le resin de térébinthe (sonter) chez les anciens égyptiens.* Cairo: Imprimerie de l'institut français d'archéologie orientale.

Lorimer, H. L. (1950). *Homer and the Monuments.* London: Macmillan.

Loveday, L. J. (1996). *Language Contact in Japan: A Sociolinguistic History.* Oxford: Clarendon.

Löwstedt, A. (1995). *Kultur oder Evolution? Eine Anthropologische Philosophie: erster Band.* Frankfurt: Peter Lang.

———. (1997). Letter to Bernal, Vienna, 13 Nov.

———. (1998). "Konstanz, Veränderung, Evolution und Ethik: Einfuhrung in die altägyptische Philosophie und ihr Verhältnis zum abendländischen Denken" (Constance, Change, Evolution and Ethic: Introduction to Ancient Egyptian Philosophy and Its Relation to Western Thought). Privately circulated paper.

Lu X. (1998). *Rhetoric in Ancient China, Fifth to Third Century* B.C.E.: *A Comparison with Classical Greek Rhetoric*. Columbia: University of South Carolina Press.

Ludendorf, H. (1938). *Astromische Inschriften in Palenque*. Berlin: Akademie der Wissenschaft, de Gruyter.

Luft, U. (1987). "Der Tagesbeginn im Ägypten." *Altorientalische Forschungen* 14: 3–11.

Lumpkin, B. (1980). "The Egyptians and Pythagorean Triples." *Historia Mathematica* 7: 186–187.

———. (1984). "Mathematics and Engineering in the Nile Valley." *Journal of African Civilizations* 6.2: 102–19.

———. (1987). *African and African American Contributions to Mathematics, a Baseline Essay*. Portland, OR: Portland Public Schools.

———. (Forthcoming). "An Ancient Egyptian Concept of Zero and the Egyptian Symbol for Zero: A Note on a Little Known African Achievement."

Lung, G. E. (1912). *Memnon: Archäologische Studien zur Aithiopis*. Bonn: H. Ludwig.

MacGaffey, W. (1966). "Concepts of Race in the Historiography of Northeast Africa." *Journal of African History* 7: 1–17.

Macrobius. (1952). *Comentarii in somn. Scipio*, i, 19, 5–6. Trans. W. H. Stahl as *Macrobius, Commentary on the Dream of Scipio*. New York: Columbia University Press.

Majno, G. (1975). *The Healing Hand: Man and Wound in the Ancient World*. Cambridge, MA: Harvard University Press.

Malamis, G. (1997). "Εισαγωγή." pp. 21–23. In Αρχαιο-λογήματα, ed. G. Malamis. Special section of ΣΥΓΧΡΟΝΑ ΘΕΜΑΤΑ 19.64: 21–112.

Malamud, M. A. (1989). "Review of *Black Athena*, Vol. I." *Criticism* 31.3: 317–322.

Malkiel, Y. (1990). *Diachronic Problems in Phonosymbolism: Edita and Inedita, 1979–1988*. Vol. 1. Amsterdam: Benjamins.

Mallory, J. P. (1989). *In Search of the Indo-Europeans: Language, Archaeology and Myth*. London: Thames and Hudson.

Malone, D., ed. (1935). *Dictionary of American Biography*. Vol. 17. New York: Scribner's.

Manning, S. (1990). "Frames of Reference for the Past: Some Thoughts on Bernal, Truth, and Reality." *Journal of Mediterranean Archaeology* 3.2: 255–274.

Marchand, S. L. (1996). *Down from Olympus: Archaeology and Philhellenism in Germany, 1750–1970*. Princeton, NJ: Princeton University Press.

Marchand, S., and A. Grafton. (1997). "Martin Bernal and His Critics." *Arion* 5.2: 1–35.

Marcovitch, M. (1995). *Tatiani Oration ad Graecos*. Patristische Texte und Studien. Berlin: De Gruyter.

Marinatos, N. (1984). *Art and Religion in Thera: Reconstructing a Bronze Age Society*. Athens: Mathioulakis.

Marinatos, S. (1968). "Mycenaean Culture within the Frame of Mediterranean Anthropology and Archaeology." In *Atti e memorie del 1° Congresso Internazionale di Micenologia*. 3 vols. Rome: Edizioni dell'Ateneo, pp. 227–296.

———. (1969). "An African in Thera." *Analekta Arkhaiologika Athenon* 2: 374–375.

———. (1973). "Ethnic Problems Raised by Recent Discoveries on Thera." In *Bronze Age Migrations in the Aegean: Archaeological and Linguistic Problems of Greek Prehistory*, ed. R. A. Crossland and A. Birchall. London: Duckworth, pp. 199–201.

Markowsky, G. (1992). "Misconceptions about the Golden Ratio." *College Mathematics Journal* 23.1: 2–19.

Martel, E. (1997). *Questionnaire on the Extent of Afrocentric Programs, Curricula, and Books Currently in Use in U.S. Schools*. Washington, DC.

Martijn, J. R. (1989). "Ideological Critiques and the Philosophy of Science." *Philosophy of Science* 56: 1–22.

Martin, G. T. (1992). *The Hidden Tombs of Memphis: New Discoveries from the Time of Tutankhamun and Ramesses the Great*. London: Thames and Hudson.

Martin, T. (1993). *The Jewish Onslaught: Despatches from the Wellesley Battlefront*. Dover, MA: Majority Press.

Marwick, A. (1971). *The Nature of History*. New York: Knopf.

Marx, K. (1973 [1939, 1953]). *Grundrisse der Kritik der politischen Ökonomie*. Trans. Martin Nicolaus. London: Allen Lane.

Massa, A. (1977). *The Phoenicians*. Trans. D. Macrae. Geneva, Switzerland: Minerver.

Masson, E. (1967). *Recherches sur les plus anciens emprunts sémitiques en grec*. Paris: Klincksieck.

Maxwell-Stewart, P. G. (1981). *GLAUKOS: Studies in Greek Colour Terminology*. Vol. 1. Leiden, Netherlands: Brill.

Mazlish, B. (1975). *James and John Stuart Mill*. London: Hutchinson; New York: Basic Books.

Mazzarino, S. (1989 [1947]). *Fra Oriente e Occidente: Richerche di storia greca arcaica*. Milan: Rizzoli.

McCarter, P. K. (1975). *The Antiquity of the Greek Alphabet and the Early Phoenician Scripts*. Harvard Semitic Monographs 9.

McGuire, J. E., and P. M. Rattansi. (1966). "Newton and the Pipes of Pan." *Notes and Records of the Royal Society* 21: 108–143.

McNeal, R. A. (1992). "Review Essay, *Black Athena*, Vol. I." *History and Theory* 31: 47–55.

———. (1993). "Review-Discussion: Bernal Once Again." *American Journal of Ancient History* 10: 137–154.

Mellaart, J. (1965). *Earliest Civilizations in the Near East*. New York: McGraw-Hill.

———. (1979). "Egyptian and Near Eastern Chronology: A Dilemma?" *Antiquity* 53: 6–18.

Meltzer, E. S. (1974). "Egyptian Parallels for an Incident in Hesiod's *Theogony* and an Episode in the Kumarbi Myth." *Journal of Near Eastern Studies* 33.1: 154–157.

Mendelsohn, E. (1995). "Science and the Construction of the Idea of Europe." *VEST* 8.4: 59–64.

Merkelbach, R. (1987). "Die Unschuldserklärungen und Beichten im ägyptischen Totenbuch." *Der römischen Elegie und im antiken Roman. Giessener Papyrus-Sammlungen* 43. Gießen, pp. 5–34.

————. (1995). *Isis Regina–Zeus Sarapis: Die griechische-aegyptische Religion nach den Quellen dargestellt.* Stuttgart, Germany: Teubner.

Messer-Davidow, E. (1993). "Manufacturing the Attack on Liberalized Higher Education." *Social Text* fall: 40–80.

Meyer, E. (1907). "Nachträge zur ägyptischen Chronologie." In *Abhandlung der Königlichen Preußischen Akademie der Wissenschaft: philosophisch-historische Classe* III, pp. 1–67.

————. (1928–1936). *Geschichte des Altertums.* 3d ed. 4 vols. Stuttgart, Germany: Cotta.

Meyer, M. W., ed. (1987). *The Ancient Mysteries: A Source Book. Sacred Texts of the Ancient Mediterranean World.* San Francisco: Harper San Francisco.

Michelini, A. N. (1993). "Comment: The Debate over *Black Athena.*" *Journal of Women's History* 4.3: 95–105.

Mill, J. (1804). "Review of Thomas Taylor." *Literary Journal* 3: 449–461, 577–589.

————. (1809a). "Review of De Guignes *Voyages à Peking, Manille et l'île de France, faits dans l'intervalle des Années 1784–1801.*" *Edinburgh Review* Apr.–July: 407–429.

————. (1809b). "Review of Thomas Taylor's Translation of the Works of Plato." *Edinburgh Review* Apr.–July: 187–211.

————. (1840). *History of British India.* 3d ed. 10 vols. Ed. Horace Hayman Wilson. London: James Madelen.

Mill, J. S. (1850). "The Negro Question." *Fraser's Magazine* Jan.: 25–31.

————. (1924). *The Autobiography of John Stuart Mill.* New York: Columbia University Press.

————. (1986 [1823]). "The Debate on East and West India Sugars." *Globe and Traveller* 7 June. Repr. *Collected Works of J. S. Mill: Newspaper Writings, December 1822–July 1831.* Ed. J. M. Robson. Toronto: University of Toronto Press, pp. 25–30.

Miller, E. (1991). "Viewpoints II." *Washington View* Mar.–Apr.

Miller, E. F. (1987). *David Hume, Essays: Moral, Political and Literary.* Rev. ed. Indianapolis: Liberty Classics.

Mitford, W. (1784–1804). *The History of Greece.* 8 vols. London: T. Wright.

Momigliano, A. (1952). "George Grote and the Study of Greek History." Inaugural Lecture given at University College London. London: H. K. Lewis.

————. (1966). "Vico's *scienza nuova*: Roman 'Bestioni' and Roman 'Eroi.'" *History and Theory* 5: 3–23.

————. (1982). "New Paths of Classicism in the Nineteenth Century." *History and Theory*, Beiheft 21.

————. (1994a [1966]). "George Grote and the Study of Greek History." *Studies in Historiography*. New York: Harper and Row. Repr. Bowersock and Cornell, pp. 15–31.

————. (1994b). "Julius Beloch." Trans. T. J. Cornell. In Bowersock and Cornell, pp. 97–120.

Montet, P. (1946). *La vie quotidienne en Égypte au temps des Ramsès*. Paris: Hachette.

Montfaucon, B. (1719–1724). *L'antiquité expliquée et representée en figures*. 10 vols. Paris: de l'aulne.

Moore, David C. (1994). "Routes: Alex Haley, Roots, Routes, and Rhizomatic Identity." *Transition* 64: 4–22.

————. (1995). "African Philosophy vs. Philosophy of 'Africa.'" In *Philosophy and the Postcolonial: African Philosophy in North America*, ed. E. C. Eze. Cambridge, MA: Blackwell.

Moran, W. L., ed. and trans. (1992). *The Amarna Letters*. Baltimore: Johns Hopkins University Press.

Morgan, L. (1988). *The Miniature Wall Paintings of Thera: A Study in Aegean Culture and Iconography*. Cambridge, England: Cambridge University Press.

————. (1995). "Minoan Painting and Egypt: The Case of Tell el-Daba'a." In Davies and Schofield, pp. 29–53.

Morley, S. G., and G. W. Brainerd. (1983). *The Ancient Maya*. 4th ed. Rev. by R. J. Sharer. Stanford, CA: Stanford University Press.

Morpurgo-Davies, A. (1986). "The Linguistic Evidence." In *The End of the Early Bronze Age in the Aegean*, ed. G. Cadogan. Leiden, Netherlands: Brill, pp. 93–123.

Morris, S. P. (1989). "Daidalos and Kadmos: Classicism and 'Orientalism.'" In Levine and Peradotto, pp. 39–54.

————. (1990). "Greece and the Levant." *Journal of Mediterranean Archaeology* 3.1: 57–66.

————. (1992). *Daidalos and the Origins of Greek Art*. Princeton, NJ: Princeton University Press.

————. (1995). "The Sacrifice of Astyannax." In *The Ages of Homer: A Tribute to Emily Townsend Vermeule*, ed. J. B. Carter and S. P. Morris. Austin: University of Texas Press, pp. 221–245.

Moscati, S. (1968). *The World of the Phoenicians*. Trans. Alastair Hamilton. New York: Praeger.

————. (1985). "I Fenici e il mondo Mediterraneo al tempo di Omero." *Rivista di Studi Fenici* 13: 179–187.

Moscati, S., et al. (1969). *An Introduction to the Comparative Grammar of the Semitic Languages: Phonology and Morphology*. Wiesbaden, Germany: Harrasowitz.

Moses, W. J., ed. (1996). *Classical Black Nationalism: From the American Revolution to Marcus Garvey*. New York: New York University Press.

————. (1998). *Afrotopia: The Roots of African American Popular History*. Cambridge, England: Cambridge University Press.

Motley, J. (1903–1904). *The Rise of the Dutch Republic: A History.* London: T. Murray.

Mudimbe, V. (1988). *The Invention of Africa: Gnosis, Philosophy and the Order of Knowledge.* Bloomington: Indiana University Press.

Muhly, J. D. (1990a). "Black Athena versus Traditional Scholarship." *Journal of Mediterranean Archaeology* 3.1: 83–110.

———. (1990b). "Discussion and Debate: Special Review Section." *Journal of Mediterranean Archaeology* 3: 51–137.

———. (1990c). Preface. *Journal of Mediterranean Archaeology* 3.1: 53–55.

———. (1991a). "Is There Evidence of Egyptian Colonization in Central Greece?" *Challenging Tradition: Cultural Interaction in Antiquity and Bernal's Black Athena,* tape 4B. Departments of African American Studies and Classics, Temple University, Philadelphia, PA.

———. (1991b). "Where the Greeks Got Their Gifts." *Washington Post Book World* 21 July: 3.

Müller, C. (1841–1870). *Fragmenta Historicorum Graecorum . . . Apollodori Bibliotheca cum Fragmentis Auxerunt notis et prolegomenis illustrarunt.* 5 vols. Paris: Didot.

Müller, K. O. (1820). *Orchomenos und die Minyer.* Silesia, Poland: Josef Max.

———. (1825). *Prolegomena zu einer wissenschaftlichen Mythologie.* Göttingen, Germany: Vandenhoek and Ruprecht.

———. (1844). *Introduction to a Scientific Mythology.* Trans. D. Leitch. London: Longmans.

———. (1848). "Ueber den angeblichen ägyptischen Ursprung der griechischen Kunst." *Kunstblatt, Beiblatt zum Morgenblatt* no. 79. Repr. *Karl Otfried Müller, skleine deutsche Schriften.* Ed. Eduard Müller. Breslau, 2: 523–527.

Murray, G. (1934). *The Rise of the Greek Epic.* London: Oxford University Press.

Murray, M. (1941). "Connections between Egypt and Russia." *Antiquity* 16.60: 384–386.

Murray, O. (1993). *Early Greece.* 2d ed. Cambridge, MA: Harvard University Press.

Muss-Arnolt, W. (1892). "Semitic Words in Greek and Latin." *Transactions of the American Philological Association* 23: 35–157.

"Mutability of Human Affairs." (1827). *Freedom's Journal* Apr. 6.

Mylonas, G. E. (1966). *Mycenae and the Mycenaean World.* Princeton, NJ: Princeton University Press.

National Research Council. (1989). *Everbody Counts.* Washington, DC.

Naveh, J. (1973). "Some Semitic Epigraphical Considerations on the Antiquity of the Greek Alphabet." *American Journal of Archaeology* 77: 1–8.

Needham, J. (1972). *The Grand Titration: Science and Society East and West.* London: Allen and Unwin.

Needham, J. W., et al. (1954–1994). *Science and Civilisation in China.* 6 vols. Cambridge, England: Cambridge University Press.

Neugebauer, C. (1990). "The Racism of Kant and Hegel." In *Sage Philoso-*

phy: *Indigenous Thinkers and Modern Debate on African Philosophy*, ed. H. Odera Oruka. Leiden, Netherlands: Brill, pp. 259–272.

Neugebauer, O. (1957). *The Exact Sciences in Antiquity*. Providence, RI: Brown University Press.

———. (1969). *The Exact Sciences in Antiquity*. 2d ed. New York: Dover.

———. (1975). *A History of Ancient Mathematical Astronomy*. 3 vols. New York: Springer-Verlag.

———. (1983a). *Astronomy and History: Selected Essays*. New York: Springer-Verlag.

———. (1983b [1980]). "On the Orientation of Pyramids." *Centaurus* 24: 1–3. Repr. Neugebauer (1983), pp. 211–213.

———. (1988). "A Babylonian Lunar Ephemeris from Roman Egypt." In *A Scientific Humanist: Studies in Memory of Abraham Sachs*, ed. E. Leichty et al. Philadelphia: Samuel Noah Kramer Fund, The University Museum, pp. 301–304.

Newberry, P. E. (1906). "Crossed Arrows, an Emblem of Neith from the Ist to the IVth Dynasty." *Proceedings of the Society of Biblical Archaeology* 28: 71–72.

———. (1907). *Scarab Shaped Seals*. London: Constable.

Newton, I. (1947). [*Principia Mathematica*.] *Sir Isaac Newton's Mathematical Principles of Natural Philosophy and His System of the World*. Trans. F. Cajori. Berkeley: University of California Press.

Niebuhr, B. G. (1852). *Lectures on Ancient History from the Earliest Times to the Taking of Alexandria by Octavius*. Trans L. Schmitz. Philadelphia: Blanchard and Lea.

Niemeier, H.-G. (1984). "Die Phönizier und die Mittelmeerwelt im Zeitalter Homers." *Jahrbuch des römisch-germanischen Zentralmuseums* 31: 1–94.

———. (1988). "Les Phéniciens dans l'ouest." *Revue Archéologique* 31: 201–204.

Niemeier, W.-D. (1991). "Minoan Artists Travelling Overseas: The Alalakh Frescoes and the Painted Plaster Floor at Tel Kabri (Western Galilee)." In *Thalassa: l'Egée préhistorique et la mer; Actes de la troisième Rencontre Egéenne Internationale de l'Université de Liège*. Aegaeum 7. Liège, Belgium: Université de Liège, Histoire de l'Art et Archéologie de la Grèce Antique, pp. 189–201.

Nightingale, F. (1987). *Letters from Egypt: A Journey on the Nile 1849–1850*. Selected and introduced by A. Sattin. New York: Weidenfeld and Nicolson.

Nilsson, M. (1941). *Geschichte der griechische Religion*. Vol. 1. Munich: Beck.

———. (1964). *A History of Greek Religion*. 2d ed. New York: Norton.

———. (1972 [1932]). *The Mycenaean Origin of Greek Mythology*. Berkeley: University of California Press.

Nims, C. F. (1968). "Second Tenses in Wenamun." *Journal of Egyptian Archaeology* 54: 161–64.

Noegel, S. B. (1996). *Janus Parallelism in the Book of Job*. *Journal for the Study of the Old Testament*, Supplement Series 223.

Nonnus. (5th C.E.). *Dionisiaca*.

Nott, J. C. (1844). *Two Lectures on the Natural History of the Caucasian and Negro Races*. Mobile, AL: Dade and Thompson.

Nussbaum, A. J. (1976). "Caland's "Law" and the Caland System." Ph.D. diss., Harvard University.

———. (1986). *Head and Horn in Indo-European*. Berlin: de Gruyter.

O'Connor, D. (1971). "Ancient Egypt and Black Africa? Early Contacts." *Expedition: The Magazine of Archaeology/Anthropology* 14.1: 2–9.

Oded, B. (1974). "The Phoenician Cities and the Assyrian Empire in the Time of Tiglath Pileser III." *Zeitschrift des deutschen Palästina-Vereins* 90: 38–49.

Odera Oruka, H., ed. (1990). *Sage Philosophy: Indigenous Thinkers and Modern Debate on African Philosophy*. Leiden, Netherlands: Brill.

Onians, R. B. (1988 [1951]). *The Origins of European Thought: About the Body, the Mind, the Soul, the World, Time and Fate*. Cambridge, England: Cambridge University Press.

Oppolzer, T. (1962). *Canon of Eclipses*. New York: Dover.

Orel, V., and O. Stolbova. (1995). *Hamito-Semitic Etymological Dictionary*. Leiden, Netherlands: Brill.

Ortiz de Montellano, B. (1991). "Multicultural Pseudoscience: Spreading Scientific Illiteracy among Minorities Part I." *Sceptical Inquirer* 16.1: 46–50.

———. (1992). "Avoiding Egyptocentric Pseudoscience: Colleges Must Help Set Standards for Schools." *Chronicle of Higher Education* 25 Mar.: B1–B2.

Osborne, Robin. (1993). "À la greque." *Journal of Mediterranean Archaeology* 6.2: 231–237.

Otto, E. (1975). "Bastet." In Helck and Otto, vol. 1, cols. 627–630.

Outlaw, L. (1992–1993). "African, African-American, Africana Philosophy." *Philosophical Forum* 24.1–3: 63–93.

Pagliaro, H. E. (1973). Preface. In *Racism in the Eighteenth Century: Studies in Eighteenth-Century Culture*, ed. H. E. Pagliaro. Cleveland, OH: Case Western Reserve University Press.

Pallotino, M. (1956). *The Etruscans*. London: Penguin.

Palter, R. (1993). "Black Athena, Afro-Centrism, and the History of Science." *History of Science* 31.3: 227–287. Repr. Lefkowitz and Rogers, pp. 209–268.

———. (1994). "Comment on Bernal 1994." *History of Science* 32.4: 464–468.

———. (1995). "Hume and Prejudice." *Hume Studies* 21.1: 3–23.

Pang, K. D. (1985). "Extraordinary Floods in Early Chinese History and Their Absolute Dates." Paper presented to the U.S.-China Symposium on the Analysis of Extraordinary Flood Events, Nanking, Oct.

———. (1987). "Extraordinary Floods in Early Chinese History and Their Absolute Dates." *Journal of Hydrology* 96: 139–155.

Pang, K. D., and H. H. Chou. (1984). "A Correlation between Greenland Ice-Core Climatic Horizons and Ancient Meteriological Records." *Eos* 65: 846.

———. (1985). "Three Very Large Volcanic Eruptions in Antiquity and Their Effects on the Climate of the Ancient World." Paper abstract, *Eos* 66: 816.

Panofsky, E. (1955). "The History of the Theory of Human Proportions as a Reflection of the History of Styles." In *Meaning in the Visual Arts*, ed. E. Panofsky. New York: Doubleday, pp. 55–107.

Pappademos, J. (1983). "An Outline of Africa's Role in the History of Physics." In *Blacks in Science: Ancient and Modern*, ed. I. Van Sertima. New Brunswick, NJ: Transaction Books, pp. 177–196.

———. (1984). "The Newtonian Synthesis in Physical Science and Its Roots in the Nile Valley." *Journal of African Civilizations* 6.2: 84–101.

Pappé, H. O. (1979). "The English Utilitarians and Athenian Democracy." In *Classical Influences on Western Thought* A.D. 1650–1870: *Proceedings of an International Conference Held at King's College Cambridge March 1977*, ed. R. R. Bolgar. Cambridge, England: Cambridge University Press, pp. 295–307.

Parke, H. W. (1977). *The Festivals of the Athenians*. Ithaca, NY: Cornell University Press.

Parkinson, R., and L. Schofield. (1993). "Akhenaton's Army?" *Egyptian Archaeology* 3: 34–35.

———. (1995). "Images of Mycenaeans: A Recently Acquired Painted Papyrus from El Amarna." In Davies and Schofield, pp. 125–126.

Patterson, O. (1991). *Freedom in the Making of Western Culture*. New York: Basic Books.

Patterson, T. C. (1977). *Civilization*. New York: Monthly Review Press.

Pausanias. *Description of Greece*. See Frazer, Levi.

Pedersen, H. (1931). *Linguistic Science in the Nineteenth Century*. Trans. J. W. Spargo. Cambridge, MA: Harvard University Press.

Pedersen, O. (1974). *A Survey of the Almagest*. Odense, Denmark: Odense Universitetsforlag.

Pembroke, S. (1967). "Women in Charge: The Function of Alternatives in Early Greek Tradition and the Ancient Idea of Matriarchy." *Journal of the Warburg and Courtauld Institutes* 30: 1–35.

Pendlebury, J. D. S. (1930). *Aegyptiaca*. Cambridge, England: Cambridge University Press.

Penglase, C. (1994). *Greek Myths and Mesopotamia: Parallels and Influence in the Homeric Hymns and Hesiod*. New York: Routledge.

Peradotto, J. (1991). Letter to the editor. *Chronicle of Higher Education* 4 Sept.: B5.

Perpillou, J. L. (1973). *Les substantifs grecs en* —$ευς$. Paris: Klincksieck.

Petrie, W. M. F. (1905). *A History of Egypt from the XIXth to the XXXth Dynasties*. London: Methuen.

———. (1908a). "Historical References in Hermetic Writings." In Section III, "Aspects of Egyptian Religion," ed. W. F. Petrie. In *Transactions of the International Congress for the History of Religion*. 2 vols. Oxford: Clarendon Press. Vol. I, pp. 224–225.

———. (1908b). "Presidential Address." In Section III, "Aspects of Egyptian Religion," ed. W. F. Petrie. In *Transactions of the International Congress for the History of Religion*. 2 vols. Oxford: Clarendon Press. Vol. I, pp. 185–210.

————. (1909a). "Historical References in the Hermetic Writings." *Transactions of the Third International Congress of the History of Religions*. Oxford: Oxford University Press.

————. (1909b). *Personal Religion in Egypt before Christianity*. New York: Harpers.

Pettinato, G. (1981). *The Archives of Ebla: An Empire Inscribed in Clay*. Garden City, NJ: Doubleday.

Pfeiffer, R. (1976). *History of Classical Scholarship 1300–1850*. Oxford: Clarendon.

Phillips, J. S. (1991). "The Impact and Implications of the Egyptian and 'Egyptianising' Material Found in Bronze Age Crete ca. 3000–1100 B.C." Ph.D. thesis, University of Toronto.

Philostratos. (1969). *Life of Apollonius of Tyana: The Epistles of Apollonius and the Treatise of Eusebius*. Trans. F. C. Conybeare. 2 vols. London: Heinemann.

Picard, C. (1927). "Sur la patrie et les pérégrinations de Demeter." *Revue des Etudes Grecques* 40: 330–369.

Pickering, Andrew. (1995). *The Mangle of Practice: Time, Agency, and Science*. Chicago: University of Chicago Press.

————, ed. (1992). *Science as a Culture and Practice*. Chicago: University of Chicago Press.

Pierce, R. (1971). "Egyptian Loan Words in Ancient Greek?" *Symbolae Osloenses* 46: 96–107.

Pingree, D. (1990). "Hellenophilia versus the History of Science." Lecture given at the Department of Science, Harvard, 14 Nov.

Planck, M. (1949). *Scientific Autobiography and Other Papers*. Trans. F. Gaynor. New York: Philosophical Library.

Plato. (1919). *The Dialogues of Plato*. Vol. 2. *The Republic*. Trans. B. Jowett. New York: Bigelow, Brown.

————. *Hippias Major*.

————. *Timaeus*.

Pliny. *Natural History*.

Plutarch. (1927–). *Moralia*. 16 vols. Trans E. C. Babbit. Cambridge, MA: Harvard University Press.

Podvin, J.-L. (1988). "Aegyptiaca du Nord de la Gaule." *Bulletin de la société d'égyptologie* 12: 61–70.

Poe, R. (1997). *Black Spark White Fire*. Rocklin, CA: Prima Publishing.

Pokorny, J. (1959). *Indogermanisches Etymologisches Wörterbuch*. 2 vols. Bern, Switzerland: Franke.

Poliakoff, M. (1991). "Roll over, Aristotle: Martin Bernal and His Critics." *Academic Questions* 4.3: 12–28.

Poliakov, L. (1974). *The Aryan Myth: A History of Racist and Nationalistic Ideas in Europe*. Trans. E. Howard. London: Chatto and Windus.

Pollinger Foster, K. (1987). "Snakes and Lions: A New Reading of the West House Frescoes from Thera." *Expedition* 30: 10–20.

Polybius. *The Histories*.

Pope, M. H. (1965). *Job: A New Translation with Introduction and Commentary, Anchor Bible* 15. Garden City, NJ: Doubleday.

Pope, M. K. (1952). *From Latin to Modern French with Especial Consideration of Anglo-Norman.* Manchester, England: Manchester University Press.

Popham, M. R. (1988–1989). "Further Excavation of the Toumba Cemetery at Lefkandi, 1984–1985." *Archaeological Reports for 1988–1989:* 117–129.

Popkin, R. (1973). "The Philosophical Basis of Eighteenth Century Racism." In Pagliaro, pp. 245–262.

———. (1978). "Pre-Adamism in Nineteenth Century American Thought: 'Speculative Biology' and 'Racism.' " *Philosophia* 8: 205–239.

———. (1980a). "Hume's Racism." In *The High Road to Pyrrhonism,* ed. R. Watson and J. Force. San Diego: Austin Hill Press, pp. 251–266.

———. (1980b). "The Philosophical Bases of Modern Racism." In *The High Road to Pyrrhonism,* ed. R. Watson and J. Force. San Diego: Austin Hill Press, pp. 79–102.

———. (1992). "Hume's Racism Reconsidered." In *The Third Force in Seventeenth-Century Thought,* ed. R. Popkin. Leiden, Netherlands: Brill, pp. 65–75.

Porada, E. (1981). "The Cylinder Seals Found at Thebes in Boeotia." With contributions from H. G. Güterbock and J. H. Brinkman. *Archiv für Orientforschung* 28: 1–78.

———. (1984). "The Cylinder Seal from Tel el Daba'a." *American Journal of Archaeology* 88: 485–488.

Posener, G. (1960). *De la divinité du pharaon. Cahiers de la Société Asiatique* 11.

———. (1982). "A New Royal Inscription of the XIIth Dynasty." *Journal of the Society for the Study of Egyptian Antiquities* 12: 7–8.

Postgate, J. N. (1992). *Early Mesopotamia: Society and Economy at the Dawn of History.* London: Routledge.

Potter, D. (1994). *Prophets and Emperors: Human and Divine Authority from Augustus to Theodosius.* Cambridge, MA: Harvard University Press.

Poulsen, F. (1912). *Der Orient und die frühgriechische Kunst.* Leipzig, Germany: Teubner.

Pound, R. L. (1984). "The Origin of *theoi* in Inscription Headings." In *Studies Presented to Sterling Dow on His Eightieth Birthday,* ed. W. T. Loomis et al. *Greek, Roman and Byzantine Monograph* 10: 243–250.

Pounder, R. (1992). "*Black Athena II:* History without Rules." *American Historical Review* 97: 461–464.

Powell, B. (1991). *Homer and the Origin of the Greek Alphabet.* Cambridge, England: Cambridge University Press.

"The Predynastic of Egypt." (1988). *Journal of World Prehistory* 2: 135–185.

Preiswerk, R., and D. Perrot. (1978). *Ethnocentrism and History.* New York: NOK Publishers International.

Preus, A. (1992–1993). "Greek Philosophy: Egyptian Origins." *Research Papers on the Humanities and Social Sciences* 3. Binghamton, NY: Institute of Global Cultural Studies.

————. (1997). *Thoth and Apollo: Greek Myths of the Origin of Philosophy.* Paper given at the SAGP/SSIPS Conference, Binghamton, NY 24–26 Oct.

Prichard, J. C. (1845). *The Natural History of Man: Comprising inquiries into the modifying influence of physical and moral agencies on the different tribes of the human family.* 2 vols. London: Baillière.

————. (1851). *Researches into the Physical History of Mankind.* Vol. 2. *Researches into the Physical Ethnography of the African Races.* 4th ed. London: Houlston and Stoneman.

Pritchard, J. B. (1969). *Ancient Near Eastern Texts: Relating to the Old Testament.* 3d ed. with supplement. Princeton, NJ: Princeton University Press.

Proclus. *In Platonis Timaeum Commentarii.*

Proclus Diadochus. (1958). *Hypotyposis Astronomicarum Positionum IV.* Repr. ref. 74. In *A Sourcebook in Greek Science*, 2d ed., ed. M. R. Cohen and I. E. Drabkin. Cambridge, MA: Harvard University Press.

Proctor, R. A. (1883). *The Great Pyramid: Observatory, Tomb, and Temple.* New York: R. Worthington.

————. (1896). *Myths and Marvels of Astronomy.* London: Longmans, Green & Co.

Ptolemy. *The Almagest, Books I–V.* Chicago: Encyclopaedia Brittanica, Great Books of the Western World, vol. 16.

Public Security Bureau, People's Republic of China. (1989). *Fandong Hui-Dao-Men Jianjie.* Trans. as "Main Activities of the Sects and Societies in Recent Years." *Chinese Sociology and Anthropology* summer 1989: 49–84.

Puhvel, J. (1980). "The Indo-European Strain in Greek Myth." In *Panhellenica: Essays in Ancient History and Historiography in Honor of Truesdell S. Brown*, ed. S. M. Burstein and L. A. Okin. Lawrence, KS: Coronado Press, pp. 25–30.

Pulak, C. (1994). "1994 Excavation at Uluburun: The Final Campaign." *Institute of Nautical Archaeology Quarterly* 21.4: 8–16.

Pulleyblank, E. G. (1984). *Middle Chinese: A Study in Historical Phonology.* Vancouver, Canada: University of British Columbia Press.

Purdy, L. (1997). "What We Shouldn't Be Learning from the Greeks." In Coleman and Walz, pp. 291–310.

Raaflaub, K. (1985). *Die Entdeckung der Freiheit: zur historischen Semantik und Gesellschaftsgeschichte eines politischen Grundbegriffs der Griechen.* Munich: Beck.

————. (1989). "Die Anfänge des politischens Denkens bei den Griechen." *Historische Zeitschrift* 278: 1–32.

Raine, K. (1969). "Thomas Taylor in England." In *Thomas Taylor the Platonist: Selected Writings*, ed. K. Raine and G. Mill Harper. London: Routledge and Kegan Paul, pp. 49–104.

Rawson, E. (1969). *The Spartan Tradition in European Thought.* Oxford: Clarendon.

Ray, J. D. (1990). "An Egyptian Perspective." *Journal of Mediterranean Archaeology* 3.1: 77–81.

————. (1991). "Levant Ascendant: The Invasion Theory of the Origins of European Civilization." *Times Literary Supplement* 18 Oct.: 3–4.

————. (1997). "How Black Was Socrates? The Roots of European Civilization and the Dangers of Afrocentrism." *Times Literary Supplement* 14 Feb.: 3–4.

————. (1998). "Egyptian Cosmology, Ancient." *Routledge Encyclopaedia of Philosophy*. London: Routledge, pp. 248–250.

Redfield, M. W. (1990). "The Politics of Reception: Aesthetic Ideology and the *Bildungsroman*." Ph.D. thesis, Cornell University.

Redford, D. B. (1992). *Egypt, Canaan, and Israel in Ancient Times*. Princeton, NJ: Princeton University Press.

Rehak, P. (1997). "Interconnections between the Aegean and the Orient in the Second Millennium B.C." *American Journal of Archaeology* 101.4: 399–402.

Reisner, G. A. (1931). *Mycerenus, the Temples of the Third Pyramid at Giza*. Cambridge, MA: Harvard University Press.

Reiss, T. J. (1992). "Review of *Black Athena*." *Canadian Review of Comparative Literature* 19.3: 429–435.

Reitzenstein, R. (1904). *Poimandres*. Leipzig, Germany: Teubner.

Rendsburg, G. A. (1981). "Diglossia in Ancient Hebrew." In *Bono Homini Donum: Essays in Historical Linguistics, in Memory of J. Alexander Kerns*, ed. Y. Arbeitman and A. R. Bomhard. Amsterdam: Benjamins, pp. 665–677.

————. (1989). "*Black Athena*: An Etymological Response." In Levine and Peradotto, pp. 67–82.

Renfrew, C. (1972). *The Emergence of Civilisation: The Cyclades and the Aegean in the Third Millennium B.C.* London: Methuen.

————. (1987). *Archaeology and Language: The Puzzle of Indo-European Origins*. New York: Cambridge University Press.

————. (1991). "Before Babel: Speculations on the Origins of Linguistic Diversity." *Cambridge Archaeological Journal* 1: 3–23.

————. (1992). "Archaeology, Genetics and Linguistic Diversity." *Man* 27.3: 445–478.

————. (1998). "Word of Minos: The Minoan Contribution to Mycenaean Greek and the Linguistic Geography of the Bronze Age Aegean." *Cambridge Archaeological Journal* 8.2: 239–264.

"Review of the 2nd Volume of 'Black Athena': The Afroasiatic Roots of Classical Civilization." (1991). In "Among New Books." *Antiquity* 65.249: 977–986.

"Review of William Tennant's *Indian Recreations: Consisting Chiefly of Strictures on the Domestic and Rural Economy of the Hindoos and Mahommedans*." (1804). *Literary Journal* 3: 326–334.

Reyes, A. T. (1994). *Archaic Cyprus: A Study of the Textual and Archaeological Evidence*. Oxford: Clarendon.

Richard, C. J. (1994). *The Founders and the Classics: Greece, Rome and the American Enlightenment*. Cambridge, MA: Harvard University Press.

Ridings, D. (1995). *The Attic Moses: The Dependency Theme in Some Early Christian Writers*. Gothenburg, Sweden: Acta Universitatis Gothoburgensis.

Ringe, D. (1995). "'Nostratic' and the factor of Chance." *Diachronica* 12.1: 55–74.

Ripley, W. Z. (1899). *The Races of Europe: A Sociological Study*. New York: Appleton.

Robertson, M. (1975). *A History of Greek Art*. London: Cambridge University Press.

Robertson, W. (1777). *The History of America*. London: Strahan.

Robins, G. and C. Shute. (1986). "Predynastic Egyptian Stature and Physical Proportions." *Human Evolution* 1: 313–324.

———. (1987). *The Rhind Mathematical Papyrus*. London: British Museum Publications and New York: Dover.

———, eds. (1985). "Mathematical Bases of Ancient Egyptian Architecture and Graphic Art." *Historia Mathematica* 12: 107–122.

Robins, R. H. (1990). *A Short History of Linguistics*. London: Longman.

Robson, A. P. (1986). Introduction to *Collected Works of J. S. Mill Newspaper Writings, December 1822–July 1831*, ed. J. M. Robson. Toronto: University of Toronto Press and London: Routledge and Kegan Paul, pp. xix–ciii.

Romer, J. (1989 [1981]). *Valley of the Kings: Exploring the Tombs of the Pharaohs*. New York: Henry Holt.

Rose, P. L. (1990). *Revolutionary Anti-Semitism in Germany from Kant to Wagner*. Princeton, NJ: Princeton University Press.

Ross, A., and A. Lea, eds. (1997). *Were the Achievements of Ancient Greece Borrowed from Africa? Proceedings from a Seminar sponsored by the Society for the Preservation of the Greek Heritage and Co-sponsored by Georgetown University and Held at the Intercultural Center, Georgetown University, Washington, D.C. on November 16, 1996*. Society for the Preservation of Greek Heritage.

Ross, P. (1991). "Hard Words." *Scientific American* Apr.: 138–147.

Rössler, O. (1964). "Lybische-Hamitische-Semitische." *Oriens* 17: 199–216.

Roth, A. M. (1995). "Building Bridges to Afrocentrism: A Letter to My Egyptological Colleagues." *Newsletter of the American Research Center in Egypt* 167, 168.

Rouse, I. (1986). *Migrations in Prehistory*. New Haven: Yale University Press.

Rudolph, F. (1977). *Curriculum: A History of American Undergraduate Course of Study Since 1636*. San Francisco: Jossey-Bass.

Ruhlen, M. (1987). *A Guide to the World's Languages*. Vol. 1. *Classification*. Stanford, CA: Stanford University Press.

———. (1994). *On the Origin of Languages: Studies in Linguistic Taxonomy*. Stanford, CA: Stanford University Press.

Russman, E. (1989). *Egyptian Sculpture: Cairo and Luxor*. Austin: University of Texas Press.

Saggs, H. N. F. (1962). *The Greatness That Was Babylon*. New York: Mentor.

Saghieh, M. (1983). *Byblos in the Third Millennium*. Warminster, England: Aris and Phillips.

Sallust. *Jugurtha*.

Sammons, V. O. (1990). *Blacks in Science and Medicine*. New York: Hemisphere.

Sanders, E. (1969). "The Hamitic Hypothesis: Its Origins and Function in Time Perspective." *Journal of African History* 10: 521–532.

Sandys, J. E. (1908). *A History of Classical Scholarship.* 3 vols. Cambridge, England: Cambridge University Press.

Santillana, G. de. (1962). "On Forgotten Sources in the History of Science." In *Scientific Change: Historical Studies in the Intellectual, Social and Technical Conditions for Scientific Discovery and Technical Invention, from Antiquity to the Present,* ed. A. C. Crombie. New York: Basic Books, pp. 813–828.

Sapouna-Sakellerati, E. (1998). "Finds at Kymi." *Ta Nea* 11.5: 66.

Sarton, G. (1936). "The Unity and Diversity of the Mediterranean World." *Osiris* 2: 406–463.

———. (1952). *A History of Science: Ancient Science through the Golden Age of Greece.* Cambridge, MA: Harvard University Press.

———. (1959). *A History of Science: Hellenistic Science and Culture in the Last Three Centuries* B.C. Cambridge, MA: Harvard University Press.

Sartre, J.-P. (1948). "Orphée Noir." In *Anthologie de la nouvelle poésie nègre et malegache de langue française,* ed. L. S. Senghor. Paris: Presses Universitaires de France.

Saunders, J. B. de C. M. (1963). *The Transitions from Ancient Egyptian to Greek Medicine.* Lawrence: University of Kansas Press.

Saunders, J. B. de C. M., and R. O. Steuer. (1959). *Ancient Egyptian and Cnidian Medicine.* Berkeley: University of California Press.

Sauneron, S. (1959–1970). *Le Temple d'Esna.* 10 vols. Cairo: Institut français d'archéologie Orientale.

Saussure, F. de. (1879). *Mémoire sur le système primitif des voyelles dans les langues indo-européennes.* Leipzig, Germany: B. G. Teubner.

———. (1916). *Cours de linguistique générale.* Lausanne, Switzerland: Payot.

Schachermeyr, F. (1967). *Ägäis und Orient: Die überseeischen Kulturbeziehungen von Kreta und Mykenai mit Ägypten der Levante und Kleinasien unter besonderer Berücksichtigung des 2. Jahrtausend v. Chr.* Vienna: Böhlaus.

———. (1984). *Griechische Frühgeschichte: Ein Versuch frühe Geschichte wenigstens in Umrissen verständlich zu machen.* Österreichische Akademie der Wissenschaften: philosophisch-historische Klasse Sitzungsberichte, 425 Band. Vienna.

Schaeffer, C. (1948). *Stratigraphie Comparée et Chronologie de l'Asie Occidentale.* Oxford: Oxford University Press.

———. (1953). "Les fouilles de Ras Shamra-Ugarit." *Annales Archéologiques de Syrie* 3: 117–44.

Schaffer, E. S. (1975). *Khubla Khan and the Fall of Jerusalem: The Mythological School in Biblical Literature and Secular Literature 1770–1880.* Cambridge, England: Cambridge University Press.

Scharff, A. (1922). "Ein Rechnungsbuch des Königlichen Hofes aus der 13' Dynastie." (Papyrus Boulaq Nr. 18). *Zeitschrift für Ägyptische Sprache und Altertumskunde* 57: 58–59.

Schindler, J. (1976). "On the Greek Type—ευς." In *Studies in Greek, Italic and*

Indo-European Linguistics Offered to Leonard R. Palmer, ed. A. Morpurgo-Davies. Innsbruck, Austria: Institut für Sprachwissenschaft, Universität Innsbruck, pp. 349–352.

Schlesinger, A., Jr. (1992 [1991]). *The Disuniting of America*. Knoxville, TN: Whittle Direct Books. Repr. New York: Norton.

Schliemann, H. (1878). *Mycenae: A Narrative of Research and Discoveries at Mycenae and Tyrins*. London: John Murray.

Schmeil, Y. (2000). "Democracy before Democracy." *International Political Science Review* 21. 2: 99–120.

Schmidt, O. (1980). "On Plimpton 322, Pythagorean Numbers in Babylonian Mathematics." *Centaurus* 24: 4–13.

Schmitz, T. A. (1999). "*Ex Africa lux? Black Athena* and the Debate about Afrocentrism in the U.S." *Göttinger Forum für Altertumswissenschaft* 2: 17–76.

Schoelcher, V. (1977 [1840]). *L'Abolition de l'esclavage, examen critique du préjugé contre la couleur des Africains et des sang-mêlés*. Paris: Pagnerre. Repr. in Joyau, pp. 74–85.

Schoffeleers, J. (1992). *River of Blood: The Genesis of a Martyr Cult in Southern Malawi, c. A.D. 1600*. Madison: University of Wisconsin Press.

Schot, R. (1982). "Neith." In *Lexikon der Ägyptologie*, ed. W. Helck and W. Westendorf. Wiesbaden, Germany: Otto Harrassowitz, 4: 392–394.

Schulman, A. R. (1982). "The Battle Scenes of the Middle Kingdom." *Journal of the Society for the Study of Egyptian Antiquities* 12: 165–83.

Schwartz, J. (1950). "Le cycle de Petoubastis et les commentaires égyptiens de l'Exode." *Bulletin de l'Institut Français d'Archéologie Orientale* 49: 75–83.

Scott, R. B. Y. (1965). *Proverbs, Ecclesiastes: A New Translation with Introduction and Commentary*. Anchor Bible. 18. Garden City, NJ: Doubleday.

Scott, T. M. (1991). *Egyptian Elements in Hermetic Literature*. Th.D. thesis, Harvard University (U.M.I., 1991. 3058).

Seligman, C. G. (1957 [1930]). *The Races of Africa*. 3d ed. London: Thornton Butterworth.

Semple, L. T. (1905). "Address given in 1904 to The Eighth International Geographical Union Congress in Washington D.C." Washington: Government Printing Office.

Seneca. (1971). *Naturales Quaestiones*. Trans. T. H. Corcoran. Loeb Classical Library. Cambridge, MA: Harvard University Press and London: Heinemann.

Sethe, K., and G. Steindorff. (1903–1935). *Urkunden des ägyptischen Altertums*. 7 vols. Leipzig, Germany: Hinrichs.

Sextus Empiricus. (1933). *Outlines of Pyrrhonism*. Trans. R. G. Bury. 3 vols. Loeb Classical Library. Cambridge, MA: Harvard University Press.

Shaw, J. W. (1977). "Excavations at Kommos (Crete) during 1976." *Hesperia* 46: 199–240.

———. (1979). "Excavations at Kommos (Crete) during 1978." *Hesperia* 48: 145–173.

———. (1980). "Excavations at Kommos (Crete) during 1979." *Hesperia* 49: 211–251.

———. (1981). "Excavations at Kommos (Crete) during 1980." *Hesperia* 50: 207–250.

———. (1982). "Excavations at Kommos (Crete) during 1981." *Hesperia* 51: 164–195.

———. (1984). "Excavations at Kommos (Crete) during 1982–1983." *Hesperia* 53: 251–287.

———. (1986). "Excavations at Kommos (Crete) during 1984–1985." *Hesperia* 55: 219–270.

Shaw, M. (1995). "Bull Leaping Frescoes at Knossos and Their Influence on the Tell ed Daba'a Murals." *Egypt and Levant* 5: 91–120.

Shelmerdine, C. W. (1995). "Shining and Fragrant Cloth in Homeric Epic." In *The Ages of Homer: A Tribute to Emily Townsend Vermeule*, ed. J. B. Carter and S. P. Morris. Austin: University of Texas Press, pp. 99–108, pll pp. 221–245.

Shore, D. (1979). "From Babylon to Brown: The Department of the History of Mathematics." *Brown Alumni Monthly* 79.5: 14–23.

Sigerist, H. E. (1967 [1951]). *Primitive and Archaic Medicine.* New York: Oxford University Press.

Simpson, W. K. (1966). "Introduction" to A. Erman, *The Ancient Egyptian: A Sourcebook of the Writings.* Trans. A. M. Blackman. New York: Harper and Row.

Sivin, N. (1976). "Eloge, Giorgio Diaz de Santillana." *Isis* 67: 439–443.

Skon-Jedele, N. (1994). "Aigyptiaka: A Catalogue of Egyptian and Egyptian-izing Objects Excavated from Greek Archaeological Sites ca. 1100–525 B.C. with Historical Commentary." Ph.D. diss., University of Pennsylvania.

Slousch, N. (1913). "Representative Government among the Hebrews and Phoenicians." *Jewish Quarterly Review* 4: 303–310.

Smith, A. (1795). *Essays on Philosophical Subjects by the Late Adam Smith to Which Is Prefixed, an Account of the Life and Writings of the Author by Dugald Stewart.* London: Cadell and Davies.

———. (1971 [1759]). *Theory of Moral Sentiments.* London: Garland.

Smith, A. D. (1986). *The Ethnic Origins of Nations.* Oxford: Blackwell.

Smith, B. H. (1988). *Contingencies of Value: Alternative Perspectives for Critical Theory.* Cambridge, MA: Harvard University Press.

———. (1991). "Belief and Resistance: A Symmetrical Account." *Critical Inquiry* 18: 125–39.

———. (1992). "Making (Up) the Truth: Constructivist Contributions." *University of Toronto Quarterly* 6.1: 4.

Smith, B. H., and A. Plonitsky, eds. (1995). "Mathematics, Science, and Post-classical Theory." *South Atlantic Quarterly,* Special issue, spring 94: 2.

Smith, G. E. (1923). *The Ancient Egyptians and the Origin of Civilization.* London: Harper and Brothers.

Smith, J. McC. (1987 [1855]). Introduction to *My Bondage and My Freedom*, by Frederick Douglass. Urbana: University of Illinois Press.

Smith, W. S. (1965). *Interconnections in the Ancient Near East.* New Haven: Yale University Press.

Smyth, H. W. (1956). *Greek Grammar.* Rev. ed. Cambridge, MA: Harvard University Press.

Snodgrass, A. (1971). *The Dark Age of Greece: An Archaeological Survey of the Eleventh to the Eighth Centuries B.C.* Edinburgh: Edinburgh University Press.

———. (1980). *Archaic Greece: The Age of Experiment.* Berkeley: University of California Press.

Snowden, F. M., Jr. (1970). *Blacks in Antiquity: Ethiopians in the Greco-Roman Experience.* Cambridge, MA: Harvard University Press.

———. (1983). *Before Color Prejudice: The Ancient View of Blacks.* Cambridge, MA: Harvard University Press.

———. (1989). "Bernal's 'Blacks,' Herodotus, and Other Classical Evidence." In Levine and Peradotto, pp. 83–95.

———. (1993). Response [to S. O. Y. Keita]. *Arethusa* 26: 319–327.

Spalinger, A. (1991). "An Unexpected Source in a Festival Calendar." *Revue d'Égyptologie* 42: 209–222.

Springborg, P. (1984). "Aristotle and the Problem of Needs." *History of Political Thought* 5.3: 393–424.

———. (1990). *Royal Persons: Patriarchal Monarchy and the Feminine Principle.* London: Unwin, Hyman.

———. (1992). *Western Republicanism and the Prince.* Cambridge, England: Polity Press.

Spyropoulos, T. (1972). "Aigyptiakos Epoikismos en Boiotiai." *Archaiologika Analekta ex Athenôn* 27.2: 307–326.

———. (1973a). "Archaiotetes kai Mnemeia Boiotias-Phthiotidos." *Archaiologikon Deltion* 28.2: 247–281.

———. (1973b). "Eisagoge eis tên Meleten tou Kopaikou Chorou." *Archaiologika Analekta ex Athenôn* 6: 201–214.

———. (1981). *Ampheion: Ereuna kai melete tou mnemeiou tou Ampheiou Thebôn.* Sparta, Greece: N.p.

Stanley, T. (1656). *History of Philosophy.* London: Moseley and Dring.

Stanton, W. (1960). *The Leopard's Spots: Scientific Attitudes toward Race in America, 1815–59.* Chicago: University of Chicago Press.

Starke, F. C. (1831). *Immanuel Kant's Menschenkunde: philosophische Anthropologie / nach handschriftlichl. Vorlesungen.* Leipzig: Die Expedition des europäischen Aufsehers.

Starr, C. G. (1961). *The Origins of Greek Civilization* 1100–650 B.C. New York: Knopf.

———. (1977). *The Economic and Social Growth of Early Greece 800–500 B.C.* New York: Oxford University Press.

Steiner, Richard C. (1977). *The Case for Fricative Laterals in Proto-Semitic.* New Haven: American Oriental Society.

———. (1982). *The Affricated ṣade in the Semitic Language*. New York: American Academy for Jewish Research.

Stella, L. A. (1955). *Il Poema d'Ulisse*. Florence, Italy: Nuova Italia.

———. (1965). *La civiltà micenea nei documenti contemporanei*. Rome: Edizioni dell'Ateneo.

Stephen, L. (1900). *The English Utilitarians*. 3 vols. London: Duckworth.

Stephens, S. (1993). "Plato's Republic: Innovation or Allusion?" Paper given at the American Philological Association annual meeting, Washington, DC, Dec.

Steuer, R. O. (1948). "The Aetiological Principle of Pyaemia in Ancient Egyptian Medicine." *Bulletin of the History of Medicine*, suppl. 10. Baltimore: Johns Hopkins University Press.

Steuer, R. O., and J. B. de C. M. Saunders. (1959). *Ancient Egyptian and Cnidian Medicine: The Relationship of Their Aetiological Concepts of Disease*. Berkeley: University of California Press.

Stewart, C.-B. (1993). "The Powers and and Pitfalls of Parsimony." *Nature* 361: 603–607.

Stieglitz, R. R. (1971). "The Ugaritic Cuneiform and Canaanite Linear Alphabets." *Journal of Near Eastern Studies* 30: 135–139.

———. (1981). "The Letters of Kadmos: Mythology, Archaeology and Eteocretan." In Πεπράγμενα του διέθνους Κρῆτολόγιχου Συνεδρίου (Ἡράκλειο, 29 Αὐγούστου-3 Σεπτεμβρίου 1976.) Athens: N.p., 1: 606–616.

Stocking, George W., Jr. (1973). "Researches, from Chronology to Ethnology: James Cowles Prichard and British Anthropology, 1800–1850." Introduction to *Researches into the Physical History of Man*, by James Prichard. Chicago: University of Chicago Press.

Stonor Saunders, F. (1999). *Who Paid the Piper: The CIA and the Cultural Cold War*. London: Granta.

Strabo. *Geography*.

Stricker, B. H. (1950, 1953). *De egyptische Mysteriën Pap. Leyden T. 32 Oudheidkundige Mededelingen uit het Rijksmuseum van Oudheden te Leiden*. Vols. 31, 34. Leiden, Netherlands: Brill.

Struve, V. V. (1930). "Mathematischer Papyrus des staatlischen Museums der schönen künste in Moskau." *Quellen und Studien zur Geschichte der Mathematik*. Vol. 1, part A. Leiden, Netherlands: Brill.

Stubbings, F. (1973). "The Rise of Mycenaean Civilization." In *The Cambridge Ancient History*. 3d ed. Cambridge, England: Cambridge University Press, II.I: 627–658.

Suret-Canale, J. (1974). *Sur le "Mode de Production Asiatique."* Paris: Institut Maurice Thorez.

Swadesh, M. (1971). *The Origin and Diversification of Language*. Chicago: University of Chicago Press.

Swann, B., and F. Aprahemian. (1999). *J. D. Bernal: A Life in Science and Politics*. London: Verso.

Sweetman, D. (1993). *Mary Renault: A Biography.* New York: Harcourt Brace.

Symeonoglou, S. (1985). *The Topography of Thebes from the Bronze Age to Modern Times.* Princeton, NJ: Princeton University Press.

"Symposium: Racism in the Eighteenth Century." (1973). In Pagliaro, pp. 239–243.

Szemerényi, O. (1958). "The Greek nouns in -ευς." In MNHMIΣ XAPIN, *Gedenkschrift P. Kretschmer* 2. Wiesbaden: Harrassowitz. pp. 159–181.

———. (1960). "The Origin of the Name Lakedaimōn." *Glotta* 38: 4–17.

———. (1966). "The Labiovelars in Mycenaean and Historical Greek." *Studi micenei ed egeo-anatolici* 1: 29–52.

———. (1974). "The Origins of the Greek Lexicon: *Ex Oriente Lux.*" *Journal of Hellenic Studies* 94: 144–157.

Sznycer, M. (1975). "L'assemblée du peuple' dans les cités puniques d'après es témoignages épigraphiques." *Semitica* 25: 47–68.

———. (1979). "L'inscription phénicienne de Tekké près de Cnossos." *Kadmos* 18: 89–93.

Takaki, R. (1993). *A Different Mirror: A History of Multicultural America.* Boston: Little, Brown.

Tate, G. (1989). "History: The Colorized Version, or Everything You Learned in School Was Wrong." *Village Voice*, 28 Mar.: 48–50.

Taylor, A. E. (1929). *Plato, the Man and his Work.* 3d ed. London: Methuen.

Taylor, T. (1969 [1799–1801]). "Mr Taylor the Platonist." In *Public Characters of 1798.* 3 vols. printed for J. Miliken: Dublin. Vol. 3, pp. 100–124. Repr. K. Raine and G. Mills Harper. London: Routledge and Kegan Paul, pp. 105–121.

Théodoridès, A. (1971). "The Concept of Law in Ancient Egypt." In *The Legacy of Egypt*, ed. J. Harris. Oxford: Oxford University Press, pp. 291–322.

Thernstrom, S., and A. Thernstrom. (1997). *America in Black and White: One Nation Indivisible.* New York: Simon and Schuster.

Thirlwall, C. (1834–1844). *A History of Greece.* 8 vols. London: Longman.

Thomas, N., ed. (1995). *The American Discovery of Ancient Egypt.* Los Angeles: Los Angeles County Museum of Art.

Thomason, S. G., and T. Kaufman. (1988). *Language Contact, Creolization and Genetic Linguistics.* Berkeley: University of California Press.

Thompson, E. P. (1966). *The Making of the English Working Class.* London: Penguin.

Thompson, L. (1989). *Romans and Blacks.* London: Routledge and Norman: University of Oklahoma.

Thomson, G. W. (1966). *The Greek Language.* Cambridge, England: Heffers.

Thucydides. *The Peloponnesian War.*

Thurneysen, R. (1946). *A Grammar of Old Irish.* Trans. from the German by D. A. Binchy and O. Bergin with supplement. Dublin: Institute for Advanced Studies.

Tökei, F. (1979). *Essays on the Asiatic Mode of Production.* Trans. W. Goth, Budapest: Kyodo.

Toomer, G. J. (1974). "Meton." In *Dictionary of Scientific Biography*, ed. C. C. Gillispie. New York: Scribner, 9: 337–339.

Trask, R. L. (1996). *Historical Linguistics*. London: Arnold.

Trefousse, Hans L. (1969). *The Radical Republicans: Lincoln's Vanguard for Racial Justice*. New York: Knopf.

Trigger, B. G. (1978). "Nubian, Negro, Black, Nilotic?" In *Africa in Antiquity: The Arts of Nubia and the Sudan*, ed. S. Hochheld and E. Riefstahl. New York: Brooklyn Museum, vol. 1.

———. (1980). *Gordon Childe, Revolutions in Archaeology*. London: Thames and Hudson.

———. (1992). "Brown Athena: A Postprocessual Goddess?" *Current Anthropology* 33.1: 121–123.

Tritle, L. A. (1992). "Review Discussion of Black Athena 2." *Liverpool Classical Monthly* 17.6: 82–96. Repr. Lefkowitz and Rogers, pp. 303–332.

Trolle-Larsen, M. (1987). "Orientalism and the Ancient Near East." *Culture and History* 2: 96–115.

Tsirkin, J. B. (1986). "Carthage and the Problem of Polis." Trans. L. Christonogova. *Rivista di Studi Fenici* 4: 129–141.

Turner, F. M. (1981). *The Greek Heritage in Victorian Britain*. New Haven: Yale University Press.

———. (1989). "Martin Bernal's Black Athena: A Dissent." In Levine and Peradotto, pp. 97–109.

Tyldesley, J. (1998). *Hatchepsut: The Female Pharaoh*. London: Penguin.

Ullman, V. (1971). *Martin R. Delany: The Beginnings of Black Nationalism*. Boston: Beacon Press.

Vaio, J. (1996). "George Grote and James Mill: How to Write History." In Calder and Trzaskoma, pp. 59–74.

Vallance, J. (1990). "On Marshall Clagett's *Greek Science in Antiquity*." *Isis* 81.309: 713–721.

Van Andel, T. H., and E. Zangger. (1990). "Landscape Stability and Destabilisation in the Prehistory of Greece." In *Man's Role in the Shaping of the East Mediterranean Landscape*, ed. S. Bottema et al. Groningen: Netherlands: Nieberg and Van Ziest, pp. 139–157.

———. (1992). "Land Use and Soil Erosion in Prehistoric and Historical Greece." *Journal of Field Archaeology* 17: 379–396.

Van Binsbergen, W. M. J. (1997). "*Black Athena* Ten Years After: Towards a Constructive Reassessment." *Black Athena: Ten Years After*. Special issue of *Talanta*, ed. W. Van Binsbergen. 28–29:11–64.

Van Coetsem, F. (1988). *Loan Phonology and Two Transfer Types in Language Contact*. Dordrecht, Netherlands: Foris Publications.

———. (1994). *The Vocalism of the Germanic Parent Language: Systemic Evolution and Sociohistorical Context*. Heidelberg, Germany: Winter.

Van de Mieroop, M. (1997). *The Ancient Mesopotamian City*. Oxford: Clarendon.

Vandersleyen, C. (1995). "Les guerres de Mérenptah et de Ramsès III contre les peuples de l'ouest, et leurs rapports avec le Delta." In *Proceedings of the*

Seventh International Congress of Egyptologists: Cambridge 3–9 Sept. 1995, ed. C. J. Eyre. Leuven, Belgium: Peeters, pp. 1197–1204.

Van der Waerden, B. L. (1974). "The Birth of Astronomy." In *Science Awakening*. Leyden, Netherlands: Noordhoff and New York: Oxford University Press, Vol. 2.

Van Windekens, A. J. (1986). *Dictionnaire étymologique complémentaire de la langue Greque*. Leuven-Paris: Peeters.

Varille, A. (1954). "Stèle de Baki: Turin no 156." *Bulletin de l'institut français d'archéologie orientale* 54: 131–132.

Velikovsky, I. (1960). *Oedipus and Akhenaten: Myth and History*. Garden City, NY: Doubleday.

Ventris, M., and J. Chadwick. (1973). *Documents in Mycenaean Greek*. 2d ed. Cambridge, England: Cambridge University Press.

Verbeke, G. (1983). *The Presence of Stoicism in Medieval Thought*. Washington, DC: Catholic University of America Press.

Vercoutter, J. (1948). "Les Haou Nebout." *Bulletin de l'Institut Français d'Archéologie Orientale* 46: 125–48.

———. (1956). *L'Égypte et le monde égéen préhellénique*. Institut Français d'Archéologie Orientale, Bibliothèque d'Étude 22. Cairo: Imprimérie de l'Institut Français d'Archéologie Orientale.

———. (1963). "Egypt: Mathematics and Astronomy." In *Ancient and Medieval Science: From the Beginnings to 1450*, ed. R. Taton. New York: Basic Books, pp. 17–44.

———. (1976). "The Iconography of the Black in Ancient Egypt from the Beginnings to the Twenty-Fifth Dynasty." In Vercoutter et al., pp. 32–88, 291–292.

Vercoutter, J., J. Leclant, F. M. Snowden, and J. Desanges. (1976). *The Image of the Black in Western Art*. Vol. 1. *From the Pharaohs to the Fall of the Roman Empire*. New York: William Morrow.

Ver Eecke, P. (1960). *Les Oeuvres Complètes d'Archimède*. Paris: Blanchard.

Vergote, J. (1959). *Josephe en Egypte: Genèse chap. 37–50 à la lumière des études égyptologiques récentes*. Louvain, Belgium: Publications Universitares.

———. (1971). "Egyptian." In Hodge (1971), pp. 40–66.

Vermeule, E. T. (1964). *Greece in the Bronze Age*. Chicago: University of Chicago Press.

———. (1975). *The Art of the Shaft Graves at Mycenae*. Cincinnati: University of Cincinnati.

———. (1979). *Aspects of Death in Early Greek Art and Poetry*. Berkeley: University of California.

———. (1986). "'Priam's Castle Blazing': A Thousand Years of Trojan Memories." In *Troy and the Trojan War: A Symposium held at Bryn Mawr College October 1984*, ed. M. J. Mellink. Bryn Mawr: Bryn Mawr College, pp. 77–92.

———. (1992). "The World Turned Upside Down." *New York Review of Books* 26 Mar.: 40–43. Repr. Lefkowitz and Rogers, pp. 269–279.

Vermeule, E., and C. Vermeule. (1970). "Aegean Gold Hoard and the Court of Egypt." *Curator* 13: 32–42.

Vickers, M. (1987). "Review of *Black Athena I*." *Antiquity* 61: 480–481.

Vitruvius. *De architectura.*

Volney, C. F. (1979 [1802]). *A New Translation of Volney's Ruins.* Repr. New York: Levrault.

von Staden, H. (1989). *Herophilus: The Art of Medicine in Early Alexandria.* Cambridge, England: Cambridge University Press.

———. (1992). "Affinities and Elisions: Helen and Hellenocentrism." *Isis* 83: 578–595.

Vycichl, W. (1983). *Dictionnaire étymologique de la langue copte.* Leuven, Belgium: Peeters.

Wace, A. J. B., and F. Stubbings. (1962). *A Companion to Homer.* London: Macmillan.

Wachsmann, S. (1987). "Aegeans in the Theban Tombs." In *Orientalia Lovaniensia Analecta* 20. Louvain, Belgium: Peeters.

Waddell, W. G. (1940). *Manetho, with an English Translation.* Loeb Classical Library. Cambridge, MA: Harvard University Press.

Walcot, P. (1966). *Hesiod and the Near East.* Cardiff: University of Wales Press.

———. (1992). "Review of *Black Athena 2*." *Greece and Rome* 39: 78–79.

Walcott, D. (1974). "The Caribbean: Culture of Mimicry." *Journal of Interamerican Studies and World Affairs* 16: 3–14.

Wallerstein, E. (1999). "The West, Capitalism and the Modern World System." In *China and Historical Capitalism: Genealogies of Sinological Knowledge,* ed. G. Blue and T. Brook. Cambridge, England: Cambridge University Press, pp. 10–56.

Ward, W. A. (1978). *Four Egyptian Homographic Roots.* Rome: Studia.

———. (1986). "Review of Giveon, *Egyptian Scarabs in Western Asia*." *Bibliotheca Orientalis* 43: 703–705.

Warren, P. (1980–1981). "Stratigraphical Museum Excavations, 1978–1980, Part I." *Archaeological Reports for 1980–1981.* 1980: 73–92; 1981: 155–167.

———. (1995). "Minoan Crete and Pharaonic Egypt." In Davies and Schofield, pp. 1–18.

Warren, P., and V. Hankey. (1989). *Aegean Bronze Age Chronology.* Bristol, England: Bristol Classical Press.

Washington, M. (1993). "Revitalizing the Old Argument: Black Athena and Black History." Comment. "The Debate over Black Athena." Special section of *Journal of Women's History* 4.3: 106–113.

Watrous, V. (1987). "The Role of the Near East in the Rise of the Cretan Palaces." In *The Function of the Minoan Palaces: Proceedings of the Fourth International Symposium at the Swedish Institute in Athens 10–16 June 1984,* ed. R. Hägg and N. Marinatos. Jonsered (Sweden): Paul Åströms Förlag, pp. 65–70.

Watrous, L. V. (1992). *Kommos III: The Late Bronze Age Pottery.* Princeton: Princeton University Press.

Watson-Williams, E. (1954). "ΓΛΑΥΚΩΠΙΣ ΑΘΗΝΗ." *Greece and Rome* N.S.
1:36–41.

Webb, V. (1978). *Archaic Greek Faience: Miniature Scent Bottles and Related Objects from East Greece 650–500 B.C.* Warminster, England: Aris and Phillips.

Weber, M. (1976). *The Agrarian Sociology of Ancient Civilisations.* Trans. R. I.
Frank. London: New Left Books.

Webster, A. (1993). "Review of *A Sociology of Monsters: Essays on Power, Technology and Domination,* edited by John Law, 1991." *Sociological Review* 41.1:
156–159.

Webster, T. B. L. (1958). *From Mycenae to Homer.* London: Methuen.

Weingarten, J. (1990). *The Transformation of Egyptian Tawaret into the Minoan Genius: A Study of Cultural Transmission in the Middle Bronze Age.* Studies in Mediterranean Archaeology 88. Göteborg, Sweden: Paul Åströms Förlag.

Weinstein, J. (1992). "Review of *Black Athena 2.*" *American Journal of Archaeology*
96.2: 381–383.

Welmers, W. E. (1973). *African Language Structures.* Berkeley: University of California Press.

Wender, D., trans. (1973). *Hesiod and Theognis.* Harmondsworth, England:
Penguin.

West, C. (1982). *Prophesy Deliverance! An Afro-American Revolutionary Christianity.*
Philadelphia: Westminster.

West, M. L. (1971). *Early Greek Philosophy and the Orient.* Oxford: Oxford University Press.

———. (1978). *Hesiod, Works and Days.* Oxford: Clarendon.

———. (1997). *The East Face of Helicon: West Asiatic Elements in Greek Poetry and Myth.* Oxford: Clarendon.

Westbrook, R. (1988). "The Nature and the Origin of the Twelve Tables."
Zeitschrift der Savigny Stifftung für Rechtsgeschichte 105: 72–114.

———. (1992). "The Trial Scene in the Iliad." *Harvard Studies in Classical Philology* 94: 53–76.

Westendorf, W. (1992). *Erwachen der Heilkunst: Die Medizin im Alten Ägypten.*
Zurich: Artemis.

Westfall, R. J. (1980). *Never at Rest: A Biography of Isaac Newton.* Cambridge,
England: Cambridge University Press.

———. (1982). "Newton's Theological Manuscripts." In *Contemporary Newtonian Research,* ed. Z. Bechler. Dordrecht, Netherlands: D. Reidel, pp. 15–
34.

———. (1993). *The Life of Isaac Newton.* Cambridge, England: Cambridge University Press.

White, A. D. (1896). *A History of the Warfare of Science with Theology in Christendom.* New York: D. Appleton and Company.

Whitney, G. (1990). "Is the American Academy Racist?" *University Bookman*
30.2: 4–15.

Who Was Cleopatra? (1992). Film. Produced by N. Valcour and T. Naughton,
directed by B. Morin for The Learning Channel and the Archaeological

Institute of America, Arkios Productions. 23 minutes, color. Distributed by Films for the Humanities (#FFH 3983), Box 20. 53, Princeton, NJ, 08543-2053.

Wiesen. D. (1980). "Herodotus and the Modern Debate over Race and Slavery." *Ancient World* 3: 3–16.

Will, G. (1996). "Intellectual Segregation." *Newsweek* 19 Feb.: 78.

Williams, B. (1980). "The Lost Pharaohs of Nubia." *Archaeology* 33.5: 14–21.

———. (1986). *The A-Group Royal Cemetery at Qustul: Cemetery L. University of Chicago Oriental Institute Nubian Expedition III*. Chicago: University of Chicago.

———. (1987). "Forebears of Menes in Nubia: Myth or Reality?" *Journal of Near Eastern Studies* 46: 15–26.

Williams, B., and T. Logan. (1987). "The Metropolitan Museum Knife Handle and Aspects of Pharaonic Imagery before Narmer." *Journal of Near Eastern Studies* 46: 245–285.

Williams, C. (1987 [1971]). *The Destruction of Black Civilization: Great Issues of a Race from 4500 B.C. to 2000 A.D.* Dubuque, IA: Kendall/Hunt. Repr. Chicago: Third World Press.

Williams, E. (1964 [1944]). *Capitalism and Slavery.* London: Deutsch.

———. (1970). *From Columbus to Castro: A History of the Caribbean 1492–1969.* New York: Harper and Row.

Williams, J. H., Jr. (1996). *Fundamentals of Applied Dynamics.* New York: John Wiley.

Wilson, J. A. (1949). "The Oath in Ancient Egypt." *Journal of Near Eastern Studies* 7: 129–56.

———. (1962). "Medicine in Ancient Egypt." *Bulletin of Historical Medicine* 36.2: 114–123.

———. (1964a). "Ancient Egyptian Medicine." Editorial. *Journal of the International College of Physicians* section 1, vol. 41, 6 June: 665–673.

———. (1964b). *Signs and Wonders upon Pharaoh: A History of American Egyptology.* Chicago: University of Chicago Press.

Wilson, J. K. (1995). *The Myth of Political Correctness: The Conservative Attack on Higher Education.* Durham, NC: Duke University Press.

Winkler, J., D. Halperin, and F. Zeitlin. (1990). *Before Sexuality: The Construction of Erotic Experience in the Ancient Greek World.* Princeton, NJ: Princeton University Press.

Winter, I. J. (1995). "Homer's Phoenicians." In Carter and Morris, pp. 247–271.

Witzel, M. (1999). "Early Sources for South Asian Substrate Languages." *Mother Tongue* special issue Oct: 1–71.

Wolff, H. W. (1974). *Anthropology of the Old Testament.* London: S.C.M. Press.

Woodard, R. D. (1997). *Greek Writing: From Knossos to Homer.* Oxford: Oxford University Press.

Wright, L. (1994). "One Drop of Blood." *New Yorker* 25 July: 46–55.

Wright, R. (1991). "The Quest for the Mother Tongue." *Atlantic* 267.4: 39–68.

Wright, W. C., trans. (1922). *Philostratus and Eunapius: Lives of the Sophists.* London: William Heinemann.

Wyatt, W. F. (1968). "Greek names in -σσος/-ττος." *Glotta* 46: 6–14.

Xenophanes. 1901. Fragments 21B 10–16. In *Poetarum Philosphorum Graecorum Fragmenta,* ed. H. Diels. Berlin: Weidmann, p. 29.

Xenophon. *Anabasis.*

Yan Li and Shiran Du. (1987). *Chinese Mathematics: A Concise History.* Trans. John N. Crossley and Anthony W. C. Lun. Oxford: Clarendon.

Young, G. D. (1953). "The Origin of the Waw Conversive." *Journal of Near Eastern Studies* 12: 248–252.

Yurco, F. J. (1989). "Were the Ancient Egyptians Black or White?" *Biblical Archaeology Review* 15.5: 24–29, 58.

———. (1991). Letter to the editor. *Chronicle of Higher Education* 4 Sept.: B4.

Zaccagnini, C. (1981). "Modo di produzione asiatico e vicino oriente antico,' appunti per una discussione." *Dialoghi di Archeologia* 3: 3–65.

Zangger, E. (1992). *Flood from Heaven: Deciphering the Atlantis Legend.* New York: Sidgewick and Jackson.

———. (1994). *Ein Neuer Kampf um Troia: Archäologie in der Krise.* Munich: Droemer.

Zilfi, M. C. (1993). "Martin Bernal's *Black Athena.*" Comment. "The Debate over Black Athena." Special section of *Journal of Women's History* 4.3: 114–18.

Index

538   Index

Martin Bernal is Professor, departments of Government and Near Eastern Studies at Cornell University. He is the author of *Black Athena: The Afroasiatic Roots of Classical Civilization* (vol. 1, 1987; vol. 2, 1991), *Cadmean Letters: The Transmission of the Alphabet to the Aegean and Further West before 1400 B.C.* (1990), and *Chinese Socialism to 1907* (1976).

Library of Congress Cataloging-in-Publication Data

Bernal, Martin.
Black Athena writes back : Martin Bernal responds to his critics / Martin Bernal ; edited by David Chioni Moore.
p. cm.
Includes bibliographical references and index.
ISBN 0-8223-2706-6 (cloth : alk. paper) — ISBN 0-8223-2717-1 (pbk. : alk. paper)
1. Bernal. Martin. Black Athena.   2. Greece—Civilization—Egyptian influences.
3. Greece—Civilization—Phoenician influences.   4. Greece—Civilization—
To 146 B.C.   I. Moore, David Chioni.   II. Title.
DF78 .B3984   2001
938—dc21   2001023173